The plight of the IDP

The response of the Nigerian Military
X JTF

ABDULBASIT KASSIM
MICHAEL NWANKPA

(*Editors*)

The Boko Haram Reader

From Nigerian Preachers to the Islamic State

With an Introduction by
PROFESSOR DAVID COOK

OXFORD
UNIVERSITY PRESS

OXFORD
UNIVERSITY PRESS

Oxford University Press is a department of the
University of Oxford. It furthers the University's objective
of excellence in research, scholarship, and education
by publishing worldwide.

Oxford   New York

Auckland   Cape Town   Dar es Salaam   Hong Kong   Karachi
Kuala Lumpur   Madrid   Melbourne   Mexico City   Nairobi
New Delhi   Shanghai   Taipei   Toronto

With offices in

Argentina   Austria   Brazil   Chile   Czech Republic   France   Greece
Guatemala   Hungary   Italy   Japan   Poland   Portugal   Singapore
South Korea   Switzerland   Thailand   Turkey   Ukraine   Vietnam

Oxford is a registered trade mark of Oxford University Press
in the UK and certain other countries.

Published in the United States of America by
Oxford University Press
198 Madison Avenue, New York, NY 10016

Library of Congress Cataloging-in-Publication Data is available
Abdulbasit Kassim and Michael Nwankpa.
The Boko Haram Reader: From Nigerian Preachers to the Islamic State.
ISBN: 9780190908300

Printed in India on acid-free paper

For our parents, who sacrificed so much for all of us.

CONTENTS

CONTENTS

PART THREE
MAKING NIGERIA UNGOVERNABLE (2009–2012)

CONTENTS

PART FOUR
BOKO HARAM STATE (2013–2015)

PART FIVE
WEST AFRICAN ISLAMIC STATE (2015–2016)

CONTENTS

ACKNOWLEDGEMENTS

We would like to acknowledge a wide range of scholars who have helped this project come to fruition. First and foremost, the Baker Institute for Public Policy at Rice University, with its director, Ambassador Edward Djerejian, and Professor Allen Matusow, who have been instrumental in obtaining funding and fellowships for the study of Boko Haram since 2011. We would also like to acknowledge the Department of Religion at Rice University, and most especially Professor Elias Kifon Bongmba, who has helped us in innumerable ways, patiently and with vast knowledge of Africa. Additionally, we are indebted to the Mosle Funds endowed to the Faculty of the Humanities at Rice University.

A special thanks to the Kanuri translating team headed by Atta Barkindo (Ph.D., Politics and International Studies, School of Oriental and African Studies, University of London) and Hurso Adam (Ph.D. candidate, Environment, Conflict and Security—Lake Chad Border region, London South Bank University). We are indebted to this team for translating the two Kanuri texts (nos. 4 and 16).

We would like to acknowledge the gracious aid of Jacob Zenn, at the Jamestown Foundation, who helped us clarify many issues and obtain texts and videos, as well as that of Alex Thurston, at Georgetown University, who kindly supplied us with a copy of Muhammad Yusuf's *Hādhihi ʿaqīdatunā wa-minhāj daʿwatinā* (text 2). We would like to thank Aaron Zelin of jihadology.net from whom we have obtained several documents and videos. Professor Abdulla Uba Adamu, Vice-Chancellor of National Open University of Nigeria, Abuja, very kindly supplied us with the audio of text 9 and text 25 with his translation, in addition to clarifying several helpful issues linguistically and ideologically (all translator notes in text 25 are his). Professor Charles Abiodun Alao, of the African Leadership Center at King's College, University of London, also supported the scholarship of Abdulbasit Kassim, and deserves to be acknowledged. Jana Hutchinson of Emory University traveled with David Cook on an Africa overland trip during 2009. We passed through Maiduguri on 8–10 May 2009. She read over the manuscript and made corrections.

We would like to thank Professor Siraj Abdulkarim at Ahmadu Bello University, Zaria; Dr Usman Bugaje at the Arewa House, Kaduna; Professor Mukhtar Bunza at Usman Dan Fodio University, Sokoto; Professor Farooq Kperogi at Kennesaw State University, Georgia; and Mallam Ibraheem Suleiman at the Center for Islamic and

ACKNOWLEDGEMENTS

Legal Studies, Ahmadu Bello University, Zaria, who have made helpful suggestions and given us feedback. Dr Carmen McCain of Westmont College also gave us several linguistic corrections. We would also like to thank Professor Murray Last, of University College, London, and Professor John Voll of Georgetown University for providing insights into West African Islam.

It is our hope that this book will provide a basis for the study of Salafi-jihadism in Nigeria. The Boko Haram insurgency has led to the slavery and slaughter of enormous numbers of Nigerians and other West Africans, both Christians and Muslims. We hope that when this insurgency is resolved, the common experience of this horror will at least result in the strengthened unity of Nigeria. May justice be rendered to the victims of Boko Haram.

A NOTE ON THE EDITORS

Abdulbasit Kassim is a PhD student in the Department of Religion at Rice University. His research focuses on the Intellectual History of Islam in Africa, Contemporary Islamic Movements in Africa, Postcolonial African States, African Religions, and the International Relations of Sub-Saharan Africa. His publications have appeared in *Politics, Religion and Ideology*, *Combating Terrorism Center* and *Current Trends in Islamist Ideology*.

Michael Nwankpa has a PhD in Sociology from the University of Roehampton. His research focuses on the dilemma of security, development and human rights. His publications have appeared in *Behavioural Sciences of Terrorism and Political Aggression* and *Journal of Terrorism Research*.

David Cook is Associate Professor of Religion at Rice University, specializing in classical Islam, apocalyptic movements and literature and contemporary Salafism. His books include *Understanding Jihad* (Berkeley: University of California Press, 2005) and *Martyrdom in Islam* (Cambridge: Cambridge University Press, 2007).

GLOSSARY

bayʿa: the formal pledge of allegiance to the imam or a caliph.

fatwā: a solicited legal opinion binding upon the questioner, but often used by others as well.

ḥadīth: the record of the sayings and doings of the Prophet Muhammad and the basis for the Sunna.

hijra: emigration, used to describe the emigration of the Prophet Muhammad from Mecca to Medina.

ḥisba: morality police, often vigilante groups.

Imam: usually prayer leader, also a legitimate leader of the Muslims.

irjāʾ: the doctrine of the Murjiʾa (see below).

Islamic State West African Province, ISWAP (Boko Haram's title after 7 March 2015)

izhār al-dīn: the public manifestation of religion.

jāhiliyya: pre-Islamic period of ignorance. Salafis frequently believe that the current period is one of renewed *jāhiliyya*.

Jamāʿat Ahl al-Sunna li-Daʿwa wa-l-Jihād: Boko Haram, abbreviated to JASDJ.

Jamāʿat Anṣār al-Muslimīn fi Bilād al-Sūdān: Ansaru, a splinter group from Boko Haram, resolved to attack non-Muslim and foreign targets, abbreviated to JAMBS.

jihād: God-sanctioned warfare, with the object of either defending Islam or expanding it.

Kato de Gora: Civilian Joint Task Force, a locally raised vigilante group, tasked by the Nigerian forces with patrols and guard functions. Frequently accused of human rights violations.

Kharijites: a puritanical, egalitarian Islamic group from the seventh and eighth centuries, whose violence was focused solely upon other Muslims. Contemporary Salafi-jihadis are often, because of their use of *takfir*, called "Kharijites" by other Muslims, which angers them considerably.

kufr dūna kufr: "disbelief without disbelief", a category of *takfir* that is accorded to lesser offenses, by which one is designated an unbeliever, but not considered to have apostacized from Islam.

GLOSSARY

Mallam: an honorific accorded to the Muslim religious elite in West Africa.

Marabout: a Sufi holy figure, the focus of popular religion throughout West Africa.

mujāhid, pl. *mujāhidīn*: fighters in a *jihād* (see above).

mujtahid: a person with high status who is qualified to reinterpret Muslim law.

murji'a: a group in early Islam that believed in postponing judgment as to the truth of an apparent Muslim's belief or unbelief. Contemporary mainstream and quietist Salafis are often accused by Salafi-jihadis of being Murji'a.

mushrik, pl. *mushrikīn*: polytheists, those who associate other entities with Allah, often used for Christians.

nashīd: a martial ditty, set to a musical cadence yet permissible according to Salafi-jihadis.

salaf: the pious forefathers, the emulation of whom is a basis for Sunnism.

salām ʿalaykum: peace be upon you, a standard Muslim greeting.

shariʿa: system of Islamic law, traditionally an aggregate of the Sunni schools of law, today perceived as a unified code by many Salafis.

Sunna: the way of the Prophet Muhammad, normative for all Sunni Muslims.

ṭāghūt, pl. *ṭawāghīt*: originally in the Qur'ān the name of an idol, but in Salafi terminology meaning "illegitimate ruler, authority, one associated with an intrinsically evil system."

takfīr: the ability or willingness to designate an apparent Muslim to be an unbeliever, for which the punishment is death.

tawḥīd: monotheism, a basis for Islam.

ʿulamā': the Muslim religious leadership.

umma: the Muslim community.

al-walā' wa-l-barā': "loyalty and enmity", a primarily Salafi doctrine by which all actions are judged in terms of polarity: one should demonstrate loyalty to Muslims and Islam and disassociation from non-Muslims and anything other than Islam.

Arabic words and names from the pre-modern period are given with full transliteration, but those from the contemporary period are given without. Names common in English (Osama bin Laden, al-Qaeda, etc) are spelled in their common form. Nigerian words and names are spelled as they would be in Nigeria, even if they are Arabic in origin (such as names like Abubakar, Dan Fodio, etc.).

INTRODUCTION

David Cook

Since its emergence in approximately 2002, the Boko Haram insurgency has morphed from being a local quietist Salafi group (2002–8), to a local Salafi-jihadi movement (in 2009–10), to a group capable of striking at will across northern and central Nigeria (2011–13), to an established Islamic state (2014), and finally to a declared affiliate and branch of the Islamic State (IS, also known as ISIL and ISIS) as its "West African Province" (7 March 2015)[1]—all during the course of some twelve years.

A great many issues concerning Boko Haram are in dispute, including its name. While officially the group is titled *Jamā'at Ahl al-Sunna li-Da'wa wa-l-Jihād* (The Sunni Group for Preaching and Fighting, abbreviated as JASDJ), popular Nigerian terminology for it quickly latched on to its declared opposition to any form of Western education—hence the title Boko Haram (meaning "Western education is forbidden"). Like other prominent Salafi-jihadi groups, such as ISIS, Boko Haram has resisted its popular name, to no avail.[2] Though it currently refers to itself as Islamic State, West African Province (ISWAP), the name Boko Haram will be employed for the group throughout this book.

Physically, Boko Haram's location is in the northeastern section of Nigeria, primarily in three states: Borno, Yobe and Adamawa states. From an ethnic point of view, Boko Haram's present base is amongst the Kanuri people, who are not confined by Nigeria's borders, but spill over into northern Cameroon and western Chad, and historically are the heirs to the pre-modern Sultanate of Borno. This state was established in approximately the year 1000, when its people were converted to Islam, and has been traditionally characterized by raids southwards, mainly for the purposes of slaving.[3]

However, the region of Borno suffered several major blows during the nineteenth century. The first of these was the influence of the *jihād* of Shehu 'Uthmān Ibn Fūdī or Dan Fodio (1804–12) that established the locus of West African (and most specifically Nigerian) Islam considerably to the west of Borno (in Sokoto).[4] Because the

1

Regions of Nigeria

Re Kanuri

jihād was led by the Fulani people, who have gradually fused with the much more numerous Hausa, in the north Nigerian Islam has come to be dominated by those who, from the Kanuri point of view, are comparative newcomers. Although present-day Nigerian Islam has several different loci—the caliphate in Sokoto being merely one of them—the northeastern Borno region is quite a backwater.

Secondly, the colonial boundaries drawn by France and Great Britain at the end of the nineteenth century effectively divided the Kanuri homeland, placing some of its people in Cameroon and Chad, and even cut the Nigerian Kanuris off from their previous home around Lake Chad (which has been gradually drying up throughout the twentieth century). Thus, the Kanuris could be seen to be ripe for a radical group like Boko Haram to appear.

Muhammad Yusuf, Boko Haram's charismatic leader, was a product of the main-line Salafi Nigerian group of *Jamā'at Izālat al-Bid'a wa-Iqāmat al-Sunna* (Society for the Removal of Innovation and the Reestablishment of the Sunna), popularly known as Yan Izala.[5] Like with so many other doctrinal splits in highly ideological groups, that between Yan Izala and Boko Haram has led to a heavy dose of polemic directed against the former (texts 3, 10, 26). But Yusuf also spent several years in Saudi Arabia, which clearly influenced him considerably.

The teachings of Yusuf (texts 1–6, 8–13, 15, 17–20) are derived largely from Saudi Arabian and Syrian books, mostly those circulated during the later 1990s and early 2000s. Presumably Yusuf obtained them when he went on hajj in 2003 and 2004. He also cites the well-known Syrian quietist Salafi Nāṣir al-Dīn al-Albānī (d. 1999), and the Jordanian Salafi-jihadi Abu Mus'ab al-Zarqawi (d. 2006). But despite Yusuf's and other Boko Haram figures' frequent use of the title *hādhihi 'aqīdatunā* (This is our Creed), he does not cite Abu Muhammad al-Maqdisi (b. 1959), Zarqawi's mentor, who is the key contemporary ideologue in the jihadi intellectual universe.

One should note that parts 1–2 reveal Yusuf, despite his lack of a formal (secular) education, to have been quite well-read and informed. Although his interpretation of African and Nigerian history is tinged with conspiracy theories (see texts 11, 15b and 15c), and he presents his facts selectively, his range is quite broad. Watching his videos, it is easy to see the reasons why he gained such a following.

Texts 1–6 can be considered to be the formative ones for Boko Haram's ideology, and essentially, they document how the group went through a period of ideological exploration and debate concerning its beliefs. Boko Haram interacted extensively with the northern Nigerian quietist Salafi elites during this period (2006–08); indeed, the material translated in this section is almost a microcosm of the debates inside Nigerian Salafism.

Yusuf takes the line that anything which cannot be attested in the Qur'ān or the *ḥadīth* (tradition literature) is an innovation, and needs to be excised. This rather uncompromising attitude is characteristic not of Salafism, but of Wahhabi (Saudi Arabian) Islam. A good example of this trend is the belief that the sun orbits the earth, which is based upon highly literal readings of the Qur'ān (e.g., Q18:86, 90), and is not accepted by any stream of Muslim exegesis outside of Saudi Arabia. However, during the 1980s and 1990s the two dominant Saudi religious figures, 'Abd al-'Azīz b. Baz (d. 1999), and Muhammad b. 'Uthaymīn (d. 2001) both penned religious opinions supporting this anti-Copernican idea. A good example of this is Ibn 'Uthaymīn's *fatwā* (solicited religious opinion), which states:

> "The summary of our opinion concerning the orbit of the earth is that it is one of those things that cannot be either denied or affirmed in the Book or the Sunna... As for what the contemporary astronomers say having described it, this does not approach in our opinion the level of certainty, so we will not abandon the plain meaning of the Book of our Lord and the Sunna of our Prophet for it."[6]

Ibn 'Uthaymīn is frequently cited by Yusuf.

Muslim scholars debated Yusuf during the early part of the 2000s to challenge him—albeit with no success.[7] It is interesting also that the texts translated below preserve a continuous series of challenges raised to the leaders of Boko Haram, Yusuf and Shekau, during the question and answer periods that followed major lectures. These Q&A sessions demonstrate that the audience was far from being cowed, even asking Shekau concerning the use of electricity (text 14), among other issues.

Radical Salafi groups like Boko Haram usually veer between some type of withdrawal from wider society and a violent confrontation with it.[8] Boko Haram under Yusuf went through both phases, establishing small commune-like enclaves throughout Borno and Yobe States during the early part of the 2000s, and then entering into a violent confrontation during June–July 2009 (text 19), apparently as a result of his followers' unwillingness to wear helmets while riding motorcycles (as this would constitute a *bid'a*, a blameworthy innovation). After a period of violence in Boko Haram's home base of Maiduguri (capital of Borno state), the group was brutally suppressed and Yusuf murdered.

Violence associated with Boko Haram goes through several cycles: the period 2010–11 is characterized by low-level local violence, usually continuing with the "commanding the good and forbidding the evil" theme as under Yusuf, but occasionally with the addition of attacks upon Christian targets. 2011–12 marked the breakout of Boko Haram into the larger Nigerian arena, and a considerable stepping up of its attacks upon Christian targets, most probably with the goal of provoking a civil war between Nigeria's Muslims and Christians. The summer of 2011 marked the beginning of Boko Haram's use of suicide attacks, hitherto unknown in West Africa.

The period 2012–13 marked a retrenchment of Boko Haram, as it was contained in the three northeastern Nigerian states of Borno, Yobe, and Adamawa. Nonetheless Boko Haram carried out many attacks during this period, most of which were low-tech in nature. However, with the collapse of the Nigerian army, especially during the first half of 2014 (when there were several mutinies),[9] Boko Haram was able during

3

2014–15 to briefly establish an Islamic state, before the revival of the military campaign against it during the spring of 2015 brought the territorial phase of its existence to a close.

In retrospect, it is easy to demarcate the phases of Boko Haram's activities by the methodologies it utilized to achieve its goals. During the first phase, its means and methods were very low-tech, and it did not utilize suicide attacks. The second phase marks a heightened prominence of the group, and the beginning of outsiders noticing it.[10] The retrenchment period of 2012–13 reverts to the low-tech methodologies, but there was more of a globalist aspect to Boko Haram as it frequently carried out kidnappings in Cameroon, and established connections with West African Salafi-jihadi groups. Following this was the Islamic State phase, which opened with a series of massacres in January–February 2014, and continued with large-scale kidnappings of women and children for slavery.

One frequently finds speculation in the research on Boko Haram that the group's primary goal may be alleviation of Nigeria's poverty or that one of the driving forces behind the group's activities might be economic.[11] This speculation does not find any support within the translated Boko Haram texts, as poverty or economic issues are not mentioned (except within the context of morals and ethics, such as not cheating one's customers).

We should understand that Boko Haram is a Salafi-jihadi group, and that although one can find it to be an outlier within the context of the mostly Sufi or mainstream Salafi strands of Nigerian Islam, it is not without its precedents or ideological justifications for the actions it takes. Every action taken by Boko Haram thus far can be justified in terms of the Salafi-jihadi ideology.

With its setbacks during spring 2015, we should understand that Boko Haram has entered a new incarnation—one that is much more focused upon territoriality, is globalist Salafi-jihadist in nature, and is characterized by grand goals of an apocalyptic transformation of Nigerian society. It would be very premature to speak, as some incautious Nigerian politicians have already done, about Boko Haram's demise. It is interesting and indicative of this most recent period that despite its set-backs, no major Boko Haram figures have defected to the Nigerians (or other coalition forces), or have offered serious negotiations. Boko Haram may very well be defeated, but it does not see itself as being defeated.

Materials translated below constitute most of the authenticated source-base for the study of Boko Haram or the West African Province of the Islamic State. They are primarily videos and audios issued by the group during the period 2006–2016, but also include published documents, *anāshīd* or *nashīds* (martial ditties allowable from the perspective of Islamic law), sermons and interviews. The primary languages are Hausa, Arabic and Kanuri, with a small amount of material in English and French. There may be additional source-materials for the study of Boko Haram, principally interviews and original documents which might be found in the region of Gwoza (the capital of Boko Haram's state) and other territories once conquered by the group.

INTRODUCTION

Much work remains to be done on Boko Haram. Of all the current Salafi-jihadi groups it is probably the least well-documented, as it is not closely associated with the internet culture, throughout much of its existence has not cultivated relations with groups outside of Nigeria—quite aside from being in one of the technologically least-developed sections of the country—and does not have a group of Muslim scholars that supports it through written materials (as most Salafi-jihadi groups have). For this reason, the documentation of Boko Haram seems to be desirable.

Most of the translations were the responsibility of Abdulbasit Kassim, but I translated the Arabic documents (texts 2, 22, 24, 27, 32, 36–37, 44, 48, 58 and 61), and annotated the other materials. Professor Abdullah Adamu translated no. 25, while the Kanuri materials (texts 4 and 16) were translated by a team headed by Atta Barkindo. The Qur'ānic translation is that of Majid Fakhry, *The Qur'an: A Modern English Version*. All *ḥadīth* selections and other citations are the responsibility of the translators. For the sake of consistency, the word "God" has been rendered Allah throughout. Places and names known in English (Mecca, Muhammad for example) will be kept in those forms; others will be written in the forms commonly used in Nigeria.

Because of the constraints of space, it was not possible to publish all these materials in full, especially those in parts 1–2. Priority has been given to materials detailing Boko Haram's history and ideological development, as well as to those developments which are specific to Nigeria. Regretfully, materials that are common to Salafi-jihadi groups have had to be excluded. However, in parts 3–5 covering the period 2010–16, most of the texts are translated in full. In general, this material is far less theological, and more political, but the basic ideas remain those of Salafi-jihadism, and nothing that is said is out of the mainstream of that belief-system.

PART ONE

NIGERIAN PREACHERS
(2006–2008)

Michael Nwankpa

The Jamā'at Ahl al-Sunna li-Da'wa wa-l-Jihād (The Sunni Group for Preaching and Fighting, JASDJ), popularly known as Boko Haram, or from March 2015 the Islamic State, West Africa Province, as it now calls itself, is a proscribed group which has terrified Nigeria and its West African neighboring countries of Niger, Chad and Cameroon since 2009. Since its establishment it has overseen a reign of terror that has been marked by the deaths of over 20,000 people and the displacement of almost 3 million people,[1] making it one of the deadliest Salafi-jihadi groups presently operating.

The ideological basis for the group's teachings is well-documented in the translated videos and sermons of this book, but it is my argument that one needs to consider other social, economic and political factors as well when explaining Boko Haram's appeal. I do not suggest in any way that ideology is absent in Boko Haram's campaign, rather that this ideology needs to be placed within a larger context.[2]

2002 is widely cited as the year Boko Haram emerged. However, Boko Haram may have first appeared under a different name around the mid 1990s.[3] It was not until July 2009, however, following the extrajudicial killing of Muhammad Yusuf, the leader of Boko Haram, while he was in police custody (text 20), that Boko Haram transformed into a full-blown terrorist group. To understand the emergence of Boko Haram and how it has morphed from a social movement into the deadliest terrorist group in the world,[4] we need to discuss some more distant but important history as well as the immediate political conditions that influenced its emergence and trajectory.

One important historical event is the Iranian Revolution of 1979 under the leadership of Ayatollah Khomeini (d. 1989). Khomeini established an Islamic Republic and sparked a new wave of Islamic radicalism (that seeks to reinstate either one Islamic state or in practice several Islamic states) as can be seen across the Muslim world up to the present day. The influence of Ayatollah Khomeini in Nigeria is evident in the establishment of the Islamic Movement of Nigeria (IMN)—a pro-Shi'a sect led by Shaykh Ibrahim el Zakzaky, which constitutes about 5 per cent of Nigeria's Muslim population of 80 million and is Africa's largest Shi'a movement.[5] IMN is also influenced by the ideology of the leaders of the Muslim Brotherhood—Hasan al-Banna (d. 1949) and Sayyid Qutb (d. 1966).[6] Perhaps these eclectic ideologies and influences account for the appeal that some of the messages (especially the anti-Western messages) of IMN have for both Sunnis and Shi'ites in Nigeria.

The *Jama'at Izalat al-Bid'a wa-Iqamat al-Sunna* (Society for the Removal of Innovation and Reestablishment of the Sunna), known as the Izala or Yan Izala, is by far the most prominent Sunni group in Nigeria.[7] Unlike IMN, this Sunni group receives support from the Saudi Arabian government and stands in opposition to Iran's Shi'ism (represented by IMN), in their promotion of Sunni Islam and Salafism.[8] The external influences from Iran and Saudi Arabia polarized Nigerian Muslims along sectarian lines—Shi'a versus Sunni—in addition to the conservative Sufi Brotherhoods.

Despite the susceptibility of Nigerian Muslims to external influences, northern Nigeria, home to Nigeria's largest concentration of Muslims, has a longer history of Islamic revivalism rooted in the successful *jihād* of 'Uthmān Ibn Fūdī or Dan Fodio (1804–12). 'Uthmān Dan Fodio's *jihād* continues to be relevant and "provides a rallying point for political and religious legitimization for many Islamic activist groups in Nigeria, including both conservative (traditional Sufi Brotherhood) and insurgent groups (Boko Haram)."[9] However, contemporary Islamic activism in Nigeria has an internal dimension that is likely sympathetic to the northern Muslim elites.[10]

The internal dimension of religious crisis in Nigeria is reflected in the *shari'a* debate of 1977–1978 in the Constituent Assembly that ushered in the Second Republic and Nigeria's first ever democratically-elected administration. The *shari'a* debate is considered the first of Nigeria's religious crisis that polarized Nigerians along religious lines.[11] Although an ethno-religious war was averted at that time, shortly afterwards in 1980–1985 northern Nigeria was unfortunately gripped by the violent apocalyptic Maitatsine uprising.[12]

Another demonstration of the politicization of *shari'a* in Nigeria is found in the full enrolment of Nigeria as a member of the Organization of Islamic Cooperation (OIC) in 1986 during President Ibrahim Babangida's military regime (1895–93). The non-Muslim population, especially the newly-formed Christian Association of Nigeria (CAN)—an umbrella body for Christians and churches in Nigeria, and a

Obasanjo's policies

PART ONE: NIGERIAN PREACHERS (2006–2008)

counterweight to the Muslim leadership—vehemently protested Nigeria's inclusion, as it perceived such an initiative as an attack on Nigeria's secular status. However, the Muslim population, including the Yoruba Muslims in the southwest and the Muslim Students Society of Nigeria (MSSN), supported the move, not so much for its religious importance but for the perceived economic benefit that the membership would yield. *how boko haram came*

All the suppressed protests and agitations erupted following Nigeria's return to democratic government in 1999 (the Fourth Republic) after a long spell of military rule (1983–1999). The dawn of the Fourth Republic was marked by a heightened state of insecurity, criminality and disorder. The security apparati, especially the police, had been severely underfunded and incapacitated during the military era. Therefore, government was simply overwhelmed and incapable of providing security, leading to the emergence of state-endorsed vigilante groups across the geo-political zones. Groups such as the O'odua People's Congress (OPC) operated in the southwest; the Bakassi Boys provided security in the southeast, as did several *hisba* (non-state Islamic police enforcing *sharī'a*) groups in the north.

Traditional tribal/ethnic conflicts also re-emerged in the southwest between Ife *yes* and Modakeke, between Ijaw and Itsekiri in the Niger Delta, and between the Tiv and Jukun in the Middle Belt. The administration of President Olusegun Obasanjo (1999–2007) had to utilize the army frequently to quell some of these internal security problems with manifestations of massive human rights violations.

It is against this somewhat chaotic background that Boko Haram emerged. The hopeful feelings of this time were squandered as the newly established democratic government failed to meet the expectations of the vast numbers of unemployed youths, not to speak of its inability to peacefully resolve the various conflicts between warring ethnic groups. Furthermore, some of President Obasanjo's policies (the compulsory retirement of key military officers, who were largely northern Muslims) were considered anti-north and a strategic attempt to undermine the north's geo-political advantage.

Hence, the adoption of the *sharī'a* penal code in 1999 by the Governor of Zamfara state, Governor Sani Yerima, was perceived as a response to the geo-political threat to the north's political survival.[13] Shortly after the introduction of the *sharī'a* penal code in Zamfara, eleven other northern states including Sokoto, Kano, Gombe, Jigawa, and Kaduna adopted *sharī'a*, with varying degrees of success, and without considering very closely the implications of such a move.[14]

The northern political elites pursued a narrow political agenda with the adoption of *sharī'a* in the wake of Nigeria's Fourth Republic. But this narrow political objective was lost on the radicalizing youths and groups who only saw a golden opportunity to realize their dream of an Islamic state.

Here the idea of an Islamic state is distinct from the one pursued lately by Boko Haram and non-Nigerian groups like the Islamic State in Iraq and Syria (ISIS).

9

Rather, it was the product of frustration with the inequality and poverty brought about by globalization and the democratic government of Nigeria.[15] Unfortunately, globalization and democracy are widely seen as Western legacies. *Sharī'a* proffers an alternative route to prosperity, as it purports to discard the corruption, inequality and poverty that Western-oriented secular states engender. The Boko Haram leader, Muhammad Yusuf played a crucial role during this period as he was the Borno State representative on the Supreme Council for *sharī'a* in Nigeria.[16]

Yusuf later became a disciple of Abu Abdur-Rahman Muhammad Ali al-Barnawi, (the leader of the Nigerian Taliban, the predecessors to Boko Haram) in approximately 2002 after Ali's Shaykh and mentor Abu al-Bara al-Daurawi fled out of fear of being arrested to Saudi Arabia with the initial seed money received from members of al-Qaeda in the Arabian Peninsula.[17] By 2004, Ali led the Nigerian Taliban into conflict with the Nigerian authorities, especially around the group's commune located near Kanamma (close to the border with Niger). Yusuf took over Ali's followership after his death and led the movement until 2009. During this period, Yusuf and his followers rejected participating in democratic elections; thus, the accusation sometimes leveled at them that Yusuf and his followers were instrumental in the electoral victory of Ali Modu Sheriff, the Governor of Borno state from 2003 to 2007, seems controversial.

However, the failure of government to provide security (the most prominent of its attempts was "Operation Flush"—a security policy that aimed to bring discipline and orderliness to the state, but that was being used to collect bribes) led to several clashes between the state forces and the Boko Haram group, leading to the deaths of about 800 members of the group, the destruction of the Ibn Taymiyya Center (its headquarters), and the murder of Muhammad Yusuf on 30 July 2009 (text 20). These interlacing factors radicalized the group and set it on the path of violence.

DEBATE ON THE STATUS OF WESTERN EDUCATION AND WORKING FOR THE NIGERIAN GOVERNMENT BETWEEN MALLAM ISA ALI IBRAHIM PANTAMI AND MALLAM MUHAMMAD YUSUF MAIDUGURI

25 JUNE 2006

[Trans.: Abdulbasit Kassim]

During the period 2004–2008, there were several debates between Muhammad Yusuf and other Salafi scholars, but this is the first whose video is extant. His opponent, Isa Pantami is western-educated and much better prepared than Yusuf, either because the latter was not told of the subjects to be debated (part 7) or because his thoughts were not well-developed. The debate lasted for six hours, of which approximately three hours have survived on video. The full text of the extant videos is approximately forty-six pages long in ten parts.[1]

Part 1: Available at: https://www.youtube.com/watch?v=h-nhmj3faHc

Darul Islam Centre for the Propagation of the Religion of Islam, Bauchi Presents: *Debate on the Status of Western Education and Working for the Nigerian Government* between Mallam Isa Ali Ibrahim Pantami and Mallam Muhammad Yusuf Maiduguri.

[*Covering the logistics of the debate.*]

Part 2: Available at: https://www.youtube.com/watch?v=JlTOPgOzGkc

Pantami [P]: What I want both of us to start with first and foremost is a question to Mallam. [Pantami wants to confirm what he heard from Yusuf's lectures] My question is regarding the position of Mallam on Western education in Nigeria? What is Western education? Secondly, in brief, if Mallam provides us with answers to these questions then we will proceed with the debate on the issue of working with the government.

Muhammad Yusuf [Y]: [Introduction] Based on my understanding, Islam views all knowledge from three perspectives. According to the first perspective, there is knowledge that conforms to the teachings of the Qur'ān and the Sunna. The second perspective, there is knowledge that contradicts the Qur'ān and *ḥadīth*. The third perspective, there is knowledge that neither contradicts nor conforms to the teachings of the Qur'ān and the Sunna.

This is akin to the saying of the Prophet concerning the People of the Book [Jews and Christians]: "If they bring what conforms to what I brought accept it. If they bring something that contradicts what I brought, you should reject it. If they bring something that neither contradicts nor conforms to it, you have the privilege to take it or reject it." This is my understanding of Western education. If there is one benefit I would derive from this education, it is the knowledge itself and not the system as it operates in Nigeria. If it is the system, as Mallam said, because of the issues of morality I do not agree that we should enroll our children in [the system]; because of some reasons I have stated. This is my position based on the question asked by Mallam. Secondly, what is Western education? Western education is contemporary knowledge that came to us through European colonialism and it includes medicine, engineering, agriculture, geography, physics, biology, chemistry, and so on. All these disciplines together, and even the English language itself, once it does not contradict the Sunna of the Prophet, in its capacity as knowledge, there is no blame [in learning it]. If it contradicts the Sunna of the Prophet or the Qur'ān, it would be rejected. If it does not contradict or conflict with the Qur'ān then it is acceptable. If we have our schools, we can adopt those disciplines and teach them in our schools. The reason they cannot go to those schools, as I said, is not because of the disciplines, but because of the system. Allah knows best. I hope Mallam understands me.

P: What Mallam intends by this explanation is that if a student wants to go to Maiduguri, for example, to the University of Maiduguri, or Bayero University in Kano, to study either medicine or engineering or any other discipline—according to Mallam's understanding, is it permissible or forbidden?

Y: In my understanding, with the system that we have in Nigeria, it is not permissible.

P: "It is not permissible" is different from "forbidden." What I want to hear: is it permissible for him to go or is it forbidden?

Y: The verdict can be changed because of a reason.[2]

12

P: Yes.

Y: If I say it is forbidden then it means the verdict cannot be changed. Even if it can change we can still call it forbidden. Is it not so?

P: Alright! This is it.

Y: However, you should understand that the verdict can still change but there is a reason at present that prevent it from being changed.

P: For instance, in this month, if a student secures an admission and wants to go to BUK (Bayero University, Kano) to study.

Y: That is what I said that it is not permissible.

P: "It is not permissible" is equivocal.

Y: If I may ask, what is the difference?

P: There is a difference. What is not permissible may be, in the first place, something that is discouraged, it can be completely forbidden, and it can even be austere than that. Its non-permissibility can create a study of Islamic jurisprudence.

Y: Okay, it is forbidden.

P: Forbidden. This is what I needed to hear. Secondly, there is also the issue of teaching in Western education or working with the government. A Muslim working here at the Bauchi specialist hospital and his intention is to assist his people—this is one case. A second case is someone who teaches in a Comprehensive or Government Science Secondary School in Gombe, or works at the Radio House or lectures at Advanced Level Colleges; is this permissible in Nigeria or forbidden in this system?

Y: This system is bilateral. There are some occupations that have ties of loyalty to the laws of the land. There are other occupations that affect the people (social services) but do not have ties of loyalty to the laws of the land. The occupations that have ties of loyalty to the laws of the land are not permissible, they are forbidden. On the contrary, the occupations that do not have ties of loyalty to the laws of the land directly, there are diverging views of scholars on them.[3]

[Discussion about the permissiblity/non-permissibility of the third category of occupations.]

Y: I am pleased that Mallam brought us to this field [of evolution]. Firstly, among the subjects there are some topics in biology, these topics, as it is well-known they are based on Darwinism or the theory of Charles Darwin. In these topics, they believe that the origin of man is not as Allah says: "We created man out of an extract of clay." (Q23:12) They see the origin of man as a chemical that evolved into an insect, and became so-and-so until it became human. From there, they even anticipate that man will still evolve, according to their own thinking.

Secondly, there is a topic in *Geography*, the theory of revolution. In their perspective, the world moves in a way they understand, not in the way that Allah created the world, with the sun. They have what they call the "ten planets," just as Ibn Taymiyya[4] narrated, or nine planets—with the addition of the sun they become ten. These ideas, after they invented them, in their own research, do not conform to the sayings of the Qur'ān and *ḥadīth*. Furthermore, they gave them the names of the Greek idols such as Mercury, Venus, Earth, Mars, Jupiter, Saturn, and Uranus and so on. This way of thinking contradicts the Qur'ān and Sunna. The study of these ideas cannot be made permissible based on this contradiction.

The second reason is the subject of sociology where they have a problem with the existence of Allah. In their view, they are not sure whether Allah exists or not. One of their substantial [pieces of] evidence is based upon the claim that since Allah is invisible then there is no Allah. Then again there is the subject of geology. They have what they call the Big Bang theory. In this theory, they postulated the idea that Allah...

Part 3: Available at: https://www.youtube.com/watch?v=4tXxFxHKqv8

Y: Allah created the world during 1,600,000,000 years, three minutes and one second.[5] This contradicts the saying of Allah: "Indeed We have created the heavens and the earth and what is between them in six days and We were not touched by weariness." (Q50:38) There is also a topic in geography at the university level that deals with the time scale. This time scale reveals the things that Allah created, for example, within the range of four million years.

P: On what page is that?

Y: *Geography*, the time scale. These years they mentioned contradict the saying of Allah: "Say: 'Do you really disbelieve in Him who created the earth in [two days] and assign equals to Him? That is the Lord of the worlds.' And He set up immovable mountains upon it and blessed it, and ordained therein varied provisions in four days equally to all those who ask." (Q41:9–10)

What this verse [selection] is saying is: will you disbelieve in Him who created the land in two days, and take partners with Him? He is the creator of all living things and He put stones (mountains and hills) on the land in two days. He places the stones from above and blessed it. Then He foreordained the food that people will eat inside during four days.

In chemistry, there is a topic on energy. They claim that its origin was not created, it does not have an end, nor will it ever become extinct. Allah knows best. This characterization is like an attribute of Allah, who was not created and He does not have an end. [Yusuf cites Ibn Taymiyya's book *al-Furqān bayna awliyā' al-Raḥmān wa-awliyā' al-Shayṭān (The Distinction between the Friends of the Merciful One and those of Satan)* to back his claim.]

DEBATE ON THE STATUS OF WESTERN EDUCATION

P: Peace be upon you. Just as Mallam is identifying these topics, before we move further in the debate, I want us to clarify some of them like the issue of biology, Charles Darwin and his theory. What is your position on education in general—particularly regarding the student who studies other subjects unconnected to this theory?

Y: I do not understand.

P: For example, I can enroll in the university to study and not study any of these theories.

Y: What you are saying is which field is he [Darwin] against and why is he against such a field?

P: For example, if Charles Darwin is not included in the study, is it permissible for a student to go and study it?

Y: If there is no such ideology, right! What will prevent it?

[Discussion about Yusuf's evidence that the theory of evolution and revolution is disbelief.]

Y: May Allah's blessing be on you. The saying that there are nine planets—does the Qur'ān or the Sunna confirm it?

P: Whether they have confirmed it or not, where is the proof that they contradict it? Bring the evidence that they contradict it. And what exactly *are* the nine planets, how are they contradictory?

Y: Listen to me. Be sure that you have proof that says the Qur'ān and Sunna accept the nine planets.

P: And do you agree that even if the Qur'ān and Sunna did not accept them, once they are silent regarding the matter, without contradicting it, then that can be used as evidence. Do you agree before I start to talk? Because you have divided knowledge into three: there is the category that conforms to the Qur'ān, the category that contradicts the Qur'ān, and the category that neither conforms nor contradicts. You agree with this division; may Allah reward you?

Y: If it does not contradict it, yes.

[*Discussing the issue of the planets according to Ibn Taymiyya.*]

Y: This is what I wanted to explain to you. I said that these nine planets; in their own system, that is what they said. And what Ibn Taymiyya said about 'ten planets', they are the same creation the atheists [non-Muslims] confirmed to be nine,[6] together with the sun which made it ten. Secondly, I said there are those who say it means the number of the worlds. There are those who say they are nine worlds. Then I said, if we take it to be so [the worlds], but Allah said the worlds are seven, seven heavens. That is what you heard.

[Pantami insists that the nine planets is not referring to the seven heavens.]

Part 4: Available at: https://www.youtube.com/watch?v=Ox3VPUYRj7s

[*Discussing the planets and the theory of evolution. Pantami states that there is no necessity for a Muslim to study evolution in the university, as he himself did not.*]

P: Mallam, between you and Allah, did you attend primary school in your life?

Y: I did not.

P: You did not attend. So, in principle how can a person give a religious ruling on the permissibility or non-permissibility of something when he did not even attend primary school in his life? [Yusuf says his position is modeled after Ibn Taymiyya's position.]

Part 5: Available at: https://www.youtube.com/watch?v=G_UVaYu3dIA

Y: [Discussion about how context shape religious rulings.] Here is the ruling of the Permanent Committee for Islamic Research and Religious Edicts[7] dated on the third of the second month (Safar) of 1420 AH [19 May 1999]. They said, "This Permanent Committee for Islamic Research and Religious Edicts" which I am certain you know, they said that "they have read several books and questions that came to them ..."

P: Mallam, please can you start over from the beginning?

Y: They said: "They researched the books that came to them and several questions, as well as further explanations because of the way foreign schools and other alien colleges were spreading in the land of Muslims." Since the question, they asked Ibn 'Uthaymīn ...[8]

P: In a land of Muslims.

Y: In *the* land of Muslims.

P: In a land of Muslims, it is not *the* land of Muslims. You added a definite article, Mallam.

Y: "...in a land of the Muslims, and the mission that they intend to spread with those schools that they [non-Muslims] have built—not because of piety and not for the pleasure of Allah—but were established only according to the Europeans' methodology."

P: What is the Europeans' methodology?

DEBATE ON THE STATUS OF WESTERN EDUCATION

Y: The methodology of Western Europeans.

P: Continue...

Y: You understand, "it does not relate to Islam, the language of Islam and the history of Islam."

P: They do not relate. Take note of these words.

Y: "...the language of Islam; they do not relate to the history of Islam." You should take note of these two things.

P: Yes.

Y: They do not relate to Islam in language and history. "It does not escape any Muslim, upon whom Allah has bestowed understanding, the severity of the Jews' and Christians' enmity towards the Muslims. They will never stop their onslaught on Islam and Muslims day and night. They have taken different measures and attempted to find every means to wreak havoc on the Muslims. They want to remove the Muslims from their religion of truth towards the abyss of misguidance. They fought Muslims with weapons for many years during the time of colonial rule. Then they came to teach the lessons of skepticism, in the minds of Muslims, skepticism about their religion, their Qur'ān and their Prophet [Muhammad].

This is what they call intellectual warfare or the battle of hearts and minds, until the issue came down to accusing the Muslims concerning their affairs, their minds and consciousness, through the process of establishing these foreign schools and alien colleges where atheistic beliefs are taught. A person, who takes some type of instruction in one path, finds other things permissible that were forbidden in other paths. They have tried to create a system, overt and covert, to attract many Muslims to misguide and destroy them. They have tried hard to increase the number of schools, inviting people to them, until those schools are now present in all societies of Muslims, where Muslim boys and girls are now trained."

P: Hmmm, no, I am not challenging your statement. I am only paying attention to your pronunciation.

Y: I made a mistake in the pronunciation. Are you satisfied?

P: I am not mocking you. This is all about brotherhood.

Y: If a person should make a mistake, it is better to correct him. "They were training Muslim children, male and female to the point where Muslims were in doubt because of their training. That is one part of questioning religious knowledge and manners. Western education also destroys ethics and the Islamic creed, and moreover it places the *umma* at the mercy of its adversaries." Allah is sufficient for us and He is the best disposer of all affairs!

"There were some scholars of Islam, may Allah accept their good deeds, in the Levant, Egypt, the Arabian Peninsula and other regions who explained the dangers of these schools in the land of Muslims. These schools are a preparation or a reinforcement on the part of Islam's adversaries to extend their attempted elimination of Islam from the minds and lives of the Muslims.

Firstly, the establishment of foreign schools and alien colleges in the land of the Muslims is a problem, together with other problems of systematic warfare which the Muslims face at their adversaries' hands, particularly in the missionary schools. This is a dangerous measure. Those who were confused, here is the step that the scholars and the Committee took to reveal the facts of this deception and the solution for the *umma*. We have once provided the ruling of the Committee no. 2096, which is dated on the twenty-second of the twelfth month (Dhū al-Ḥijja) of 1418 AH [20 April 1998] in the book where we discussed the problem of the Christians' threats. Besides the problems of the Christians, there is also the problem of the establishment of foreign schools in the Muslims' land.

Secondly, in addition to the discussion, this is the ruling: "It is not permissible for Muslims to allow the establishment of foreign schools and alien colleges. It is not permissible to strengthen or allow them to be entrenched. It is not permissible for them to be accepted. It is not permissible to enroll Muslim children in them, because they are a medium for destroying the teachings of Islam and ethics. This is an apparent danger and a confirmed source of corruption. It is compulsory to debunk [the idea of foreign schools] and block all doors which bring them into existence. The issue will even increase with the establishment of such schools, particularly in the Arabs' land, because the Prophet said, 'Two religions should not be together in the Arabian Peninsula.'"[9]

The unrecorded section probably opens with the question of governance and the necessity for Muslims to participate in the government. This is a crucial difference between Yusuf and the Salafi scholars, and Pantami immediately brings out the Qur'ānic proof of Joseph, who according to Q12:55, had control over Egypt, and worked for Pharaoh, an "unbeliever".

Part 6: Available at: https://www.youtube.com/watch?v=Rq-OgUWMAVA

P: The Prophet Joseph held authority in the land of the Pharaoh [Egypt]. At that time in the land of Pharaoh, they said, "He was taking charge of its monetary affairs and its likes; he acted in the capacity that a finance minister would act today." Because "He said: 'Put me in charge of the treasures of the land; I am a keeper who knows'" (Q12:55) as a minister of finance in Egypt, in place of al-'Azīz [Potiphar],[10] who was dead at that time. One should note that the exegetes explained that the "treasures"— which are storehouses—are things related to property. They said: "It is well known that being a member of parliament or holding a ministerial post affords an individual the political power to protect the people against injustice"—they said this [position] is permissible. "This power is synonymous to the power that was held because of tribal affiliation—of some people in the past."

[*Pantami gives several other examples of Qur'ānic participants in government, and the reasons Muslim scholars have held such participation to be beneficial based on the experience of the Prophet Shu'ayb, who was persecuted by his people, until Yusuf finally interrupts him.*]

[Yusuf interrupts Pantami for interfering in his attempt to explain his position on how religious rulings are issued.]

P: May Allah forgive you, Mallam. I did not intend to take over the conversation. Once you draw my attention, I did not get angry; that was why I stopped.

Y: Secondly, the issue that they discussed, as I said, this is not the issue we are critiquing. Thirdly, you skipped into what we intended to discuss ahead—which is the issue of working with the Nigerian government. You said they gave a ruling that the Prophet Joseph worked under a secular government, but they brought only one opinion. By bringing one opinion—honestly, that is not how scholars have been interpreting—that it is acceptable, [merely] because the Prophet Joseph worked under a secular government, [concluding that working under the Nigerian government] is certainly acceptable.

P: This is the reason I want to read al-Qurṭubī, *al-Jāmiʿ*...

Y: But they are not the people who said so.

P: The reason is because they are qualified to give their deliberations in understanding the issue. If al-Qurṭubī cited one ruling, then scholars are qualified to deliberate. Can they not deliberate?

Y: It is not the opinion of one scholar he cited.

[Discussion of the drawback of having contrasting views.]

Part 7: Available at: https://www.youtube.com/watch?v=Uv4kfkzxlNw

[Yusuf complains about the organization of the topics of the debate.]

Y: Secondly, the explanation that Shaykh ʿAbd al-Raḥmān b. Nāṣir Saʿdī brought regarding the verse of *sūrat Hūd* (Q11:91)—we have read it. I mean, the verse that Allah says, the people of Shu'ayb said: "Were it not for your family, we would have stoned you, for you are not too dear [to be stoned]." (Q11:91) He established a proof based on this verse that there can be a Republic. And Allah knows best. I do not know what they mean by a republic. They did not say that one should work with the secular government. He only talked about the existence of a Republic.

P: This is the response that they gave you, I cannot do the exegesis now, but among them there were students who studied directly with him. I came with the [text of the] *Taysīr* where he talked about a Republic.[11] I came with it.

Y: This is what I am telling you I saw. What is here contradicts his *Taysīr*.

P: The word "Republic" is his statement, and so I can read what he meant by that word.

[*Discussion about the different version of Taysīr al-Karīm al-Rahman and the meaning of a republic.*]

Y: May Allah reward you. Secondly, about the issue of the field of medicine or doctors, on this subject we do not have anything to say. It is these disciplines you are discussing. We are not condemning the discipline itself; it is the method that we debated. These disciplines are the ones regarding which you said that you have evidence—if they are true or not?

P: May Allah forgive Mallam, here they are. I did not mean to interrupt you. The things you said are what? They are theories?

Y: Yes, they are.

P: Since they are theories, what I meant was that there is no way someone can study medicine without studying biology. It is never possible. There is no one who can study engineering without studying chemistry—that is what you were talking about. The issues you brought up regarding geography—sometimes as you talked about solar energy, for instance, mixing up things like biology, medicine, and engineering—there are places where they studied all these things with geography or geology as prerequisites. Because they are intertwined, if you are studying one you must study the other.

[Pantami read the ruling of Ibn 'Uthaymīn on the permissibility of studying theories that contradict Islam in order to critique it. He also spoke about the Islamization of knowledge at different higher institutions in Northern Nigeria. In his book "Beyond Timbuktu: An Intellectual History of Muslim West Africa", Professor Ousmane Kane provided detailed explanation of the Islamization of knowledge in West Africa see chapter 7 pp. 140–159.]

Part 8: Available at: https://www.youtube.com/watch?v=I03W3mlRf98

P: Let me ask you one question. There is a *hadīth* I know you usually read, because I know, though I did not hear it myself. It was a student who told me about it, but I said I was not convinced, and he should bring me the cassette [in which it was cited]. Until now, he has not brought it to me. In the *hadīth*, the Prophet said "Rulers will come to you, bringing the evillest people close by, who will delay the set-prayers from their set-times. Whoever reaches this time let him not be a tribal chieftain ('arīf), a policeman (*shurṭi*), a tax-collector, or one who seals documents."[12] [Discussion about the weakness of the Hadith.] We have already examined the *ḥadīth* and it is not authentic. The way we understand the research which I did, this *ḥadīth* is among the pillars upon which you build your preaching.

Y: This [tradition] is not part of the pillars of my preaching. Certainly, you said you are conversant hearing this *ḥadīth* from me.

P: No, I am not conversant hearing it from you.

Y: Did you not say you use to hear it from me?

P: I have heard from someone who attributed it to you, but I have not heard it from you. This is the reason I am asking you.

Y: Then why did you say it is among the pillars of my preaching?

P: The reason is that I once had a debate with some students who studied in your place [school] and I heard them reciting the same *ḥadīth*. I researched the *ḥadīth* and what scholars wrote about it. This is it. If you said so, I want us to clarify the *ḥadīth* and proceed if possible?

Y: Let me explain to you. Firstly, we have been discussing this *ḥadīth* in question and the way al-Albānī classified it after some five years of research.

[Yusuf discusses his research on the weakness of the hadith.]

P: But did you tell the people [that you do not agree with it]?

Y: Yes, indeed.

P: Okay, praise be to Allah. We previously sat here with some students, and I said the *ḥadīth* is not authentic. They said no! They said it is authentic.

Y: It's been long, since [the month of] Shaʿban[13] when we received *al-Nāṣiḥa fī tahdhīb al-Silsila al-Ṣaḥīḥa*. We came to Abuja at the time and I think we came to either this town or somewhere else. We also came to Kano, then we got the book and we went to check it. It was in the month of Shaʿban that we did the sitting [for discussion]. Then they brought this new abrogation of al-Albānī;[14] so we went on to refute that scholar because of what we read. Thereafter, we called our students in the university on the phone, but they said they do not know this book. The student we called said he has never seen this book, but that the book, if it is acceptable in Saudi Arabia, should be allowed into the country. If it is not allowed into the country, then the scholars did not certify it. However, he gave us three names of scholars who critiqued al-Albānī, but his name was not among the three. Therefore, after this Great Festival [at the end of Ramadan, October 2005] we received the book of Shuʿayb [al-Arnaut] here. Then we saw what al-Albānī relied upon...

P: This is the book.

Y: It is in the book; it was at this point we dropped the *ḥadīth*.

P: Yes, as it is, I had wanted us to talk about it. Based on my understanding, if I am not mistaken, most of the students can accept that interpretation.

[Pantami discusses his research on the weakness of the hadith.]

Y: We are speaking about the issue that scholars have explained, pertaining to the affairs of the predecessors. Because of that, what should we leave?

P: Sorry, this *ḥadīth*, is there a cassette where you openly stated that the *ḥadīth* is not authentic?

Y: Yes, indeed.

P: Because the reason is there is a brother who said you know that it is not authentic but you conceal it and I told him: no. I do not want suspicion. To avoid suspicion like this, I will want you to send me the cassette so that I can convince him and maybe there is something I want to take from it.

Y: By Allah's permission. I believe even yesterday I was asked here in Bauchi and I gave this explanation. Even yesterday, in the study we did or did you not hear it?

[Pantami is satisfied with Yusuf's response.]

Y: As such, let us proceed with the explanation on the issue of working with the government and the understanding of the predecessors. You said something with which I am going to disagree. I mean what you talked about the scholars who discussed [the legitimacy of obtaining a] passport—if we take their discussion on passports and their discussion on working with the government and relate it to the predecessors...

P: This is not what I mean. You did not understand what I mean. Every time we want to talk, let us talk with facts. The time has changed and there is no scholar among the Sunnis who is in a doubt that when an environment changes there are religious issues that can change. There are those who say it can change including the issue of declaring Muslims to be unbelievers (*takfīr*) or other issues. This is what I mean. [Pantami says this subject should only be discussed by scholars.]

Y: Yes, so bring their explanation.

P: It is you who should bring your explanation.

Y: Me? I *have* brought my explanation.

P: Which one did you bring?

Y: I brought the explanation of Ibn Qayyim [al-Jawziyya][15] and the explanation that you mentioned concerning verses and *ḥadīths* that I brought, but you said that is not how you understood them. Anyway, that is the principle of debate. If I bring verses and you say that is not how you understand them, then you should clarify them according to your own understanding. May Allah help me—I will take your own interpretation, if it turns out to be correct.

[Pantami quotes the ruling of Dr. Abd al-'Aziz b. Ahmad al Bajadi on the permissibility of working with an un-Islamic government as long as the work does not have ties to constitution.]

Part 9: Available at: https://www.youtube.com/watch?v=-LidIYH-eI4

[Pantami support the permissibility of working with an un-Islamic government to ease the suffering of other Muslims. Yusuf considers it forbidden as long as the job is tied to the constitution.]

P: What is the position of those who work in these [civil service government] jobs; is this permissible or forbidden? If it is forbidden, are you going to impose some religious rulings on them or will they be pardoned? [*Pantami and Yusuf burst into laughter*] Take note, I said it only in a lighter mood, not for mischief. It is nothing, just light discussion, so do not take it as something serious, because it is nothing. There is no negativity about it.

Y: The issue that concerns the *sharī'a* or working with the security [forces], as we said. Firstly, all the followers of Sunna have reached a consensus on the principle of declaring a Muslim an unbeliever (*takfīr*). Anything that constitutes unbelief, if an unbeliever does it; he is already an unbeliever, no query. He does not have to do it to become an unbeliever. But if a person is a practicing Muslim and he performs the actions of unbelief, we need to follow the principles [of apostasy].

One, it should be that the person does not have an interpretation that he hides behind, whether it is a verse or *ḥadīth*, even if it is weak, as long as he does not know it is weak. Two, it should be clear that he does not have doubt that makes him see his action as good and there is no reason to eliminate that doubt. Three, we also need to be clear that he received no message at all notifying him that his action is wrong. Fourth, there is also the case of doubt, misinterpretation, and coercion.

P: Yes, there is the condition of coercion.

Y: There is coercion. But if a person is being coerced, we cannot call him an unbeliever. But if a person is committing unbelief, and you inform him this is unbelief, but he says: "No, it is not" [then he needs to be labeled]. This is our position on declaring a Muslim an unbeliever.

[Discussion of the principles of takfir. Yusuf argues that the judges in the Shari'a courts do not rule according to the Shari'a rather they rule on the basis of the penal code.]

Part 10: Available at: https://www.youtube.com/watch?v=PFhYWeLWEyk

[Discussion of the requirements of Shari`a judges.]

Y: These requirements which were written, I have known about them even before I understood my current belief. In the past, I have participated in the Committee of *sharī'a*, therefore...

P: Sorry, I am confirming that you indeed participated in the committee. We have sat together with you in previous meetings within the past four to five years. Can you remember the time?

Y: Yes, I remember in Gombe, right? At that time, the job we were given was to investigate the judges they have in Borno state and to determine whether or not they are qualified to render *sharī'a* rulings or not, and on what basis they rule at that time. We went around and investigated. It is based on my investigation that I concluded that they are not working with the *sharī'a*. Based on what I know.

P: They do not work with the *sharī'a*?

Y: At that time and based on my knowledge. For example, you can see a judge who does not have any business with the books of the *sharī'a*.

P: Yes, mostly there is no doubt because of the immorality of the people, like the one I know, in one town. Sorry, there are judges whom we have confidence of their probity such as Mallam Abdullah Sadiq. If a woman goes in front of him, she must put on a veil before he allows her to sit. According to his own principles of *sharī'a*, he does not need to see her face. [Discussion about the virtuous and dishonest judges.] Furthermore, what is Mallam's understanding regarding the occupation of the individual who studied law, for example?

Y: It is not permissible for the individual who studied law to perform the job of a lawyer.

P: Okay, what is the reason?

Y: The reason is the work he does and the court to which he goes to do those jobs—firstly, just as you cited those rulings of scholars, he is working directly with the constitution. He has studied the constitution and he is working for the constitution; it is the constitution he is defending and the constitution he knows, and all other things derive from it. The way they honor judges and so forth—that is not what Islam teaches and then the words... the profession changes the rulings of Islam in favor of the laws of the constitution.

P: Words like what?

Y: For example, honorifics like "My Worship" or "My Lord."

P: Okay. Honorifics like "My Worship"—between Allah and myself, I cannot speak about them, because I did not investigate them. But other words like "My Lord"—I asked a lawyer, who knows what is taught to Muslims, and he said what they mean by this honorific is not excessive praise. Simply what they mean is "May Allah help the law." That is how they say it. May Allah help the law. That is the interpretation of the honorific.

Y: But I heard a meaning contrary to that interpretation.

P: The lawyer who interpreted it to me is sitting there; he is a lawyer.

Y: My lawyer is not...

P: If you say your lawyer, we understand what you mean because you may be relating to him as a trusted friend of yours, or this may be a blood relation. It can take any form.

Y: He said what they mean is praise that exceeds limits (ḥudūd) of Allah

[Yusuf insists that the principles of takfir should be applied to lawyers before excommunication.]

P: The principles [of *takfir*]; no doubt, no ignorance, no misinterpretation. He is part of an occupation, but does not agree with it, except to advocate on behalf of Muslims, due to certain conditions.

Y: No! This is not what I am talking about.

P: Then what do you mean?

Y: The issue of the occupation, is it permissible or not? I said it is not permissible if it is related to the constitution. Is that not true? If it is not related to the constitution, there are contradictory views. And we took these different views and proceeded with them. Then we proceeded into a discussion where there are those who said even with the constitution they do not agree with [being a lawyer]. That is why we are discussing the issue of the occupation.

[Pantami asks Yusuf about the permissibility of practicing Law as a profession.]

Y: I am not seeing the permissibility of this type of job. Because I told you that all occupations directly related to the constitution, I do not consider them permissible.

P: Okay, what is the reason, Mallam?

Y: The reason is the job shows obedience to the master of the constitution.

P: Obedience to it? If someone works with it, then it means he is obedient?

Y: Yes, that is obedience.

P: It is possible regarding certain conditions, which are not his free will.

Y: How?

P: Because of the need of his fellow Muslims who cannot do anything other than that. The reason is, the word of condition, it is important that we clarify, perhaps we may achieve consensus or maybe we will disagree with each other. [...] here is a Muslim who has been cheated; there is no other way for him to claim his rights except through what I have studied. I will not advocate for him because of my conviction, but then they might cheat him. He will not have any means of claiming his rights, except through me. This is my point.

Y: For instance, you studied [law], you do not have a position in the Bar, you do not have anything you were just sitting, someone was cheated and you went to help him.

P: There are those who do not have a position in the Bar. Look at him [the lawyer, sitting in the audience]—he studied law, but there is nothing that brings him together with the occupation. [Discussion about those who study Law and do not practice it.]

Y: It is not permissible. It is not permissible for him to do the work.

P: What is the reason?

Y: The reason is he will be following the constitution. [The debate did not end on a satisfactory note. Both parties disagree on the concept of obedience and how it should be applied to the constitution.]

2

TRANSLATION OF SELECTIONS FROM MUHAMMAD YUSUF

HĀDHIHĪ ʿAQIDATUNĀ WA-MINHĀJ DAʿWATINĀ
(*THIS IS OUR CREED AND METHOD OF PROCLAMATION*)[1]

(c. 2006/2007)

[Trans.: David Cook]

This text is 168 pages, written in Arabic, and was most likely composed in late 2006 or 2007, as it mentions the work of Abu Musʿab al-Zarqawi (killed 2006). It was probably composed because of Yusuf's poor showing in the debate against Pantami (text 1), to justify his views. Much of the text is methodological in nature, and is heavily dependent upon the Saudi Salafis previously noted. The important sections concern democracy—identified as "the idol of this age"—education, the national symbols of the police and army, the Shiʿa, the Sufi orders, and the full implementation of shariʿa. As far as Salafi-jihadi writings go, it is not particularly original, especially as much of it consists of quotations, but within the context of northern Nigerian Muslim thought it stands out because of its radical anti-national and anti-educational emphasis.

[Introduction]

And then, the truest discourse is Allah's words, the best guidance is the guidance of Muhammad, the worst of matters are the newest, as everything new is an innovation, and every innovation is an error, and every error is in the Fire.[2] [Standard Islamic opening]

(p. 16) Everyone who claims that new inventions and technology are inventors and creators without taking Allah into account is one of the materialist philosophers, who do not believe and do not affirm the existence of Allah—who is far raised above their corrupt creed. Whoever divides between the [divine] creation of living beings, humans and jinn, quadrupeds and cattle, sun, moon and stars, [seas] and the mountains, and the heavens and the earth [on one side], and the new contemporary technological inventions in the act of invention, creation and origination is one of the heretics (ahl al-ahwā). [...]

(p. 31) Whoever associates anything with Allah in his worship, as if he prays to Allah and to others, or venerates Allah and others, or works for honor and this world, or studies for a worldly purpose, is a polytheist unbeliever. The Almighty said: "Let him who hopes to meet his Lord do what is good and associate none in the worship of his Lord." (Q18:110) [...]

(p. 33) Those who follow their legal system, and resort to illegitimate rulers (ṭawāghīt) for judgments are polytheists, as the Parliament and representatives combine deifying themselves and associating others with Allah. This is because they have a "mace"[3] which they venerate by various means, like bowing, submission, and humiliation by which they deify it as a system, because they do not follow any [other] system.

(p. 37) We do not believe in democracy, which has appeared on the face of the earth at the hands of Allah's enemies, the Jews and the Christians. In the name of freedom, and popular rule, they claim to be Allah, but we know absolutely that justice resides in that which Allah has revealed, not in that which humans have made as a system.

(pp. 51–2) We follow the Imams of the Muslims and "those in authority over them," but do not accept perfection from any other than Allah's Messenger, and the prophets. We are with the Sunna and the grouping; in our preaching, we do not vary an inch from them. [52] Nor do we revolt against our imams, even if they are unrighteous and do wrong as long as they do not commit infidelity. This is just as Allah's Messenger has ordered us: "Umm al-Ḥasīn said: "I performed the pilgrimage rite with Allah's Messenger at the Farewell Pilgrimage. Allah's Messenger said many things, but then I heard him say: 'If a mutilated slave is made commander over you'— she [Umm al-Ḥasīn] thought he said: 'black—'who leads you with the Book of Allah, then hear and obey him.'"

I [Yusuf] say: Allah's Messenger made that conditional upon his leading with the Book of Allah.

(p. 53) Ibn Baṭṭāl said [...] the jurisprudents have a consensus to obey the dominating ruler and to fight together with him. Obeying him is better than rebelling against him, to avoid shedding of blood and to calm disturbances (duhma). Their proof is this report, and others that support it. They only excluded from this prohibition when the ruler has fallen into open unbelief. Then it is not permissible to obey him;

indeed, it is obligatory to fight him, to the best of one's ability [from Ibn Ḥajar's *Fatḥ al-bārī*, book of tribulations, 13/9].

Al-Qāḍī [al-ʿIyāḍ] said: If unbelief and changing the Law, or innovation have gotten into him, then he is outside the law of rulership, and obedience to him falls away. Revolting against him is incumbent upon the Muslims, and the appointment of a just imam, if it is within their power to do so. If this is only possible for a group, then it is incumbent upon them to rise and remove the unbeliever. But this [removal] is not incumbent for the innovator, other than if they think that they have the power over him—if impotence is apparent, then it is not necessary to revolt. [In that case] let the Muslim emigrate from his land to another, and flee with his religion. [54]

I [Yusuf] say: From this open unbelief, the ruling is according to the law of the *jāhiliyya*, which has become dominant over the lands of the Muslims. Ibn ʿUthaymin said: "Whoever does not rule according to what Allah has revealed, makes light of it, treats it with contempt, or believes that something other than it is better or more beneficial for the people, is an unbeliever, whose unbelief has expelled him from the *umma*."

[...] I say, with the aid of Allah, this is one of the basis of the belief of the Sunnis—I mean, obedience to those given authority—of which many people today are ignorant or pretend ignorance. Many of them speak about the obedience of those given authority as an absolute, but do not distinguish between committing unbelief and disobedient actions, despite the clarity of the traditions and statements of the forefathers concerning that issue. [59]

[...] Ibn Taymiyya stated in his *Majmūʿat al-fatāwā*, [vol.] 38, p. 277: "This is the way of the best of this community past and present." [...] On this basis, we follow the rulers of the Muslims according to the Book and the Sunna, even if they are unjust, iniquitous and do wrong, as long as they do not command rebellion against Allah. Al-Bukhārī cites a tradition on the authority of [ʿAbd Allāh] b. ʿUmar: "Hearing and obedience is incumbent upon the Muslim man in that which he likes and dislikes unless he is commanded to a rebellious action. When he is commanded to a rebellious action, then there is no further hearing or obedience." [60]

When they commit unbelief then rebelling against them is obligatory to the one who is capable; for the one who has no capability then it is incumbent upon him to emigrate, just as we cited previously from the statement of al-Qāḍī ʿIyāḍ.

At that time, we must revolt against them and not obey them, but when they do wrong or are iniquitous, as long as they lead us by the Book of Allah, we will obey them, so long as they do not order a rebellious action against Allah. When they order a rebellious action against Allah, then there is no further hearing or obedience. This is our proclamation, and we announce it to the *umma*. We call the people to reform the creed, application of the Law and to *jihād*.

We do not follow the Jews or the Christians: "O believers do not take the Jews and the Christians as friends; some of them are friends of each other. Whoever of you takes them as friends is surely one of them. Allah indeed does not guide the wrongdoers." (Q5:51) We do not associate with them in any of their methods, such as democracy, dictatorship, communism, or capitalism. We are not with them in their Parliament, and do not learn Aristotelian or Platonic knowledge from them.

We will clarify some of their methods and unbelief in the different schools that is completely contradictory to the Islamic method and teachings, because many of the people have been deceived under the name [61] of knowledge, advancement and civilization, so have gone astray and led astray many from the *umma*. The one who is protected, is protected by Allah. After this section, the clarification concerning democracy will come, because democracy is the shadow of unbelief, atheism, permissiveness and the dawning of Western education. [62]

(pp. 64–65) The difference between Islam and democracy or secularism is huge, and is apparent in the basic principle, the result, the method, and the goal of these supposed freedoms.

1. Freedom of religion, [65]
2. Freedom of opinion
3. Freedom of ownership
4. Personal freedom

against democracy too

The fighter, Abu Mus'ab Ahmad al-Zarqawi,[4] may Allah have mercy upon him, said: "Democracy has come to us saying: The people in the democratic system are the ruler and the point of reference, and have the decisive word in all decisions. But the truth in this infidel illegitimate system is that it says to the one who desires the people's decision...his will is sacred to the democrats, his choice compulsory, and his opinions progressive. His rule is wise and just according to the unbelievers, and whoever he exalts is exalted, whoever he humbles is humiliated, so that whatever the people forbid is forbidden, and whatever they permit is allowed." [...]

(p. 69) Second, democracy is founded upon the freedom of religion, so that the man in the shadow of democratic organizations can believe what he wishes, and follow whatever religion he wishes, apostatize from whatever religion whenever he wishes, even if this apostasy leads to leaving Allah's religion for atheism and worshipping something other than Allah—a matter that is without a doubt void, corrupt, and in opposition to most of the legal texts. These affirm that for the Muslim, if he apostatizes from his religion and *sharīʿa* in favor of unbelief, his penalty in Islam is death, just as in the *ḥadīth*, which al-Bukhārī and others have related: "Whoever changes their religion—kill him, but if not, then leave him."[5] The apostate cannot make a covenant, receive protection, nor hospitality—there is nothing in Allah's religion for him, other than the demand for his repentance or the sword. [...]

(p. 72) Fifth, democracy is founded upon the separation of religion from the state, politics and from life. What is Allah's is Allah's, which is fulfillment of worship among the Sufis and in the prayer rooms—whatever else in the political, economic

penalty

and social domains is, according to them, in the province of the people, just as the Almighty said: 'They assigned to Allah a share of the tilth and cattle he created, saying: "This is for Allah"—as they declare—"and this is for our associate gods." (Q6:136) [...] You will find them preferring the Law Court over what they have called the *sharīʿa* Court. Whatever is adjudicated by *'High Majesty Court'*[6] [sic!] is not adjudicated by the *'sharīʿa/Customary Court,'*[7] according to their claim.

(pp. 84–91) These foreign secular colonialist schools contain elements that are opposed to *sharīʿa*, which forbids practicing, announcing, studying and teaching in them, as in what follows:

First, the spread of the Freudian, Darwinian, Marxist, belief in development of ethics (Lévy-Bruhl),[8] and for the development of society (Durkheim),[9] with the focus upon existential secular thought, and the supposed freedom. [85] These are in opposition to the *sharīʿa* texts, which concentrate upon following the thoughts of the prophets and the *sharīʿa* of Muhammad. The Almighty said: "Whoever seeks a religion other than Islam, it will never be accepted from him, and in the Hereafter, he will be one of the losers." (Q3:85) ...

Second, spread of materialism, in that they believe in atheism, but the Almighty has said: "They say: 'There is nothing but this our present life. We die and we live and we are only destroyed by time.' However, they have no certain knowledge of this; they are only conjecturing." (Q45:24) These people believe that things were created through natural selection (Nature), but this is nothing but the essence of unbelief, since there is no Creator or Designer, nor Life-giver or Death-causer, so this theory is the theory of polytheism.

Third, the theory of Charles Darwin, who concentrated upon natural selection and survival of the fittest. This infidel theory makes the origin of humanity a tiny microbe dispersed through a stagnant swamp millions of years ago, which evolved through quadrupeds to monkeys, and finally into humanity. Glory to You, this is a monstrous falsehood, when Allah affirms that the origin of humanity is creation from earth and water... [86]

Fourth, the belief that the sun is stationary, not moving, and does not orbit, but that it is the earth which orbits around the sun. This is what they call the "globality of the world," because the world in their belief is a globe. Glory be to You, this is a monstrous falsehood, [as] the Almighty states: "And the sun runs to its fixed destination. That is the decree of the All-mighty, the All-knowing." (Q36:38) ... [87]

Fifth, the belief that the rain comes in the summer and returns in the spring. This is a void belief which contradicts the belief that Allah is the Bestowal, the Praised-one, so they think that the rain is like the waterfalls that they make for people. The Almighty said: "And We send down water from heaven in measure, then lodge it in the ground." (Q23:18) And the Almighty said: "Have you not seen that Allah drives the clouds, then brings them together, then piles them into a heap, from which you can see rain coming." (Q24:43) ... [88]

31

Sixth, being like the Jews and the Christians in their dress and manner, such that some of the losers believe that the religion of the Jews and the Christians or their method is the most progressive for humanity. This is like secularism, regionalism, nationalism, tribalism, and capitalism, such that you find some of the Muslims abandoning their names, by which they were named legally, and taking on infidel Jewish or Christian (*masīḥiyya*) nicknames or descriptions. The Almighty said: "O believers, do not take the Jews and the Christians as friends; some of them are friends of each other. Whoever of you takes them as friends is surely one of them. Allah indeed does not guide the wrongdoers." (Q5:51) [The Prophet Muhammad] said: "I was sent with a sword just before the Hour so that they would worship Allah alone, who has no associate and [89] my sustenance was placed beneath the shadow of my spear. Humiliation and contempt were placed upon those who oppose me, and whoever likens themselves to another group becomes one of them."[10]

The Muslim youth have likened themselves to the unbelievers in their manner; there is no longer any difference between them and the sons of the unbelievers. This is leading to something despicable in the religion, as it leads to something forbidden or unbelief, as is described in the books of *al-walā' wa-l-barā'* (loyalty and disassociation based on Islam).

Seventh, the belief that *"energy can neither be created nor destroyed."*[11] This is complete unbelief, as this is one of the descriptions of Allah Almighty, "Nothing is like unto Him, He is the All-hearing, the All-seeing," (Q42:11) and the Almighty said: "Everything on it is perishing; but the Face of your Lord, full of majesty and nobility, shall abide." (Q55:36–7)

Eighth, the belief that the drop of sperm has a spirit inside of it is a lie against Allah the Almighty... [the Prophet Muhammad] said: "Creation is done for you in your mother's belly for 40 days as a drop, then a clot for the same time, then as a small chunk, the [90] same time, then He sends an angel to it, which blows its spirit in it, and is commanded with four words—to be decreed for it its sustenance, its duration, its occupation, and whether it will be felicitous or infelicitous."[12] Consider, O Muslim, it is without a spirit for two out of the three trimesters, as a drop and as a clot, until He sends an angel to it to blow its spirit into it.

Ninth, ignoring the Islamic months, and the Islamic days [of the week]. There are [vacation] breaks according to the Jews, Christians and secularists...

(pp. 92–93) The reprehensible actions in the foreign schools are:

1. Mixing of the sexes, which is forbidden in our Islamic religion and its forbiddance is well-known as a necessity. [93]
2. A woman adorning herself, in spite of what Allah said: "Stay in your homes and do not display your finery as the pagans of old did." (Q33:33)
3. Physical exercises which distract from religion, like football (soccer), handball and the Olympic competitions.

4. For the woman to travel alone, without a (male) guardian or a husband, in spite of the forbidding of the Prophet of her, saying: "It is not permitted for a woman who believes in Allah and the Last Day to travel day or night without a (male) guardian or her husband."[13]

5. Spreading of illicit sexual relations, and disgusting actions, like forbidden sexual relations (*zinā*), lesbianism, and homosexuality."

(p. 108) Our preaching forbids working under the government that rules by some [source] other than what Allah has revealed, according to French, American or British law or any constitution, or system that is contrary to Islam and contradicts the Book and the Sunna.

Accepting any work under the likes of this unbelieving government would imply complete obedience to its system, and be in accord with its polytheistic principals. The Almighty said: "And do not incline towards the wrongdoers, lest the Fire should touch you," (Q11:113) and the Almighty said: "Surely, those who have turned upon their heels after the Guidance was manifested to them, it was Satan who insinuated to them and deluded them. That is because they said to those who disliked what Allah has sent down: "We shall obey you in part of the matter," but Allah knows their secretiveness." (Q47:25–6) "They take their rabbis and monks as lords besides Allah, as well as the Messiah [Jesus], son of Mary, although they were commanded to worship none but one god. There is no god but He, exalted He is above what they associate with Him." (Q9:31)

(pp. 164–65) al-Shaykh Hamid b. ʿAtīq said: The Almighty said: "You have had a good example in Abraham and those with him, when they said to their people: 'We are quit of you and what you worship apart from Allah. We disbelieve in you. Enmity and hatred have arisen between you and us forever, till you believe in Allah alone'." (Q60:4) The land, whenever the rule belongs to the worthless people, those who worship graves, drinking alcohol, [165] and gambling. These are not satisfied with just the outer manifestations of polytheism and the rule of illegitimate rulers. Every land which is like this, there is no doubt that this is the lowest form of practice, and that its people are in opposition to that upon which Allah's Messenger stands.

The final page(s) are missing.

3

CLEARING THE DOUBTS OF THE SCHOLARS
BY MUHAMMAD YUSUF

(C. FALL 2006/SPRING 2007)

[Trans.: Abdulbasit Kassim]

Several Islamic scholars, mostly Salafi and scholars affiliated with the Izala movement, held a series of discussions with Yusuf both in Nigeria and Saudi Arabia where they attempted to persuade him to change his ideological leanings. Of specific interest is the discussion between Ja'far Adam and Yusuf, which enables us to date this audio to the period prior to 13 April 2007, when Adam was murdered. The outcome of the series of discussions is usually followed up with the dissemination of different accounts about Yusuf and his group. This lecture is based on a two-part audio recording recorded in Kano where Yusuf made an attempt to clarify the following misconceptions to his followers: his relationship with the Nigerian Taliban (he referred to them as the Kanamma brothers in the recording); the report that he was sponsored by the Jews to infiltrate and destroy the Ahl al-Sunna movement in Nigeria; that he uses takfir *against Islamic scholars and refers to them as* ṭāghūt *and unbelievers; and that he withdrew his religious rulings on Western education and working with the government.*

Part 1: Available at: https://www.youtube.com/watch?v=dWfv28iSEZQ

[Questioner]: There are some doubts that are being circulated and I will like you to clarify the doubts so that those who give evidence with the doubts can gain a feeling of tranquility. I heard an allegation against you that Mallam Ja'far Mahmud [Adam]

engaged in a conversation with you and you agreed in his presence that your preaching is specious, but you find it difficult to publicly declare this to your followers. There is also an allegation against you that Mallam Abba Aji[1] engaged in a conversation with you, and that you agreed in his presence that your preaching is specious, but you find it difficult to publicly declare this to your followers. They also said Mallam Abba Aji publicly declared to the people that your preaching is on the path of destruction and your intention is to destroy the people. This is the doubt I want you to clarify for us so that we can be free of it, and eliminate all the misunderstandings.

[Yusuf's response]: I was confronted with the same doubts in Bauchi, and I believe it was in Bauchi they circulated these doubts. Allah knows and the brothers with us know that I do not like to respond to personal attacks except when it is necessary. I deemed it necessary to respond based on the disposition of our brothers we met in Bauchi. Therefore, it is not wrong if I repeat my response here.

Firstly, Mallam did something, but he failed to recall. I mean Ja'far. What he failed to recall is the fact that since I started this preaching, Mallam Abba Aji and I have never sat together to discuss this preaching. This is the third time I am repeating this statement. I said it in Maiduguri, Bauchi and here. Mallam Abba Aji and I have never sat together to discuss this preaching. [Yusuf reiterates his speech] We have never discussed these questions. What I know is the fact that he has ever invited me to his Jum'a (Friday) mosque since I sometimes pray my late-afternoon and evening prayers there. He said to me: "What are they saying in your place?" and I said, "Look at the evidence." He said: "You should be sincere and make sure you have evidence for whatever you say."

Secondly, there was a period during which some people at the Imām Malik Center[2] and others met him and sought his advice for a discussion with me. He replied them that rather than discussing with him, they should meet and discuss with me. They came and we sat together to discuss. They were sixteen in number, and if you include me, we were seventeen in total. If he is referring to that discussion, the recording is available. The discussion was recorded in the Kanuri language. I believe there are many people who understand the Kanuri language. If I withdrew [from the preaching], people would know. Therefore, Mallam Abba Aji and I have never sat together to discuss this preaching.

Thirdly, there was a period we sat and discussed with him [Ja'far] in Maiduguri with some students of knowledge. Afterwards, we travelled together to Gwoza for preaching, and we discussed it again there. We came back to Maiduguri and continued with our discussion. We parted, both of us disagreeing. I believe Mallam can recall [now], except that he might have forgotten because of the length of time. Nevertheless, if both of us failed to recall, the angels must have written about it.

There was another period when he came together with Mallam Abdulwahhab [Abdallah] to Maiduguri.[3] They told us they came to attend a marriage ceremony. At that time, there was a speech that I heard they delivered. By Allah, I did not discuss it with anyone, because I did not believe they delivered such a speech until I heard the recorded speech myself. In the recorded speech, he said there is someone who believes in our preaching, but afterwards he took his wife for child delivery in the hospital. There, it was an unbeliever who supervised the [baby] delivery.

At that time, they visited us on Friday, and they invited us for a discussion but I declined. I told them I needed to visit my wife in the hospital, but that I would return for the discussion once she was discharged. My wife has not even been put into a hospital bed, let alone for someone to claim that it was an unbeliever who supervised her delivery. There were two ladies who took my wife to the hospital—they are my students and they both believe in my preaching. There was no one who went there to see my wife, let alone for someone to bring the news to them. [Yusuf validates himself.]

There was also another recorded speech he delivered and some people said the speech was directed against me. I said no. It was directed against the brothers who emigrated to Kanamma based on the events he narrated in the speech. I overlooked the speech to the point where some brothers said I was too lenient and soft on people, but I said it is not like that.

Thereafter, they came with Mallam Abdulwahhab, and we sat and discussed extensively. Mallam Abdulwahhab asked me: "Where exactly did you come to understand this type of preaching?" I mentioned some books to him, specifically the book of Aḥmad Shākir that deals with the topic of 'Almāniyya (secularism) [Yusuf is likely referring to Aḥmad Shākir's book 'Ḥukm al-Jāhilīyah']. He asked me: "Have you read the book of Shākir 'Abd al-Raḥmān dealing with the same topic"? [Mallam Abdulwahhab is likely referring to the book of Shākir 'Abd al-Raḥmān 'al-Thawrah al-ishtirākīyah al-'ālamīya'] I said no. Then he said: "You do not know anything. This book covers every issue about unbelief far better than the book you read." In fact, he asked me: "Where are you from?" I kept quiet. He said: "If you reply that you are a Nigerian, then you are an unbeliever." He also asked: "Do you have a passport or not?" It is also unbelief. Then he said: "There is a need to consider certain factors in these issues." So, I said everything that I heard from him only strengthen my arguments.

[Yusuf validates himself.] When we finished eating, we entered the kitchen to wash our hands. Mallam Abdulwahhab held my hand, and he said: "Please withdraw from your position and preaching because of Allah, so that you will not be alone, without supporters." The person who defeats you with evidence does not need to plead with you. We departed from there after the discussion.

In the last discussion we had, he told me he heard that I am proclaiming takfīr against the people. I replied him that the youths are the people who carried out such act. He told me: "Why will you not caution them about the way they proclaim takfīr against the people?' I replied him that I gave several lectures to caution the youths. He asked me to bring the recorded lectures so I brought three cassettes of my lectures. I was coming to meet them, but they did not inform me they had already planned to engage me in discussion. The only thing they told me is to come along with some people, so I went together with two other scholars.

We met them with some other people and started a discussion. The discussion was about the *hadīth*: "Rulers will come to you, bringing the evillest people close by..."[4] We did not cite any verses during the discussion. I know it was not only me—the entire world knows—this *hadīth* was not the only issue I discussed. We discussed the saying that the principal [task] of *hadīth* scholars is to collect all the *hadīths* together. At the time, we both agreed that the *hadīth* was authentic. We were the first people who later declared that the *hadīth* was not authentic by Allah's power, but at that time we both reached an understanding that the *hadīth* was authentic.

[*Proof cannot be on the evidence of one* hadīth *alone.*]

Secondly, they also said my students are calling the [other] scholars *ṭāghūt*, unbelievers and so on. I said this is untrue. One of the scholars said he was informed that they call scholars *ṭāghūt*. I replied to him that I will agree with his statement, but I am unable to make such a proclamation. I told them by Allah's permission, I would speak on the issue, and discuss the *hadīth* after looking at other *hadīths*. When I returned that day, I delivered a lecture and the recording is available. In the lecture, I gathered the people, and I said anyone who calls a scholar *ṭāghūt* or unbeliever, I disassociate myself from him. It is not on my behalf that you declare scholars *ṭāghūt* or unbeliever. I clarified this point to them. However, I do not know whether that is their understanding, and Allah knows best.

There is also another claim that we sat and discussed with Muhammad Sani Rijiyar Lemo.[5] By Allah, we did not discuss with him. Although we have a closer relationship with him, we did not sit face-to-face to discuss [anything]. When I travelled for the lesser pilgrimage [to Mecca], I went to Medina. The twelve to thirteen days I spent there, I lived in his house, together with other students of knowledge. Some of them were from Birnin Kudu, Kano and Maiduguri. We stayed together. By Allah, we did not discuss the issue of our preaching—whether it is right or wrong, or whether we should withdraw from it or not.

They only asked me about the situation in Nigeria. They said there is no peace in Nigeria, and that I am responsible for the division among the people of Sunna. I narrated the entire story to them, and they also talked about this *hadīth*. At the time, Dr Ibrahim Jalo gave an admonition, and he spoke about the brothers who emigrated [to Kanamma]. When I explained my stance to him and what I was told, he directed me to read what he wrote on democracy, and afterwards we would discuss the topic.[6] This was what transpired between us before we parted, but we did not sit together to discuss [anything].

It was only when I came to Mecca that I discussed with Mallam Ja'far at Mina.[7] Our discussion centered on the brothers of Kanamma. I narrated what I saw to him and he said: "By Allah, that is the nature of people. They will attribute it to you." He advised me to inform the security agencies. I told him: "Why should I inform them?" At that time, Mallam Abba had told me not to inform anyone; rather I should pray to Allah. By Allah, that was what he told me. I told him [Mallam Ja'far] what Mallam

Abba Aji told me. He said there is a reason he was advising me, because all the security operatives are my fellow Muslims. He said: "If you inform them, you would have denied them any proof against you. Even if you return after they know that they wronged you, you would be free." This was what he told me, but I did not act upon it because I thought it was a trap.

Thereafter, we went together with some people and we sat together to discuss. One of them said: "Why do scholars usually climb the pulpit and censure your preaching?" He said: "It is expected that you should caution yourself." He also said they would speak with Mallam Abba Aji so that they can warn the people to stop saying what they are saying, and exonerate me. He informed me what they plan to do so that they would not be misidentified as people supporting me. He advised me to write a critique to demonstrate that all what they are saying is false. He told me to write the letter, send it, and later we would talk about it. Then he also said: "If you plan to write the letter, you should hire a lawyer to write the letter on your behalf so that you would not entrap yourself."

After we parted, we agreed with him that we should write the letter and include the letter where the youths said I have become an apostate because I follow the government. They said they do not care about me, so they have emigrated [to Kanamma]. He said it would suffice. Consequently, we talked about writing a letter. We did not write the letter let alone hire a lawyer. However, since we had discussed it, he thought we had hired a lawyer. He did not receive any further information—then he proceeded to speak about how we hired a lawyer. [Yusuf says he is compelled to speak about these details.]

There is another serious allegation that I previously did not speak about, but I was later asked in the place we preached. They alleged that I said that the Jews are the people who sponsored me. This is the reason I have a big car,[8] I have so many students and other things. This is not sufficient evidence for you to claim that the Jews sponsored me. By Allah, before I embarked on my travels, before these incidents happened, my funds declined, notwithstanding my house and other possessions. We were limited to farming. You would be surprised that we were engaging in such activity. Up till now, we have not abandoned farming.[9]

My brother oversees the farming and trading. I also have funds with other brothers with whom we engage in business transactions. Just because you do not know the source of a person's funds is not sufficient evidence to claim that he is being sponsored from abroad. Thus, we said in Bauchi that if I or anyone is being sponsored from abroad to infiltrate the people of Sunna, and sow discord among the Sunnis or destroy the religion, may Allah penalize him. In fact, I said: "You, the people of Bauchi, you know what a *mubāhala* is?[10] I will do it here, then," and some people among us said: "Amen." I said: "If I, Muhammad Yusuf, sat together with the security forces either at home or abroad planning to destroy the Sunnis, even on one occasion, may Allah do to me what He did to a *zindīq* [heretic]. On the other hand, if I did not plan with anybody, but someone said I did, and may Allah forgive him." This is the same thing I repeated there.

Part 2: Available at: https://www.youtube.com/watch?v=BxZXhOpmqSU

[Yusuf laments on how he was banned from preaching in the mosque of the rival scholars.] There are none of my recorded cassettes available for anyone to listen to where I did not speak about Western education. I hope it is understood. Therefore, we have discussed with so many scholars. We discussed with some of them in their houses, mosques and we also discussed with some people in the corridor of the mosque at Medina. We discussed frequently, but I never said I withdraw from this preaching. I have never said so. By Allah, this is a false accusation. I never told anyone I withdraw.

[Yusuf laments over the treachery of the rival scholars. He insists on his ruling on western education.] The ruling on Western education is my ruling. I confirmed it as my ruling in all my discussions with the scholars and the elders.

The issue of working with the government and democracy is exactly what I said and there is no one who has contended with my opinion. It is either they say the time is not yet suitable, or there are other contexts that need to be considered. None of them has ever told me that I am wrong or what I am saying is a lie. There is a Mallam who is alive and is in this town.[11] He referred me to a book I previously did not know on this issue. I told him I read the book on 'Almāniyya. He said: "Which of the books on 'Almāniyya?" I said: "The one written by Aḥmad Shākir." He said: "Have you read the one written by Safar Ḥawālī?"[12] [Mallam Abdulwahhab is likely referring to the book 'al-'Almāniyya: nash'atuhā wa-tatawwuriha wa-āthāruhā fī al-ḥayāh al-Islāmīyah al-mu'āṣirah' written by Safar Ḥawālī] I said: "No." He said: "You do not know anything. Go and get a copy of Safar al-Ḥawālī's book, and increase your knowledge on this issue."

In fact, he asked me: "Where are you from?" I kept quiet. He and his friend laughed at me. He said: "By Allah, if you had said you are a Nigerian then you would have become an unbeliever." By Allah, that was what he told me. He is alive and he is here in this town. He told me: "If you say you are a Nigerian, you will be an unbeliever." But then he said: "There are some issues we need to consider." I told him that the issues we need to consider are exactly what I am not seeing. Sorry until you show me and I see it, I will hold onto what you said that it is unbelief and Allah said we should abandon all unbelief. Allah says: "He does not approve of unbelief in His servants." (Q39:7) In fact, Allah wants us to hate unbelief "He has made you to hate unbelief, sin and disobedience" (Q49:7) and to have complete faith [verse unclear in the recording.] [Yusuf speaks about his tenacity and readiness to uphold his ideology.]

Yusuf finishes by saying that he will continue with his preaching.

4

EXEGESIS CONCERNING *SŪRAT HŪD* (QUR'ĀN 11:84–90)

BY MUHAMMAD YUSUF

(c. FALL 2006/FALL 2007)

[Kanuri trans. team and Atta Barkindo]
Available at: https://www.youtube.com/watch?v=Mxrt07Gl6G0

This is one of several exegeses of the Qur'ān by Muhammad Yusuf, delivered in Kanuri. Although the content is basic, and is little more than a homily, it is easy to see Yusuf's ability to relate the Qur'ānic story of Hūd to the realities of contemporary Nigeria. The translators tentatively date it to October 2006 or 2007 (during Ramadan, mentioned in the text), when Yusuf was concerned with the morality of Nigerian society. It was probably delivered at the Ibn Taymiyya Center, Maiduguri.

My beloved brothers in Islam, peace be upon you. Today, by the permission of Allah, our exegesis will focus on *Sūrat Hūd* (Qur'ān 11). Today is the twenty-ninth day of Ramadan and we pray that Allah will grant us the opportunity to complete the remaining day successfully. Allah, the most merciful, instructs us in Qur'ān 11 concerning the prophets Noah, Abraham, Lot and Shu'ayb. In verse 84, Allah speaks specifically about Shu'ayb: "And to Midian [We sent] their brother Shu'ayb. He said: 'O my people, worship Allah; you have no other god but Him." (Q11:84) Thus, there is no other god who has created you, enriched you or brought you to life except Allah.

Then, the Prophet Shu'ayb asked the people whether they have other gods who can provide what Allah has provided for them? Of course, the answer is no. Thus, it is better for us to worship Allah, who gave us life than worshipping other idols. He also said to the in the same verse:

> Do not skimp the measure and the weight. I see that you are prospering, but I fear for you the punishment of an encompassing day. And my people be just and give full measure and full weight; and do not cheat people out of things due to them, and do not sow corruption in the land by committing evil. What remains for you from Allah's provision is better for you if you are true believers, and I am not a watcher over you. (Q11:84–86)

The people to whom the Prophet Shu'ayb was sent, the Midianites, apart from being apostates, had imbibed the culture of extortion and interfering with the weights and measurements of goods to make profits in their commercial dealings. They had lost any sense of guilt in the exaction of illegal profit during a transaction which Allah has forbidden. One of the strategies they used was revealed in an open market during the life time of the Prophet Muhammad. The prophet came across a seller who spread his grain out for sale and was awaiting buyers. The prophet dipped his hands into the grain, only to discover that the topmost part of the grain was dry but underneath it was wet and soggy, for the grain was not ready to be sold to the public. It was raw and unripe. The prophet said to the trader: "'O servant of Allah, why did you do this?'" The man replied: "O Messenger of Allah, I was caught up in the rain, and the grains became wet and soggy." The Prophet told him: "It could have been good and better for you if you had made it visible for your customers to see both the dry and wet/soggy part of the grain at the point of purchase. This would also allow the wet grains to dry up quickly."

Another method embraced by the people of Prophet Shu'ayb is their trick of soaking food items in water, making the size increase by a few inches. Sometimes the size of the items, depending on the food stuffs, was tripled. Some market-sellers [today] also use broken pieces of wood, grass and sand dunes to increase the quantity of sack/bag of food items. In this way, customers assume the bags/sacks are filled up with more food items than is the actual case. In response to these commercial tricks, some customers have designed a pair of shoes called *chukman*. This pair of shoes is made with animal skin, with inserted iron tips that protrude at the front of the shoes with a sharp edge. Once customers have arrived at the market, they hit the tip of the shoes hard against the bag/sack of grain. Thus, the customer ascertains if the sack contains wood, grass or stones. At the same time, it was also possible to tear the bag/sack by the side to reveal the type of grain in the sack, wet or dry. In fact, using this method, customers can now know which traders are cheats and should be avoided.

Yet, the people of Prophet Shu'ayb refused to listen to him. They continued their worship of trees. Allah said in another verse: "Woe to the skimpers! Who, when they measure for themselves from others exact full measure; but when they measure or weigh for others actually skimp. Do not those people thnink that they will be resuscitated?" (Q83:1–4) The people asked the Prophet Shu'ayb: "O Shu'ayb! Does your prayer (*salāt*) command that we should abandon what our fathers worshipped and that we should not do with our wealth what we wish? You are indeed the clement and right-minded one" (Q11:87), they said to the Prophet Shuʻayb sarcastically.

Before the arrival of our Prophet Muhammad there were some Jews who were initiated in the knowledge of the Prophet's coming and of his mission. They promised to accept and follow him but when he arrived or appeared, they denied his prophethood and rejected him. Our movement will not consider anything from Imām Ḥanafi, Mālik, Shafiʻī and Ḥanbali (the four legal schools of Islam) and others, not to speak of the Jews. We only submit to the Qur'ān and Sunna of the Prophet Muhammad. The Prophet Shuʻayb replied:

> O my people, do you think that if I have a clear proof from my Lord and He has granted me a fair provision from Him [I would commit any of those evils]? I do not want to do what I forbid you to do. I only want to do what I can to set things right. My success comes only from Allah. In Him I have put my trust and to Him I turn. O my people let not my disagreement with you bring upon you what the people of Noah, the people of Hūd or the people of Salih brought upon themselves. The people of Lot are not far away from you. And ask forgiveness from your Lord; then repent to Him. My Lord is truly Merciful, Kind. (Q11:88–90)

5

WHO IS THE PROPHET MUHAMMAD?

BY MUHAMMAD YUSUF

(c. 2007/2008)

[Trans.: Abdulbasit Kassim]
Available at: https://www.youtube.com/watch?v=m9P5C6mdWyU

Although the Danish cartoons are not referenced, most likely this sermon should be associated with the various controversies about the Prophet Muhammad during the period 2006–2009. The primary subject of the sermon is the exegesis of Qur'ān 4:48–54. In his exegesis of these verses, Yusuf accentuated the theme of the polytheism of obedience and focused on the criticism of the constitution, democracy, and working with the secular government as well the schisms between his group and other Islamic groups, particularly the Salafis. In addition, Yusuf also demonstrated his admiration for the jihadists who fought in Tora Bora. There were some missing parts at the beginning and the end of the video.

Who is the Prophet Muhammad? [Description of the Status of the Prophet]

Let us ask ourselves, when Allah says: "I have not created the *jinn* and mankind except to worship Me" (Q51:56)—is it true or false? If it is true; then what is the worship of Allah? What is our lifestyle? Is there any difference? Why do we take several hours to satisfy our own needs, without commensurate time in knowing how to worship Allah?

45

Why would you go to Western school from 7am to 5pm or till 1pm or 3pm, but do not have the time to study the religion? Why would you go to the market from morning to evening, but do not have the time to study the religion which is the main purpose of your creation? You were created for the sole purpose of worshipping Allah. You were not created for these other activities; rather they are only there to help you to fulfil the purpose of your creation. Trading, socialization, marriage would only help you to fulfil the purpose of your creation, but they have now preoccupied our time and diverted our attention from the sole purpose of our creation.

[*Yusuf comments on how easy it is to fall into polytheism.*]

Therefore, by Allah, the [Nigerian] Constitution is polytheism. It is idol worship. By Allah, anyone that works under the Constitution is committing polytheism. Democracy is polytheism. By Allah, anyone working under the government is committing polytheism. It is the polytheism of obedience. You should ask the scholars the meaning of the verse: "but if you obey them, then you will surely be polytheists." (Q6:121) What is the meaning of the verse: "And do not obey the orders of the extravagant." (Q26:151) What is the meaning of the verse: "Do not obey the unbelievers and the hypocrites?" (Q33:1)

Obedience! What is the meaning of the verse: "They take their rabbis and monks as lords besides Allah, as well as the Messiah [Jesus], son of Mary, although they were commanded to worship none but one god. There is no god but He; exalted He is above what they associate with Him." (Q9:31) What is the meaning of the *hadīth* of the Prophet: "Rulers will be appointed over you—so you will enjoin the good and forbid the evil. Whoever does good is innocent [of sin], while whoever forbids is safe, but whoever is satisfied [with them] and swears allegiance [is in the wrong] ..."?[1] [Citation of Q33:66–67]

You see that obedience can become polytheism. Any action which leads to obedience to the government is polytheism. Obeying the flag they hoist is polytheism. Honoring their mace is polytheism. Those legislators in the National Assembly are all polytheists. They are idols. They are *tāghūt*. They are associates worshipped together with Allah. Brothers! If we do not do disassociate from them, Allah will not accept your Islam. Allah says until you say you believe only then would I accept it:

"Say: 'We believe in Allah, in what has been revealed to us, what was revealed to Abraham, Ishmael, Isaac, Jacob and the Tribes, and in that which was imparted to Moses and Jesus, and the other prophets from their Lord, making no distinction between any of them, and to Him we submit.'" (Q2:136) Until you testify thus, you are not a Muslim. I hope it is understood. It is in this that you manifest Islam. It is in this that you become safe from polytheism. And may Allah protect us.

[Quranic reciter reads Q4:49-52 and Yusuf cautions against self-praise.] I cannot speak about myself because Allah taught us manners and he forbade us from praising ourselves. It is not even ideal to give names of praise to your child. For example,

Barratu is a name of praise. I hope it is understood. You should not give yourself names of praise. This is the reason why some scholars critiqued those past names that they gave people such as Shams al-Dīn, or Nūr al-din are among the names of praise.[2]

[Yusuf laments on partisanship] However, we have been interpreting the Qur'ān together for almost fifteen years but they have never told us we have misinterpreted it. Throughout the time, we were together until we parted, no one ever showed us a verse we have misinterpreted. I hope it is understood. We will be grateful to Allah and we will accept it as charity, if they will show us our error. We will accept that and amend it. We are also willing to show other people their error so that they can accept that and amend it. We will not help the religion of Islam and we will not be guided, if we were not correcting one another.

[Yusuf cautions against injustice and oppression] You may be together with a friend of Allah or a pious slave of Allah, but because you see him like that, you talk to him angrily, it is not right. No doubt if you become angry at the pious slave of Allah, then Allah would be angry with you. You should respect Allah's slaves—they are all the same. You should be good to them and do what is right. The one who commits an error like the Salafis, you should admonish him. If he needs to amend his action, you should advise him to do so. Allah says: "Have you not considered those who have received a portion of the Book? They believe in idols and demons [jibt and ṭāghūt]," (Q4:51) after Allah has given them the Book.

Inside the book, Allah says they should disbelieve in ṭāghūt, but instead they believe in ṭāghūt. I hope it is understood. They would look at the unbelievers and say that they are more civilized and peaceful than the believers and their path is better, "and they say to the unbelievers: 'Those are more rightly guided than those who believe.'" (Q4:51) This deception has afflicted the people. Some scholars defined jibt as marabout and ṭāghūt as Satan, but there are other scholars who defined jibt as Satan and ṭāghūt as marabout.[3] I hope it is understood. Jibt is magic and ṭāghūt is Satan. Is it understood? Whoever Allah has given the Book, either the [true] Bible or the Qur'ān, then he goes to the marabout or engages in magic or is following the ṭāghūt is included in the definition of this verse.

[Yusuf explains that Ibn 'Abd al-Wahhāb taught that some among the Muslim community would also worship idols.]

Yes! You were also given the Book, but some of you would believe in jibt and ṭāghūt. Why? The Prophet said, "Surely you will follow the ways of those who were before you exactly…" Those people worshipped ṭāghūt, and so some of you will also worship ṭāghūt, what is the proof? "Surely you will follow the ways of those who were before you exactly…" Those people built a mosque upon the [holy man's] tomb and worshipped it, so some of you would also worship tombs, what is the proof?

"Surely you will follow the ways of those who were before you exactly…"—did it happen or not? It happened. People are worshipping ṭāghūt by following a law other than the law of Allah. People are going to the tombs of [Sufi] holy men to worship there. Some people among this *umma* will worship idols, and will say about "the unbelievers: 'Those are more rightly guided than those who believe.'" (Q4:51)

Now, everyone who comes to this mosque prays five times a day—or is it six times we pray? We pray five times a day. We are fasting in the month of Ramadan, or do we fast in the month of Shawwal? We perform hajj, or do we not perform hajj? We are giving charity (*zakāt*), or do we not give charity? We are reciting the Qur'ān, or is it the Bible that we read? We are doing everything expected of us in Islam—yet in the view of someone who calls himself a scholar the unbelievers are better than us. He thinks we constitute a threat. In fact, some of them said that there is no danger that has befallen the proclamation of Islam in Nigeria like our preaching. Haha!

What about CAN (Christian Association of Nigeria)? What about the Jews? Two days ago, the Jews surrounded this town, is that not a danger?[4] Ruling by other than Allah's laws for several years, is that not a danger? All these churches, do they not constitute a threat? According to them, it is this preaching that constitutes danger. "They believe in idols and demons, they believe in *jibt* and *ṭāghūt*, and say to the unbelievers: 'Those are more rightly guided than those who believers'" (Q4:51)—do you see the meaning of this verse?

[Yusuf emphasizes the message of the verse] [Qur'ānic Reciter]: "Or do they have a share in the kingdom? If so, they will not give the people a speck on a date-stone. Or do they envy the people for what Allah has given them of His bounty? For We have given Abraham's family the Book and the Wisdom and bestowed upon them a great kingdom. Some of them believed in him, others rejected him. Sufficient is the scourge of Hell." (Q4:53–4)

[Yusuf continues]: [Discussion of *the ṭāghūt*]

You see, inside Tora Bora,[5] they said that America made a bomb that inhales oxygen, and so they would use it to inhale the oxygen of the *mujāhidīn* who were inside the mountain. When the bomb inhales the oxygen, the *mujāhidīn* would suffocate and die. So, this type of people; what if they had control over the air and oxygen? Then they would withhold it. When they created the bomb, and dropped it upon the mountain, perhaps it even increased the oxygen rather than inhaling it. I hope it is understood.

[Yusuf repeats the verses] The person whom Allah left misguided there is nothing you can do for him. All the caterpillar[6] and mortal insults, there is nothing they can do to the person who is guided by Allah. That is how you would leave him on Allah's path. Similarly, the person whom Allah has left misguided, praise and compliments will not advance him anywhere. That is how you would leave him in his misguidance. "Or do they envy the people for what Allah has given them of His bounty?"

[Yusuf discusses about envy and how it relates to the acquisition of Islamic knowledge. He also speaks about the elevation of foreign-trained scholars above the locally-trained traditional scholars.]

6

EXEGESIS OF *SŪRAT AL-TAWBA* (QUR'ĀN 9:9–16)

BY MUHAMMAD YUSUF

(c. SPRING 2008)

[Trans.: Abdulbasit Kassim]

This exegetical sermon is undated, but as it references the Danish cartoons, most likely it should be associated with the assassination plots against the cartoonist Kurt Westergaard in February 2008, and the subsequent reprinting of the cartoons. It can probably be dated to spring or summer 2008. Yusuf uses this material to prove that non-Muslims are irredeemably hostile to Muslims. The beginning is a bit rough.

Part 1: Available at: https://www.youtube.com/watch?v=Y33rL_D_6pw

[Qur'ānic reciter]: "How [can that be]? If they overcome you, they will observe neither kinships nor pacts with you. They only give you satisfaction with their mouths, while their hearts refuse; and most of them are sinners." (Q9:8)

[Yusuf lectures]: [Non-Muslims do not honor blood ties or agreement] Even if you were born in the same house, once you are a Muslim, they will slaughter you. Even if he is the one who fathered you, once you are a Muslim he will slaughter you. They do not care about the family ties. They do not care about any agreement. Once they have an opportunity against you, they would not care about any agreement or family ties. I hope it is understood.

[Yusuf speaks about conflict in the Middle Belt of Nigeria] If they have power over you, they would not honor any agreement or family ties. It is for this reason you should never be a pacifist. You should never lay down your weapons. Allah says: "O believers, be on your guard; so, march in detachments or march all together." (Q4:71) You should hold your weapons firmly and go out in small groups or as a whole. We should never lay down our weapons. I hope it is understood.

[Yusuf emphasizes the last point]

Regarding love, you should not love them because if they have any opportunity over you they would not spare you. Allah says:

> O believers, do not take My enemy and your enemy for supporters, showing them friendship, when they have disbelieved what has come to you of the Truth. They expel the Messenger and expel you because you have believed in Allah, your Lord. If you have gone out to struggle in My cause and to seek My good pleasure secretly showing them friendship, while I know very well what you conceal and what you reveal. He who does that among you has surely strayed from the right path. (Q60:1)

You should not love them, you should not love them at heart and you should not show them that you love them. You should hold them as enemies. I hope it is understood. They are the people that drove you and Allah's Messenger from your town. Yes, they are the people. It is not necessary for you to say that those people are the people of Quraysh.

[The unbelievers of the past and present are the same] So, the unbelievers of today are the same people Allah's Messenger is speaking about. They are the people who drove out Allah's Messenger from their town.

Are they not the people drawing his [Muhammad's] image? So, they are the same people. If they had met him they would have driven him out of their town. Would the people who are drawing Allah's Messenger's image have left him in their town? They are the same people that drove Allah's Messenger from their town. Why do you love them? Is it because they can play football? What is football? Why do you love him [the non-Muslim]? Is it because of politics? Why do you love him? Is it because of movies, drama or because you have lost your sense of reasoning? The person who does not love Allah's Messenger, you put his image on your cloth and you add his name, Ronaldo,[1] and you are walking around with it.

[Yusuf cites Q60:2] Look at what they are doing to Muslims in Guantanamo. Look at the Abu Ghraib prison inside Iraq. The prison was built with the money of the Iraqi people in their own land and property, yet they are the same people that are being incarcerated in the prison. They would put people as prisoners, and a dog to assault the prisoners, while they were completely naked. They would also force a dog to sleep with the female prisoners. That is exactly what they do to the people.

"If they come upon you, they will be enemies of yours"—will you agree with this humiliation by saying words of peace and let there be no violence until you die? Allah will say why did you not elevate His religion? "Do you, then, believe in one part of the Book, but disbelieve in another? The reward of those among you who do that is nothing but disgrace in this world, and on the Day of Resurrection they shall be turned over to the most severe punishment." (Q2:85)

What you should be doing is clarifying, seeking knowledge, and preparing day and night—"And make ready for them whatever you can of fighting men and horses, to terrify thereby Allah's enemies and your enemy, as well as others besides them whom you do not know." (Q8:60)

At the time when there is no arrangement and opportunity to engage them, do not engage them. Although they will harass you, scare you, confuse you, arrest you, beat you, or even kill you, throw firecrackers or teargas at you, do not allow their actions make you to leave your religion. By Allah, these are some of the things we need to know. One day if they see that they have an opportunity, for example, if they know that there is nothing you can do, then they will start firing teargas at you and your little children. You will be sneezing together with these little children who you see walking around. By Allah, do not be surprised, because they can do it the same way they did it in the other lands.

[Yusuf narrates the persecution of Muhammad and his followers] We know that at a point in time we will experience similar tortuous experiences [as the Companions] here. At a point in time you may be on the road when they will catch you without even knowing where you are coming from. They will say they do not even know and did not see you. But there is nothing they will do—even if they kill you Allah will save some people. Killing a martyr on Allah's path is like sowing a seed. I hope it is understood.

"...are like a grain [of wheat] which grows seven ears, each carrying one hundred grains..." (Q2:261)—you are sowing a seed, then seven more people will emerge, and each of them will be tougher than the martyr. If the martyr has one stubborn head, the people who will emerge will have one hundred stubborn heads. I hope it is understood.

[Yusuf narrates the persecution of the early Muslims like Yasir, Sumayya and Zinnira] Because of that, we should also be prepared to face similar trials if we are indeed sincere. Allah will test us. Let no one think that he will come just like that, perform the religion's rites, praise and be happy with honor and courage, that they will be afraid of him, and allow him to go and establish the Islamic state? By Allah, this is not true. The truth is "Have the people supposed that they will be left alone to say: 'We believe,' and then they will not be tested." (Q29:2)

Notwithstanding the honor they bestow, you see they are still coming to humiliate you. You are feeling that because he [Yusuf] is a scholar they will not do anything to him, but one day you will see him on the table [at the security forces]. They will come and put handcuffs on him. We know that this trial will happen, and we know that it is not humiliation, but rather it is the path of the religion. [Yusuf speaks about patience in the face of trials and the necessity of preparation for jihad.]

You would hear them saying that war is not good, you know you are a Muslim, I am a Christian, but since we have come to this town, so we should live happily. By Allah, it is a lie. What is the evidence for this? Allah says: "They only give you satisfaction with their mouths, while their hearts refuse, and most of them are sinners." (Q9:8) Most of them are violators of agreements. They are rebels and they do not have the truth.

Part 2: Available at: https://www.youtube.com/watch?v=R3NcgQv-LVM

You may hear one of them saying that he is a security or police officer and his main duty is to protect lives and to ensure peace and stability: "You see we are Christians who were transferred here to protect your lives." It is a lie; you came here to kill us. That was the same way 'Umar Mukhtār replied to the Italians.[2] They invited him to a meeting, but he refused to attend. They invited him again but he refused to go to them.

[Discussion of 'Umar Mukhtār's meeting with the Italians] Then they told him that they brought new civilization to this land. They said they are not here to humiliate the people; rather they want them to be civilized, to progress, to learn to understand the world and enjoy it. 'Umar Mukhtār replied them by asking, "Who owns the land?" They replied him that it belongs to him and his people.

Then he said: "We do not want your new civilization." They told him: "We want to integrate your land to the world so that trade would flourish." He told them: "We have our own system of trade." He later gave them a condition that they can go across the water, settle [temporarily] and be permitted to enter the land for trade, but not be permitted to settle there. They (Italians) disagreed with him. They wanted to settle in the land while 'Umar Mukhtār would be made the king.

They promised to give him 50,000 Italian *lira* of that time.[3] They also promised to build a house for him but he said: "What about the other people?" They said: "But you are the king." He said: "I am fighting because you have humiliated the other Muslims. How can I enjoy myself while the other Muslims are being humiliated?" [Yusuf narrates how Italians try to woe 'Umar Mukhtār.]

The person who understands Allah and recites the Qur'ān will not waste his time [with non-Muslims]. It is only when you do not recite the Qur'ān that their statements appear good to you. For instance, if you are working and a Christian infuriates you. A police officer would call him and reprimand him: "Why would you say he should work and cannot go and pray? Go and pray!" When you leave, they would laugh and make fun of you.

By Allah, that is how they are: "When they meet you, they say, 'We believe'. But when they are alone, they bite their fingertips with rage." (Q3:119) If they meet you they would say: "We are one, let us live in peace, one country, one people, but when they are alone they would hold their tongues." This is what the Qur'ān says. If you do not understand the unbeliever as he is portrayed by Allah, you are a fool. You do not know the Qur'ān. You are insane.

The way the Qurʾān says is how it is. There is no one who loves you when you are stronger than him, except when he is afraid of you—but for him to love you? No! Allah says: "How [can that be]? If they overcome you, they will observe neither kinships nor pacts with you. They only give you satisfaction with their mouths, while their hearts refuse; and most of them are sinners." (Q9:8)

[Qurʾānic reciter]: "They have sold Allah's revelations for a small price, and have barred [others] from His path. Evil indeed is what they do! They observe with the believers neither kinships nor compacts. Those are the real transgressors. Yet, if they repent perfom the prayer and pay the alms, they will be your brethren in religion. We expound the revelations to a people who know." (Q9:9–11)

[Yusuf continues]: [Unbelievers do not honor agreement] There is no agreement with Israel that has ever been made which the Israelis have honored. All the agreements for the past sixty years, the Israelis have not honored them. Once they write an agreement that they would withdraw from a place; they would withdraw from the Gaza Strip, they would withdraw from Bethlehem; the agreement ends there. At the time of writing the agreement, the Muslims would think they are being truthful in their agreement, but at night they would come and occupy the place. Then the Muslims would say: "But you said so-and-so?"

Yasir Arafat would go to America, go to Russia, he would go here and there, then they would promise him that after some days he should be patient, "but tell your terrorists not to attack." He would order the arrest of some people now, and then they would become angry and attack. Since they [the Israelis] have attacked, it means they were not truthful. Then they would further their occupation. They killed him [Arafat] and installed another one called Mahmud Abbas. These are all pointless schemes. There is no agreement or family tie that they would honor other than gunfire.

By Allah, a Jew only honors an agreement when he sees gunfire. Regardless of the years you spend with him, you cannot make an agreement that he would honor except when he sees gunfire. Once he is injured, he would surrender instantly. That is why Allah says: "And if they incline to peace, incline to it too, and put your trust in Allah." (Q8:61) If they repent, we are not expected to be people with one eye. Once they say fight, then should you take it only as a fight?

No! You are inviting [them] and anticipating that they will become Muslims. Once they become Muslims, then you will change your stance. This is the reason why Allah quickly told us, if they repent, they observe the prayers and pay the alms, then they are your brothers in religion. You should give them status, mix with them and do everything together. We reveal our signs bit by bit to people of knowledge.

[Qurʾānic reciter]: "But if they break their oaths after their pledge [is made] and abuse your religion, then fight the leaders of unbelief; for they have no regard for oaths, and that perchance they may desist." (Q9:12)

[Yusuf continues]: [Yusuf speaks about the violation of peace agreement] At the time they were speaking about *sharīʿa* in Zamfara State, there was a southern legislator who was invited on the television network and he blasphemed the religion of Islam. They phoned him and he was saying that they cannot be feeding the North [Muslims] while they are speaking about [implementing] *sharī'a*. Yet, one Islamic scholar with a blind heart, who does not know what he is doing—if you ask him he would say that they are trusted unbelievers.

[Yusuf censures the quietist scholars] Mallam said [*reading from a book*] it is from this verse that they deduce the law on the person who blasphemes against Allah's Messenger, because there is no blasphemy against the religion that is worse than insulting Allah's Messenger or drawing his image. Whoever blasphemes against Allah's Messenger should be killed. Or the person who denigrates the religion of Islam by saying that there is no knowledge in it, no progress in it, no politics in it, or he demonstrates that the religion of Islam is confining.

[Yusuf censures the quietist scholars] Allah says you should fight the leaders of the unbelievers, if they attack your religion. Once they attack your religion then you should look for their leader and slaughter him. You should look for the person on top and slaughter him; the person in the fore-front should be killed. Why? This is because they do not keep their promises. If you do that they would desist. If you kill the leaders, they would stop attacking your religion. I hope it is understood.

You should not have any business burning churches. Who is [behind] building and sustaining the churches? Who initially built them? Would you leave him then burn the churches or demolish them? When there is a limit, you should stop doing things without observing the limits. You cannot travel from your area and burn other places. No! Islam did not teach us to neglect the limits. The religion emphasizes limits, leadership, calmness, knowing what is right because if you start going forward there is no going back. I hope it is understood.

You should not burn churches—no, leave them, so after the *jihād* they will become stores. You should kill the leaders of the unbelievers [instead] because they do not keep their promises, so perhaps they will desist from attacking your religion. Then Allah says...

[Qur'ānic reciter]: "Will you not fight a people who broke their oaths and intended to drive the Apostle out, seeing that they attacked you first? Do you fear them? Surely, you ought to fear Allah more, if you are real believers." (Q9:13)

Part 3: Available at: https://www.youtube.com/watch?v=rf1TCBXLtWc

There is obviously a section missing here.

[Qur'ānic reciter]: "Fight them, Allah will punish them at your hands, will disgrace them, give you victory over them, and heal the hearts of a believing people. And He will remove the rage from their hearts. Allah shows mercy to whomever He pleases, and Allah is All-Knowing, Wise." (Q9:14–5)

[Yusuf continues]: One day a scholar was preaching and surprisingly he criticized us for always reciting the *jihād* verses. I was completely dumbfounded. Maybe whenever we approach these verses, he would like for us to skip over them. If we skip over them, is he also going to skip over them, too, or would he [like to] change the meaning of these verses? See what Allah says, will you not kill? Then what should I say? Should I skip the verses? Or after explaining the verses, maybe I should say that Allah is not referring to us. How will I handle these verses? Will you not kill a people who violated their oaths? They plotted to expel Allah's Messenger and they are the ones who started attacking you in the first place.

By Allah, some Muslims in this country do not even know the country called Denmark. They do not know. Who initiated the attack between the people who started drawing the image of an idol and a cartoon, and labelled them Allah's Messenger, while you are residing in your town? Allah says: Will you not kill them, when they are the people who started the attack on you and your religion?

[Yusuf censures the quietist scholars who equate jihad as violence and rebellion] The only thing we say is that what the Europeans brought is unbelief, so let us abandon it. What is our fault? It is democracy we have condemned, but we did not condemn your town, Maiduguri. It is not your language Kanuri that we condemned. It is not your wares or trading, not your people, not your women who we condemned.

This democracy that came from America is unbelief. The football that they play is damaging to the manners of family. The films they produce are corrupting the morals of the society. Those are the ills we are fighting. These soldiers are deceitful; it is not the religion of Islam they are protecting. These police are bogeymen—it is not Islam, but the law of the land that they are protecting.

Because of that, it is not permissible for a Muslim to enlist [in the police] and protect the law of the land. It is not permissible for a Muslim to go and die because of nationalism. So why are you fighting us? How does it affect you? What is your own belief? Are you a worshipper of the land? Or are you a democrat? Is it your religion? It is the religion of George Bush that I am condemning. You and Bush, are you the same? Have pity on yourself. [Yusuf censures the quietist scholars]

But it is not only me who says so; why would you concentrate on me alone? It is what Allah says that we will say and we are hoping that Allah will allow us to wage *jihād*. By Allah, we want to wage *jihād* even if we do not reach that stage; if we see those who have reached the stage we will join them in the *jihād*. There is nothing we hide from you. The *ṭāghūt* should know, and you too should know.

Allah says that you should kill them. To be honest, there is no other interpretation I know of, if not this interpretation. In Hausa, there is no other interpretation that I know of, aside from this interpretation. Allah will punish them with your hands. With your hands, in this verse; is it with your rosary? It is with your gun you will shoot, and He will disgrace them and assist you over them, and heal the hearts of the Muslims.

What happened in Iraq, did it not enrage you? What is happening in Palestine, Kashmir, what happened in Chechnya did it not enrage you? What happened in this country on different occasions, in Zango Kataf, Kafanchan and other places—did it not enrage you? There is no day that you will heal from this anger until that day in which you wage *jihād* for the sake of Allah.

As a result of the lack of knowledge of religion, a governor instigated the killing of over 500, 600 to 1,000 Muslims, then they said he has been suspended for six months. The people were saying that this suspension is good. It is good in what way? They did not kill him; in fact, they did nothing—but you said suspension is good? After they have killed more than 1,000 Muslims, then they said he is suspended for six months. When normalcy is being restored they would return him back to his position. Indeed, they returned him to his position and he continued to govern, while the Muslims felt they have been healed. They forgot those [Muslims] who they drove from their town fifty, forty and thirty years previously, those whose wealth was looted and kept in the field of a primary school. They have all been forgotten.

You do not know their whereabouts. The people who captured their women and children—you do not know their whereabouts. That is it—they have all been forgotten. Then they would wait for the next one. When they do it again then they will shout and shout, that is it and they will all be forgotten. Is that the life? There is no day upon which the heart will heal, except the day they wage *jihād*. Allah will ease the anger of the believers' hearts through the path of *jihād* and Allah will accept the repentance of the ones He wants among them by accepting Islam. [...]

[Qur'ānic reciter]: "Do you imagine that Allah would leave you alone before knowing who of you fight [in the way of Allah] and do not seek supporters besides Allah and His Apostle? Allah is fully aware of what you do." (Q9:16)

[Yusuf continues]: Since it is possible for you to feel that the previous verses are too harsh, then Allah says to you, what do you think they would do? If it is not like that, what do you expect they would do? Now, most people are saying this is not the period of *jihād*. This period is the era of dialogue. Look at the television and the radio, go there and explain. After all, they did not prohibit the preaching of the religion. Look at women wearing the *ḥijāb*, look at the Islamic schools that have been built. These are also forms of *jihād*. Look at politics; if you participate, you can elect a good leader. Allah says, "Do you imagine that Allah would leave you alone before knowing who of you fight [in the way of Allah]?"

Is Allah referring to political *jihād*? No! Go back to the previous verse: "Will you not fight a people who broke their oaths." Do you think they do not know those who came out and drove the unbelievers away? Do you think we will leave you just like that? Those who fight *jihād* did not hold anything that is not from Allah. They do not have any idol that they love. They do not have any *ṭāghūt* which they love. They do not have any mace that they worship. They do not have anything upon which they rely upon except Allah. They do not follow the laws of anyone except Allah's Messenger. They do not have any friends, either for consultation or love, except the believers.

If they do not know that you fought *jihād*, that you love Allah and Allah's Messenger, you love the believers, and you do not have any close friend except the believers—if they do not know all the above, you will not be spared until they know. Until they bring the test of disavowal from the unbelievers: "And We shall test you to know who are the fighters among you and who are the steadfast; and We will test your news." (Q47:31) We will not leave you until we see those who are the true jihadists, until we see in his heart that his loyalty is to no one except Allah, His Messenger and the believers.

[Yusuf explains the meaning of loyalty] Certainly, Allah will narrate all the things that you did, good or bad, Allah will narrate them on the Day of Resurrection. What we said that is correct, may Allah reward us and may He forgive our errors. Every person who wants to attain that level, by Allah he should go and study the Qurʾān both during both the day and night. He should engage in the night prayers and fasting. He should repent and avoid sinning against Allah and leave those that draw him to sin. By Allah, He will put you at that level. And may Allah aid us to attain that level.

7

EXPLANATION OF THE MEANING
OF ISLAMIC MONOTHEISM

BY ABUBAKAR SHEKAU

(c. SUMMER 2008)

[Trans.: Abdulbasit Kassim]

Available at: https://www.youtube.com/watch?v=vxW9Pl1rZs8

This video lecture by Abubakar Shekau is based on the book Mirāth al-anbiyā' (Inheritance of the Prophets), *and is the first documented presentation by Yusuf's successor. It covers the three types of* tawḥīd, *namely:* tawḥīd al-rubūbiyyah, tawḥīd al-asmā' wa-l-ṣifāt *and* tawḥīd al-ulūhiyyah. *Although it is undated, the lecture was most likely delivered at the early stage of preaching, mid-2008, based on the content of the lecture and Shekau's style of presentation. There were some missing parts at the beginning and the end of the video.*

[Standard Islamic opening] This lecture will focus on the topic: "how can a servant become a monotheist?" How can a servant possess *tawḥīd* (Islamic monotheism)? This is the topic I intend to discuss in my lecture based on the explanation of the scholars of the religion, Allah willing and may Allah assist us. The reason [I am delivering this lecture on this topic] is because of the questions that are often put to me, notwithstanding my student status, and to Mallam [Yusuf]. It is for this reason I decided to read the explanation of scholars on this topic—perhaps the people who always ask questions about this topic will buy this cassette, or we can give them refer-

he claims to be a student

ences to the books of eminent scholars. [Questioners can check the references for research.] The book I intend to read, Allah willing, is *Mirāth al-anbiyā'*. I hope it is understood.[1] The explanation of this topic is based upon this book since the author referred to the citations he relied upon for his explanation.

[Explanation of the meaning of a monotheist. *Tawḥīd is the capital*]

Allah is the only one who creates from nothing. Whoever possesses the thought that it is not Allah who creates from nothing; he should know that he has appropriated the right of Allah and given it to [someone] other than Allah or he has belied the right of Allah as often taught in Western education. I hope it is understood. In Western education, they believe that the heaven and earth are not created by Allah. Right from the onset, they dispute in the right of Allah based on *tawḥīd al-rubūbiyyah*. Is this understood? The same way the people of *alūhiyyah* sees everyone as god, I mean the people of Ibn al-'Arabī,[2] is the same way their creed is wrong.

[Explanation of the qualities of Allah]

The second category among the three rights of Allah is the right of Allah based on *tawḥīd al-asmā' wa-l-ṣifāt* (oneness of Allah's names and attributes), which include some names and features that are the attributes of Allah. These names and attributes belong to Allah alone. It is not permissible for anyone among mankind to give those names and attributes to anyone not even a near angel or a prophet that was sent to mankind. [Examples of the names of Allah]

Among the features of Allah that no one shares with Him is His feature of having complete power. Allah alone is the one who has complete power and judgment over everything. Is it understood? There is no one who has complete power over everything except Allah. Now, you see that all these laws are lies. There is no king except Allah, and if He desires, He will judge us now. Everyone in this world follows Allah. There is no one who does not follow Allah, including the unbelievers.

[Explanation of the rights of Allah] Among the rights is Allah's possession of complete knowledge. Allah has complete knowledge about us "...and that Allah has encompassed everything in knowledge." (Q65:12) Allah has complete knowledge about everything. He knows the life cycles of lice, ants, spiders, and mosquitoes and even how they copulate. He knows their movement as well as the movement of trees not just in Borno, Africa, Asia, Middle East, Europe, but in the whole world since the time of the Prophet Muhammad until the Day of Resurrection. Allah knows their movements. He knows what they did and it is all documented. Allah has this complete knowledge. He sees us everywhere we are. You must give Allah this right.

You should agree it is only Allah who knows what is hidden. There is no one who sees you while you are seated. It is a lie. Do not allow them to deceive you with [the knowledge of the] CIA and [the] SSS. It is a lie. There is no one who can know what you are doing until he sees you or someone informs him. It is a lie. Even if he comes there, he must see you. If he says on so-and-so day, you wore a specific cloth. It is a lie. It is not from his office he saw you. It is a lie. I hope it is understood.

[Allah is all-Seeing, all-Knowing not the *ṭawāghīt*] The third right is the right of Allah based on worship *tawḥīd al-ulūhiyyah* [oneness of Allah in worship]. Is it understood? Good and pure worship is for Allah alone. No one should be worshipped other than Allah. You must accept that Allah is one. Even if you accept that there is no creator except Allah, if you accept that there is no one that provides except Allah, even if you accept that there is no one that afflicts except Allah, if you accept that there is no one that has complete power over everything except Allah, even if you affirm the names of Allah, but you do not worship Allah you are an unbeliever.

[Explanation of the rights of Allah] Since you know that there is no one like Allah, why would you follow the laws of [anyone] other than Allah? It is surprising that you are saying you would not follow the Jews, but you are using speakers, cameras and cars? Will you not feel some sense of shame?

You should remember from the time of the Prophet Adam till today, science and technology have not progressed to the level of producing one seed of grain, one seed of guinea corn, or one drop of water. All of us who have gathered here today, how many seeds of rice have we swallowed today? Yet, there is no one who can produce a seed of rice, even if it will involve some research. So why would we not follow Allah who created the seed of rice? Allah has eased the process for us. He does not want us to engage in research; rather we should follow Him, His Book and His prophets. Yet you contend without any evidence. [Explanation of the rights of Allah]

8

EXEGESIS OF *SŪRAT AL ʿIMRĀN* (QURʾĀN 3:165–175)
BY MUHAMMAD YUSUF

(9 SEPTEMBER 2008)

[Trans.: Abdulbasit Kassim]
Available at: https://www.youtube.com/watch?v=aXXX5–49TtA

This selection is interesting because it demonstrates the jurisprudential side of Boko Haram, as it is preceded by a series of twelve legal (and other) questions. But the most interesting exegesis is that of Yusuf's martyrology, which is fairly well-developed in accord with that developed by Abdallah Azzam during the Afghanistan war (1979–89). There were some missing parts at the end of the video.

[Standard Islamic Opening]

Peace and blessings of Allah be upon you. Today is Tuesday, 30 Ramadan 1429 [9 September 2008], after the migration of Allah's Prophet from Mecca to Medina. We are presenting our daily evening study in this blessed month and we will start today from the verse 165, *AI ʿImrān*, the third chapter of the Qurʾān. This is the thirty-ninth lesson since we started.

[Yusuf reads and answers questions]:

Question 1: One of the questioners asks whether prayer is valid behind a prayer leader whose trouser hem lies below the ankle?

A: Allowing the trouser hem to lie below the ankle is among the major sins,[1] but a major sin does not render the prayer of a person invalid. If the prayer of a person is not invalid, then it is not prohibited to follow him in prayer; you can follow him in prayers. [Admonish him]

Question 2: Another questioner asks in Arabic about the ruling on a person who was fasting and had sexual intercourse with his wife during the month of Ramadan, but did not ejaculate before he withdrew from intercourse.

A: His fasting is negated. [Explanation of how to payback fasting]

Question 3: This questioner asks about whether the Bible, the Torah, and the Psalms are divided into sixty parts like the Qur'ān? And over how many years were they revealed?

A: I do not know into how many parts the Torah, Psalms and the Bible are divided, because I have never read them before, and I have never met a scholar who told me the number of parts into which they are divided. So, I do not know, but what I know is the fact that they are also divided into verses. They were revealed all at once, not piecemeal like the Qur'ān.[2] This is what Allah says in the Qur'ān: "He has revealed the Book to you in truth confirming what came before it, and He revealed the Torah and the Gospel [as guidance to mankind]." (Q5:3) "Revealed" in the verse means it was revealed at once. [Discussion of the meaning of revelation]

Question 4: This questioner asks whether Allah created the world because of His own volition or He created it because of the Prophet Muhammad.

A: [Explanation of Allah's volition] He did not create the world because of the Prophet Muhammad. He created the world so that people will worship Him and ascertain the truth: "We have not created the heavens and the earth and what lies between them save in truth." (Q15:85) [Discussion of the purpose of creation]

Question 5: This questioner is asking about the meaning of [the name] Abū Bakr al-Ṣiddīq.

A: The meaning of *bakr* is a newly born calf. The owner of cattle is Abū Bakr. Al-Ṣiddīq is the one who always confirms the truth. His name is Abū Bakr 'Abdallah bin Abī Quḥāfah al-Ṣiddīq.

Question 6: This questioner is asking about the ruling on fasting for a traveler. Should he suspend his fasting?

A: The traveler can suspend his fasting. [Yusuf cites Q2:184]

Question 7: This questioner is asking about the ruling on working in the house of an unbeliever, such as washing, ironing and other things. Is it permissible or not?

A: Washing and ironing for an unbeliever, if it does not affect your religion or interfere with the time of your religion, is permissible. However, I will not be able to provide a religious ruling on the other things you did not mention.

Question 8: This questioner is asking about the ruling on working for a banker in his house. Is it permissible or not?

A: A banker, if he does not have any other source of income, it is not permissible to work for him. [Yusuf cites Ibn Taymiyya's ruling on usury] If his sources of income are both permitted and forbidden at an equal level—for example, he earns 10,000 *naira* ($80) from permitted and forbidden [sources], then there is doubt, and it is advisable to break away from doubt, otherwise it will put you in danger.

Question 9: This questioner is asking about the ruling on following the caller to prayer during the call to prayer? Is it any caller to prayer that we should follow?

A: Yes, you are expected to follow any caller to prayer who calls to pray according to the way of the Prophet Muhammad. You should repeat whatever he says. [Yusuf says it is not mandatory to repeat the call to prayer over the radio.]

Question 10: This questioner is asking about the ruling on a person who registered with the company called Gold Shift Ltd, the company that registers people and at every month's end they pay you without your having worked. Is this permissible?

A: Is this the only detail you can provide? You just register with them and at the end of every month they will pay you without doing any work?! Perhaps there is a catch, so until you provide the details of the type of agreement the question cannot be answered. However, for those who bargain with you to bring five customers, and then they will pay you based on the value of those five customers, this type of bargain is a means of gambling. You should ignore them. [until their motives become clear.]

Question 11: He said he is satisfied with my explanation concerning Western education because there is a mosque in his university they nicknamed the mosque of "carryover."[3] He said he swears by the One who holds his soul in His hand, if you go to the mosque after the night prayer you would see them praying the evening prayer congregationally when nothing prevents them from praying at the appropriate time other than [going to] their lectures. [He] is asking about the permissibility of going for *iʿtikāf* [seclusion during the last ten days of Ramadan] for twenty days.

A: It is permissible by Allah's will.

[Question 12 regarding prescription of books on Arabic grammar.]

Question 13: This last question is not really a question. [Yusuf cautions against partisanship] If you hear someone saying on the radio that we order people to go to the farm, or any other claims, if you want to believe this claim then you can because the aim is to win over your heart. On the other hand, if you think their claim is a lie then you should ignore it. If you have any further questions, ask the people going to the farm whether we collected money from them. This questioner is asking about the claim he heard that anyone who does not go to the farm we are collecting 2,000 *naira* [$15] from him. He also said in his question that he heard I have a lot of farm equipment, so anyone who comes to me without any equipment I would usually order them to pay 50 *naira* [30 cents] before allowing them to go to the farm. So, since the claim is a lie, there is no need for anyone to write a question about it.

[*Yusuf denounces irrelevant questions in an irked manner...*]

[Qur'ānic reciter]: "And when a misfortune befell you after you had inflicted twice as much, you said: 'Whence is this?' say: 'It is from yourselves.' Surely Allah has power over everything. And what befell you on the day the two armies met was by Allah's leave, that He might know the true believers. And that He might know the hypocrites. When it was said to them: 'Come, fight in the way of Allah or defend yourselves,' they replied: 'If only we knew how to fight, we would have followed you.' On that day, they were closer to unbelief than to belief. They say with their tongues what is not in their hearts; and Allah knows best what they conceal! Those who said to their brethren, while they themselves stayed at home: 'Had they obeyed us they would not have been killed,' say: 'Then ward off death from yourselves if you are truthful.'" (Q3:165–8)

[Yusuf continues]: [Discussion of the battles of Badr and Uhud] If you go out for *jihād* and you observed every rule and followed Allah's Messenger's Sunna, but you were afflicted by defeat, this defeat is because of your deeds. You should find out: maybe you stole from the booty, such as in the example we read yesterday, or maybe you admired some of their women. If you are fighting *jihād*, then anyone you see are enemies of Allah. The same way you detest the sight of a beast, that is the same way you should detest the sight of their women. However, if you stay back and admire their women, then you should be prepared for a disaster. I hope it is understood.

How would you prepare and admire their women at the same time? Even if they are gathered together, they should be viewed as beasts. They are property and booty.[4] If you see wealth and money, and are attracted to them, then you are crying out for an impending disaster by which Allah will test you. Allah has power over all things.

[Yusuf discusses the battle of Hunayn and Q9:25] You see from this statement alone that we have a large number who can test you. Now, someone could invite you to join these soldiers, the soldiers of ignorance [the Nigerian army], when he is making a claim that by joining them you will assist the religion.

This type of statement is a statement of unbelief. The soldiers worship the cross. The metal indicating their rank is the image of a cross. Each time they conduct a parade in the presence of an important personality, they usually make the sign of a cross with their swords. If you look at their military paraphernalia for each of their parades, they are all the property of the church, including their drums, belts, etc. So, is it this type of army you will join and help the religion, how? And you will kill a person that Allah and His Prophet did not order to be killed.

All the people who were killed by the Nigerian army—not one of them falls into the category of people who Allah ordered to be killed. And Allah does not allow you to kill even an unbeliever or an animal without His permission. I hope it is understood.

Therefore, this army is an army of unbelief. The army of Nigeria, and others of the ignorant systems, is not the army of Islam. Anyone who advises you to join the army has deceived you. The scholar who gave you the ruling allowing you to join the army to help the religion should lead by example by also joining the army. Let him also become a soldier. Let us see the scholars coming back with their belts [in the form of crosses]. After all, whenever the Prophet preached about the religion, he was known for leading by example.

[Discussion of the jihad of hypocrites] This is the reason why these scholars are hostile to us because they do not want the *jihād* to become a reality. Should it become a reality, they will also be affected. If the American soldiers arrive here, they will not see any difference between you and me. They will see us as the same people—our beards are the same, our mosque is the same, and our prayers are the same. If they instruct them [American soldiers] to shoot the Muslims, they will shoot anyone without differentiating between us, except when you pledge your allegiance to them. Only then will you earn their protection. [Discussion of those who possess faith and unbelief in them.]

[Qur'ānic reciter]: "And do not think those who have been killed in the way of Allah as dead; they are rather living with their Lord, well-provided for. Rejoicing in what their Lord has given them of His bounty, and they rejoice for those who stayed behind and did not join them; knowing that they have nothing to fear and that they shall not grieve. They rejoice in Allah's grace and His favor, and that Allah will not withhold the reward of the faithful." (Q3:169–71)

[Yusuf continues]: [...] Allah revealed the verse: "And do not think those who have been killed in the way of Allah as dead." Therefore, anyone who desires the medicine of death, he should strive to be martyred. Martyrdom is the medicine of death. Even if you die, you are not dead.

[Discussion of the martyrdom of Haram Ibn Milhan al-Ansari at Bir al-Mauna and the death of Muhammad] He is the person who told us that the martyrs do not feel the pain of death, not more than the sting of an ant. If an ant or a bug stings you, you will feel a small pain. But once you remove it, the pain is gone. That is the similitude of a martyr's death. It is for this reason you would see a martyr while he is dying, he would still be calm and admonishing.

Shaykh Abdallah Azzam was narrating to us about an incident that occurred during the Afghan War [against the U.S.S.R.] in Afghanistan. He said while they were fighting, the stomach of a martyr burst, and all his intestines poured onto the floor. Yet, he was sitting and admonishing, so the people that gathered around him were crying. He asked them, why were they crying? They said: "Do you not see that your stomach has burst?" He said: "So it has burst!" And it was like that he died. There were many of the martyrs whose stories they narrated, who after two weeks of death their corpses were seen to be as fresh as new.[5]

That is martyrdom that makes you see your blood smelling sweet. It was a bomb that they put in the body of the car of 'Abdallah Azzam while he was driving with his son for the Friday prayer. The bomb exploded and it shattered them.[6] They found one leg on a tree, another one on a different tree. They were all shattered, yet for several months if you visit the place of the explosion you would perceive the fragrance of musk.[7] The place is scented [by his martyrdom]. I hope you understand.

[Virtues of Martyrdom] "They are rather living with their Lord, well-provided for." Allah's Messenger said their souls are kept in a bird—specifically the birds whose nest is attached to the Throne [of Allah]. There is something like a bulb around the Throne in a circle. They will put the soul of the martyr inside a bird. It is the main part of the body that is changed. It is still that person, but in the body of a bird. Then you will enter paradise, roam about freely from this tree to that tree, and then come back to the Throne to sleep. When the day breaks, then you will continue roaming paradise freely, according to your wish, and then return to the Throne to sleep.

[Virtues of Martyrdom] So, this special treatment in paradise is the reason why the martyrs desire to return to earth and be martyred again. The Prophet said: "If not for the fact that I do not want to make things difficult for my *umma*, I would not have stayed at home while some people go out and fight. Each time I want to go out and fight, they would also want to go out but they cannot [because of lack of mounts]. This is the reason why I sometimes stay back home, and instruct other people to go out and fight. By Allah, I would want to be killed, then returned to the earth, and be killed again more than ten times on Allah's path."[8] The Prophet admired the death of a martyr. I hope it is understood.

Therefore, Allah's Messenger said, the soul of a believer is kept in a bird that will be eating food inside paradise until the Day of Resurrection when Allah will return the soul [of the martyr] to his body. I hope it is understood. That is martyrdom. Indeed, martyrs are the ones who will enjoy this special privilege: on the Day of Resurrection they will stand on the same pulpit with the prophets. The prophets will ask a question: "Who are these people?" This is because of their status, the pleasure and the acceptance Allah has given them. They are those who offered their lives and their blood for the sake of Allah, and for the sake of uplifting the religion. I hope it is understood. This is the reason why there is no one who will desire to return to the earth except the martyr.

[Yusuf cites Q36:14, 27] From the point when the martyr is killed, Allah will forgive all his sins. His first drop of blood will fall inside paradise. Allah will marry him to any virgin of his choice, and give him the opportunity to intercede for the people of his household.[9] I hope it is understood. Martyrdom is not a small status. And may Allah grant us the status of martyrdom. [Yusuf cites Q3:171]

[Qur'anic reciter]: "Those who responded to Allah's call and the Messenger's after they had incurred many wounds. To those of them who do what is right and fear Allah, a great reward is in store. Those to whom the people said: 'The people have been arrayed against you, so fear them.' But this increased their faith and so they said: Allah is sufficient for us. He is the best Guardian! Thus, they came back with a grace and bounty from Allah. No harm touched them, and they complied with Allah's good pleasure. Allah's bounty is great! That indeed is the Devil frightening his followers; but do not fear them, fear Me, if you are true believers!" (Q3:172–5)

[Yusuf continues]: [Yusuf narrates the battle of Uhud] This is *jihād*. It is not now when you are comfortable in the town. You may have fought and been injured, but you would still be commanded to move forward and continue the *jihād*. You have been injured, and without food, yet you would still be commanded to move out for *jihād*. Why? No matter the situation, if the unbelievers are left alone, they will gain strength. This is the reason why we should go and break them, so that our children will grow and practice Islam. There is no retreat. I hope it is understood.

Therefore, a Muslim should increase his saying of "Allah is sufficient for us. He is the best Guardian!" Despite any evil plot or scheme against us, we are Muslims, and we should always say "Allah is sufficient for us. He is the best Guardian!" Once we say it, we have overpowered the danger. Despite the plot of the Jews, the Americans or any worldly plot against us, we should always say "Allah is sufficient for us. He is the best Guardian!" with sincerity.

[Discussion of the meaning of the prayer "Allah is sufficient for us. He is the best Guardian!"] "Thus, they came back with a grace and bounty from Allah. No harm touched them, and they complied with Allah's good pleasure. Allah's bounty is great!" They came and told you that people have gathered to harm you, and they are many, and more powerful than you. They are prepared to do this and that to you. America will come.

"That indeed is the Devil frightening his followers; but do not fear them, fear Me, if you are true believers!" It is only Satan who suggests to you the fear of his supporters and friends. What is the difference between an American and a Nigerian soldier? They are all the same. I hope it is understood.

The *mujāhidīn* will deal with them. The people defending the country, tradition, custom, political party, constitution can never defeat you while you defend the Qur'ān, except when you do not have faith. This is the creed Allah wants us to hold and believe. "The case of those who took up other protectors, apart from Allah, is like that of the spider who built a house. Truly, the most brittle of houses is the house of the spider, if only they knew." (Q29:41) [Yusuf discusses about those who take America, China and Russia as protectors besides Allah.]

9

BBC HAUSA SERVICE INTERVIEW
WITH MUHAMMAD YUSUF

(c. 15 OCTOBER 2008)

[Trans.: Abdulbasit Kassim]

This is probably the only interview of Yusuf by a foreign media agency. The interview was moderated by Bilkisu Labaran of BBC Hausa service in Kano and it should be dated to approximately 15 October 2008 (according to the reference to the moonsighting, which would have been 30 September 2008, said to have been "two weeks ago" in the text). In the interview, Yusuf reiterated his opposition to Western education, the polio vaccination, and the Nigerian government. He expounded the source of his creed and refuted the Kharijite label pinned upon him by Izala scholars. He also advocated the prophetic (pseudo-)medicine and gave a detailed account of the moonsighting controversy between his group and the Islamic authorities as well as the dispute between his followers and the Izala movement.[1]

Bilkisu Labaran [B]: Right now, I am here together with Mallam Muhammad Yusuf with whom we shall discuss some issues. Let us start with what you said that Western education is forbidden. Is this true?

Muhammad Yusuf [Y]: [Standard Islamic opening] It is true that I said that Western education under this current system and curriculum which was introduced to us by the Europeans is forbidden. It is antithetical to monotheism. There are different elements [in Western education] we have found out to be specious because they are antithetical to the principles of monotheism. We are not the first people to

71

espouse this view. There are notable scholars in the past like Ibn Taymiyya and other contemporary scholars who also espouse similar views that there are certain elements in Western education that are antithetical to monotheism.

For example, the belief that rainfall is caused by the process of evaporation is erroneous. That belief is antithetical to the word of Allah in *sūrat al-Mu'minīn*: "And We send down water from the heavens in measure, then lodge it in the ground, although We are able to allow it to drain away." (Q23:18) There is also a *hadīth* of the Prophet where he narrated that whenever it rains, the Prophet would go out so the rain would fall on him, and he would say "Allah has created you anew."

Likewise, the belief that the world is spherical is merely a hypothesis and any hypothesis that contradicts the principles of the Qur'ān is considered null and void. There is also the theory of Darwinism and of evolution, which states that man evolves through different stages. This theory is unbelief and it is antithetical to the Qur'ānic account of the creation of man.

All these constitute disbelief in the revelation of Allah. These are the elements we said should be expunged, while we can appropriate the true knowledge, and teach it in accordance with the principles of Islam. For example, when a person studies medicine, he should be allowed to practice it professionally. You studied journalism and now we are giving you information. When a person studies and later discovers that what he studied was erroneous, he is expected to repent. For the people who have yet to study, it is important that they should be taught the true knowledge, for them to learn what is right from the inception. However, it is inappropriate to study erroneous knowledge when one is aware of the error. Allah does not hold anybody responsible for that about which they are ignorant.

B: This leads me to another question. There is a purported account that you made some of your followers and students to destroy their [school] certificates. Most of them are now hawking dates, selling shoes and have abandoned their educational pursuits.

Y: As I previously stated, Western education under this current system and curriculum, which was introduced to us by the Europeans, contains different elements, some of which are antithetical to Islam and some of which concur with the principles of Islam. It is not permissible to study Western education until one understands those elements that are permissible to study.

For example, gender-mixing in schools and universities is antithetical to Islam. This verdict is based on the religious rulings of notable scholars and it is not just my own opinion. Therefore, it is not permissible to study what contradicts the principles of Islam.

On the issue of the certificates, if a person becomes learned in a field, that person cannot take the knowledge from his brain. A certificate is just a form of symbolism. We did not counsel anyone to destroy his certificate. We only counsel people not to embrace this system of education in its entirety. Accept what is beneficial and refrain from what is antithetical to Islam.

In this country or anywhere in the world, we agree with the educational systems that do not contradict Islam. Right now, we also engage in teaching. We are building primary and secondary schools that will be administered strictly in accordance with the principles of Islam. We support progressive education for Muslims on the condition that it is permissible [and not antithetical to Islam].

We did not encourage people to practice only one form of trade. We have people who engage in different forms of business like clothing, selling of perfume, those who import and export, those who sell books—and those who sell dates are not prevented from engaging in other trade. It is fallacious to say that we encourage people to engage only in selling dates. Selling dates is a form of trade, and if a person is interested in it, he can go ahead with the trade. Whatever form of trade that is permissible in Islam, we encourage people to engage in it. We are self-sufficient and we do not receive any form of support from the government or any organization either at home and abroad. Trading in dates is not the only means of our livelihood. We are self-sufficient and our provision cannot come from the profits of selling dates alone.

As for my creed, I believe in the creed of the Prophet Muhammad. I follow the Book of Allah and the Sunna of the Prophet. On the issue of my creed, I developed my understanding from the book *al-'Aqīda al-ṭaḥāwiyyah* (*The Creed of Imam Ṭaḥāwī*) by Abū Jaʿfar al-Ṭahawī.[2] I share the same creed with him. I share the same creed with Imām Aḥmad b. Ḥanbal, Imām Shafiʿī and Imām Mālik. I share the same creed with the author of *Risāla* in the chapter "what is uttered by a way of speech." I have read *Kitāb al-tawḥīd* (*The Book of monotheism*) and *al-Uṣūl al-thalāthah* (*The Three Foundations of Truth*).[3] I share the religious rulings of scholars like Ibn Taymiyya and Ibn Qayyim al-Jawziyya. This is my creed and Allah knows best concerning my creed.

I am not a Kharijite. Kharijites are the people who rebel against legitimate Islamic government, like the caliphate of 'Uthman and 'Ali. They also plotted against the caliphs, used *takfīr* against them, and killed the Companions. I hold the belief that caliphs 'Uthman and 'Ali were both Muslims and legitimate leaders. I hold them in high esteem and I disagree with the creed of the Kharijites.

The people who accuse me of being a Kharijite erroneously equate my dissent against this government with the rebellion of the Kharijites against caliphs 'Uthman and 'Ali. This is the main reason they call me Kharijites. Imām Shahrastānī[4] said that Kharijites are those who rebelled against the true leader. On this basis, any government that rules by means of the constitution, democracy, military dictatorship or monarchy cannot be classified as a government ruled by the true leader, so long as it does not govern by means of the Book of Allah and the Sunna of the Prophet.

The Prophet enjoined the Muslims to follow a leader, even if he is a slave, as long as he rules by means of the Book of Allah, and even if he betrays them. If he fails to uphold the Book of Allah, he does not deserve to be followed. It is on this basis that we dissociate ourselves completely from this government.

As for those who label us as Kharijites, if indeed we are Kharijites Allah will make this clear, but if they are merely being mischievous, Allah will make it clear. And Allah knows best.

B: There was a time some medical officials from the government visited to give the polio vaccination.[5] Is it true that you objected to their mission?

Y: Yes. We do not believe in such medications because there are many preventive drugs which the Prophet explained to us of which the people are not aware. As an Islamic teacher, it is my duty to educate the people concerning the medications the Prophet explained to us rather than supporting the medication offered by the government. The government, America and the United Nations have the means of propagating their plans.

For instance, the black seed, the Prophet said it can cure any disease.[6] The Prophet also said whoever drinks Zamzam water with a good intention,[7] it can cure any disease. There is also the olive about which the Qur'ān and the Prophet said contains many blessings (Q24:35). There are also supplications which as a Muslim I should promote, because the Qur'ān attests to their efficacy.

The polio vaccines, on the other hand, there are indications that they have limitations and adverse effects on children, even here in Kano. The side effects of these vaccines are known and I should not be supporting what is known to be detrimental to the *umma*.

B: Let us now talk about the 'Id celebration that took place about two weeks ago. The *Jama'atu Nasril Islam* (JNI) announced the sighting of the moon and declared Monday as the day of 'Id, but you did not accept that, so had your 'Id on Tuesday. What was your evidence for that?

Y: According to the principles of Islam, moonsighting is the responsibility of all Muslims. Because the government we have is a democratic government, we are saddled with the task of sighting the moon and informing the government to have it announced. Under an Islamic government, it would be the responsibility of the government.

According to the principles of Islam, any leader who does not govern with the Book of Allah and the Sunna of the Prophet should not be described as an Islamic leader. On this basis, we do not view the Sultan as the leader of the Muslims; rather, we view him [merely] as the Sultan of Sokoto.

For over fifteen years, we have been engaging in moonsighting. In fact, when we were fasting alongside the government, we used to convey information about moonsighting to them and they would announce it. Three years ago, we were the ones who sighted the moon, and conveyed the information to the government for them to announce it. Last year, when we sighted the moon, we conveyed the information to them, yet they refused to announce it. We proceeded to commence the fasting, since we have seventeen people who have confirmed that they sighted the moon and there is no contrary evidence. When 'Id approaches, fortunately we did not sight the moon so we fasted the thirtieth day and we celebrated 'Id the same day with them.

However, this year we had differences in our moonsighting, so we celebrated 'Id based on our sighting, because it is obligatory based on our belief and the opinions of some scholars of *ḥadīth*. Ibn Taymiyya... brought evidence from Allah's words: "Say: 'My Lord has only forbidden open and secret indecencies, sin, unjust aggression, and your association with Allah that for which He sent down no authority, and your saying about Allah that which you do not know.'" (Q7:33)
Ibn Taymiyya said according to this verse, Allah has enumerated four things that under no circumstances should a Muslim commit; polytheism, unlawful sexual intercourse—homosexuality, lesbianism—lying against Allah and oppression.

B: What is the reason behind the controversy between you and the authorities?

Y: There are some of my students in Monguno who were initially together with the Izala members. They jointly owned three mosques. When misunderstandings erupted between us, two of the mosques came under the control of my followers, while the remaining one came under the control of the Izala members. The Izala members prevented my followers from attending their Friday congregational mosque because they disagree with my followers. It therefore became a necessity for my followers, due to their harassment, to open a mosque for their Friday congregational prayers, since the mosque where they previously performed the Friday prayer came under the control of Izala members, who had also embezzled the finances of the mosque. Without any investigation, the police arrested sixty-four of our members and they sealed off their mosque.

B: What is your position regarding the arrest of your followers?

Y: I will follow due process and legitimate means prescribed by Allah to secure their release because we do not take illegal steps unless it becomes necessary. The people have misunderstood us as a set of people prone to fighting. We are only against the government and not the people. Indeed, if truly we are prone to fighting, the oppression from the government is enough to spur us to start fighting.

10

FILM

BY MUHAMMAD YUSUF

(c. DECEMBER 2008)

[Trans.: Abdulbasit Kassim]
Available at: https://www.youtube.com/watch?v=xthVNq9OKD0

This lecture, tentatively dated to early December 2008, is a supplement to Yusuf's polemic against the government and the scholars who argued against his methodology. The lecture can be classified into three sections: the first section covers the theme of spirituality, seeking knowledge, and the censure of artifice in films; the second section covers the theme of ideological justifications for tagging the government as illegitimate and criticism against the Islamic scholars who support the government, while the final section covers an explanation of the different creeds in Islam. Here, Yusuf explained how the ideology of his group is based upon the creed of Ahl al-Sunna wa-l-Jamāʿa which he argues is antithetical to other creeds in Islam. There were some missing parts at the beginning of the video.

He came out and declared to the world that they cannot carry out this task. This is the meaning of victory. If you love a person who opposes the Prophet Muhammad, Allah will not love you. If you love a person who opposes the Prophet Muhammad, the Prophet Muhammad will not love you. How will you secure his intercession while you know that when a person dies he will have no other provision in heaven apart from his religion? You will not have any provision or savior except your religion.

Brothers! The films we watch, whichever genre: Indian films, American, Chinese, Nigerian films, Hausa films—they are all deception. They are complete deception from the beginning to the end. From the beginning, you will understand their deception by the names of the cast. The actual names of the cast are not the names they are assigned in the film. This is the first deception. The second deception is the deception of assigning a spouse to a person who is not an actual spouse in real life. If they claim this is the son of a character, he is not his son in real life. If they claim that a character is affluent, it is a deception because in real life the character is destitute. I hope it is understood. This is how they produce the films. It is deception. The greatest deception is when you watch a film and they narrate to you that the cast all died, but the next day you would see them alive.[1] There is no idiocy that surpasses this deception. It is the Jews who are playing with the intellect of Allah's slaves.

Therefore, brothers, let us return to our senses. There are stories that can give your mind tranquility in the books and not films or fictions. This is true. Allah says this Qur'ān is story we gave you in truth: "We narrate to you the fairest narratives in revealing to you this Qur'an." (Q12:3) You should recite the Qur'ān for you to hear the story of the people of the past, the story of the people that have forged ahead and those that entered the paradise. [Discussion of the virtues of paradise.]

However, you should exercise patience with the present world. You should relinquish the enjoyment of this world and worship Allah. If, however, you choose to follow your desires in this world, you will not be entitled to your desires in the hereafter. The religion in a nutshell is for you to obey the commands of Allah in this world, even when it is not delightful to you. In the hereafter, Allah will leave you to satisfy your desires. In this world, if you choose to follow your desires and disobey the commands of Allah, Allah will do as He wishes with you in the hereafter. This is the religion, brothers.

[Discussion of the virtues of jihad, worship and seeking for Islamic knowledge] By Allah, the life we are living today and all these governments that we have are governments that reject Allah and His Messenger. They have abandoned the Book of Allah. They have invented their own laws with their hands and intellect. The law of ignorance is the same law about which Allah says: "Now, is it the judgment of the 'period of ignorance' [jāhiliyya] that they desire? Yet who is a better judge than Allah for a people who believe with certainty?" (Q5:50) The law of ignorance is the law that contradicts the book of Allah and the Sunna of His Messenger. This is the law of ignorance and people should learn how to differentiate between ruling with some [source] other than Allah's laws and ḥukm jāhiliyya (the laws of ignorance).

The law of ignorance is the secular constitution while ruling with [something] other than Allah's laws is when a judge, who is following the book of Allah and the Sunna of His Messenger, mistakenly follows his selfish desires in a ruling. This is the meaning of ruling with other than Allah's laws. The law of ignorance, on the other hand, has no relation to the Qur'ān and ḥadīth at all. In Nigeria, they do not govern based on the laws of the Qur'ān and *ḥadīth*. They govern with other laws, and their system of ruling is like the worship of an idol. In idol worship, they would compel the people to contribute money, slaughter camels, but the devotees of the idols are the [true] beneficiaries of these donations—the likes of Abū Jahl, 'Utba, Shayba and others.[2]

Similarly, if they compel you to help the land and be patriotic towards the country, the country does not represent the masses, rather it symbolizes the elites. If you pay taxes, is it the country that benefits? Where exactly do they channel those taxes? They channel them into their private pockets. They are the country. Whenever you hear them saying "help the country," they are calling for help for themselves. They want to rule over you and control you. Therefore, brothers, we have not been ordained to serve any country; rather we are expected to be served by the country/land: "It is He who made the earth level for you; so, stroll through its regions and eat of its provisions. Unto Him is the Resurrection." (Q67:15)

The land has been made subservient to you so that you can use it to worship Allah. You should neither serve the country nor the government, except in what has been ordained by Allah. Any government that contradicts Allah's laws is falsehood: "The judgment is truly Allah's." (Q12:67) Allah forbade us from following a government that contradicts His laws. We should only follow the government that rules with Allah's laws. The government of Allah will be achieved through preaching.

[Discussion of Islamic monotheism and criticism of Izala scholars] Whoever follows the obedience, law, politics, education and knowledge that contradict the way of the prophet Muhammad will be driven away from al-Kawthar[3] on the Day of Resurrection. Therefore, we should practice the religion brothers, so that we will not be driven away on the Day of Resurrection. We should practice the religion, brothers. [Discussion of Q2:21.]

By Allah, this non-Islamic government will be defeated. This [defeat] is presently being decreed. It is not compulsory that this government will be defeated at our hands, but it must be defeated, it will be defeated by the call of monotheism. What is expected is for people to stop hanging onto the tree [of the government], because the day will come when they will finish chopping down this tree, so you will fall with it.

[Yusuf admonish his listeners to join the struggle to establish Islamic monotheism] Therefore, just as we announced yesterday, these people are just ranting on the radio stations with a claim that they called me for a debate, and I declined. Is that not their claim? This is the reason we said we announced a ten-day series of admonition. Yesterday was the first of the series. Today is the second. We are inviting anyone. Initially, we said we do not want to debate issues with the scholars of Islamic schools—is that not what we said? However, from today we accept everyone including them before the end of these ten days' admonition. [Yusuf challenges his critics for a public debate.]

[Moderator announces]: [Announcement] Allah willing tomorrow there is going to be another admonition at night at the Borehole Lane, along the byway of Ustaz by Allah's permission after 'ishā' (evening prayer), and Mallam Muhammad Yusuf will be present. Afterwards, there is going to be another admonition on Tuesday at Mafoni, at the lane of the leader of Daraman, and on Wednesday in Gamboru near the pharmacy of Ibn Mas'ud, inside Gamboru.[4] On Thursday, there will be another admonition at Bulabulin around the area of Tsamia Lane, Allah willing.

[Abubakar Shekau reads a question]: [Islamic prayer] Mallam, this questioner is asking you to provide a detailed explanation about the Shi'ites because there are some youths who are following their creed based on the belief that Shi'ism is a way to express love of the household of the Prophet. [Discussion of Shiites persuasion of Muslim youths.]

[Yusuf responds]: As we previously mentioned in the lecture, there are different variants of Shi'ism. The variant that is prevalent in this land is the Ithna' 'Ashara Ja'fariya Shi'ites. This variant of Shi'ism is outside of the religion of Islam. In their creed, they do not agree that the Qur'ān is complete. They have a book called *Uṣūl al-kāfī*, which we have once took to Bama, but they[5] declined to engage us [in debate]. We still have the book up till this time, and in it they argue that the Qur'ān is incomplete, and they also cite many *hadīths* to support their claim.

[Discussion of the Shiites creed] Whenever you see them doing their procession—very soon they will conduct their procession[6]—and they place a *hijāb* on a black or female dog, they are referring to our mother 'A'isha. [Yusuf explains Shiites vilification of Aisha.] They are not practicing the religion of Islam and Allah knows best.

[Shekau reads a question]: [*a question on the issue of* maṣlaḥa]

[Shekau reads a question]: The last questioner is asking for an explanation of the creed of the Mu'tazila, Kharijites, Ahl al-Sunna, and Murji'a: which one of these creeds listed is closer to the truth and which one is closer to unbelief? May Allah elevate you and reward you for your sermon.

[Yusuf responds]: This question should be amended. If you are seeking for an explanation of the creed of the Mu'tazila, Kharijites, Ahl al-Sunna, and Murji'a, then you should not ask which one of these creeds is closer to the truth—rather you should ask which one of them is the truth. This is because Ahl al-Sunna is the truth and you should not say it is closer to the truth. It is the truth.

[Discussion of the Mu'tazila creed] There are different variants of the Kharijites. There are those who revolt against the Book of Allah and the Sunna of His Messenger. The government of Nigeria is Kharijite! I hope it is understood. Ibn Taymiyya explained that if a government does not govern with the Book of Allah and the Sunna of His Messenger, the government is Kharijite. I hope it is understood. [Yusuf explains why the Nigerian government is Kharijite.]

Imām Shahrastānī said Kharijites are those who refused to follow the true leader. I hope it is understood. He said: "Kharijites are those who deviate from following the true leader."[7] The true leader—and who is a true leader? The true leader is the leader that governs with the Book of Allah and the Sunna of His Messenger the leader that governs like 'Uthman, 'Alī because those are the leaders against whom that the Kharijites first revolted. Does [President] Yar'adua govern like 'Uthman? The people who are calling us Kharijites because we declined to follow Yar'adua, they consider the government of Yar'adua to be on the same level as that of 'Uthman. This is the main reason we are called Kharijites. I hope it is understood.

Whoever refuses to follow the true leader is a Kharijite. Is this leader a true leader? Is he a leader who governs with the book of Allah and the Sunna of Allah's Messenger? I hope it is understood. The people who refuse to follow the Muslim leaders ruling with the Book of Allah and the Sunna of His Messenger are the Kharijites. This is the first creed.

[Discussion of Kharijites belief on major sins] Therefore, we do not share any of the creeds of the Kharijites. The wives of the Kharijites, even when they are menstruating, they must pray according to the understanding of some of the Kharijites, and there are others who believe they must pay back the prayers they missed during their menstruation. The Kharijites declared 'Uthman and 'Alī to be unbelievers. We do not believe in any of their creeds.

[Discussion of the Murji'a creed] This is the last question. Therefore, let us pray may Allah guide everyone that He wishes to be guided. Anyone who has sincere intention, may Allah guide him. Every Mallam whose thought is for the religion may Allah guide him. Anyone who has corrupted thoughts, may Allah distance him. O Allah! We are beseeching you, the youths we admonished, please help them and help us. O Allah! Guide them and place us all together on the true path. O Allah! Grant us the ablity to help your religion.

PART TWO

REACHING A VERDICT
(2008–2009)

David Cook

After the deliberations and discussions of Part 1, by the end of 2008 Boko Haram had reached its verdict about Nigeria. While the group's initial phase was characterized by the group having close connections to the northern Muslim religious elites, and frequently debating with its leading lights, starting in late 2008 a marked change appears within the extant materials. Violence was not foreign to Boko Haram before this time (then known as the Yusufiyya or the Nigerian Taliban), such as during the 2004 Kanamma clashes with Nigerian police.[1] Yusuf's preaching, though, during the period 2006–2008 demonstrates a breadth of topics that is alien to the period 2008–2009 culminating in the June–July 2009 uprising.

Starting with the dramatic video History of the Muslims (text 11), Yusuf's focus is almost exclusively upon *jihād* and violence. Nor is he alone in this change of tone, as both his subordinates, Abubakar Shekau and Mamman Nur, are fully participant in the ferocious language. Although the proximate cause of the Boko Haram uprising were the restrictions placed by the security forces associated with the anti-crime initiative called "Operation Flush" on Boko Haram members riding motorbikes without helmets, this was merely a pretext.

In early 2009, the Nigerian government, like other African governments, had begun to crack down on the high numbers of unprotected motorcycle drivers and passengers, making them wear helmets and take other safety precautions. This crackdown was resented somewhat, and ultimately provided the spark that set off Boko Haram's first revolt. One cannot reasonably doubt, however, given the paranoia surrounding Yusuf and his subordinates, his continual denunciation of the

Nigerian government as unbelievers, and the apocalyptic atmosphere attested in the videos, that there would have been a major clash sooner or later. However, it is worth noting that Yusuf emphasizes his continuous contact with the government and police until text 19.

One of the most remarkable aspects of the videos is that they preserve question and answer periods (sometimes at the beginning, sometimes at the end) in which a great many of the basic doctrines of Boko Haram are challenged. While Yusuf tends to answer in a scholarly, measured manner, Shekau answers by bullying the questioners.

Thematically, the videos are straightforward. Starting with History of the Muslims (text 11), and continuing with the Sermons (text 15), Yusuf tries to prove that African Muslim history is closely associated with *jihād*. The only reason why the Nigerian government and others can dominate the Muslims is because the latter have abandoned *jihād*. In this part, Yusuf covers all aspects of *jihād*, including its relationship to the family, the spiritual and monetary basis for fighting (text 17), and then in the Declaration of War (text 19) he gives the reasons for the conflict, and what the stakes are. Shekau's and Nur's speeches are nowhere near as eloquent as those of Yusuf, but make up for that lack with a surprisingly folksy, albeit bombastic, tone.

11

HISTORY OF THE MUSLIMS

BY MUHAMMAD YUSUF

(c. DECEMBER 2008)

[Trans.: Abdulbasit Kassim]
Available at: https://www.youtube.com/watch?v=eUQYNucjqUE

This video lecture proves that Yusuf's goals were oriented towards Salafi-jihadism, and pointed towards the militant stage of Boko Haram. His bodily bellicosity in the video is obvious, and his methodology at this stage is modelled after that of al-Qaeda. Tentatively it should be dated to post-29 November 2008, as the document speaks of the Jos riots at that time. It is a great pity that the first section is not extant. This document should be compared in its methodology to 'Abd al-Salām Faraj's The Neglected Duty, and should be considered in its importance to be Yusuf's political and religious testament.

There should be no personal concern from you for anyone who performs evil acts, even if he claims to have faith. Once his action demonstrates that he has invalidated what he said, you should not have any further business with him. Anyone who says he believes in Allah and goes to a [Sufi] *marabout* is deceitful. If he participates in democracy, he is deceitful. If he enrolls in the army, he is deceitful. He does not have the right to any form of loyalty. As a result, these strange matters happened and the *umma* deviated from their religion—most of them, except the group about which Allah spoke (*al-firqa al-nājiyya*), and a few of the people who Allah protected.

They deviated from the Prophet's teachings on monotheism, on worship, and on social relations. They combined the practice of Sunna with [blameworthy] innovations. They combined the practice of monotheism with polytheism. They combined the social relations of Islam with some cultural practices and then they adopted nationalism. There was a period when the Muslim states protected nothing but the Arabic language, the mastery of Arabic. They did not care about learning the Qur'ān; they did not care about learning the *ḥadīth*—they only cared about learning Arabic literature. They called it "the dawn of Arabic civilization." They only taught people Arabic, and Arabic songs which were taught in the musical clubs. They had no circles for the recitation of the Qur'ān.

You see this is displeasing to Allah. Then they also elevated the scholars of innovation since the year 900 AH [1494 CE]; they became close to the authorities because they did not challenge the king. However, the scholars of the Sunna made their position clear concerning their [the kings'] amorality, but they were humiliated and distanced [from power]. You see this is displeasing to Allah. I hope it is understood.

During this period, they also began to seek for advice from the land of Europe and Western Europe, especially from France. There was a relationship between them and Egypt, and a similar relationship between the Ottoman state in Istanbul, and the French government in France.[1] They had agreements concerning enlightenment and educational transfers from both sides. This is one of the reasons why Allah withdrew His help from these Muslims; after the Muslims embarked upon [blameworthy] innovations. I hope it is understood.

It was reported that for 300 years, the Muslims were not practicing the Sunna; they were following the Sufi brotherhoods and Shi'ism. Those two sects were the leading sects all over the [Muslim] world. For three hundred years, from 900 to 1100 AH [1494–1689], there was no loyalty to the practice of the Sunna anywhere in the [Muslim] world. From 900 AH, all the Muslim leaders belonged to the Sufi brotherhoods. They humiliated the scholars and students of the Sunna. This was the same situation in the Muslim world in 1000–1100 AH [1591–1689]. It was only from the year 1100 AH that the Muslim world began to hear the voice of the likes of Shaykh Muhammad b. 'Abd al-Wahhāb.[2] I hope it is understood.

There were other scholars who emerged in the land of India and other places. Many of them called to the Sunna; some were killed and others had their affairs weakened, but Allah assisted him [Ibn 'Abd al-Wahhāb] till he established an Islamic state, and his writings have been made available by his students.

Right from that period, the practice of the Sunna has been flickering, but the world was determined to exterminate it. Right from that period, the European colonial masters have been engaging in different hideous schemes to exterminate the practice of the Sunna. The unbelievers, hypocrites, and apostates began to write—specifically those who were good at writing. They drafted a series of falsifications and they interpreted, for example, the verse of the Qur'ān: "O believers, obey Allah and obey the Messenger and those in authority among you," (Q5:59) as the westerners they brought from England, together with other Europeans from France, who came to the Arab lands to study the religion to desecrate it.

They were the ones who misinterpreted the different verses of the Qur'ān with their selfish interpretations, particularly Qur'ānic verses such as: "Whosoever does not judge according to what Allâh has revealed—those are the unbelievers!" (Q5:44) And: "O believers, obey Allah and obey the Apostle and those in authority among you" (Q5:59) in a bid to change the history of Islam. They proclaimed that Allah's Messenger came to fight for nationalism. You would often hear them saying: "It was for nationalism that the Prophet Muhammad fought—did you not hear when he said the 'succession' should not be removed from the [tribe of] Quraysh? So why would he prevent nationalism?"[3] They promulgated this idea to destabilize the minds of those who do not have faith and Islamic knowledge.

As a result, they introduced the idea that if you want to practice your religion, you can do so within your private domain, but do not bring your religious practices into the public domain, because it would sow disunity. Then you would often hear them saying: "Did you not see how the successors of the Prophet were engaging with in-group fighting? It was by coercion they agreed to enthrone Abū Bakr; they also enthroned 'Umar using coercion. Then they selected 'Uthmān, but they were not satisfied with him so they killed him. They selected 'Alī, but they were not satisfied with him so they killed him. They were just engaging in wars. Look at a good system here, you elect someone. So, after some time if his performance is not good you elect someone else."

That was how they introduced democracy. This is the scheme of the Jews and the Christians. It is for this reason that Allah said they should not be followed. If they are followed, they will make you disbelieve. "O believers, if you obey a group of those who have received the Book, they will turn you, after you have believed, into unbelievers." (Q3:100) I hope it is understood.

In another verse, Allah says: "O believers do not take the Jews and Christians as friends; some of them are friends of each other. Whoever of you takes them as friends is surely one of them. Allah indeed does not guide the wrongdoers." (Q5:51) But surprisingly, you will see people going to them: "Yet, you will see those in whose hearts is a sickness hastening toward them, saying: 'We fear that a misfortune will befall us.' However, it may be that Allah will bring a victory or some other matter from Him; whereupon they will regret what they concealed within themselves." (Q5:52)

The hypocrites would say we are afraid to oppose them because they are the leaders and they can prevent us from praying. If we do not follow them, we might not be able to offer our prayers—it is for this reason we are following them. However, Allah responded to them by saying He will bring a way out for his servants easily. The way out is to fight them and be victorious over them. These followers of the Jews and

Christians will realize what they concealed in their hearts, in bitter regret. They will see that the servants of Allah have become victorious. Then afterwards they will regret it, but it will not benefit them. I hope it is understood. These are the innovations that were promoted which prompted Allah to withdraw His mercy [from the *umma*].

If you carefully look at the situation, you would acknowledge Allah's patience. For 300 years, the Muslims were given the opportunity to repent, amend their ways, and follow those who call to the Sunna. Yet they refused, and so the Europeans entered the Muslim lands. When they invaded a land, they destroyed it, and then colonized it. I hope it is understood.

The Muslim state of al-Andalus [Spain] was partitioned. The Muslim states that were located within Africa were also partitioned—for example, Libya. The Ottoman state was also partitioned and other Muslim states in the Arab region were also partitioned. When the Europeans fight, and invade a Muslim state, then other states would claim it is none of their business. They would claim that the Europeans are not fighting them [the Muslims]. These actions have paved the way for European domination, after a series of strategic and hideous schemes. When the Europeans explore a Muslim land with resources, they would amalgamate this land with a non-resourced land, whose people can easily be enticed by wealth [because of the resources].

The Muslim lands that proved resilient to their enticement of wealth were amalgamated with non-resourced lands. They carried out all these hideous schemes based on their wisdom. For example, present-day Niger and the northern part of Nigeria were one territory, originally. They belonged to one single territory and there was no boundary between them. It was all an Islamic territory. There were places in Niger where the *jihād* of 'Uthman Dan Fodio [1804–12] penetrated. There were also places in Niger where the preaching mission of the Mais' [title of Borno rulers] penetrated before al-Kanemi.[4]

You should know that it was not al-Kanemi that brought Islam to this land; in fact, he even destroyed Islam in this land, as did his son.[5] During the reign of his son—he was the one who initiated the appointment of slaves as kings throughout the lands—he appointed judges and prevented people from studying. This was to the point where in the Kanuri [language], you would often hear people saying: "They do not want anybody to study beyond the alphabet in *al-Risāla*."[6] They said that was sufficient. He also instructed that they should teach the people the language of Kanu, not the dialect of Kanuri. The dialect became difficult [for people]. If you do not know the dialect, it becomes hard to study. The people would take a long time to learn. The ruler and his entourage were the only ones who had the knowledge to control the people. They also killed the scholars.

It is only the rulers known by the title of "Mai," like Mai Idris Alauma[7] and other Mais, who practiced Islam. The preaching mission of the Mais penetrated Niger, Chad and other places.[8] With the arrival of the Europeans, they amalgamated the Muslims of northern Nigeria with unbelievers [of southern Nigeria]. In Niger, they left them without amalgamation [any other state], because of their belief that if the people are exposed to wealth they would prosper, but if they are left without amalgamation their prosperity will be unrealized.[9] It does not mean that Niger does not have resources, but the Europeans did not explore [those resources]. If their technology states that a land does not have resources, [this conclusion] will be generally accepted.

The Europeans executed the same hideous scheme in Chad. They amalgamated the Muslims of Chad with some unbelievers [in the south], and then they ignited ethnic war amongst them. The European colonial masters left the people there with a system based upon a rotation of power. If a specific group ruled for a period, then another group will take over power. Once a group refuses to rotate power, others would attempt a forceful seizure of power. This scheme started since the era of [François] Tombalbaye.[10] I hope it is understood.

This was the same scheme during the era of Goukouni [Oueddei],[11] Hissène Habré[12] and Idriss Déby. At this moment, some efforts are being made by other groups to seize power from Idriss Déby.[13] So, if a group seizes power, then another group is standing by to take over power. The people of Kanembu want to rule the land, people of Gorane want to rule, people of Bulala want to rule, as do the Shuwa people as well.

Everyone wants to rule the land. This is the mentality that the Europeans have inculcated into the minds of the people. Once a group seizes power, they would start encouraging other groups to prepare for a takeover. It is for this reason that the land has been plunged into crisis, such that you can hardly separate one crisis from another.

This scheme was also repeated in the Sudan, where they amalgamated the country with the South and people like John Garang[14] and his ilk [to the Muslim north]. If a land proclaims Islam, they would offer their duplicitous support, but then they would argue that other Muslims will not support the country, "so therefore accept our offer of support." Saudi Arabia would offer their support and the people will concur, since they believe their offer of support is an agreement.

These are all the schemes they adopted to divide the Muslim lands, kill the Muslims, as well as the scholars. After these initial schemes, they hired those Muslims they [the Europeans] taught from Western Europe, and then they trained the latter in Islamic traditions. These types of people became the scholars who issue religious rulings, and write books on Islam. They also hired people from the Western and Eastern regions [of Nigeria] and took all of them abroad to be trained. These Muslims are scholars, but they were indoctrinated into secularism during their training abroad. They are the ones who return to promote new ways of thinking.

You would often hear them saying that "democracy is Islam" and *jihād* is so-and-so. They all studied abroad in Western Europe. How can you take someone from Egypt, where they founded the first university,[15] to England, to study the religion? Is this not foolishness? How can you abandon an Islamic scholar from your community, and travel to England to study religion, Islamic studies? Where and in which university?

These are all the schemes of the Europeans which have corrupted the people's thinking. These are the destructive ideas with which they came, so we have found ourselves in this present condition.

After colonialism, when they were about to grant independence to the country, they inculcated the people with the thought that there is no religion. They argued that political authority should preclude religion, which is what is known as secularism. They argued that there should be no religion in political authority. This is the ideology they left behind for those who took power after them. They gave them democracy, capitalism or communism as substitutes that should be promoted in different places.

As such, since they have eliminated the flag of "there is no god but Allah," they introduced the flag of nationalism. They eliminated the laws of the Qur'an and the Sunna, and they brought the laws of ignorance in their place. They also brought the love of Western Europe, Western education and those different political systems. Even after independence and the aftermath of the post-war period of the Biafran conflict,[16] the Europeans came and argued that the merger between the Muslim North and Christian South is weak. They claim that there is no brotherhood between the two regions, since the eastern region supported secession, while other regions opposed it, leading to civil war. Thus, they came up with a better approach to further integrate the two regions, which is based on the idea they call federalism.

The first approach which they brought is the National Youth Service Corps (NYSC). In the future, all students who have successfully finished from the university will enroll in this service. If a student studies in Maiduguri, they will transfer him to Aba for service. I hope it is understood. If a student studies in Sokoto, they will transfer him to Enugu for service. If a student studies here, they will transfer him there for service.[17] If a student also studies there, they will transfer him here for service, including their women and others. The purpose of the service is to strengthen the spirit of brotherhood because if a student comes here for service, maybe someone will marry her here. Similarly, a student who was transferred there for service, maybe someone will marry her there. The student who served here and feels comfortable here might stay here after the service and maybe marry here. The student who served there might stay there as well. This is the intent of the program.

The second approach they brought is the JAMB exam.[18] The third approach they brought is the establishment of Federal Government Colleges. If a child finishes his primary school here, they will take him to Federal Government College, Enugu. And if a child finishes over there, they will bring him here to promote unity in the land, which is the goal of the federalism program.

However, Allah did not agree with their program because He has His own intention. Their ambitions did not materialize. They were only able to succeed with those who were already part of or like them. I hope it is understood. Just as Allah says that Satan and those who are misguided: "Over My servants you have no authority, except

for those sinners who follow you. Hell shall be the appointed place for them all."
(Q15:42–3) I hope it is understood.

They run their affairs based on the ruling of ignorance. In this state and condition,
the scholars of Islam like Ibn Ḥazm,[19] Ibn Ḥajar [al-ʿAsqalānī], and Imām al-Nawawī[20]
have issued religious rulings in their books concerning what is expected from the
Muslims. Ibn Ḥazm in al-Muḥallā, Imām al-Nawawī in al-Minhaj bi-sharḥ Ṣaḥīḥ
Muslim and Ibn Ḥajar in Fatḥ al-bārī have stated that if a leader becomes an unbeliever or an apostate, it is mandatory to change him and install a Muslim leader, if the
Muslims have the capability or if they have the power.[21]

What if the Muslims do not have the power? Then they should do two things:
either they must emigrate since they are powerless, or they must explore all means to
acquire power to overthrow the unbelieving or apostate leader and install an Islamic
caliphate. I hope it is understood.

This action is compulsory on all Muslims and no one is exempted. This is the law
of Allah incumbent upon both male and female [Muslims]. I hope it is understood.
And all praise is due to Allah that in this land [Nigeria] we have had preaching
towards Islamic reform, and even all over the world, the preaching of Hasan al-
Banna[22] of the Muslim Brotherhood. They did their best based on their own efforts,
but Allah tested them with innovations and other errors.

Notwithstanding, you would understand that those who started the preaching
towards Islamic reform had good intentions, but a lack of scholars and books
deprived them of the people who would have shown them the Sunna. In that land
[Egypt], they were spreading innovations, and in all the books were published there,
so that was where they had a problem.

Still, they had many preachers like Abul Aʿla Mawdudi.[23] They called the people to
return to the religion and law of Allah. They informed the people that the English
law is not Allah's religion. They also made some statements concerning Western education and democracy, and a call to Islamic reform. Allah gave them a privilege that
no one ever denied them. But there were those who later deviated; some of them
became the members of al-Takfir wa-l Hijra[24] and others became democrats in the
Muslim Brotherhood under the name of Hasan al-Banna. I hope it is understood.

So be careful with those small books that they brought from Saudi Arabia which
insult Hasan al-Banna and Sayyid Qutb.[25] Be careful with them, the people who
produce such books are the ones that if you give them Osama [b. Laden] too, that is
how they will treat him. Be very careful. We did not say they are infallible or that they
do not make mistakes, but it is important to know where they erred or made mistakes. That is what should be considered. I hope it is understood.

The reason we do not take these figures as models in the preaching towards Islamic
reform is mainly because their scholarship is less than the predecessors like Ibn
Taymiyya, Ibn Qayyim and Muhammad b. ʿAbd al-Wahhab, who also issued similar
rulings. So, for religious rulings, these predecessors suffice for us. However, we do not

say what some use to say. We agree that among the members of the Muslim Brotherhood there are innovators and those who follow the Sufi brotherhoods, but what they wrote that demonstrates their ideas concerning the preaching towards Islamic reform is a subject in which we do not accuse them of error. Anyone who tells you that they are innovators, tell them not in the subject of preaching towards Islamic reform—at least those who I mentioned by name.

As such, in this preaching towards Islamic reform, we do not accuse them of errors. There are other issues in which they erred, and if anyone wants to refute them he can, or write a book about it. There are those who say they are unbelievers, and they write books about them. These same people also wrote against Osama. However, those who are true scholars, you would see that they take what is accurate in their books, and say, for example, that Sayyid Qutb said so-and-so. That is exactly what the true scholars do, and even in Saudi Arabia you would find scholars like that.

[Discussion of the Murji'a creed] But again al-Albānī said in this era, there is no one who interpreted the phrase *lā ilaha illā Allah* (there is no god but Allah) the way Sayyid Qutb did. You see that is fairness. In his book *Milestones*, he interpreted *lā ilaha illā Allah* exactly the way it should in this era. This is fairness. Wherever a person has erred, it is important to identify the error, but you do not condemn the person in totality. Qutb is the one to whom Allah gave the privilege of understanding the errors inherent in communism and all those polytheistic systems. It was from his books that the people who started the preaching towards Islamic reform, like Osama in Saudi Arabia and others who emigrated from Egypt first gained their inspiration. I hope it is understood.

As a result, the laws of ignorance have become pervasive in the world. [Discussion of the weakness of Muslim Brotherhood's ideology] Even those who saw themselves as followers of the predecessors believed that they could proclaim and work together with people of different ideologies. The Shi'ites among them would tell you now: "It is the Jews we want to fight so we should stop the infighting. If you belong to the Sufi brotherhoods, you can come along with your rosary,[26] but we should stop the infighting." It is this type of unity on which they embarked upon that eventually led to their disintegration. I hope it is understood.

As a result, Allah did not allow the emergence of movements that will exclusively preach for the return of the Sunna until recently—like the al-Qaeda movement, the Taliban and so on. The intention of the members of these movements was purely aimed towards the Sunna. It is only the books of Sunna that they study. At this present time, the people of Algeria have also returned to the likes of these movements. These are the movements that preach towards Islamic reform based on the Sunna, which you will see. I hope it is understood.

There are people in this land who were also following similar steps. First, they were following [Ibrahim] Zakzaky,[27] who said he wanted to revive the *sharī'a*, but he eventually drifted towards Shi'ism. Then later they formed another group *Jama'atul Tajdid al-Islami*, but eventually they drifted towards democracy. Now, they have all become democrats, and some of their members are local government chairmen and counsellors. All these deviations are not Islam. I hope it is understood.

And it is the consequence of that type of unity which engendered these deviations. Then again, they formed the group called the Salafis. The members of this group are those who preach that everything should return to the Sunna of the Prophet. You would often hear them saying: "Pray according to the way the Prophet prayed." Although they want everything to be based on the Sunna, when they approached the issue of democracy, they found the basic concepts in Islamic monotheism difficult to understand. They were struggling to uplift the Sunna without understanding that the starting point is to uplift Islamic monotheism. It is compulsory that you conjoin *lā ilaha illā Allah* along with *Muḥammad rasūl Allah*.

There are many things happening in this land that make me worried. It is as if the unbelievers have perfected a plan to accumulate weapons, money and veteran soldiers, elites and chairmen [of committees] who will help them achieve their plan. These people would come together secretly and they would select a town to foment chaos against the Muslims. Once they are successful, they would kill and kill until they are tired of killing. Then they would dispatch soldiers to mediate the chaos.

When they kill the Muslims, the Muslims are angered and prepared for vengeance, it is only at that point they would intervene. At that point, the Muslims are furious—they have seen the wanton killing perpetrated by the unbelievers, the way they killed a pregnant woman, immolated the Muslims, including the children—but then they are prevented from carrying out their retaliation. If the Muslims insist they must retaliate, then the [federal Nigerian] soldiers would arrest them and declare them to be trouble-makers. You would hear them saying: "We are making attempts to halt the chaos, but they [the Muslims] are bent on carrying out acts of violence."

That was exactly what they did in Kafanchan and Zango Kataf. At the time, they started fighting at Zango Kataf on Thursday [14 May 1992], during the era of Mohammad Dabo Lere, the governor of Kaduna state,[28] [when] he refused to dispatch police to stop the massacre. The unbelievers had three field-days of killing the Muslims on Thursday, Friday and Saturday. On Saturday when they took the corpses and the injured to Kaduna, the Muslims were angered about the killings. They were about to come out and retaliate, when they [the government] dispatched the soldiers into the town to stop them [from doing that].

In the first place, they said there are soldiers, but they have no vehicle [to come to the rescue]. However, on Sunday, since they knew the Christians would go to church, they sent soldiers and vehicles to protect the Christians and their churches. I saw this and tried to understand it. Then they arrested Zamani Lekwot, an army general, who was an accomplice and involved in the killings. He even shot, with his pistol, one man called Alhaji Garba. He shot this man, who later fell to the ground, then he removed his liver and bit it. They were announcing all these events on the radio, and then he was taken to the court.[29]

They said so-and-so person did this and they were all arrested and charged to court but in the end, [President Sani] Abacha said they should release them all. And even he, Lekwot, was made the king of the town. That was what they did. See what they also did in [the town of] Tafawa Balewa at Kwata. See what they did in Bauchi because a lady became a Muslim! See the aftermath of what they did in Shagamu, in Lagos and other places! See what they have been doing in Jos, the whole state! These events gave me the understanding that there is no time when these events would stop, because they only want to eliminate Muslims and Islam.

Then again there is also the unequivocal insult of the Prophet of Allah, like the one that *Fantime* newspaper did. They insulted the prophets Jesus and Muhammad. They believed that since they combined the two prophets, the people would not worry. They are Christians, but they said the Prophet Jesus had a prostitute (*karuwa*), and the Prophet Muhammad, too, had a prostitute. That was what they said. But they said the Prophet Muhammad married his prostitute while the Prophet Jesus did not. That was what they wrote.

At the time, the only reaction was the burning of the newspapers, but they were neither arrested nor charged in court. This event came to pass. Then one rash lady at the time of beauty pageant [Miss World] [Isioma] Daniel also perpetrated the same injustice.[30] And before that period, in Kafanchan one Reverend [Abubakar] Bako also insulted the Prophet as well.[31] So they would just insult the Prophet, then kill the Muslims and live in peace.

Look at the recent event in Jos, they did what they wanted and continued in peace while their governor was always there protecting them.[32] If this were in a town of Muslims, and they did similar actions, he would be up front arresting people and handing them over [to the police], but he said they would not arrest his people. They are not at fault. "It was the people from Niger who came here to fight them." Any Muslim now is from Niger!

Now that all these events are happening, all the time I am always thinking: Why is it that whenever these events happen, they would just say: "Sorry, you should exercise patience, wait for what the government will do or let us plead to the government to take measures." Always that is what they say. Then Allah made me to understand that it is not like that. What will stop them from insulting the Prophet or killing the Muslims is *jihād*. But how are we going to carry out the *jihād*? With whom are we going to carry out the *jihād*? Allah made me to understand that first and foremost, we must embark upon the preaching towards Islamic reform. Then, we will have to be patient until we acquire power. This is the foundation of this preaching towards Islamic reform. It was founded for the sake of *jihād* and we did not hide this objective from anyone.

Our preaching towards Islamic reform is a reaction to what the likes of Isioma Daniel said, and that is what has made us come out saying that we should revolt against democracy, we should revolt against Western education, and we should return to the way of the Prophet [Muhammad]. We should build ourselves.

The issue of those other paths helping us will not work; we should come back to our own. In fact, we are seeing that if we do not follow our own path, we will not be successful. That is how we saw it at the beginning. Then Allah said: "Since you are serious about your mission," then He started pushing books at us that we did not have before now. Honestly, we would just go to a market, for example, Kurmi market [in Kano], see one [new] book and buy it. Then Allah enriched our understanding concerning preaching towards Islamic reform, and we did not hide it from anyone.

Before we came, we were studying different books earnestly. On [the topic of] this preaching towards Islamic reform, we studied different books like the book dealing with *Almāniya* written by Aḥmad Shakir, which I taught both in the Hausa and Kanuri [languages]. Mallam [Abubakar] Shekau has also been teaching this book. They have been debating with him. Usually, they would go and select a small part from the book and then come back to debate with him. They have been doing this with him.

We also read and taught *Taḥkīm al-qawānīn* written by Muhammad b. Ibrāhīm Āl al-Shaykh. We also read and taught *Wujūb taḥkīm sharī' Allah wa-nabdh mā khala-fahu* written by 'Abd al-'Azīz b. Bāz. We also read and taught the second chapter of the book on *Nawāqiḍ al-imàn qawliyyan wa-'amaliyyan*, both in Hausa and Kanuri. We also read and taught the two volumes and the chapter on *Taḥkīm shar' Allah* in the book *Mushkilat al-ghulūw fī al-dīn fī al-'aṣr al-ḥāḍir*.[33] We also read and taught the sections that discussed working with the government and the misconceptions concerning the Prophet Joseph in *Madārik al naẓar fī al-siyāsa bayna al-tatbīqāt sharā'iyya wa-infi'lāt ḥamasiyya*.[34] We studied different sections of *Majmū'āt al-fatāwā*.[35] We also read some sections in *Mirāth al-anbiyā'*, and delivered lectures on them. We read and taught the book *Kitāb al-tawḥīd* and the explanations in *Fatḥ al-majīd*. We also read and taught *al-Uṣūl al-thalātha* and the explanations of Ibn 'Uthaymīn. We also studied *Ḥukm al-jāhiliyya* and *Mukhtaṣar 'umdat al-tafsīr ['an Ibn Kathīr]* by Aḥmad Shakir. We also read the religious rulings of the Permanent Committee for Islamic Research and Religious Edicts. [Discussion of the benefit of the books mentioned.] I hope it is understood.

[Discussion of kufr dūna kufr]

And Allah gave us the power, victory, and the evidence became apparent. Even the uneducated person understands that there is a difference between the judgment in which there is no Islam at all, and the judgment that is Islamic, but mistaken. Therefore, *kufr dūna kufr* [lesser apostasy] only applies to the judgment that is based on the law of Islam, but is mistaken in the issuing of a ruling. If the judge or ruler believes that the judgment made is identical to that of Allah, then he has become an apostate. If he considers his own law to be better [than that of Allah] he has become an apostate. If he sees such a thing as permissible, then he has also become an apostate—the only exception is if he sees it as a mistake, he is at fault, and he is regretful, then we can say it is *kufr dūna kufr*. And even at that level, [Muhammad b. Ibrāhīm]

Al al-Shaykh said it is worse than illicit sexual relations, worse than gambling, worse than all other major sins. This is because what Allah calls unbelief is worse than what He did not call unbelief. I hope it is understood.

Based on this explanation, we understood that [loyalty to] the constitution by which they judge the people in this land [Nigeria] is clear unbelief. The judge who rules with constitution cannot be categorized under *kufr dūna kufr*, he is a clear unbeliever. The ruler who rules by means of a constitution is an unbeliever. That is how we understand this issue. If there is something that will make us to exempt someone then it is one of the *thawābit al-takfīr* [the establishment of the fact of apostasy]. Since the start of our preaching towards Islamic reform, this condition has been accorded only to me, namely to make an exemption in declaring a person to be an unbeliever. Some students would go to extremes, but we would call them out and say: "No, you will not declare someone apostate until you follow this process."

There was an occasion where the people of one community came all the way from Gombe to debate because they did not agree with us. We sat and discussed the issue of declaring a person to be an unbeliever for eight hours and all the people were there seated. I was not even in good health at the time, as I just came back from Saudi Arabia.[36] I said I do not agree with them about how they understand the issue, so then they left.

Some other group of people came from Daru and I said I do not agree with them on the same issue, so they also left. Then we went to them in their town and discussed the same issue of declaring a person to be an unbeliever. Then they said we are also unbelievers, so we left. All the brothers are aware of these discussions. I hope it is understood.

Then in this time someone would come and say: "Whosoever does not judge according to what Allah has revealed—those are the unbelievers!" (Q5:44) the way it is interpreted here is not correct. It is now that he understands it. So, have you been sleeping? What people do not understand is that we are usually going to places they do not go. These people, if they know our preaching towards Islamic reform we will know it, and if they do not know, we will also know. We did *iqāmat al-ḥujja* [call for evidence] for them but you might not know since you have never gone to the presence of the Divisional Police Officer to discuss this issue.

On the other hand, I have been called several times to their office. There was a time when it was the Director-General of the State Security Service who invited me—Ibrahim and others were the ones who escorted me. I went to their office and we sat with him to discuss the mission of our preaching towards Islamic reform. We explained to them what we are doing and they told us: have we taken our complaint to the Divisional Police Officer of our locality? There was a time that it was the Inspector General who called me. Together with Ibrahim and others, we went to his office.

And we also met with the Deputy Inspector General twice. There was a time when they sent an invitation that the President wants to invite us and we called a consultation meeting (*shūrā*). We called the meeting because of the need to establish *iqāmat al-ḥujja*, but they declined the invitation. [Yusuf narrates his experiences of the invitations.]

As a result, our creed is established upon the principle that all judgments or rulings not formulated in accord with the Book of Allah—the people who formulate such judgments or rulings, that constitutes *thawābit al-takfīr* for them. Anyone about whom we are certain to have establish evidence upon is an apostate from Islam. But established evidence, no matter how extensive it is, we are unconcerned [with punishment], since Allah says: "We do not punish until We have sent a Messenger." (Q17:15) Even the black unbelievers,[37] our evidence will suffice for them. If it is the *ṭāghūt*, you should present evidence to him, but when you present your evidence it is over. I hope it is understood.

Allah does not punish anyone, even Pharaoh, till evidence is established against him. When he hears it and refuses [to repent]—then that is it. I hope it is understood. [Discussion of Allah's judgments]

We also discussed the ruling concerning Western schools and education. It is the Europeans who brought these Western schools, and they handed them over to the missionaries. Everyone who reads history knows this fact, except a fool. They inculcated their ideology in the schools, and they always indoctrinate people with their manners and training. Inside these schools, as we have taught several times, the understanding they have about Allah's creation is not the same as Allah says. The creation of man, the creation of heaven and earth, the jinn, the angels, Allah Himself, the rainfall, the stones—I hope you understand.

Everything—their entire understanding of these things—is not Islamic. If they talk about stones, then you can be sure that it is not what Allah says. If they talk about the earth it would not be what Allah says. If they talk about heaven, stars, air, water, trees, angels, jinns, the origin of man, everything they say, it is not what Allah says. This is the ideology that they inculcated into Western education. They brought it based on the system of unbelief. For example, the idea of a weekend on Saturday and Sunday is theirs. And all the Christmas holidays, Good Friday, and Easter Monday, which you celebrate. And those holidays, if you observe them, you will be assisting them in what they are doing, because that is what you have learned.[38]

Even if you love the Qur'ān and the Sunna, how will you aid the Qur'ān and Sunna? If you will not open the Qur'ān, sit down, but just be speaking English, with what will you aid the Qur'ān since you cannot study it? With what will you aid the Sunna since you did not study it? And they will not give you the time to study it. You are under pressure. Everyone who has been studying in Western schools when he recites some verses, you would see that English is preferable to him. Even if he comes to admonish, he speaks more impressively in English, not with the religion just as Shaykh Abubakar Mahmud Gumi said in *al-ʿAqīda al-ṣaḥīḥa bi-muwāfaqat al-sharīʿa*.[39]

So, because of this, we have seen what we saw, and we discussed it with these people. And the day I came, I said: "I have never seen any time like this when they understood my preaching towards Islamic reform." They understood this preaching very well. You would hear them saying that "these people say that the constitution is not true, and are preparing to fight the constitution." That was what they said, and they themselves said they know that it is not true.

There is a person who identifies as a Christian, but he said he agrees that this constitution is not true. He told me that they also believe that all laws which contradict the Bible constitute unbelief.[40] As a result, this preaching is not wrong but the government does not want it. That person is an unbeliever! He is the one I said that told us that there would be no reform, except through the path we are following.

We also discussed the ruling concerning working with the government under an unbelieving ruler. Based on the contradictions of scholars—some said it is permissible but with certain conditions, while some said it is not permissible and the example of the Prophet Joseph is different, and so forth. Some scholars also said it is not permissible at all. Allah has made us to understand that working with the government under an unbelieving ruler is obedience [to an entity other than Allah]. As a result, all forms of obedience [to the government] are not permissible. There is no difference between minor and major obedience, it is simply obedience. I hope it is understood.

As a result, we do not agree to work with the government under an unbelieving ruler. There is no difference between all kinds of work and service which assists the unbelieving ruler. All of them lead to following a *ṭāghūt* and worshipping him. This is the preaching towards Islamic reform. We do not agree with this Western education at all. This system of Western education, we do not agree with it at all. If it is scientific knowledge that conforms to the [Islamic] religion, that should be studied, good. We are also willing to study it.

And it is best that we study it with the language of our religion [Arabic] or our mother tongue [Kanuri]. This is what we will study, we will study ours, on the condition that it conforms to Islamic monotheism and does not contradict the *ḥadīth*. [Discussion of the classification of knowledge] We do not agree with working with the government under an unbelieving ruler, who is not under an Islamic government; the government whose flag is not *lā ilāha illā Allah* and who does not rule by the *sharīʿa* of Islam. We do not agree with it at all. I hope it is understood.

And the verse: "Whosoever does not judge according to what Allah has revealed— those are the unbelievers!" (Q5:44) in reality is applicable to this type of government. I hope it is understood. I mean, this type of government which rules and judges by means of the constitution. The case that is regarded as *kufr dūna kufr* is when a ruler or judge rules by the Qurʾān, but made a mistake or deviates in the process of issuing a ruling.

What we are saying is that for the person who does not understand us, if he has the opportunity of possessing some knowledge, he should come and let us discuss the issue with those who know. If he does not have that opportunity, everyone should withdraw according to what he understands and act accordingly. At the time when we arrived at this understanding, those who were saying *kufr dūna kufr* is not like that, those who were saying a *jāhiliyya* law is not like that; it is a condition under which they can practice democracy. When we realize that they are not correct, then we withdrew and started our own preaching towards Islamic reform. I hope it is understood. *his declaration for Islam*

The person, too, can withdraw and start his own preaching. Let no one feel that this statement is too harsh—this is the religion. As for me, I am ready to part with my mother and father, and all my children, wives and money because of this religion.[41] As such, I come, you come, and you will not make light of our suffering. I hope it is understood. Here is a system; it is not mine, it is not ours, it is not my father's: it is that of the Prophet laid out for us to follow. If you see any mistake, then come let us check it—here is a book, let us check it and discuss it. I hope it is understood.

[No compromise in ideology] If someone works with the police, is a soldier, in immigration, customs, the Navy, the Air Force, the Army or SSS [State Security Service]—no one who works in these professions will assist the religion [of Islam], except by destroying them. He will waste his time, and will spoil the religion. As I told you the SSS and the Homeland Security of all countries were created only to fight against the religion of Islam. There is nothing that makes them nervous like the religion of Islam, and the jealousy and wickedness in them is only known to Allah. [Discussion of police brutality] *loyalty is demanded*

At the time they held me there, I spent five days in their headquarters in Abuja. When they were about to take me to the police; I had about 36,000 *naira* [approximately $250] with me; then they collected it and said they would bring along the money. Then we went to their headquarters without the money. It was after a week they called Bayero,[42] and they gave him the money. It was then I understood that here in the police station, they eat and drink with your money. They do not give out any food and I had no money. At last they called Bayero and gave him my money and all my belongings. I was thinking: Why did they hold my money and belongings? But they did not know that the place to which they took me [prison], Allah has made it like a home for me (cf. Q12:33).

I arrived and I entered inside, there I met Mallam Abubakar Katsina,[43] who said I should go and take my bath. I said to him that I just had my bath not long ago. Then we came out and then he said: "Here is some food." You see, but what they wanted was for you not to leave with any money. Since they eat with money, then they wanted me to sit and say: "Please help me beg the SSS to bring my money since I cannot go hungry for so long." Allah refused that situation because it did not happen to me. I am saying it so that they would hear.

Because of that, all these professions, by Allah, we have rejected them. The government in its entirety, we have rejected them. We have also rejected Western education. We have rejected working with the government under an unbelieving ruler. We are following according to this methodology, and the path of the forefathers. Any ruling that is brought forth which contradicts the position of the Salafi scholars, by Allah, we are going to welcome it, once there is evidence, not just a ruling. No matter how highly rated is the scholar, we will say: what does he rely upon for his ruling?

[*Evidence must be supported by a* ḥadīth *to be accepted.*]

As I told you, the Hausas say: "Friendship with a chicken does not prevent the chicken from being slaughtered." Notwithstanding the friendship you feel for it, you will still slaughter it. By Allah, we will do what is unpleasant for you because it is our religion. This is our salvation on the Day of Resurrection. We do not want anyone to touch it. There is nothing that has made us ignore our friends and fellow-scholars, from whom we studied or with whom we studied. It is solely because they said this understanding is false. And for us, if there is no reason you say our understanding is false, then we will leave you. I hope it is understood.

[Discussion of religious exchanges] If it is your understanding—you are black and I am black, you are here, and I am here; it is not compulsory for me to follow your understanding. As a result, you will hear some people saying that our understanding is different from that of so-and-so scholar. It is just a way of spreading corruption. Some will say this explanation is just the understanding of Mallam. This is nonsense because it is not the understanding of Mallam, rather it is the saying of Allah.

[Yusuf cautions against gossips] Anyone who goes to a secret corner and calls people to tell them something, they should come with him. It is not that we said he should say there is a mistake, or that we have problem of declaring a person to be an unbeliever, or the way we prioritized *jihād*, or whatever, is not correct. Let him come let us discuss what is correct. Allah says: "Help one another in righteousness and piety, but not in sin and aggression," (Q5:2) but that backbiting is "helping in sin." Let him come to us to discuss it at any time. We welcomed a scholar of democracy when he travelled from his destination to engage us in a discussion inside our school.[44] We sat and discussed with him, and there were brothers there who surrounded us heatedly. He spoke and we listened to him, so why wouldn't we listen to you? We will listen to you. Do not think we will not listen to you.

But the corruption, because we saw what happened in the past—the likes of the dissention during the time of [the caliph] 'Uthman,[45] and the dissention of the Kharijites—since we know what happened in the past, it is a lesson for us. Because of that, we will take strong measures to prevent any form of dissention. I hope this will be a remedy [for that ailment]. But for now, there is no one who we suspect. Let nobody preempt so-and-so. If it becomes necessary, there is nobody with hair on his head to whom we will be afraid of saying so-and-so. We will call his name specifically, if conditions warrant us to do so, but now let no one anticipate this. As you see, everyone should be left like that. If the time comes we will say this person has brought something contrary to our movement. I hope it is understood.

You see there are people who trespass the boundaries. We have delivered our admonition to everyone. This path—it is not as if I am telling people I have my own path that all of you should follow. No! Even if I myself am the one who deviates from the path, you should follow the path and leave me. And do not agree if I cite something contrary to what we have read in the books. Let no one accept it from me. This is not like I am telling someone: "This is it, so let no one interprets it and say '*hmmm* Mallam, it is this-and-that people'; it means you are among them." Anyone who tells you it is so-and-so people—he too is among them. Is this well understood?

So, Allah willing, tonight there will be an explanation like this in the Kanuri language. Tomorrow morning, I will deliver a lecture on *jihād*. What is *jihād*? When will we start *jihād*? This lecture will be tomorrow morning, Allah willing.

[Islamic prayer] And may Allah make us die as martyrs, and accept those whom He did not destine for martyrdom with a righteous death. We are praying to Allah to guide our women to do what is right. We are praying to Allah not to raise our biological children and the ones in the future, O Allah, do not raise them in the condition in which we were raised. O Allah, do not give them love of football or Western education or this democracy, do not put it in their minds. O Allah, as we are despising [those things], and the children are also despising, please raise them like that, O Lord of the worlds.

[Islamic prayer] Tonight, Lawal Bukar will deliver a lecture in the Kanuri language. It is akin to this lecture, since everyone understands Kanuri and Hausa. Allah willing, we will explain more about this for the benefit of the people who are in the village. Then tomorrow morning we will deliver a lecture about what is *jihād*. And we will speak and elaborate our understanding.

They were not raised well

12

ADMONITION

BY MUHAMMAD YUSUF

(c. JANUARY 2009)

[Trans.: Abdulbasit Kassim]
Available at: https://www.youtube.com/watch?v=kHG6f5cWjKs

Darwin, old old man

In this lecture, Yusuf stressed the takfir *of the Nigerian soldiers by demonstrating how their paraphernalia constitutes symbols of unbelief. This lecture explains the group's strong antipathy towards the Nigerian army even before the 2009 conflict. Yusuf touched upon the theme of* al-walāʾ wa-l-barāʾ *in his discussion of Muslim participation in Christian festivities and he also refuted the "Kharijites" appellation penned on his group. Because Yusuf mentioned his indictment in the court for training the people of Niger and bringing them to Nigeria, this lecture can be dated to the period after his indictment on 12 January 2009.[1] There were some missing parts at the beginning of the video.*

The claim of Darwinism is that man will evolve into another variation in the future. Darwin's theory was postulated by an old man in the distant past, but his theory is still being studied. Go and read the Arabic or English dictionary for more information about him. This theory is unbelief in Allah because Allah provided a detailed explanation in the Qurʾān about the origin of man and how man was created. In *sūrat al-Baqara*, Allah explained to us about the creation of the Prophet Adam.

Allah added more explanations about our forefather Adam in *sūrat al-Aʿrāf, sūrat al-Isrāʾ, sūrat al-Kahf, sūrat Ta-Ha* and He completed the explanation in *sūrat al-*

The issue of holidays [handwritten annotation in left margin]

Zumar. There is no place in the Qur'ān in which Allah did not explain that the origin of man is water: "It is he who has created you from clay," (Q6:2); "And of His signs is that He created from dust..." (Q30:18); "So let man consider what he was created from. [He was created from flowing water]." (Q86:5) This is the origin of your creation, but someone has come to tell you the contrary. [Yusuf repeats himself]

What you are being taught about the origin of animals in biology is contrary to Allah's explanation. Everything has been changed, and their understanding is different from the explanation of Allah. Why were those who introduced dialectical theology (*'ilm al-kalām*) always trying to show the people monotheism in the sphere of lordship (*rubūbiyya*)? Yet, because their teaching contradicts the teaching of Allah's Messenger the teaching of dialectical theology became prohibited.

Why is it that those that teach philosophy claim that the subject is beneficial and they can develop the field of Islamic philosophy? They developed the field of Islamic philosophy with the claim that it will aid the knowledge of Islamic jurisprudence, yet scholars declared it to be an innovation, which has no origin in Islamic knowledge, and they prohibited it. Let alone the people who teach Christianity to you directly! They have not changed the Christian knowledge or the curriculum which the missionaries brought along with them. You should read the history of the coming of Europeans' and their introduction of Western education.

Ask the secondary school students which holiday they prefer: Christmas holiday or the *'Id* holidays? I hope it is understood. If you have a secondary school student in your house or area, call him and ask him which holiday he prefers between the two school holidays: Christmas or *'Id* holidays? I am sure some of you know the answer when you were enrolled in Western education. In a year, they would give you a one-month holiday for you to remain at home and relax.

However, during the *'Id* celebration, they would hardly give you a one-week holiday. (*Someone in the audience mentions that they give only three days' holiday.*) They deliberately arranged the holidays in that pattern. Once the month of December approaches, they would give you a long break for you to observe the Christmas and New Year's holidays before school resumes. Children are always happy during these holiday periods.

However, during the *'Id* celebration, they would only give you a short holiday, and you would not be able to enjoy [eating] meat and new clothes. Then you would start feeling angry because of the short holiday. This is the reason why whenever you ask a student which holiday he prefers: Christmas or the *'Id* holidays, of course, he would choose the Christmas holiday. You prefer the same holiday as Jacob and John.[2] You would see someone travelling all the way from Abuja, and when you ask him the purpose of his travel, he would reply that he came for the Christmas holiday.

Are you a Christian? You also observe Good Friday and Easter Monday holidays in your work place. These happenings are because of our refusal to study the creed of our predecessors. Take the book *Iqtiḍā' al-ṣirāṭ al-mustaqīm: li-mukhālafat aṣḥāb al-jaḥīm* (*Following the Straight Path in Opposition to those going to Hell*) of Ibn Taymiyya. By Allah, you will realize that these things they are doing are blunders which contradict *tawḥīd*. They are celebrating the unbelievers' festival, and you also join them in this holiday. They do not work; you also do not work. You do everything possible to indicate that you celebrate with them during these holidays, since you give good wishes to your boss by presenting him with a card, or he presents one to you.

Therefore, my brothers, by Allah, it is incumbent upon us to understand the present state of our religion. We should not allow our weakness to make us lowly. We made ourselves inferior. After we had honor, we are going to look for honor from the unbelievers. Everyone is looking for honor from America. Everyone is looking for influence from the government of his town. "Do they seek glory from them? For all glory belongs to Allah." (Q4:139)

[*Only non-Muslims seek the honor of being football players or members of parliament; true Muslims will seek honor by following the example of the Prophet Muhammad and his Companions.*]

Therefore, we should do the work of Allah and not be working for the *ṭāghūt*. All over the world there are only two parties: there is the party of Allah and there is the party of *ṭāghūt*. I hope it is understood. "Those who believe, fight in Allah's cause, and those who disbelieve, fight in the cause of *ṭāghūt*. "Fight then the followers of the Devil. Surely the guile of Satan is weak." (Q4:76) The believers are those fighting on Allah's path for the supremacy of the word of Allah and the unbelievers are those fighting in the path of the *ṭāghūt*. The person who is fighting for the country, fighting for nationalism, or fighting for the law of the land is not fighting because of Allah. [Yusuf derides Muslims working in the security forces]

Do not allow them to make you to worship what ought not to be worshipped. It is stressful. It is a useless work. Do not let some people deceive you that they are scholars, go and ask them Allah has prevented some things in *sūrat al-anʿām*; firstly, he prohibited polytheism:

Say: "Come, I will recite what your Lord has forbidden you: that you associate nothing with Him; that you show kindness to your parents; that you do not kill your children for fear of poverty; We will provide for you and for them; that you do not approach indecencies, whether open or secret; and that you do not kill the living soul which Allah has forbidden you to kill except for a just cause. This is what Allah commands you to do, so you may understand." (Q6:151)

The soldiers violate all these prohibitions. "That you associate nothing with Him"—he is already worshipping the country. "That you show kindness to your parents"—it was from this town they transferred him to Enugu[3] so he has no ability to cultivate good relations with his parents, is that not so? "That you do not kill your children for fear of poverty; We will provide for you and for them"—you should not do family planning, even though already they do not agree with having many children. "That you do not approach indecencies, whether open or secret"—except if he is not deployed to fight in Liberia or Darfur, is that not so?[4] "And that you do not kill the living soul which Allah has forbidden you to kill except for a just cause"—you should not kill a soul which Allah has forbidden, except for a just cause.

Who said they should kill a soul? Who has the command? Who gave the command? Now the soldiers who are shooting, are they shooting those Allah commanded to be shot? You will pay to Allah for shooting His slaves. By Allah, even if it is an unbeliever you do not have the power to shoot, except when it is based on the clear permission and explanation of Allah and the Prophet. The Prophet looked at the Companions and said: "Any one who killed an unbeliever who had a peace agreement with us; we will testify in front of Allah on the Day of Judgment." An unbeliever! But you shoot a Muslim and then you expect to gain the intercession of the Prophet, who will testify with the Companions if they kill an unbeliever!!

[*Yusuf explains that it is the Islamic scholars who have been inciting people to call his followers Kharijites.*]

You cannot fight against Allah's light. They have been engaging in this name-calling for long. You hear them shouting "Kharijites! Kharijites! Kharijites!" In fact, one of the scholars, because of his penchant for using the name "Kharijites," each time he walks around the children call him a Kharijite scholar. (*Yusuf burst into laughter.*) Up to this time, the name "the Kharijite scholar" has stuck to him. You would hear the children saying "the Kharijite scholar" said so-and-so. They have never had that name. If the name applies to us, it would be pinned on us automatically. But since it is not our name, it backfired.

The Hausas would say that the ant returns to the mound. So, ask those scholars, since you are close to them because this is the neighborhood of soldiers. Go and ask your scholar when Allah says in the Qur'ān "and that you do not kill the living soul which Allah has forbidden you to kill except for a just cause"—what is a just cause?

Allah's Messenger said: "It is not permissible to spill the blood of a Muslim except in three cases: first, when a married person commits forbidden relations," and he should not be killed with gun; "second, the person who commits murder," and an Islamic judge must issue a death sentence for him; "then the third case is the person who leaves the religion of Islam, the one who became an apostate," and the Prophet said he should be killed, with Allah's permission.

These are the three cases where it is permissible to spill the blood of a Muslim. Another case where it is permissible to spill the blood of a Muslim is when the person has committed the act of sodomy. The Prophet said both the penetrator and the one penetrated should be killed. The Prophet also said the *marabout* should be killed. Other than these cases, Allah and his Prophet did not command the spilling of the blood of a Muslim.

ADMONITION

You say your name is Ibrahim, or 'Abdallah, but each time you come to pray you remove your official [military] cap. Each time the soldiers want to pray they remove their official caps. Even the police and the *Dan Agaji* do the same,[5] because they are imitating the soldiers and do not understand the main reason they remove their official caps. The main reason they remove their caps during their prayers is because of the coat of arms symbol on the cap. The symbol has an idol with two horses and a bird. That is the symbol Nigerians worship. That idol cannot bow to Allah because it is their god. They cannot bring it down close to the ground. It must be raised all the time. They do not want to humiliate it.

Even if it is an offense one has committed so they brought you to a superior officer, if he asked you to do a frog jump, you would have to remove the cap. The cap is above doing a frog jump. So, if they come to pray, they would keep [the cap] because they cannot put it on the ground. How can a police officer take this elephant and put it on the floor? It is you that is ignorant of the fact that even the elephants bow to Allah. If you do not know go back and ask. If a soldier leaves that cap on and prays with it, let us see if he will not be punished. *prayer above occupation*

If you have seen a soldier or policeman, and even *Dan Agaji* who prayed with his cap, please inform us. They will not pray with the cap on because the cap is above bowing down to Allah. [Yusuf derides the uniform of security forces]

Therefore, we should fear Allah and follow our religion. We are calling upon you. You should sit down and think about your occupation. We are calling you to think about your engagement with Western education. We are calling on you to think about your engagement with politics. They are all contrary to what the Prophet Muhammad brought for us. It is not even the Prophet Jesus who brought it. Wait and hear this surprise: the real religion that the Prophet Jesus brought— not that of the Christians, I mean, the Islamic monotheism with its *shari'a*—today after the coming of the Prophet Muhammad if you say you want to follow it then you have become an unbeliever.[6]

The Torah and the Bible are the books of whom? They are the books of Allah. To whom were they revealed? They were revealed to the Messengers of Allah, Moses and Jesus—and they are among the messengers endowed with resolve.[7] By Allah, if the Torah was here and you said you want to derive law from it, then you become an unbeliever, according to the Prophet Muhammad. Let alone the paper [Constitution] that some people sat and wrote together with prostitutes, fornicators and unbeliev- ers.[8] They were the ones that sat down and wrote the law. And it is what they honor; it is with it that they judge the people with their blood and their wealth. You should think about this.

[Discussion of Umar's exchange with prophet Muhammad about the Torah] The Prophet Moses himself today could not learn something from us except by becoming a follower of the Prophet Muhammad. So how is it that you follow a book that is not even revealed from Allah? It is not Islamic, rather it is the unbelievers who sat and wrote it. It contradicts Allah's religion—and you said no one can preach against it, no one can criticize it, and no one should pray that Allah should protect us from it. Then we respond with the saying of the Prophet where he said that the nations of the world will gather against you from everywhere.[9] In Palestine, they kill women and children and they bomb them. They said bombs were thrown at a scholar with his four wives and eleven children.

Muslims are on their own when they come and kill them. They would invade a land and kill the residents. The Prophet said: "You will become like a meal for hungry people." The companions were surprised by this statement then they asked: "Are we going to be so few for them to do this to us, O Allah's Messenger?" The Prophet said: "No, you will be many. Your population will occupy every Friday mosque and every market, but you will be like foam in the water. You will not have the power to stop water." Does leather on water have the power to stop the water? It flows anywhere the water takes it. They do not have a say in anything, except in following the unbelievers.

Look at the way everywhere in Maiduguri is usually empty on Sundays, as if it is Enugu. You have become foam on water because of what "Allah has removed the fear the heart of the unbelievers has for you." Previously, you were following the commands of Allah, following *tawḥīd*, fasting and practicing disassociation and loyalty (*al-walāʾ wa-l-barāʾ*), and you were doing everything right. Then Allah put fear in the heart of the unbelievers. But now that you have left Allah and gone back to your customs, you have gone back to innovation, polytheism, so then Allah removed that fear, and the unbelievers are no longer afraid of you. You know foolishness and ignorance is traumatic.

Some years back, there was a governor who said he would sign the bill for the teaching of Christian religious knowledge in primary and secondary schools. Do you remember that time? We revolted against the idea with the claim that they would inculcate unbelief as part of Western education. So, at the time teachers went to seek the counsel of a scholar. We said we are seeking his counsel, so he replied: "Counsel for what?" We want the scholars to speak about the issue and the plan of the military governor. What is his name? (*Audience responds.*) Ningi Haruna.[10] His name is even Haruna [Aaron], and yet he wanted to sign the bill claiming they must teach these subjects, because it is their [students'] right.

We informed this scholar and he attested to the veracity of our claim, but he asked us what type of unbelief would they inculcate into the education? We explained to him. He asked the question again and we explained to him. We thought he did not understand, so then we told him they would inculcate their Christian practices. He asked us: "What practices were they doing before?" By Allah, there is no one who explained that to him. No one gave him the answer to the question. We went together with those scholars who are now fighting us. The scholar said: "What practices were they doing before?" He said: "They were already practicing unbelief and now you are saying so-and-so." We left and called him an uncivilized scholar and so forth.

So, you see at that time they came prepared, as if they would revolt. They prayed at the gate of the Shehu. However, when they had a meeting which was attended by the Inspector General of Police, ministers, elites, Islamic scholars and the Christians, one of the Christians named Kana Mani[11] stood up inside Borno, in front of all these scholars, and said that the Muslims are gradually pushing them to the wall. He warned that when they [Christians] fight back the Muslims would regret it. When the Muslim representative stood up to give a response, he started pleading that the religion of Islam does not advocate violence but peace. He said the religion of Islam is derived from the word *salām*, which means "peace."

You see the fear that they had for the Muslims—Allah has removed it from their hearts because you have become like them. When they remove the fear and you become equal [to the non-Muslims], then they will start throwing fear in your heart. What is the fear, the Prophet said to the Companions: "The love of this world and fear of death." You see they do not want distress. This is the reason why you would see someone praying, but because of fear he is praying in his office to conceal his Muslim identity. But since it is their place and their religion, they are never shy to show you their cross.

The ideology of the people of Nigeria, the government of Nigeria, and the Christians of Nigeria, sees the religion of Islam as a stranger in this land. Christianity was introduced just about hundred years ago, but now the religion of Islam is the stranger.[12] Now, they are referring to the people who attend our gatherings as "the people who migrated from Niger." They said we are migrants from Niger because the people of Nigeria do not practice Islam, only the people of Niger practice the religion. That is how they refer to us as migrants from Niger.

I was indicted in the court for training the people of Niger and bringing them to Nigeria. They are all Nigeriens. The governor of Jos said: "The people of Niger came and fought, but they were overpowered." What they mean is that the Muslims are powerless except when they receive assistance from foreigners. They said they [Muslims] are foreigners. They have driven out your religion and now they want to drive you out as well.

It is for this reason they are preoccupied with killing as they wish. Now, we are saying: enough is enough. This land is the land of Islam. What we are saying is Allah who took the Arabs from their desert to conquer the empire of Rome is here, the religion they followed to achieve that victory is still here and Allah's power is also here. Therefore, this land is the land of Muslims. If a person wishes to accept Islam, he should accept Islam. If a person does not wish to accept Islam, then he should gather his transport fare and prepare to go to a new destination. [Islamic prayer]

Question and Answer Session

[The question reader reads]: The first question is what is the difference between a messenger and a prophet?

[Yusuf responds]: The main difference is that Allah has elevated the position of a messenger over that of a prophet. [Messengers came with a revealed book and *sharī'a* while prophets follow the teachings of messengers.]

[The question reader reads]: The second question is what is the meaning of the knowledge of *tawḥīd* [monotheism]?

[Yusuf responds]: The knowledge of *tawḥīd* is the knowledge that will show you the unity of Allah. It will show you that Allah does not have a partner, He does not have a friend, He does not have an assistant, and He does not have a son or a daughter. You should understand that Allah is one and He does not look like anyone. This is *tawḥīd*.

[The question reader reads]: The second to last question concerns *iẓhār al-dīn* (open display of the religion). Is it only incumbent upon the scholar or is it also incumbent on the people as well?

[Yusuf responds]: It is incumbent upon all the Muslims. The meaning of *iẓhār al-dīn* is for you to make apparent the Allah who you are worshipping. [iẓhār al-dīn is related to tawḥīd.]

[The question reader reads]: The last question is a question from a person who repented from playing football, watching films and gambling. He was told by someone that all the sins he committed in the past would not be forgiven because he has attained the age of puberty. He is asking about the truth of this claim.

[Yusuf responds]: The claim is incorrect. The person who told the questioner this response does not understand Islam. Once a person sincerely repents, which Allah mentioned in the Qur'ān, his sins are forgiven on the condition that he regrets his sins and promises never to return to them.

13

EXEGESIS OF *SŪRAT AL-BAQARA* (QUR'ĀN 2:284–286)

BY MUHAMMAD YUSUF

(14 FEBRUARY 2009)

his prayers

[Trans.: Abdulbasit Kassim]
Available at: https://www.youtube.com/watch?v=OD0tWMhZSkY

The key theme in this video lecture is the phrase in Qur'ān 2:285 "we hear, and we obey."
In his explanation of this verse, Yusuf discussed the significance of obeying Allah's com-
mandment concerning hijra *and* jihād. *Yusuf censured the Islamic scholars for being sub-*
servient to the dictates of the illegitimate rulers', as well as their cooperation with the State
Security Service to blackmail and impede his preaching. He challenged their authority
and scholarship by claiming that their opposition to his preaching stemmed from their fear
of America, France and England. This lecture should be considered as part of the rebuttal
from Yusuf to the Islamic scholars who argued against his methodology of jihād.

O Allah, annihilate unbelief, destroy the unbelievers, weaken them and decimate
them! O Allah, sharpen the sword of the *mujāhidīn*. O Allah, sharpen the guns of the
mujāhidīn. O Allah, help the *mujāhidīn* to shoot their guns. O Allah, you are the one
who helped the Prophet Muhammad to shoot during his battle. O Allah you are the
One who said: "when you threw [arrows] it was actually Allah who threw..." (Q8:17)
O Allah, help the *mujāhidīn* to shoot. O Allah, you are the one who killed the unbelievers—kill the unbelievers of this era. O Allah, you are the one who destroyed the

111

states of Persia and Rome, O Allah you are the one that destroyed Pharaoh, O Allah destroy these states of unbelief that surround us. O Allah, gather them and destroy them. O Allah, shake them and scatter them. O Allah, weaken all the people that strengthen them.

[Standard Islamic opening] Just as we presented in the first introduction, today is Saturday the nineteenth of Safar, the year 1430, after the migration of the Prophet of Allah from Mecca to Medina. Today's lesson was initially scheduled for the study of the book on the Prophet's biography *al-Raḥīq al-makhtūm*,[1] but because of the short time and the problem of electricity,[2] we will continue with the Qur'ānic exegesis which is the second lesson. We will start from verse 284 in the blessed chapter of *al-Baqara*. And may Allah lead us through.

[Qur'ānic reciter reads]: "To Allah belongs whatever is in the heavens and on the earth. And whether you reveal or conceal what is in your hearts, Allah will call you to account for it. He will then forgive whom He wills, and punish whom He wills. He is able to do everything." (Q2:284)

[Yusuf lectures]: Allah says all what is in the seven heavens and the seven earths and the things that are between them are His dominion.

[Discussion of Allah's attributes] Once Allah instructs us, the discussion is over. If you perform *hijra* for your own sake either for worldly benefits or to marry a woman then your *hijra* will be rewarded based upon your intent. However, if you perform *hijra* for the sake of Allah, then your *hijra* will be rewarded by Allah.

[Discussion of prophet Muhammad's migration from Mecca to Medina] Similarly, if Allah instructs you to fight *jihād*, but you argue that it is not realistic, you will never understand when the *jihād* is realistic. Allah will deny you that understanding. Why? This is so because it is like the action of the Jews. Allah commanded the Prophet Moses to inform his people about the holy land He ordained to them. The instruction was not for them to fight but to enter the holy land: "My people, enter the Holy Land which Allah ordained for you, and do not turn back, lest you become the losers." (Q5:21) It is none of your concern how you will enter. Allah instructs you to enter and you are expected to follow the instruction.

This [*the refusal of the Jews to enter Israel at the command of Moses*] is akin to the present-day utterances of the people. Allah instructs us to fight *jihād*. They concur with this instruction yet they claim that America and other countries are mighty people. You would hear them saying, "we will not fight them, until they leave." This utterance is akin to what the people of Moses said: "We shall not enter it, until they leave it." (Q5:22) We will not stop practicing democracy until they stop practicing it, "if they leave it, then we shall enter" and practice the *sharīʿa*.

These scholars will not instruct the people to practice the *sharīʿa*. They will not instruct the people to wage *jihād*. However, if the *ṭāghūt* announces that *sharīʿa* should be practiced from now, they will agree and follow the instruction. When we understood this scheme, Allah showed us that although these scholars are the people who should be leading us, but we need to stop waiting for them because they will never stand up to lead us. We were waiting for them to lead us when suddenly a *ṭāghūt* announced that *sharī'a* should be practiced so they concur and follow the instruction.

You would hear them quoting the statement of Allah: "Or do they have associates who enacted for them as a religion that for which Allah did not give leave?" (Q42:21) You would also hear them saying concerning any governor or minister who impedes the practice of *sharī'a*: "May Allah curse him—and *qunūt* should be recited against him."[3] Anyone who refuses to practice the *sharī'a* should be killed. These were their words and statements. Later, the governor announced that this *sharī'a* is not practical so then they also concur that the *sharī'a* is not practical.

Consequently, Allah says: "And had We commanded them: 'Slay yourselves or go forth from your homes,'" (Q4:66)—if Allah instructed you to pick a knife and slit your throat, you are obligated to kill yourself. This is the *sharī'a* of Allah. You should obey the instruction to kill your children. This is the *sharī'a* of Allah. [*Recounting the story of Abrahim's almost-sacrifice of his son.*]

This is exactly what Allah wants from us. If Allah instructs us to perform an action and we hear and obey the instruction, He will make the execution of the instruction easy for us by a way we did not expect. However, if Allah instructs us to do an action but we contend with Allah, saying it is not realistic, we will never understand the instruction and we will end up like the Jews. Why the apprehension about following the commands of Allah to enter the holy land? They said they would not enter because they [fear] people of great strength in the land.

[Prophet Ibrahim obeyed the instruction of Allah] In this town, they were busy insulting us on the radio and calling us bastards. They said they were the people who caught me. I read their multiple plots to them. I told them I knew the person to whom the scholars usually go to to collect money for blackmailing us. I gave them his name. I told the SSS that they are behind all these plots. They have an expert who specializes in blackmail. His name is Fulan Garba Shinkafi. I told them that his office is responsible for overseeing all these evil people.

By Allah, none of them argued with me, but asked: "How did you get this information?" I told them that they are the people who informed their students and their students informed us. Then they asked me, whether I believe the information or not? I responded that why would I not believe it after all I have seen? Before I returned to the town, they switched all of them, including their director—"They schemed, and Allah schemed, but Allah is the best of schemers." (Q8:30) Which expert did they bring? If you hold fast to Allah, everyone will come challenging you.

Therefore, I said that we know the Qur'ān memorizers, and even an angel is not wiser than Him. By Allah, they were the people who arranged all these plots. When I told them, their bodies froze. I told them: "You are the people who sponsor them by giving them money. You are claiming the authority to govern, yet why would you bring a poor man to fight another poor man? What type of authority or governance is that?" They all kept quiet. Similarly, I mentioned the name of this official who disputed with me, then mentioned the name of another official. When they disputed with me I mentioned the name of the official who oversaw the discussion. Before I returned to the town, they removed him.

By Allah, they are the people who paid these scholars to insult and blackmail us. By Allah, they are the people who paid them and we know their scheme. We know! He is an expert and his expertise is in blackmail. You should watch him; any town he visits, his mission is to devise different schemes and plots. He is either blackmailing a person using drama and film, or plotting with scholars to insult and blackmail them. The moment the [blackmailed] person no longer enjoys popular sympathy, they arrest him. It is not possible for people like him to work alone.

During Ramadan,[4] they carried out this blackmail and insulting, and then thinking that I no longer enjoy popular sympathy, they arrested me. However, when we were returning to the town, everyone—those who had heard of the insulting and blackmail and those who had not—cheered us. By Allah, we do not feel ashamed and afraid. We do not feel ashamed or fear any person. Once you carry out an action for the sake of Allah, the worst thing they can do is to kill you. We have already accepted this fate. We have already bought it. So, with what will you scare us, death?! We have bought and paid for it. We have finished the transaction between us and Allah.[5] It is either you kill or shoot us here, or do as you wish. [Discussion of the People of the Ditch Q85:1–22.]

[Yusuf delegitimizes his rival scholars for issuing false religious rulings] By the way, who is a scholar? Anyone who issues false religious rulings has ceased being a scholar. If you claim that he is a scholar, then this verse is also referring to him: "And tell them [O Muhammad] about the man to whom We gave Our revelations, but he renounced them and was followed by the Devil." (Q7:175)[6] Some people claim that people like me do not have the sufficient knowledge to label a person an unbeliever (*takfīr*). They said it is only the scholars of *ṭāghūt* that have the knowledge to do so. What if I read Ibn Qayyim's definition of *ṭāghūt*? What If I read Imām Muhammad b. 'Abd al-Wahhab's explanation of the five types of *ṭāghūt*? Is that not sufficient?

[Knowledge of tawhīd is important] The liars will persist in their ways. Once they finish a scheme, they will keep quiet, pretend and feign ignorance while they make plans for a new scheme. This is how they will continue until they become overwhelmed. I hope it is understood. This is the reason I always repeat the Hausa adage: "the rope is beyond the power of a chicken." This preaching is the rope. It is beyond the power of a chicken. Everyone in the world is a chicken. From Satan to America, they are all chickens. So, there is no one who can halt the rope—rather it will be released to kill them. I hope it is understood.

[Yusuf explain Q2:286] There is no unbearable law for which we do not have the strength. Take for example the *ḥijāb* of women. There is nothing as easy as the *ḥijāb*. You should wear the *ḥijāb*, a thick and wide *ḥijāb*. You should drag it on the floor in a way that when you are walking no one can see any part of your body.[7] Even if the wind blows on it, your body will be intact and covered. This is the law of Allah. Is it beyond our capability? Is it not possible to obey this instruction?

[Discussion of the meaning of *tawhīd*] You said you cannot put *tawhīd* into practice. You cannot fight *jihād*. Is it until you allow them to replicate what they did to the Palestinians? For sixty years, they are slaughtering their children. Their situation will gradually be replicated here. Look at what happened at Kafanchan in 1987. They killed the Muslims—mostly men who were capable of fighting. In Zango Kataf, they killed both men and women. They gathered the women and they instructed them to say "Jesus." After they obeyed, they forced them to drink alcohol, poured petrol on them and set them on fire. This is what they did in Zango Kataf here in Nigeria. They carried out the same action in Yelwa Shandam. They gathered the women and fled with them. There are those who are yet to be found, and others who returned, but came back with two children or a child. They forced them to drink alcohol and fornicated with them.

Now, they have also killed children, burnt and roasted them. In the face of all these killings, they still claim that we do not have power to do anything. It is a condition. Is it until they finish their killings? There is nothing that will prevent these killings except *jihād* in Allah's path, but they said they will not allow us. They made all efforts to prevent us by taking reports about us to the SSS. They will inform the SSS to be careful about us. Yet, you claim to be an Islamic scholar. You visit different places with your schemes and plots to prevent this preaching. They said our preaching will trigger a crisis. So, on which day will they stop all their destruction?

In fact, these scholars consider our preaching to be worse than the destruction they carried out in Jos. [This scholar] is not concerned with that destruction at all. It is not his concern that they slaughtered small children. The only issue that draws his attention is the implementation of democracy. Usually when you see him, he is busy making noise about his grievances against the governor, who did not swear in his preferred candidate. Once the governor swears in his preferred candidate, the discussion is over. He is not bothered about the little children and memorizers of Qur'ān who were slaughtered.

The only issue that draws his interest is the implementation of democracy, yet he claims to be a Muslim. Now, they are praising Obasanjo. They said may Allah bless him because he is a good person. He impeached the Governor after he observed the aftermath of the fighting. There are those who also praised [Musa Umaru] Yar'adua.[8] They said in the aftermath of the fighting, the Governor visited the presidency, but Yar'adua hissed and shunned him, and this is the reason they praised him. The case of these people is like a camel outdoor who saw a camel indoor with a cargo moving back and forth, and said: "Allah forbid that your possessions would decay."

With your strength, honor and all your religion and Islam, they still play on your intelligence like a donkey or a brainless fool. We said: "O brothers, since we have secured an opportunity, all what we predicted is happening; let us come together for admonition." They opposed our admonition and counseled the people to enlist with the soldiers. They said these events occurred because they did not enlist. They counseled them to enlist *en masse*. What they failed to understand is the fact that the same people they counseled to enlist with the soldiers are the people who will slaughter them.

[Obedience in word of mouth should be combined with actions.]

14

WESTERN CIVILIZATION IS ATHEISM AND ANTI-ISLAM

BY ABUBAKAR SHEKAU

(16 FEBRUARY 2009)[1]

[Trans.: Abdulbasit Kassim]
Available at: https://www.youtube.com/watch?v=eQY4GLtzLdU

This video lecture should be considered in its importance to be the political and religious statement of Abubakar Shekau, who would become Yusuf's successor. The content of the lecture is closely related to the content of text 11 delivered by Yusuf. The themes covered in this lecture would later feature in many of the writings and multimedia messages of Shekau after 2009. Of specific interest in this lecture is Shekau's parody of the national pledge and anthem which represents his anti-national ideology and revulsion of the Nigerian state. Shekau's style and his rather bullying attitude, during the question and answer period, contrast with that of Yusuf (see texts 10, 12). There were some missing parts at the beginning of the video.

[Missing parts]

Allah can bear witness for me regarding my explanation of this issue. This is the scheme they designed for our women. The same scheme also applies to our male children. This is the reason Allah's Messenger said a child should be taught how to pray at the age of 7, and should be whipped if he refuses to pray at the age of 10.

When a child passes the age of 7, his mind is like a magnet that attracts everything. This is the reason the Europeans choose this age for beginning primary school so that they can infuse their way of thinking into our children from their early years. A child is enrolled in the school at the age of 7. After six years of primary school, he is close to the age of puberty. This is their scheme. I hope it is understood.

At the onset, the duration of primary school is seven years. It was later reduced to six years. At that time, you would be speaking English fluently by primary level six or seven. Everyone who attends this system would understand my explanation. I hope it is understood.

There is a popular song they taught children at the school: "Class 1 he is a dullard, Class 2 he is a dullard, Class 3 he is a dullard, Class 4 he is close to being adroit, Class 5 [unclear], Class 6 he has become an European." This is the song they taught children. We were enrolled, but our grandparents bemoaned so they removed us. We were enrolled in a school in Damaturu called Bindigari. The school was constructed with aluminum. Is it understood? Our grandparents bemoaned that their children are being kept in a fireplace, and so they removed us.

A child attains adolescence at 16–17, so after primary school, these stages usually fall between Form 1 to Form 3. Allah's Messenger said when a child attains adolescence, he will be untamed if there is no one to give proper training. He can either become a miscreant or virtuous. Is this understood? This is the scheme they designed.

This description has also been confirmed by both unbelieving and Muslim psychologists. If you place a child in a course until he reaches 25, it will be difficult to change his education again. This is their scheme. That is why once you start discussing this issue, Muslims are the first people to disagree with you. They have already been molded during this course into a pattern in which minds have been cloaked. This is their scheme.

When you approach 16–17, you proceed from Form 1 to 3, 4, 5 and 6, so by then, you have reached 23–24, and have been taught the harmful knowledge. Even at that stage, their scheme has not reached its finale, because then they will enroll you into the university. You will learn all the noxious behavior before you enroll into the NYSC.[2]

At the NYSC, you will be compelled to serve a camp-fire [at night]. You will start belittling the people who did not undergo the same type of training as hicks. They are ignoramuses. The only people they will consider intelligent are those who have studied Western education. They are the guys. By Allah, you will start viewing other people as illiterates.

This is exactly what they have written in their books, saying every person who cannot read or write is an illiterate. That is why if you cannot speak English or cannot write what you are saying, they will consider you to be an ignoramus or a dolt. This is their creed and this is what they inculcate in you. Is this understood?

Brothers! This is their scheme of destruction against our children, friends, women and our brothers at the level of social behavior and at the level of ideological indoctrination in education. Do you understand? They have cloaked our mind with thoughts contrary to Allah's injunctions. They have ruined our lives with teachings that are contrary to Allah's Messenger. They have imposed a law on us that contradicts the law of Allah. Do you understand the scheme they designed for us? This is the scheme.

There are other schemes they have designed for us such as the national pledge, the national anthem and the annual celebrations. I hope it is understood. Each day of celebration in Christianity where Christian worship is usually designated as a holiday by the government. Do you understand the scheme they designed for us? Boxing Day, Children's Day, Easter Monday, Good Friday, Happy New Year, Christmas etc. have all been declared as holidays. Do you understand? When December approaches, the holidays in this month are different from the holidays in all other months. During the 'Id al-Aḍḥā celebration, do you experience the same type of holiday as those in December? You do not experience the same type of holiday.[3] I hope it is understood. This is their scheme.

Then you will recite the national pledge:

[National Pledge]	[Shekau's Parody of the National Pledge]
I pledge to Nigeria my country	I give allegiance to Nigeria my country. The same type of allegiance or covenant you give Allah "those who pay you homage are actually paying Allah homage. Allah's hand is above their hands." (Q48:10)
To be faithful, loyal and honest	to be faithful (with faith), loyal (true followership) and honest (with sincerity)
To serve Nigeria with all my strength	to serve Nigeria, meaning I will worship Nigeria. "Serve" here means worship. This is the reason the prophets are called servants of Allah. You are declaring that you are a servant of the country. With all my strength, meaning I will serve the country with the wherewithal Allah bestows upon me.
To defend her unity,	I will protect her wholeness. I will protect Nigeria united between Muslims and non-Muslims. There is no difference between Muslims and non-Muslims because they are all under the rules and regulations of this country. This is the unity you must protect. You will take severe measures against anyone who tampers with this unity. That is why once you meddle with the law of the land, you will be treated by people as seri

	ous offender. However, when you sin against Allah, they will consider it as a joke.
And uphold her honor and glory	I will uplift her honor, value and glory. I will glorify her. There is no one who should be praised with this word "glory" except Allah.
So, help me God	you are saying: "O Allah assist me."

Allah says everywhere you see them worshipping other gods besides Him, they are invoking nothing but female deities.[4] As you can see, they also refer to Nigeria as a female deity. They use the feminine word "her" to describe the Nigerian government. In the English language, the pronoun "her," such as "to defend her unity" is feminine, which is different from the pronoun "his" which is masculine. They said, "her unity and to uphold her honor."

Allah says: "Apart from Him they only invoke the goddesses of Quraysh." (Q4:117) If you substitute the word "Nigeria" in the national pledge with Allah, you will realize that they have given Allah's attributes to Nigeria. The pledge should only be made to Allah. I pledge to Allah, my Lord, my Allah, whom I worship. Is it understood? To be faithful, loyal and honest; to serve Allah with all my strength; to defend His unity; and uphold His honor and glory; so help me Allah. This is *tawḥīd*.

Furthermore, look at [the national anthem]:

[National Anthem]	[Shekau's Parody of the National Anthem]
Arise, O compatriots, Nigeria's call obey	Arise; they are calling the people of the land. Nigeria is calling you. You should come and obey. Obey! Obey!! If they say obey Allah, what do they mean? Nigeria is calling you to obey her.
To serve our fatherland	We should serve our father's land. We should work for the land of our grandfathers and great-grandfathers
With love and strength and faith	with love, the strength in our body, and faith
The labor of our heroes past	the labor of our parents and grandparents in keeping Nigeria unified.
Shall never be in vain	the labor, for which our scholars were slaughtered, they urinated on the Qur'ān, and invented the constitution which governs us up till today, shall never be in vain. We will not allow. This is unbelief.

WESTERN CIVILIZATION IS ATHEISM AND ANTI-ISLAM

This is Western education. January, February, March, April, May, June, and July are all names of idols which people worship. Up till now, the government usually prepare a gathering to celebrate the idols of each month. They might disguise and call it civil service, but they are engaging in the worship of their idols. You might not know. They speak about May Day, but they are gathering together to celebrate the idol of the month. The people are mostly unaware.

For instance, January is for the god of love and other months are for the god of praise, god of war etc. This is exactly the meaning of these months. The days of the week Sunday, Monday etc. are also names of idols. They are all names of idols. This is unbelief and they have surrounded us with it.

They left us with prayers, fasting and alms-giving but you should know that if you are engaging in polytheism, all other acts of worship are null and void. Allah told Allah's Messenger: "If you associate any others with Allah, He will frustrate your work and you will certainly be one of the losers." (Q39:65)

[Shekau cites Q6:83–88] This begs the question why is it that the scholars, particularly those in this town, would agree that Western education is unbelief, democracy is unbelief, the constitution is unbelief, but then would say that because there is nothing we can do about that fact, we must engage with them. You agree that it is unbelief but then you said there is nothing you can do about it even though Allah has commanded you to abstain from it.

[Prophets were killed because of their preaching against polytheism] You! You! You! By Allah, let us be thoughtful. By Allah, we do not understand unbelief. We do not understand polytheism. For instance, if someone insults his parents, we would all agree that he has committed an offense. However, polytheism is worse than insulting your mother. It is worse than insulting your father. How come we do not understand this flaw?

Polytheism is worse than everything. If you are practicing polytheism and die believing in it, you will not be forgiven. Even if people come together to seek forgiveness for you, Allah will not accept their prayer. O people! Polytheism is dangerous. If you are practicing polytheism and die believing in it, if people approach your tomb and pray that may Allah increase your punishment, they will be rewarded. O people! Polytheism is dangerous. Now, we are in the world of polytheism, the polytheism of the people who disbelieve in the existence of Allah.

[Christians believe in Jesus as the son of God, and cannot be trusted.]

However, Allah says: "Since I do not have a son and you said I have a son, you have become unbelievers. All the love you have for me, I reject it." Do you understand my explanation? "Unbelievers are those who say: 'Allah is the Messiah, son of Mary.'" (Q5:17) "Those who say that Allah is the Messiah, son of Mary, are unbelievers." (Q5:73).

So the people that accept the existence of Allah, but because they refuse to follow Allah's injunctions, He called them unbelievers. What about the people who referred to the government as a secular government? Secularism! The godless world! The world of no religion! Even the people that believe in religion, Allah called them unbelievers because they refuse to follow Allah's injunctions. Do you understand my explanation?

[Discussion of the polytheism of of Abū Jahl and Walīd b. Mughīrah] Today, they say the Qur'ān is no longer effective. They also disagree with the Prophet and the religion. It is the New World Order, the new system of running the world. Globalization! This is what they are spreading across the globe. Will you follow this people and still hope to enter paradise? Do you understand this scheme?

O Muslims! This is exactly what we are fighting. It is this belief that we oppose and fight. By Allah, we were not the first people to embark on this type of preaching, as I have presented to you the explanation of past scholars on this issue. However, even if there are no scholars who spoke about this issue, the Qur'ān and the Prophet preceded the scholars. Is it not so?

[Discussion of implicit and explicit Quranic verses] In fact, we were commanded not to follow our parents in polytheism: "but if they strive with you to associate with Me that of which you have no knowledge, then do not obey them." (Q29:8) So how can someone say that democracy is not polytheism? What is the meaning of government of the people by the people and for the people? Whatever the people want, even if it contradicts the law of Allah, will be accepted. Is that not democracy?

Whatever the people reject, even if it contradicts the law of Allah, will be accepted. Is that not democracy? Is this what you believe is not polytheism? Several scholars have made explanations concerning this issue. According to Ibn 'Uthaymīn, he said democracy is the methodology of the unbelievers. It is not permissible for a Muslim to participate in democracy. He did not say that it is good, let alone for a person to participate in it, or let alone for Muslims to be encouraged to participate in it. This is what Ibn 'Uthaymīn said.

He said, among the principal creed of the Sunnis is the belief that aiding the unbelievers nullifies Islam. He said whoever does not call the unbelievers and polytheists unbelievers (takfīr), aids them or says they are benevolent has become apostate from Islam. This is what Ibn 'Uthaymīn said. You can check *Fatāwā al-mar'ah*, part one, p. 7, written by Ibn 'Uthaymīn and 'Abd al-Raḥmān b. Jibrīn.[5]

Another scholar Saʿīd ʿAbd al-ʿAẓīm said in his book *Qawāʿid wa-uṣūl muhimma li-qirāʾāt al-turāth* that democracy is the idol of this era. He said if you desire to know the idol of this era, it is democracy. He said democracy is a religion for those who follow it, and they want to compel this religion upon Muslims through force. Look at what he said here. These are scholars who have explained this issue.

There is another scholar who is still alive his name is Muhammad Ḥassān. In his book *Khawāṭir ʿalā ṭarīq al-daʿwa* he said in this era there are false scholars who have emerged, and that even if a king rules by some [source] other than the law of Allah, they will say it is legitimate. If a king permits something, they will follow him and say it is permissible. If he forbids something that is permissible in Allah's sight, they will follow him and say it is forbidden. Even if he is a democrat, they will say what is democracy? Is democracy not also Islam?

There are people who have made similar statements in this town. There is a scholar in this town who wrote a book titled *Islam and the Contemporary World System*.[6] In the book, he said democracy is not against Islam. This is exactly what he said and we have the book. Is it understood?

These are the type of statements you would hear from these types of scholars. He said that [the medieval scholar] Ibn Qayyim has explained in-depth concerning these scholars who call to falsehood. Ibn Qayyim said they are evil scholars sitting on the gate of paradise. While they are calling people to paradise with their statements, they are calling people to hellfire with their deeds. Do you hear this explanation?

[Criticism of rival scholars who support democracy] At first when you listen to their preaching, you would assume that they are pathfinders. On the contrary, they are armed robbers. This is the explanation of Ibn Qayyim—and the period between him and us is 700 years. Look at his book *Badāʾiʿ al-fawāʾid*, p. 12. If you want the name of the publisher, it is Dar al-Bayan. We do not want you to say: "I went to crosscheck but I did not see this explanation." Check the publication of Dar al-Bayan.[7] Do you understand this explanation?

Look at this book, the title is *al-Muḥallā* and it is written by Ibn Ḥazm.[8] It is a well-known book. The volume I am going to quote from is the twelfth, pp. 128–129. In the book, Ibn Ḥazm said: "If an entire town that is completely Muslim is invaded by a crusading unbeliever, who is victorious over the town of the Muslims, then says: 'I have defeated the town, but you can stay in your town and follow the laws of your Qurʾān. However, you must accept that I am the leader of the land.'" Ibn Ḥazm said: "If you stay in the town, you will all be unbelievers." Do you hear his statement? This is what Ibn Ḥazm said.

For example, America has captured Iraq, so if they would allow the people of Iraq to follow the Qurʾān, but insisted that America is the country which would run the affairs of the land, both foreign and domestic affairs, including ambassadors and ministers—according to Ibn Ḥazm whoever stayed in the land would become an unbeliever. This is the explanation of Ibn Ḥazm. He is not a contemporary scholar. [Ibn Ḥazm's scholarship is profound]

Ibn Taymiyya said polytheism is not included as part of the necessity that allows for omitting incumbent laws or doing something illegal. Once an action is labelled polytheism, it must be abandoned without any condition. Another scholar said rather than engaging in polytheism for a day because of necessity, it is better for everyone to die. When they inquired from him the reason for his statement, he said:

"Sedition (*fitna*) is worse than slaughter." (Q2:191) He said if the entire world would perish, it is better than to engage in polytheism for a day.

It is because I do not have sufficient time that is why I prefer to be brief. In this book, I brought for this lecture, there are twenty-five scholars who have brought evidence that if you report a case to the court of the unbelievers, you have become an unbeliever, without any pardon. The first scholar is Ibn Ḥazm, the second is Ibn Taymiyya, the third is Ibn Qayyim, the fourth is Ibn Kathīr, the fifth is the author of *Fatḥ al-majīd*, who is also the grandson of Muhammad b. Abd al-Wahhāb.⁹ The sixth scholar is Imam Shinqīṭī.¹⁰

He said [Imam Shinqīṭī] the person who reports a case to the constitutional court, there is no one who would doubt if he is a Muslim or not except the person that Allah has denied him clear insight or the person that Allah has blinded from his revelation.

Based on the references cited, my fellow Muslims, we see all these scholars and their writings as the truthful scholars that the entire world agrees with their scholarship and they attested that they said all the above statements. They are the scholars we follow. After the Qur'ān has explicitly informed us, we do not need to go the extent of bringing the views of these scholars. However, there are those who have said we are interpreting the Qur'ān according to our own understanding. That is the reason we are saying look at the statements of the scholars. This is what we saw.

Fellow Muslims! I will like to end this discussion with this book. I have often read the book, and cited the titles of the previous books because they are new. In the book, Ibn 'Uthaymīn said if a school is mixed with both genders—even if it is the only school in the town—it should be abandoned. I always read this statement, as well as the ruling of the Permanent Committee [for Ruling]. Is it not so? I do not need to repeat their ruling.

[Discussion of *Kufr dūna kufr*] Therefore, we are not the people making up these explanations. We saw these explanations written in the books. The Qur'ān also made these explanations as well as the *ḥadīth* of the Prophet. O Muslims! This is the total of our explanation.

[Shekau cites the chapters on tribulations and leadership in '*Tafsīr al-Manār*', '*Fatḥ al-bārī bi-sharḥ Ṣaḥīḥ al-Bukhārī*' and *Ṣaḥīḥ Muslim*.] Even if he drinks alcohol, once the law they follow is the law of the Qur'ān and the Sunna, and he sends soldiers to fight *jihād*, we do not care about his flaws—and it is compulsory to follow him and his land is a land of the Muslims. However, the leader who governs with the constitution, even if he was born in the middle of the Ka'ba [in Mecca], it is forbidden to follow him. Do you understand my explanation?

This is our explanation. All what we are saying, we saw it written in the book. Surprisingly in this book... May Allah protect our secret, may He make us firm on the path of truth, may He make us to work with the truth and may He make us to die on the path of truth.

Otherwise, my brothers, if only they will understand! If the government really loves Islam, how is it possible that in a town like [Maiduguri] Borno they used the Qur'ān to wipe feces? Afterwards, they kept weapons in front of the school to fire on anyone who protests. You should remember this incident. You should also remember what they did to the Muslims in Jos recently where they set an entire school ablaze, killed the people and threw infants to burn in the fire. They carried out all these actions, but we must follow [them].

[Discussion of Umar's exchange with prophet Muhammad about the Torah] Now, even if it was the Prophet Moses we follow we would still not be guided. Yet, we are following [Lord Frederick] Lugard. We are following the constitution. Yet, we still call ourselves the people of Sunna.

[Criticism of rival scholars] As you all know, they cannot alter the arrangement of the heaven and earth or night and day. Regardless of your dominion, you cannot force the day to dawn, and that is exactly why you cannot take any measures against the Muslims. By Allah, whatever action you do to your brother because he practices the religion, the harm of your evil will affect only the person who plotted such evil. This is what Allah said: "Yet the evil cunning will only recoil upon its perpetrators." (Q35:43)

Here, we are male, but this preaching cannot transform us into females. This is the same way the person who plots evil will be encompassed by the evil he plotted. Do you understand? By Allah, this is certain. You should understand that we do not wield knives or sticks yet today we have been preaching for the past seven years. It is not our power. It is not our knowledge. It is not our capability. It is Allah that brought us far till today. If He desires, He will allow us to reach our goal tomorrow, but if He desires, He will annihilate us tonight.

However, you should remember that there are so many people who anticipated that they will kill us, but now they are dead. There are so many people who prepared to take severe measures against us, but Allah took measures against them. You cannot count them because they are many. There are those we know and those we do not know. Allah knows them. He knows what He did to them. We do not have the capability. We are nothing! We are nothing! It is the preaching. Allah has tested you with us. In your own view, you are seeing us. Yet, if you attempt to harm us, it is the preaching you will harm. There is no doubt that among us there are flawed people, but Allah will not allow them to earn any reward.

As such, you cannot change the preaching because it is different from the preaching of Maitatsine,[11] from the preaching of the Shi'ites and from the preaching of the Izalas. Is it understood? It is different. It is the preaching of the Qur'ān, ḥadīth of the Prophet and the explanation of the forefathers. We are also hoping that Allah will sustain us in this preaching. I hope it is understood.

[Prayers for success] O people! By Allah, do not attempt to fight against this preaching. If you attempt to harm this preaching, it is against Allah you will be fighting. We can also derive some lessons from the events that are happening inside and out of this town on this issue. It is not surprising to us. A prophet himself was killed and nothing happened. It is not surprising to us that they will kill us and still go ahead and eat food, drink and continue living.

[Discussion of the stakes ahead] Look at the People of the Trench![12] What did Allah say about them? They had nothing against them, except that they believed in Allah. We are only praying that we will end up well. However, I am preaching to anyone who prostrates in prayers never to attempt to fight against Islam. Never should you fight against Islam.

Even if he is a traveler, you should never fight against him to help an unbeliever. Do you understand my explanation? Even if he is a traveler, once he declares that he is a Muslim, you should never help an unbeliever against him. Do you understand my explanation? It is only permissible for both of you to join hands together and fight the unbeliever and thereafter you can both fight each other. Do you understand? This is the teaching of Islam.

> ...but those who have believed, yet did not emigrate, you will not be responsible for their protection until they emigrate. Should they seek your support for religion's sake, you ought to support them, but not against a people with whom you have a compact. Allah is fully aware of what you do. (Q8:72)

[We are being persecuted because of our beliefs] Look at the level of insults they hurled at us on television during Ramadan. The day before yesterday, Mallam [Yusuf] was saying that they were recruited and paid money to hurl insults and blackmail us. They were hired to "catch them and kill them." He went there to Abuja and he told the SSS that they were the ones who hired people and paid them to hurl insults against us. They gave them money to insult and blackmail us so that everyone would view us as the wrongdoers, whereupon the government can take severe measures against us. It is shameful for you to say that you are a follower of Sunna. By Allah, it is shameful.

[Criticism of rival scholars and closing prayer]

[Moderator reads a question]: This questioner is asking about the treaty of Hudaybiyya, and he wants you to explain the misconceptions about the treaty? Another questioner is asking for a clarification whether it is permissible or not to engage in a friendly relationship with an unbeliever, if he does not prevent you from your worship?

[Shekau responds]: If they do not prevent you [personally] from your worship, they prevent [the rest of] us. They have prevented us from ruling with the Qur'ān. This is the reason we will not engage in friendly relationships with them [unbelievers]. So, thank you. Is it not so according to his explanation?

With regards to the treaty of Hudaybiyya, people ought to understand that Allah's Messenger was in Medina with his followers and he was the leader. Then he came to

WESTERN CIVILIZATION IS ATHEISM AND ANTI-ISLAM

Mecca, right? Abū Jahl and Abū Sufyan were the leaders of Mecca.[13] Mecca was ruled by an unbelieving government, while Medina was ruled by an Islamic government. The treaty was between an Islamic and an unbelieving government.

So, you should wait for the time when we will have an Islamic government, then come together signing a treaty with the unbelieving government. Right now, you should understand that you are under the rule of an unbelieving government. What will you use to sign a treaty? You are only a serf. Treaties are signed between leaders. The Prophet was a leader who signed a treaty with the leaders of Mecca. Is it not so? Now, you should also look for an Islamic leader when the government is established—then we will proceed to sign a treaty. Do you understand? This is the first clarification about the treaty of Hudaybiyya.

[*Explanation of the treaty.*]

[Moderator reads a question]: This questioner is asking about your position concerning the impermissibility of Western education, but he said you are making use of loudspeakers, mobile phones and microphones. If Western education is impermissible, how would they invent all these appliances? What is the ruling on using these electrical appliances?

[Shekau responds]: Yes, Western education is impermissible, but these electrical appliances are good. This light is good because it brightens this place. These speakers are good because you can all hear my voice. These appliances are good. However, Western education is impermissible because they have said the sun is stationary. Is it impermissible in your own view? Is it permissible to say that the sun is stationary? The sun is not the speakers. If the same view was said about the speakers, I can also leave them.

This is not Western education. Even if there is no Western education, the people can learn how to create all these appliances. Yes, even without Western education. They do not even learn about these things in Western education, they only learn deception. It is deception. You would see someone with a master's degree in engineering, but cannot manufacture even an engine to produce pasta.

Yet, there is another person coming from the village who has not attended primary school, in fact he does not understand "go and come," but he can dismantle a machine and cobble it together. The so-called engineer cannot do this, yet someone who did not attend primary school can do this. Is it Western education which taught him this knowledge? Therefore, even without Western education, this knowledge can be learnt.

Western education is not a revelation. The only thing that cannot be learnt except in front of a scholar is the Qur'ān. Western education is just about the brain. Whatever someone's brain knows; another person can also know the same thing. Is it understood? We will go in an easy mode. Whatever the brain knows, the brain of other people can also know the same thing.

[Discussion of the repression of the brain's capability to invent] If the brains of the people were not repressed, they would have shut down Western education in its entirety. Do you understand my explanation? Up till now, it is not even Western education they are learning. If only they gave everyone the opportunity to invent what will benefit the people, then they will do away with all these medications. Even in the village, they will bring paracetamol for you to take, and by Allah they would just deceive you, put it in the leather pack, wrap it and paint it and you would think it is something beneficial.

All these inventions are nothing special. If you can invent a gun, will they allow you to? They will not allow you. This is how they repressed the ability of people. If only they would have given everyone the opportunity to invent what will benefit the people, among the black people you will see someone who will invent a flying plane without attending Western education. It is deception and repression. Even with an automobile, there are big companies which invent cars and motorcycles, but if you invent they will not buy. The ability of people has been repressed. This is deception. This privilege is only designed for them forever.

You do not know, but all these inventions do not emanate from them. This is for you to know in terms of fairness and detailed explanation. These inventions do not come from them, they belong to Allah. [Discussion of Allah's unity]

Even the European himself belongs to Allah—or is he the one who created himself? He belongs to Allah. These inventions do not emanate from Western education, they all belong to Allah. Let me say that the European should put an engine inside himself and turn himself into a motorcycle so that I will go around with it. What will prevent it? What I said is that even if it is in the house of a scholar that there is a flaw, they should desist from it. Anywhere there is a flaw, it should be fixed. We are only trying to prevent destruction.

Moreover, since I said Western education is impermissible and you disagree with my position, saying that I should not use electricity, then you should not use it as well, since if you did, it would mean that you are not following Allah. You are expected to withdraw from living under this sky. Is it not so? Since you will not follow Allah, and want to follow the adherents of Western education then you should acquire your own world. You should withdraw from the world of our Creator.

[Everything belongs to Allah] Now, you see the speakers, you see electricity, those are the inventions you see, right? If all the world gather together because of science and technology, can they create one grain? If the whole world should come together, can they create one grain of rice? If the whole world should come together, can they create one seed of maize, one seed of beans or one drop of water?

Before you came for this lecture, did you not swallow hundreds of rice seeds? If you will follow the inventor of electricity, then you are expected to follow the maker of rice seeds too, that is, if they are the inventor of electricity. If you will follow the inventor of the speaker, then you should also follow the owner of the water, of which you must drink at least one keg when you return home. This is water of which the whole world cannot create even one drop. You should soak a car and consume it. We should fear Allah. And may Allah assist us and may He curse the Jews. They have destroyed us. You see we are fighting ourselves.

[Moderator reads a question]: These are the last questions. The first question the questioner said there is no scholar who said democracy is permissible. He said what you mention about a scholar in this town [Maiduguri] who wrote that democracy is not against Islam is untrue. The second question the questioner said what is the meaning of Kharijites and why do they call you Kharijites?

[Shekau responds]: Yes, there is a scholar that wrote it and the name of the book is *Islam and the Contemporary World System*. The name of the author is Aḥmad ʿAbd al-Qadir. Now have I confirmed to you that there is a scholar who wrote it? You can go ahead and inquire from the scholar whether he wrote the book or not? That is it!

What is the meaning of Kharijites? The Kharijites are the people who label a government ruling with the Qurʾān unbelievers (*takfīr*). Each time you find a set of people who label a government ruling with the Qurʾān unbelievers, they are the Kharijites.

[Shekau cites *Milal wa-al-niḥal*ʾ by Imām Shahrastānī.] We did not say a Muslim government is an unbelieving government. Is Nigeria an Islamic government? You see, it is an unbelieving government we called an unbelieving government. You should exercise patience till the day you have an Islamic government—we refer to it as an unbelieving government—only then can you refer to us as Kharijites. This is it. Kharijites labeled ʿAlī as an unbeliever, and they slaughtered the Prophet's Companions. The wives of the Kharijites were also praying even during their menstruation. The day you see us with these characteristics, even if we do not accept the label, you can call us that name. Otherwise, when we go to heaven, we will see who is truthful.

[Moderator]: In the end, there are those who requested for prayers. There is also a woman who died in this house and they are requesting for prayers for her, may Allah forgive her. [*Shekau says the closing prayers.*]

15(A)

GROUPING OF SERMONS OF THE IMAM ABU YUSUF MUHAMMAD BIN YUSUF JAMĀ'AT AHL AL-SUNNA LI-L-DA'WA WA-L-JIHĀD

(RELEASED 3 MARCH 2015)

[Trans.: Abdulbasit Kassim]
Available at: http://jihadology.net/2015/03/03/al-urwah-al-wuthqa-foundation-presents-a-new-release-from-jamaat-ahl-al-Sunna-li-l-dawah-wa-l-jihad-boko-%E1%B8%A5aram-grouping-of-sermons-of-the-imam-abu-yusuf-mu/

This trio of written sermons in Arabic was released by Boko Haram six years after the murder of Yusuf. They are a thematic group, concerning the Muslim personality, a call to jihād, and covering colonialism. Most likely they were delivered separately as the tone of the first sermon differs markedly from the hysterical tone of the last two. It is of course possible that the first sermon was delivered together with the others, but as there are no internal indications as to its date, it has been placed separately. The final two sermons are placed chronologically prior to the Declaration of War (text 19). Most probably the release of these sermons on 3 March 2015, as the Nigerian army was defeating Boko Haram and just four days before the amalgamation of Boko Haram with the Islamic State, was designed as a rebuke to Shekau from disaffected elements of the group who wanted to stress the legacy and leadership of Muhammad Yusuf.

Short Biography of Imam Muhammad Ibn Yusuf al-Barnawi

His name, family origin and birth: Imam Abu Yusuf Muhammad b. Yusuf b. Muhammad b. Aḥmad al-Dagheri al-Badawi al-Barnawi. He was born in Yobe state [Nigeria] in 1967, corresponding to the year 1388 AH.

His worship, piety and spirituality: He performed the hajj pilgrimage three times and also *'umra* [off-season pilgrimage], the lesser pilgrimage. He loved the poor so much that his house was a residence for them. He memorized the Qur'ān, but he was not among those who read the Qur'ān, but do not reflect on its meaning. He prayed and recited the Qur'ān extensively, especially in Ramadan. He was also a devout in his logic and words.

His religious education and preaching: He started seeking religious education since he was a child. He started by memorizing the Qur'ān at the age of 10. His father helped him with the memorization of the Qur'ān. Later, he traveled to different places seeking additional religious education. He used to read books, and he dedicated his life not only to reading the religious books, but also to propagating religious education. He wrote books on *Fiqh al-jihād* (Islamic jurisprudence concerning *jihād*) and other fields.

He opened religious schools and centers in different cities and areas such as al-Salafiyya School, Abū Hurayra School, 'Ubāda b. al-Ṣāmit School, al-Ṭā'ifa al-Mansūra Center, and others. He also opened the Ibn Taymiyya Center, which was the headquarters for all the schools and centers, and he accepted students from all over Africa to study at the Center.

His mission: He developed a strong will after the Battle of Manhattan [11 September 2001] when the world was divided into two separate categories.[1] He dissociated himself from the Islamic scholars who act as "palace lackeys." He started calling people to the creed of Sunna, and he called them to Allah's path based on wisdom. He traveled to all the cities in Northern Nigeria, and some cities in the South. After doing this patiently for nine years, opposed by different obstacles, the tyrants' scholars realized that he had success in his preaching, so those who preferred the earthly life above the next world issued a *fatwā* (religious edict) to kill him and extirpate his preaching. His center, the Ibn Taymiyya Center, was destroyed and his students were killed after four days of brutal fighting. He was taken as a captive and then he was executed on 8 Sha'ban 1430 AH (30 July 2009) in Maiduguri.

—From the son of Abu Yusuf Muhammad b. Yusuf b. Muhammad

First Sermon [Part 1]
"The Muslim Personality'

[Standard Islamic opening]

And thereafter:

O servants of Allah!

I urge you to make your souls conscious of faith in Allah and warn you from violating His commands or doing what He has prohibited. Verily, faith in Allah is the best practice, and Allah does not accept good deeds, except from those who have faith in Him. Faith in Allah will protect you from hell, and it is the reason for knowledge and guidance. Faith in Allah gives strength after weakness and it is a means of livelihood. Verily, the good end is for those who do the right deeds.

O servants of Allah!

Allah desired for the Muslim personality to be strong and perfect so that a Muslim can face, and change, his circumstances. He can do that because Allah is with him, since Allah loves the strong Muslims more than the weak ones. The true Muslim should not have an interest in certain things while neglecting others. He should not focus on certain things but neglect others, such as a Muslim who stands in the front row during the prayer, but does not take care of his bad breath or bad smell. Another example is a Muslim who loves, obeys and fears Allah, while neglecting his family and relatives.

You may find a Muslim who is interested in knowledge and spiritual devotion while he neglects the education of his children, unaware of what they are reading or with whom they have made friends. You may find a Muslim who is taking good care of his children, while not taking care of his own parents and treating them badly. You may find a Muslim who is obeying his parents, but oppressing and mistreating his wife. You may find a Muslim who is treating his wife and children kindly, but he is mistreating his neighbor. You may find a Muslim taking care of his own business and doing whatever is good for him, but he is very bad in his social interactions and careless about other Muslims. You may find a Muslim who is practicing the rituals of Islam, but does not observe the Islamic etiquette of greeting, eating, drinking and being in company of others.

A true Muslim should not do any of those things, and should not act in any of these ways. A true Muslim will know that Almighty Allah orders the believers to have faith in Him, His Messengers, establish the prayer, pay the charity tax (*zakāt*), do good deeds and fight *jihād* for his sake. Allah said:

> O believers, kneel, prostrate yourselves and worship your Lord and do good, that you may perchance prosper. And strive for Allah as you ought to strive. He elected you, and did not impose on you any hardship in religion—the faith of your father Abraham. He called you Muslims before and in this that the Messenger may bear witness against you and you may be witnesses against mankind. So, perform the prayer, give the alms and hold fast to Allah. He is your Master, and what a blessed Master and a blessed Supporter! (Q22:78–79)

O servants of Allah!

The Muslim should not be like this, nor should his personality be like this. The true Muslim should do whatever Allah ordered him to do, feel responsible for his flock, accept Allah's decree, obey Allah, perform the obligations and the Sunna, do the five prayers, pray in the mosque, follow the Sunna, spend the whole night praying, while fasting the whole day, and reciting more of the Qur'ān.

He should be faithful, sincere, and act the way the Prophet acted. By doing this, renewing and changing his personality will be achieved and this is how he will become one of the *mujāhidīn*. "Allah does not change the condition of a people until they change what is in their hearts." (Q13:11) The Prophet said: "There is a piece of flesh in the body which, if it becomes good (reformed) the whole body becomes good, but if it is spoiled the whole body is spoiled—and that is the heart."

The true personality of the Muslim should encompass Islamic morals, as we mentioned—we cannot say that he is a true Muslim who can lead, master and command unless he observes this etiquette. He should not observe one while abandoning the other. Doing this, however, requires accepting the orders of Allah and his Messenger completely without differentiation. He should also avoid anything that Allah and the Prophet has forbidden without differentiation. "Now, what of one whose breast Allah has opened unto Islam, so that he basks in light from his Lord? Woe betides then the hard-hearted, upon Allah's mention. Those are in manifest error." (Q39:22)

To reach "the true Muslim personality," one should train his soul and purify his heart. "He has succeeded who purifies it, and he has failed who instills it [with corruption]." Doing this will help him to face the serious matters—the most important things which should be taken care of by him. One of those things is establishing the right spirit for *jihād* against his soul, as well as the meaning of determination, seriousness and the patience in his mind, heart and feelings; especially in this era, the era of unbelief, where Islamic laws are no longer ruling the Islamic and Muslim countries.

The "sun of Islam" has faded in the present day, and the tyrants have become the rulers. They have nothing to do in the Muslim countries except to implement the schemes of Allah's, Islam's and Muslims' enemies—whether those schemes are communist, colonial, Jewish, or Christian ones. Because of those schemes, the Islamic caliphate has been extirpated, and materialism has become pervasive in Islamic societies.

Massive hurricanes of erotic pleasure and pornography have spread here, as well as streams of invalid principles and atheistic thinking. The Islamic countries have become targets for every greedy unbeliever, whether they are Americans, the UN, or others. The goal of those groups is to control the Muslims and change them towards unbelief. They wanted to kill the Muslims so no one can apply the meaning of "there is no god except Allah," the *sharīʿa*, and *jihād* in order the fight their current situation.

O servants of Allah!

It is obligatory to find bravery in a Muslim personality. We need a Muslim who fears nothing. A Muslim, who perfects his personality and who can bravely teach this *umma* the patience and the endurance as well as giving life to the spirit of *jihād* within them. Maybe this spirit of *jihād* will help to retain the glory of Islam and the Muslims.

O servants of Allah!

Did you see how [Umayyad caliph] 'Umar ibn 'Abd al-'Aziz[2] managed to bring back the caliphate of the "Rightly Guided" caliphs?

Did you see how Aḥmad b. Hanbal managed to stop the *Mu'tazila* and the creed of *i'tizal*?[3]

Did you see how Ibn Taymiyya managed to repel the *Jahmiyya*, the *Rafida* [Shi'ites], and the plots of the Tartars [Mongols]?[4]

Did you see how Salaḥ al-Dīn al-Ayyubi managed to save the *jihād* and establish it among the Muslims?[5]

Did you see how Muhammad b. 'Abd al-Wahhab spearheaded the resurgence of Salafism?

And here in Nigeria, is the Caliphate of Dan Fodio from amongst you, which has now become a thing of the past?[6]

Where is the true Muslim, who perfects his personality and his belief, spirituality, ideology, culture and education, to stand firmly against Judaism, unbelief, democracy, pornography, and corruption in a strong and brave manner so that he can become the inheritor of those great leaders?

O my Muslim brother! Be brave, courageous and protective of your religion. Give victory to your religion, the book of your Lord and the Sunna of your Prophet with your soul and your wealth.

Where are you, O female Muslim?

Be one of those great Islamic figures. Give victory to Allah's religion with your faith, your prayer, your supplications and your support of the men of the religion.

Where is the house of the Muslim?

The house where the flag of Islam is recognized by its denizens' sacrifices, *jihād*, and blood.

Where is the Muslim family?

Where is the *umma*?

"Answer you Lord's call before a day comes from Allah that cannot be turned back. Upon that day, you will have no shelter, no disclaimer." (Q42:47)

The true Muslim, who is committed to this religion and recites the Qur'ān continuously, can—with his personality—be the reason behind the establishment of the true Muslim sister, the Muslim house, the *umma*, the puritan city and the Islamic State. He can do that with his *jihād*, sincerity, hard work, faithfulness, sacrificing, and spending his soul and money in fighting.

"So, fight for Allah's cause; you are charged only of yourself. Urge the believers on that Allah may perchance restrain the unbelievers' might. Allah's might is greater and greater is His retribution!" (Q4:84)

The Prophet said: "He who loves to meet Allah, Allah also loves to meet him, and he who dislikes meeting Allah, Allah also abhors meeting him."

He also said: "Every person starts his day as a vendor of his soul, either freeing it or causing its ruin."

Allah said: "He who expects to encounter Allah, surely Allah's term shall come; and He is the All-Hearing, the All-Knowing. He who strives, only strives for himself. Allah is the All-Sufficient, in need of no being." (Q29:5–6)

First Sermon [Part 2]

[Standard Islamic opening]

a true muslim

And thereafter:

Fear Allah O the servants of Allah! Increase your provisions, and verily the best provision is piety. Do the good deeds for the greatest day: "Do not be like those who forgot Allah, and so He made them forget themselves. Those indeed are the sinners." (Q59:19)

O servants of Allah!

If we desire reformation, it is obligatory upon us to start by reforming our inner selves through raising the personality of a Muslim. We can do that firstly by the knowledge of monotheism and the shunning of polytheism (in all its kinds and categories). We should believe in the doctrine of the forefathers.

After that, we should learn from the Qur'ān and the Sunna regarding what will help us to know how to perform our obligatory duties. We should also reject the psychological defeat in the areas of education, curricula and the media. We should not practice democracy, but we should fight to death with those who practice it. We should be pleased only by the religion of Islam, the Qur'ān and the Sunna of our Prophet, because there is no way to get rid of the evils of democracy, nationalism and atheism, except by committing ourselves to this religion, steadfastness in monotheism, and the defense of our principles.

The true Muslim is the one who acts according to the disciplines of Islam, such that he attains the personality of a true and brave Muslim. This person will be the one who will support our religion. Allah promised those who give victory to His religion with good rewards. The Prophet says: "Islam will reach every place, the same way as do the day and the night, and Allah will send Islam to every house, by themselves or by force; by themselves when they believe in it and support this religion, or by force through humiliating unbelief."

The true Muslim refining the personality of Islam is the one who deals with others and exercises patience towards the harm they cause, because he is the one with a cause, a carrier of a message, a tongue of the propagation of the religion, and a man of *jihād*.

For anyone who wants to face these challenges, he must teach himself about sacrificing for the sake of that cause, and be patient towards the costs of this cause, the consequences of this call, and the work resulting from the *jihād* for the sake of Allah. Another thing is to handle the rudeness and the unacceptable opinions of the rest—their misbe-haviors, their misconceptions, their bad temper and their self-involvement.

The true Muslim is the one who thinks positively of Allah and asks Him to grant him victory against his enemies without feeling disappointed. We ask Allah to help every one of us to become a better Muslim and to call and fight for his sake. We should also confer blessing upon the Prophet, as Allah told us: "Allah and His angels bless the Prophet. O believers, bless him and greet him graciously, too." (Q33:56)

O Allah! Exalt the mention of Muhammad and the family of Muhammad as You have exalted the family of Abraham. You are Praised and Glorious. O Allah, bless Muhammad and the family of Muhammad, as You blessed the family of Abraham. You are Praised and Glorious! O Allah, bless the four Righteous Caliphs, and the other six of the Ten [who were promised heaven].

O Allah! Bless the family of Muhammad and all his Companions. O Allah the greatest!

O Allah! Forgive ourselves, our parents, all male and female Muslims, all male and female believers, alive or dead.

O Allah! Show us the right path, give us the ability to follow it and show us the evil path and give us the ability to avoid it.

O Allah! Guide us to defeat our enemies; guide this *umma* to help those who are obeying you, and punish those who are disobeying you; guide them to enjoin good, and forbid evil.

O Allah! Help us to help other Muslims and do not let us disappoint them.

O Allah! Let our *jihād* be for Your sake and make it purely dedicated to You.

O Allah! Help us win over Your enemies, our enemies, and Islam's enemies.

O Allah! Support Your *sharīʿa*.

O Allah! Punish the angry Jews, the Americans, the secularists, the hypocrites, and the apostates. O Allah! Handle them because You can, kill them all, and do not leave even one of them.[7]

O Allah! Destroy democracy, the foreign schools and all the centers of corruption.

O Allah! Tear up those earthly infidel laws, those who put them in place, and those who apply them to Muslims.

O Allah! Defeat every government who does not rule according to Your Qur'ān and the Sunna of Your Prophet.

O Allah! Establish the Islamic State and strengthen it with monotheism, save it with Your *jihadi* servants, and improve it with the Sunna of Your Prophet, O Almighty.

16

HĀDHIHI ʿAQĪDATUNĀ (THIS IS OUR CREED)

BY ABUBAKAR SHEKAU

(c. SPRING 2009)

[Kanuri trans. team and Atta Barkindo]
Available at: https://www.youtube.com/watch?v=Jeowy05QfBw

This video is a lecture of Shekau, leader of Boko Haram after 2009, in the Kanuri language, and is undated. From the contents, speaking as it does of Yusuf having been in Abuja, it was probably delivered during the early spring of 2009 (on the evidence of him alluding to "seven years" of the group's history, as it was founded in 2002). The style of this lecture is folksy, hortatory, and, comparatively speaking, there is little citation of the Qurʾān or exegesis.

Without wasting much of your time, my fellow brothers and fighters of Allah, I am going to speak in Kanuri. My speech will be followed by the speech of Muhammad [=Mamman] Nur, who will also speak in Kanuri. Mallam Yusuf will conclude the session in Hausa. However, remember that our language is Arabic, and other languages are simply used out of choice.

Our lesson before the arrival of Mallam Yusuf today is on *taḥadiyyāt* (challenges) and those things that require an absolute level of patience and sacrifice to resist. That is why Allah says: "You will not find a people who believe in Allah and the Last Day befriending those who antagonize Allah and His Messenger, even if they are their fathers." (Q58:22) [...]

It means fighting those who reject Allah's laws, construct human laws and stand by them. We stand firm by our own laws, which are Allah's laws and so we stand firm by them. We are aware that they [followers of the constitution and democracy] will never accept Islamic law and we shall never accept democracy or constitutions. We stand by Allah's laws just as they stand by the laws and values of the constitution and democracy. So, the task we have ahead of us is not a small task. What is expected is for us to exercise patience, fear Allah and be ready to face bitterness and confrontation.

If a person is suffering from sickness, no matter how bitter a medicine is, he will take it because he knows that he will be healed again. Today the only disease known worldwide is democracy and the constitution. The only known contemporary medicine for this disease, now and forever, is Islam. Yes! It is only Islam—and so if you take Islam as the appropriate medicine, you will be healed. Islam is the only medicine and once you maintain the injunctions of Islam in accordance with the teaching of the Qur'ān, you will be healed instantly—there is no doubt about it.

So, the modern sickness that has infected Islam and Muslims is unbelief, and what is the medicine for unbelief? It is *tawḥīd* [monotheism]. Another disease that is destroying Islam and affecting us Muslims today is *shirk*, and the only medicine for it is *tawḥīd*. The third disease is *al-munāfiq* [being a hypocrite], and its medicine is also *tawḥīd*. Generally, therefore, we all require *tawḥīd*, the oneness of Allah, for ourselves. If we as Muslims possess *tawḥīd* in our hearts, we have the obligation to guard it, protect it and revolt against those who want to insult, abuse, destroy or misuse the *tawḥīd* of Allah.

A rich man is always careful about his wealth, and employs every means possible to guard and protect his possessions. So, it follows, we must be careful about *tawḥīd*, to guard it and protect it. It is the essential and the central core of Islam. Consequently, *mushrikīn* are subject to bombs. *Munāfiqūn* [hypocrites] are subject to bomb blasts and must be eliminated. Unbelievers must be bombed, so they have no option but to accept Islam and follow the principles of *tawḥīd*.

Therefore, if Allah has bestowed upon us the wisdom of *tawḥīd*, then we have an obligation to guard it using war and bombs. In other words, *jihād* is necessary to protect the *tawḥīd* of Allah. Yes, if Allah has secured this faith for us, then we must not allow infidels and unbelievers to steal and destroy it. We must promise Almighty Allah that we shall defend this faith by fighting and by shedding our blood. This method is the only remedy leading to the success we desire, the goal we aim to achieve, protecting the purity of the Islamic faith. We must therefore stand and fight to ensure that *tawḥīd* is the central focus of this movement.

Consequently, it is not easy to be part of this movement without making sacrifices and overcoming challenges. That is why I said, we must all prepare to make sacrifices. Believe me, even if you have no full knowledge of what we are doing now, you can still stand firm, and be committed as long as you are ready to learn and be humble to accept. Thus, nobody will be overcome by any pressure even if he is ignorant of what he is doing, nobody! If you know to what you commit yourself, and know it well in your hearts, brutality and killings will just be like a story! A story [*titimi*]![1]

[...] Therefore, I call on all Muslims, and the entire people of Yerwa (Maiduguri), and the whole of Borno [state] including other Nigerian cities, towns and villages to listen to us, and to understand our vision and goals. Our goal is nothing but to call people to follow Allah's path, the Qur'ān and the Sunna of the Prophet. It is important for all Muslims to know that what we are doing is not contrary to the teaching of the Qur'ān. Anyone who thinks what we preach, teach and propagate is contrary to the Qur'ān—such a person should not talk, but should come forth with verses from the Qur'ān that contradict us. Do not come with commentaries and opinions, but with facts as stated in the Qur'ān.

This is because Allah has simplified His verses for everyone to understand. We equally bear witness to what is written in the Qur'ān, and in bearing witness, we preach and make it easy for many to understand the Qur'ān, remember it and practice its principles. A few years ago, we were nothing but street-roaming adherents of the Qur'ān, who were unknown and unrecognized. We were only identified by our begging bowls, while we were begging for food like travelers without a destination.

It is Allah's mercy that has brought us this far, given us the confidence and the commitment to preach to you, cites the Qur'ān and makes it easier for you to understand. It is because of Allah's mercy that what we preach pricks your conscience and rattles their brains (*makes an eerie noise—"lraw, raw, raw"*). Mind you, it is not of our making, but because Allah's words from the Qur'ān penetrate every heart He has created. Therefore, for all of you that are here, the Qur'ān must serve as the only manual you have. Even if you are a *dajjāl* [Antichrist], the Qur'ān must be your guide. The Qur'ān must reflect in your life, affect your personality and through you, take hold of those around you.

Therefore, what we want to say here is that our constitution is the book of Allah. But the Torah, the book of Jews, is not from Allah, nor Allah's Prophet and was not prepared by the Imams. The Torah was constructed and put together by unbelievers. Allah, in the Qur'ān, instructed us that "we should not follow any book except the Qur'ān."[2] As such, believers now find themselves under the jurisdiction of the Qur'ān. Therefore, you should not drive away a person who comes to you to seeking Allah's words.

And those of you who have already obtained the knowledge of the Qur'ān should be patient and not hasty. You will be delivered from your enemies by Allah's grace. You will enjoy His mercy and help. Believe me, we depend on Allah's words in the Qur'ān, and "whoever does not judge according to what Allah has revealed—those are the unbelievers," (Q5:44) meaning the real unbelievers (*al-kāfirūn*). No matter how so called "moderate" commentators twist the facts, the truth does not change—they are known as unbelievers and the verse will never present them as virtuous. That is why the verse in the Qur'ān ends with the fact that they are *mushrikīn*.

Therefore, when Allah says that something is bad, that thing remains bad no matter what the interpretation. If you are to sum up what Allah has said and indicated as bad in the Qur'ān, there is nothing as bad as unbelief. People of Yerwa (Maiduguri), I call on you. If you see an unbeliever in your midst, investigate him. If he is not a visitor, but belongs to the city, inform him that we are Muslims living in a Muslim city, and we are proud to be Muslims in a Muslim city. However, since we are Muslims, living in a Muslim city [Maiduguri] and are proud of Islam, how can our children and those of the unbelievers be going to same school? How can we and the unbelievers participate in the same political system, and go to the same judge to obtain justice?

In fact, by these practices, we neither claim to be followers of the Prophet, nor compare ourselves with His Companions. For the sake of Allah, can we really be compared with the friends of the Prophet? Mind you, we must live like the followers and friends of the Prophet before we can get access to paradise. Again, remember, the Prophet said: "This community (*umma*) will divide into seventy-three groups, of which seventy-two will be thrown into hellfire." When the Prophet was asked, which group will enter paradise, he said: "Those who hold firm according to my teaching."

My friends, we should ask ourselves whether we are qualified to be like the Companions and friends of the Prophet. Mind you, I am just guiding you, brothers. You should do nothing bad or fight yourselves. I am not asking you to fight yourselves or allow division to emerge within the group. It is important for you to note that after the Holy Prophet and the first Companion, Abū Bakr,[3] the word of our group, *Ahl al-Sunna wa-l-Jamāʿa*, does not have any other person like ʿUmar. These are the people we should listen to and strictly follow the legacy they left for us.

The problems we have been facing in Borno state for the past seven years could have been solved with only one *hadīth* of ʿUmar, even without supporting that by Qur'ānic verses, I swear by Allah. ʿUmar took a verse from the Torah, in the [original] book of Moses, a verse which did not contradict the Qur'ān. The verse was in support of other verses in the Qur'ān. ʿUmar said to the Prophet, "I found this verse in Torah and I think it supersedes that of the Qur'ān." Upon hearing this, the Prophet was discomforted by the words of ʿUmar and he frowned. Then a fellow among the Prophet's Companions cautioned ʿUmar and said: "Don't you see you have discomforted the Prophet?"

ʿUmar instantly prostrated himself before the Prophet and said: "For the sake of my father and my mother, O Prophet of Allah, I accept that Allah as my lord, Islam as my religion, and Muhammad as Prophet and Messenger. O Prophet of Allah, I apologize as I did not know that what I said was wrong." Then the Prophet said: "Will you people bring [blameworthy] innovations while I am still alive?" He continued: "Had Moses been alive, and if you decided to follow him—staying away from me—you would have been lost."

So, think about this. If Moses as a prophet is not to be followed in the same way and manner the Prophet Muhammad is followed, it means those who abandon the teachings of the Prophet Muhammad, and prescribe innovations following other gods are lost, doomed and headed for hellfire. This means that all unbelievers are headed for hell. This also indicates that even believers who submit to the constitution and democracy cannot be called *Ahl al-Sunna*, the righteous followers of the Prophet's traditions.

So why should we stand by and continue to suffer over these issues for so many years in Borno, Nigeria and beyond? Is this *ḥadīth* fake or weak? If not then why argue against it, why hide the fact of it from the public and the community? The community that decides to follow Moses, the constitution and other human beings is headed for hell and not paradise.

Why for the sake of Allah shall we be fighting each other for five to six years, rather than fighting against the constitution? How is it that Muslims fight for politics, and work so hard to obtain political offices, while claiming to be members of Yan Izala, a group [supposedly] dedicated to fighting against innovations and errors being brought into Islam, and to uphold the traditions of the Prophet? If that is what Islam stands for, and what our movement is working to achieve, it is important to ask whether democracy is [in accord with the] Sunna, or whether the constitution *is* the Sunna?

If democracy and the constitution are not the Sunna, then why can't we get rid of them? If we all agree that celebrations of the Prophet's birthday constitute an innovation, and that the three days' funeral prayers are an innovation, why is the constitution not an innovation? These [former] things are declared innovations and you have distanced yourselves from them, but why not from the constitution? Why can't we reject the constitution outright?

Brothers, we should fear Allah and follow His injunctions. I need you to pay attention to this book. (*Shekau holds up a book about how the Nigerian constitution is written, followed by thunderous applause and shouts of "Allahu akbar!"*) Are you seeing this book? OK. The title of this book is *How our laws are made.* That is how the laws of the country [Nigeria] are created. Now look at this again and you will see the constitution. It reads: "how powerful the constitution is," that is, it is above all other forms of law. What this means is that it is above all laws, including the law of Allah. If you read what is written in the constitution, you will be surprised. Let's go through a little. Surprise—"the constitution of the Federal Republic of Nigeria is the most powerful law of the land." It says, "this constitution is meant to guide Nigeria and Nigerians in everyday proceedings."

The truth about this constitution is found in the introductory part of the 1979 constitution, which is still in force. It speaks about the supremacy of the constitution. It states that this constitution is supreme and shall have binding force on all authorities and persons throughout the Federal Republic of Nigeria (*shouts from the listeners saying, "It's a lie, lie, lie!"*). In another section, it says, if any other law is inconsistent with the provision of this constitution, the constitution shall prevail. (*Shekau holds up the book, with the cover picture showing the picture of the mace above the picture of the Qur'ān.*)

Just as you can see (*Shekau holds the book cover up for everyone to see*), the picture of the mace is above the picture of the Qur'ān. This is intended to create a simple understanding that state authority is above the authority of Allah. Equally, it means that man-made laws are above divine laws. This also means that in Nigeria, the Qur'ān and Allah's laws are nothing. It means we are subservient to the constitution and not to the injunctions of Allah.

Although I do not have an interest in the book of madmen, I still read it so that I can explain it to you, and the dangers the constitution presents to our faith, to Islam and our desire for paradise. (*Smiling and muttering "nyaure—nyaure," "funny, funny," Shekau continues*), why should I read a book which claims that no law shall go against it? That any law that violates the constitution is null and void.

Thus, the unbelievers have their constitution, written and kept as a document. These unbelievers are asking us to read the constitution, regardless of the way we read it, and telling us we should not go against it, deny it or say the constitution is lying. Well, see it for yourself that the constitution is what the unbelievers stand for, yet, we shall be lucky to be killed while fighting against the constitution.

We have seen people die without faith, so if we die fighting against the constitution, fighting to enthrone the law of Allah, then we have a reason to die. So, if we die doing this, believe me, we will be lucky to have died on a good path. So, you cannot follow the constitution, judge by means of the constitution and do things according to the constitution—a collection of man-made laws—and then stand before the people on Fridays to lead them in prayer.

What are you leading them for? If you follow the constitution, you have become a lord of yourself, creating laws and neglecting Allah's laws. What do you read in your prayers? Is it the constitution? Such Muslims should just stay at home. They should stay indoors rather than come to the mosque to mislead people. Those who follow the constitutions have declared themselves as gods.

My dear Muslim community, we should turn toward Allah's path, we should stand by Allah and His words, and we should not get tired. This movement that we initiated must be fulfilled and completed. We must transform this group and complete our mission. Allah willing, nobody will take the hoe away from us! We must start our farm work and bring the cultivation to completion in due season. Whoever loses his hoe and the grasses have overgrown [his farm] cannot harvest with his bare hands. The farmers here will understand my illustration better—good.[4]

Mind you, we have been calling your attention toward this issue of model schools. For instance, Ibn Taymiyya has said several times that churches are better than model schools. He said: *boko*, model schools, are anti-Islamic.[5] The teachings of these schools contradict the existence of both the heavens above and the earth below. All the theories taught in these schools are against Islam and contradict Allah's laws in the Qur'ān. I will like to give all of you this assignment, demonstrate to me where Western education shares a common ground with the teachings of Allah.

Let me be sincere with you: I swear by Allah, even those who have obtained Western education [*boko*] and have gone deep into its principles still express doubts about the morality of Western education. Truthfully, they know that the teachings of Western education go against the *tawḥīd*, the oneness of Allah. This includes not only subjects as sociology, but all other course of human sciences. That is why you will hear them use concepts as nature in place of Allah. This is meant not only to convince you but also to mislead you.

They say things to favor their individual narratives, arguments and intellectual pursuits, but they do not believe in Allah or the nature that they claim has replaced that Allah. That is why today you find the promotion of absolute freedom and liberty has become commonplace. Illicit sexual relations are permitted, gay marriage (homosexuality) is allowed and lesbianism is promoted. You will hear unbelievers tell you, geography is this, and geography is that. Such sayings are among the many hundreds of vices these unbelievers and promoters of faithlessness rail against Allah. To be sincere those that have gone deeper into Western education think they know everything and some with the aid of religious scholars have obtained both Islamic knowledge and Western education.[6]

As such, we have two categories of *boko*, both of which do not agree with the existence of Allah. The first group is the one steeped in Western education and do not at all believe in the existence of Allah. The second category is steeped in Western education, and believes in the existence of Allah, but their activities are contrary to the injunctions of Allah. So, let me read from the book of wizards and witches. (*Shekau brings out a book, followed by applause*).[7]

And I read it out for you here again, "When Westerners started on how to crack Islam, they send one of their men to Egypt to study the secret powers of the Muslims. The person came back with a copy of Holy Qur'ān, stating that as long as Muslims read and practice the injunctions in the Qur'ān they will be powerful. The Western world began to deliberate on how to make the Qur'ān insignificant and unimportant. At the end of their meeting, they outlined many programmes which were centered on occupying the minds of Muslims so that they will have little or no time for the Qur'ān. The programmes include secular education, sports and music." (*Shekau pauses*). Please listen to this.

"I mean to educate people without referring to the creator Allah." (*He repeats this twice*). This is our point of dispute that we said they do not believe in Allah. In this education, they make reference to mathematics, geography, physics, biology, geology and many other sciences. From the beginning to the end of their program, there is no reference to Allah. Allah is excluded from the litany of science. No reference is made to the Prophet and his tradition.

In most of the books written about Ibn Taymiyya, democracy and the constitution are presented as products of Western education. Therefore, Western education is the most nonsensical form of education. If you have a son in school, you should immediately withdraw him. If you are a secondary school student, you should withdraw immediately without wasting any time. If you are up to level four or any year in the university, you should quickly withdraw, withdraw, withdraw. If you are hoping for paradise, withdraw. I swear by Allah: Western education is a lie and a deception.

Listen, a missionary, by the name of Samuel[8] said, the most expensive way of distorting the Muslim mind and character is through secular education. "Encourage Muslims to obtain Western education and their thinking will change. The result is evident today as many Muslims have lost their Islam, while others claim to be Muslims, but have lost traces of Islam—all in the name of being educated." (*Shekau reads the missionary's words twice*). These words, these words, I do not care to read it a million times without stress, even trillion times, because that is the main issue trying to destroy Islam today—Western education.

A book written in Hausa by Sanusi Yuguda, from Kofar Nasarawa, Kano State, is called Dafin Boko (The Ills of Western Education). The summary of Sanusi's book includes the aims of Western secular education, which is to produce set gentiles whose characters and mindset will be of secular values not Islamic norms. Sanusi is a lecturer at Bayero University, Kano. He wrote his book when Babatunde Fafunwa was minister of education.[9] Fafunwa himself has written an article titled, "The History of Education in Nigeria."

Confirming Fafunwa's article, Sanusi clarifies that the aim of Western education is to force black people to adopt western mindsets and character. He argued that when this is achieved, then the aim of Western education would have succeeded. Let us ask ourselves, has this been achieved or not? In my opinion, yes, it has been achieved. That is why you see unbelievers who promote Western education with their bald heads everywhere.[10]

Another aim of Western education is to separate religion from politics, promote the rights of women, a so-called gender ideology, when Allah himself has restricted women. But Western education gives women unlimited freedom and the right to go anywhere, and do what pleases them. Additionally, another aim of Western education is the promotion of nationhood above Allah's laws. The worst of it is that the nation not only denies Allah, but takes over the place of Allah.

In this context, Allah is excluded from the values of Western education. Other nations are forced to imitate the Western world in trading, free thinking and the adoption of Christian values, like funeral rites and wedding ceremonies.[11] While the Western world learns by listening to others and selecting what will profit them, we learn by imitating and copying what is offered by the West in an uncritical manner. The Westerner and anyone who has adopted the Western mind know only himself and his family. He roams the street like a hyena, trying to convince others to become faithless and godless. Is it true or false? (*Audience erupts: "It's true! It's true!"*) Thank you all for today. This book of mine is so voluminous and I have many other things to say. However, I will reserve them for another time. Let me step aside and allow others to speak as you ponder on what I have said today.

17

PROVISION OF THE MUSLIM FIGHTERS

BY MUHAMMAD YUSUF

(14 MARCH 2009)

[Trans.: Abdulbasit Kassim]
Available at: https://www.youtube.com/watch?v=VWCNdqwGU-M

This video was delivered in Hausa and Arabic by Yusuf, and is based upon the well-known hagiography of the Prophet Muhammad, al-Raḥīq al-makhtūm (*The Sealed Nectar*), *and is aimed at the spiritual training of Boko Haram. It discusses the necessity of following the commands of Allah as opposed to the desires of the soul, purification of the soul prior to* jihād, *spending money in Allah's path, fasting during the dry season, standing the night in prayer, good morals, and love and disassociation* (al-walā' wa-l-barā'). *In its complete form, it is approximately twenty-four pages long, although the video itself is incomplete.*

[Standard Islamic opening]

Today is Saturday, 1 Rabi al-Thani 1430 AH. We announced that all the brothers should attend this study. In the past, the pattern we employed to study the Prophet's biography is by reading *al-Raḥīq al-makhtūm: baḥth fī al-sīra al-nabawiyya* by Ṣafi al-Raḥmān al-Mubārakfūrī followed by Qur'ānic exegesis. However, Allah drew my attention to some observations about our lives, and then I saw the necessity for a lesson on some of the topics we have previously studied. We need to isolate some of these lessons because they are the capital for a person that seeks an entry to paradise. If they are lacking in an individual, such individual will not be called among the believers or those who possess sincerity. And you will not succeed in the hereafter, you will not overcome your soul and you will not be able to worship Allah.

[Discussion of the lessons aimed at soul purification] Some of these lessons include *al-Infāq fī sabīl Allāh* (spending in Allah's path), *tahdhīb al-nufūs* (purification of the soul), *taqraʿ al-qulūb* (subdual of the heart's desires) and *yuḥibbu Allāh* (love of Allah). Secondly, there is also fasting during the period of the dry season.[1] You fast today and fast tomorrow and you repeat the same on Mondays and Thursdays.[2] These types of activities, neither our souls nor our bodies want them but Allah loves them. Thirdly, there is also *qiyyām al-layl* (standing up for late night prayers). A person should stand up at night and stretch his legs and pray. [Discussion of the benefits of late night prayers and the fourth lesson—brotherhood for the sake of Allah] The fifth lesson is the love of Allah. Then [the sixth is] patience with its three branches: patience in following Allah, patience to leave what Allah detests and patience when Allah tests you with your brothers: "We have made some of you tempters of each other." (Q25:20) The seventh lesson is *ḥusn al-khuluq* (moral character and good behavior).

These seven lessons, a person will not succeed and will not enter the paradise until he safeguards these lessons. There is no place where the jihadists succeeded over their enemy except by abiding with these lessons.

[Yusuf cites and explains Q2:189; 3:15–17; 3:200; 4:135; 33:4; and 73:20] You should know that the wealth you gave for the sake of Allah is your own and you will be rewarded with it in the hereafter. However, what you enjoyed here in the world ends in this world. This is what the Prophet was alluding to when he said: "You will hear someone saying, 'My money! My money! My money!'" Do you have any money except that which you spend here in the world on your body, and you will eventually become old, or that with which you give alms, and which they took for you to the hereafter? The latter is the money that belongs to you. I hope it is understood.

As such, you should buy your paradise just as you are hoping to buy your house here. Everyone you see aspires to buy a house and he reproaches himself for not building a house, despite all his years of living in the world, or someone reproaches him for not building a house despite all his years of living in this town. That should not constitute what should be reproachable. What is reproachable is for you to look at the Qur'ān and the *ḥadīth*, and yet you do not have a house in paradise. You will die and be buried in the grave without enjoying any benefits is what should be reproachable.

[Spend in Allah's cause] "Spend [money] in Allah's cause, and do not cast yourselves with your own hands into destruction, and be charitable. Surely Allah loves the charitable." (Q2:195) You should spend in Allah's cause so that you will not throw yourself into destruction, according to Allah. This is also how [the Companion] Abū Ayyub Al-Ansari interpreted the verse. Abū Ayyub Al-Ansari said at the time they went in [the Battle of] Qadisiyya in the heat of battle,[3] a Muslim soldier penetrated deep into the enemy ranks. People exclaimed, "*Subhan Allah* (Praise God)! He has contributed to his own destruction." Abū Ayyub al-Ansari stood up and answered:

> O people! You give that interpretation to this verse, whereas it was revealed concerning us, the Ansar. [...] Allah revealed to the Prophet Muhammad: "Spend [money] in Allah's cause, and do not cast yourselves with your own hands into destruction," refuting what we had said. So, destruction lay in staying with our wealth and repleting it and abandoning combat.

As such, we should give out for the sake of Allah. Allah says: "Who is it that will lend to Allah a generous loan, so that He might multiply it for him manifold? Allah provides sparingly and generously, and to Him you shall be returned." (Q2:245) Then Allah also says: "You will not achieve piety until you spend part of what you cherish; and whatever you spend, Allah knows it very well." (Q3:92)

[Spend in Allah's cause to gain paradise] We should spend to uplift our religion and not be greedy. Allah does not want us to be greedy. We should spend to uplift the religion. We should uplift the religion with our wealth. That is one of the activities that the human body does not like. You can do everything that concerns you and everything that concerns a person because of praise. You can help a person because now he will praise you. You can help your brother because he will praise you now. You will intend to squeeze 5,000 *naira* [about $35] to give it to him, but you cannot give anything out of that 5,000 *naira*. You will intend to squeeze 10,000 *naira* to give it to a lady, or to your family, but you cannot give it out as charity. I hope it is understood.

[The companions did not sit at home when Islam is in need of them] The second lesson is fasting. Many of us have anxiety regarding fasting. There are two benefits that we will derive from fasting in the world and the hereafter. There is the benefit of good bounty in the world and eternal bounty from Allah in the hereafter. Fasting also helps to improve the state of health of our body. All the major worries we have concerns about such as piles, stomach pain, etc. occur because of the lack of proper arrangement in our feeding and the infrequency of fasting.

[Benefits of fasting and late night prayers for the Muslim fighters] In Algeria, they delved into secular politics before they later understood that secular politics is not the religion. They later returned to the mountains with close to 40,000 people. However, because not every one of them was nurtured with the training of the religion, they were there until their population decreased to a number between 1,000 and 2,000 people.[4] It is only those who possess faith that are still following the path now, but majority of those who initially returned to the mountains have all withdrawn. Some of them even came back and launched a witch-hunt against Allah's slaves while others became the soldiers of the *ṭāghūt*. They knew all the places where

Allah's slaves followed and where they sleep, and they are the ones who led teams in their search and witch-hunt.

[Benefits of fasting and late night prayers] In addition, we should establish brotherhood for the sake of Allah. Allah is the one that brought us together as brothers, it is not our parents, it is not our mosque, it is not our people, it is not our town, it is not our language, and it is not the color of our skin. Everyone who is on the path of Allah's religion, whether he is here or in Afghanistan, or in America, wherever he is, he is our brother. And it is until we give him the love that Allah says we should give him only then are we going to gain entry to paradise. Because of that, Allah gave us example with the Companions of Allah's Messenger, Allah says: "Muhammad is Allah's Messenger, and those who are with him are hard on the unbelievers, merciful towards each other." (Q48:29)

[Yusuf ends with a long discussion on the essence of brotherhood in Islam.]

18

RETURNING TO THE QUR'ĀN AND SUNNA:

LECTURE BY MUHAMMAD MAMMAN NUR AND MUHAMMAD YUSUF

(15 MARCH 2009)

[Trans.: Abdulbasit Kassim]
Available at: https://www.youtube.com/watch?v=cUot3BrT0FE

Just three months prior to the July 2009 uprising the violent rhetoric of the circle around Yusuf has grown exponentially. Mamman Nur's talk is especially filled with incitement and threats—one suspects that he went first to channel the anger of the group. This anger was apparently brought on, as Yusuf says in his later address, by the rumor that one of the members of the group had been killed and his body dumped in Gwange Cemetery in Maiduguri. Although this rumor turned out to be false, it seems clear even before the 26 July 2009 uprising that elements of Boko Haram were spoiling for a fight with the Nigerian security forces. Probably Yusuf's more moderate follow-up address was supposed to calm the situation somewhat after Nur's more fiery address.

Lecture From Muhammad (Mamman) NUR[1]

[Standard Islamic opening] My fellow Muslims of this blessed community who came here for this lecture, I will start by greeting you in the Islamic way by saying: "May the peace and blessing of Allah be upon you." We pray to Allah to grant us the opportunity

151

of repeating this form of greeting in the paradise. Today is the night of nineteenth of the third Islamic month, Rabiʻ al-Awwal, 1430 [15 March 2009]. [Islamic prayer] We pray that He should allow us to say what He wants and not someone else wants; that we should say what His verses have confirmed, and not what democracy has confirmed; that we should say that with which the angels of Allah will agree and not that with which the soldiers of *ṭāghūt* will agree. And may Allah grant us success.

It is general knowledge that in this condition we have found ourselves today, it is compulsory that we return to the path of the Qurʼān and the Sunna of the Prophet of Allah. This is the reason Allah says that all the time that you keep engaging in immorality, democracy and Western education, Allah says: "Return to your Lord and submit to Him before punishment visits you," (Q39:54) so you should gather and return to your Creator, according to Allah. "Return to your Lord and submit to Him before punishment visits you," is the turning back to your Lord alone satisfactory? No! When you turn back to your Lord there are many clarifications, such as *jihād* and bloodshed in the Qurʼān.

Then Allah says: "And submit to Him" when you return, so you must also surrender to Allah. It should not be that after you return to your Lord, they say something and then you withdraw. No, "and submit to Him" means returning to your Lord. When you return, Allah will explain to you: "Thus he who disbelieves in *ṭāghūt* and believes in Allah grasps the firmest handle that will never break." (Q2:256)

Allah will explain to you: "Those who believe fight for Allah's cause, and those who disbelieve fight on behalf of *ṭāghūt*." (Q4:76) Allah will explain to you: "Charge forth, on foot or mounted, and struggle with your possessions and yourselves in the way of Allah. That is far better for you, if you only knew." (Q9:41) For you not to feel the weight [of being mounted] then Allah says, "and submit to Him," you should surrender to Him by accepting His clarifications and following His commands.

Allah says here: "O believers, enter into complete peace." (Q2:208) O you, who believe, enter Islam completely; do not put one foot in Islam while the other is out. Do not say your prayers according to the Qurʼān, but then refuse to wage *jihād* according to the Qurʼān. Do not pray and fast according to the Qurʼān, but refuse to disbelieve in *ṭāghūt*; the Qurʼān has said it. I hope it is well understood.

[Nur cites Ibn Kathir] The trials of Allah are of two types: there is the trial of this world, of great tribulation, and severity of life, suffering, lack of peace of mind and [Operation] Flush;[2] these are some examples of the trials of the world. What led to this condition that in the land of Islam they brought some miscreants with [uniforms made of] tick cloths to come and make life difficult for people, why? What did we do to them? You did nothing, but see how they are dealing with you. What happened? It is your fault—yes, you, you, you, you return to your Lord, "and submit to Him" before that trial comes.

The time we went to Sokoto, we saw the original flag with which they waged the *jihād* of "There is no god but Allah" in the museum.[3] It was our forefathers who waged it at the time when the Europeans came. They fought at that time. They have folded the flag. It is folded and in fact they would not even open it for you to see the inscription "there is no god but Allah." It has been folded and kept in the museum.

At that time, they had honor, pedigree and power. When they heard they [the British] had brought Western education, they said: "By Allah we will not accept it!" They waged *jihād* against this. They waged *jihād* against this Western education yet today you are forcibly enrolling your son into Western education?! And seeing it as the epitome of civilization? And saying that your heart is in good condition so you attend Western education? Our forefathers waged *jihād* against Western education— against the Europeans. It is because of democracy that they killed them. It is because of democracy that they [Europeans] killed [Muhammad] Attahiru I[4] and all of them were fought and killed. I hope this discussion is well understood.

When we return, we should surrender to Allah before the trial occurs. Then even after that, you won't see that they disturb you with [Operation] Flush; they will disturb you with high cost of food. Do not think if you go to heaven you will have a share if you did not disassociate yourself and revolt against this government, I hope it is understood. "Then you will not be helped," Allah says, and so if that happens, we will not help you. "Follow what has been revealed to you from your Lord." (Q7:3) Ibn Kathīr says it is the Glorious Qur'ān. I hope it is understood.

[Nur cites Q8:53] Shehu 'Uthman Dan Fodio waged the *jihād* to establish a state of the Qur'ān. Is this not so? They waged *jihād* and established the state of the Qur'ān—then what happened? Allah did not change it for them until the time when they told the Europeans to bring what they brought; they received it, and *then* Allah took away peace and stability. Then they brought trials and severity: "that is because Allah never changes a favor He confers on a people until they change what is in their hearts." I hope it is well understood.

This is the reason why Allah said to us: "Then you will not be helped," since then a soul will say: "O this is my regret for not following the truth. See they have shown you Allah's path, the path of monotheism (*tawḥīd*), but you refused to follow it." On the Day of Resurrection, you will say: "If Allah had guided me, I would have also disassociated from this *ṭāghūt*; I would have also followed the Qur'ān. I would have been among the pious ones and so on and so on." It is correct, right? Or he will say: "If I have a few seconds to return to earth, I would be among those who change their behavior but the time has passed." I hope it is well understood.

So, because of that, my brothers, let us return to the path of Qur'ān and Sunna, and we will not be humiliated. There is nothing that will give you honor in the earth except following Allah and His Messenger. If you follow Allah and His Messenger; you will have honor, elevation, and progress. However, do not think that when you intend to go out, you should not tell someone about it. No, you should say it. It is mandatory that you read, know, and you should tell people. You should be patient concerning the harm that will be done to you. I hope it is understood.

[Nur cites Q5:105] You have said the truth, it is compulsory that you admonish people: you should admonish your wife, your relatives, your people—you should admonish the people of your region, the people in your town, your land and so forth. You should admonish all of them, the police, the soldiers, all of them, you should admonish them, including [Operation] Flush. You should stand in front of them and when they say you should kneel, reply to them by saying, "No!" "And the mosques are Allah's." (Q72:18) You should tell him [the policeman] this to his face. It is not enough that you have been guided—admonish him as well, so that he can take Allah's path. Abū Bakr said: "I have heard Allah's Messenger saying, 'People when they see evil...'"—bad things, polytheism, democracy, the constitution, worshipping graves, seeking assistance from entities other than Allah, these are all evil. Relying on someone other than Allah; these are all evil.

These systems of Western education are all evil; you cannot take female children to boarding school to become lesbians with fellow females. The females are now even engaging in marriage [with each other].[5] The government of Nigeria has now given them permission; if you want a woman to marry a woman they have given them permission. If a man wants to marry another man they have given them permission. So, will you not destroy this government of prostitution?!

You are seated [here]—what are you waiting for?! Do not come and say that they brought only one car; they put a red flag on it, so it is blood red. Do you not see that our turbans too are red! From blood to blood! It is Allah who says so—He said: "So let those who sell the present life for the life to come fight in the way of Allah. Whoever fights in the way of Allah and is killed or conquers, we shall accord him a great reward" (Q4:74)—either you kill or you are killed, it is a reward for you. Allah says, "If you are suffering, they are suffering, too" (Q 4:104). If you are feeling anxious, as they [the police] have shot you, then you feel you are going to fall and die, "they are suffering, too"—they, too, if you hit them, they feel it in their bodies. But the difference between them and you are: "but you hope from Allah what they cannot hope" (Q4:104)—there is something you hope to receive from Allah that they do not. I hope it is understood.

You would hear them saying: "You know, if you put on the helmet, if you fall [off the motorcycle] your head will not be injured." "If you wear the cloth [on the motorcycle], when night approaches and a car flashes its lights at you, they will see the reflection and not hit you." What type of compassion and pity is this? Is it not better for them to allow a person to fall and for a car to run him over than the beating that those people [police] give to the people? How many people did they kill at the time when they brought them into the police [for breaking the helmet laws]? The one who brought them in [the governor], may Allah curse him. And may Allah destroy him. And may Allah demolish him.

[Admonish the people and let us run and survive together] There is a reason I believe that the people of [Operation] Flush are foolish. The person who instructed them to do this work is in his house sleeping.[6] If we start to work, we will start from people like them, but the person who instructed them will be hiding in his house. Do you not have sense? When the situation becomes tense and severe, do you know what he will do? He will take a plane and flee from the country. So, do you not have sense? A person is supposed to think and be careful. Return and follow Allah—even you, the person who introduced Flush. Let us all come and follow Allah. Leave the thing that you are doing. If you do not know that, if you remain adamant, then Allah is the remedy of everything. Allah is the remedy of all things. I hope it is understood.

We did not say we have might, strength or honor. No! Honor is for Allah. It is not our possession. Honor is not in our turban; honor is not our courage—honor is not our bodies, not of anybody or anything. Honor is for Allah! This is the reason why the hypocrites when they told Allah's Messenger, in secret, "They say: 'If we return to the City [Medina], the mightiest will drive out the lowliest therefrom.'" (Q63:8) Allah said, no, it is not like that. "Might belongs to Allah, His Apostle, and the believers, but the hypocrites do not know." (Q63:8) I hope it is well understood.

As a result, let us return and admonish people. We should not say: "When you are guided then you are saved." No! You should explain to people and let them understand Allah's religion. I hope you all understand. Abū Bakr said: "If you see evil, you should change the evil." These things that we highlighted are all evil. I hope you all understand. Then he said: "If they saw evil and they did not change it, Allah will cause His trial and punishment to descend upon them." Allah will send down tribulations. You are here now and you have understood this warning. The government of unbelief is the government of *ṭāghūt*. O my brother, you should leave this infidel system; come let us destroy it, you, me and him. I hope it is understood.

If we do not do so after we understood that this is unbelief; after we understood that the remedy is *jihād*, after we understood, then retreated and sat down, then certainly Allah will bring down a trial which will overwhelm all of us. "And fear a calamity (*fitna*) which will not only afflict the wrongdoers among you, and know that Allah is severe in retribution." (Q8:25) So we should come back to Allah's path. We should demolish the path of unbelievers, the path—that is not Allah's path and His Messenger. I hope it is understood.

All these things that are happening—it is not only democracy, it is not only the constitution, and it is not only Western education. Aside from these evils, there are many crimes against Allah that are committed in the towns. The people in the market are cheating; the person selling vegetables would add a kola nut inside the vegetables.[7] What type of injustice is this? You should also look at the banks and the taking of interest, they have occurred everywhere in town. From different places, they came here to build banks. Even in your [mobile] phone, they are advertising gambling to you! They will remove you from Allah's path.

Illicit sexual relations have also become rampant. You would see someone walking on a street, if he sees a man and a woman displaying illicit amorous affection, he would comment by encouraging them to display their illicit affection in hidden places, but just not in public. This is exactly what Allah's Messenger mentioned as one of the signs of the last Hour. As a result, we will remove the evil. Allah's Messenger said: "Whoever sees an evil should remove it with what?" He said: "With his hand." I hope it is understood. "You should change it with your hand." Let us change it. I hope it is understood.

[Nur cites Q35:10; 8:62; and 3:26] Therefore, Allah mentioned that: "Those who take the unbelievers as friends, instead of the believers..." (Q4:139)—those who take unbelievers as colleagues, friends, [marriage] partners and so forth and love them. I am not saying that trading with them is forbidden. No, but for your system and [theirs], for everything to become equal with their unbelief. I hope it is understood.

What is the use of seeking status from them? For example, those who have doubts, what do they say? If we do not enter and join them, they will not allow us to pray. If we do not enter and join them, our admonition and sermons will be banned—is that not what they say? If we do not enter and join them, they will kill us. Now, if we leave the unbelieving government, then they will impose an unbelieving governor, an unbelieving councilor, or an unbelieving chairman upon us. Should we sit and allow unbelievers to rule over us? Since we have told you, it is only because we saw your name was Abū Bakr, 'Abd Allāh, 'Uthman and 'Alī—that is why you wasted our time. If only we peeped and saw that the governor's name is John, the chairman's name is Joseph, that official's name is Peter, then the talk is over. The talk would have been declared over for a long time.

It is the love we have for you that made us wait till now. It is the need to make you understand—that is what made us to wait till now. The desire for you to come and let us go together is what made us to wait till now. Whether you like it or not, whether you love them or not, we will commence the *jihād*! If you are not aggressive, you left us and go, we will be aggressive towards you. This task is obligatory. That is the main reason why we made it clear that what we are saying is not just verbal proclamation. It is not Zakzaky's type of preaching; it is not like his preaching. Even for him, they understand that it is only verbal—that is why they [the authorities] arrest and release him because they have no guns, but here they are. They know a *mujāhid* must have [a gun]. But even though there is [a gun], because a fighter does not part with it, they should go to the traditional scholars, so that they can obtain protective medicine to drink against guns.[8]

You know the weapon of a fighter—he is not the one who shoots, it is Allah who shoots: "When you threw it was actually Allah who threw..." (Q8:17) It is not him who shoots; it is Allah who fires [the gun]. What is required of you is that you have good manners and adhere to Allah. Seek honor from Allah. Do not be arrogant and selfish, but just follow Allah and His Messenger. When you do so, then you will have victory on the path [of Allah]. Allah has done it for those before us and He says: "I will do it for you, too." "Allah promised those of you who have believed and done righteous deeds that He will surely make them successors in the land and He made those who came before them successors..." (Q24:55)

As such, they should not deceive people that we must enter and join these people to have honor and religious status. No! We are saying that they cannot prevent us from our prayers. They cannot put a halt on our admonitions and sermons. In fact, their scholars are feeling intimidated by our admonitions! All of them, including their scholars, their mobile police, their SSS [State Security Service] are hurt by our admonitions. That is why they say it is unbelief. You know the nature of man, if a thief steals, he still wants to be called a good person, doesn't he? If they call him a thief, he does not want to be called that name.

This is similar with those in unbelief. If you call them *ṭāghūt* and say that what they are doing is unbelief, they do not want you to say that, but the fact that they do not believe is the main issue. The holidays of Saturdays and Sundays—Saturday is for Judaism; Sunday is for Christianity. They give you a Christmas break; it is a holiday for Christianity. They give you a break on Good Friday and Easter Monday—they are holidays for Christianity. They taught your children the national pledge and anthem. They are singing it with them, even though those are words of unbelief. That is the problem. The type of education they are studying is based upon Christianity. Football is idolatry. Their education shows that there is no god. Some disciplines, like philosophy, show that there is no god. Sociology also shows that there is no god. I hope it is understood. They contradict the verses of Allah.

You would hear them saying that man was just an insect, then became an ape, then the fur of his body fell off and he became human. Do not take these types of claims as jokes. You know there are exams you will write and if you say you disagree with these claims, you will not pass. It is not just writing an exam, even if you say these claims with your mouth, the angels [recording your deeds] have written it [in heaven]. After saying it, you must still write it out in exams. You see the day [of Resurrection] they will say: "Read your book"—it is the one you would have written yourself [of your actions] that they will give you to read. Read your book yourself! Do you not know that this is unbelief? Oh, but they [establishment scholars] say it is a necessity (*darūra*). This is the main reason why we are telling you it is unbelief.

It is not that we do not want you to work and collect a salary; that is not the problem. The problem is about the grave, the hereafter, and paradise. The problem is that they have desecrated our Qur'ān. If you are not disturbed, we are disturbed. How can we forget this thing? It is not possible. They have it and it is necessary that we do what we do. We will never forget! They killed our people in Yelwa Shandam,[9] we do not forget. Palestine, Jews, your people have killed our people—we do not forget. If we start, we are not going to go to Israel because Allah says: "Fight those of the unbelievers who are near to you." (Q 9:123). It is obligatory for us to start with you.

Even if we have the same parents as you, but you became a police officer or a soldier; if we come out, we will not say: "We want to wage *jihād*, so go and hide."

No! We will say: "Repent, so come let us implement the Qur'ān and the Sunna. If you return then we will go together, otherwise it is with you that we will start." This is the main reason why it is obligatory for all of us to learn disassociation (*barā'a*). Because by Allah, if you do not learn disassociation, you will meet someone and say that he is your father, brother, relation or friend. He is fighting Allah's government and Allah's religion. There is no relation [to him] except based upon Islam. Allah says: "O believers, do not take your fathers and brothers as friends, if they prefer disbelief to belief. Those who take them as friends are the wrongdoers." (Q9:23). I hope it is understood.

[Nur cites Q4:102] They were given the method of praying in the battlefield of *jihād*. Allah says when you meet [in battle] with the unbelievers; they are firing, you should also be firing. The only condition [for prayer] is for you to be saying *Allahu akbar*, and the movement with your head. That is it—and your prayer is complete. So, who will prevent you from prayers? There is no one who will prevent you from praying. You will be firing and they also will be firing, while you are praying. When it is time for afternoon prayer, then you should say *Allahu akbar*, and start reciting *sūrat al-Fātiḥa*[10] then you turn there and fire [at the enemy]. You also should turn to the side and destroy them.

The unbelieving soldier is easy to destroy. You do not understand. Once you say *Allahu akbar*—Allah is greater than everybody, Allah is greater than everything, Allah is greater than his [the enemy's] uniform, Allah is greater than his gun, Allah is greater than his commander, Allah is greater than his government and greater than everything he has. As a result, honor is from Allah and we can only seek it from Him. It is for this reason Allah says: "And let not what they say grieve you. All power is Allah's. He is the All-Hearing, the All-Knowing." (Q10:65) Those who oppose us, Allah says: "Those who take the unbelievers as friends, instead of the believers—do they seek glory from them? For all glory belongs to Allah." (Q4:139) I hope it is understood.

There is nothing that will make us successful except when we return to Allah's path [*jihād*]. It is only by returning to Allah's path that you will be able to trade in tranquility, you will be able to do your work in tranquility; you will climb on your motorcycle and do three-on-one [motorbike].[11] Based on the practice of Allah's Messenger, you will be able to move around in tranquility and no one will touch you. There is no way we will obtain this tranquility, except when we go back to Allah's path. And there is *jihād* in Allah's path. I hope it is understood. *Jihād* is among the means of seeking honor from Allah. It is compulsory for all to comply.

Now you see how things have been disrupted. They kill this person and shoot that person. One of our female relatives phoned me earlier. She said: "They say you have started trouble in the town?" I said: "No. We did not start any trouble." "Did they touch one of you?" I said: "Yes, they did. They have always touched us and have not stopped, but we did not start any trouble yet, though maybe in the future we will." I hope it is understood.

RETURNING TO THE QUR'ĀN AND SUNNA

It is not called trouble, but is called worship of Allah. They should not touch us. They should leave us alone to worship Allah. Leave us to proclaim the religion. Leave us to do admonition. They should leave us to remove our relatives, family and colleagues from this unbelief, so that they can come back to the path of the Qur'ān and the Sunna. They should not compel or pressure us. You know what the Hausas say: "When pushed to the wall, you can only turn back," isn't it? You cannot break the wall and pass through it, except by turning back and escorting them to where they came from. And may Allah make us successful. Because of the limited time, my time is up. What I have said that is correct, may Allah reward us.

Lecture from Muhammad Yusuf

[Standard Islamic opening]

And thereafter, may the peace and blessing of Allah be upon you. Praise be to Allah. Today is Sunday, 18 Rabi' al-Awwal, the night of the nineteenth [14–15 March 2009], isn't it? This is a lecture that we organized in haste because they did not announce it on Friday or Saturday. It was today in the morning that the lecture was announced after the morning study because today people were anticipating different things.

It is for this reason we said it is right that we come and tell the people whatever it is they should know then Allah changed the affairs because He does His things as He likes, not as a person likes. What we have been calling the people to is for them to be aware that sinning against Allah—when it becomes too much in the lives of the people—Allah will try them [with tribulations]. From that tribulation there will be poverty, from that tribulation there will be mutual despising, from the tribulation there will be fear; Allah will try them with fear. From the tribulation, there will emerge terrible tyrants; from that tribulations, there will be misconceptions and so many things that can occur.

So, because of this Allah is urging us to improve our deeds, so that Allah can improve our lives. Anyone who does not improve his deeds, his life will not be improved in this world and the hereafter. But the one who improves his deeds, his life will be good in this world and in the hereafter. Therefore, Allah says:

> Whoever does a good deed, whether male or female, while a believer, we shall make him live a good life, and We will give them a better reward than what they have done. (Q16:97)

[Yusuf cites Q20:124 and 20:52] This is the reason why the condition in which we found ourselves today has happened, with everyone cheating one another. Some are cheating their wives. Anyone who did not teach his wife religion has cheated her. Anyone who did not teach his children religion has cheated them. Anyone who did not admonish his neighbor has cheated him. Anyone who did not admonish his younger siblings has cheated them. Anyone who did not try through appropriate ways to admonish his parents about the religion has cheated them. You cannot just sit down and say that you know they are old people, from yesterday. No! You should preach to them about the religion with good manners and character. Let us run together and be saved together. There is nothing as good as seeing that your parents have entered paradise. Is it not so?

Just imagine the pity they felt for you. This is the reason why Allah says when you pray for them you should say: "Lord, have mercy on them, as they took care of me when I was a child." (Q17:24) O Allah! You should have pity on my parents as they had pity on me. Your parents felt a great deal of pity for you, so there is nothing you can do for them like seeking for them the path of salvation through prayers and admonition.

But since we have cheated ourselves by our refusal to admonish, by giving ourselves rights, by lack of this, lack of that, then Allah imposed on us cheaters again: "And thus We cause some of the evil-doers to dominate the others, because of what they used to do." (Q6:129) We will impose some unjust leaders upon a people because of the crimes and sins which everyone is committing. And this injustice will not end until the day in which we improve upon our habits, because Allah says: "Allah does not change the condition of a people until they change what is in their hearts." (Q13:11) Allah does not change the condition of people—their lives, the high cost of things, envy between themselves—until they change their behavior by returning to monotheism, returning to faith, and returning to doing good deeds. Whenever they return to this path then Allah will assist them. He will raise their status and distinguish them. I hope it is understood.

[Yusuf cites Q6:123] Yesterday, they brought the news to us that they had killed one of our students. They [the police?] came to us, and said that they killed him and took him to the Gwange cemetery. They abandoned him to the cemetery people, and then left. This was the news—what happened really? We went and found out, then we realized that certainly they engaged in a fracas, but that there was no one killed. But when we sent people to go and find out what happened—when they got there, they [the security forces] engaged them in another fracas. I hope you understand.

They brought out their guns, and instructed them [Boko Haram] to leave the place. When we received this report, we replied by saying that there is a remedy for their lunacy. However, when the day broke, all of us came back to our senses and we resolved the issue. Now we are together with our brothers—look at them here. So, this is the reason why the topic of the admonition changed [suddenly]. Initially, we had wanted to discuss the arrest of our brothers, but now they have returned. So, we will admonish everyone to fear Allah. I hope it is understood.

[Our proselytism is for the emancipation of the followers of Allah's messenger] Allah's Messenger said it is not permissible to flog someone more than ten times, if it is not because of the judgment of Allah. It is not permissible for a scholar or any other person. They said that one police officer said he went to this scholar and that scholar to ask about the issue, and they said what they [the police] are doing is acceptable. However, the Prophet said it is not permissible. Allah's Messenger said anyone flogged more than ten strokes, that has exceeded the limit. All the flogging that you want to do to either your child or student, it should not even reach ten strokes. If it reaches ten strokes, then you must have a [Qur'ānic] verse or *ḥadīth* to support your action.

Then Allah's Messenger said in the end time there will be policemen be carrying a cane, like the tail of a cow, and they will be flogging the people.[12] The scholars did not tell you about this *ḥadīth*. The Prophet said these types of people are going to hellfire. You police, you [Operation] Flush! Allah's Messenger said at the end time there will be unjust kings, their police will have long canes, they will flog the people without reason, and they are all dwellers of hellfire! You see your scholars did not tell you about this. The scholars only desire to give you rulings that would make you happy and leave, but we will give you rulings that will make you sad, but they will be the truth because we also took the rulings upon ourselves.

[Be patient and follow the prophet's path] Now these events are tribulations that befell us, but we did not know. They are the consequences of refusing to follow Allah. They are calling people to come and follow Allah and His Messenger, but some people close their eyes and say it is not true. This is the reason why the [Operation] Flush in this state is more powerful than anywhere else in Nigeria. Although you refused to follow the truth, it will not work on those who follow the truth. It will not work, Allah willing and Allah knows even you too, you know. I hope it is understood.

But since you denied the truth, after understanding it, is it not compulsory that the tribulations should be inflicted upon you? I hope it is understood. By Allah, we should follow Allah. He will ease everything for us. This is a tribulation and injustice. It is evil for a person who is in a town and can admonish, to keep quiet. You have a person who is just like a donkey, a Muslim who has declared the *shahāda* [declaration of faith] in the land of Muslims, and an unbeliever [policeman] who will pick up his shoes and use them [to beat him]. A Muslim will be standing by, saying: "Look at the beating they took!"

Is this not humiliation? Is this not disrespecting? Is this not injustice? And they said they brought them [the policemen] for your benefit. But if you do not put on a helmet and fall from a motorcycle, should your punishment be one of beating? Because the reason for the helmet is that should you be injured when you fall, it is for your benefit. But why should they beat a person and abandon him to die? Should the punishment be that severe? Some people do not know their worth and there are some who are even happy with this. In their area, if they have a quarrel with their neighbor they would go and bring [Operation] Flush. He is happy and people would be clapping for them. It will not work. They should not beat people just like that like donkeys.

Since you said you went to scholars and they said that it is acceptable, why have they not come out to tell the people? If a scholar tells you that it is good then they should broadcast that fact to the people, that this helmet is good, then we will understand. Every person who does not want trouble should know that everything that is not the law of Allah that was imposed on them is not obligatory. Why the flogging? What is the benefit of the flogging?

The governor of the town—governor, what did the people do to you? What did they do? What did they eat? Or did they eat the *tuwo* in his house?[13] Is there any fault that the people erred? Or is it the vote that they cast for him that is at fault? Or are the people that voted for him at fault? That is the dividend that he is bringing to them because they voted for him. He should give them what he has accumulated. Give houses to those who have none, so that the people who are not married can also marry. Instead you brought insane soldiers inside the town who are flogging the people. Because of his nature, they keep him in the bush. He is a madman and knows nothing except how to open fire. I hope you understand. There is nothing he knows except to open fire. If you want to alert him just open fire at him, and he will be alerted.

Secondly, you are not following your own ideology. The ideology of democracy does not permit soldiers to enter the town. This is the main reason why if you go to Abuja you would not see soldiers, because that is where the Europeans visit. If they see soldiers in the town they would question them: "Why do you bring soldiers into the town when you are practicing democracy?" It is not allowed to see a soldier roaming about, except when he wants to go to the office or something else. But roaming about in the town and arresting the people—this you should not see. Here, however, you would see it, because they have seen [people as] animals they can humiliate. If they arrest people and are humiliating them, are you not supposed to say that these are the people who elected me, therefore they are not supposed to be humiliated like this? I hope it is understood.

[Injustice is not allowed even on an infidel] Why then would they bring insane people to beat the people without reason? Disorganized people who do not know what they are doing, and they would just be beating the people. This is injustice! It is not acceptable! They should stop it. Since you have said some scholars said it is acceptable, they should admonish the people to understand this fact, but this reckless action is animalistic. It is not humane. It is an explanation that we humans need to understand, but beating a man and especially a Muslim is not right. This action is not right. It is not authority but dictatorship. It is dictatorship, not democracy. Even in the tenets of democracy, dictatorship is considered as a form of unbelief. Those who practice the religion of democracy view dictatorship as unbelief. It is wickedness: "And when you attack, you attack like giants?" (Q26:130)

You will still see people who are praising them, when they should be shifting away from them. You do not flog people. What will you get from flogging the people? What will you get from flogging the people? The soldiers who you stationed in one town or village, by the time the day breaks they would have flogged at least 100 people. Do you have the back [for flogging] on which the angels will take vengeance for these 100 people? If not, Allah that instructed you to beat them, then they will take revenge on you. As a result, for all the chickens that you have eaten, are you prepared to be flogged 100 strokes? Allah does not do injustice. By Allah, He will avenge the masses.

And while you are alive you will see. This action is injustice. Stop injustice! But the person who is engaging in unbelief, if you stop him from doing injustice, how will it be? The movement is the same. But maybe if you stop cheating people perhaps Allah will have mercy upon you and guide you. But look at you, you are the leader of democracy, you are the leader of those ruling with laws other than those of Allah, and to add to that, you are the leader of those flogging the people. Sooner or later, you will be the person who is flogged. I hope it is understood.

[Criticism of Ali Modu Sheriff] Look at the people fornicating, even if you do not know Allah and his Messenger but they are fornicating and transmitting AIDS. It is a disease that the Messenger had already foretold when he described the time when people are fornicating indiscriminately; Allah will bring a disease for which you will not have a remedy. And He brought it. So why do you not flog the people to stop illicit sexual relations? Anyway, Allah said you should flog, so flog them now to stop illicit relations because of the disease.

If they challenge you on what grounds they are being flogged, tell them it is because of the disease. But if a person did not put on the helmet, which disease will infect him? None! You perpetrate injustice against the people and now the people are not in a normal state. If they put on the helmet which is so big upon the head, they will ask again where is the cloth [for signaling]? This is the reason we say you should practice Islam. Slaves of Allah, they are in peace, but you went and voted for them. They are the ones who went to vote for them. You said you agree with all the things that they did for you. Look at you, before he was thinking that he needed your vote, so he would not act recklessly towards you, but now that he knows that he does not need your vote, so he will maltreat you! Why did you vote for him? I hope it is understood.

After they [Modu Sheriff] have finished the second term, this is the same person to whom they were giving his donkey water, when he said they should stop giving his donkey water because it is not thirsty. Then he started fighting the people who brought water for his donkey. The people gathered and campaigned for you shouting and screaming. They did everything for you, but this is the consequence of what they did, flogging, as if they committed illicit sexual relations. Even in the *sharī'a* of Islam, the person who committed illicit relations cannot be punished without bringing four witnesses (Q24:4, 13)—otherwise the flogging cannot be applied. If you misbehave, the *sharī'a* of Islam will only give you five or four strokes, it will never reach ten because the Prophet has forbidden it. But these people [police] will flog you anyhow

163

with their canes. Allah will take revenge on these people because He does not overlook injustice. I hope it is understood.

Allah says, "O people, your aggression shall recoil upon yourselves." (Q10:23) "In fact, the wrongdoers only promise each other vanity." (Q35:43) I hope it is understood. So, because of that, stop being unjust! Stop cheating people! You should leave the people to thrive to do their business. Leave them to look for their food since you do not give them anything to eat. The youths searched while riding on motorcycles, you did not give anything to them, yet you come telling them that they must buy a helmet and wear it? They must buy a cloth and wear it? What type of "help" is this? I do not understand. What type of help is this?

[Yusuf cites Q6:129] This is the admonition that I have for us today. I hope it is understood. The arrangement is not what I had planned, but Allah changed it. As such, we will keep the original plan till another day. I hope it is understood.

[Muhammad Nūr]: Just as they have presented the lecture to us, may Allah reward the presenters and the listeners. [No time for questions] There is a member who is seeking prayers from us, another person is sick and requests our prayers. And may Allah make us successful.

[Muhammad Yusuf]: We should pray to Allah to actualize all our needs. (*Prayer in Arabic closing the session.*)

15(B)

GROUPING OF SERMONS

[Trans.: Abdulbasit Kassim]

While the first sermon (text 15(A) above) cannot be dated according to internal evidence, the mention of the murder of Yusuf's followers in this second sermon make it certain that it was delivered during the crisis point between March to July 2009. It was probably due to this fact that the sermon was not released until March 2015. The themes of this sermon are strikingly akin to those of texts 6 and 13 above.

Second Sermon (Part 1)
"Come to *Jihād*"

In the name of Allah, the Most Beneficent, the Most Merciful.

[Standard Islamic opening]

And thereafter:

O servants of Allah!

I urge you to make your souls to be conscious of faith in Allah and I warn you against the violation of His commands or the perpetration of what He has prohibited. Allah said: "Do not make a mockery of Allah's revelations; and remember the grace Allah has bestowed upon you, and the Book and the wisdom He has revealed this to you to admonish you. Fear Allah and know that He knows everything." (Q2:231) "Splendid is Allah's exhortation to you. Allah is All-Hearing and all-Seeing." (Q4:58) "He admonishes you that you may take heed." (Q16:90)

O servants of Allah!

Among the advice, Allah gave His believing servants was for them to be careful and beware of their enemies, be fully prepared to defend themselves against the aggression of their enemies, guard the creed of Islam, rescue the weak and the oppressed, and make the Word of Allah supreme on the surface of the earth. Allah said: "And fight them so that sedition might end and the only religion will be that of Allah. Then if they desist, Allah is fully aware of what they do." (Q8:39) Ibn Taymiyya said: "If the prevailing religion is not Allah's religion [Islam], war is obligatory until Allah's religion alone prevails."

Verily, the Muslims of today have abandoned this obligation, and their act of abdication gave rise to the tyranny of the unbelievers, the rise of the banner of polytheism, the pervasiveness of Jews' and Christians' laws ruling over the community of Muhammad, the spread of corruption, makeup, illicit sexual relations, homosexuality, lesbianism and the consumption of liquor. These are the great tribulations that have become widespread within the Islamic nation. "And fear a calamity (*fitna*) which will not only afflict the wrongdoers among you; and know that Allah is severe in retribution." (Q8:25)

Because of this weakness, laziness, complacency, and attachment to this world on the Muslims' part, the unbelievers launched their tyranny over the Muslims all over the world. They forced the Muslims to obey the unbelievers' laws and systems in Palestine, Algeria, the Philippines, Afghanistan, and more recently in Iraq. You can see how they hit the Muslims with sticks, and whips as well, sending them into exile from their cities. The houses of the Muslims were burnt and destroyed. Muslims were killed with rifles, different types of torture, and they also stepped upon the heads of the Muslims, those who are prostrating to Allah. They also perpetrated worse atrocities by harassing the Muslim women.

O servants of Allah!

What we are now facing is a new catastrophe like what Allah has told us: "And fear a calamity (*fitna*) which will not only afflict the wrongdoers among you; and know that Allah is severe in retribution." (Q8:25) In Nigeria, specifically in the northern region, multiple misadventures have occurred, such as the organized war against the Muslims by the Christian group in Nigeria, the Christian Association of Nigeria (CAN), with the help of the infidel government. This happens for example, in places like Kafanchan, Tafawa Balewa, Zango Kataf, Kaduna, Bantaji, Wabi, Numan, Plateau [State], Yelwa Shendam, Shagamu, Ikoyi Lagos, and other locations. All these misadventures were organized by CAN with the help of the Nigerian government.

They killed thousands of Muslims, burnt their wealth, kidnapped their daughters, forcing them into unbelief, and even forced them to do despicable things. Now, they have come up with a new system in Borno, in Maiduguri. The state governor under this system is an impious man, an oppressor, and an apostate who does not rule with Allah's laws, like the unbelieving Tartars [Mongols].

There is no good in keeping silent towards those who do not want Islam and the Muslims, who do not love Islamic clothing, or any of the Islamic symbols such as the turban, chewing stick (*miswāk*),[1] and pocket-size Islamic devotionals. They hit all our Muslim brothers with whips and sticks. During the previous week, these unbelievers [the police] shot our brothers with bullets and they injured twenty brothers while they were heading towards the cemetery for a funeral of three people, who died because of a car accident, as well as that of a child who died because of a nose injury.

Those people, O Muslims! They are our enemies. Should we allow them to carry out such actions against the Muslims? Where is the call for *jihād*? Where is the faith in Allah? Where is the authentic creed?

> And why don't you fight for Allah's cause and for the downtrodden, men, women and children, who say: "Lord, bring us out of this city whose inhabitants are unjust and grant us, from You, a protector, and grant us, from You, a supporter." Those who believe fight for Allah's cause, but those who disbelieve fight on behalf of the Devil (*ṭāghūt*). Fight then the followers of the Devil. Surely the guile of the Devil is weak. (Q4:75–76)

O servants of Allah!

Verily, *jihād* is obligatory upon each one of you (*farḍ ʿayn*) if the unbelievers invade Muslims' lands, if the imam mobilizes you for *jihād*, or if you encounter your enemies face to face. We are now facing all these conditions. And on this basis, it is obligatory upon us to respond to the call of Allah to wage *jihād* and the incitement of his Prophet. Allah says:

> O believers, what is the matter with you? If you are told: "March forth in the way of Allah," you simply cling heavily to the ground. Are you satisfied with the present life rather than the hereafter? Yet the pleasures of the present life are very small compared with those of the hereafter. If you do not march forth, He will inflict a very painful punishment on you and replace you by another people, and you will not harm Him in the least; for Allah has power over everything.

> If you will not support him, Allah will not support him, when the unbelievers drove him out—he is the second of two, while they were both in the cave. He said to his companion: "Do not grieve; Allah is with us." Whereupon Allah sent down His tranquility upon him and assisted him with soldiers you did not see, and made the word of the unbelievers the lowest. The word of Allah is indeed the highest and Allah is Mighty and Wise. Charge forth, on foot or mounted, and struggle with your possessions and yourselves in the way of Allah. That is far better for you, if only you knew. (Q9:38–41)

In these verses, we can hear a call from Allah to his believing servants to go out for *jihād* to make His Word supreme and to overturn the words of the unbelievers. If the Muslims should stop this *jihād*, if they become weak and accept those unbelieving laws, it will result into a great tribulation and huge corruption on this earth like what is happening now.

The unbelievers, on the other hand, will continue to occupy the land of Muslims. Because of that, Allah ordered the believers to be prepared:

And make ready for them whatever you can of fighting men and horses, to terrify thereby Allah's enemies and your enemy, as well as others besides them whom you do not know, but Allah knows well. Everything you spend in Allah's path will be repaid in full, and you will never be wronged. (Q8:60)

This preparation that was mentioned by Allah includes spiritual preparation such as belief in Allah, knowledge of the unity of His worship, being faithful in once worship to Him and not ascribing partners to Him, affirmation of His unity of Lordship, the unity of His names and attributes, belief in His Prophet, following his Sunna, his path, and commitment to his *sharī'a*, as well as the adoption of the manners of Islam. It also includes material preparation such as learning the act of shooting, buying rifles, bombs, as well as training the Islamic soldiers to fight the unbelievers.

You should sacrifice your souls, your homes, your cars and your motorcycles for the sake of Allah. Do not be stingy with your blood and your family in making the Word of Allah supreme. Allah's Messenger said: "He who dies without having fought in Allah's cause or without having thought of doing so, will die with one characteristic of hypocrisy inside of him." He also said: "He who neither takes part in fighting nor equips a warrior nor looks after his (the warrior's) family, will be afflicted by severe calamities." Yazīd b. 'Abd Rabbihi said in his own narration: "before the Day of Resurrection."

Based on these narrations, the one who does not make his preparation will be a hypocrite: "Had they wanted to go forth, they would have prepared for that; but all was averse to their going forth, and so He held them back, and it was said to them: 'Sit back with those who sit back.'" (Q9:46)

Part of the preparation includes obtaining a horse to fight in Allah's path as well.

O servants of Allah!

Verily, this *jihād* and those *mujāhidin* will not be left alone, except when Allah will reward them. Their reward shall be the victory over the enemies. He is the possessor of all strength and the Victorious, the Knower of all and the Judge, the rewarder of thankfulness and forbearance. Allah's Messenger said:

Allah guarantees that he who goes out to fight in His way believing in Him and affirming the truth of His Messenger, will either be admitted to paradise or will be brought back to his home [safely] from where he has set out, with whatever reward or share of the booty he may have gained.

By Him who holds my soul in His hand, if a person is wounded in the way of Allah [*jihād*], he will come on the Day of Resurrection with his wound in the same condition as it was on the day when he received it; its color will be the color of blood, but its smell will be the smell of musk.

By Him who holds my soul in His hand, if it were not to be too hard upon the Muslims to be left behind, as I do not have enough [steeds] on which to mount them, I would not lag behind any expedition to fight in Allah's cause. By Him who holds my soul in His hand, I would wish to fight in the way of Allah and be killed, to fight again and be killed and to fight again and be killed.[2]

Mu'ādh b. Jabal also reported from the Prophet that he said: "Paradise becomes incumbent for a Muslim who fights for Allah's cause for a period as long as the time between two consecutive turns of milking a she-camel. He who receives a wound or a bruise in Allah's cause will appear on the Day of Resurrection as fresh as possible, its color will be the color of saffron but its fragrance will be that of musk."

Abū Hurayra also reported from the Prophet when he said:

One of the Prophet's Companions came upon a valley containing a rivulet of fresh water and was delighted by it. He reflected: "I wish to withdraw from people and settle in this valley; but I will not do so without the permission of Allah's Messenger." This was mentioned to Allah's Messenger and he said [to the man], "Do not do that, for when any of you remains on Allah's way, it is better for him than performing prayer (*salat*) in his house for seventy years. Do you not wish that Allah should forgive you and admit you to paradise? Fight in Allah's way, for he who fights in Allah's cause as long as the time between two consecutive turns of milking a she-camel, will be surely admitted to paradise."

Allah says: "Of the believers, three are men who fulfilled what they pledged to Allah; some of them have died, some are still waiting, without changing in the least." (Q33:23) Among the benefits of *jihād* is the fact it does not have any equivalent among the voluntary acts of worship. Abū Hurayra reported from the Prophet when he was asked the question: "What other good deed could be an equivalent of *jihād* in Allah's path?" He replied, "You do not have the strength to do it." The question was repeated twice or thrice, but every time he answered, "You do not have the strength to do it." Then he said, "One who goes out for *jihād* in Allah's path is like a person who observes fasting, stands in prayer constantly, recites the verses of the Qur'ān, while not break his fasting and prayer until the participant of *jihād* in Allah's path returns [from battle]."

O servants of Allah!

Verily, *jihād* and watching the borders (*ribat*) for the sake of Allah have a great reward. *Jihād* cannot be done without guarding and watching the borders and martyrdom operations (*istishhad*).[3]

O Muslims! Islam needs your blood and wealth.

Allah has bought from the believers their lives and their wealth in return for paradise. They fight in the way of Allah, kill and get killed. That is a true promise from Him in the Torah, the Gospel and the Qur'ān, and who fulfills His promise better than Allah? Rejoice then at the bargain you have made with Him for that is the great triumph. Those who repent, worship, praise, fast, kneel, prostrate themselves, enjoin what is good and forbid what is evil, and observe the ordinances of Allah—to [such] believers give the good tidings. (Q9:111–12)

Guarding the borders for the sake of Allah is better than this earth and all that is in it. Salman reported that he heard when Allah's Messenger said: "Keeping watch (*ribāṭ*) in the way of Allah for a day and a night is far better than fasting for a whole month and standing in prayer during all [the month's] nights. If a person dies, while performing this duty [of watching], he will perpetually receive the reward for his meritorious deeds, and he will be saved from Satan (*al-fattān*)." Faḍāla b. 'Ubayd also reported that he heard when Allah's Messenger said: "The actions of every dead person come to an end with his death, except those of the one who is on the frontier in Allah's way. This latter's deeds will be made to go on increasing for him till the Day of Resurrection, and he will be secure from the torment of the grave."

'Uthmān also reported that he heard when Allah's Messenger said: "A day on the frontier in Allah's way is better than one thousand days in any other place." Ibn 'Abbās also reported that he heard Allah's Messenger when he said: "Two eyes will not witness hellfire: the eye that wept from fear of Allah, and the eye that stayed in patrol overnight for the sake of Allah."

It has also been narrated on the authority of 'Abdallāh b. Abī Qatāda on the authority of his father Abū Qatāda that he heard the narration of Allah's Messenger when he stood up among them [his Companions] to deliver his sermon in which he told them that *jihād* in Allah's path and belief in Allah are the most meritorious acts. A man stood up and said: "O Allah's Messenger! Do you think that if I am killed in the way of Allah, my sins will be removed from me?" Allah's Messenger said: "Yes, if you fight in the way of Allah and you were patient and sincere, and you always fight facing the enemy, never turning your back upon him. [*This is repeated.*] Gabriel has told me this."

Abū Hurayra also reported from Allah's Messenger: "Whoever believes in Allah and His Apostle, offers prayers perfectly, and fasts [the month of] Ramadan, it is incumbent upon Allah to admit him into Paradise, whether he emigrates for Allah's cause or stays in the land where he was born." They [the Prophet's Companions] said, "O Allah's Messenger! Should we not inform the people of that?" He said, "There are one hundred levels in paradise which Allah has prepared for those who carry on *jihād* in His cause. The distance between every two levels is like the distance between the sky and the earth, so if you ask Allah for anything, ask Him for [the paradise called] *firdaws*,[4] for it is the central and the highest part of paradise. At its peak, there is the Throne of Beneficence, and from it gushes forth the rivers of paradise."

Second Sermon (Part 2)

[Standard Islamic opening]

And thereafter:

O people! Fear Allah and obey Him. And know that He made dying as a martyr a thing of joy for the *mujāhidīn* in the past and the ones in the future: "And do not think those who have been killed in the way of Allah as dead; they are rather living with their Lord well-provided for. Rejoicing in what their Lord has given them of His bounty; and they rejoice for those who stayed behind and did not join them; knowing that they have nothing to fear and that they shall not grieve." (Q3:169–70)

> Anas also reported that the Prophet said: "No one who has entered paradise will desire to return to this world, even if he should be given all that the world contains, except a martyr. For he will wish that he could return to this world and be killed ten times over, because of the dignity that he will experience by his martyrdom." In another narration, it ended with: "Because of the excellence and distinction he will experience because of his martyrdom."

Anas also reported: "So Allah's Messenger and his Companions proceeded towards Badr[5] and reached there, forestalling the polytheists of Mecca. When the polytheists also reached there [to Badr], Allah's Messenger said: 'None of you should step forward to do anything unless I am ahead of him.' The polytheists now advanced towards us, and Allah's Messenger said. 'Rise up to enter paradise which is equal in width to the heavens and the earth!' 'Umayr b. al-Humām al-Anṣārī said: 'O Allah's Messenger, is paradise equal in extent to the heavens and the earth?' He said: 'Yes.' 'Umayr said: 'My goodness!' Allah's Messenger asked him: 'What prompted you to utter these words?' He said: 'O Allah's Messenger, nothing but the desire that I should be among its residents.' He said: 'Verily, you are among its residents.' He ['Umayr] took out dates from his bag and began to eat them. Then he said: 'If I were to live until I have eaten all these dates of mine, it would be a long life.' So [then] he threw away all the dates he had with him, and he fought with the enemies until he was killed."

It has been reported on the authority of 'Abdallāh b. 'Amr b. al-'Āṣ that Allah's Messenger said: "All the sins of a *shahīd* (martyr) are forgiven except debt." And in another chain of transmission Allah's Messenger said: "Death in the way of Allah blots out everything except debt." Abū Hurayra reported that Allah's Messenger said: "The martyr experiences no more pain in being slain than one of you experiences from the stinging of an ant." Sahl b. Hunayf reported that Allah's Messenger said: "He who asks Allah sincerely for martyrdom, Allah will elevate him to the station of the martyrs, even if he dies on his bed."

Abū Bakr b. 'Abd Allāh b. Qays reported: "I heard my father saying in the presence of the enemy: Allah's Messenger said: 'The gates of paradise are under the shades of the swords.'[6] A man with a shaggy appearance got up and said, 'O Abū Musa [al-Asha'ri]! Did you hear Allah's Messenger say that in person?' Abū Musa replied in the affirmative; so, he returned to his Companions and said: 'I give you farewell greetings.' Then he broke the scabbard of his sword and threw it away. He rushed towards the enemy with his sword and fought with it till he was martyred."

O servants of Allah!

Martyrdom for the sake of Allah is a great sign of those who will live in Paradise. It was the status Allah's Messenger had wished for himself when he said: "By He in whose hand my self is! I would like to fight in the way of Allah and be killed, then be brought to life again so I could be killed, and then be brought to life again so I could be killed."

GROUPING OF SERMONS

[Trans.: Abdulbasit Kassim]

The themes of this sermon on colonialism (third sermon in the series) parallel the themes in the History of Muslims (text 11). It also parallels a speech delivered by Osama Bin Laden titled "Crusader Wars."[1]

Third Sermon (Part 1)
"A Sermon on Colonialism"

[Standard Islamic opening]

And thereafter:

O servants of Allah!

I urge you to make your souls to be conscious of faith in Allah: "We have enjoined those who received the Book before you, as well as yourselves: Fear Allah, and if you disbelieve, surely to Allah belongs what is in the heavens and on earth." (Q4:131)

O believers! The fear of Allah will help you against your enemies, the unbelievers and the hypocrites: "And if you forbear and fear Allah, their wiles will not hurt you at all. Allah knows fully what they do!" (Q3:120)

The enemies of Islam—the Jews, the Christians and the polytheists as well as their hypocrite and the orientalist lackeys—have ignited the fire of a 'world war' since their occupation and colonialization of the lands of Islam. They have desecrated the sacred dwellings of Islam and changed the *sharī'a* by enforcing the oppressive constitutions, the laws of the *jāhiliyya*, their tyrannous regimes, their devilish banners, their twisted secular studies, as well as their atheistic colleges and universities. Not only did do they

173

do all the above, but they also recruit people from us [Muslims] to carry on their goals: "And they will continue to fight you until they turn you back from your religion if they are able." (Q2:217)

O believers!

What are the reasons behind these world wars against Islam and the Muslims? If we look at the map of both the Islamic region and the world, you would see that all Islamic states have suffered from wars, blood, and killings. Remember what happened between India and Pakistan, where they killed dozens of Muslims in that train.[2] Remember what happened in Bosnia—Herzegovina, and Palestine in 1948—in all these places, they killed Muslims, destroyed their houses, and demolished their mosques.

Do not forget O believers, that when the British, French and the Japanese [sic] colonialists reached the Hausa State [the state of Ibn Fūdī] and the Borno empire under the rule of [Frederick] Lugard (may Allah's curse be upon him and those who follow him), they killed the Muslims, destroyed their houses and mosques, burnt the flag of "There is no god except Allah," urinated on the Qur'ān, and ended the state that was established by Shaykh 'Uthmān Ibn Fūdī.[3]

All these actions were carried out under the command of Britain. They attacked Muslims in Sokoto State and the nearby area, until they forced its caliph Muhammad Tahir I to immigrate. He immigrated with some Muslims fleeing with their religion to Burmi. Those Jews followed him, destroyed the area and the mosque there. They killed Prince Muhammad Tahir I as well as those who were with him.

And for how long, O believers?

And for how long are we going to keep following those who killed our fathers and ancestors and fought Islam?

And for how long are we going to remain slaves to those criminals?

And for how long are we going to remain students to those enemies?

How many [Muslim] girls have been turned into girls without a veil, decency or modesty!

How many Muslim boys have they changed their beliefs to that of the unbelievers till the point that they now act like them in their unbelief!

"Whoever acts like a community, he is part of them."

O believers!

Do you still remember the saying of Allah: "O believers, do not take the Jews and Christians as friends; some of them are friends of each other. Whoever of you takes them as friends is surely one of them. Allah indeed does not guide the wrongdoers." (Q5:51) Did you forget how the infidel Hindus captured 400 Muslim girls? Then when the Muslims went out to save them, they killed 3,000 Muslims, and they were not satisfied with that until they burned their bodies.

"Hatred has already been manifested in what they utter; but what their hearts conceal is greater still. We have made clear Our signs to you if only you understand." (Q3:118) O believers! Jews and Christians work all the time to hurt the Muslims: "If they come upon you, they will be enemies of yours and will stretch out their hands and tongues against you with malice, and they wish that you would disbelieve. Your kinsmen or your children will not profit you on the Day of Resurrection. He shall separate you one from the other; and Allah perceives well what you do." (Q60:2–3)

O believers!

Do Jews and Christians love the Muslims? How can they love the Muslims while they killed their prophets in the past?

How can we follow them after what they did to our female Muslims?

"Showing them friendship, when they have disbelieved in the truth that has come to you." (Q60:1)

They did not believe in the Qur'ān, and they called the Prophet Muhammad a liar. They burned the Qur'ān and the other Islamic books, and they killed the Muslims. Are these people your allies and protectors? Do you consider them like that? Don't you think? Don't you remember? When will you act?

O believers!

Verily, there are some Muslims among those who are knowledgeable and pious who follow those polytheists in their disbelieving democracy, parliaments, and constitutions. They are doing these actions because of misconceptions, their desires, and their love of this world and their hatred of death "Will they not ponder the Qur'ān, or are there locks upon their heads? Surely, those who have turned upon their heels after the Guidance was manifested to them, it was Satan who insinuated to them and deluded them. That is because they said to those who disliked what Allah has sent down: 'We shall obey you in part of the matter,' but Allah knows their secretiveness." (Q47:24–26)

O believers!

Here is Haile Selassie, the infidel for whom festivals were held whenever he visited a place. When he ruled Ethiopia,[4] he planned to eliminate Islam in the country within fifteen years. He bragged about this plan in front of the Americans. He used to force the Muslims to kneel to his Christian officials; if they did not do that, he ordered them to be killed. He also ordered that the blood of the Muslims be shed for lesser issues. He shut down the schools of Muslims and opened the schools of Christians so that the sons of Muslims would enroll in these schools and later graduate as Christians.

The Jews, Christians and their lackeys: "They observe with the believers neither kinships nor pacts. Those are the real transgressors." (Q9:10) Why do we find Muslims who are allying with them and not fighting them? Why do we follow their systems? Why do we go to the unbelievers? Why are we afraid of the unbelievers?

175

Why do Muslims enroll their sons in those schools where they are raised by the goal of the Jews and the Christians, which is to abandon the religion? "Neither the Jews nor the Christians will be pleased with you until you follow their religion. Say: 'Allah's guidance is the [only] guidance.' And were you to follow their desires after the Knowledge that came down to you, you will have no guardian or helper [to save you] from Allah." (Q2:120)

Yet, O believers!

"Yet you will see those in whose hearts is a sickness hastening to woo them, saying: 'We fear that a misfortune will be fall us.'" (Q5:52)

O Almighty Allah!

Do they seek honor with them [through power]? Those ignorant people thought that progress, development, and civilization are in the unbelievers' hands. However, Allah says: "honor belongs to Allah entirely." Allah says: "However, it may be that Allah will bring victory or some other matter from Him; whereupon they will regret what they concealed within themselves." (Q5:52) Therefore, Allah has ordered us to hate them, and prepare to fight them. Allah ordered us not to ally with them.

How is it you love the humiliated unbelievers, who are hated by Allah, His Messenger and the truthful believers? How is it you love those unbelievers, the grandsons of monkeys and pigs? How come you love them while they hate you, your religion, your Allah, and the Sunna of your Prophet? How come you love them when they do not love you, and they even hate you? They eat the prohibited meat[5] and the meat of pigs. They take the money of the people without rights and prevent people from following Allah's path. How come you love their women while they are wearing almost nothing?

O servants of Allah!

"Do you wish to give Allah against yourselves a clear case?" The only subject that Allah discussed more than other, after the belief in monotheism and the prohibition against associating partners with Him, was the prohibition of a Muslim forming an alliance with the unbelievers.

"O believers, do not take the Jews and the Christians as friends; some of them are friends of each other. Whoever of you takes them as friends is surely one of them. Allah indeed does not guide the wrongdoers." (Q5:51) "O believers, do not take My enemy and your enemy for supporters, showing them friendship." (Q60:1) "O believers, do not befriend a people against whom Allah is wrathful and who have despaired of the hereafter, just as the unbelievers have despaired of the dwellers of the tombs." (Q60:13) "O believers, do not take your fathers and brothers as friends, if they prefer disbelief to belief. Those who take them as friends are the wrongdoers." (Q9:23)

O believers! There are many text proofs that we should not ally with the unbelievers and we should not love them. How is it that some Muslims declare that they have unbelieving friends?

And that they are friends and allies? It is forbidden by Allah; rather Allah ordered the Muslims to prepare for war against the unbelievers: "And make ready for them what you can of fighting men and horses to terrify thereby Allah's enemies and your enemies." (Q8:60)

Say to them always:

"Say: 'Nothing will befall us except what Allah has decreed for us. He is our Lord, and in Allah let the believers put their trust.' Say: 'Do you expect for us anything other than one of the two best outcomes, while we wait for you that Allah will smite you with a punishment?' So, wait and watch; we are waiting and watching with you." (Q9:51–52)

O believers!

By doing this, we can face this war—this global Zionist war against our religion—not by deficiency, fear or following others, rather by belief in Allah, faith, truthful statements, actions and steadfastness. "Do not fear them, but fear Me." (Q2:150) "But do not fear them, and fear me, if you are true believers." (Q3:175) "O believers, forbear, and vie in forbearance and steadfastness; and fear Allah so that you may prosper." (Q3:200)

"Say to those who disbelieve: 'If they desist, He will forgive them what is already done; but if they go back, they [should remember] what befell those before them. And fight them, so that sedition (*fitna*) might end and the only religion will be that of Allah. Then if they desist, Allah is fully aware of what they do." (Q8:38–39)

Third Sermon (Part 2)

[Standard Islamic opening]

And thereafter:

O people! Fear Allah and you should know that having faith in Allah makes you succeed. You should seek help and patience in your prayers, your abundant fasting, night prayers and recitation of the Qur'an. You should remember Allah many times so that you may be successful. And remember to supplicate for the Prophet of Allah. You should praise Allah in the morning and evening. You should also help the orphans and treat your relatives and the needy with goodness.

Verily, this type of war you are facing requires such preparations and good morals. There is no other path to victory, splendor and stabilization except by applying the *sharī'a* of Allah and working with Allah's religion. We should work with Allah's religion. Allah will support those who support this religion and those Muslims who illuminate His Word. "Indeed, Allah will support whoever supports Him. Allah is surely Strong and Mighty." (Q22:40) "O believers, if you support Allah, He will support you and steady your footsteps." (Q47:7)

Did the Muslims around the world support Allah's religion? Did they enjoin the good deeds and forbid the evil ones? Did they call others to Islamic monotheism and the fight against polytheism? Did they raise their children according to Islamic morals? Without that—O believers—you will be humiliated. We ask for help from Allah. There is no power except from Allah, the Highness and the Great. "Allah and His angels bless the Prophet. O believers, bless him and greet him graciously, too." (Q33:56)

O Allah! Exalt the salutations of Muhammad and the family of Muhammad just as you exalted the family of Abraham. You are Praised and Glorious. O Allah, bless Muhammad and the family of Muhammad as you blessed the family of Abraham. You are Praised and Glorious.

O Allah! Whoever wants to help Muslims and Islam, aid and support him! Whoever wants to harm Muslims and Islam punish him! O Allah supports us against our enemies.

O Allah! We ask you to support us, help us and aid us to win over our enemies.

O Allah! We ask you to help Muslims, and show them the right path.

O Allah! We ask for your guidance and help. [closing prayer.]

19

OPEN LETTER TO THE NIGERIAN GOVERNMENT OR *DECLARATION OF WAR*

BY MUHAMMAD YUSUF

(12 JUNE 2009)

[Trans.: Abdulbasit Kassim]

This is the last official statement of Yusuf before the June–July 2009 uprising. It is quite easy to see his open rebelliousness, frustration and anger over the indiscriminate killing of his followers, together with his growing paranoia and apocalyptic sense. This lecture was a defining moment for Muhammad Yusuf. It ushered his movement into a new cycle.

Part 1: Available at: https://www.youtube.com/watch?v=f89PvcpWSRg

[Standard Islamic opening]

And thereafter, may the peace and blessings of Allah be upon you.

Today is Friday, 18 Jumādā Thani 1430 [2009], after the migration of Allah's Prophet from Mecca to Medina. Based on our tradition, every Friday evening we usually conduct the exegesis of the Holy Qur'ān in this mosque, al-Ṭā'ifa al-Manṣūra, located at Doki Street, here in Maiduguri. Today, Allah willing we will substitute the session on the exegesis of the Holy Qur'ān with a discussion concerning some certain issues.

Yesterday, Thursday, 17 Jumādā Thani 1430, some of our Muslim brothers were on their way to perform burial rites for four corpses of our brothers at the Gwange cemetery,[1] [after departing] from the Ibn Taymiyya Center in Maiduguri, when they ran into a detachment of Nigerian soldiers and the Mobile Police. [This unit was] under a Joint Task Force called "Operation Flush" which was introduced under the leadership of 'Ali Modu Sheriff, the governor of Borno State. They opened fire upon our brothers with their guns, shot them with their bullets and now, even as I am speaking with you, there are eighteen brothers who are currently receiving treatment in the hospital.

One of the brothers was shot at the back and two bullets were removed after they opened his back. Another brother was shot between his stomach and thigh. Another brother was shot in the head and the bullet skirted the side of his eye, such that if it had hit just a little further to the side, he would have died. Yet another brother had both of his legs destroyed. Another brother had his thigh mangled; they broke his bone, and there is a bullet lodged inside his bone. And another brother had his hand broken.

Despite the details we received about the incident, we refuse to issue any statement based on images from [mobile] phones or hearsay from people. This is the reason we said that yesterday we do not have any explanation until we visited the casualties whom we saw in pools of their blood and in pain. They did not do anything wrong. They did not insult anyone. They did not commit any fault. This injustice was meted out to them simply because it has always been the mission of the Borno State government to use "Operation Flush" to suppress our brothers, our preaching, and to humiliate the people of this town [Maiduguri]. This is their intention and they have continued to implement it. We have previously mentioned that this task force was created because of our group. Now this has been confirmed.

No matter the fate of a person, the blood of a Muslim is priceless. Allah's Messenger said: "Verily, bringing the whole world to an end is much easier in Allah's sight," that is, for the earth to burst, for the sky to collapse, for the stars to fall, for the moon and the sun to scatter, for the oceans to dry up and for the mountains to melt, "is easier in Allah's sight than spilling the blood of one Muslim."

Now, unbelievers have started shooting to kill. By Allah, the claim that they were only shooting to defend themselves and not to kill is a lie. By Allah, they did those shootings to kill our brothers, and it is only Allah who did not take their souls. It is only Allah who did not kill them. There was an unbeliever among them who was shooting, and our brothers heard him saying, "I will kill them and finish them off"— that was what he said.

So, listen to me, I am the person delivering the admonition, not you, so let no one interfere. Why would a person who does not intend to kill the people utter such words? Right from the beginning, the hatred that an unbeliever and a hypocrite have for a believer is everlasting and long-standing for as long as the heaven and earth continue to exist. There is no way that they will love you or that you will love them. It will never happen because they do not love us and Allah has said it in the Qur'ān.

DECLARATION OF WAR

It is only the foolish people among us that keep loving or supporting them or keep seeing them as people of integrity and justice, but there is no one among them who is just. They did not build the government of Nigeria to guarantee justice. They did not build it to allow the practice of Islam. They did not build it to protect Islam and the Muslims. They built it to fight Islam and kill the Muslims. This is the work of the government which they are now implementing in Plateau State, and it is well-known. Even the people living there were driven out and it is akin to the period of crisis in Kafanchan, in case you have forgotten. This is the step that they are taking to avenge what they did in Kaduna twice or thrice and what they did in Zango Kataf twice. They are the ones who initiated all the crises without any reason.

This enmity, as we have previously mentioned, Allah said it is forever. It will not end because a believer will not compromise his faith, while the unbeliever and the hypocrite will not abandon his polytheism and evil plotting. Allah says: "Many of the People of the Book wish, out of envy, to turn you back into unbelievers after the truth had become manifest." (Q2:109) That is, if you do not succumb to their desire, you will never have good rapport with them. There is nothing that will make you agree with an unbeliever and hypocrite on an equal level except if you become like him.

There is no day you would wear different clothes from him, look different from the way he does, your wife is unlike his wife, your children are unlike his children—and you think he would agree with you? He would not agree with you! Whether you touch him, or do not touch him; whether you agree with him or do not, he will never love you. I hope it is understood.

Allah says: "Neither the Jews nor the Christians will be pleased with you until you follow their religion." (Q2:120) The Jews and Christians will never agree with you until you follow their religion. If you follow their religion, then you will become their ally. If you do not follow their religion, there will be enmity between the both of you, and their hope will be to kill you or separate you from this world. Allah says, "They wish that you disbelieve, as they have disbelieved, so that you will all be alike." (Q4:89) They wish that you, the believers, will disbelieve as they have disbelieved in Allah so that you can all become equal with them, your clothes will become equal, your laws will become equal, your politics will become equal, your schools will become equal. That is what they want.

Once you differ with them then they will continue with their enmity. They will continue to mention your faults. You are a person with faults. They have never agreed with a Muslim. There is no day in which the unbelievers will agree with a Muslim. There is no day in which the hypocrites will agree with a Muslim. I hope it is understood. There is no day in which they will agree with the Muslims. They will never agree with the Muslims. The plan of the hypocrites and unbelievers in this world is to extinguish Islam and to destroy it.

Should we sit and remain quiet, when all the carnage that occurred in Iraq during the time of the Mongols is exactly what they will replicate here? They saw some brothers going to the funeral and shot them. This is exactly how they will come to our [Ibn Taymiyya] study center and shoot, if we allow them. This is also exactly how they will abuse our women and terrorize them if we leave them. I hope it is understood. Instead of us to sit and keep quiet while they humiliate our women, or they will come to our study center and humiliate us, we will rather sacrifice our lives.

It is better we do not live in the world at all. Allah says: "They wish that you disbelieve, as they have disbelieved"; they want you to disbelieve. Allah says, whether you like it or not, they will not agree with you. "They observe with the believers neither kinships nor pacts." (Q9:10) They will never protect a believer, a family tie or promise. When you have made a promise with them, they are not concerned with keeping the promise. Your family ties—whether you are a cousin or nephew—is not their concern. They will not protect these ties.

"They only give you satisfaction with their mouths." (Q9:8) They will sweet talk you and let you know that they are with you, and that they are doing the work to protect you, "while their hearts refuse, and most of them are sinners." (Q9:8) I hope it is understood. Allah says: "If they overcome you, they will observe neither kinships nor pacts with you." (Q9:8) "They observe with the believers neither kinships nor pacts. Those are the real transgressors." (Q9:10)

Therefore, we will not tolerate anyone who treats us as they wish and just goes back to sleep. After one of them [Operation Flush] drinks alcohol, you would see him sitting under the tree, without any sign of remorse holding his gun and threatening the people. Last night, our brothers went to donate blood to those who needed it. When they reached the hospital, they searched them and told them to go and eat before donating blood, but before they departed they told the security man what they were told. He assured them that they can go without any problem. However, when they returned to the hospital, the security man denied them entrance to the hospital.

Part 2: Available at: https://www.youtube.com/watch?v=elVjD7znMik

The brothers asked him, as they had informed him before leaving, but he indicated that the "Operation Flush" people are the ones who instructed him to deny them entrance to the hospital. At this point, the brothers delegated a leader to go and talk to them. The leader left the other brothers behind, and went to meet them [the security] on the road. But when he approached them they cocked their guns warning him that if he dared to cross the road they would shoot him. They do not care about your leadership because they are only out to terrorize. They would shoot him; that was exactly what they said to him. After they shot twenty people yesterday, they still have the audacity to threaten to kill another person if he dare cross the road to meet them? I hope it is understood.

Is this how you want to leave them and just watch them to continue their atrocities? It should not happen! We will not take that nor will we agree with that, because we have witnessed these types of atrocities. Since the beginning of this preaching, many things have happened and passed. They have leveled many allegations against us, incarcerated us and taken us to court without any justifiable reason. This is exactly what is happening to all our brothers in different places.

As I am speaking right now, in Argungu in Sokoto State, they said they will confiscate the mosque of our brothers. They also said they have banned them from preaching anywhere, and have issued an order to arrest them wherever they see them. They said the Izala sect should be given more opportunity to preach against them [Boko Haram] so that the people will reject them. This order was issued by the traditional emir of the town.[2]

Similarly, in Sokoto, I have been informed that the governor of the state[3] has issued an order for my arrest whenever I visit the town. Yesterday, we were also informed that our brothers were brought in by the SSS [State Security Services] in Kaduna. This is the same situation in Bauchi State. In fact, this is the treatment we get everywhere and it is all because we built our preaching on calming the people, instilling patience and strengthening them.

And praise be to Allah, even in our state of being "ignorant and childish," we are grateful to Allah for the path He chooses for us. We are grateful to Allah. Yesterday, our brothers saw their other brothers lying in their blood, with one of the brothers' legs broken and another brother rendered speechless [from shock]. They saw their brothers while they were on their way to the funeral, yet they did not retaliate or say they would do anything on their own.

The scholars called them and they exercised patience. Honestly, this is the work of Allah. We are grateful to Allah. But what we are saying here is what we have mentioned several times, that we will never sit down and watch anyone humiliate us and go free. They have achieved what they wanted by shooting the people. We took them to the hospital and have paid the bills, while [the shooter] goes to sleep and show no remorse. He does not even care about us. This cannot go on. By Allah, it cannot go on.

Because of that, Allah has granted us the opportunity to deliver His message. At the time, they were disturbing us with too many calls so that we can explain to them what our preaching is all about and why the security forces were harassing us. We wrote a bulky letter and sent it to the so-called president during the era of [Olusegun] Obasanjo so that he can read what our preaching is all about and what we are preaching versus what they are doing to us. We also sent a similar letter to the House of Representatives, the Senate and governor and so on. We sent it to all of them.

Similarly, when about sixty-two of our members were arrested during the commissioning of our Friday mosque at Monguno,[4] we sent them a letter and, to confirm to us that they received the letter, they sent us a reply, but ignored the issues we raised. These two events certainly happened. We also made sure that in all the meetings we had with them, we write or verbally inform them about the goal of our preaching. I can assure you that there is nothing that they do not know. After all, they also received our cassettes and they know what we are preaching to the people.

Allah has made our preaching penetrate many places. Normally, what is required is for someone to be patient, even if they spill his blood or jail him. Let the one who is ignorant of our preaching know what we are preaching but Allah made people to know by His will not by our work. The preaching has penetrated unprecedented places; they know it, have heard it, particularly those whom we want them to hear—they have heard it. Therefore, we will not just relax and watch them kill our people. It cannot go on.

We are aware that this is a war that they have planned to execute on us from time to time under the leadership of this Governor, 'Ali [Modu] Sheriff. We should also not forget there was a time that "Operation Flush" attacked three of our brothers. They injured and incarcerated them. The next day, we went and talked with them and they promised that from now on, they would not touch anyone coming for prayers or attending our preaching sessions. They also said that if it is only one person, they may not be able to recognize him, except when he is bearing our symbol or wearing the helmet. We passed this message on to our brothers.

Or is it not like that? So, tell me is a funeral not an act of worship?[5] Are the brothers not in a group? Why would they beat them? Why would they cheat them? Maybe someone would ask why they alighted [from their motorbikes]? Do you expect them to go while they [the security] are beating one of their brothers? They should go while they are beating one of them, then what is the importance of going in a group? If they catch one of the soldiers will the soldiers leave him and go?

Between the brotherhood of a soldier, and that of Islam, which one is stronger? Therefore, we will not listen to anyone. We have decided not to write any letters again. We will not discuss this with anyone, and nobody should invite us to meet with them. We do not agree and we will not forgive. And these insane soldiers who were stationed in this town, if they do not redeploy them out of this town, there will not be peace.

We are not just speaking on behalf of ourselves; we are speaking on behalf of all the people who are being cheated. When we went to discuss with Dane,[6] I told him that all the brutalities they are committing against the people without any justifiable reason should be stopped. I told him we do not agree with the soldiers because they are insane people, they lack intellect and they are drunkards. A soldier is a person who was made to be crazy, and kept on the outskirts of the town [Maiduguri] but you brought him into the town to satisfy your own personal interest. They are beating the Muslims.

All the time you would see a practicing Muslim being beaten with a cane and his rights trampled upon. Do you think this is Andalus [Spain]? Is this place Israel? Is this place Baghdad? Are you Christians fighting Christians? Therefore, by Allah we will not condone this anymore. An unbeliever shot twenty people saying that he would kill them; does that mean that this type of shooting will go unpunished? Do they expect that we will become afraid of guns and we would sit down and allow them to take law into their hands?

In Islam, when we establish a truce with a person, Allah says: "But if they break their oaths after their pledge [is made]," (Q9:12) if they violate their agreement—they agreed not to harass our people but then they harassed them, in fact they even shot to kill and they ridicule our religion—Allah says: "Then fight the leaders of unbelief; for they have no regard for oaths, and that perchance they may desist." (Q9:12) You would often hear them saying: "I am a soldier," "I am not a politician," therefore, "We do not negotiate with people." If a soldier does not see return-fire, he will not quickly agree to negotiation. Their claim is useless and nonsense babble.

Glory be to Allah—this is a lesson to us. We had initially thought that our brothers have not reached this stage, but I can confirm they have reached it. When I approached the brothers, I asked each of them when they were shooting, "Where were you?" One of them replied to me: "I was here, I took this brother, and that brother." I asked him: "Did the brothers run?" He replied to me, "No," rather than running they were advancing towards them [the security]. A small child who had come and told me that he also advanced towards them. I asked his friend: "Why did they shoot you?" He replied me that he was held back, crying.

You never know when brothers have reached this level except in a state of oppression. This is a lesson and a gift from Allah. It is a sign of progress. It is something to celebrate and to be grateful to Allah for by prostrating and showing gratitude to Him. It is not by talking that you can demonstrate the fearlessness in the face of a gun. The ability to carry a gun is not the fearlessness in the face of a gun. Let them shoot while you did not run, or when you see blood but did not run—that is the true meaning of fearlessness in the face of a gun.

[The period of patience is over] Therefore, the blood of a believer cannot be shed by an unbeliever in his own land and then he goes scot-free. In fact, he is even bold enough to threaten the brothers by saying that "between you and us is just a matter of one hour." If it is not fear, why do you attack people who were on their way to a funeral? What you should have done is to announce a specific date when we will encounter each other. You see unarmed people going to a funeral, but you attack and shoot them with your guns calling that an act of courage. An act of courage is for you to stop us from our preaching. A courageous man should tell me not to engage in my preaching.

A courageous man should come and say that in this country, Nigeria, there will never be the practice of the *sharīʿa*. Let him say so if he can! Whether you are a governor or a president, when you ban the practice of *sharīʿa*, that will be something worth fighting for. I dare say that in this land *sharīʿa* must be implemented! And I challenge you, anyone who feels he is a man, be you a governor, senator or commissioner of police or inspector general, to say the contrary. This is not funny. If they say that a person disobeyed their order, I have never received any complaint from them. Since we entered into an agreement, I have not received any complaint that our brothers disobeyed their orders and nothing happened [as a result].

They just started preparing for war by shooting our brothers with the intention of killing them. Have you ever seen someone shoot [someone] in his abdomen not trying to kill him? Have you ever seen someone shoot [someone] in the head or in the neck not trying to kill him? Have you ever seen when someone is shot in the backbone to the point where he must undergo surgery both from the front and back to remove the bullet—but you say that the shooting is not intended to kill him?

It is Allah who did not want them to die to ease our affairs. These people are our enemies. They are enemies! "They are the enemy, so beware of them. May Allah discomfit them! How they are perverted!" (Q63:4) They are the enemies, be careful with them. May Allah curse them! How will they deviate from Allah's path and commit this type of atrocity?

Part 3: Available at: https://www.youtube.com/watch?v=9nYGyYEA1Y8

They have shot our members because of their hidden agenda and so we took them to the hospital, yet they are afraid that the people they shot will run away? How can they station soldiers in a hospital? What is the meaning of this? And they were even bold enough to deny our brothers entrance into the hospital. Even then, if not that we had initially told our brothers that the Prophet said if you do not follow the instructions of your leader all your [good] deeds will become nullified, do you think your badgering [of them] or cocking of a gun will scare them or prevent them from gaining entrance if they want to? Since we said we would not agree, let us see if your guns will work or not.

This is my open letter to:

A. The political leader of the party called PDP [People's Democratic Party], the president of Nigeria. They call him Alhaji Musa Umaru Yar'adua and they also refer to him as GCFR [Grand Commander of the Federal Republic].
B. The inspector general of police. His name is Mr Mike Mbama Okiro.[7]
C. The third person I am directing this message to is the Director-General of State Security Service, Mr Afakirya Adua Gadzama.
D. The Chief of the Defense Staff, Air Marshal Paul Dike.
E. The Chief of the Army Staff, Lieutenant General [Abdurrahman Bello] Dambazau.[8] He is even from Kano.
P. The Chief of the Air[force] Staff, Air Marshal Paul Tarin.
G. The Chief of the Naval Staff, Vice Admiral Ishaya Ikoh Ibrahim.
H. Members of the National Assembly; senators and members of the House of Representatives.

DECLARATION OF WAR

I. The small authority, the so-called Governor ʿAlī [Modu] Sheriff.

I want these nine people to listen to this message.

You are all aware that our members (twenty faithful) have been shot with guns belonging to the military and they have been injured. We will not agree nor will we discuss it with anyone. That is why we called this lecture an open letter. And I know that it will reach you. I know it will reach you. There are those amongst us here who will specifically deliver the message to them since we made the invitation. So, let them deliver it to you so that you can hear it and for those who do not understand Hausa, they should translate the message for them, because I do not understand English. We do not accept this brutality they perpetrated. This shooting of twenty people—we do not accept it, and we will not forgive it nor let it be.

Secondly, we do not accept these insane people—that is what I call them—the insane soldiers of "Operation Flush" and the Mobile Police of "Operation Flush" who are roaming in the streets of Maiduguri. We do not accept them. As long as you want peace you should take them away from the people. Since they always mention peace, peace is your idol, so worship him now by taking the insane soldiers away. This is my message. I hope it is understood.

This is Islam and that is how Allah has made it. In this religion, there is disassociation (barāʾa), loyalty to the believers (walāʾ), and making the religion apparent (izhār al-dīn). Whatever we do is according to a plan. [The order to shoot came from higher officers and the elites.]

And now, if the Muslim community should say let us be patient that is how Allah destined it. "We will certainly test you with some fear and hunger, and with some loss of property, lives and crops. Announce the good news to those who endure patiently." (Q2:155) It is true that this is a test. But since a soldier opened fire, what does he have that is above opening fire? If it is a test, then that is the limit. What does a soldier have that exceeds opening fire? They arrested our members at Monguno under the pretense that the information they received was that they were trouble-makers.

Did you not know that they only restrained themselves because they were following orders? They always say: "When we encounter you, we will finish you within an hour or half," but we keep telling our members to be calm. Allah says: "Hatred has already been manifested in what they utter, but what their hearts conceal is greater still." (Q3:118) Therefore, allowing you to do what you want and keeping quiet will give you an opportunity to kill us tomorrow. On a similar note, a brother told me that at present, it is possible that we do not know all the brothers [who have been unjustly maltreated]. If we keep reticent, perhaps tomorrow they will go ahead and shoot the scholars.

The soul of a believer is worth more than anything. The blood of a believer is worth more than everything; it is worth more than your buildings. I hope it is understood. You think you are courageous, you can kill people and you are not afraid of death. Yet, it is you they protect and you are always surrounded by security men, while we freely move around. All these preachers, regardless of the harshness of their preaching, they can freely move around. Let everyone move around alone if he can. On our part, we move alone, let everyone move alone if he is truthful.

I swear by Allah, the Almighty, that there is every need for you to search your hearts! This attitude of yours is what has led to what happened in Palestine during the past sixty years.[9] Till now, Israel is still not at peace. Peace has eluded them. This type of attitude of yours is what led to what happened in Afghanistan. The injustice of Russia [invading] is what made that region the very center of endless *jihād*. This is what happened in Chechnya, in Kashmir, what is happening in Somalia, and what happened and is still happening in Algeria. And this is what is happening in Pakistan.

[Brotherhood is more important to us] if we lost just one of our brothers all of us will feel heartaches because: "A believer vis-à-vis another believer is like a building whose different parts enforce each other." (*Yusuf then clasped his hands with the fingers interlocked while speaking.*)

What makes me happy, yesterday, as I was bathing, is the fact that when I came out I witnessed the way our brothers informed each other of what had happened. The people who were shot, perhaps they did not even know them personally or maybe they are not of the same ethnic group, from a different town, or maybe only recently became acquainted, but when he [the messenger] came here, he could not even speak due to his anger. It was only after I calmed him down that he could explain what had happened, because of his love of his brothers. Our brothers are expensive. They are not useless. They will kill this person because they said he came to the bakery. They will kill the other person because they say he is not sane, so they took him to the *marabout*. That other person too, they will kill him saying that he is the one who made trouble, just like that.

By Allah, we will not condone it anymore and I know that Allah will test me with the speech I have made. "And We shall test you to know who are the fighters among you and who are the steadfast; and We shall test your news." (Q47:31) I am the person that says we will not accept them taking advantage of our brothers and keep quiet; and the belief that this is the test of Allah. [The period of patience is over.]

There is no reason why they brought "Operation Flush," except that they want to intimidate us by questioning us about the reason why people wear turbans in Maiduguri. Why are they attending Islamic lessons and sermons? Why are they preaching and declaring the *ṭāghūt* to be unbelievers? So, what do you want us to do? Do you want us to follow the *ṭāghūt* after Allah says we should not believe in it? Or because you said we should follow the *ṭāghūt* then we should agree to follow it? And do you think because you have a gun, you can kill us all and then we will stop?

Keep shooting. Keep shooting and you should know that if our brothers had wanted to devour the soldier they would have do so. By Allah, they would have eaten them up. Your bullets are how many? At the maximum, you have two magazines of which the total number of bullets would be sixty-two or sixty-three.[10] The people who came against you there exceed sixty-two. Shoot them? And if they catch you, and we say they should eat you up, by Allah they will. Therefore, it is a lie that it was our brothers who attacked you.

It is just their plan as part of their agenda to shoot our members, otherwise, they gave us their word in a meeting we held together that they will not attack us and that they will allow us to practice our religion. Why did they say they would shoot when the commander (*amīr*) went to them last night? Why did they beat our brothers the time we had to go to their place?

This is their system. They are oppressors. Allah is the one who says: "How [can that be]? If they overcome you, they will observe neither kinships nor pacts with you. They only give you satisfaction with their mouths, while their hearts refuse, and most of them are sinners." (Q9:8) If they have the advantage over you, they will not protect family ties, promises or any agreement with you.

We are human beings. We are Allah's slaves. This world belongs to Allah. Nigeria is not the house of anybody's father. Borno is not anybody's land, it is the land of Allah, and we will stay in it and worship Allah. We will not follow your land's law. We will not follow it. So, continue on your shooting spree. Since you have heard this sermon and you are in the town holding guns, you are ready, and in your capacity as leaders of unbelief engaging in meeting, go on.

The same way you know our homes, that is how we also know your homes. As you know the road that we intend to follow, we know the road that you will follow. As our brothers across the world have obtained the power to seize any *ṭāghūt* even when they are few, so also can we seize any *ṭāghūt*. Either you restrain your guns or you start firing from now—we shall see who the coward is.

As I am delivering this speech, during the next two days I will be in Abuja. Let us meet with you there. Last Tuesday, they said the inspector general wanted to see me. If only they detained me while this happened, I do not think there is anyone who would calm our brothers. It is all based on intention. Because of that, I will go to Abuja. I want you to deliver this message to them. And if you will not deliver it, I will give you a copy of the cassette both audio and video.

[Take my lecture to the names I mentioned. Our plans will soon be unveiled.]

Part 4: Available at: https://www.youtube.com/watch?v=yU7eVc-NOyE

The reality of the issue at hand is that we will not tell you because Allah says: "If you fear treachery from any people, throw back their treaty to them in a like manner. Allah does not like the treacherous." (Q8:58) When you fear that some people will take advantage of you; they are just deceiving you that we should be peaceful. "We know you are peaceful people, you are not trouble makers," then they will come back and kill our people. If we understand that betrayal, if you are afraid of such treachery, come out and tell them you will not accept it.

This is the reason why I said we will not write to anybody. We were writing [to officials] earlier because our scripture includes preaching as part of the religion. We were following those calls because each time we met and discussed with them, we also engaged in preaching the religion so that everybody can gain the knowledge of it, as Allah has mandated us to do.

And praise be to Allah, based on the Islamic understanding that Allah gave us, we believe that our preaching has reached your ears. You have heard our preaching, you know exactly what we are preaching and you know our intention. The people of the town have also heard our preaching, so also those of you who call yourselves scholars but have become surrogates to this government—you have heard and understood our preaching—that is why you decided to turn a blind eye to the truth by opposing us.

[*Describing the Prophet going to Khaybar.*] So, you see, sometimes it is just the preaching of one day we would accomplish, we would say: "Everyone should come. We have come with our weapons, but come and hear the preaching first."

If they come and hear the preaching and say it is not true and turn away to leave, then we will follow them and attack. This is our message. There is nothing to hide. We will not condone the shooting of our members. We will not stop nor hold any meetings with anyone again. And if you want to arrest me for this, I will be on my way to Abuja during the next two days. It is easier for you there. It is entirely your problem, but just bear in mind that whether you arrest me or not, you will not go unpunished. Allah will avenge us through the hands of the believers! I hope it is understood.

Therefore, my admonition to the brothers is for them to obey. There are some people who have their own desires and see that *jihād* is not the answer. If they are truthful, may Allah give them victory, but if they are lying, there is no way they will succeed. Do not let them to divert your attention or overwhelm your mind. It is not on the edge of the station that they do real planning. Anyone you see on the street or who sits on the bench and claims that he is planning is lying, you should know he is just a street man. Allah's Messenger is better than anyone in planning. I hope it is understood.

Let us be obedient. Whatever you are commanded to do, do it, and leave that which you are asked not to do. We should abide by the limit that was placed. We have limits. Islam has more limits than any other thing. I hope it is understood. Do not allow those deceivers who are in the habit of deceiving people to lead you astray. I hope it is understood.

[Establish a stronger connection with Allah] Brothers! Let us imbibe the culture of fasting. Night prayers should never stop us. Although it is difficult, and there is bodily tiredness, but it is the quickest means of gaining Allah's reward and martyrdom. That is how one can get a sense of courage and overcome fears. You should engage in fasting, it will increase your patience. If you engage in fasting, you will gain the spirit of endurance. You will go on for three days without eating but you will not care. I hope it is understood.

This is contrary to the soldier of *ṭāghūt* who cannot go on for one day without eating. That is why all their bags are filled with food. If you imbibe the culture of fasting like the Prophet David, who ate one day and rested the next day, or fasting Mondays and Thursdays, you can withstand any strenuous act without looking for food for three days. I hope it is understood. If you obey Allah, you will work with the strength of Allah. If you go far from Allah, Allah will leave you to yourself. I hope it is understood.

Therefore, my brothers, repent to Allah. Everyone has faults. "Every human commits sin," Allah says in a *ḥadīth qudsi* (tradition narrated from Allah). "O my servants, you sin day and night, but I forgive all sins—seek My forgiveness and you shall be forgiven." You should repent. You should improve your relationship with Allah through constant repentance.

Allah mentioned the characteristics of the *mujahidin*: He says that they are "the ones who constantly repent, constantly worship and constantly praise and thank Him." They also practice "wandering asceticism" (*siyāḥa*), which some scholars interpreted as fasting, while others said it is *jihād* in Allah's path. They are those who constantly bow and prostrate. You do not see them sitting pointlessly. Once they see that it is time for prayers they pray, recite the Qur'ān and engage in the remembrance of Allah. The time has passed for you to sit with a doubtful person, whose conversation is pointless. His doubts are dead; they have entered the grave and rot. I hope it is understood.

Now, here in Maiduguri if a person should approach you and attempt to dissuade you from crossing a tarred road, I believe it is not expected of you to waste your time sitting and conversing. There is time for everything. Therefore, you should forget about those people. Leave them to their insults. The period of their obstruction has come to an end. Hasn't it? It has come to an end.

They made an effort. Some of them came from the east, some from the west, some from the other towns, but they all collaborated as if they cannot die. But where is the truth? The hard effort of a whole year, and still you cannot find the truth. In one year, they have ended their verbal counterattack on everyone and returned to their normal way of life, except for those who engage the village people whom we preached to with the aim of refuting our preaching.

By Allah, those people tell lies. The other day I heard the cassette of someone who went to Kano to refute our preaching. He narrated an incident where the soldiers of "Operation Flush" confronted our members who refused to wear the [motorcycle] helmets, and he said: "[Yusuf] went to the office of the SSS to plead for their release." According to his story, when I approached the officers of the SSS, I was directed to the soldiers and I fell on my knees begging the soldiers. This person who told this story identified himself as a preacher.

So why would you waste your time with this type of people who are consummate liars? Forget about them and close the chapter with them. Now we have closed this chapter! We do not want anyone to approach us with all the statements of doubtful people. Do not tell us what that scholar said—and by the way who is that scholar? Who is he? Right now, our discussion should focus on Allah's enemies, who have risen now.

Today, look at the Palestinians: they have just stones in their hands, but Allah has removed fear from their hearts. You would see a young boy of 13–15 years pursuing an armed soldier holding a gun with thirty-six bullets, but the soldier would still run away. Even though the Palestinians are not operating a completely Islamic system, yet they still frighten their adversaries. It is better for us to sit and watch you kill us than for us to accept your un-Islamic system of governance.

In your case, you are engaging in acts of unbelief while you are also killing the people. Is it not even better to be killed? "Sedition (*fitna*) is worse than slaughter." (Q2:191) But you combine the two crimes, you kill, then you also disbelieve. All the atrocities Allah mentioned about the people of Quraysh—"Indeed, those who disbelieve and debar others from Allah's path have gone far astray" (Q4:167)—they have also committed it with the help of their traditional scholars.

Each time we mention the traditional scholars, I do not want you to think that I am referring to the teachers who use pen and ink (*zawre*). No, the Izala scholars are the traditional scholars. Never again should you refer to the teachers of pen and ink as traditional scholars. The traditional scholars are the Izala, the scholars of democracy, and George Bush's students. They are the traditional scholars and the hypocrites. These traditional scholars should know that the harm they cause, and that of their mentors, is on the forefront of our agenda. We will no longer be deceived by them.

They should go and give their masters advice because now the time has passed for study, preaching or rebuttal. They should change their strategy and inform their masters to change their strategy, because our movement has changed. We are not the people who changed the situation; you were the people who changed it with your hands. You shot our members but you are bent on repeating this again? Since you shot our brothers, they consoled themselves, took those injured to the hospital and they also took the corpses for funeral without confronting you. Why would they gather soldiers to cork their guns and come back? Is it not for killing more people?

I want to inform the people whose names I mentioned earlier, the so-called leader, the inspector general of police, the director-general of SSS, and others, and the governors, the soldier who shot our members, we will soon know whether he is a patriot of Nigeria or not: You have no sense at all. So, you will not understand my statements alone.

However, let me inform you in clear terms that he started something which is beyond him. Because our initial agreement with you, what we have been saying is that we will practice our religion, not caring about anyone else, as long as they did not harass us or prevent us from our religion. Any day in which they prevent us from our religion, we will look for another place and migrate there. If there is no place to which we can migrate, then we will stay where we are, finding a place to practice our religion.

Or is it not so? And let me tell you that this attack that was launched upon our members, if there were women among them, they would not have hesitated [to shoot them]. They can even shoot a pregnant woman the way we witnessed how they shoot children. A soldier, who aimed a killing-shot at people indiscriminately, can shoot a pregnant woman.

In our study center, women do attend with their *hijāb*. Some brothers carry women on their motorcycles but then they would say that the soldier was afraid [of them attacking]. Why would he be afraid? Why would he claim to be a soldier? He claims to be afraid [of being attacked]—so that was why he shot? You are the people giving him this proof that he saw plenty people, but he was afraid and so he shot [at them]. Why would he be afraid? Is he not a soldier?

So tomorrow they will shoot a woman and her child, and say that he was afraid— that was why he shot [at them]. He can shoot a pregnant woman just the same way as a boy. He shot our brother between his groin and stomach. He can also shoot a pregnant woman, and the bullet will penetrate deep into her body. Then you will say that he was afraid—that was why he shot.

Therefore, we need to put an end to these tribulations. We do not want you to say that they should not take the law into their hands, because you have already taken the law in your hands. You have perpetrated atrocities and brutalities. What crime did we commit? Is it wrong to perform a funeral? People have gone to bury their dead, but you attacked them. And they were taken to hospital, yet you prevented our members from donating blood to those in mortal need? We will go and donate blood, so you should come out and shoot. You should come out and shoot.

Inform your soldiers of "Operation Flush" that we will go and donate blood, so they should come out and shoot. We will no longer be bothered by your intimidation or harassment. You shoot, you kill. It is martyrdom!

Part 5: Available at: https://www.youtube.com/watch?v=mMYkSvxxOtA

Brothers, you did nothing to warrant their disdain. You do not belong to the opposition, PDP, nor do you belong to either the ANPP or the AD.[11] It is simply because of your faith in Allah and your conviction that it is only Allah's laws which should be followed, and not their democracy—that is why they display their hatred towards you. At no point in time should any soldier or nationalist fight you nor should you look for any other reason why they are fighting you. Do not even waste your time looking for alternative reasons.

Do not say: "If we had done it like this, it would have..." No! He [the soldier] does not love you simply because you love Allah. There is nothing that connects us to them: "They did not begrudge them except that they believed in Allah, the All-Mighty, the

All-Praiseworthy." (Q85:8) There are so many people in this town, why is it that they do not harass them? Why is it that they are not pressured? Whose corn flour did you ever pour away? Whose milk have we spilled? Whose belongings did we take from their house? Whose home have we looted? What did we ever take or loot?

Just because we said what Allah says, the Prophet says anytime they see us they would insult the turban [we wear] and our sticks. Once they see us, the discussion would turn to us. That is not enough, now again they shoot us with guns, just like that? They killed our brothers for no justifiable reason. This is my explanation. We do not agree, and we are not going to talk to anyone. I will not call anyone on the phone nor will I write letters to anyone as I used to do. That time has passed; now is not the time for writing. We will not write a paper or broadcast for anyone to read.

This is the explanation. I wanted to bring it out in the sermon, but not everyone would hear. As a result, my explanation is that we will not forgive the shooting of our twenty brothers. We will not allow them [soldiers] to go scot-free, nor will we withdraw. We will not leave nor will we listen to anybody. This is the original chaos that you have been talking about, and you were the ones who initiated it. You did it! You brought insane people, gave them guns with bullets, and the permission to shoot us. No soldier will shoot a gun without permission. Do not take us as fools or people who do not know what they are doing. "The soldier became scared and he shot."

No, you gave them the permission to shoot so they did. We will not condone this brutality because if we overlooked it, we have brothers in many other places with smaller population [who would be vulnerable]. We have brothers in Niger, Sokoto, Kano, Abuja—you have all their records. You know where they are. If you can shoot twenty people in Maiduguri and go scot-free, what do you think they will do to our brothers in other places whose population is not more than twenty people?

They are good at calling people and threatening them. Is this what is going to be happening to our members in other places? There is no trust. It is not only today they started promising us with their claim that: "In the future this will never happen again." It is a lie. Since we saw our members' blood, since we saw bullets being removed from their bodies, since we saw the types of pain they suffered, since we have faced what we faced because of our care for them, we will not condone this anymore. I keep repeating myself because I want people to know that we have been pushed against the wall.

There was a time they initiated useless and humiliating calls. That period was a time of testing. We condoned and tolerated their brutalities. At that time, they would phone me, and inform me that I am being invited to the office of the SSS. Then I would visit their office and wait for three hours, only for them to tell me that they were having a meeting and that the director is not around. They would then ask me to go, but come back the next day. Then I would come back and the next day they would call me.

Why did I do that? I wanted them to understand the goal of our preaching. That is the nature of the Sunna, and we exercised the required patience. But I thank Allah our preaching has reached many places, some through audio cassette, while some people heard about our preaching through word of mouth alone. Now they just inform us that someone has gone ahead to commission [the building of] a Friday mosque. The questions he asked us were not more than two hours. He came and asked us, "this preaching that you do...?" We gave him the evidence.

What if I am asked so-and-so? We gave him the evidence. That is it—then he accepted it and told the truth to his people. However, his people denounced him, and claimed that the religion of the land should only be based upon the Izala. They told him that if he refuses to follow the Izala, he should leave. The man went ahead and opened a mosque with his followers and he continued with the preaching. So this example; is it by our preaching? Is it by our teaching? Allah has spread the message and everybody has heard. I hope it is understood.

[Our brothers have passed the test] We saw a brother with bullets in his body, while he was being admonished to be patient. He told us that he has now understood the truth. This is the Sunna. Another brother said that, by Allah, "We are enjoying [this]." He was asking his brothers about other brothers while we were all feeling sorry for him. We are grateful to Allah that we were not among the people Allah describes "of mankind are some who say":

> There are some people who say: "We believe in Allah," but if one of them is injured because of Allah, he reckons the persecution of men like Allah's punishment. If, however, victory comes from your Lord, they will say: "We were with you." Does not Allah know better what is in the breasts of the whole of mankind? (Q29:10)

Our brothers were only concerned about their other brothers. Among the devotional acts that are encouraged after prayers is the visitation of the wounded, because they need rest and sleep. But the way our brothers love each other, you will see they want to visit them all the time. This is good but they require rest therefore we must organize the visitation [times]. If you see the way our brothers love one another and you still do not understand, then Allah will give them [the police] the opportunity to further brutalize them.

You should prepare your guns, because we know you are preparing. Some days back, during their training, one of them said that they would get rid of us very soon. We know for sure that, even if you attack us with all your military strength and planes, those who will survive will continue, and not hesitate to wage *jihād*. Whether you attack us openly or by surprise, whether you arrest us or open fire on us at our study center, or when we are going home, it makes no difference. We do not trust these insane people who are beating our brothers without reason.

Even if you do not attack, it is Allah who protected us, not you. It is not as if you did not intend to attack. We know that every single bullet you brought out today was meant for us. There is a brother who does not have a motorcycle, so he does not have anything. A soldier approached him and told him *salām 'alaykum*, but he did not respond. Why would he respond to a cursed unbeliever? We say it, unbeliever! The soldier arrested and beat up the brother because of his refusal to respond to his greetings. We do not forget this incident.

The soldier's name is 10–10.[12] Let him add ninety-ninety to become hundred-hundred. You know him, you soldiers. There is no reason to humiliate people in the town because they are practicing their religion with their Book and the practice of the Prophet of Allah. We are practicing our religion without oppressing anyone; our members were attacked on their way to the burial ground. If you visit them, they smell only like blood.

And someone will come and tell us that it is predestined. Did the one who wounded our members tell you something about predestination? If Allah tries someone, He cautions the believer to be patient, but not the person who wounded him. Do you understand? Since you have shot our members, sit down in your capacity as soldiers—let them sit down, and enjoy what they did the same way the governor is enjoying what he did.

Their leader said that they were only defending themselves; they are not at fault. He said our members are guilty, why did they alight from their vehicles? But why would they not alight when you [soldiers] are attacking their brothers? If they had remained where they were, it would have meant that they defied the order of the Holy Prophet when he said believers are like one single body.

We agree with this notion that soldiers do not engage in politics and reconciliation. Let them refrain from reconciliation. We will not stop repeating ourselves that we are not going to condone the shooting of our brothers, and we will not let it go scot-free. If this sermon is too harsh for you, then, I am here. It is easy to arrest me or kill me. We do not agree, and we will not let him go scot-free. I hope it is understood.

We are tired of this deception. I am also tired of giving excuses to the cow without seeing the horn. Do you understand that? So, follow the movement, follow the path of the Sunna, submit to the leaders, and you will be surprised, by Allah's permission. I pray to Allah to help us. This is the message. What we have said that is correct, may Allah give us the reward and may He forgive us our errors.

And before we pray, I want to emphasize the importance of repentance, night prayers, fasting, as well as the praising of Allah, and the recitation of the Qur'ān. Everyone should stay where he is—we are not yet finished. We should be steadfast with the congregational prayer, remembrance of Allah, recitation of the Qur'ān and most importantly, obedience. Whatever you are instructed to do, even if you will die, go ahead and do it. Whatever they forbid you from doing, even if you will die, do not do it.

Do you understand this? Everything that you are asked to do, even if you will die, go and do it, do not come back and say: "When I went...?" No! When you go, *its an act of terrorism* [handwritten annotation]

even if you will die, go and do it. Don't you see how they put bombs on people, instructing them to leave, so they will go and explode [in suicide attacks]? And yet they are happy.

You should be like that. Whatever they forbid you from doing, even if you will die, do not do it. [*Describing the necessary obedience.*]

The brothers who were injured, may Allah heal them. And may Allah make their blood which they shed to be the blood that will earn them a reward from Allah. And may Allah make their injury, an injury with which they will be resurrected, fresh on the Day of Resurrection, with the fragrance of musk. Those who donated blood from their bodies, may Allah grant them the reward of paradise based on their brotherhood.

Those who perpetrated this act of terrorism against us, may Allah avenge for us, together with those who supported them by sending these insane people into our city. We pray to Allah to destroy them. Let us all pray towards that.

After that, I will instruct our security men, the *ḥisba* people, and our brothers who collect donations, to do so from each row on behalf of our brothers who are in the hospital. I repeat, only those who I mentioned: the security men and the people of *ḥisba*. They should seek assistance because of these injured brothers. Aside from the fractures they sustained, every single one of them—if they need to undergo an operation to remove the bullet in their bodies, it will cost 35,000 *naira* [$250], apart from the blood test and other costs. Even now, we paid for one brother before we came for this lecture. Since they are your brothers, whatever happens to them is your responsibility, so I implore everyone to show his brotherhood here between him and Allah.

Then again, please help them with prayers. And may Allah strengthen their minds. Now, these brothers if you wage *jihād* with them, they will not listen to the people who inflicted this pain on them. Anyway, this is the benefit of trials. And may Allah improve their health, strengthen their bodies, and increase their enthusiasm. Discussion of the bravery of early Muslims]

Therefore, this is the miracle of the religion of Islam, and Allah will raise them to work for the religion of Islam. The person who crippled you because you said you want to work for your religion, he did not kill you? He said, "I will kill them, finish." We can only kill ourselves, the two parties, finish.

As a result, the people of the town should know the people who are the initiators of this chaos. You are saying to us that we are the initiators of this chaos, but now you have seen your governor, who brought the soldiers of the land, who are following his command—he created it and bought cars for them. They blocked our brothers who were going for a funeral and shot twenty people, and they did not feel any remorse. Therefore, we said we do not accept the presence of these soldiers in the town. They should remove them immediately, if they want peace. If they do not remove them, then you, the people of the town, should know those who are the initiators of chaos. Even if they remove them, the blood of our brothers will not be spilled in vain. This is my message.

During the period 26–29 July 2009 approximately 1,000 Nigerians, mostly members of Boko Haram, were killed in Maiduguri, as well as other cities, and their complex at the Ibn Taymiyya Center was destroyed. Muhammad Yusuf was taken captive.

20

INTERROGATION OF MUHAMMAD YUSUF

BY NIGERIAN SECURITY FORCES

(30 JULY 2009)

Just before his extrajudicial killing by Nigerian security forces, Yusuf was interrogated in Maiduguri. This interrogation contradicts statements by the Nigerian Police that Yusuf was executed because of a shoot-out between him and the security forces. Below is a transcript of the interrogation.

Interrogator [=I]: We went to your house yesterday and we saw a lot of animals, syringes and materials used for making bombs, why were you keeping those materials?

Yusuf [=Y]: Like I told you, to protect myself...

I: [Cuts in] To protect yourself how? Are there not the authorities, the law enforcement agencies [who can protect you]?

Y: The authorities, the law enforcement agents are the same people fighting me...

I: What did you do?

Y: I don't know what I did... I am only propagating my religion, Islam.

I: But I am also a Muslim...

Y: I don't know why you refuse to accept my own [Islam].

I: Why should you say *boko* is *ḥaram* (forbidden)?

Y: Of course, it is *ḥaram*.

I: Why did you say that?

Yusuf: The reasons are so many...

I: The trousers you are wearing...

Y: [Cuts in] ...they are pure cotton, and cotton belongs to Allah

I: But Allah said in the Qur'ān *'iqra'* (read),[1] that people should seek knowledge...

Y: That's correct, but not the knowledge that contravenes the teachings of Islam. All knowledge that contradicts Islam is prohibited by the Almighty... *sihiri* (sorcery or magic) is knowledge, but Allah has forbidden it; *shirk* (polytheism or sharing or associating partners with Allah) is knowledge, but Allah has forbidden it; astronomy is knowledge, but Allah has forbidden it...

I: At your place we found computers, syringes—aren't all of them products of knowledge?

Y: They are purely technological things, not *boko*... and westernization is different.

I: How come you are eating good food—look at you, looking healthy—you are driving good cars, and wearing good clothes while you are forcing your followers to sell their belongings and live mostly on *dabino* (dates) and water?

Y: That is not true. Everybody is living according to his means. Even you are different. Whoever you see driving good cars that is because he can afford them, and whoever you see living in want, that also means that the person doesn't have the wherewithal.

I: Why did you abandon your mosque and your compound?

Y: Because you went and opened fire there...

I: But you sent your people there to die in the fire?

Y: No, my people have left the place.

I: What about those who came to fight for you... where and where do you have followers?

Y: You have chased all of them away.

I: Apart from Maiduguri...

Y: There are some in Bauchi but police chased them away even before now; there are some in Gombe, police went to their house and chased away; there are some in Yola, Adamawa, police attacked them, same with those in Jalingo, Taraba State. It was after they chased them away that they turned to us here in Maiduguri.

I: What happened to your hand?

Y: I fell.[2]

I: In this town [Maiduguri], how many areas do you have?

Y: The headquarters is right here.

I: What about other branches?

Y: We have in Gwange, Bulunkutu...

I: Where they intercepted weapons the other day, right?

Y: [Laughs] Intercepted weapons?

I: What about your 2IC [second-in-command]... because they said you have soldiers, police, etc?

Y: That is not true...

I: But don't you have a 2IC, who acts in your absence?

Y: I have...

INTERROGATION OF MUHAMMAD YUSUF

I: What is his name?

Y: Mallam Abubakar Shekau.

I: Where is he now?

Y: I don't know.

I: Who and who escaped with you?

Y: I did not run with anybody.

I: Who are your sponsors, here at home or abroad?

Y: Nobody.

I: No, tell us the truth...

Y: *Insha Allah* (if Allah wills), I won't lie to you...

I: You have a farm around Benishek?

Y: Yes.

I: Now, you have made us kill people who are innocent. What do you have to say?

Y: You bear responsibility for all those you killed.

I: What about those killed by your followers?

Y: My followers did not kill anybody.

I: What about those killed among your followers?

Y: Those killed among my followers, whoever killed them are those who committed the crime.

I: Where are you from originally?

Y: I hail from Yobe State.

I: Where in Yobe State?

Y: Jakusko.

I: What about your father?

Y: He is also from Jakusko.

I: What about your mother?

Y: She is from Gashua.

I: Have you ever travelled abroad?

Y: Only on hajj (pilgrimage).

I: What year was that?

Y: 2003 and 2004.

Muhammad Yusuf was executed sometime after this interview on 30 July 2009.[3]

PART THREE

MAKING NIGERIA UNGOVERNABLE
(2009–2012)

Michael Nwankpa

It is difficult to prove that Boko Haram would still have embraced terrorism regardless of whether Yusuf was killed.[1] Those who support the idea that Boko Haram was headed in that direction base their argument on evidence of some radical views in Yusuf's preaching (texts 11–19). Such extreme views appear incompatible with the Nigerian federal secular state, but Murray Last argues that *sharīʿa* can operate successfully within the Nigerian constitution, although not as interpreted by supremacist groups like Boko Haram.[2]

To some extent, we can argue that *sharīʿa* already exists alongside the Nigerian constitution. Therefore, it is not so much about allowing Muslims the freedom to choose to be judged by *sharīʿa* rule; rather it is the politicization of *sharīʿa*—the manipulation of *sharīʿa* to whip up religious sentiments among disaffected youths for political advantage to the elites—that constitutes a danger. The response of the northern Muslim intellectuals, religious and political elites to Yusuf's claims are equally interesting. While frequently admitting the validity of these claims, we can see that they prefer to remain quietist rather than taking them to their logical conclusion. All too often, as in text 3, Yusuf was confronted by appeals to respect authority, rather than an actual refutation of what he believed.

The Boko Haram crisis attracted legislative response from government (both domestic and external). In 2011, the Nigerian senate passed the new anti-terrorism legislation,[3] and by June 2013, Boko Haram became the first group to be proscribed under this law. At the request of the Nigerian government, the United Kingdom blacklisted Boko Haram in July 2013, while the United States followed suit in

November 2013. Other countries and alliances, such as Australia and the European Union, only declared Boko Haram to be a terrorist organization in 2014, following Boko Haram's brazen kidnapping of boarding-school girls in Chibok area of Borno State on 14 April 2014.[4]

The outlawing of Boko Haram by the Nigerian government and external governments has had very minimal effect on the group, as Boko Haram has ramped up its terrorist attacks and transformed itself into the deadliest terror group in the world.[5] Proscription of Boko Haram only increased the group's international visibility, and earned it the (belated) attention of Salafi-jihadi groups such as al-Qaeda, al-Shabab and ISIS (see text 60). Undoubtedly, Boko Haram continues to benefit immensely from the media coverage and the cooperation (ideological, operational and tactical/ strategic) with other affiliated terrorist networks.

During this period, Boko Haram's strategic attack on the security forces and government symbols shifted to terrorist attacks against civilians. This shift in targets and the brutality of these attacks represent a strong external influence and indicate Boko Haram's little need for popular support. Nevertheless, the group divided towards the end of this period, as its leaders are not all agreed on this new strategy, especially the attacks on Muslims (text 35). Before examining the next batch of translated texts that show how Boko Haram transmuted into a full-blown violent group, it is important to analyze the economic factors and warfare strategy that evolved during this period of the insurgency.

Economic Factors

Effects of the Nigerian industrialization projects of the 1970s and the austerity program of the 1980s are still visible today. For example, the large-scale irrigation schemes and damming process carried out in most northern states during those decades have contributed to the drying up of Lake Chad (an important source of water and economic survival to northern Nigeria and the neighboring countries of Chad, Cameroon and Niger). This has, in addition to the desertification of the Sahel, produced a long-term devastating effect on the economic livelihood of people in the northeast region (scarce water and scarce grazing land to support the core northern economy of fishing, farming and cattle rearing) and contributed to the social and ethno-religious tensions across the whole of the north, including the Middle Belt.

Globalization, which is coterminous with Western capitalism, is viewed in a negative light in the north, as it has contributed to the underdevelopment of countries like Nigeria.[6] In Nigeria, however, the economic marginalization was more palpable in the north than the south. "If in global terms, Nigeria was on the periphery, Northern Nigeria was the periphery of the periphery."[7]

Among the results there have been recurrent clashes between Hausa-Fulani herders and the sedentary non-Fulani (largely Christians) farmers in the Middle Belt states of Kaduna and Plateau in their contest for scarce arable land. These conflicts predate the Boko Haram crisis and are commonly (but wrongly) characterized as ethno-religious conflicts. The reality is that these conflicts are economically based, but capable of taking on a religious dimension.

While the north has produced more Nigerian presidents and heads of state than the other regions, this fact has not translated into economic wealth for the northern masses. They have remained poor and alienated with little hope of economic and social mobility. One is tempted, therefore, to see Boko Haram as the reflection of the region's poverty. This may be the case indirectly; however, such a stance finds little to no support within the Boko Haram texts (the exception is text 35 from Ansaru). Yusuf and Shekau hardly ever mention poverty, nor do they promote a vision of society that would alleviate northeastern Nigeria's basic economic issues.

If Boko Haram was partially influenced at the initial phase by grievance, including harsh socio-economic conditions, teeming youth unemployment, lack of economic and social mobility, elite greed and corruption and religious complacency, this is no longer the case. The vision of Yusuf, in his claim before his death, to "set up a new society whose sole purpose was to be close to Allah,"[8] is no longer tenable. Rather, Boko Haram, in its current form, is driven by a wanton desire for power.

While the conflict of interest between local and global objectives and choice of tactics, especially violence against the local Muslim civilian population, may have fractured Boko Haram into several factions, the huge economic benefits from ransom money and other illicit economic activities help to patch the relationship between them. For instance, Boko Haram and Ansaru (see texts 31, 35–6) may have cooperated in the 2013 kidnap of the French family of seven in northern Cameroon, with Boko Haram providing cover in its Borno-controlled base for the share of the $3.14 million ransom paid for the release of the abductees.[9] It is also not unlikely that Boko Haram is used for paid-to-kill missions. Many locals may have hired Boko Haram to settle personal scores, including business owners and local politicians, especially for eliminating their rivals (see synopsis, text 29).

The insurgent economy extends to the government and its officials. For instance, it is quite alarming to see a ten-fold increase in Nigeria's defence budget allocations, from 100 billion *naira* ($625 million) in 2010 to 1 trillion *naira* ($6.25 billion) in 2014.[10] Ostensibly, the war against Boko Haram is the main motivation for this increase, as this period marked an escalation in the group's activities.

Evidently, the Nigerian government benefited from the proscription of Boko Haram as an international terrorist organization as it enables them to tap into the Global War on Terror. Branding Boko Haram an international terrorist group means that international cooperation is needed to counter Boko Haram's threat. As such, the Nigerian government receives external support ranging from counter-terrorism training, surveillance equipment, and security aid. However, the aid has produced unhelpful consequences as it has fueled corruption among public officials including politicians and top military personnel. The external loans and aid, as well as the ever growing defence budget (with an apparent lack of transparency and oversight mechanism), keep the wheels of corruption well-oiled.

Warfare Strategy

It is difficult to give an accurate number of Boko Haram fighters. At the end of 2014, most Boko Haram analysts put the figure at 5,000–15,000.[11] But this number has surely fluctuated. In 2013, at the height of the state of emergency, Boko Haram was forced to return to the guerrilla tactics of hit-and-run, as the heavy presence of the military with the curfews, military check-points and house-to-house searches made it difficult for Boko Haram to operate in Maiduguri and the major cities in the northeast. Boko Haram attacked mainly villages on the outskirts of Maiduguri during this period, using armed assault (firearms) and other incendiary devices (that involved torching houses).

It is not uncommon in Nigeria for private car owners to use their vehicles for public transportation, as there are fewer state-owned vehicles. Boko Haram has taken advantage of this. Some of the northern states have banned the use of certain means of transportation, such as motorbikes, and also made efforts to identify genuine transport workers, but these measures have had very little impact, just like the military checkpoints sprawling across the major roads. It is also not uncommon for soldiers at the checkpoints to collect bribes from motorists.

Boko Haram utilized a wide variety of tactics during this initial period, including ambush, assassination, kidnapping and hostage taking, armed assault mainly via firearms, explosives—largely improvised explosive devices (IEDs) (including car bombing, and remote-controlled bombing)—arson, and finally suicide bombing for its diverse targets. Its targets included private property and citizens, security personnel (military, police and navy) and security bases (such as military barracks and police stations), government, religious institutions and leaders, and educational establishments. Each target often (but not always) attracted a distinct form of tactics and a variety of tactics could be used in any one sequence of terrorist attacks.

Although the now-defunct Joint Task Force (JTF) arrested and killed several Boko Haram top commanders in 2012 (including Abubakr Adam Kambar, Abu Qaqa, Muhammad Suleiman, Mallam Ghali and Kabiru Sokoto—who is currently serving a life sentence),[12] the group managed to rebound during 2014. Boko Haram's statements during this period reveal the group to be in search of a mission, and still a bit unsure of itself. Some of the documents here lack the extensive Qur'ānic citations characteristic of the other phases of the group's existence.

21

STATEMENT OF SANI UMARU

(9 AUGUST 2009)

This statement was the first sign that Boko Haram did not actually disappear with the murder of Muhammad Yusuf. However, Sani Umaru did not remain the leader of the group for very long, and it took several years for the threats listed in this missive to become a reality. The continuity of language and enemies with the pre-July 2009 Boko Haram materials is obvious. For the first time, however, the group begins aligning itself with al-Qaeda (point no. 2) and protesting the name accorded to it by the wider world. It is significant that in Umaru's statement this alignment with al-Qaeda and protest takes precedence even over the veneration of Yusuf (point no. 3).

1) First of all, that Boko Haram does not in any way mean "Western education" as the infidel media continue to portray us. Boko Haram means "Western civilization" is forbidden. The difference is that while the first gives the impression that we are opposed to formal education coming from the West, that is Europe, which is not true, the second affirms our belief in the supremacy of Islamic culture (not education), for culture is broader, it includes education, but is not determined by Western education. In this case, we are talking of Western ways of life which include: constitutional provisions if these relate to, for instance, the rights and privileges of women, the idea of homosexuality, lesbianism, sanctions in cases of terrible crimes like drug trafficking, rape of infants, multi-party democracy in an overwhelmingly Islamic country like Nigeria, blue [pornographic] films, prostitution, drinking beer and alcohol, and many others that stand in opposition to Islamic civilization.

2) That the Boko Haram is an Islamic Revolution whose impact is not limited to northern Nigeria, in fact, we are spread across all the 36 states in Nigeria, and Boko Haram is just a version of al-Qaeda which we align with and respect. We support Osama bin Laden, we shall carry out his command in Nigeria until the country is totally Islamized, which is according to the wish of Allah.

3) That Mallam [Muhammad] Yusuf has not died in vain and he is a martyr. His ideas will live forever.

4) That Boko Haram lost over 1,000 of our martyred members killed by the wicked Nigerian army and police [who were] mostly of southern Nigeria extraction. That the southern states, especially the infidel Yoruba, Igbo and Ijaw unbelievers will be our immediate target.

5) That the killing of our leaders in a callous, wicked and malicious manner will not in any way deter us. They have lost their lives in the struggle for Allah.

Having made the following statement, we hereby reinstate our demands:

A) That we have started a *jihād* in Nigeria which no force on earth can stop. The aim is to Islamize Nigeria, and to ensure the rule of the majority Muslims in the country. We will teach Nigeria a lesson, a very bitter one.

B) That from the month of August, we shall carry out a series of bombings in both southern and northern Nigerian cities, beginning with Lagos, Ibadan, Enugu and Port Harcourt. The bombing will not stop until *sharī'a* [is implemented] and Western civilization is wiped from Nigeria. We will not stop until these evil cities are turned into ashes.

C) That we shall make the country ungovernable, kill and eliminate irresponsible political leaders of all leanings, hunt and gun down those who oppose the rule of *sharī'a* in Nigeria and ensure that the infidel does not go unpunished.

D) We promise the West and southern Nigeria a horrible pastime. We shall focus on these areas which are the empire of the devil, and have been those encouraging and sponsoring Western civilization on the shores of Nigeria.

E) We call on all northerners in the Muslim States to quit following the wicked political parties leading the country, the corrupt, irresponsible, criminal, murderous political leadership, and join the struggle for [an] Islamic society that will be corruption-free, sodomy-free, where security will be guaranteed and there will be peace under Islam.

f) That very soon, we shall stir Lagos, the evil city, and Nigeria's southwest and southeast, in a way no one has ever done before.

Allahu Akbar!

Either you are for us or against us!

Mallam Sani Umaru, acting leader, Boko Haram

Signed: 9 August 2009[1]

22(A)

DOCUMENTS FROM ADVICE
AND SHARI'I INSTRUCTION

BY SHAYKH ABU AL-HASAN RASHID AL-BULAYDI
TO THE FIGHTERS IN NIGERIA

(RELEASED 13 APRIL 2017)

[Trans. David Cook]
Available at: https://azelin.files.wordpress.com/2017/04/shaykh-abucc
8wal-hcca3asan-rashicc84d-22sharicc84ah-advice-and-guidance-for-the-
mujacc84hidicc84n-of-nigeria22.pdf

This group of documents is associated with Abu al-Hasan Rashid al-Bulaydi, the shari'a advisor for al-Qaeda in the Islamic Maghreb (AQIM), and details the close relations between Boko Haram and al-Qaeda affiliates that date to the period of the July 2009 uprising, if not before. However, the most interesting documents are not the lengthy exposition by al-Rashid to Boko Haram concerning the relationship between Islamic legal principles and combat (dated 18 October 2011), but the letters indicating the close relations between AQIM and Boko Haram during this early period. Why precisely this document cache was released in April 2017 is something of a mystery, as the latest document in the trove is from 2011. However, when one considers the now public nature of the internal Boko Haram disagreements over how to treat Muslims and apply the shari'a, it seems likely that these documents are designed to highlight AQIM's early support for Boko Haram during its fledgling years (2009–11), both from a training as well as a financial point of view—note the inclusion of a receipt for 200,000 euros from 5 July 2010, which seems irrelevant at present other than as a reminder—as well as to possibly convince some elements of Boko Haram dissatisfied with Shekau's leadership to join al-Qaeda.

This latter possibility finds support in the narrative created in the documents: there are letters from 'Abd al-Wadud, who of AQIM is the one person most closely associated with a policy of gradualism in the application of sharīʿa, *as well as an undated letter from elements of Boko Haram's core members critiquing Shekau's leadership and Islamic knowledge along the lines that will be developed by Ansaru (texts 32, 36–37) and Mamman Nur (text 72). This letter is placed in its approximate chronological order after text 27 as text 22(B). Al-Rashid's* Advice, *which has not been translated due to its length, also takes this more moderate line. If this interpretation is correct, then while these documents are valuable, they are also highly selective, and designed to bolster AQIM's position as an elder organization in the jihadi family, having helped Boko Haram during its formative years, now wanting to help (or take advantage of) it again at its current low point. Note that through all the texts published in this cache Boko Haram is referred to as "the group," never by its actual name(s).*

From Abu Zayd 'Abd al-Hamid to our shaykh and commander Abu Musaʿb 'Abd al-Wadud:[1]

Subject: A message from the commander of Nigerian Group.

Three brothers sent from the commander of the Nigerian group, who is Abubakar Shekau, arrived as a delegation to us. He is the one who took command after the killing of the Imam Muhammad Yusuf. The three are the brother Abu Muhammad, the commander of the troop, and the two brothers Khalid al-Barnawi and Abu Rayhana. They had previously lived with us in this border region [with] the Tariq b. Ziyad Battalion, so we know them well, and they have mentioned for us the reason for their coming, which was the event that happened recently in Nigeria. With that, they agreed to come to us so that they could study with us the possibility of a union, refuge or connection that would exist between us.

The contents of their message were:

1. They request that there be a connection between their commander and the commander of AQIM, and under that

a. The establishment of a [safe] place between us to be delineated in Niger.

2. Request for mutual assistance between us and they mentioned that they have a large problem with weapons and money.

3. Extracting the brothers from Nigeria to here [the Malian desert] in order to train with us.

4. Receiving advice from us on how to carry out *jihād* in the land of Nigeria.

DOCUMENTS FROM ADVICE AND SHARI'I INSTRUCTION

We advised them of the following points:

1. First of all, with regard to the question of training, I mentioned to them that training is divided into two parts: True training, in which the fighter after completion of the training period, has to translate what he has learned in the training camp into the field. This cannot be time-limited. As for the theoretical training it is dependent upon the training materials obtainable in the training camp, so its benefit for the fighter is less.

2. As for the question of safe house between us in Niger, this will be easy by Allah's grace. But from experience, its existence will be short, if news of it spreads among the brothers, so it would be better if it were kept in complete secrecy, known only to a small number of the brothers and not written down anywhere.

3. As for the question of the union, I mentioned to them that this was an easy matter and could be accomplished at any time and quickly, if Allah wishes.

Written on Monday 3 Ramadan 1430 [24 August 2009]

This message is part of the response from the Shaykh 'Abd al-Wadud.

Date: 10 Ramadan 1430 [31 September 2009]

As a starter, we lift, from me directly, and from all the fighters indirectly, our condolences and consolations to you and all your armies, and to the rest of the Muslims in Nigeria in the wake of the killing of the prominent Imam Muhammad Yusuf, who we consider to be a martyr, although we do not state anyone to be pure before Allah, and the killing of the hundreds of our innocent brothers, who had no crime, other than they said: "Our Lord is Allah." (Q22:40)

We affirm to you with regard to this violent action that your brothers in AQIM stand with you, supporting you and assisting you, and sharing in your joy and sadness.

We promise to you that we will transform this pure blood into a fire that will burn the bodies of the tyrants (*tawāghīt*), and a light by which our brothers will illuminate their path to raise the Word of Allah to the highest (Q9:41), and make the word of the unbelievers the lowest, by a more penetrating resolution and a firmer will.

We are happy at the arrival of your delegation, and we see it as an initiative for good towards a new era which will confound the Crusader Jewish plan of aggression towards Islam and its people in the coastal [African] nations and in Africa generally: "Do not be faint-hearted and do not grieve; you will have the upper hand if you are true believers." (Q3:139)

As for the aid and support you have requested of us, we ask the Master to place us at the service of our brothers, as we consider it possible and welcome. For further detail:

1. The question of continuous and firm union between us, we welcome it, and see it as a hasty necessity to strengthen it, alter it, and raise it to a continuous level.

2. The question of defining the point of union is among the important necessary issues, and we consider this problem to be left to the efforts of the guiding brothers and the people of knowledge in the land, from both of us.

3. The question of receiving waves of Nigerian brothers for the goal of training: to start we agree to supply what aid we can in this way, and we will leave the entry ranks, numbers of the first wave and the length of training up to the brothers who are responsible in the southern sector. They know their abilities best.

4. The question of monetary support is not a problem to the extent that we have it, so we have added some extra. The limited support can be the responsibility of the Saharan commander or whoever he deputizes but the larger outlays will remain under the realm of our possible obtaining of them, so the issue is unclear. Soon we will spend all our efforts in this matter.

5. As for what is specifically connected to weaponry support, this is not a problem, because of their abundance. The matter will be studied by the specialized leadership as to the amount in stock and the methods of supply.

6. The question of the proclamation of the *jihād* in Nigeria, we advise not to take any decision or to proclaim anything under the influence of shock, but to put it off until the time is ripe from all perspectives with calm nerves, together with a comprehensive consultation with the jihad leaders in the Islamic world. The present stage is one of good preparation, watching and planning.

    It is necessary to mobilize the Muslim community in Nigeria to embrace the *mujāhidin*; then it is necessary to prepare well by training and educating the *mujāhidin*, and also gathering all the requisite military equipment, especially explosive materials. [...]

7. As for the types of mutual cooperation we see as possible, subordination of our media to the interests of your issue, such as publication of your news and distribution of your speeches and communiques, making your group known, and exposing the crimes of the *ṭawāghīt* in Nigeria. [On 2 October 2010, al-Andalus media published a sermon by Abubakar Shekau. The sermon, which celebrated 'Id al-Fitri was the first observed AQIM dissemination of an official message attributed to a group other than al-Qaeda or an affiliate.]

There remains the question of the union between us, but this is an easy matter, and we advise taking the necessary security measures: keeping complete secrecy in communication both in content and in the manner of delivery. And not publishing news of which there is no need among the *mujahidin*.

This, and do not forget to convey our greetings to all the brothers with you and to tell them that our hearts are with them, that they should be patient, and take heart. Victory comes with patience, and ease with hardship.

—Your brother Abu Musa'b 'Abd al-Wadud, commander of AQIM

[...]

In reality, the waves of youths coming from Nigeria to the Sahara for training were in the tens, and the brothers in the Sahara trained and sent, and the cadres of Nigerian brothers who were in the Sahara returned there, and came under the commandership of Abubakar Shekau.

In the same way, the mujahidin rendered support by keeping roads and bridges open, and with money, which is illustrated by this missive from Shaykh Abu Mus'ab 'Abd al-Wadud to the Shaykh 'Abd al-Hamid concerning the first financial outlay paid to Shekau's group. The financial situation for AQIM at that time was difficult.

> From the commander of AQIM to his brother Abu Zayd [...]

I have sent a missive to you previously to ask for your advice concerning the outlay which we will pay to the Nigerian brothers as an aid to them and to establish them as we had written to them in our missive to them previously. It is possible that this request for advice did not reach you or got held up for some reason, but I am able to aid them initially to the sum of 200,000 euros. Then we will see in the future whether to add to that. If you don't have guidance or objection, then pay their commander this sum from the AQIM account.

Tuesday 23 Rajab 1431 [5 July 2010][2]

> —Your brother Abu Musa'b ['Abd al-Wadud]

Shekau wrote a letter of gratitude to Abu Zayd 'Abd al-Hamid on 7 October 2010, telling him that he was beholden to him for the training and financial generosity. Most of the letter is a long treatise on the Islamic quality of patience (ṣabr). The narrative continues:

The issue continued in this manner with delegations coming and training, then returning, and weapons, money and support, until it was first noticed that Abubakar Shekau allowed and took the possessions of Muslims under the rationale that they lived under the rule of unbelievers by choice. The martyr shaykh 'Abdallah Abu al-Hasan al-Shinqiti wrote Abubakar Shekau a letter of advice, but there is no mention of any response from Abubakar Shekau. It is apparent that Abubakar Shekau did not benefit from this letter, but instead increased allowing the [forcible] taking of Muslims' possessions and signs of deviance and extremism began to appear in him, so a group of those closest to him[3] began to oppose him.

Other warnings from AQIM leaders and spiritual mentors are cited. The letter from Boko Haram members critiquing Shekau is translated as 22(B), placed after text 27.

23

DECLARATION OF WAR AGAINST CHRISTIANS AND WESTERN EDUCATION

BY ABUBAKAR SHEKAU

(c. JULY 2010)

[Trans.: Abdulbasit Kassim]
Available at: https://www.youtube.com/watch?v=Okrm2ZryK90

This video is undated, but judging from its quality of production and contents, restating some of the themes in texts 7 and 14, the extra-judicial killing of Boko Haram members, allegation of the collaboration between the Izala scholars and the government—a common early theme in the aftermath of the 2009 conflict—and mentioning the arrests of Muslims because of the World Cup event (which presumably is the 2010 FIFA World Cup in South Africa), it should be dated to July 2010. In this video, Shekau reiterated the ideology of the group and its declaration of war against the Christians, Western education and secular constitution as well as the goal of establishing shari'a *in Nigeria.*

You should remember what happened in the city of Maiduguri. They cleaned feces with the Qur'ān in your Western schools. They perpetrated that action in the city of Maiduguri. When they perpetrated this action, no measure was taken against them. Rather, they stationed weapons at the scene so that whoever intended to instigate chaos because of the incident can be curtailed.[1] Today, we have risen and want to practice our religion and remain steadfast on Allah's path. Yet, they kept plotting to spill our blood. They employed different tactics to provoke us. Afterwards, we rose to defend ourselves and our religion.

At that time, the elders were sitting. Although their mouths are filled with hatred of the unbelievers, their [the elders'] actions are filled with love for them. This is so because they are the people who arrest a Muslim, and hand him over to the unbelievers and in their presence, the Muslim will be shot. For instance, the governor of Bauchi[2]—Allah is king! so if you do not repent, you are in trouble. Is it because of the World Cup you order the arrest of Muslims, and put them in prison? Is this the type of approach you employ? You should wait and see the consequences [of your actions], by Allah's permission. Certainly, we have begun *jihād* in Nigeria. This is just a tip of the iceberg. We have not begun *jihād* [fully] yet by Allah's permission. We are grateful to Allah. Generally, something will have to happen before something else will follow.

Because of Allah's support and the path to victory Allah has bestowed upon us, we do not see any power that can destroy us, by Allah's permission. This is so because we are working with Allah's power, and He has given us the means of which you are afraid. That is exactly what we will use to fight all the people who do not believe in Allah, and all the hypocrites who come between us and the unbelievers, or who act as their attack-dogs. Whenever we identify such people, certainly, we will use a sharp knife to cut their necks, by Allah's permission.

This is our path and what we preach to the *umma*. O you Izala scholars! O you scholars who are trying to form a coalition with the government leaders appointed by European colonialism to impede the religion of Islam! Your mouths are filled with the love of the Prophet, the Qur'ān and the claim of being Sunnis. Yet, your actions demonstrate that your group is the same as Pharaoh! Your group is the same as [Frederick] Lugard! This is so because you are always happy whenever the unbelievers gain victory over the Muslims, and always sad whenever the Muslims gain victory over the unbelievers: "If you are visited by some good fortune, it vexes them; and if you are visited by some misfortune, they rejoice at it; but if your forbear and fear Allah, their wiles will not hurt you at all." (Q3:120)

Allah also told us that there is nothing we are expecting except two best outcomes: "Say: Do you expect for us anything other than one of the two best outcomes; while we wait for you that Allah will smite you with a punishment, either from Him, or at our hands? So, wait and watch, we are waiting and watching with you." (Q9:52) There is nothing we expect except these two outcomes. In the first outcome, we are killed and go to paradise [...] In the second outcome, Allah will sustain our lives and give us the opportunity to gain the victory over you. This is what Allah promised us in His Book. This is what you should know. This is the path we are upon and follow in establishing the *sharī'a* of Allah in this land. Allah is the king.

Surprisingly, the Christians printed a newspaper in Nigeria with the name that some people call us: "Boko Haram." In the newspaper, they argued that we are not "Boko Haram;" rather we are people who want the pure implementation of Islam's *sharī'a*.

They said: "Do you not see that when they started their war, they did not start by attacking the schools; rather they started by attacking churches and other places where they engage in unbelief, such as the police stations? If they were only interested in opposing Western education, they would have been attacking only the Western schools." Therefore, they said they would not be deceived that indeed we are Muslims and in the future if we rise, they would also rise. They said those Muslims who unite with the Christians are dissimulators because they want to appease their brothers, the Christians. They are saying, by Allah, our goals and actions are not focused towards Islam.

You Christians should understand that indeed our goals are focused towards Islam. We want to fight you. You should rise with your weapons, because we want to break your cross. We want to demolish all the churches, throw aside the constitution, and bring the law of Islam [into force], or else we will perish. When we perish, then you can eat your chicken, drink your juice, and go ahead and vote, but if we are alive, your blood will be spilled. This is so because they want to separate us from our religion. We are ready to defend our religion by ourselves. Let us enter the field and see who will eat sand in this wrestling-match! This is what Allah has told us, so this is our path and the path upon which we will meet our Creator.

The Izala people have met and agreed that henceforth they will take severe measures against any attempt to propagate Muhammad Yusuf's cassettes. They said whoever is trying to propagate Muhammad Yusuf's books and cassettes—they will take severe measures against him, including our cassettes. This type of action is minor. You should even go ahead and conceal our message from the entire world, even after we preached to the *umma* for eight to nine years. Yet, you claim you did not understand our goal. Our goal is not directed towards killing people; rather it is focused towards following the Qur'ān and Sunna and ensuring justice, saying the truth and following Allah's path.

After the coming of the Europeans, you collaborated with them and damaged the lives of our youths with football-playing, watching films and illicit sexual relations. They have also damaged the lives of our females with prostitution, and giving birth to bastards, which they consider civilization. They also injected the Jews' and Christians' training into the minds of the Muslim children through Western education. This is the plot they have executed. Yet, some people claim there is good in it. There is no good in it.

By Allah's permission, the people you killed, you assumed that you have killed them, and the first among them is our leader Muhammad Yusuf. You did not kill him, according to Allah: "And do not say of those who are killed for Allah's cause that they are dead. They are alive, but you are unaware [of them]." (2:154) Then again, it was largely the civilians in the town [Maiduguri] you killed. You did not meet those who were holding weapons: they are here. About 95 per cent of them are here and they are making their preparations. Whether you die or stay awake, we must practice Allah's

217

religion. Whether you die or stay awake, we must fight. Whether you die or stay awake, we must have revenge. We must have revenge! We must have revenge! We must have revenge!

There is no group of people who is afraid of spilling blood like us. However, since it has become a type of religion, bloodshed is now a celebration for us. If we were asked to slaughter our chiefs, we will do so, according to command of Allah the same way the Prophet Abraham's son surrendered to his father for slaughter, as Allah says: "Then, when they both submitted and he flung him down upon his brow; And we called out to him: O Abraham!" (Q37:103) This is the task Allah has placed upon us.

If it is SSS or a spy you are worried about, look for [the angels] Raqīb and ʿAtīd,[3] look at Allah the Knower of the Unseen. Whatever they [government agents] know, either they saw you or someone told them. It is not possible that they sit in their offices and obtain information about you. It is a lie. There is no one who can know something while sitting in a place, except Allah. Whoever told you that you did so-and-so on so-and-so day, he heard it from someone. If you fall into my hand, I will carry out the judgment of Allah against you. The day that you fall into my hand, you shall see, by Allah's permission. This is the path we are on and may Allah help us. May He place us on the truth and direct our intentions solely to Him.

O Muslim! We do not forbid anything, except what Allah and His Messenger forbade. Likewise, we do not make permissible anything, except what Allah and His Messenger make permissible. This is what we believe. We have revolted against Western education, against democracy, against any system that contradicts the system of Allah and His Messenger. We hold firmly to the system of Allah, based on the Qurʾān, the Sunna of the Prophet, and in accordance to the path of the Sunnis.

We revolt against the Shiʿites, Maitatsine, and all other groups to which we do not belong. However, if you look for the path of the Qurʾān and the Sunna, you will find us there by Allah's permission. If you say these people are Maitatsine, we are not. If you say they are Shiʿites, we are not. If you say they are Kharijites, we are not. If you say they are Jahmiyya, we are not. If you say they are Muʿtazila, we are not. If you say they are Sufis, we are not. If you say they are [the Sufi brotherhoods] Naqshbandiyya, Shadhiliyya, [the theological tendency] Maturidiyya or any other group to which you try to relate us, you will not make a match, because in the first place you do not know the characteristics of those groups.

It is only because you are jobless—that is why you call us "Boko Haram." In the past, you will see elders fleeing with their children to the villages, in protest of Western education. You did not call them by any name, yet you call us "Boko Haram" because we understood how dangerous you are to the people. We are grateful to Allah. Is it not in Western education that they teach that there is no God? It is in Western education that they teach all forms of unbelief. Whatever I said that is right, may Allah reward us, and for my mistakes may Allah forgive us.

May Allah bring the day when we will put into action what our mouths have uttered. This is so because admonition is not admonition when it is [merely] mouthed, but not translated into action. We pray to Allah to allow us to act upon our statements and safeguard the weapons beside us. Let us put our words into actions. O Muslims! This weapon is nothing. They have only spread lies to you. In thirty minutes or one hour, you can handle a weapon. Some people will say that they cannot learn how to handle a weapon in one day. They have only spread lies to the people.

In Western education, they deceive you the same way the police and soldiers are trained to be deceived. They would take them and give them six months or several years of training until they completely mold them. Once they have been indoctrinated, they give them the weapons. You know this reality and your commanders also know. The day we will meet each other [in battle], you will know whether we can handle weapons or not. On the day of celebration, we will fire [guns], and on the day of fighting we will know who is superior. Whatever I said that is right, may Allah give us the reward, and forgive my mistakes.

[*Note on the video screen.*]

O Muslim people! You should know that *jihād* is obligatory today on every Muslim. Therefore, you should come out and let us build strength to defend our religion and avenge the blood of our brothers who were killed by the Christians and the oppressive government.

This message is from *Jamāʿat Ahl al-Sunna li-Daʿwa wa-l-Jihād* [JASDJ] in the land called Nigeria.

24

MESSAGE OF CONDOLENCE TO THE *MUJĀHIDIN*

BY ABUBAKAR SHEKAU

(12 JULY 2010)

[Trans.: David Cook]
Available at: http://jihadology.net/2010/07/12/new-message-from-the-
leader-of-buku-boko-%E1%B8%A5aram-in-nigeria-risalat-taaziyyah/

Following the 1 February 2010 announcement of support, training and provision of weap-
ons to Boko Haram by the leader of al-Qaeda in the Islamic Maghreb (AQIM) Abu
Mus'ab 'Abd Wadud,[1] al-Andalus media produced a video on April 23, 2010 titled "The
Raid of al-Damous"[2] to avenge the extra-judicial killing of Boko Haram members by the
Nigerian Army, which was aired by al-Jazeera.[3] Two other al-Qaeda affiliates, al-Shabab
in Somalia and al-Qaeda in Iraq, also each dedicated a video concerning extra-judicial
killings of Boko Haram members ("A Gift to the people of Tawheed in Nigeria" by
al-Katā'ib Media[4] and the eighth series of the video "Fursān al-Shahāda" by al-Furqān
Media).[5] On 13 March 2010, Ansar al-Mujāhidin network also produced a video titled
'Nigeria, the New Wound' with similar themes. An article titled 'The Misery of Muslims
in Nigeria' also appeared at the back cover of the 16th issue of Sada al-Malahim
Magazine produced by al-Malahim Media of al-Qaeda in the Arabian Peninsula and
distributed by al-Fajr Media Center. The article described the conflict in the Middle Belt
region of Nigeria, precisely Jos, as an organized Crusader attack against Muslims spon-
sored by the International Union of Churches in Nigeria with the support of U.S.

221

Microsoft corporation. The article ended with an outline of five duties of Muslims towards the Muslims in Nigeria which include the provision of support with money and weapons, the preparation of the Muslims on a military and faith level and the spread of the culture of martyrdom. This condolence message at the one-year anniversary of Yusuf's death (according to the hijri *calendar) is a sign of reciprocity from Shekau to the global* jihād *community, particularly in response to the deaths of al-Qaeda leaders in Iraq in April 2010. The message marked an early sign of ideological alignment between Boko Haram and al-Qaeda.*

"And do not think of those who have been killed in the way of Allah as dead; they are rather living with their Lord, well-provided for. Rejoicing in what their Lord has given them of His bounty; and they rejoice for those who stayed behind and did not join them, knowing that they have nothing to fear and that they shall not grieve." (Q3:169–70)

Prayers and peace upon our Prophet Muhammad, who said:

"Allah has guaranteed for those who go out in His path, 'When nothing but fighting in My path, faith in Me and belief in My messengers causes him to go forth, then it is guaranteed that I will cause him to enter Paradise or return him to the place from which he came with the reward or spoils he has gained.' By the One who holds Muhammad's soul in His hand, every wound suffered in Allah's path will be brought on the Day of Resurrection in the form in which it was on the day the wound [was received], its color the color of blood, while its fragrance that of musk. By the One who holds Muhammad's soul in His hand, if it was not a bother for the Muslims, I would not have sat out a single raid that you carried out in Allah's path ever, but I did not find the wherewithal to mount them,[6] nor did they, as it bothered them to be left behind [when I went forth]—and by the One who holds Muhammad's soul in His hand, I would have loved to have raided in Allah's path, be killed, then raided, be killed, and then raided and be killed."

And now, I am sending my message as a deputy on behalf of my brothers, the fighters in one of the lands of Africa called Nigeria as a condolence to the fighters in Allah's path in general, and to the troops in the Islamic State of Iraq particularly. It is a condolence to the leaders of the Muslims and the fighters, and their learned ones (*'ulama'*), such as Abu 'Abdallah, the shaykh, the fighter, Osama b. Laden, Dr. Ayman al-Zawahiri, Abu Yahya al-Libi,[7] Abu 'Abdallah al-Muhajir, and the emir of the Islamic State in Somalia, Aweys (Hassan), Abu Mansur, and Abu Musa'b 'Abd al-Wadud, emir of the al-Qaeda organization in the Islamic Maghrib, and the emir of the fighters in Pakistan, Chechnya, Kashmir, Yemen, and Muhammad's [Arabian] Peninsula, in addition to our learned ones who I did not mention.

I will like to bring this reminder to my brothers' attention, that this is the way, as Shaykh Abdallah Azzam said: "O brothers, the path of proclamation is loaded down with adversities, filled with dangers—prison, killing, expulsion and rejection, so whoever wants to take it upon himself or to fulfill its calling (in one of the paths of the *jihād* or in the proclamation), let him take this into account."

> Or did you suppose that you will enter Paradise, before Allah has known who were those of you who have struggled, and those who are steadfast. You were yearning for death before you met it. Now you have seen it and you are beholding it. Muhammad is merely a messenger, before whom many messengers have come and gone. If he dies or gets killed, you will turn on your heels? Should any man turn on his heels, he will not cause Allah any harm; and Allah will reward the thankful. (Q3:142–44)

> We will cast terror into the hearts of the unbelievers because of their associating with Allah that for which He sent down no authority. Their abode is the Fire and wretched is the dwelling-place of the evildoers! (Q3:149)

We pray to Allah on behalf of the Commander of the Believers, Abu 'Umar al-Baghdadi and Abu Hamza al-Muhajir,[8] and ask that Allah have mercy upon them and cause them to enter the highest Paradise. We hope that Allah will honor them, accept them as martyrs, and give them a generous reward and stipend. And be good to their families and close ones—Allah is greatest! Allah is greatest! Allah is greatest!

May Allah have mercy upon Abu 'Umar al-Baghdadi, and may Allah reward him well. Among his statements concerning patience, "O soldiers of Allah, we have resolved by the might and power of Allah not to leave you in fetters, and we will sacrifice ourselves to free you from prison. By Allah, if they placed you behind 1,000 walls that will not prevent us from seeking to liberate you by any means." He also said: "O monotheist, O fighter, I am sending you my good advice, because I love you, and by loving you I am closer to my master; indeed, I cannot find any more hopeful action that calms me more in the presence of Allah than loving you."

By Allah, rise, wage *jihād*, fight, "that the only religion will be that of Allah." (Q8:39) For this, rise, for this, resist and for this, be killed, and then be rightfully one of the princes of the martyrs, just as we consider them to be, even though we do not declare any of the Muslims to be pure before Allah.

To Allah belongs that which He takes and that which He gives, and everything with Him is proceeding to a set date [cf. Q13:2], so you should take that into consideration and endure. O unbelievers, hypocrites and apostates, do not think that the *jihād* has finished; rather, now the *jihād* has just begun. O America, die in your rage! [cf. Q3:119] Allah helps His religion! Do you not remember and think about when the commander of martyrdom-seekers Abu Musa'b al-Zarqawi was martyred; you thought that the *jihād* was finished, but Allah brought Abu 'Umar al-Baghdadi [in his place]. So, do not be too overjoyed as the Islamic State of Iraq is firm with the aid of Allah.

Allah will bring others, just as the Almighty said:

> And when the punishment for the first became due, we sent forth against you servants of Ours possessing great might who went after you in your country. Thus, our threat was

accomplished. Then, we gave you back your turn against them and aided you with wealth and children and increased you in number. [And We said:] 'If you do good, you do good for yourselves, and if you do evil, you do it for yourselves, too. And when the punishment for the second [making of mischief] became due, [We sent Our men] to afflict you, and to enter the Mosque as they entered it the first time and to destroy what they conquered. (Q17:4–8)[9]

We ask Allah Almighty to help our brothers the fighters in every place, and to destroy America and its allies, and let the world witness generally, and America, Britain and other Crusader [states], and the Jews of Israel who kill Muslims in Palestine every day, the polytheists, the apostates and the hypocrites specifically, that we are with our fighter brothers in Allah's path in every place—those who have sacrificed themselves in order to raise the Word of Allah and to save the downtrodden Muslims under the humiliation of the Jews and the Crusader Christians, like in Afghanistan, Chechnya, Pakistan, Iraq, Muhammad's [Arabian] Peninsula, Yemen, Somalia, Algeria and other countries.

I will remind our brother Muslims of what Shaykh Abu 'Abdallah Osama b. Laden has reminded them in his message to our Muslim brothers in Iraq, when he said: "I entrust myself to you in God-fearingness, secretly and openly, in patience and endurance in *jihād*, for victory is [the result of] an hour's patience. I entrust myself to you in much recollection [of Allah] and prayer." Allah Almighty said: "O believers, if you encounter an enemy host, stand fast and remember Allah frequently, that perchance you may prosper." (Q8:45)

Lastly, I send my greeting of peace to the fighters' commanders, and to the Commander of the Believers in the Islamic State of Iraq, Abu Bakr al-Baghdadi,[10] and I ask Allah to help His religion through us, to grant us martyrdom (*shahāda*) in the battle, looking forward, not turning back, being saved by His mercy and grace. O most merciful! And prayers upon our Prophet Muhammad, and upon his family and Companions altogether. Our last prayer is praise be to Allah, Lord of Worlds.

—Your brother, Abu Muhammad Abu Bakr b. Muhammad Shekau, the imam of JASDJ in one of the African countries [Nigeria].

25

LEAFLET FROM THE BAUCHI PRISON BREAK[1]

(7 SEPTEMBER 2010)

On 7 September 2010 (28 Ramadan, during the traditional period of Laylat al-Qadr (cf. Qur'ān 97)), which was also the same day that the 2011 election was announced), there was an attack on the Bauchi Federal Prison by approximately fifty members of Boko Haram. 721 prisoners were set free, among whom were approximately 150 Boko Haram members. Two leaflets were distributed by the group on that day. The first leaflet was a small paper which just mentioned that the real name of the group was not Boko Haram, but JASDJ. This translated text is the second leaflet, and the event constitutes the group's second birth. The sophistication of the attack evinced the likelihood of transnational support from other jihadist groups mainly in the Sahelian-Sahara region, where several key members of Boko Haram had migrated in the aftermath of July 2009.

If the perpetrator has forgotten (the victim will not).[2]

Peace and blessings of Allah be with you. In the name of Allah, who has power over everything and who commands to worship only Him and nobody else. Muslim brothers, we send special condolences on the recent events in this country, particularly in the city of Suldaniya (Jos).[3] May Allah bring rest to those who died and grant us His special protection. Amen.

After this, we will like to issue a warning about what happened in the past. Everyone can attest to the fact that since we started our activities about eight to nine years ago, we have never molested anyone. We only preached that it was forbidden to follow any path contrary to what Allah through his Messenger (Prophet Muhammad) commanded us to follow. You are all witness to the sudden attack on our mosque [in Maiduguri] during the early dawn prayer by this oppressive government, shooting and killing our members and arresting others. And yet there are, among our Muslims brothers, those who act as government agents to help the security forces kill or arrest us.[4]

This is a general notice to all [believers]: fighting this government is mandatory. Whoever refuses will be accountable to Allah. For us, we will rather die than fail

Allah on account of our deeds. Whoever can, join us. If not, shut up, for [this] does not concern you, leave us alone, and watch what will happen.

We are warning those who inform the security forces. We have certainly not forgotten, and we will never forget. By Allah, we will not leave the matter. Do not think we will ever forget how you made it possible for them to kill innocent Muslims at Tashar Mass Mosque[5] and the Dutsen Tanshi Police Station [both in Bauchi town].[6] How you helped them demolish our mosques and houses. How you helped them by lying and accusing us of provoking the attacks, simply because you have the media to express any view you want.[7] Therefore, get ready to run for your life if you were involved in one way or the other in the massacre of our people. From state officials to ward heads do not report us to the security forces or your wife will become a widow, your children orphans, and your mother will have to give birth to another to replace you after your death. You will certainly see things you will not want to see. Your only recourse is to repent and stop collaborating with the security forces. If you do not, there is a heavy punishment waiting for you.

You have been warned.

Signed: JASDJ, waging a *jihād* in this country called Nigeria.

26

HAUSA *NASHID* "WE ARE NOT BOKO HARAM, WE ARE THE PEOPLE OF SUNNA"

BY JAMĀ'AT AHL AL-SUNNA LI-L-DA'WA WA-L-JIHĀD

(c. FALL 2010)

[Trans.: Abdulbasit Kassim]
Available at: https://www.youtube.com/watch?v=u2bEHaA0iX0

This nashīd *is not dated, but from the contents, referencing Yusuf extensively, and protesting the use of the name Boko Haram—a common early theme—and mentioning the commencement of martyrdom operations, it should be dated to the fall of 2010. The* nashīd *also laid out the goal of the preaching of Yusuf, rebuked the Kharijites name ascribed to the group, censured the complicity of Izala scholars and the Nigerian government in the killing of its members and advocated jihād as a solution to the religious conflicts in Nigeria. One should note the affiliation of the new leader of Boko Haram (Shekau) to Abu Musa'b al-Zarqawi (see text 2), and Osama bin Laden.*

In the name of Allah, the most Beneficent, the most Merciful,

Our name is not Boko Haram, O people of Nigeria, we are Muslims, the people of Sunna, and you should understand the truth [*repeats in chorus*].

In the name of Allah, the most Beneficent, the most Merciful. Allah is the Lord of the world and the One who created everything in it. O Lord, help me to narrate this poem concerning the events that occurred in this land of Nigeria.

Our name is not Boko Haram, O people of Nigeria, we are Muslims, the people of Sunna, and you should understand the truth.

O Lord, send blessings upon the Prophet Muhammad. The one to whom you gave the Qur'ān and said we should all hold on to it. O Lord, make us to follow him in all our affairs. Let us not deviate from his path; the path of truth.

Our name is not Boko Haram, O people of Nigeria, we are Muslims, the people of Sunna, and you should understand the truth.

O Lord, include the companions in the blessings, all of them and add all those who follow them, all of them. O Lord, you should separate us from those who deviate, all of them. Those who leave their path have gone astray, all of them.

Our name is not Boko Haram, O people of Nigeria, we are Muslims, the people of Sunna, and you should understand the truth.

After I have finished sending the blessings, then here is an explanation of the message that the martyred scholar, Muhammad Yusuf, came with to the people of Borno and other towns that have stopped following Your path; the call of all the world.

Our name is not Boko Haram, O people of Nigeria, we are Muslims, the people of Sunna, and you should understand the truth.

We will not follow a system that the Qur'ān did not describe. We should leave all the systems that are not structured by Allah's Messenger. There is no fault if we follow the one who does not contradict the Book, because that is justice to check self-centeredness.

Our name is not Boko Haram, O people of Nigeria, we are Muslims, the people of Sunna, and you should understand the truth.

We should not follow the system of America, the world's unbelievers. We should not follow the constitution created by the world's unbelievers. The only system that we will follow is only that of Allah. This is the crux of our preaching you should understand; the world's Muslims.

Our name is not Boko Haram, O people of Nigeria, we are Muslims, the people of Sunna, and you should understand the truth.

Our scholar, Muhammad Yusuf, may Allah have mercy on him; the one who was propagating that we should follow the Prophet, the leader of the *umma*. He is the brave one who faced the *ṭāghūt*. O Lord, join him with the Prophet on the Day of Judgment.

Our name is not Boko Haram, O people of Nigeria, we are Muslims, the people of Sunna, and you should understand the truth.

You are also a lion, Mallam Shekau, may Allah assist you. Lead us to follow the system of Allah, we do not oppose you. Everyone who wants to fight *jihād* should follow you. This is the representative of Zarqawi and Osama in Nigeria.

Our name is not Boko Haram, O people of Nigeria, we are Muslims, the people of Sunna, and you should understand the truth.

Government of Nigeria: the unbelieving, the unjust. You have collaborated with the scholars to cheat the *umma*. Ignorant scholars, heroes of Iblis [the devil] and *billama* (local government),[1] those who cheated Allah's Messenger; the best of the prophets...

Our name is not Boko Haram, O people of Nigeria, we are Muslims, the people of Sunna, and you should understand the truth.

These Izala scholars, we have listened to the words of this world. Those who say that politics is better than prayers, you have heard. No doubt this is just a saying of a selfish person. Tomorrow in the Day of Judgment, he will burn if he does not repent in the world.

Our name is not Boko Haram, O people of Nigeria, we are Muslims, the people of Sunna, and you should understand the truth.

You said to us that we are Kharijites and they know that we do not follow the Kharijites. Allah is able, the Izala people—you have cheated us in this world. Tomorrow on the Day of Judgment, Allah will judge us all.

Our name is not Boko Haram, O people of Nigeria, we are Muslims, the people of Sunna, and you should understand the truth.

Then they just gave a message that they should kill the believers. Soldiers, mobile police and police, see them killing the believers. Then they tagged us with the name Boko Haram to deceive the people of Nigeria.

Our name is not Boko Haram, O people of Nigeria, we are Muslims, the people of Sunna, and you should understand the truth.

In the first place, it was in the state of Borno that they upset our brothers. They shot twenty people without fault. Our brothers were on their way to the cemetery to bury a brother when the soldiers of Nigeria opened fire on them.

Our name is not Boko Haram, O people of Nigeria, we are Muslims, the people of Sunna, and you should understand the truth.

Borno and Bauchi, Kano and Yobe, you have killed our brothers. They have killed the adults and even the children and they put many others in the prison, our Muslim brothers. They killed Mallam Muhammad Yusuf too; you heard about it.

Our name is not Boko Haram, O people of Nigeria, we are Muslims, the people of Sunna, and you should understand the truth.

They have been committing acts of terrorism against us in this land for a long period of time. Just like that they will kill Muslims, male and female. Look at that land; remember what they did at Tafawa Balewa and Zango Kataf—all in Nigeria.

Our name is not Boko Haram, O people of Nigeria, we are Muslims, the people of Sunna, and you should understand the truth.

The group of Christians in this land called CAN [Christian Association of Nigeria] has been plotting in this land for a very long period of time. They have been gathering weapons and killing Muslims in the land. Look, Muslims have been displaced all over Bauchi.

Our name is not Boko Haram, O people of Nigeria, we are Muslims, the people of Sunna, and you should understand the truth.

If you blaspheme Allah's Messenger like the day we all heard that *Thisday* newspaper has done so in this world. We do not forget this and we do not forgive anyone who blasphemes the Prophet.[2]

Our name is not Boko Haram, O people of Nigeria, we are Muslims, the people of Sunna, and you should understand the truth.

Gideon, the action he perpetrated in this land, he wiped feces with the Qur'ān in this land. Our Muslim brothers who struggle in the land quickly took a severe action on the accursed unbeliever.

Our name is not Boko Haram, O people of Nigeria, we are Muslims, the people of Sunna, and you should understand the truth.

Now look at Plateau State, you have heard what they are doing. You heard in the media that they have killed many Muslims. There is no way to end this, the Muslims of this world except through *jihād* in Allah's path in Nigeria.

Our name is not Boko Haram, O people of Nigeria, we are Muslims, the people of Sunna, and you should understand the truth.

We have intended to fight *jihād* to intercede for the *umma* in Nigeria. We will fight the Christians who are killing the *umma* in the land and even the *ṭāghūt* misleading the *umma*, and all those that support the unbelievers inside Nigeria.

Our name is not Boko Haram, O people of Nigeria, we are Muslims, the people of Sunna, and you should understand the truth.

We have prepared dangerous fire of trials against the *ṭāghūt* of the land with you and all the disbelievers in the land. See us with RPG and DShK (Dushka)[3] in the land. See us with Kalashnikov for wiping out the unbelievers of Nigeria.

Our name is not Boko Haram, O people of Nigeria, we are Muslims, the people of Sunna, and you should understand the truth.

We will carry out "martyrdom operations" you have heard; that is the act of suicide bombing in Nigeria. We will share it to your barracks and your churches and against the Christians and *ṭāghūt* that are in Nigeria.

Our name is not Boko Haram, O people of Nigeria, we are Muslims, the people of Sunna, and you should understand the truth.

We will attack the towns in front of Nagira [?] filled with beasts. We will scatter the beasts that are in the town. It is you that I am referring to *ṭāghūt*, we will scatter you into pieces then the angels will fill the hell through your necks.

Our name is not Boko Haram, O people of Nigeria, we are Muslims, the people of Sunna, and you should understand the truth.

O you, governor of Borno, "apostate" with the behavior of dogs, ignorant slave of the Europeans and America. You will understand your fault on the day the *mujāhidīn* will descend on you. You will see the power of the One and Only; the King of the world.

Our name is not Boko Haram, O people of Nigeria, we are Muslims, the people of Sunna, and you should understand the truth.

You will see the power of the One and Only; the King of the world.

Our name is not Boko Haram, O people of Nigeria, we are Muslims, the people of Sunna, and you should understand the truth.

You, [governor] of Borno tell the one [governor] of Jigawa that we are close. You, [governor] of Bauchi tell that unbeliever [governor] of Plateau that we are close. You, [governor] of Kaduna you should come if you are afraid that we are close. You should come let us clash with the *ṭāghūt* of Nigeria.

Our name is not Boko Haram, O people of Nigeria, we are Muslims, the people of Sunna, and you should understand the truth.

You should come and attack the unbelievers and *ṭāghūt* of Nigeria.

Our name is not Boko Haram, O people of Nigeria, we are Muslims, the people of Sunna, and you should understand the truth.

You will see the power of the One and Only; the King of the world.

Our name is not Boko Haram, O people of Nigeria, we are Muslims, the people of Sunna, and you should understand the truth.

From your *mujāhidīn* brothers in Nigeria; put us in your prayers.

[*Throughout the video, scenes are shown of Osama b. Laden, Ayman al-Zawahiri, Abu Mus'ab al-Zarqawi, Ahmad Yasin, Samir bin Salih bin 'Abdullah al-Suwaylim (Ibn al-Khattab who fought in Chechnya), and al-Shabab fighters. These scenes demonstrate that even at this early period Boko Haram saw itself as being part of the world Salafi-jihadi network. There are also scenes from the fighting in Middle Belt, Nigeria, and al-Jazeera clips of the murder of Boko Haram members from July 2009.*]

27

A LETTER TO OSAMA BIN LADEN'S DEPUTY

BY ABUBAKAR SHEKAU

(c. FALL 2010)

[Trans.: David Cook]

Available at: https://www.dni.gov/files/documents/ubl2016/arabic/
Arabic%20Praise%20be%20to%20God%20the%20Lord%20of%20
all%20worlds.pdf

This undated letter is probably from late 2010 or early 2011, prior to Osama b. Laden's death on 2 May 2011 at the hands of U.S. forces in Pakistan. Most of the letter's contents are requests for Islamic advice, and are not translated here. There has been some commentary on the significance of the letter; its pleading tone and absence of self-confidence indicates a leader (Shekau) who has not yet decided what to do with Boko Haram. Notwithstanding, this letter evinced the early transmutation of Boko Haram from a local group into a transnational actor and its gradual co-optation into the al-Qaeda jihadi universe via the middlemen from the Sahelian-Sahara region.[1] Even though there is no clear evidence of how Shekau's letter from Nigeria was delivered to bin Laden in Pakistan, a connection existed during this period (see text 22). Some of the Boko Haram fighters knew operatives of AQIM such as Abdallah Abu Zayd 'Abd-al-Hamid, Mokhtar Belmokhtar and Yunus al-Mauritani; the latter was in contact with al-Qaeda, but was arrested in 2011.[2]

Praise be to Allah, since the time when Allah granted us this understanding, we have been united according to one belief, sworn to one imam, Abu Yusuf Muhammad b. Yusuf, desiring union and harmony to the command of our Lord until this very day.

Praise be to Allah, we have listened carefully to your videos, and heard your news, meaning the videos of the knowledgeable and senior ones of the al-Qaeda organization, like Osama b. Laden, may Allah protect him, Dr Ayman al-Zawahiri, Abu Mus'ab al-Zarqawi, may Allah have mercy upon him, and other knowledgeable ones such as Abu Yahya al-Libi and Abu Qatada al-Filistini,[3] may Allah protect and shepherd them.

There is nothing remaining but for us to know its [al-Qaeda's] order and organization, because the one who does not know the way in which he trods will be helpless after the journey. When he is helpless, whether returning backwards or making another mistake in judgment—but one who knows the ways in which he trods, will not be helpless because he knows them.

O Allah! We desire to be under one banner, although it is necessary to consider closely before this, as our religion is one of close consideration and knowledge. We desire to have this close consideration, and our goal is the raising of the Word of Allah upon the face of the earth, and seeking His favor. We ask Allah Almighty to aid us in this goal, and to place us among those who are fighting in Allah's path, not among those who are unbelievers fighting in the path of the *ṭāghūt*.

Please, I will like particularly to speak with a representative of Osama b. Laden, may Allah protect him, because the group is a trust from Allah, who will ask me concerning it on the Day of Judgment.

Your brother in Allah, Abu Muhammad Abubakar b. Muhammad al-Shekawi, the Muslim in Shakau, leader of the JASDJ.

22(B)

LETTER FROM DISAFFECTED MEMBERS
OF BOKO HARAM TO AQIM CRITIQUING SHEKAU

[Trans. David Cook]
Available at: https://azelin.files.wordpress.com/2017/04/shaykh-abucc
84-al-hcca3asan-rashicc84d-22sharicc84ah-advice-and-guidance-for-the-
mujacc84hidicc84n-of-nigeria22.pdf

*This letter is undated, and was released as part of the AQIM documents from 13 April
2017, purporting to date to 2010–11. Osama bin Laden, mentioned in the letter, does
not have the Islamic blessing of "may Allah have mercy upon him" after his name, so it is
most likely that the letter was composed prior to his death, probably in early 2011. The
contents of this letter are very critical of Shekau from an Islamic standpoint, as far as his
leadership and strategic vision, and strongly echo themes that will be developed by Ansaru
in texts 36–37, and by Mamman Nur in text 72.*

To the *mujāhid* shaykh 'Abdallah al-Shinqiti [...]

Your valuable letters have come to us, and we have benefited from them hugely, and
were made happy by them. Among that which made us overjoyed was the encourage-
ment towards the characteristics of good, and incitement to taking the right way and
the middle straight method. This was quite apropos of the circumstances in which we
are, and we wish that Abu Muhammad al-Shekawi (the commander of our group)
would act in accord with them in order to correct our affairs that have gone wrong.

He has begun, as you have seen in his message, to manifest some of the signs of
extremism and deviation from the straight methodology, thinking evil of those

brothers who exhort him and caution him from his error. Would that he believed what was in it and acted in accord! But far from it, different types of tribulations have strung along rattling the brothers, so in what follows we will clarify some of them so that you can visualize their reality, and guide us in what is appropriate to do about the situation.

1. Among the most serious is the extremism in labeling (Muslims) unbelievers (*takfir*), for Abu Muhammad al-Shekawi uses *takfir* for all who participate in the elections (specific *takfir*) disregarding the principles and rules of *takfir*. He holds to those who believe that there is no excuse because of ignorance with regard to the greatest *shirk*, and relies upon their words and writings such as Shaykh ʿAli al-Khudayr's *al-Mutammima*, in spite of the fact that there are errors in it and clear contradictions with regard to other religious leaders.

Likewise, Diya' al-Din al-Qudsi's book, *La ʿudhr bi-l-jahl fi al-shirk al-akbar*, which is famous for extremism, and mistreatment of religious leaders together with plagiarism, which has caused him to be in disrepute—for example Abu Basir al-Tartusi, after he stole his book *al-Ṭāghūt* without its name and claimed to be the author.

He is also intellectually dependent upon Bashir Abdallah's book *al-Afaq al-mubin*, from which him and other members of his group have obtained deviant ideas. These are famous for extremism and going overboard, and do not see any other than themselves as Muslims, in spite of their small number. The greatest religious principle among them is "Whoever does not use *takfir* against an unbeliever is himself an unbeliever," in spite of the great damage in the use of this principle. Among their statements is the *takfir* of the shaykh Osama bin Laden, and even the majority of the *mujahidin* in Allah's path today, because they do not use *takfir* against the masses.

Indeed, they call them "Muslims" and consider them to be brothers, and are sorry about the *tawāghīt* and the Crusaders who oppress them, and they fight for their [the masses'] salvation. All of this, according to Bashir and his group, is unbelief and enough to warrant expulsion from the [Islamic] community! Because it demonstrates loyalty to the unbelievers.

Our shaykh Abu Yusuf [Muhammad Yusuf] debated them during his life, of which the result was the declaring of Yusuf to be an unbeliever, so that they as a result of not being willing to use *takfir* against him would not become unbelievers themselves. This was because he refused to declare *takfir* against the [Nigerian] people as a whole. "Whoever does not use *takfir* against an unbeliever is himself an unbeliever."

Al-Shekawi makes things worse by not stopping at this point, but adding to this the permitting of bloodshed and possessions, just as you saw at the beginning of this letter, as if he was a student of [Antar] al-Zouabri[1] and a graduate of his school!

2. Among the things from which the brothers suffer also is Shekau's strange opinion concerning the imamate. He claims that he is at the level of the greatest Imam, and is only satisfied when we treat him as if he was a caliph. He does not permit anyone to disagree with him, to argue with him, and in this he is like the Jews. Just like withdrawing from him, removing one's hand from obeying him after the gravest

of forbidden actions, and even if he brings terrible innovations—those things that cause the call to *tawḥīd* and *jihād* to be sullied and lost, failure and destruction, "other than when you see open unbelief among you; this is a proof from Allah."[2]

Whoever dirties himself with any of this, his sentence is death. He is killed because he is one of the Kharijites or the rebellious (*bughāt*). The obligation upon us all (according to his opinion) is to obey him through thick and thin, and it is all on us—even if he beats the back or takes possessions or imputes against one's (sexual) honor, even if he revokes proclamation and *jihād*!

Among the things that clarify his intent as to the obligatory obedience for the Imam is that he would sometimes demand from the brothers that they hand over whatever they have for the *jihād*, refusing them even one round of ammunition—just as he has proclaimed—but the obligation is to turn it all over to the obedience of the Imam. His proof for this is that Abu Bakr al-Siddiq spent all of his wealth in Allah's path, and did not leave anything for his family!

Under this principle he has sent some of the leadership of our fighting youths (those who do not agree with his views) out, and then taken all their weapons and left them out to dry. For it is permitted to the Imam, according to his understanding, to do this, by any means. This is in spite of the fact that they only began fighting it with what they had acquired on the day it became clear that he was uninterested in the matter of preparations!

As for payment of the spoils and the fifth of the booty to him is one of the major responsibilities for which pages are printed and cassettes are recorded for publication and distribution among the members of the group. This is to make them aware of the rights of the "Imam" to which they are obliged. It is nothing short of amazing that in these self-same leaflets he proclaims that preparation for fighting the enemies is not among his responsibilities! [*Citation of Q9:92, 2:188 and some exegesis.*]

Among all that precedes there is one other great principle: "No *jihād* without the Imam's permission," so if someone is martyred in battle without his permission then he is a rebel! And his martyrdom, as he has proclaimed about some of them, is not accepted! Indeed, it is not permitted for any of the members of the group to travel to one of the lands of *jihād*, like Somalia or Algeria to fight with his brothers there. If he does this without his permission then he gets the death sentence.

3. [*Shekau also runs the group in a high-handed manner, and completely ignores his* shūrā *council—note how many of the signatories below are members of it—and makes the claim that "Matters of the jihād are entrusted to the Imam."*] He has confessed to us more than once, in spite of his suitability for the imamate, he does not know anything about the war stratagems.

He has exiled the best of us, religious leaders and commanders, and indeed proclaimed his removal of the commander of the army—all of this because of warning over error, conflict over opinion or arguing concerning some right. [...]

4. Among the worst of his crimes connected with our *jihād* is his spreading secrets, and even betraying confidences, withholding money, and refusing to prepare for

battle. The last of this was three cassettes released under the name *al-Bayān al-kāmil* (*The Complete Exposition*) in which he squandered our efforts in clarifying everything! Now it is in the hands of the *ṭawāghīt*! Among the results was the loss of some plans and the *ṭawāghīt*'s arresting some commanders.

This should suffice with the caution that there is much more...

[*Shekau is also responsible for loose morals, division of families, incorrect religious practices, and encouraging lying and deceit. According to the critique, instead of paying attention to these issues, Shekau spends his time proclaiming* takfīr *rather than cleaning up the behavior of his supporters. All of this has led to the Nigerian people bad-mouthing the religion and jihād, and causing general chaos. Citation of Q3:174.*]

These are some of Shekau's crimes, and their fruits. Efforts have been expended, and attempts have been made to remedy the matter, but have not been successful. Either the one repents and begs forgiveness from the Imam or is accused of grave sins, among which are being Kharijites or rebels, and is sometimes threatened with death.

Among what we have sent are some of the brothers' efforts attempting to make things right or to caution from these errors.

For this reason, we have ceased to work with Shekau, as he has already expelled many of us previously, and does not allow us to fight at his side unless we agree with him in all of his opinions among other conditions. Despite this he flees from students of (Islamic) knowledge and avoids them.

We have mandated an operation of making people aware and advising the youth, waking up those who sleep, restraining those who have risen to not pass the point—and in the same way we are also cautioning from the methods of excess and laxity, encouraging holding to the midmost straight method, with an element of preparation, to the best of our ability, as we have considered and continue to consider this the best way.

[...] Our only problem right now is the imamate of Shekau, that alone. [...]

Your brothers in Allah:

Abu Muhammad al-Hawsawi, commander of the army, and member of the *shūrā* council

Abu Ahmad al-Kishnawi, commander of the northern sector, and member of the *shūrā* council

Khalid al-Barnawi, commander of the Tariq b. Ziyad battalion

Abu al-Bara' al-Nurini al-Akinawi, commander of the al-Bara' b. Malik battalion

Abu 'Ubayda al-Kanawi, commander of the Nur al-Din battalion

Abu 'Abdallah al-Imam, member of the Research and *fatwā* committee

Abu Muslim al-Ibrahimi, member of the *shūrā* council

Abu Khalid al-Yerawi, commander of the proclamation and guidance division, member of the Research and *fatwā* committee

Abu Nusayba al-Bushawi, battalion commander

LETTER CRITIQUING SHEKAU

Abu Maryam al-Yaʻqub, commander of the Musʻab b. ʻUmayr battalion
Abu ʻAsim al-Hasani, member of the Research and *fatwā* committee
Rashid's letter of advice is a reply to this letter.

28

MESSAGE FROM SHEKAU

(17 APRIL 2011)

[Trans.: Abdulbasit Kassim]
Available at: https://www.youtube.com/watch?v=9ChTgAjpoyY

In the aftermath of the July 2009 conflict, Nigerian security officials claimed that Shekau had been killed along with other Boko Haram members in clashes between the group and the security forces, a recurring phenomenon of premature Shekau death statements. He re-emerged in a video interview with a local Nigerian journalist from Daily Trust Newspaper. *In the interview which was filmed on 19 April 2010, Shekau said that although he had been shot in the thigh during the fighting with the security forces, he was rescued by "fellow believers and protected by Allah."[1] This video is the second "revival" of Shekau and most likely a response to the report that he was killed by security forces in Kano after an exchange of fire in a Kano neighborhood in 2011.*

[Standard Islamic opening] All praise be to Allah who says: "Allah will defend the believers; Allah surely does not like any thankless traitor. Permission is given to those who fight because they are wronged. Surely, Allah can give them victory. Those who were driven out of their homes unjustly, merely for their saying: 'Our Lord is Allah.'" (Q22:38) [Islamic prayer.]

Thereafter, may the peace and blessings of Allah be upon you. Today, I am sending my salutations to my Muslim brothers. There is nothing that spurred my message to you, other than needing to dispel a false story. It is for this reason I consider it necessary to send a message to you, my Muslim brothers, to clarify the truth to you. I was not killed. There is no surprise at all if I was killed, arrested or departed. Allah's prophets were also killed, others were arrested, while yet others departed. An example of a prophet who departed is in the Qur'ān: "So, he departed from it fearful and vigilant. He said: 'Lord, deliver me from the wrongdoing people.'" (Q28:21)[2] There are also multiple examples of the prophets who were killed. The Prophet Joseph is a prophet who was arrested: "My Lord, prison is dearer to me than that to which they call me." (Q12:33) Allah is great. He said the prison is dearer to him if they would call him to engage in unbelief. There are also more examples in the life of the Prophet Muhammad.

Therefore, if I was arrested, it will not be a surprise. Rather, I pray that Allah will bestow steadfastness upon me. And may Allah conceal our secrets. As a result, it is important for our brothers to understand the nature of this people—I am referring to the world government of the day, the unbelievers, the hypocrites and the polytheists and those who control the world government today—you should know that whatever action they do is aimed at advancing their agenda. There is nothing they do that is surprising.

As a result, we should understand that all these radio organizations such as the BBC, Germany, France, or anywhere they are in the world were established to promote a specific agenda. Have you ever heard them saying they would promote Islam or the *umma*? However, you would always hear them promoting democracy as a creed. Therefore, you should know that whatever you hear from them is not a surprise. It is aimed towards advancing their agenda. You should know. So, when they came out to announce that I was killed, it is not surprising. All the news reports that claimed that I was arrested are false. They also said they arrested the protector of Abubakar Shekau.[3] It is a lie. They did not arrest him. We know what transpired when you visited the servant of Allah's house, but you will not say anything about it.

We know what has been happening, by the mercy and power of Allah, in the city of Maiduguri, where we were oppressed initially. We know what has been happening by the way [certain] soldiers are dying—specifically, the soldiers who took up weapons to attack us. We have been killing them and we know, but you will not say anything about it. There was a time when one of them was speaking with a pleading tone, yet he still came out to say: "We are being killed."

On this basis, my brothers, I am not saying you should not listen to the radio, but whoever wants to listen to it should also be aware of their agenda. You should know that none of their reports conform to the Qur'ān. It is a lie. Rather, their goal is to advance the agenda of the United Nations and the members of the Security Council, such as America and England. That is their agenda. Therefore, it is important for a person to acquaint himself with this knowledge.

My concluding message to you, my brothers, is for you to remain steadfast on the path of the truth. This is the path! This is the path! The news that I was arrested is a lie. It is a lie and it is not a surprise if I was arrested. And may Allah grant us the opportunity to be killed on this path. Martyrdom is my ultimate desire. I am also using this medium to encourage my brothers to be patient. Whoever wants to establish the religion must face some trials. This is the reason the Prophet said: "The people who receive the highest tests among mankind are the prophets, those who follow, and those who follow them." The Prophet's Companions approached him and they told him to pray to Allah so that He can bestow victory upon them. The Prophet replied them that there were those who came before them who held firm to the religion. There were those whose flesh was mutilated, yet they did not turn away from the religion.

Therefore, my brothers, please exercise patience. We thank Allah this war is just starting. Now, we are grateful for the strength Allah has bestowed upon us. It is not by our doing, but it is Allah who provided us with strength. We do not rely upon our weapons. Rather, we rely on the strength of Allah. It is better for them to kill all of us than for us to be in a state [Nigeria] that lacks monotheism. The religion is far better than the life of this world. This is our path. I am sending my salutations to my brothers in the religion. And may Allah aid us on this path and accept our prayers. My brothers, be steadfast in your closeness to the Qur'an and the *ḥadīth* especially in this period of trial. And may the peace and blessings of Allah be upon Prophet Muhammad. All praise be to Allah, the Lord of the worlds.

29

MESSAGE TO NIGERIA'S PRESIDENT GOODLUCK JONATHAN

BY ABUBAKAR SHEKAU

(11 JANUARY 2012)

[Trans.: Abdulbasit Kassim]
Available at: https://www.youtube.com/watch?v=umkj50SUzck

From September 2010 to January 2012, Boko Haram stepped up the sophistication of its attacks and most of its threats became reality. Of particular interest during these periods are three suicide attacks—all claimed by Boko Haram: one on 16 June 2011 at the Abuja police headquarters, which was allegedly carried out by Muhammad Manga;[1] on 26 August 2011 at the United Nations compound which was allegedly carried out by Muhammad Abu Baraa;[2] and on 25 December 2011 against the Catholic church in Madalla, which was allegedly masterminded by Kabiru Sokoto.[3] There were other attacks and a string of assassinations during these periods, some of which were claimed by Boko Haram, while others were unclaimed, but bear the signature of the group. These include the assassination of politicians (Awana Ali Ngala,[4] Modu Fannami Gubio,[5] Modu Gana Makanike),[6] Islamic clerics (Shaykh Bashir Mustapha,[7] Ibrahim Ahmad Abdullahi,[8] Ibrahim Birkuti,[9] Mallam Dala),[10] village heads (Muhammad Tukur,[11] Abba Anas Ibn Umar Garbai),[12] and a journalist (Zakariyya Isa).[13] There were attacks upon police stations, barracks, prisons, churches, polling stations, hospitals, sellers of non-halal meat, and beer gardens. Although this video was addressed to former Nigerian president Goodluck Jonathan, Shekau also reiterated the group's beliefs and targets, listed as Christians, security personnel and those who betrayed the group.

[Standard Islamic opening] All praise be to Allah, the One who says: "Allah will defend the believers; Allah surely does not like any thankless traitor. Permission is given to those who fight because they are wronged. Surely, Allah can give them victory. Those who were driven out of their homes unjustly, merely for their saying: 'Our Lord is Allah.'" (Q22:38) Allah also says: "It was not you who slew them, but Allah; and when you threw, it was Allah who actually threw, so that He might generously reward the believers. Allah is all-Hearing, all-Knowing." (Q8:17) Allah also says: "Sedition [*fitna*] is worse than slaughter." (Q2:191) May the peace and blessings of Allah be upon Prophet Muhammad who said: "This matter [Islam] will surely reach as far as the night and day, and Allah will cause this religion to enter every city and tent-dweller's dwelling, either with glory or by humiliation—glory by which Allah glorifies Islam, and humiliation by which Allah humiliates unbelief,"[14] and his family, Companions and those who follow him till the Day of Judgment.

And thereafter:

Salutation to the *umma* in its entirety, this is a message and summons to Goodluck Jonathan and the President of CAN (Christian Association of Nigeria),[15] as well as a piece of advice to the *umma* in its entirety.

All praise be to Allah, we are those who call ourselves JASDJ, but some people refer to us by the derogatory name "Boko Haram." [Our message is clear]

Our conflict is not targeted towards the entire population [of Nigeria], except the security personnel, Christians and those who betrayed us. Everyone is well acquainted with the actions the Christians have perpetrated against the Muslims in more than one or two instances. There is nothing that compelled me to deliver this speech, other than the speech that Jonathan and the CAN president delivered about us and the various opinions different people espouse about us—including the portrayal of us as a cancer and an evil in this country called Nigeria.[16]

We are not a cancer, nor are we evil, and we do not attack people indiscriminately. If people do not know us, Allah has knowledge of everyone: "Allah suffices as Knower," (Q4:70) "Allah is the All-Sufficient Witness!" (Q4:79) Everyone has knowledge of the way our leaders were executed. Everyone has the knowledge of the brutality that was inflicted upon our members, and was meted out to the Muslim population in this country from time to time—for instance in Zango Kataf, Tafawa Balewa, in different villages in Kaduna, in Langtang, Yelwa Shendam, the events that occurred in Lagos, and so many other brutalities that were perpetrated against the Muslims in this country.

For that reason, it is unbelief that is indeed devilry, just like Allah says: "Sedition is worse that slaughter." According to Allah, sedition and defiance is unbelief. Everyone knows that democracy and the constitution constitutes unbelief.

Everyone knows that there are some actions Allah has prohibited in the Qur'ān and the Prophet in the *ḥadīth* which are prevalent in Western education. We have not said anything other than calling the *umma* to Allah's path, which is the only path by which we can attain peace, and live according to Allah's tenets. This is the core objective of our preaching, because of which our members were killed and mosques destroyed.

Afterwards, we decided to defend ourselves. Allah has promised that if you follow His commands, He will bestow strength upon you. This is what transpired. And on this basis, Jonathan, you should know that this affair is beyond your capability. It is not our undertaking, but Allah's. It is beyond your capability.

I swear to Allah, what you are saying is just like you have not been saying anything at all. This is so because before Allah created the earth, He had omniscient knowledge of what will happen on earth, and He has promised in His Book that He will aid His religion. It is beyond your capability, and this is not [merely] our undertaking. Whatever you see happening, Allah allowed it to happen because you have refused to follow Him, and have betrayed His religion. It is for this reason you should understand, Jonathan, that this affair is beyond your capability.

If there are few people in your government who have good opinions about us, it is not surprising.[17] It has happened many times, and our hands are open. Whoever says he will not follow Allah, even if he loves us, Allah has commanded us not to love such a person. Rather, Allah said we should preach to such a person, show him the right path and embrace him on our path. You Christians should know that Jesus is a servant and prophet of Allah. He is not a son of Allah.

This religion of Christianity you are practicing is not Allah's religion; it is unbelief, and Allah forbade it. What you are practicing is not religion. Apart from that, you Christians have cheated and killed us to the point of eating our flesh. You perpetrated all that you desired against us while we were preaching and calling you to become Muslims, so that we can follow the religion that Allah bestowed upon us. Even during peaceful preaching without violence, you went ahead slaughtering us, taking our wives and humiliating us.

Now, the CAN president said his people should also come out and do whatever they want to do.[18] Any right-thinking individual knows the meaning of his statement. We are not going to do whatever we desire to do; rather we will follow what our religion commanded us to do. That is the reason I am calling you and other Christians to repent. This undertaking of ours is Allah's undertaking. Fellow Muslims! Understand our objective. We do not aim to kill, humiliate, or confiscate anyone's property. This clarification has become necessary, but even if I do not clarify it, I can keep silent because Allah, whose pleasure I seek, knows my intention. We have clarified our intention, so if we breach our trust, Allah has knowledge of everything. There is no one who can breach the trust of Allah. Allah will punish severely anyone who breaches the trust of the *umma*.

Therefore, the *umma* should understand that we do not have any objective other than to give victory to Allah's religion. [This is my message to you] However, if you want further clarification, you can go ahead and listen to our tapes to understand our objectives and the goal of our preaching. This is also my message to the president of Nigeria, Jonathan, who came out to say negative things about us, and has also spearheaded ruthless actions against us. Now that we have succeeded taking vengeance and Allah has given us victory, they are protesting, and have forgotten the ruthlessness perpetrated against us for the past eleven years when our members were being killed.

Allah is great! Allah is great! Allah is great! "Allah suffices as Knower," "Allah is the All-Sufficient Witness!" Allah is sufficient for us. [We serve Allah and we are following His path.] We do not harm anyone except the person who harms us. This undertaking of ours is Allah's religion. Our undertaking is based upon established evidence in the Qur'ān and the *ḥadīth*. He commanded us and we follow His commands. Whoever thinks that he can fight Allah should not think that his prayer or praying in the mosque will save him. [*Discussion of the* "Masjid al-Ḍirār".][19]

Therefore, any Muslim who deceives or hides under the cloak of the religion—if we come across such a person, we will not hesitate to kill him. Yes, I mean what I am saying. We will kill him, because it does not take five minutes to kill, just as we are being killed. We pray to Allah to be killed during this war so that we can reap the reward of martyrdom. This is our goal. We are working to achieve victory for the religion and are being killed. Our goal is to achieve victory and enter paradise. Yet, you are saying that we are not following the religion. This is all nonsense-talk. We read and follow the teachings of the Qur'ān. All praise be to Allah. This is what Allah has instructed me to explain to the *umma*.

In conclusion, all the discussions about peace overtures—we will accept peace overtures only if it will help us on the path Allah has commanded us to follow. We will not accept peace overtures that suit the unbelievers' interests. Rather, we will accept a peace overture that adheres to Allah's command. There is a peace overture that is acceptable, and one that is not. Both instances are in the Qur'ān. The first instance is in *sūrat al-Anfāl* (Q8), while the other is in *sūrat Muḥammad*, also called *sūrat al-Qitāl* (Q47). Allah has clarified all these explanations to us. The *ḥadīth*s have also clarified them to us and we are following the actions of the Prophet and the path of the pious forefathers. This is our path and the core of my explanation.

30

WE ARE COMING TO GET YOU, JONATHAN!

BY ABUBAKAR SHEKAU

(12 APRIL 2012)

[Trans.: Abdulbasit Kassim]

Available at: https://videos.files.wordpress.com/ebCevT2X/boko-haram
_s-jamc481_at-ahl-al-sunnah-li-da_wah-wa-l-jihc481d-amc4abr-
imc481m-abc5ab-bakr-shekau-22we-are-coming-to-get-you-
jonathan22_std.mp4

In a bid to redeem the image of Nigeria, President Jonathan, while in South Korea, gave an interview on 27 March 2012, where he assured the international community that his government would defeat Boko Haram by the middle of the year.[1] This video of Shekau is a response to Jonathan's statement. During this phase of Boko Haram, another Northern Nigeria jihadist group that shared a common ideology with Boko Haram but differed in tactics had emerged. This new group in conjunction with al-Qaeda in the Islamic Maghrib (AQIM) focused on the kidnapping of western expatriates in Nigeria. There are two events which drew the attention of the international community to the transnational cooperation between this new jihadist group (later identified as Ansaru) and AQIM: (a) the kidnapping and subsequent killing of a British and an Italian hostage (Chris McManus and Franco Lamolinara).[2] The two men were kidnapped on 12 May 2011 in Kebbi State and killed on 8 March 2012 in Sokoto State, after a failed rescue attempt by British and Nigerian forces; and (b) the kidnapping of the German expatriate Edgar Fritz Raupach in Kano on 26 January 2012. AQIM claimed the kidnapping with video evidence filmed in Kano and produced by al-Andalus media[3] and demanded that the hostage be freed only if the German government freed Umm Saifullah Al-Ansariya (Filiz Gelowicz) from a German prison.[4] Raupach was later killed on 31 May 2012.[5] Although Boko Haram denied links to the kidnappings,[6] the group would later join Ansaru in the trade following the kidnapping of the Moulin-Fournier family on 19 February 2013 at Waza Park,[7] the kidnapping of Father Georges Vandenbeusch, the parish priest of Nguetchewe, on 14 November 2013, near the town of Koza, both in northern Cameroon[8] and the kidnapping of the Catholic priests (Giampaolo Marta and Gianantonio Allegri) and Nun (Gilberte Bissiere) on 4 April 2014 in Tchéré-Tchakidjebé Catholic parish in northern Cameroon.[9]

[Standard Islamic opening]

And thereafter:

From the humble servant seeking Allah's mercy, Abu Muhammad Abubakar b. Muhammad al-Shekawi to the President of the People of Unbelief and Polytheism, specifically [President Goodluck] Jonathan, who is addressed in English as the president of Nigeria, and to the *ṭāwaghīt* of the world in general

O people! O people! I want you to listen to me attentively. Listen to this servant of Allah, who has no other duty to pursue on earth as a Muslim except the propagation of the *sharīʿa*, and striving towards its implementation. May Allah help us all.

O people! We have listened to the proclamation of the unbelievers' president, Jonathan, that we will be defeated within the next three months. There is no one who speaks like that, except the person who has strayed from his Creator's path. We want him to know that we have certainty and committed faith in Allah that nothing can be done to subdue us.

All praise be to Allah, our ultimate desire is that all of us should be killed as martyrs on Allah's path, so that we can all be blessed with the rewards of Allah, as promised in His holy Qurʾān. This is the ultimate mission before us and we pray that Allah should purify our minds, strengthen us and guide our intention upon His path.

I swear by Allah that there is nothing you can do to stop us. Your predecessors since the era of Pharaoh, and those who succeeded him, until the present time, were unable to do anything to us, even though they bragged like you. If you see a person not treading Allah's path, you will always hear him making many empty threats. May Allah grant you fortitude as you continue to proclaim your empty threats. As for us, we have nothing but the worship and trust in Allah. Allah is enough as our protector.

We want people to understand that we have no intention of killing people indiscriminately. Some people may be disguising under our name to terrorize and extort people, but we are not with them, and we do not know them. Now, it might be difficult for people to understand or differentiate us from those that disguised under our name, but surely there will be a day when Allah will make His *sharī'a* clear for the whole world to understand where we stand.[10]

As for the people we have killed, it has been established that they constituted an affront to Allah's path and His Messenger in themselves. This is our message to the world, and specifically to those who proclaim empty threats about us. We will not bother ourselves engaging in too much talk, nor will we feel uneasy about people's opinions. Rather, we will only comment on issues that we consider beneficial to the people. We pray to Allah to continue supporting us on this path and make us to continue this path with no purpose other than His worship. We also pray to Allah to bestow upon us the privilege of being amongst the martyrs, who will be killed on the path of the struggle for the establishment of His dominion.

It is surprising that you are boasting about the way you killed and attacked us. Have you forgotten what Allah says:

> Do not be faint-hearted and do not grieve; you will have the upper hand, if you are true believers. If you have been afflicted by a wound, a similar wound, a similar wound has afflicted the others. Such are the times; we alternate them among the people, so that Allah may know are the believers and choose martyrs from among you. Allah does not like the evildoers! (Q3:139–140)

How we wish that the believers would ponder the meaning of these verses! Anyone who understands the meaning of these verses will understand that any time an unbeliever arrests or kills a believer, he will laugh at the idiocy of such an unbeliever. This is so because Allah has said such persecution will not last for a long period, so do not be faint-hearted and do not grieve because of whatever challenge you face on this path. You will gain the upper hand, if you are true believers.

I want the world to know that, even if I were to be trampled upon, with my head pressed to the ground, and people beating me, I would gain the upper hand in Allah's sight, if I am a sincere believer. Even if we were killed or maimed on this path, Allah said many people who fought similar *jihād* have suffered worse persecution.

On this path, Allah said if we kill 1,000 people today, and by tomorrow they kill 100 people amongst us, Allah said that He is the one who alternates among the people to test our faith, so that those who have professed faith in Allah will be able to know the people from amongst them who are the sincere believers and Allah can choose martyrs from amongst us. If all the arrests and killings of our people we have witnessed in recent times did not happen, how are we going to know the people who have weak faith from the people that are the true believers in Allah? Allah alternates among the people, so that He may know the believers and choose martyrs from amongst us (Q3:140). Indeed, Allah does not like the evildoers. This is my message.

31

REASONS FOR ATTACKING *THISDAY* NEWSPAPER
BY JAMĀ'AT AHL AL-SUNNA LI-L-DA'WA WA-L-JIHĀD

(4 MAY 2012)

[Trans.: Abdulbasit Kassim]
Available at: https://videos.files.wordpress.com/SdjA7vo7/boko-haram-jamc481_at-ahl-al-sunnah-li-da_wah-wa-l-jihc481d-22reasons-for-attacking-thisday-newspaper22_std.mp4

On 26 April 2012, Boko Haram carried out one of its long-standing threats—a suicide attack on the office of Thisday newspaper in Abuja, and a car bomb explosion outside a complex housing several newspaper offices, including Thisday, in Kaduna.[1] Boko Haram justified the attack as retaliation for blasphemy against the Prophet Muhammad during the Miss World Beauty Pageant in November 2002 by a journalist. Prior to his death, Yusuf had proclaimed jihād against anyone who committed blasphemy against the Prophet,[2] and later the group had made its intention clear to carry out retribution against Thisday.[3] In this video, Boko Haram also threatened to attack other media organizations for acting as accomplices to the government, for claiming the group conducted the kidnappings of foreign expatriates, for misinterpreting the statements of its leaders, and for the false report regarding the arrest of its purported spokesman. Towards the end of the recording, the group also claimed attacks on universities in Kano and Gombe.

[Standard Islamic opening]

And thereafter:

By Allah's permission, this is a message from the Department of Public Enlightenment of JASDJ, a group waging *jihād* in Nigeria.

We wish to provide an explanation of the attack we conducted on *Thisday* newspaper. The reason we decided to attack the media organizations, particularly *Thisday*, is because the newspaper was used in the past to commit blasphemy against our Prophet of mercy, Muhammad, during a beauty pageant in Kaduna in November 2002.

At the time the event occurred, some people who referred to themselves as the Muslims' leaders came out saying that they have forgiven those who committed the blasphemy. However, based on our knowledge, we know that there is no one who has the power to forgive anyone for an offence concerning which Allah Himself has stipulated a judgment, especially a grave offence such as blasphemy against the Prophet Muhammad. No one has the power to forgive this type of offence in Islam, and the judgment for the blasphemers is for them to be killed.

The judgment concerning the lady who committed the offence [Isioma Daniel] is for her to be killed, whenever there is an opportunity. Likewise, the media organization should also be decimated whenever there is an opportunity to do so. The evidence for this has been well explained in the preaching of Mallam Muhammad Yusuf in Maiduguri on the issue of blasphemy against the Prophet. Now, we can attack the media organization, and we are hoping to continue these attacks until we decimate them. It is our hope that Allah will help His religion.

The Muslim *umma* should also understand that the type of action perpetrated by *Thisday* newspaper is the reason Allah says: "Fight them, Allah will punish them at your hands, will disgrace them, give you victory over them and heal the hearts of a believing people." (Q9:14) By Allah's permission, this verse is the principal evidence that has spurred us to attack *Thisday* newspaper. We know that any sincere Muslim, who possesses faith in his heart during this era, must have been deeply touched by the blasphemy against the Prophet by *Thisday* newspaper. Likewise, any Muslim who possesses faith in his heart must be delighted by our attack on the newspaper. Therefore, Allah said: "heal the hearts of a believing people." As a result, we pray to Allah to heal the hearts of the believers through our retribution against the unbelievers in this land.

Furthermore, *Thisday* newspaper and other media organizations mentioned later [in this video] have also acted as accomplices by helping the unbelieving government in their war against us. Some of the offences of *Thisday* newspaper and other media organizations include: firstly, during the botched attempt to rescue some kidnapped foreign expatriates, who were later killed in Sokoto, these media organizations questioned us as to whether we were responsible for the kidnapping, when we had stated it clearly that we disassociate ourselves from the kidnapping and have nothing to do with it. Yet, these media organizations went ahead reporting that we were responsible for the incident, lying about us.

Secondly, when we sent out a video of our leader, Imam Abubakar Shekau, the media organizations reported what our leader did not say. They said he threatened to annihilate this government in three months—the same way the government made its empty threat of annihilating us in three months. However, the truth of the matter is that nowhere in the video does our leader utter the statement they attributed to him.

Thirdly, on the purported arrest of Abu Qaqa by the State Security Service.[4] We have explained to them that the person who was arrested was not Abu Qaqa. Yet, the media continue to portray us as liars, and they said that our leader had ordered Abu Qaqa II to be executed, so now we are searching for Abu Qaqa III. Recently, they also came out with another lie that someone known as Muhammad Awwal Kontagora was Abu Qaqa II, who was ordered executed by our leader, and they said his parents also confirmed it that he is Abu Qaqa II. That was just a big lie to convince the world. This is our explanation to the Muslim *umma* so that they can understand the purpose of our *jihād*.

The media organizations also said that we killed the father of Abu Darda to send a message to him for revealing our secrets after his arrest by the security agencies, and they wanted him to believe that he is one of our targets. These are all lies, and there are many such lies. These media organizations have committed numerous offences that are detrimental to Islam and we do not have the power to forgive them. We will take revenge on them, by Allah's permission.

Some of these media organizations have been categorized into three groups: the first group includes organizations like *Thisday* whose offences are mammoth. The second group is the newspaper organizations we will soon attack, such as *Punch*, *Daily Sun*, *Vanguard*, *Guardian*, *Nation*, *Tribune*, *National Accord* and VOA Hausa radio. We will attack all these media organizations, including their staff and offices, by Allah's permission. For instance, VOA Hausa radio has recently launched a campaign for people to support the government against us. The third group is the media organizations that are on the verge of joining the first two categories, and if they are not careful, we will attack them very soon. These include *Leadership*, *Daily Trust*,[5] *People's Daily* and Radio France International (RFI).

There is also an online medium, Sahara Reporters,[6] whose office is based in New York. They have made their website, particularly the comment section, into a platform where unbelievers attack Islam, Allah, the Prophet Muhammad and the Qur'ān. We are warning them to desist from making their website a platform for attacking Islam; otherwise we will find a way of attacking them as well.

We resorted to this medium of communication to send our message, as opposed to our previous telephone conferences, because of journalists' fear of conducting telephone conferences. This is an explanation of why our *mujāhid* brother attacked the *Thisday* office. We are grateful to Allah for the success recorded through the attack on *Thisday* and we hope to continue with such attacks.

Finally, the unbelieving government has resorted to the arrest of our wives and children, and the demolition of our houses like they did in Biu [Borno] and Hotoro [suburb] in Kano recently. For this reason, we decided to start attacking government schools, and specifically tertiary institutions. We promise to demolish 500 buildings for every one of our houses that the government demolishes. We have already started with Gombe and Kano and we will continue, by Allah's permission.[7]

32

FORMATION OF JAMĀ'AT ANṢĀR AL-MUSLIMIN FI BILĀD AL-SŪDĀN

(GROUP OF THE MUSLIMS' HELPERS IN THE LAND OF THE BLACKS)

BY AMIR ABU YUSUF AL-ANSARI

(9 JULY 2012)

[Trans.: David Cook]

Available at: http://azelin.files.wordpress.com/2012/07/jamc481at-ane1b9a3c481r-al-muslimc4abn-fi-bilc481d-al-sc5abdc481n-22first-statement22.pdf

On 20 January 2012, there was a mass Boko Haram attack in the main northern Muslim city of Kano, during which approximately 185 people were killed indiscriminately. In retrospect, it was most likely this event which led to a split between the largely Kanuri-dominated, Borno-centered Boko Haram under the command of Shekau, and the Hausa-dominated Ansaru. This split was later partially papered over when Boko Haram swore allegiance to the Islamic State (spring 2015), but the differences between these two groupings were very real during the period 2012–14. In the video debut of Ansaru, which emerged on YouTube on 2 June 2012, in Hausa and English, the group emphasized the inexcusability of killing Muslims (a critique of Boko Haram) and the need to protect Nigerian Muslims against violent Christian organizations.[1] Although Ansaru and Boko Haram were steeped in the same jihadi *ideology, utilize similar nar-*

ratives and have common adversaries, some of the operations of Ansaru, such as the attack on Nigerian soldiers heading to Mali,[2] the killing of seven foreign hostages,[3] and the kidnapping of Francis Colump,[4] demonstrate that the group had broader transnational objectives. The transnational scope of Ansaru was further demonstrated when a member of the group who identified himself as Abu Ali al-Nijiri featured in a video titled 'Battle for Shaykh Abd al-Hamid Abu Zayd' produced by the Sahelian branch of AQIM. This statement is its founding proclamation and its contents are akin to the group's video debut. The statement also serves as a prototype to the group's charter which was later released in 2013.[5]

For the first time, we are happy to announce the formation of this group possessed of true foundations. For us it will be an unblemished look at everything: we will enjoin the good, and work towards spreading it, while forbidding the wrong, and try to put an end to it.

The full name of the group: Group of the Muslims' Helpers (Ansaru) in the Land of the Blacks, which means the vanguard of aid and protection for the Muslims, particularly in Black Africa.

The motto of the group: "Jihād in Allah's path," which means fighting in Allah's path.

The emblem of Ansaru shows the Qur'ān, with two machine guns surrounding it. A black flag upon which is written "There is no god but Allah and Muhammad is His Messenger" is hung upon each machine gun. The Qur'ān is the sign of knowledge and guidance, while the weapons are the sign of *jihād*. The two banners are the sign of the Islamic caliphate. By this emblem, it shows that correct knowledge and the power of *jihād* are the two bases for righteous rule and its defense.

The goals and aims of the group:

1. Preaching the straight path and raising the consciousness of the people.
2. Protection of the lives and property of the Muslims.
3. Quick response and retaliation against any unjust or terroristic action against the Muslims.
4. Return of glory and nobility, which was during the time of the caliphate, to the Muslims, just as it was during the caliphate of Dan Fodio.

The means of attainment of these goals:

The means by which these goals and aims will be attained is "*jihād*," because the word "*jihād*" just as Allah and His Messenger clarified it, includes everything that it is possible for one to utilize in order to aid and protect the religion of truth and to overcome injustice and unbelief—whether by knowledge, by weapons or by wealth.

The reasons for the foundation of the group:

The foundation of Ansaru is the result of injustices, the plethora of violent and barbaric actions against the Muslims in this country (Nigeria). Everyone knows that the unbelievers in this country, especially the Christian Association of Nigeria (CAN) and its helpers were the first to arouse internal strife in this country, which led to the loss of an uncounted number of souls. The likes of these terroristic organizations continue to hold to their initiative in which their target is terrorizing the Muslims and conspiracies against Islam. The proofs of their crimes are well known to everybody, and what happened in Plateau [State] lately, before the Feast suffices for one to understand the situation. The unbelievers besieged the Muslims while they were in the prayer-place for the Feast, praying the feast-prayers. Then the unbelievers began to throw rocks upon the Muslims, opened fire on them, killing them, destroying their homes, and burning women and children. The worst is that they began to roast the bodies of the killed Muslims as food for the unbelievers! Everything that is mentioned the camera registered for the entire world to see—how they are experts in terroristic actions. But the startling thing is that neither the government nor any other body did anything.

This is only an example, and we do not forget the rest. Similar violent actions that happened in Kafanchan, Zango Kataf, Saminaka, Zonqwa, Yelwa Shandam, Langtang, Tafawa Balewa, Bauchi, Shagamu and other places. This has become such a real issue when you see a refugee camp in this country, and it is camp for Muslims.

During these conflicts, there was no Muslim organization which became militarized, while on the other side there are several armed organizations from the unbelievers. Some of these organizations were founded forty years ago, and their purpose is to terrorize the Muslims and conspire against Islam. The terroristic organizations include CAN, AKHWAT AKWOP,[6] OPC, AFENIFERE, MASSOB, MEND, IPC, IYC and others.[7]

Since there are the likes of these organizations fighting Islam and terrorizing the Muslims, when the government is not prepared to defend our rights because it is not an Islamic government, it is incumbent upon the Muslims to found their own organization specially to fight terror.

We know that many have said that is the responsibility of the government—so why do you not call upon the government to fight the terrorists? Why do you not follow the legal paths to obtain the rights that the government guarantees?

Our answer to the likes of this question is as follows:

During all the conflicts that were perpetrated against the Muslims in this country, the government did not manifest, even once, any interest or come to our aid. The government took part in aggravating the situation. Aren't they the killers of Mallam Zubairu and his family in Hotoro in Kano State? And aren't they those who attacked the Qur'ānic schools (*madrasas*), humiliating our teachers, throwing the sacred scriptures in sewers? And aren't they the killers of Mallam Muhammad Yusuf and more than 700 Muslims?

Despite the historical facts, the Nigerian government and what is called the Crusader powers (which are led by the terrorist Christians) in the lands were both founded by the British victors who sent them (the government and the Christians) to terrorize the Muslims and conspire against Islam.

We do not forget the evil actions and words that the (British governor-general) [Frederick] Lugard said in Kano after he killed many Muslims, including Attahiru I, who was the sultan of that time, and many of the protected personalities—he subjugated our heroes and humiliated the signs of our religion.

According to what has been mentioned, it is clear to us that both the government and the Christians inherited the war against Islam from their masters, who founded terror in our land. For that reason, the idea of an alliance with the government against the Christian terror or seeking our rights by means of the government is pointless and not up for discussion.

The firm proofs from the Qur'ān and the Sunna indicate that the one correct solution for the likes of this situation is *jihād*. Allah Almighty said: "And why don't you fight for Allah's cause and for the downtrodden, men, women and children, who say: 'Lord bring us out of this city...'" (Q4:75) Just as He said: "Allah will defend the believer; Allah surely does not like any thankless traitor. Permission is given to those who fight because they were wronged. Surely Allah can give them victory. Those who were driven out of their homes unjustly merely for their saying: 'Our Lord is Allah.'" (Q22:38–40)

The Prophet said: "When you conduct transactions using *'ina* [a type of interest], have taken to following the tails of cattle, are satisfied with agriculture, and have abandoned *jihād*, then Allah will give you over to lowliness which will not be removed until you return to your religion."

In closing, we call all Muslims, wherever they are, that it is incumbent upon them to render aid to us, to liquidate the unjust rulers (*tughat*), and exchange them for peace and justice, and returning the nobility of Islam is the one true way to establish justice—since whenever the unbelievers are those who are leading with the greatest strength, there will never be peace, as that is their nature.

Our brothers and sisters, always remember the reward and merits of *jihād*, and do not accept lowliness ever.

—Abu Yusuf al-Ansari

33

MESSAGE TO THE WORLD

BY ABUBAKAR SHEKAU

(1 OCTOBER 2012)

[Trans.: Abdulbasit Kassim]
Available at: https://videos.files.wordpress.com/DBYgNcIP/imc481m-
abc5ab-bakr-shekau-22a-message-to-the-world22_std.mp4

In this video, Shekau delivered three concise messages to the government. He reiterated the group's commitment to retribution against blasphemy of the Prophet Muhammad. He also threatened to attack the wives of Nigerian security officials because of the arrests of the Boko Haram members' wives, and finally, he denied any negotiations or signing of a peace treaty with the government. It is important to mention that before this video, Shekau had previously delivered a 30-minute video on 5 August 2012 (this video could no longer be accessed), in which he reiterated a similar message that his group would not negotiate with the government, and demanded that the Nigerian president convert to Islam.

[Standard Islamic opening] All praise be to Allah who decreed *jihād* as an act of worship and the peak of Islam. And may the peace and blessings of Allah be upon the Prophet Muhammad who said: "Your provision has been placed under the shade of a spear, and humiliation and contempt upon all who oppose me."[1]

Thereafter, may the peace and blessings of Allah be upon you. This is not intended to be a prolonged explanation to save time. This is my abridged message to the people, particularly the leaders of unbelief, fighting against our religion. In this country called Nigeria, they are fighting us day and night, for no other reason than our proclamation to practice and give victory to the religion as well as holding firm to the commands of Allah. It is for this reason Allah says: "They did not begrudge them except that they believed in Allah, the All-Mighty, and the All-Praiseworthy." (Q85:8)

All praise be to Allah. This is my abridged message to those who act as kings. They are the recipients of my message. By Allah, you are not free and you do not have peace of mind. Whether we are here or not; by Allah, you are not free. By Allah, you have invited woe upon yourselves. We are only praying for help from our creator whose religion we uphold. And may Allah help anyone who possesses the love of the religion in his heart.

My abridged messages are threefold: firstly, concerning the blasphemy against the Prophet—plotting and acting in a film to humiliate our Prophet Muhammad.[2] This plot will not affect Islam. However, whoever is engaging in such reprehensible act should await our reaction. Everyone already knows what I mean by my statement and you should wait to see our reaction.

Secondly, this government was initially holding our brother in prison. They arrested and humiliated him with all the different levels of humiliation. We did not protest. Allah is the king and we were practicing our religion. However, they have stepped up from the humiliation of our men to the incessant arrest of our women. Allah is the king. In this week alone, they arrested seven women and no one knows their whereabouts or what they are doing to them.

You, the Muslims, you know what the unbelievers, Allah's enemies, do to women. By Allah, some of the women were [forcibly] undressed and they also fornicated with some of them. We know what they do to women. In one place, they arrested seven women. In another place, they arrested three women. Allah is the only one who knows the actual number of women they arrested. The women whom we know were arrested are more than ten. They arrested them and now we do not know their whereabouts.

These women are married women belonging to our religion. Yet, they [the government] would come out and demonstrate to the people that they want to establish a peace treaty. You would hear them saying: "Now we want a peace treaty." It is a lie. There is no one with whom we can sit to sign a peace treaty. Rather, you planned and sat together with some people, and afterwards you declared that you arrested the leaders of that nonsense name you call us, "Boko Haram," and now you are engaging them in negotiations. They said they have caught the edge of the rope. You have not caught the edge of the rope—rather you caught the edge of nonsense, and may Allah forbid that.

There is no one with whom we sat for negotiations. They are just engaging in their usual lies. While they humiliate and kill people, they deceive the people by claiming that they are engaging in negotiations with us. By Allah, we are not engaging in any negotiations. Rather, they are just killing us, but we will not leave the religion. For you to understand their deception, listen to what they broadcasted on the radio— Abu Qaqa, who they said is our spokesman, was arrested, later died the following morning at the hospital, and returned to his Lord. However, he is alive. Since deception is your major preoccupation, it will not be a surprise if my speech to you will spur you [the government] to kill him to satisfy your need for broadcasting, since you worship the people. This is the third message.

These are my short messages. Since you hold our women in captivity, you should wait and see what will happen to your women in line with *sharīʿa* injunctions. No, we will not become enraged and seize your women. You should wait and see what will happen to your women in line with *sharīʿa* injunctions. If it is delightful, wait and see: "...wait then. Surely, I shall be, along with you, among those who wait." (Q7:71; 10:20) You are SSS, right? Shekau will stand on your throats. Yes, SSS, right? You should wait and see how Allah will put Shekau on your throats. You are in trouble since it is Shekau you are fighting, and Allah is by the side watching. It is Allah we follow, and Shekau is nothing.

Yes, the religion is what we want to practice. Look at me, I am in good health and am alive. In fact, I desire the death you wish for me, bastards. All praise be to Allah. This is the end of my explanation. O Allah! Help me to deliver this message to all the people of the world. O Muslim *umma*! It is the religion and the Muslims we are defending. We do not kill or humiliate Muslims. Even the unbelievers, we lay out the reasons we are attacking them before we attack. It is the victory of the religion that is our ultimate desire and may Allah aid us.

34

CLARIFICATION OF THE FALSE REPORT ON NEGOTIATIONS WITH THE NIGERIAN GOVERNMENT[1]

BY ABUBAKAR SHEKAU

(c. NOVEMBER 2012)

[Trans.: Abdulbasit Kassim]
Available at: https://www.youtube.com/watch?v=XQumMx6mfK4

Following the scuttled peace talks between Boko Haram and the Nigerian government, which were facilitated by Dr. Datti Ahmed[2] in March 2012, the consistent rebuttal of media reports on negotiations between Boko Haram and the government became a recurring phenomenon. Prior to this video, Boko Haram's purported spokesman Abu Qaqa on 7 June 2012 debunked media reports associated with Shaykh Dahiru Bauchi that he was moderating such a dialogue.[3] On 14 August 2012, Abu Qaqa also debunked the claim by Abu Muhammad Abdulaziz that Boko Haram had initiated dialogue.[4] This is the second video in the series of rebuttals by Shekau. It was released as a rebuttal to the 1 November teleconference delivered by Abdulaziz during which he stated that Shekau mandated that five members of the group (himself, Abu Abbas, Ibrahim Yusuf, Sani Kontagora and Mamman Nur) liaise with General Muhammadu Buhari and a five-member committee of Borno elders (Dr Shettima Ali Monguno, Senator Bukar Abba Ibrahim, Ambassador Gaji Galtimari, Barrister Aisha Wakil and her husband Alkali Wakil) in order to begin dialogue with the Nigerian government in Saudi Arabia.[5]

Abdulaziz made new calls for negotiations and a ceasefire on 26 November 2012[6] and 28 January 2013.[7] However, both calls were debunked by Shekau through a flyer posted in different parts of Maiduguri on 20 February 2013[8] and a video sent to journalists in Maiduguri on 2 March 2013.[9] It is noteworthy that, although Shekau and Abu Qaqa debunked all these reports, some members of Boko Haram seemed to support negotiation with the government in 2012–2013. This claim is evidenced in the video by Abu Mansur al-Fulani al-Adamawi delivered on 28 Dhu al-Qa'da 1434 (2 October 2013), which featured the opening clip of al-Sahab Media (the official media arm of al-Qaeda) and images of Salafi-jihadi scholars such as the Saudi Arabian Sulayman al-'Ulwan, the Jordanian Abu Muhammad al-Maqdisi and the Palestinian Abd al-Latif Musa (Abu Nur al-Maqdisi), leader of the Palestinian group Jund Ansar Allah.[10] In the video titled "Message to Imam Shekau," Abu Mansur advised Shekau to engage in dialogue with the government for the benefit of the umma, *and also in order to free the imprisoned Boko Haram members. He mentioned some names, such as Mallam Lawal, Abu Awza'i and Hassan al-Banna.*

[Standard Islamic opening]

And thereafter:

All praise be to Allah. O Muslim *umma*, may the peace and blessings of Allah be upon you. I want to make an unblemished explanation to the *umma* in general because of the fabricated report which has been disseminated to the *umma* which is baseless.

[Mentioning the issues to be discussed] I do not intend to take much time, O *umma*, you should know that the person you had his name in the radio, even though he is an impersonator, he calls himself Abu Muhammad Abdulaziz, or Abu Abbas, and he said we have chosen the likes of Muhammadu Buhari and Bukar Abba Ibrahim for negotiation to put an end to our *jihad*. This proclamation is false and is baseless.

We do not know any Abu Abbas or Abdulaziz who belongs to our group. We did not delegate anyone to go to Saudi Arabia or anywhere in the world to represent us in negotiations. How can we even go towards that direction giving the fact that our aim is to establish an Islamic State that will be governed solely by the Book of Allah and the Sunna of His Messenger? Was this not our message and the goal of our preaching before our mosque was destroyed? Afterwards, they massacred the Muslim *umma* without any restraint, and it was this persecution that spurred us to avenge and give the victory to the religion of Islam.

Are we going to put aside the obligation Allah bestowed upon us because we want them to rebuild our mosque for us? We do not worship the mosque. We worship Allah alone and we uphold the Sunna of His Messenger. We do not have any business with Ali Modu Sheriff to the point where someone claimed that we demanded prosecuting him. Ali Modu Sheriff, all those individuals and others who serve in this disbelieving government, by Allah's permission, if they fall into our hands they should immediately know they will lose their lives, except those who repent or follow Allah's path. This is our creed and this is the path we follow.

I am the leader of JASDJ, and I am the one expressing this utterance. I do not need to tell you my name or show you my picture. All praise be to Allah. Everyone knows me. I swear by Allah this is the explanation I have for you.

There are verses where Allah encouraged the Muslims to engage in a peace treaty with Allah's enemies, and there are also other verses where Allah forbade the Muslims to engage in a peace treaty with Allah's enemies. These two instances are in the Qur'ān, and we know when it is appropriate to work with either of the verses in these two instances which were revealed to His Messenger. There is a verse where Allah says, after seeking refuge from the accursed Satan: "And if they incline to peace, incline to it too, and put your trust in Allah. He is truly the Hearer, the Knower." (Q8:61) On the other hand, there is another verse in which Allah says: "So do not weaken and call for peace, while you have the upper hand and Allah is with you. He will not stint you your actions." (Q47:35) These are the verses from Allah.

The only time we will ever consider a peace treaty is when we have successfully established an Islamic State with a Muslim leader, and the unbelievers living under the control of the state incline towards peace and agree to live in peaceful relations with us without resenting us while we govern them with the *sharī'a*. This is the only time we can engage in a peace treaty as Muslims. You can go ahead and verify that from the Book of Allah.

[No peace treaty during jihad] Therefore, it is important for everyone to understand that the report they [the SSS] disseminated is false. I swear by Allah they are nothing to us. Allah will make this clear to you in this world or the hereafter. This is my explanation to you. All those individuals who cooperate with the unbelievers like themselves should wait for us. They should wait because there will surely be a day during which you will witness what will befall, by Allah's permission.

As a result, I have made it clear that we did not engage in any negotiations with anyone for signing a peace treaty or laying down our weapons. It is a lie. We did not plan to [open] dialogue with Bukar Abba Ibrahim, Muhammadu Buhari or Senator Ali Modu Sheriff. It is a lie and a spurious assertion. Whoever governs with democracy and a secular constitution is our enemy, and I swear by Allah, there is war between us. The only exceptions are those who repent and follow Allah's path. Likewise, whoever reveres the ungodly system in this land can never do us any harm: "Allah will not give the unbelievers the upper hand over the believers." (Q4:141) This is the verse Allah revealed in His book.

For that reason, this is my concluding explanation. The report they disseminated is false. It is false. This explanation of mine is intended to serve as a rebuttal to their false report. And may Allah conceal our secrets. In conclusion, I want to comment on the people who were killed in Maiduguri. I swear by Allah they are Muslims who were killed while praying. Although you may be unaware, those people who dress in the uniforms of the police and soldiers are unbelievers who have successfully infiltrated the government. They are responsible for killing the Muslims. We are upon the path of the religion, and have come out to fight *jihād*. We do not attack those who pray, fast or hold firm to the religion. We follow whatever Allah has commanded us to do. We will never give up our path. We will continue the path even if we are alone. All praise be to Allah, there will surely be a day when Allah will make clear whatever He wishes to make clear. This is the explanation that Allah foreordained for me to deliver to you to make clear the events happening in this land.

35

GLAD TIDINGS, O SOLDIERS OF ALLAH

BY ABUBAKAR SHEKAU

(29 NOVEMBER 2012)

[Trans.: Abdulbasit Kassim]

Available at: https://videos.files.wordpress.com/nUniRM5n/shaykh-abc
5ab-bakr-shekau-22oh-soldiers-of-god-you-are-mortals22_dvd.mp4

In this video, Shekau declared an ideological bond with other groups waging jihād. *It is possible to conclude that what Shekau really wanted at this stage was for Boko Haram to be declared an al-Qaeda affiliate in West Africa. al-Qaeda has always made explicit its long-term goal of a jihadi battlefront in Nigeria, as illustrated in a tape purportedly released by bin Laden in 2003 in which Nigeria was mentioned as a country where Muslims needed to be liberated.[1] Similarly, Abu Bakr Naji in* Idārat al-Tawaḥḥush *(Management of Savagery) classified Nigeria as a region of priority.[2] The counterproductive violence of Boko Haram similar to that in Algeria not only spurred the formation of Ansaru but also weakened the legitimacy of the group in the eyes of al-Qaeda.[3]*

[Standard Islamic opening]

And thereafter:

From the poor servant, seeking the mercy of Allah, Abu Muhammad Abubakar b. Muhammad al-Shekawi, to my honorable *mujāhid* brother, may Allah protect and preserve you, and may He make our steps and yours successful.

[Salutation]

Here we are in a country called Nigeria, where we sacrifice for the sake of Allah, and in Allah's path we fight those who disbelieve in Allah, by Allah's permission, Allah willing. This is a message of glad tidings to our *mujāhidīn* brothers in the world.

O our brothers and shaykhs in the Islamic Maghrib, may Allah preserve and protect you. O soldiers of Allah, the soldiers of the Islamic State in Mali, glad tidings to you, and may Allah reward you on our behalf in the best way. And glad tidings to our brothers and shaykhs in beloved Somalia, to our brothers and shaykhs in Libya, to our brothers and shaykhs in oppressed Afghanistan, to our brothers and shaykhs in wounded Iraq, to our brothers and shaykhs in Pakistan, to our brothers and shaykhs in blessed Yemen, to our brothers and shaykhs in usurped Palestine, and to other places where our brothers are waging *jihād* in Allah's path. Glad tidings to you, and may Allah reward you on our behalf in the best way.

We ask Allah to make us the victorious sect (*al-ṭāʾifa al-manṣūra*), which is from among the Sunnis in terms of creed, speech, knowledge, actions, qualities, guidance, preaching and *jihād*. Allah is great! Allah is great! All honor belongs to Allah! Allah is great! Allah is great! All honor belongs to Allah!

The religion will be victorious until the Day of Judgment, and its support is an obligation, Allah willing. Allah says: "Allah has not intended this except as good news to you and that your hearts might be reassured thereby. Victory comes only from Allah, the Mighty, the Wise!" (Q3:126)

Allah said that He only sent the angels to help the Muslims at [the Battle of] Badr as glad tidings to Muslims. Allah says:

> Allah will defend the believers; Allah surely does not like any thankless traitor. Permission is given to those who fight because they are wronged. Surely, Allah can give them victory. Those who were driven out of their homes unjustly, merely for their saying: "Our Lord is Allah." Had Allah not repelled some people by others, surely monasteries, churches, synagogues and mosques, wherein the name of Allah is mentioned frequently, would have been demolished. Indeed, Allah will support whoever supports Him. Allah is surely Strong and Mighty. Those who, if We establish them firmly in the land, will perform prayers, give the alms, command the good and prohibit evil. To Allah belongs the outcome of all affairs. (Q22:38–41)

Allah's Sunna promises that the pious people will have a good finale, and that Allah's righteous servants will inherit the Earth. However, it is also part of His Sunna, that when the people of faith forfeit it, He replaces them with others and Allah brings people whom He loves and they love Him:

> O believers, whoever of you renounces his religion, Allah will certainly bring forth a people whom He loves and they love Him, humble towards the faithful, but mighty towards the unbelievers. They fight in the way of Allah and do not fear anybody's reproach. That is a favor from Allah which He confers on whomever He pleases. Allah is Munificent, All-knowing. (Q5:54)

We ask Allah to make us from among them.

O my brothers in Allah, we did not forget this *ḥadīth* concerning sincerity to Allah:

Abu Hurayra said: We witnessed along with Allah's Messenger the battle of Khaybar. Allah's Messenger told his Companions about a man who claimed to be a Muslim, "This man is from the people of hellfire." When the battle started, the man fought very bravely and received a great number of wounds and was crippled. Then, one of the Prophet's Companions came and said: "O Allah's Messenger! Do you know what the man you described as being from the people of hellfire has done? He has fought very bravely for Allah's cause and he has received many wounds." The Prophet said, "But he is indeed one of the people of hellfire." Some of the Muslims harbored some doubt about that. But while the man was in that state, the pain caused by the wounds vexed him so much that he put his hand in his quiver, took out an arrow and committed suicide with it. Some men from among the Muslims went to Allah's Messenger and said, "O Allah's Messenger! Allah has made your statement true." Allah's Messenger said, "Allah is Great! I testify that I am Allah's slave and His Messenger." Then he ordered Bilal to announce amongst the people: "None but Muslims will enter the paradise, and Allah may support this religion even with a wicked (disobedient) man."[4]

O Muslims! Do not panic, for victory is very near. Allah says: "It is He who sent His Messenger forth with the guidance and the religion of truth, to make it triumph over every religion, even though the idolaters may be averse." (Q61:9) Allah's religion will be victorious either through you or others. Allah says: "If you do not march forth, He will inflict a very painful punishment on you and replace you by another people, and you will not harm Him in the least; for Allah has power over everything." (Q9:39) The truth will rise! The truth will rise! The truth will rise! Allah says: "O believers, whoever of you renounces his religion, Allah will certainly bring forth a people whom He loves and they love Him, humble towards the faithful, but mighty towards the unbelievers. They fight in the way of Allah and do not fear anybody's reproach. That is a favor from Allah which He confers on whomever He pleases. Allah is Munificent, All-knowing." (Q5:54)

[*Shekau recites a poem but it is not audible because of the waves in the background.*]

O *mujāhidīn* brothers! This is proof that our *jihād* is a *jihād* in Allah's path, because it is impossible for us to kill every day and not be killed. Allah says: "They fight in the way of Allah, kill and get killed. That is a true promise from Him in the Torah, the Gospel and the Qur'ān; and who fulfils His promise better than Allah? Rejoice then at the bargain you have made with Him; for that is the great triumph." (Q9:111)

O honored brothers, our Lord, the Glorified, and the Almighty says:

Do not be faint-hearted and do not grieve; you will have the upper hand, if you are true believers. If you have been afflicted by a wound, a similar wound, a similar wound has afflicted the others. Such are the times; we alternate them among the people, so that Allah may know are the believers and choose martyrs from among you. Allah does not like the evildoers! And that Allah might purify the believers and annihilate the unbelievers. Or did you suppose that you will enter paradise, before Allah has known who were those of you who have struggled, and those who are steadfast. You were yearning for death before you met it. Now you have seen it and you are beholding it. Muhammad is merely an apostle, before whom many apostles have come and gone. If then he dies or gets killed, you will turn on your heels? Should any man turn on his heels, he will not cause Allah any harm; and Allah will reward the thankful. It is not given to any soul to die, except with Allah's leave at a fixed time. He who desires the reward of this world, we will give him [part] of it, and he who desires the reward of the life to come, we will give him [part] of it; and we shall reward the thankful. How many prophets with whom large multitudes have fought; they were not daunted because what befell them in Allah's cause? They did not weaken or cringe; and Allah loves the steadfast. (Q3:139–146)

We ask Allah to place us among the patient ones. O Allah: "Their only words were: 'Lord, forgive us our sins and our excess in our affairs. Make firm our feet and grant us victory over the unbelieving people.' Therefore, Allah granted them the reward of this life and the excellent reward of the life to come, and Allah loves the Beneficent!" (Q3:147–148)

Allah is great! Allah is great! Allah is great! May Allah accept our martyred brothers, as we consider them, but we do not declare pure any before Allah. May Allah release our imprisoned brothers. Endure in patience, O soldiers of Allah! Endure in patience, O soldiers of Allah! O you who follow the men of Badr, Uḥud, Aḥzāb, and Hudaybiyya's examples, the conquests of Mecca and Tabūk, and the rest of the battles! O you who long for paradise! O you who long for paradise! O you who long for paradise! O you who abandoned worldly pleasures and desires, families, and neighbors in pursuit of paradise, you who left your fathers, mothers, children, siblings, spouses, clans, all of that for the pleasure of Allah and to raise His Word high! Patience upon patience, O soldiers of Allah! Patience upon patience, O soldiers of Allah! Allah is great!

O Britain, America, Israel and Nigeria! Do not think that *jihād* stops with the death of imams, because they are individuals. *Jihād* has just started! *Jihād* has just started! O enemies of Allah! Do you not see and think how many shaykhs and men were martyred—like Shaykh Abdallah Azzam, Abu Musʿab al-Zarqawi, Abu ʿUmar al-Baghdadi, Osama bin Laden, Abu Yahya al-Libi, Abu Yusuf Muhammad b. Yusuf al-Nigiri,[5] and others, may Allah have mercy on them, and we ask Allah the Almighty to make us among the martyrs. Did *jihād* stop? Did *jihād* stop? No, a thousand noes, a thousand noes! *Jihād* does not stop until Allah wills it to be stopped, and with the glory of Allah the Almighty, O unbelievers, O apostates, O hypocrites, die in your frustration. Allah will support His religion with us or other than us. Allah says:

If a good fortune befalls you, they are displeased, and if a disaster befalls you they say: "We have taken our precaution before." Then, they turn away rejoicing. Say: "Nothing we befall us except what Allah has decreed for us. He is our Lord, and in Allah let the believers put their trust." Say: "Do you expect for us anything other than one of the two best outcomes; while we wait for you that Allah will smite you with a punishment, either from Him, or at our hands?" So, wait and watch, we are waiting and watching with you. (Q9:50–52)

The world should bear witness—America, Britain, Nigeria and other Crusaders, meaning America and Britain, should witness—the Jews of Israel who are killing the Muslims in Palestine should witness, the polytheists should witness, the apostates and the hypocrites, and Nigeria in particular, should witness, that we are with our *mujāhidīn* brothers fighting in Allah's path everywhere, those who did their best to raise high the Word of Allah and helped the weak Muslims who are humiliated by the Jews and the Crusader Christians, by Allah's permission. We are with our *mujāhidīn* brothers fighting in Allah's path everywhere, in Afghanistan, Chechnya, Pakistan, Kashmir, Iraq, the Peninsula of Muhammad [Arabian Peninsula], Yemen, Somalia, Algeria, and other places that I did not mention.

O police, O so-called police and soldier camps in this country, repent to Allah; otherwise, we will kill you, as Allah commanded us. Your blood is permissible! Your blood is permissible! Your blood is permissible! Allah has made your blood permissible to us, because you worship the laws of the government and not Allah's laws. Democracy is an unbelieving system. O Obama! O Jonathan! O Obama! You will soon see what we are seeing, by the power and permission of Allah.

Finally, you do not have power to do anything to us: "Surely, neither you nor what you worship can ever turn anyone against Him; except he who will be roasting in hell." (Q37:161–163) Our Lord, the Almighty, says: "Our word unto our messengers has already gone out. They will surely be supported. And our hosts are the true victors." (Q37:171–173)

We ask Allah to place us among His victorious soldiers. O Allah, those oppressive Jews, O Allah, shower your wrath and punishment upon them, O Lord of truth! O Allah, the Revealer of the Book, the Mover of the clouds, the Defeater of the confederates (*aḥzāb*), defeat the usurping Jews who occupy, and shake them! O Allah, destroy their unity and disperse them and shake their feet. O Allah, we place you against them and seek refuge in you from their evil! O Allah, grant victory to our brothers everywhere! O Allah, grant victory to our brothers everywhere! O Allah, grant victory to our brothers everywhere! O Allah, support and aid us, help and back us! O Allah, we are weak, so strengthen us and our will, and preserve our faith, O Lord, O Generous One! Unite us, O Allah, there is no shelter except in You, O Allah! O Allah, harm has touched us, so remove it from us, and from all our Muslim brothers everywhere! O Allah, whoever wants to harm us, return the harm unto them! And may the peace and prayer of Allah be upon our Prophet Muhammad, and upon his family and his Companions. Praise be to Allah, the Lord of the worlds.

[Video continues with fighters in their military training.]

36

DISASSOCIATION OF THE JAMĀʿAT ANṢĀR AL-MUSLIMIN FROM TARGETING MUSLIM INNOCENTS

(14 MAY 2013)

[Trans.: David Cook]

Available at: http://azelin.files.wordpress.com/2013/05/jamc481at-ane1b9a3c481r-al-muslimc4abn-fi-bilc481d-al-sc5abdc481n-22innocence-of-the-mujc481hidc4abn-from-the-blood-of-the-innocent-muslims22.pdf

*On 18 March 2013, there were bus bombings in Kano, during which approximately sixty-five people were killed. On 13 April 2013, the first Baga massacre occurred, during which at least 187 people were killed (it is still unclear whether this was the work of Boko Haram). In the light of these massacres it is not surprising that Ansaru felt the need to proclaim its disassociation (*barāʾa*) from the killing of innocents.*

[Standard Islamic opening] Our Muslim community, your *mujāhidīn* sons in the Land of the Blacks continue to trace the most fantastic sacrifices, expending their lives after they have spent their wealth—and the expression of their situation is:

Leave us to travel the pathways of our fathers	as we have provision from the awe-inspiring endeavors.
Our appointment is with a clear victory, but if	death, then the appointment is with our God.

Leave us to die so that we can attain   as death in the path of guidance is birth.
martyrdom   [2]

So be, O dear community, an aid to the *mujāhidīn*, and do not be with our enemy against us, an enemy that does not watch over a believer, nor accords protection as long as he testifies that there is no god but Allah and that Muhammad is Allah's Messenger. Do not be deceived by the boasting of the Genghis Khan [Nigerian] government to which you have fallen victim. This is an attempt to sugarcoat their supply losses after their spiritual defeat. They only desire to make you take part in the struggle.

The reality is that your salvation from that labyrinth and loss, and poverty and injustice is the reason for the struggle—so how can you believe the likes of these monstrous lies about the *mujāhidīn*? When they have left their wealth and families only to become a protective barrier against the Christian march, both locally and externally, against the Muslims' lands? The Truth [Allah] said: "Had Allah not repelled some people by others, surely monasteries, churches, synagogues and mosques, wherein the name of Allah is mentioned frequently, would have been demolished..." (Q22:40)

The enemies of God, the hateful Christians, would think 1,000 times before targeting the Muslims, fearing that the *mujāhidīn* would take vengeance upon them. The blessed and raised One said: "So, fight for Allah's cause; you are charged only of yourself. Urge the believers on that Allah may perchance restrain the unbelievers' might. Allah's might is greater; and greater is His retribution." (Q4:84)

On that note, we in the JAMBS [Ansaru] proclaim our disassociation from targeting the masses of Muslims who have spoken the two declarations of faith (*shahāda*s), manifesting outwardly the signs of Islam. So as long as they entered Islam in complete certainty, we will not expel them without complete certainty—not with imagination, innovative interpretations, nor with legal discussions in which there is room for disagreement and about which the Muslim can be ignorant.

This is clear in our working reality that we do not intend [to attack] a Muslim whose blood, wealth and [sexual] honor are protected by the Law-giver. That operations where defenseless Muslims are targeted, and which end in the killing of people and children, and the destruction of protected homes that the venal media purport to convey are actions of Satan's armies, and those who do not understand the Law's policy or its intentions. There are those who profit from this for political purposes or private whims, but how would we dare to carry out these loathsome actions, when we recite the words of the leader of the Anṣār and the Emigrants [from Mecca to Medina], the one who was sent as a mercy to the worlds [Muhammad]: "Destruction of the world is less in Allah's eyes than the unjustified killing of a believer..."

May Allah have mercy on the commander of the martyrdom-seekers, Abu Mus'ab al-Zarqawi when he said: "We will never, by Allah, be satisfied that Muslims' blood would be shed without a sincere reason. Because I would come and allow you to cut off my head rather than kill a Muslim man without a sincere reason." What words, and how awe-inspiring they are! O Allah, we disassociate before You from the actions of those, and ask forgiveness from You from the actions of those.

As for us, the *mujāhidīn*, the only thing we are trying is to cause people to abandon the worship of creatures for the worship of the Lord of creatures, that they would say: "Our Lord is Allah." But they [the Christians] are the ones who began this war—and the beginner is the one at fault—when they obtained the support of the atheist government, which has taken democracy as a religion, and international law as the law and method. The massacres by those disgusting rabbles are not concealed either from near or far, such that they have become video selections on handheld phones passed back and forth among the people.

After all of that, does anybody think that we would remain hands-tied in the presence of these planned and orchestrated crimes? Does anybody think that we will bow to the *ṭāghūt* who thinks the forbidden is permitted and the permitted forbidden? A *ṭāghūt* which spreads corruption on the earth? And forbids the people the most specific of their rights? And thinks of obtaining its own advantage before protecting the souls of the people?

Does anybody think that we will be lowly to every vile person? Establishing unbelief, while the *ṭāghūt* is among us?

Thinking that the issue of the forbidden is permitted and not allowing us the permitted to humiliate us.

O descendants of 'Uthman Dan Fodio and al-Hajj 'Umar al-Futi,[1] rise as one man, as there is no good in us if our [sexual] honor is violated, our religion and symbols are held in contempt, and the best of our brothers and sons are killed, while we are quiescent, unmoving, since "the root of humiliation is only demolished by a shower of lead."

Form a line around your *mujāhidīn* brothers so this will be a popular revolt against the corrupt rulers, the expert thieves, who will not leave religion to the people to make their next world righteous or this world to make a livelihood for them. Death of nobility is better than life of humiliation!

Our Muslim brothers, how can you abandon your *mujāhidīn* sons when they lie awake at night as well as day to return your glory and nobility to you, and because of your harming the *mujāhidīn*. Accusing them is harder on them than the darts of the enemy—and how, when these are added to joining with the army of the unbelievers in fighting the monotheists under the flag of the head of unbelief, America—after it announced in the full light of day, that it was "a crusader war" and that "you are either with us or with them [the terrorists]," meaning that there is no third camp. It is either Islam and *jihād* or unbelief and apostasy. Our Creator, praise be to Him, said: "Those who believe fight for Allah's cause, while those who disbelieve fight on behalf of the Devil (*ṭāghūt*). Fight then the followers of the Devil. Surely the guile of the Devil is weak." (Q4:76)

O Allah! Strengthen Islam and the Muslims, and weaken polytheism and the polytheists! Destroy Your enemies, the enemies of the religion! Help us against them altogether! O Allah, the Revealer of the Book, the Mover of the clouds, Defeater of the confederates (*aḥzāb*), defeat them, and help us against them. O Allah, be with the downtrodden in the Syrian lands, and give them power over Your enemy Bashar [al-Assad], his *shabiha* (militia) and his armies! O Allah, prepare the matter of Your guidance for this community, strengthening in it those who obey You, and weakening in it those who disobey You. Finally, praise be to Allah, Lord of the worlds!

37

SERMON FOR 'ID AL-AḌḤĀ 1434/2013

BY ABU USAMA AL-ANSARI

(14 NOVEMBER 2013)

[Trans.: David Cook]

Available at: https://azelin.files.wordpress.com/2013/11/abc5ab-usc481
mah-al-ane1b9a3c481rc4ab-e2809ckhue1b9adbah-e28098c4abd-al-
e28098ae1b88de1b8a5c481-for-the-year-1434-he280b3.pdf

It is interesting that Ansaru tended to use more inclusive, revolutionary language, albeit with an obvious Islamic supremacist focus, than does Boko Haram. Only from Ansaru can we find examples of what could be attempts to reach beyond the boundaries of the most literal form of Salafism to other Muslims in their own language, and even to Nigerians as a whole.

Praise be to Allah, who empowers Islam by His aid, who weakens polytheism by His force, who directs events by His command, who gradually lowers the unbelievers by His cunning, who foreordained the days one after the other by His justice, who tests His servants with evil and good in tribulation by His wisdom, and who makes the finale for the God-fearing by His grace, and prayers and peace upon the one whom Allah raised as a lamp of Islam by his sword.[1]

And afterwards:

So, the struggle between truth and falsehood is ancient, and the testing is a history and lengthy story since "There is no god but Allah" was revealed on the earth. The prophets and the righteous ones were tested, as were the monotheistic imams. The Almighty said, telling of the sons of Adam: "And recite to them in all truth the tale of Adam's two sons, when they offered a sacrifice, which was accepted from one, but not accepted from the other. The latter said: 'I will surely kill you'; the other replied: 'Allah accepts only from the God-fearing.'" (Q5:27) Falsehood will never be satisfied with the existence of truth nor will [falsehood] accept it [truth]—they are opposites that cannot coexist.

Among Allah's tests of His servants is that enemies of the prophets' preaching, the preaching of monotheism, could raise doubts because of the lusts in their hearts. The Truth [Allah], blessed and raised, said: "Likewise, we have assigned to every prophet an enemy, the devils of men and jinn, revealing one to the other tawdry speech in order to deceive..." (Q6:112) and also: "And that is how We appointed to every prophet an enemy from the criminals." (Q25:31)

But by the grace of Allah and His mercy the truth is clear, bright, and falsehood manifest, stuttering. "We have prepared for the wrongdoers a fire whose canopy encompasses them all. If they call for relief, they will be relieved with water like molten brass which scars the faces. Wretched is that drink and wretched is the resting place!" (Q18:28)

The signs of the struggle are clear and manifest, when the communities of unbelief throng together from all groups, to initiate an open-ended war that they call "terror." This is in corroboration with the statement of our Prophet, Muhammad, in a tradition narrated by al-Imam Aḥmad and Abū Dā'ūd on the authority of Thawbān:

> Allah's Messenger said: "The nations are about to call out to each other over you from every horizon, just as hungry people call out over a bowl of food." We said: "O Messenger of Allah, will it because we are few on that day?" He said: "On that day you will be many, but you will be scum, like the scum of the flash-flood. The fear will be taken from the hearts of your enemy, and *al-wahn* (weakness) will be placed in your hearts." We said: "What is *al-wahn*?" He said: "Love of life and dislike of death."

In another version, according to Aḥmad, it is "dislike of fighting."

Allah's enemy, [George] Bush clarified it for us with his statement: "This is a crusader war." And he said, may Allah dishonor him, that "you are either with us or against us." He was telling the truth, even though he is a liar, because belief struggles against unbelief, and the truth struggles against falsehood. Our Creator, praise Him and raise Him said: "Those who believe fight for Allah's cause, while those who disbelieve fight on behalf of the Devil (*ṭāghūt*). Fight then the followers of the Devil. Surely the guile of the Devil is weak." (Q4:76)

Our beloved Muslim community, do not be deceived by what the Western unbelieving media circulate, that they are fighting the enemies of freedom, those who are rebelling against international laws, for if the matter were like that, then why are they supporting the government of ['Abd al-Fattah] al-Sisi in Egypt, after what the entire world witnessed, that they carried out a revolution against the legally constituted government of Morsi and his Muslim Brotherhood. They came to power by democratic means, by which the West was satisfied, like the coming to power through the majority.

But the unbelievers are not satisfied with a government next to Israel that raises Islamic emblems, even if they are empty emblems. There are signs in this for those of this defeatist ideology, if only they would take heed.

Jihād is a human movement, in which there are correct and incorrect, and the *mujāhidīn* are not angels, who do not disobey Allah in anything. When the Companions of Allah's Messenger, under the leadership of the Sword of Allah, Khālid b. al-Walīd, killed close to 1,000 men in error—and the story is verified, present in the books of conduct—when such happens in the first generation, how will it be for those following it?

The mistakes of the *mujāhidīn* come to nothing in the presence of their self-sacrifice and heroism. It is possible for them to sit it out like others who rest upon this world and its adornments, they have refused anything other than to brave the dangers and difficulties—people are sleeping while they are awake. They sacrifice themselves cheaply, redeeming their religion and their community. Their situation is expressed: "They said, 'If the [army] stipend is meagerly, then we are sacrifices for the religion.'"

Our Muslim brothers and families in the land of the Sudan [Nigeria], and especially in the northeast, we would console and comfort you concerning the killing and deportation that has happened among you, in the shadow of a complete media blackout, when the communication networks are not working so it is not possible for the world to truly know of the crimes being committed against our Muslim community.

When we point out the possibility of publicizing the *mujāhidīn*'s mistakes, this does not mean, ever, that we support the purposeful attacks on them, and we do not think whoever is defending their people and families should be subject to woes and disasters, but you are brothers and families, we judge you by the manifest law of Islam, which is exemplified by the two declarations of faith (*shahādas*), that whoever says them, his blood and wealth are protected, as long as he does not openly repudiate them.

We, the *mujāhidīn* of Ansaru, have announced our disassociation from the operations that target Muslims in their markets, their fields, and even in their mosques, as we have devoted an entire epistle which we called "Disassociation of the Anṣār al-Muslimīn from the Targeting of Innocent Muslims."[2] Those who have taken responsibility for these horrible operations have appeared in the media, when their leader and imam appeared to announce in clear Hausa phrases their responsibility for the latest massacres in Benishek. This was when they set up a roadblock for travelers on the main road to kill anybody leaving Borno State without distinction. This resulted in the killing of dozens.

Previously they had announced their responsibility for the attack on Baga, in which hundreds were victims, and many of the Muslims took refuge in the thickets to die there of hunger and thirst. Since it is not right or just that such actions be ascribed to us, after their perpetrators took responsibility for them, we do not agree with them or support them, and we disassociate ourselves before Allah from them.

The one who follows the affairs of the land of the Sudan [Nigeria] will know the large number of the Muslims' sufferings in it, as the attacks of the hateful Christians are from one side, while the injustice of the organized rulers are from the other. They [the Muslims] stretch out their necks begging for someone who will aid them, and take the hand of the unjust. Then suddenly people from our own skin put pressure on them in the same way as the hateful enemy, and from more than one direction.

The rulers of Nigeria, and most of its criminals, try to sugar-coat the realities of their injustice and crimes to the people when they manifest to the world that they are reformers, who love peace and security, while we do not. Is peace and security the product of criminals' crimes? Do we not pray in our mosques, the same way as the Muslims, without attacking anybody? Are you not the ones who began this war when you killed the best of us, our elders, our men, women and children?

This is for clowns and imbeciles—rulers who do not provide for their peoples the most important of their daily needs: water, electricity and hospitals! The souls of the people are cheaper than what is around them. Then they come out and say that the [terrorists] have destroyed the land and killed the innocent [Muslims]. Where was terrorism when Muslims were killed by the thousands, their markets and homes burned, their mosques destroyed, as happened in Yelwa Shandam, Tafawa Balewa, Jos and in the south of Kaduna State? Are those who carried out those crimes not the true criminals?

Lastly, we would like to proclaim to our Muslim community that we are coming to the defense of our religion and sanctities, proclaiming the promise of Allah, which He wrote for His righteous servants, to return the glory that our ancestors, Shehu 'Uthman Dan Fodio, his children and disciples, made, by the power and might of Allah. May Allah empower Islam by it and weaken unbelief.

We would like to take this opportunity to convey peace greetings to the *mujāhidīn* and those who guard the borders on every frontier, and at their head:

1. Our precious commander, our pre-eminent elder, the leader of the community, one with constancy and zeal, Shaykh Ayman al-Zawahiri.
2. The Commander of the Believers, Mulla 'Umar.
3. The Commander of the Islamic State in Iraq and Syria, Abu Bakr al-Husayni al-Qurashi al-Baghdadi.
4. The Commander of Jabhat al-Nusra, the Victorious Front, Abu Muhammad al-Joulani.
5. The Commander of the al-Qaeda Organization in the Arabian Peninsula, Abu Basir Nasir al-Wuhayshi.

6. The Commander of the al-Qaeda Organization in the Islamic Maghrib (AQIM), Abu Musaʿb ʿAbd al-Wudud.
7. The Commander of the Shabab Movement Mukhtar Abu Zubayr.
8. The shrewd leader Khalid Abu al-Abbas.

And other commanders and elders of the *mujāhidīn*, and the rest of the Muslims who [Mulla] ʿUmar does not know, but the Lord of ʿUmar knows, and may He receive their Feast (*ʿId*) and their sacrifices. We ask Allah that He have it occur next year when our community and holy sanctuaries are liberated. Victory will be for the people of faith and monotheism, and defeat for the people of polytheism and defamation. The Feast is not for those who wear new [clothing] but for those who have rejected polytheism and defamation.

O Allah! Aid the *mujāhidīn* in every place, in the Caucasus and Khurasan [Afghanistan], in Iraq and Syria, in the Sahara and the west (*maghrib*), and in the Egyptian lands, the African regions, and in the land of the Sudan. O Allah, Revealer of the Book, Mover of the clouds, Defeater of the confederates, defeat them and aid us against them. O Allah! Destroy America, and hasten its perishing! It and whoever is allied with it. O powerful one, O mighty one, foreordain mighty victory, O merciful and compassionate one, and the last of our prayers is: Praise be to Allah, Lord of the worlds.

—Abu Usama al-Ansari

PART FOUR

BOKO HARAM STATE
(2013–2015)

Michael Nwankpa

For a brief period between July 2014 and March 2015, Boko Haram had territorial control over a large area of land in Borno, Yobe and Adamawa states (northeast Nigeria). During this time, Boko Haram became the deadliest terror organization in the world, with 6,644 deaths in 2014 alone, compared to ISIS' 6,073 and the Taliban's 3,477 during the same period. Boko Haram continued to carry out its activities in northern Nigeria and expanded its attacks to Niger, Chad and Cameroon. This was in spite of extensive Nigerian army operations, an extension of the state of emergency, and the constitution of a regional multinational counter-force comprised of the armies of Chad, Cameroon, Niger, Nigeria and Benin.[1] Additionally, Boko Haram has spurned all attempts by the Nigerian government to engage in dialogue, including those with promises of amnesty.

Most probably, a military approach to Boko Haram (armed combat) would not be suitable; rather, a criminal justice and law enforcement approach, in addition to limited political concessions, would represent the right counter-response.[2] However, law enforcement and intelligence measures alone might be inadequate in preventing and resolving conflict, especially in societies where genuine grievances exist.[3]

An economic approach may be more ideal in such an environment, as "businesses started and jobs created are as much 'indicators of success' as insurgents killed or intelligence provided."[4] Boko Haram's objective of imposing *sharīʿa* on the Nigerian state is obvious, but only true to the extent that by imposing its vision of the world, it will gain political-religious control. Hence, power is the true force behind the Boko Haram campaign of terror. Although, Boko Haram's leadership is largely Kanuri, its membership is diverse, comprising of both Hausas and Fulanis. Kanuris make up only about 4 per cent of the Nigerian population. Hence, Boko Haram's Islamic state can only materialize if it manages to forge alliances with either of the other ethnic groups, just as the alliance between the Hausas and the Fulanis helps to maintain the authority of the Sokoto caliphate, and protects the national interest of the traditional northern Muslim elites. But, such an alliance is unlikely to happen as Boko Haram's political ambition threatens not just the Nigerian secular state but even more so the traditional Muslim elites in the north.

Tactics

To a large extent, Boko Haram has preferred guerrilla warfare tactics against the Nigerian army and the regional forces. Its confrontation with the military has been largely asymmetrical, but it has laid ambush for individual military personnel as well as antipersonnel landmines targeting a whole troop. Boko Haram often gains weapons from such raids. For example, Boko Haram attacked the military artillery in Adamawa State on 30 November 2015, where it burned down a military base after carting away guns and ammunition.

Boko Haram has also assassinated sizeable numbers of the public, including Islamic clerics (who may have cooperated with the security forces against the group, see texts 9–10), members (who are considered traitors or who decide to leave the group) and, apparently, security forces and other government representatives. For instance, on 17 September 2015, Boko Haram killed three women and five men in Cameroon's border village of Aisaharde for allegedly collaborating with the Cameroonian troops against the group.[5]

The use of suicide bombing marks a resurgence of its urban guerrilla warfare. Boko Haram enabled the coordination of bomb and suicide bomb attacks in major northeastern cities such as Maiduguri, Damaturu, Potiskum, Gombe and the central capital city, Abuja. On 14 April 2014, Boko Haram bombed a bus stop in Abuja, killing nearly 100 people and wounding many more. It was on the same day that it kidnapped the 276 teenage girls at Chibok (text 40). Nigerian intelligence believes that Boko Haram fighters have infiltrated the cities and operate sleeper cells; they have supposedly identified a sleeper cell in Abuja and made some arrests.[6]

Most of the explosives are IEDs that are locally made in bomb factories scattered across the northeast. It is not surprising therefore that the use of explosives accounted for 60 per cent of all Boko Haram-related attacks in 2013 and 54 per cent in 2014.[7] The Nigerian military has destroyed several of the bomb-making factories and made useful arrests of several would-be suicide attackers, some as young as 12 years old.[8]

Boko Haram's second most-preferred tactics were armed assault using firearms. These tactics account for 30 per cent of the attacks in 2013 and more than half of all the attacks in 2014, including 67 per cent of all Boko Haram-related deaths.[9] For example, on 6 October 2015 Boko Haram killed eleven and wounded thirteen Chadian soldiers, and on 31 August 2015, Boko Haram members on horseback killed eighty (fifty, according to official sources) people in Borno State.[10]

Bombing and suicide bombings are used to inflict maximum damage by those seeking the death (and injury) of a large number. In most cases, it is often difficult to independently confirm if some of the attacks were done by bombing or suicide bombing. Nevertheless, it is true that the group has escalated its use of suicide bombing. In the first quarter of 2015 (January–March), Boko Haram had carried out eighteen suicide bomb attacks, leading to about 211 deaths.[11] Since President Buhari assumed office in May 2015, the use of suicide bombing has radically proliferated. There have been over seventy suicide bombings across northern Nigeria, Chad, Cameroon and Niger during June–December 2015 alone.

This number is staggering as it is far more than the combined number of suicide attacks carried out by the group in the five years previously. Roughly, a total of fifty-eight suicide bomb attacks were carried out in Nigeria between 2011 and the first quarter of 2015, accounting for about 5 per cent of all Boko Haram-related deaths.[12] However, in the recent escalation, 500 or more people have died from the recent hike in suicide bombings, accounting for nearly half of Boko Haram-related deaths since June 2015. Approximately 1,600 people died during the Boko Haram conflict between June and September,[13] taking the death toll in 2015 to 3,500. The number is likely to have risen since then.

The reasons for the sharp increase in both the number of suicide bomb attacks and casualties include the group's increasing use of remote-controlled suicide bombs and the staging of multiple suicide attacks, as well as its attacks on soft civilian targets such as the market and the mosque. There is a notable shift in Boko Haram's use of the suicide bomb attack from mostly single attacks to double and twin attacks. This allows the group to inflict maximum damage and achieve greater numbers of casualties. There is some difference in the gender dynamics since 2014, when Boko Haram recorded its first female suicide bomber. More females (mostly teenage girls and girls as young as 10) are used to perpetrate these acts. It has been suggested that some of these "human bombs" may not be aware of what they are doing, as the bombs are detonated remotely. Overall it is evident that suicide bombing is the most lethal weapon used by Boko Haram, and so its frequent usage does not suggest to me any signs of desperation, as the military has suggested.

Indeed, the Nigerian military has been helpless to stop the wave of suicide attacks. Soldiers at several checkpoints themselves have suffered from both armed assault and suicide attacks. For example, on 16 August 2015, a male suicide bomber killed four people at a military checkpoint in Borno State. A similar incident occurred in Borno State on 23 November 2015.

Money-Making And Sexual Slavery

Boko Haram started kidnapping local people including women, children and men in 2013. Kidnapping and hostage-taking have since become major features in Boko Haram's *modus operandi*. The number of hostages taken in 2014 alone was 1,298, more than a ten-fold increase from the previous year, when eighty-nine hostages were taken.[14] In 2014, there was a global increase in kidnapping and hostage-taking as a function of terrorist tactics; however, Nigeria, Iraq and Syria account for the majority of the over 9,400 incidents of this kind that occurred that year.[15] It was in 2014 that Boko Haram kidnapped approximately 276 boarding school girls in Chibok, a Local Government Area in Borno, Nigeria, an action that sparked international outrage and put Boko Haram firmly on the global map of terrorism. Boko Haram kidnapped over 2,000 women and girls in 2014.[16]

On 17 May 2014, a Chinese company was attacked in northern Cameroon and ten Chinese workers were kidnapped.[17] A tribal chief with his family and the wife of Deputy Prime Minister of Cameroon, Francoise-Agnes Moukouri were also abducted in northern Cameroon in July 2014. The abductors produced a video of the hostages—a pattern in all the kidnappings and a sign that the abductors often (but not always) seek to pursue negotiations.[18]

Kidnapping and hostage-taking serve many purposes to Boko Haram. They are an important source of revenue as well as of human shields, and most are also forcefully conscripted and trained to become Boko Haram spies, fighters and suicide bombers. Some of the girls and women are also kidnapped simply to be married off to Boko Haram fighters or to be used as sex slaves and carry out other administrative duties (many of the captured girls and women that have been rescued by the military corroborate this view, with many returning pregnant). There are clear cases of child soldiers, and Boko Haram is famous for allegedly using girls under the age of 12 as well as teenage girls for its suicide missions. In recent times, the Nigerian army and its counterparts in multi-national joint counterterrorism cooperation have rescued thousands of kidnapped people including children, women and men.

38

RAID ON MAIDUGURI

BY ABUBAKAR SHEKAU

(26 MARCH 2014)

[Trans.: Abdulbasit Kassim]
Available at: https://www.youtube.com/watch?v=Pba8uvuf9Is

On 14 March 2014, Boko Haram carried out a daring daylight raid on the heavily guarded military prison at Giwa Barracks in Maiduguri, freeing some of their incarcerated members. The freeing of these prisoners was important for the evolution of Boko Haram's caliphate. In this video, Shekau claimed the attack on behalf of the group, and declared war against the "Civilian JTF" (Kato de Gora)—a vigilante group formed in Maiduguri. Shekau also hinted that the group would enslave unbelievers' women and girls, a threat that was later carried out (text 40). For the first time, Shekau also admitted that his group murdered Shaykh Muhammad Auwal Adam Albani, a Zaria-based cleric of the Salafiyya movement, on 2 February 2014. He also refuted the claim that his group is fighting for a "Northern Agenda" which would be akin to southeastern-based groups fighting for a break-away state of Biafra. Shekau also issued a verdict for his followers to kill and slaughter those who oppose the group's vision. One should note that the use of Qur'ānic citations in Part 4 is much higher than in Part 3.

[Citations of Q9:52, 9:111, and 4:76.]

And thereafter:

Brothers in faith, may the peace and blessings of Allah be upon you. May Allah increase us in patience and may we be among His slaves who strive to be on the right path, the path of those Allah has favored. May Allah save us from the path of those who have incurred His wrath or have gone astray. May Allah make us among the people who follow the Prophet Muhammad. May Allah save us from following the Jews, the Christians, black unbelievers, democrats and anything that He has not commanded us to follow in His Book. May Allah protect us. There is no might except Allah's power and may Allah assist us with His might.

All praise be to Allah. We are grateful to you. We started the struggle with knives, but look today at the ammunition with which we are fighting. We can only praise you, Lord of the worlds, by your own words. This is the only praise that we will direct to You, Lord of creation. O Allah! We are grateful to You, Lord of creation. O One who created all languages, who created all the languages spoken in the world. O Allah! We thank you in the Hausa language, but we want you to teach us the language of the Qur'ān [Arabic]. O Allah! We are grateful to you.

Brothers! May Allah increase us in patience. Brothers! I am urging you to continue in patience. The message of your leader is that you should seek knowledge, purify your intentions, seek the acceptance of your Lord, and the praise of Allah. Never should you work because of a person or your leader. Whoever does that is lost. May Allah assist us. Brothers! May Allah help us. This is a message of greetings and praise. O sisters in faith! You should be patient, be patient, my sisters, be patient, small children, be patient, women! JASDJ, patience and more patience. Patience! Patience! Patience!

This is the opening message to my speech on the attack that took place today in Maiduguri, inside the barracks they call "Giwa Barracks." Allah is great! That "Giwa Barracks" is a barracks of pigs, dogs and rats. By Allah, it is a barracks of rats. Even if you were born in Ado Bayero's house in Kano,[1] this Hausa [language] must sink into your brains deeply. We are grateful to Allah. O Allah! You have shattered the barracks of pigs, dogs and rats. Allah is the greatest! We are grateful to you. We praise You as You want us to praise You. O Lord of humanity; Allah is the greatest.

We are the people who carried out the attack in Maiduguri. This is a message from the leader of JASDJ. We are the people who carried out the attack in Maiduguri, just like other attacks that you see and hear. We are the people that carried out all the attacks. It is important that we explain the attack that took place inside Giwa Barracks.

Allah has killed His enemy, decimated His enemy. Allah has killed the enemy of His Messenger and of Islam. He has shattered His enemy and has helped His servants. We are the people who carried out the attack in Maiduguri. We are the people who killed the unbelievers inside Giwa Barracks. So, look at this man calling himself "Civilian JTF." You are not "Civilian JTF"! I will give you a new name: "Civilian TBL" *trouble*. You are "Civilian TBL." You are not "Civilian JTF." We do not know any "Civilian JTF." You are "Civilian TBL." You are a *trouble-man* and by the permission and help of Allah, you shall see [what will happen].

I deliberately choose to mention those words in English, so that you will understand my intention and focus. After explaining that we are the people who carried out the Giwa Barracks attack, this speech will explain our hostility to the "Civilian JTF." Whoever aligns himself with the "Civilian JTF," if you choose to run, hold onto your weapon, wear the uniform of the soldiers or police—in fact if you like, wear the turban, *barmusu*.[2] Even if you become the grandchild of Wubchama,[3] the son of the Shehu of Borno or the children of the Borno, Yobe, Adamawa elites, and in fact Nigeria in its entirety.

You should become whatever you think you can become. Henceforth, I am launching my war against you. Before now, I did not even view you as something that exists. I did not know there was something called "Civilian JTF." But now, I have launched my war against you. *Jihād* has been declared on whoever identifies himself as "Civilian JTF." By Allah, you shall see. I have declared war against the "Civilian JTF" to enter paradise. Allah is the One who knows my intention. This is my verdict, and whoever Allah allows to hear, let him hear. If you like you can become a member of the SSS. As for me, this world is divided into two parties: either you are with us, or you are with the other side, and I will surely kill you. This is my task.

"We are quit of you and what you worship apart from Allah. We disbelieve in you. Enmity and hatred have arisen between you and us forever, till you believe in Allah alone." (Q60:4) This is my task and I, Shekau, am the person speaking. Henceforth, you will know who Shekau is. You don't know my madness, but today, you will see it. By Allah, I will slaughter you. If I don't slaughter you, I will not be contented. By Allah, I will slaughter. [*Shekau repeats the same statement in Kanuri.*]

If you like you should fry us, eat us, or do anything you wish to us; Allah has told us you will do what is worse than that. Allah is the One who created you, and He knows you. Up till now, you have not executed the things Allah told us you will do. We are waiting. Now, we are on the path. "JTF," *Kato de Gora*, the people of Borno, right? [*Shekau speaking in Kanuri.*] "Kill them wherever you find them and drive them out from wherever they drove you out. Sedition is worse than slaughter." (Q2:191) I would not mind mixing together Kanuri and Hausa, and even Yoruba, for bastards like you. I am not following your system. I am saying what I plan to do. If you like, you can choose to listen or not. This is the black book! This is the black book! My speech today is about the black book.[4]

Brothers! Wherever you are, may Allah make this cassette reach you; I have given you permission to rise, take arms and start killing them, even if you are 3. Kill! Kill! Kill! Today, our religion is nothing but killing. [*Shekau speaking in Kanuri.*] You should kill, slaughter, but do not eat them. You should leave the old, the women, the insane, and those who choose to repent. Whoever declares enmity towards Allah should be killed. Abandoning the practice of the religion is the same as enmity towards Allah.

Since I was born, I have never seen people refusing money, so why are you contending with Allah? I don't tolerate nonsense. You are contending with my Allah, but you do not refuse money, bastards! If I insult your mother, you will hate me, so why are you contending with my Allah? Why are you contending with my Allah, bastards?

You should kill. This is my speech today. Today's speech is a complicated speech. This is the speech of Shekau. By Allah, even if we kill you all, bastards like you, who did you arrest? Who would you arrest? Because you call us Boko Haram! They said that in Maiduguri, specifically in Giwa Barracks, they arrested our brothers. They caught some civilians, put tires around their necks [doused in gasoline]⁵ before killing and lynching them. Yes, we are waging a war against them.

Since you caught someone, necklacing him before lynching him to death, all the while thinking I am the one being killed, I am feeling that I was killed even though it is not me you killed. I feel like I am the person being killed. For instance, if you hold this iron and blow it up, that is exactly what you will do to me if you catch me. Right now, I have judged you as though I was the person being killed. By Allah, I must kill you. By Allah, killing is my occupation. Brothers! Let us kill them. It is better we leave the world—may Allah bring an end to the world.

May Allah curse you! May Allah curse you! May Allah curse you! O Lord of the worlds! These are your slaves helping Jonathan. They are Your slaves, they pray yet they are playing with the Qur'ān. They are Your slaves, yet they are helping Bush, Clinton and Obama. They are Your slaves, yet they are preoccupied with watching movies, playing [football] in the stadium and fornicating. O Lord of humanity! They are Your slaves, yet they are engaging in these evils. O Allah! You are the Knower. We are Your slaves and You have made pleading with You easy, so we are beseeching You with this prayer. O Lord of creation! Help us. O Allah! Expose them.

Allah made us victorious in the attack on Giwa Barracks. We broke into the barracks, burnt and killed. We rescued over 2,000 brothers—most of whom are commanders. Look at the video—they are laughing and being welcomed by their brothers. In fact, one of the commanders who was rescued stole a gun at the barracks gate immediately upon being released and started fighting right there! They have all been released. The world has changed, and the task has been begun.

By Allah, you should hear this again, Western education is forbidden. University is forbidden. You should all abandon the university. I totally detest the university. Bastards! You should leave the university. Western education is forbidden. Girls! You should all go back to your various houses. Enslaving the unbelievers' women is permissible. In the future, we will capture the women and sell them in the market. Danger! Danger! Danger!

Now, I see that you possess small sticks! The government should provide guns for them. Your soldiers could not confront us; it is the people with sticks who are feigning defiance. The sticks are small Jonathans. Provide them with guns, Kalashnikovs and Dushkas. Teach them to fly aircraft. What the soldiers could not do, the "Civilian JTF" will! Provide them with guns, because their sticks are small. Danger! We shall all see. By Allah, this is my admonition.

This is my speech. We are the people who carried out the attack in Maiduguri. The people you killed in the town were among the freed prisoners, but they were not our brothers. They are the people of the town you apprehended. They were freed, but thought the town was still the way they left it, so they left their short [prison] knickers, and were heading home when you apprehended them. You thought they were our brothers so killed them. We gathered all our brothers, clothed them, housed them, gave them cars, food, washed them and rubbed them with oil. They are now enjoying the cool breeze and are all in good condition. Praise be to Allah.

You have acquired Nigeria. Now, you are speaking about Biafra, right? The people of Biafra, too, have their land, right? That is small. You can also remove your flag. We are not only fighting the Biafrans, or the people of Cross River [State]; rather we are fighting the whole world. Whoever does not practice Islam is our enemy. Do not think we are northerners. Let me say it plainly to you, so that you can have peace of mind, because I can see that you are trying to explain on the radio. We are not fighting for the north; rather we are fighting the whole world. This is our task. May Allah help us and may He guide our intention.

Anyone who repents will be our brother. There is no one who destroys but then repents whom Allah will not accept. We also follow Allah. Thus, anyone who repents and returns to Allah's work, by Allah, he is our brother and we will accept him. But anyone who does not repent is our enemy so we will kill him. This is the religion we follow, and that is our path.

Up till now, you have failed to understand that democracy is unbelief. You insist you must practice it, right? You should go ahead, and we will also [go ahead]. We will kill all your scholars. They said I killed [Muhammad Awwal] Albani, and they even displayed the news in the newspapers. Yes, I will kill all of them! Who is Albani? Albani is trivial. I will kill all of them. I will exempt no one, except the one who follows Allah and His Messenger. Anyone who follows the Jews and the Christians is my enemy. And if that person says he is not following them, Allah knows the end judgment which we will all present in His presence in the hereafter. Just as I delivered a speech today I will carry out my task, by the permission of my Creator.

The rest of my speech is enough for you. I do not intend to deliver a long speech. I only came to deliver a speech confirming that we carried out the Maiduguri attack. This attack should be considered a low-scale attack because we went to the barracks to free our brothers. We will not reveal our intent to you, but you will see it in action. We only freed our brothers from the barracks. You should wait and see.

All the soldiers in Maiduguri are few. Bastards like you hover over one aircraft. Look at Allah above the aircraft. If you don't know, sit down now. Look at Allah above the aircraft. Look at the angels Gabriel, Israfil and Michael above the aircraft, and in fact the entire world is within one angel's handhold. I know you will not agree with my explanation because you are engaging in this nonsense. It is not my concern whether you accept or not. I know you will not accept my explanation, but that is what I believe. This is what I am striving for, and it is the work of Allah. We will preach Allah's message, by the permission of our Creator.

In this world, we must establish the Qur'ān, and burn the constitution. If Allah commands me to burn [something], I will burn it. However, right now I will only slaughter, not burn, because the time for burning has not come. Let me first commence with slaughtering. Allah's Messenger slaughtered—that is why I will slaughter.[6] I will not burn. You, "Civilian JTF," you can go ahead and burn, but I will only slaughter. Let us proceed and see if your fire will die out first or my knife will tire first. I will burn with my bombs, but I will not put tires around your necks. I will not do that; rather I will slaughter. Today, this is my speech for the JTF. [*Shekau speaking in Kanuri.*]

May Allah curse you! I don't feel pity for you even if you do for me. Bastards! Black unbelievers! You are relying on your prayers, but humiliating Allah's religion. May Allah curse you. This is my speech for today. This is where I will stop. May Allah make this speech solely for His cause, and may He make my anger for Him. My brothers! Even if you are in Abuja, Lagos, in the south or anywhere else, you should start fighting. Even if you are alone, take your knife, go and look for a person sleeping and slaughter him. Brothers! Please start slaughtering people. Take your knife, look for someone and slaughter him. We are fighting because of Allah. This attack is still a low-scale attack. Jonathan, you should bring Obama to sit together.

Brothers! There is an explanation I would like to add. This explanation is regarding the false news reported on the radio and newspapers, where they said we have been defeated in the Sambisa Forest. They said their planes burned all of us, so we ran and sought shelter in Cameroon, Chad, Niger and other bordering countries. These are all lies. Even if I did not say it is a lie, you know it is. I will not stop exposing their lies. This is my rebuttal to your claim that you killed our people and so forth. If only you will mention your people we killed, something surprising would happen in this land.

You do not mention all your people we kill. However, if you kill two people among us, you lie and broadcast that 100 people were killed. You, the people of Borno, you have seen how many people they killed in Maiduguri, but how many among us did they say they killed? Who did you kill? Give us their names—let us hear them. Bastard liars! They killed no one in Sambisa. Rather, we were the people who killed them. They cannot even enter Sambisa. Bloody liars! Our brothers have captured all their armored cars, driving them wherever they like, and you can see that from the videos. I have climbed on those armored cars myself. Even the scholars you listen to—like Solomon Dalung[7] and Abdullahi Wase—have criticized you for allowing us to loot your armored cars.

Now, when you have used up your lies, you said you are fighting white people. Maybe you saw angels [cf. Q8:9] or you saw paradise. They said they are Arabic-speaking white people. There is not a single white person among us. I am saying this because it might be beneficial. Whether you accept it or not, there is not a single white person among us. I will not swear upon this issue because of you; I will not call the name of my Allah for this. There is no single white person among us. We are all black people. We are the people Allah is using to stand on your throats. This is the true situation of our brothers—and may Allah protect and uplift them. They mentioned Sambisa, but you should understand that we have captured the whole of Nigeria.

Have I not said your refinery will soon stop working? Wait and see. We wil explode your petrol house. Whatever we say, we will do, because we are not hypocrites who speak without acting. Your refinery, your god, we will explode it. Have we not said in the past that we will go to Abuja? Did we not go? America should tell you. Let the American ambassador inform you.[8] When we said we would go to Abuja, did we go or not? So now, I am saying that we will go to the refinery. This is my task.

Therefore, there is nothing that has befallen us. We are in good health, and our brothers. Praise be to Allah, we are grateful to our Creator. He has told us: "They will only cause you a little harm; and if they fight you, they will turn their backs on you, and will have no support." (Q3:111) Allah has already told us. We agree with Allah; you will see surprises in Allah's place, not in our place. By Allah, you will see surprises in Allah's place.

My brothers! I am greeting you wherever you are. Be patient! Let us work for Allah. Those of you that came out of the prison of Giwa Barracks, may Allah increase your patience. May Allah make us love Him; may He make us stay on the Prophet's path; may He make our struggle gain us paradise and grant us the blessings of martyrdom.

39

HAUSA *NASHID* IN THE VIDEO "THE RAID ON MAIDUGURI"[1]

BY JAMĀ'AT AHL AL-SUNNA LI-L-DA'WA WA-L-JIHĀD

(26 MARCH 2014)

[Trans.: Abdulbasit Kassim]
Available at: https://videos.files.wordpress.com/8R0zcMXP/jamc481_
at-ahl-al-sunnah-li-da_wah-wa-l-jihc481d-22the-raid-of-maiduguri-
222_std.mp4

*Another approach to understanding what drives Boko Haram members is by focusing on the Hausa and Arabic poetry (*nashīds*) that speaks of the group's vision and the underlying theme of an apocalyptic battle or cosmic war between good and evil, most of which cannot be put in plain terms except through poetry. Since the early phase of 2014, Boko Haram videos have mostly featured Arabic* nashīds *produced by Ajnad Foundation for Media Production of the Islamic State. Depending on the content of a video, Boko Haram's use of poetry can be classified into four categories: (A) Praising* nashīds— Nashīds *of this genre, also known as* madih *in Arabic, are dedicated to praising the generosity, bravery and heroic deeds of fighters. (B) Martyrdom* nashīds—*This category of* nashīds *describes the joy of paradise and encourages Boko Haram fighters not to give up their fight. (C) Mourning* nashīds—Nashīds *of this genre, also known as* rithā' *in Arabic, are related to martyrdom* nashīds *but in this case are composed for people of high standing like Muhammad Yusuf. (D) Battlefield* nashīds—Nashīds *of this category are*

297

used to mobilize and encourage Boko Haram fighters. They mostly tell the stories of the heroism of their fighters, and speak of recovering lost dignity and freedom.

Some of the popular nashīds *produced by Ajnad Foundation for Media Production of the Islamic State and featured in Boko Haram videos, which can all be accessed on jihadology.net, include "The Burning Hellfire", "Caravan of the Light", "Praise be to God", "In the Way of God", "Soon, Soon", "We Will Move Forth to Excellence", "Our Shari'a", "Clanging of the Swords, Nashīd of the Defiant", "The Regiment of My [Islamic] State", "The Life of Humiliation Is Not Acceptable", "My Umma, Dawn Has Appeared", and "My Umma Was Not Satisfied With Weakness". Aside from the use of Arabic* nashīds, *Boko Haram also produces Hausa poetry (see text 26). The use of Hausa poetry is a potent tool that Boko Haram employs to infiltrate the psyche of its members, denounce the Islamic establishment that opposes their campaign and draw support and legitimacy from the Muslim population. The poetry below is a translation of one of the Hausa poems of Boko Haram featured in the video "Raid on Giwa Barracks" released on 26 March 2014.*

We will fight our *jihād* to bring back the *sharī'a*. We will defeat you, the enemies of *sharī'a*. We will kill you. We will not leave you!

We will fight on the path of *jihād*. We will shoot and cut with swords. We will kill the unbelievers so they do not engage in destruction.

We will follow [you to] your churches and demolish them. You should not take this poem as a joke. It is the truth and what we are doing. You will see us do it.

We will fight with law-making unbelievers; those unbelievers who are making obnoxious laws. There is no law except that of Islam.

O you *ṭāghūt*, all of you should come and follow Allah. You should follow the *sharī'a* and undertake your prayers. If you refuse, you will be faced with war.

You see we are here waiting for you. You and your soldiers should come, all of you. Let us have a duel and let us know those who are courageous.

Mobile police and [other] police, you should move away from our place. You are too small to hinder us, you are women. We have understood you.

We have come with disease, disease of *jihadi*. We will push aside destruction, disease and corruption. No unbelief, only Islam.

We will come out to defend our *sharī'a*. We will fight the unbelievers who want to kill us. Carry the weapons and defend the Muslims!

It is martyrdom we want. They should spill our blood; paradise is what we desire. Even if we are trounced, let them see us increasing.

O Allah! Give us firmness to kill them. We should destroy their churches and barracks. We would slaughter and shoot them.

HAUSA *NASHID* IN THE VIDEO "THE RAID ON MAIDUGURI"

O Muslims! Come let us fight *jihād*. If you refuse and prefer corruption, Allah will hear you. He will capture you.

And if you refuse, unbelievers will kill you. They will slaughter the adults and even the young ones among you. They will kill women and will engage in mischief.

You should not follow the people who will deceive you. You leave *jihād* and you are chasing after the world; Allah will hold you and no one will save you.

You should come let us fight with unbelievers, engaging in mischief. We should fight big thieves and the cheaters! We should scatter unbelievers so that they will not engage in destruction.

Whoever wants to know whether we are brave, he should ask Borno, Bauchi, Kaduna and even Abuja. There are no contentions [about that].

Or you should ask those unbelievers of Plateau; on the day of ʿId, it was a hyena that they lost. On the day of their ʿId, we burnt them.[2] Ask the unbelievers of Adamawa and Gombe, or the *ṭāghūt* that resides in Yobe. We have dispersed them and drove them away.

If you want to know we are not afraid, we do not have doubt, and they cannot win against us with their gathering [of troops]; you should ask the battlefield and it will tell you.

We will fight our *jihād* to bring back the *sharīʿa*. We will defeat you, the enemies of *sharīʿa*. We will kill you. We will not leave you!

40

MESSAGE TO THE *UMMA*

BY ABUBAKAR SHEKAU

(6 MAY 2014)

[Trans.: Abdulbasit Kassim]
Available at: https://www.youtube.com/watch?v=Vm2LdvevMBU

In this video, Shekau cited the theological exegesis for slavery in Islam to justify the Chibok girls' kidnapping, and as a rejoinder to clerics who opposed his group. Using the classic rhetoric of George Bush, "you are either with us or you are with them," Shekau also laid out the doctrine of al-walā' wa-l-barā'. *Part of the video is an exegesis of Qur'ān 109. This video is significant in understanding how Boko Haram constructs its enemies and allies and most importantly how the group justifies its actions under the rubrics of Islamic theology.*

[*Opening with a speech of Osama b. Laden and the* nashīd *"We are Osama."*][1]

[*Shekau shooting into the air and chanting jihadi rhetoric against unbelievers, including Obama, Bush, and Clinton, followed by praises of the coming Islamic caliphate.*]

[*Citation of Q9:52, 9:111.*]

Allah has also commanded the *mujāhidīn* to fight the devil's followers, including Obama, Bush, Clinton, François Hollande, Vladimir Putin and the smallest of them, Jonathan. Allah says "Fight then the followers of the Devil. Surely, the guile of the Devil is weak." (Q4:76) [Standard Islamic opening]

And thereafter:

My brothers in faith! I am sending my greetings to you, the type of greeting that Allah wants us to spread among ourselves as Muslims. Allah is guiding us, and may He make us among the believers who are guided. Allah says: "So, when you meet the unbelievers, strike their necks till you have bloodied them, then fasten the shackles." (Q47:4) Are you hearing? You claim to be believers, right? This is the command of Allah and it was neither revealed today, nor can it be subjected to any fanciful interpretation. This [word] *fa-ḍarba* (strike) is a verbal noun and it is akin to the verse in the Qur'ān: "So strike upon the necks and strike every fingertip of theirs." (Q8:12) Allah is great! Allah has commanded us to kill the polytheists, the democrats, the followers of constitution, the *marabouts*, and those who enroll in Western education, where they engage in acts of unbelief and polytheism such as reciting the pledge to Nigeria. [*Shekau continues with his parody of Nigeria's national pledge—see text 14.*]

I am defending Allah's *tawḥīd*, while you are defending the country. This is where we differ, and where I derived my evidence that Western education is unbelief. Allah has commanded the believers to fight the polytheists who disbelieve in Allah, obstruct Allah's path and spread unbelief in the land. You will hear someone claiming that there are no differences between religions. Where did you derive such an idea that there are no differences between religions? Who told you there are no differences between religions?

Allah told us that there are differences between religions. What will you say to the saying of Allah: "Neither the Jews nor the Christians will be pleased with you until you follow their religion." (Q2:120) This verse was revealed to Prophet Muhammad. So how will you say that there are no differences in religion? You sat there with Christians claiming to be scholars with your turbans to the point where you are also observing the Easter Monday and Good Friday holiday with the Christians—all in the name of peace and progress. What type of progress is that after you have disbelieved in Allah?

Allah has commanded us to slaughter and kill. If you meet the polytheists on the battlefield, my brothers, you should strike their necks. This is the command of Allah, not Shekau. According to Allah, you should strike the neck of Jonathan, Kashim and *bura-uba.*[2] It is a lie. Even if a person prays in the Ka'ba, if he is engaging in polytheism, he is an unbeliever. Truth is truth, even if the person saying it is a liar. Falsehood is falsehood, even if the person saying it is perceived as truthful. You should strike their necks, my brothers, until the time you overcome the unbelievers in the whole world, and receive victory from Allah. Allah will grant you victory. Until the time you overcome the unbelievers face to face, Allah will grant you victory.

Yes, we will capture slaves. Who told you there are no slaves in Islam? What are human rights? Bastard liars! The One who created His slaves is the One who does not know his rights? Any female who has attained the age of 12, I will marry her off. Any girl who has attained the age of 9, I will marry her off, the same way they married the

Mother of the Believers, the daughter of Abū Bakr, 'Ā'isha, to the Prophet Muhammad at the age of 9.[3] You have met your adversary: the unbelievers of the world. Allah is the greatest. We must follow Allah. You should die with anger. My brothers, you should cut the unbelievers' necks. You should capture slaves.

You are vexed that I captured those girls from their school. Did you not hear when I said they should seal off and close all Western schools? Girls! You should go and marry. I am repeating myself again: seal off and close all Western schools. I am the person who captured the girls. By Allah, I will sell them in the market. I have a market for selling people. Allah commanded me to sell. The girls' Owner told me to sell them. I will sell the girls. According to Allah: "Strike their necks till you have bloodied them, and then fasten the shackles." (Q47:4)

After we kill, and the smell of the unbelievers' blood, like Obama, George Bush, Vladmir Putin, and Jonathan, becomes unpleasant, we will open the prisons and lock up all other unbelievers if we see there is nothing better to do with them. Yes, I will imprison Jonathan's daughter[4] and the daughter of *bura-uba*. There is nothing that will make me to retract what I am saying except if you repent. If you repent, anyone who becomes a Muslim is my brother.

Ikrima, son of Abu Jahl became a Companion of the Prophet, even though he was originally the son of Abu Jahl.[5] Despite all your acts of unbelief, you have not attained the position of Abu Jahl. Bastard Jonathan! Yes, Obama, I am referring to you. Yes, by Allah you have never fought me, and I have never seen you yet I am angry with you. By Allah, I am angry with you. "Strike their necks till you have bloodied them, and then fasten the shackles." (Q47:4) Allah says fasten the shackles. We don't care to imprison them for a long period of time. If we see there is nothing to do to them, Allah says He gives us the privilege: "Thereupon, release them freely or for a ransom." (Q47:4) Yes, you will bring trillions in ransom, even though there is nothing we would do with your money. Bastards!

They said we are afflicted by unemployment. If only you know us, you will know our work. "Thereupon, release them freely or for a ransom, till the war is over." Then Allah says: "Yet had Allah wished, He would have taken vengeance upon them, but He wanted to test you by one another." (Q47:4) We who are believers said we will fight *jihād*. Allah wants to test us whether we will fight, or just try to impress other people. This is the reason Allah is bringing some difficult trials on us. This is the explanation of Allah. "Those who die in Allah's path, He will not render their works perverse." (Q47:4) By Allah, they will enter paradise. O Allah! We want to be killed on your path. O Allah! Make us fight solely for Your cause. This is my short admonition to my brothers in faith.

By Allah, you should hold firm to the religion, and practice it solely for the sake of Allah. What I will add in my speech for you to understand is that slavery is permitted in the religion. Yes, do not let them deceive you. Because we said we will capture people as slaves, you are angry? The Assembly of Manipulators [United Nations] is the name I assign to you, Ban Ki Moon's people. By Allah, why will you say there is no slavery? Why do you slaughter chicken? Who gave life to a chicken? Is it not Allah who commanded us to slaughter chickens? So, if Allah says there is slavery, is He not the one who owns the slaves? If He says women are slaves, are they not slaves? They all belong to Allah. It is in the Qur'ān, revealed by Allah. Will you argue with an object's creator? For example, is it possible for you to evacuate a person from a house with his wife and children, while the house belongs to him? Everyone in the area will say you are unjust if you do this. So where are you, Jonathan, Obama, and Ban Ki Moon, and where is Allah?

You are even calling yourselves defenders of human rights. Bastard homosexuals! They legalized homosexuality and lesbianism under the guise of human rights. What era are we living in? Even animals know humanity better than you. A ram only engages in sexual intercourse with a ewe. A goat only engages in sexual intercourse with a she-goat. A bull only engages in sexual intercourse with a cow. Look at you—a woman will proudly marry another woman, accepting that she is the woman's wife. Look at the era in which we found ourselves!

Yet, the likes of Obama will rise and say it is their right. They will claim that they should not be stopped, because it is their right. Look at the era in which we found ourselves! If we say: "We will follow Allah and the laws Allah laid down for us," you oppose us. We emigrated, yet you followed us, and have kept fighting us. Do you think we will not follow Allah? "O My servants who believe and do the righteous deeds, my earth is vast, so worship Me alone." (Q29:56) You should create your own earth, and look for your own slaves to worship you. We are on the land of our own Creator. I don't recognize Nigeria, Cameroon, Niger or Chad. By Allah, I don't have a country. Anywhere I go or wherever I stand is the country of Islam. This is my religion, creed and the path I follow.

O people! You should know that there is slavery in Islam. Allah's Messenger captured slaves. In the Battle of Badr, Allah's Messenger captured Naḍr b. al-Ḥārith and ʿUqba b. Abū Muʿayṭ prisoners, and he ordered that they be killed. As such, if I capture Jonathan, I will kill him also. The same way you said you will kill me, if you capture me. What will prevent you from capturing me? Who am I in the first place? Do you expect me to abandon Allah's work because you threatened to capture me? Do you think I am insane? You are the people who are insane. I will never abandon Allah's religion.

You are so desperate to capture me that you have announced a reward of 50 million [approx. $150,000] or a trillion *naira* for whoever captures me. [*Prophets were slaughtered...*] So, who am I if they slaughter me? Who am I if the Civilian JTF killed me? Do not think I consider myself important—even a small child can kill me. This is not a pride thing. Your threat will never make me to abandon Allah's religion. This is my creed and this is the teaching I inculcate into people even though you do not want them to do it.

Today, if I die, someone will take my place who will eclipse me. Were you not complaining about Muhammad Yusuf? Now, you consider him less fierce than me. This is what will happen when you kill me, because then someone will take my place who will eclipse me. This is Islam. By Allah, in this religion, they killed the prophets. What would you say about *aṣḥāb al-ukhdūd*?[6] That town's king dug a trench filling it with fire and burnt them. This is the religion I follow. There are periods when Allah's Messenger captured an unbeliever and freed him. Likewise, if I capture an unbeliever, and I think freeing him is better for my own system and Allah's rules and regulations that I follow, I will free him. I am a leader. I know this speech will anger you. Yes, I am a leader, and am above the president. There is no president in Nigeria and the world. I am a president in Islam. I know this speech does not sound pleasant to you. Allah's Messenger freed Thumama ibn Uthal, who was a leader of Banu Hanifa, and there are many more examples.

Imam Shinqītī said in his *tafsīr* [exegesis] that none doubt the permissibility of capturing slaves except unbelievers. Please go and check the *tafsīr* of Imam Shinqītī. There are also several verses in the Qur'ān: "But if you fear that you cannot be equitable, then only one, or what your right hands own." (Q4:3) You should go and check the interpretation of "what your right hands own" [concubines]. You only intended to prevent us from Allah's religion by claiming that there is no slavery. So where did you derive the evidence to capture and imprison people? What are your reasons? You are doing your own capturing, but do not want us to follow Allah's command. "But those favored will not give their provision to those [slaves] whom their right hands possess." (Q16:71) This verse is in *sūrat al-Naḥl* in the Qur'ān, and it concerns slavery. "Do you have among what your hands own partners in what we provided for you, so that you are equal therein?" (Q30:28) You will find this verse in *sūrat al-Rūm*.

As such, my brothers, if there is no slavery, can you practice the religion? By Allah, we should open a market and sell people. Whoever refuses to follow Allah and prefers to be an unbeliever, he is a ram ready for sale. Jonathan, Obama, and Bush, if I capture you, I will sell you. I will put you in the market for sale, even though your monetary value as unbelievers is small. Does an unbeliever have value? I am the one who has value. [...] If you repent, Allah will accept your repentance. However, if you do not repent, then you should know that you are a ram ready to be sold in the market. Afterwards, I will slaughter you, but I will not eat you, because we do not eat human beings. We are blood-letters[7] but we don't eat human beings. Khalid b. Walid also let blood. It is not as if we will drink the blood.

[*Scholars like Muhammad b. Sirin were children of slaves.*] You are nothing. Allah commanded me to sell. The Creator himself commanded me to put them for sale in the market. Do you even have the possibility of opposing? You too, with Allah's slaves, were engaging in what is not in the religion and killing themselves. You gave a person a weapon to loiter about. [*Also, Makḥūl, a Syrian scholar, was a slave.*]

Today, the people who are saying that there is no slavery, or that the verses concerning slavery have been abrogated, are secularists who aid Bush and Obama. Allah says and His Messenger explained that you must wash the plate from an unbeliever before you use it to eat. However, you are holding hands with Bush and Obama. You are here standing and laughing with them, accepting them as your advisers. I am referring to you, King of Saudi Arabia. I do not have any business with this type of people. My brothers are the likes of Zarqawi, Abu Yahya al-Libi and the brothers of the Islamic State of Iraq and Sham. Our brothers are the people of Afghanistan, Chechnya, Azerbaijan, Pakistan, Yemen, and Mali. Our brothers are those who implement the laws in the Qur'ān.

We do not follow Saudi Arabia. Until the day, we see the Islamic State of Saudi, we will have nothing to do with Saudi Arabia. This [Boko Haram] is my own revolt. I will not fear anyone. I will call anyone who does not follow Allah's laws an unbeliever. You can eat me, but I will not leave my religion. You think me to be very black, right? It is not white skin that I follow. Bastards! You deceive people with your white skin, and the claim that you are Arab. I will not follow anyone other than Allah and His Messenger. And may Allah grant us sincerity on His path.

O brothers! My message to you is even if you are alone you should feel that you are moving ahead with the group. This is the religion. You just come and deceive us with your democracy. Do you know democracy at all? Abraham Lincoln, Aminu Kano[8] and Tafawa Balewa[9] are all unbelievers. Now, you will wonder what is wrong with me. Whatever you like you can say, but they are all unbelievers. They did not rule with the Qur'ān; rather they ruled by the constitution, which is not Allah's book. Allah says: "Judgment is Allah's alone; He determines the right and He is the best decision-maker." (Q6:57) This is our religion.

If you like you can choose to understand or not understand. It is up to you—"to every one of them on that day is a business sufficing him." (Q80:37) This is the religion. "A day when no soul shall avail another soul anything and the command on that day shall be Allah's." (Q82:19) We have revolted against you, and have disassociated ourselves from you. There is no power except through You, O Lord. We pray to Allah to protect us. O Allah, make us to practice this religion solely for Your sake. And may Allah make all our actions guided by Qur'ānic dictates and the Sunna of His Prophet.

O Muslims! Permit me to interpret this verse for you: "Say: O unbelievers." (Q109:1) Can we say this verse was revealed today or we are just hearing it for the first time today? You recite this verse all the time. Who does not pray ṣalāt al-witr?[10] Do you not recite this verse when you pray? Do you not recite this verse when you read the Qur'ān? So, what will you do with this verse when you die, after you decided to follow Obama and Jonathan? You follow democracy, judge according to the constitution and work with Western education. Do you not call us Boko Haram? Yes, Western education is forbidden, it is not permissible. You, soldiers are saying that Western education is permissible, right? It is a lie. Western education is forbidden. I am not Boko Haram; rather I am JASDJ. I don't care if you call me Boko Haram.

"Say: O unbelievers, I do not worship what you worship." (Q109:1–2) Everyone knows the meaning of worship since you all say it with your mouth. You should go and interpret your national anthem and pledge to know the meaning of worship. I will not worship what you worship—democracy, the constitution and Western education. "Nor do you worship what I worship." (Q109:3) You do not believe in Islamic monotheism. You are killing us for this purpose. You are loitering around and searching for us in different hide-outs for this purpose. "Nor do I worship what you have worshipped." (Q109:4) I will not worship what you are worshipping, forever. Is your religion not communism? Are you communists? Are you not atheists? That is why you say that everything is nature. Do you think we don't know the origin of your ideology: communists, atheists, French, American, Russian, German, and Chinese? "Nor do you worship what I worship. You have your religion and I have mine." (Q109:5–6) This is the interpretation of *sūrat al-Kāfirūn*. If you think I am not correct, then you can go and check the Qur'ān yourself.

You have your religion of nationalism, democracy, the constitution, Western education, and all other acts of polytheism which you will not abandon until you die. You cannot beautify these verses even if you invented Arabic. Obama's scholars, Jingir and Gabchia[11] and all others like them, are unbelievers. Bastards! All of you, I will kill you. Whoever follows democracy is an unbeliever.

Today, I am calling all Muslims to the call of their Creator. O Muslims of the world! You should know that we have disassociated ourselves from the unbelievers, polytheists and apostates. If you don't know those who have committed apostasy, they are the people who pray, but still practice democracy. They are unbelievers. Why are you using your prayer as proof [of being a Muslim] after you have become an unbeliever? If you don't know a hypocrite, he is the one who comes to our gathering crying, with his trousers shortened, a long beard and big turban,[12] but is here as an opportunist, satisfying his own desire. He is also an unbeliever. I don't know you, but if you are not among us, you are not a believer: "There are some who say: 'We believe in Allah and the Last Day,' but they are not real believers." (Q2:8) According to my creed, a hypocrite is an unbeliever.

I am referring to the unbelievers, America and Israel; I will call you by your name, you are the people who incurred the wrath of Allah (Q1:7). Rome and Britain are those who have gone astray because they are Christians (Q1:6). I am referring to you, the French, François Hollande, the atheists, and homosexuals. I am referring to you, Germany, the likes of Margaret Thatcher, Russia and Nigeria, where I reside. All the senators are unbelievers, the likes of Ali Modu Sheriff, ['Ali] Ndume, and Saminu Turaki, who calls himself "the peacemaker."[13] If you fall into our hands, you will understand peacemaking with our knives. They are all unbelievers.

Let me draw your attention to a speech Bush once delivered when he was president. He made the speech to disbelieve in Allah, but today we will offer a rejoinder to it. Bush said the war they are fighting today in Afghanistan and Iraq is a war of the cross, a crusade and a war for Christianity. He said it with his mouth.[14] There is no one unaware of this speech. He said they must burn this country and pass judgment upon it, referring to Afghanistan where Islamic law was practiced [under the Taliban]. By Allah, the same way Bush delivered that speech, I will offer a rejoinder today. To the people of the world, everybody should know his place: it is either you are with us, the *mujāhidīn* of JASDJ, following the creed of the righteous forefathers, or you are with the Christians—the likes of Obama, Lincoln, Bush, Clinton, Jonathan and Aminu Kano. They are the fathers of your democracy, the likes of Tafawa Balewa. They are all unbelievers. It is 'Uthman Dan Fodio who is our own [example]. They are the ones who practiced the religion with sound creed, the likes of Ibn 'Abd al-Wahhab.

We know what is happening in this country. This war is a war of *tawḥīd*, disassociation, a war against Christianity, democracy, the constitution, Western education and polytheism. By Allah, we have not even started the war. In the future, we will go to Abuja and the refinery in Cross River [State], the town of Jonathan. We will go there, because it is your town; rather we will go there because it is the town of unbelievers. What is my business with Jonathan—he is just a small insect. Do you know my intention at all? Do you know why I embark upon this war? I have sworn allegiance to Allah: "Those who pay you homage are actually paying Allah homage. Allah's hand is above their hands; so, he who breaks his oath only breaks it to his loss, and he who fulfils what he has pledged unto Allah, He will grant him a great wage." (Q48:10)

You should listen to the speech of Bush. Let me repeat it in English, but I will reverse the speech referring to Allah, even though he specified the cross, not Allah. This is the reason the entire world, and even Nigeria, is fighting the Muslims. What did they do, the Muslims in Langtang, Yelwa Shandam, Kaduna and Zango Kataf? Once you are praying, they will become furious against you. It was in this country they gathered feces with the Qur'ān, right here in Maiduguri, in the university. You are here cheating Allah's religion and His Messenger but are claiming that you are practicing Islam?

Listen to this, every nation and every region now has a decision to make. It is either you are with us—I mean those of us who are following the footsteps of the forefathers—or you are with the likes of Obama, George Bush, François Hollande, and Clinton. I did not forget Abraham Lincoln, Ban Ki Moon and all the unbelievers in general. This is a *tawḥīd*. This war is against Christians and all the unbelievers, just as Allah says: "Fight them until there is no sedition (*fitna*) and the religion becomes that of Allah." (Q2:193) Allah says: "You shall fight them or they shall submit." (Q48:16) The Prophet said: "I have been commanded (by Allah) to fight people, until they testify that there is no true god except Allah, and that Muhammad is the Allah's Messenger." The Prophet also said: "Whoever changes his religion, kill him."[15] And there are many other proofs.

O democrats! You should bear witness that I have declared my disassociation from you. You should prepare for me everything you wish—I rely on Allah alone and He is also your Lord. Despite all your scheming, Allah will not allow you to do to me what He does not wish. Don't you know that Allah says: "Allah will not give the unbelievers the upper hand over the believers." (Q4:141) It is only because you don't know the promise of Allah that you are doing what you are doing. The same way you have good knowledge of money is the same way I understand the promise of Allah. You are dying because of money, but I will die because of Allah. You believe in money but I believe in Allah. "I call Allah to witness and call you to witness that I am innocent of what you associate with Him. So, try your guile on me, all of you; then do not give me any respite." (Q11:54–55)

Allah also says: "And relate to them the story of Noah, when he said to his people: 'O my people, if my dwelling [among you] and my reminding you of the revelations of Allah, is too much for you, then in Allah I have put my trust. Agree upon a course of action with your associates; then let not that course of action be a burden to you; then pass to me [your decision] and give me no respite.'" (Q10:71) Allah also says: "And if you call them to guidance, they do not follow you. It is the same, for you, whether you call them or you remain silent. Indeed, those you call, apart from Allah, are servants like you; so call them let them answer you, if you are truthful. Do they have feet to walk with; do they have hands to smite with; do they have eyes to see with; or do they have ears to hear with? Say: 'Call your associate-gods, then plot against me and give me no respite.'" (Q7:193–195)

41

MESSAGE ABOUT THE CHIBOK GIRLS

BY ABUBAKAR SHEKAU

(12 MAY 2014)

[Trans.: Abdulbasit Kassim]

Available at: http://jihadology.net/2014/05/12/new-video-message-from-boko-%e1%b8%a5arams-jamaat-ahl-al-sunnah-li-dawah-wa-l-jihad-shaykh-abu-bakr-shekau-message-about-the-girls/

On 14 April 2014, Boko Haram kidnapped 276 girls from the Government Secondary School in Chibok, Borno State. Fifty-seven of the schoolgirls managed to escape soon after their abudction and another girl, ʾAmina Ali Nkeki, escaped on 17 May 2016 after two years in captivity. Negotiations between the Nigerian government and Boko Haram brokered by the International Committee of the Red Cross and the Swiss government led to the release of twenty-one girls on 12 October 2016. Another Chibok girl, Maryam Ali Maiyanga, escaped on 5 November 2016 while another batch of eighty-two Chibok girls were released on 6 May 2017 following intense negotiations led by barrister Mustapha Zanna and the intervention of the International Committee of the Red Cross and the Swiss government. The Zanna-led negotiation involved the swapping of five Boko Haram prisoners and the payment of an undisclosed amount to Boko Haram.[1]

After the hashtag #BringBackOurGirls began to trend on twitter, international outrage was directed against Boko Haram and the Nigerian government for the kidnapping, and several protests around the world were held. Clerics in Nigeria and the Muslim world, including the Sultan of Sokoto, Sa'ad Abubakar III, and the Grand Mufti of Saudi Arabia, 'Abd al-'Aziz Al al-Shaykh, also condemned the kidnapping of the girls. Notwithstanding the international outrage against Boko Haram, the Islamic State and other clerics who share the group's ideology, have lauded Boko Haram for the kidnapping of the girls. In its official English magazine Dabiq, *issues 4 and 5 (October and December 2014), the Islamic State cited the kidnapping of the Chibok girls as a justification for its own sexual enslavement of Yazidi women in Iraq (see also text 61). Likewise, in a Q&A session posted on JustPaste, Musa Cerantonio, an Australian convert who supports the Islamic State, provided theological justifications supporting Boko Haram's action.*

In this video, Shekau provided a theological justification for the kidnapping of the girls and refuted Islamic clerics who condemned it. Shekau intended to use the girls as pawns in exchange for some of the incarcerated members of his group. In the second part of the video, the kidnapped girls were shown in hijābs *and jointly reciting the Muslim testimony of faith and* sūrat al-Fātiḥa. *Three girls were interviewed. The first two girls explained why they converted to Islam, as the evidence presented to them shows Christianity is not a true religion. They refuted the idea that they are being maltreated and they admonished their parents to convert to Islam. The third girl, who was a Muslim, called on other girls to abandon Western education, and she chided her parents for not showing her the right path. It is obvious from this video that the girls spoke under duress and said what they were instructed to say.*

Since 2010 Boko Haram has targeted schools, killing hundreds of students. Some notable Boko Haram attacks on schools include (all in Yobe State): the 6 July 2013 attack on the Government Secondary School, Mamudo, where forty-two students were killed;[2] the 29 September 2013 attack on the College of Agriculture, Gubja, where up to fifty students and teachers were killed;[3] the 25 February 2014 attack on the Federal Government College, Buni Yadi, where fifty-nine students were killed and burned to ashes;[4] and the 10 November 2014 attack on Government Science Secondary School, Potiskum, where at least forty-six people were killed and seventy-nine wounded.[5]

[Standard Islamic opening]

[*Shekau speaking in Arabic.*]

Amazing! Allah is great! And higher and more majestic is Allah. O my brothers in Allah! This message is about the girls whom we abducted from the Western schools. This message is about the girls whom the tyrants of the world, Obama, François Hollande, and Jonathan are speaking about. Allah is the greatest! And higher and more majestic is Allah. Allah is more powerful than everything.

Amazing, it is completely amazing, if you hear all I want to say, you will cry, Obama. These girls with whom you busy yourselves have become Muslims. Have you found out how they became Muslims? Those girls have become Muslims; they have become Muslims. Allah is the greatest! They have become Muslims. They have converted to Islam and left the Christian religion. They have become Muslims. By Allah, they declared by themselves the testimony of faith and bear witness in front of Allah that He is the exalted, the mighty and He is one. There is no deity worthy of worship but Allah, and Jesus is Allah's servant, Messenger and His Word which was sent down to Mary as a spirit. Praise be to Allah. This suffices, by Allah's permission, as a speech to the whole *umma* that these girls have become Muslims. There are other girls, whom we have also abducted, who are present, with Allah's permission.

And one of the tyrants' scholars, whose name is Muhammad Nujaimy, Muhammad the unbeliever, Muhammad the hypocrite, who is in Yemen, spoke. You are an unbeliever. When have I captured a free person for you to cite the Prophet's *hadīth* saying that he who sells a free person and consumes the price is damned by Allah?! You, by Allah, are one of the cursers, the accursed—wherever they are found, [they should be] seized and massacred, completely. This is Allah's established way from the forefathers. Exalted is Allah. By Allah, I have taken on the democrats, the crusaders, the unbelievers who abandon their religion, committed apostasy, left the religion of Islam, and entered the religion of the Jews—the religion of this age.

Those scholars, the tyrants' scholars in this age, by Allah, are those who have corrupted Allah's religion. Exalted are You, O Allah! It is common knowledge that many of the best tyrants' scholars, in this age, are from the states of this world which claim to belong to Islam. They have corrupted the religion and lives of the people, and have surrendered to Judaism and Christianity, uniting their beliefs with them—that is democracy.

Do you claim democracy as a religion? Democrats say: A government of the people, by the people, for the people. Have you accepted the people's rule as a religion, for you to disown us? How do you disown us? We have beaten you to it! An unbeliever among unbelievers! We disown you, and between us has arisen enmity and derision, forever, until you believe in Allah alone [cf. Q60:4]. This is the Qur'ān. You are an American, a scholar among American scholars, but you think you are Muslim? How are you a Muslim after you have become an unbeliever?! Exalted is Allah. This is enough for me. Allah is a sufficient trustee, and Allah is a sufficient witness.

Now, I want to announce to the *umma* that these girls have, by Allah, become Muslims. Praise be to Allah from whom good comes. Exalted are You, O Allah! And there are other girls who, by Allah, except for whom there is no god, we will not release them from our hands until you release our brothers in your prison. For four to five years, you have arrested our brothers, and they are now in prison. You have been doing many things to them, but now you speak about these girls! By Allah, we will not release them until you release our brothers! We will not release them until you release our brothers. By this, I mean the girls who have not embraced Islam. As for those of them who are Muslims, they are our sisters. Praise be to Allah.

[*Shekau speaking Hausa.*]

Let me give a short explanation since I don't intend to give a long speech. I just want to show you that these girls with whom you busy yourselves, those students we captured, I said I will sell them, since I have a market for selling slaves—and you even went ahead to say that I am selling Muslims? Are those Christians, Muslims or what? Obama's scholars, contemporary scholars, or is it the democrats who are Muslims? I will sell them, and I am repeating it again.

By Allah, you will be unable to rescue them until you release our brothers you have arrested and incarcerated in your prisons. The women you are humiliating. In fact, there is a woman whose baby you captured, but you left her. We know all what you do. Now, because we caught these girls, the girls who Allah helped to accept the religion, many of them have accepted the religion. There are those who did not accept the religion, and many of them are here sitting with us. Now, you make noise about Chibok, Chibok. Only Allah knows the unbelieving women we have captured, the women Allah instructed us to enslave. Yes, Allah said we should enslave them.

Those verses I recited about capturing slaves are there for you to see. I am not a Muslim who prays, then abandons capturing slaves. I will not be like those who believe in some verses while disbelieving in others. I will follow the Qur'ān in its entirety. In the Qur'ān, there are verses on capturing slaves—that is why I captured them. Is it because of these girls you are making noise? I have captured lots of men as well. In fact, I will capture Europeans, and even Obama. I only capture slaves. The person you see who did not become a slave is because he declared the testimony of faith and accepted the religion. He will cease being a slave by following the dictates of Islam. There is no way a person who is originally a Muslim can become a slave. However, the person who becomes an unbeliever can only become an unbeliever if he commits acts of unbelief in all the ways that lead to becoming an unbeliever. This is what Allah says, and this is the religion I am following.

It is amazing. Look at these girls; let them tell you with their own mouths, I will not say anything. By Allah, look at how they are reciting *sūrat al-Fātiḥa*. Look at how they are declaring the testimony of faith—so that some of them are saying it with their own mouths: "O our mother, O our father, you should repent; by Allah, the religion of Islam is the truth." This is what they said with their own mouths.

If you like, you can say that we intoxicated them or gave them some concoction to drink. We do not have alcohol. We are following the religion; Allah has forbidden us from having alcohol. There are examples in the time of the Prophet, so do not think we intoxicated them. Did you not know Sa'd b. Abī Waqqāṣ? When he became a Muslim, what did his mother say to him? She said until he reverts to unbelief, she will not eat or drink, until either he leaves Islam or she will die of starvation. What did Sa'd say to his mother? He said: "Mother, even if you had 1,000 lives, I will not leave this religion." This is the type of understanding these girls now have about Islam.

The world must change. Since we said we will follow Allah's commands, the world must indeed change. Now, have you not changed the world with your mantra of globalization? Today, the world is now global. After all, you are the people who schemed, so how would you know that the world is changing? Your hypocrites, Israel

314

and America, they said the world is now global with the assemblage of united non-sense [United Nations]. You must be angry towards me as you said I have violated the norms of international law and disobeyed your laws. I am not following nation-states; rather I am following Allah and His Messenger. This is my brief speech.

What I am saying is: if you really want us to release the captured girls who have not converted to Islam, those girls are now with us, and we are handling them in the way the prophets handled unbelievers. We will not free them until you free our brothers you imprisoned in Borno, Yobe, Kano, Kaduna, Abuja, Lagos and even Enugu. By Allah, they have imprisoned our brothers all over the country. There are those that have been imprisoned for up to five years, so they have not seen their wives or children. Even if it is for the sake of revenge, will I not capture these girls as well? Let alone the fact that Allah commanded I should capture slaves. What about you who captured my brother for five years, you captured a woman for four to five years, and prevented her from marriage. You captured our children and families, killing our brothers. Some of our brothers, you gave them poison which they swallowed and died, twenty of them at once. You perpetrated all these harms on us.

Now, we caught some girls, but you are screaming: "Shekau has captured [girls] and he said he will sell them." I will sell them. Those women, even if they become Muslims, they are still slaves. I am the person who has the right to emancipate them. This is a *ḥadīth* of Allah's Messenger. Bastards! Scholars of Jews and hypocrites! You say: "And he who kills a believer intentionally will, as punishment, be thrown into Hell, dwelling in it forever." (Q4:93) Are they believers? Even if he becomes a believer, until I manumit him, then will he become a Muslim. Look at the *ḥadīth* of Allah's Messenger in al-Bukhari and Muslim. Can you refute this *ḥadīth*? Look at it—the Prophet said, "Whichever man manumits a Muslim man Allah will deliver one of his bodily parts for [the other's] bodily parts from hellfire."[6]

You are wrong in thinking that the religion is limited to the Qur'ān. The religion is also in the *ḥadīth* of the Prophet. Therefore, your mouth cannot desecrate the religion. This logic of yours, which you call globalization, federalism, capitalism, socialism, will not desecrate the religion. You Jews, with big red eyes, those with heads like plates, those moustacheless and beardless, those with the sign of hellfire on their necks, you will never desecrate our religion for us. We will follow Allah. What will you do? Allah has heard you, and up till now you say you will gather [together] and confront us? Even Pharaoh in Nigeria, we must fight him, let alone Obama. All praise be to Allah.

[*The girls are jointly reciting the testimony of faith and* sūrat al-Fātiḥa.]

[*One of the girls standing in front of the camera is reciting alone while others are seated.*]

[Interview of the first girl]

Questioner [Q]: What is your name?
Girl: Hauwa [H].

Q: Hauwa what?

H: Hauwa Abdul.

Q: What is your original name?

H: Qwante.

Q: Qwante?

H: Yes.

Q: Are you a Christian?

H: Yes.

Q: Now that you have become a Muslim, what is your name?

H: Halima.

Q: Why did you become a Muslim?

H: I became a Muslim because I realize that the path we were upon was not the right one. That is why I accepted the right path, so that our lives will be good and Allah will be happy.

Q: Is there any evidence that they gave you that Christianity is not a true religion?

H: Yes.

Q: What evidence did they give you?

H: They explained to us that Christianity is not the right path, so they placed us on the right path so that we can continue to follow Allah. They explained to us that Jesus was born without a pregnancy. He is not the son of God.

[Interview of the second girl]

Q: What is your name?

Girl: My name is Saratu [S].

Q: Saratu, are you a Muslim or is it now you became a Muslim?

S: It is now I became a Muslim.

Q: So what is your original name?

S: My original name is Saratu.

Q: Saratu what?

S: Saratu "Saugi" [*unclear*].

Q: What name did they give you?

S: Sa'datu.

Q: Sa'datu, where are you from?

S: Emirigu.

Q: What about your area?

S: Bakin Kasuwa.

Q: Why did you become a Muslim?

S: I became a Muslim because it is the path upon which Allah will intercede for us on the Last Day.

Q: Is there any evidence they gave you?

S: Yes.

Q: What evidence did they give you?

S: The evidence is that Jesus is not the son of God; he is Allah's servant.

Q: That's who?

S: That Jesus is not the son of Allah; he was sent to come and say they should follow him [Jesus, as a messenger].

Q: If I may ask you, since you came here, they said they [Boko Haram] are mistreating you. What type of humiliation have they shown you here? Can you explain it to me?

S: We did not witness any humiliation shown to us; nothing but good.

Q: What will you say to your parents who are yet to become Muslims?

S: They should become Muslims.

Q: So how will you call them to become Muslims? What I want from you is for you to call on your parents to become Muslims. Tell them that the religion they believe is not the true religion.

S: I will tell them to also become Muslims. The path they are upon is not the right path. They should follow the path I took.

[Interview of the third girl]

Q: What is your name?

Girl: My name is … [*no audio here to hear the name*].

Q: Where are you from?

G: Chibok.

Q: You should raise your voice.

Q: What area are you from?

G: Yelwa area.

Q: Are you originally a Muslim or is it now you became a Muslim?

G: I was originally a Muslim.

Q: What about your parents?

G: They are Muslims.

Q: So, what type of call will you make to your parents?

G: I will tell them that first they did not show us the right path. They did not show us that Western education is forbidden. Now, I am thankful to Allah who showed us the right path. I will tell my parents that the path they showed us is not the right path.

Q: What will you say to other women in the world who are engaging in Western education?

G: May Allah guide them and show them the right path, as Allah showed us.

Q: Is there any form of mistreatment they did to you since you came here?

G: None.

Q: So, what things do they give you?

G: Food. We are getting food. We thank Allah. We are eating rice, macaroni, spaghetti and other delicious foods. We are grateful to Allah. Truly, you did not harm us.

42

BEHEADING OF NIGERIAN AIR FORCE OFFICERS

(22 JULY 2014 AND 15 OCTOBER 2014)

[Summarized by Abdulbasit Kassim]
Available at: https://www.youtube.com/watch?v=IZsCUEHqvLs; https://
www.youtube.com/watch?v=bNq0DIqgR5A&spfreload=10&bpc
tr=1475356331 (viewer discretion advised)

Although Boko Haram is well-known for carrying out mass casualty operations, the group also conducts other operations such as beheadings with high shock value to terrorize Nigerian soldiers. This is a summary of two beheading videos of the Nigerian Air Force officers, Umar Abubakar and Chimda Hedima.

On 22 July 2014, a 6:46 min/sec video was shared online by Sahara Reporters showing some members of Boko Haram decapitating a Nigerian Air Force officer and parading with his head. The captive, who was extensively interrogated before he was beheaded, identified himself as Umar Abubakar, and he disclosed that he was a member of Section 9 of the Nigerian Armed Forces engaged in counter-insurgency measures against Boko Haram.

In the video, Boko Haram members questioned the captive on the reasons he is serving the state rather than serving Allah. They displayed his identity card and chanted that Allah has given them "an unbeliever today!" Although the captured officer proclaimed himself to be a Muslim affiliated with Izala, Boko Haram members explicitly told him that no number of prayers could save him, because they would implement the laws of the Qur'ān upon him. While chanting "Allah is great," Boko Haram members decapitated the officer and paraded his severed head in jubilation.

In a similar fashion, Boko Haram members also shot down an Alpha jet of the Nigerian Air Force on 11 September 2014, and captured the pilot, a wing commander identified as Chimda Hedima. Although the Nigerian military initially dismissed the report that Boko Haram shot down their fighter jet, that claim was debunked by images of the aircraft's wreckage being displayed while Chimda Hedima delivered his final speech. In the 11:14 min/sec video entitled: "Shooting down the Nigerian Air Force Plane," Chimda, wearing a camouflage-print T-shirt and with a heavily bandaged hand in a sling, was seen kneeling in front of an unmasked Boko Haram fighter in combat fatigues, and saying in English:

> My name is Chimda Hedima of the Nigerian Air Force. I work in 75 SUG Yola. I am a pilot of the Nigerian Air Force and I fly the jet. On 11 September 2014, I was assigned to undertake a mission to Kauri area of Borno State. During this mission, we were shot down and our aircraft crashed. Till this day, I do not know the whereabouts of my second pilot. I never saw him. I was taken by the members of JASDJ. At the time of the crash, I sustained cuts, broken wounds and some other injuries in the head.[1]

After Chimda Hedima delivered his final speech, an unmasked Boko Haram fighter named Ali Meedan al-Gambarawi gave a short speech where he explained the religious symbolism of beheading for the group. In his speech, he stated that beheading would not only terrify the "enemy," but it would also enhance the legitimacy of the group as victorious, fighting against the unbelievers for the religion's victory. He also threatened President Goodluck Jonathan, Barack Obama, François Hollande and Izala scholars, whom he condemned for supporting the Nigerian government. Lastly, he threatened other soldiers with meeting the same fate as the captive if they continued fighting. The final scenes showed the officer's gruesome decapitation.

43

DECLARATION OF AN ISLAMIC CALIPHATE
BY ABUBAKAR SHEKAU

(23 AUGUST 2014)

[Trans.: Abdulbasit Kassim]
Available at: https://www.youtube.com/watch?v=Rl4IgD—nKg

In this video, Shekau declared that the areas of Nigeria under Boko Haram's control constituted an Islamic caliphate.[1] This declaration was followed by new names for the captured towns—Gwoza was renamed Dar al-Hikma, 'Abode of Wisdom,' and Mubi as Madinatul Islam, 'City of Islam.'[2] This video also contains footage of Boko Haram fighters raiding villages and pillaging what looks to be a military base, while Nigerian soldiers were shown running away into the mountains. Shekau also vowed to strike back at the Civilian JTF, and the final scene of the video shows gruesome footage of approximately twenty members of the Civilian JTF being executed.[3] It is unclear when this video was released whether Shekau was establishing an independent Islamic caliphate in Nigeria or attempting to link his caliphate to the Islamic State caliphate which was declared by Abu Bakr al-Baghdadi in June 2014.

All praise is due to Allah, who decreed *jihād* as an act of worship. Allah is the One who decreed *jihād* as one of the most exalted acts of worship for His servants. He has bestowed glad tidings of two best outcomes upon His servants: either His servants attain victory or martyrdom [cf. Q 9:52]. All praise be to Allah who assisted us in bombing Abuja,[4] Damaturu, Damboa[5] and Nigeria [as a whole]. All praise be to Allah who granted victory to our brothers in Gwoza,[6] where they established an Islamic caliphate. And praise be to Allah, who has saddened the grandfather of the unbelievers—that is, Israel and Britain—and angered their father, America. And praise be to Allah who cast horror in the hearts of their grandchildren and children, "because of their associating with Allah that for which they have no authority" (Q3:151), such as democracy and other secular systems.

Allah has commanded His servants in the Qur'ān to slay those who ascribe partners with Him. He said, and I quote after seeking protection from the accursed Satan: "Kill them wherever you find them and drive them out from wherever they drove you out. Sedition is worse than slaughter." (Q2:191) He also said: "And fight them so that sedition might end and that the only religion will be that of Allah. Then if they desist, Allah is fully aware of what they do." (Q8:39) [Islamic opening]

And thereafter:

O people of Nigeria and other areas, you should know that a person does not become a Muslim except through disassociation from democracy, other acts of polytheism and all those *ṭawāghīt*, from the leading *ṭāghūt* in the world. It is obligatory upon you to declare a disassociation from the *ṭawāghīt*, their servants and helpers. Allah says: "They wish to submit their disputes to the Devil, although they have been commanded to denounce him; but the Devil wishes to lead them far astray!" (Q4:60) They wish to submit their disputes to the constitution and democracy, although they have been commanded to denounce them.

Mujāhid, a Qur'ānic exegete, said: "*Ṭāghūt* is Satan in man's image, and any entity set up by the people to judge between them with laws not in accordance with the decisions of Allah and His Messenger." Shaykh al-Islam Ibn Taymiyya said: "Anyone who seeks judgment from someone unsanctioned by the Prophet has sought judgment from the *ṭāghūt*." [Ibn Qayyim on *ṭāghūt*...] Examples of *ṭāghūt* who are worshipped as partners with Allah in this era include democracy and the constitution. Allah says: "They wish to submit their disputes to the Devil, although they have been commanded to denounce him; but the Devil wishes to lead them far astray!" (Q4:60)

O people! Until now, I am standing to speak in my usual routine. I will not get tired and may Allah purify my intention and grant me steadfastness on the path of the Prophet Muhammad, who slaughtered eighty Jews in one evening. And may Allah grant me steadfastness on the path of the Prophet's Companions, who slaughtered Europeans, the grandfathers of Benjamin Netanyahu, Vladimir Putin and the fathers of Obama. The Prophet's Companions slaughtered 3,000 unbelievers.[7] Today, if I slaughter 1,000 unbelievers I am yet to start, right? I will not get tired of explaining, admonishing my brothers, seeking knowledge, and accepting the truth, even from a person not practicing the truth. I am a student of truth. And may Allah make our words match our actions, and purify our intentions—count us among the *mujāhidīn* waging *jihād*, unafraid of the blamers' blame.

DECLARATION OF AN ISLAMIC CALIPHATE

O people! Here I am, Abubakar Shekau, Abu Muhammad b. Muhammad, Abubakar al-Shekawi, the imam of JASDJ, in the land called Nigeria. We do not have any business with that name "Nigeria." We are only using the name "Nigeria" because that is the way you use it. This land is an Islamic caliphate. We do not have anything to do with Nigeria. In this land of ours, we govern by Allah's Book and the Sunna of the Prophet. O people of Damboa, Maiduguri, Damaturu, Yola, Taraba, Mubi—even if I don't know how to pronounce it properly—Gombe, Kano, Kaduna, Jigawa, Lagos and Abuja. O people! This heaven above you has a Creator, no matter whether you oppose him or become an ingrate. The same way you see your houses as your possession; so the heavens are Allah's possession. This land we are living also has a Creator. We are certainly not the people who created ourselves. We will follow the Creator of heavens and the earth, and the One who created us.

O people! Allah has granted us victory in the town of Gwoza because we rose to give victory to His religion. O people! My aim is to provide an explanation to counter the persistent lies issued by the disbelieving government. You are late. We are not working for our own interests. Who can challenge Allah? Even if you don't agree, surely there will be a day during which you will agree, though it will be of no benefit: "The day when neither wealth nor children will avail one; except for him who comes to Allah with a pure heart." (Q26:88–89)

[Shekau cites Q80:34–37] As a result, I do not intend to deliver a long explanation. Allah has granted us victory within a short period of time. Armored cars—or let me call them their popular name "caterpillar" Civilian JTF, you should take it easy on yourself. Why don't you put on a veil, women's clothes and fake breasts so you will not be identified? Why Civilian JTF? Why? Have you forgotten what you did to our brothers? You scolded them by saying: "You are Boko Haram. Have you ever carried a gun before? You should say the truth." That was how you killed our brothers. Civilian JTF, everyone will be rewarded by their actions: "Then whoever has done an atom's weight of good shall find it; and whoever has done an atom's weight of evil shall find it." (Q99:7–8)

Civilian JTF, you should repent, because I swear by Allah, you will never be successful on your path. We will not stop killing you, because Allah commanded us to kill you. We do not feel pity for you, because one day you will be known as unbelievers. Feeling pity for you is a sign of unbelief. Punishing a fornicator while feeling pity for him means you are not a believer in Allah's sight, not to speak about a person engaging in unbelief. The democracy you are supporting is worse than homosexuality and incest. Democracy is unbelief. Democracy is the law of the people, by the people, and for the people. Democracy is human rights.

By Allah, Civilian JTF, you are all unbelievers. You should understand why we are killing you. Even though you put on head-gear,[8] we will remove it, and while you shout for mercy, we will strike your head and break it. Even if you had not killed us, we would kill you, if only for revenge on behalf of the countless brothers you killed—as is evident in your video.[9] You can go and check it, brothers. Any brother who says we should feel mercy while killing these unbelievers has also become an unbeliever. We do not play in our religion: "Say: 'Were you then mocking Allah, His revelations and His Apostles?' Make no excuses; you have disbelieved after believing." (Q9:65–66)

There is no hypocrisy in our religion. We follow only the truth. As such, all these [armored] cars you are seeing, we brought them out only because you idolize them as your gods—on our part we consider them as toys. We don't care about these Jeeps; look behind Shekau [at them]. Is it not because of these Jeeps you are killing people? We are only showing them to you to enrage you. If you have 100 of these Jeeps, that is a small number. Look at the weapons you used to protect your towns. This is just one of the weapons we are showing you. We are not showing you the weapons we bought with our money[10] nor the weapons confiscated from you.

When it is time for shooting, you will see the weapons in our possessions, though we do not take pride in our weapons. Our victory was not achieved by our weapons; rather it is Allah who granted us victory. "It was not you who slew them, but Allah; and when you threw it was actually Allah who threw, so that He might generously reward the believers." (Q8:17) By Allah, we know the type of training our Creator mandated for us. We do not take pride in our weapons or anything; rather we take pride in victory bestowed upon us by Allah.

As such, you are finished, Civilian JTF. Allah has decreed woe upon you. By Allah, you will not achieve your desire. Has a lion ever fought with an ant? America, Israel, and France are nothing before Allah, unless we lack complete faith in Him. This is my explanation. Allah gave us these weapons. We were the ones who carried out the operation in Gwoza. Allah granted us victory. It is not just Gwoza; we are the ones who carried out all the other operations inside Borno State.

You claimed victory in Damboa. Bloody liars! You know the pains you faced at our brothers' hands, and you know there is no single brother of ours in Damboa town. We did not go to there to settle—rather we went there to kill, so afterwards our brothers returned to their settlement. They know the town we captured and the towns in which we settled. If Allah wants to capture Damboa, as He captured Gwoza, He knows how to do it. Allah is the One who captured Gwoza for us because He wants the Qur'ān to be implemented in the town. He wants the Qur'ān to be implemented in the whole world, not just Nigeria.

Look at America—threatening not to allow Islamic law to be practiced in Iraq. They are not even ashamed to say it. Yet, someone who claims to be praying will still go ahead and glorify America as his leader. This is the world of today. If a person is truly a believer, he will not have time to fear these people. This is the explanation Allah has decreed which I will deliver to you.

[...] My brothers, we should not imbibe love of this world. Allah says the world is cursed, and all things in it are cursed, except the remembrance of Allah and whatever relates to that. O Muslims! You should fear Allah and remove the love of this world from your hearts. Since Allah created the world, He did not turn to look at it because of the paltry value of this world. Brothers! You should fear Allah and know that whosoever imbibes love of this world is an unbeliever: "Then, as to him who has transgressed, and preferred the present life; hell, indeed, is the refuge." (Q79:37–39) In fact, Ibn Qayyim wrote a book wherein he said that anyone who imbibes love of this world, even an atom's weight, will only enter paradise on the day that a camel is able to pass through the eye of a needle.

As such, we are not in this struggle because of this world's benefits, nor because we want you to love or praise us, even though we know you cannot praise us since we are opposites. We are white while you are black. May Allah protect us and make our actions directed solely for His cause. Civilian JTF, the way we are killing you, and uncovering all the female clothing you use to disguise yourselves, you should know that a hypocrite, even while reciting the testimony of faith—"There is no god but Allah"—it is obligatory to kill him. This is my final speech. All praise be to Allah. I am Abubakar Abu Muhammad b. Muhammad al-Shekawi, the imam of JASDJ in the land called Nigeria.

[*Footage of Boko Haram fighters raiding villages, pillaging what looks to be a raided military base, while Nigerian soldiers are shown running away into the mountains.*]

[*Speech of Abu Muhammad al-Adnani and an Arabic* nashīd.]

Hausa *nashīd*

Let us fight the *ṭāghūt* with all the dangerous weapons, until they run or become Muslims.

In this land, we will fix the Islamic flag. The law of the land is close to extinction. The unbelievers' blood has spilled on the coal-tar and Muslims are now gaining an understanding. *Jihād* is for the protection of children and women. O youths! You should come and assist to be successful.

Let us fight the *ṭāghūt* with all the dangerous weapons, until they run or become Muslims.

We will attack their barracks, offices, houses and anywhere they reside. We will descend upon them, including the soldiers, police, mobile police, SSS and anyone who collaborates with them. If we meet them, we will strike them, and they will regret.

Let us fight the *ṭāghūt* with all the dangerous weapons, until they run or become Muslims.

O youths! You should exercise patience. You should advance the *jihād* and let us demolish their houses, burn their schools and offices, so that they will not forget—also destroy them with all the dangerous weapons, until they run or become Muslims.

Let us fight the *ṭāghūt* with all the dangerous weapons, until they run or become Muslims.

They are thinking that if they kill one person [then] we will rest, or if they arrest us, we will depreciate in numbers. *Jihād* cannot be stymied by the depreciation in numbers. That is why despite, all their scheming, *jihād* has not ended.

Let us fight the *ṭāghūt* with all the dangerous weapons, until they run or become Muslims.

Submit yourself to become successful. Even if you go to heaven, you will rest, but if you kill an unbeliever, it is an act of worship. If he is the one who killed you, you have succeeded. This is the *jihād* we are fighting. Allah loves those who fight with the flag of Islam and the banner of "there is no god but Allah."

Let us fight the *ṭāghūt* with all the dangerous weapons, until they run or become Muslims.

O Allah! We beseech You for blessing and guidance. Grant us sincerity and acceptance. If You help us to overpower the terrorists, we will destroy their rules and laws.

Let us fight the *ṭāghūt* with all the dangerous weapons, until they run or become Muslims.

Be patient, men of *jihād*, you should slaughter their followers without a break and fight them with all the weapons of hatred, until they run or become Muslims.

Let us fight the *ṭāghūt* with all the dangerous weapons, until they run or become Muslims.

44

INTERVIEW WITH A *MUJĀHID* ABU SUMAYYA[1]

[Trans.: David Cook]
Available at: http://jihadology.net/2014/05/24/new-release-from-al-%e
1%b9%a3awrim-media-foundation-interview-with-one-mujahid-from-
jamaat-ahl-al-sunnah-li-l-dawah-wa-l-jihad-boko-%e1%b8%a5aram-in-
nigeria-part-1/

This short text is obviously designed to introduce Boko Haram to the wider Salafi-jihadi audience, and explain their actions in a way that is comprehensible. As it appears to mention the Chibok girls, the text should be dated to the summer of 2014. It is not completely authenticated, as no identifiable names are given (the interviewee, Abu Sumayya, is not identified in terms of his position within Boko Haram for example), but more likely than not it is authentic.

Considering the media distortion which the *mujāhidīn* face in the land called Nigeria, simultaneously with the brutal campaign being carried out against them by the apostates, with Western crusader support, and because of the media weakness from which the *jihadi* arena suffers in the land called Nigeria, and the necessity to know and bridge the gap between the *mujāhidīn* and their [Muslim] community, we have decided to carry out this interview with the brother Abu Sumayya from the JASDJ.

Interviewer: Is it possible that you will honor us and tell us about yourself?

AS (Abu Sumayya): I am your brother Abu Sumayya the Nigerian, from the JASDJ.

Interviewer: Why do they call you "Boko Haram"?

327

AS: The Nigerian government and those who oppose our method (*manhaj*) were the ones who gave us this name, although our name is JASDJ.

Interviewer: And why did they give you that name?

AS: They gave us this name because we forbid the study inside the missionary schools which are found in our land, because of the nullifiers of Islam and other matters found in them that are in opposition to our Islamic values and education, and destroy the basis for our religion.

Interviewer: Could you give an example of what you just said...

AS: The sons of the Muslims study the laws of Darwin—that the origin of humanity is the monkey, that there is no hereafter or Reckoning, and that the human being, when he dies, his spirit transfers into another body. They teach them the veneration of the cross, and to perform Christian religious slogans. Additionally, they intermix boys and girls, which causes the spread of indecencies between them—so we forbid study in them [these schools].

Interviewer: Are the girls you have taken prisoner from those schools?

AS: Yes, they are Christian [girls].

Interviewer: What is the goal of taking Christian [girls] prisoner from these schools?

AS: We have wives and daughters by the thousands in the government's hands, who are subject to abuse (*intihākāt*) regarding their sexuality and bodies—and nobody asks about them. We want them to be liberated.

Interviewer: Let's return to the beginning, who is the founder of the Jamāʿa?

AS: Shaykh Muhammad Yusuf, may Allah have mercy upon him.

Interviewer: Tell me a bit about his life.

AS: He was Shaykh Muhammad, son of Yusuf from the Borno tribe, who had four wives, and twenty-one sons and daughters. He was killed when he was 40 years old. He grew and came to his prime in Islamic schools, and studied at the hand of the most select members of the Nigerian *ʿulamā* in Maiduguri. For example, the Shaykh Abba Aji Waquni Qabaja and the Shaykh Jaʿfar [Adam], may Allah have mercy on him, from whom he learned Qurʾanic exegesis, and other famous *ʿulamā*. He did not sit on the seat of teaching until his masters had vetted him regarding his religion, his knowledge and his suitability for education.

Interviewer: It is said that Shaykh Muhammad, son of Yusuf, was originally a Shiʿite according to his practice, but then became a Sunni?

AS: These are monstrous lies and rumors from the [other] Islamic groups—who know very well that he grew and came to his prime in Nigeria, and only left it to go on the hajj [pilgrimage] and for the off-season pilgrimage, then returned immediately. Originally there are no Shiʿites in the Borno tribe, and his shaykhs knew him and knew his creed.

Interviewer: So what was his method and creed?

INTERVIEW WITH A *MUJĀHID* ABU SUMAYYA

AS: He belonged to the creed and method of the Sunnis, according to the understanding of the pious forefathers in word, deed and creed. For that reason, his group was called JASDJ, and he composed a book, calling it *This is our Creed*.[2] He clarified in it the bases of his creed and method, and if it is possible we can show that at the end of this interview, if Allah wishes.

Interviewer: Some of the people accuse you of being Kharijites?

AS: We are not Kharijites, for we disassociate ourselves before Allah from the method of the Kharijites, and do not label a Muslim as an unbeliever (*kāfir*) because of a grave sin, as long as they do not see it as permitted or deny some known issue from the religion by necessity when proof is presented or in the absence of an impediment. Or [as long as] they do not violate one of the nullifiers of Islam that the *'ulamā'* of the Muslims have specified is a nullifier of the religion—which would be binding with proof being presented or the absence of an impediment with regard to individual *takfīr* that the *'ulamā'* have laid down.

Interviewer: What is your stance regarding democracy, and legislative bodies that legislate laws contrary to the teachings of Islam?

AS: These are nullifiers of Islam, and we see them as unbelief in Allah, mighty and majestic, because the meaning of democracy is "rule of the people for the people," but Allah, mighty and majestic, said: "Rule is for Allah alone."

Interviewer: What is your stance regarding the United Nations, its declarations, and its branches such as the World Bank and the International Court of Justice?

AS: We disassociate ourselves before Allah from them, and view them as nullifying Islam.

Interviewer: Towards what was Shaykh Muhammad Yusuf hastening in his proclamation?

AS: He was hastening towards the preparation of the Muslims, in creed, in knowledge and in military matters so that they could be prepared for undertaking the obligation of proclamation and *jihād* in Allah's path to raise the Word of Allah to the highest and for the *sharī'a* of the Merciful to be ruling on earth.

Interviewer: Why did the government kill him?

AS: Because they felt the danger of his proclamation, and that together with his religious teaching he was gathering weapons and preparing the sons of the Muslims for *jihād*, to fight innovations, despicable matters, sorcery, and magical arts. His opponents gathered against him, and incited the government to kill him. He was made to go to prison several times, and they offered him enticements in return for his giving up of the ruling by the *sharī'a* and the establishment of the Islamic State, so they decided to kill him.

Interviewer: Is your *jihād* presently to take revenge for your shaykh or for the ruling by the *sharī'a*?

AS: We were originally preparing for *jihād*, and we had allocated a time of approximately thirteen years for the preparation of the Muslims for *jihād*, but Allah foreordained the speeding up of the announcement of *jihād* after the passing of seven years when the shaykh was killed and most of our *'ulamā'* and students were killed. So, we saw that the proclamation programs were stopped, and had no way other than to announce the *jihād*, so we gathered our belief around Abubakar Shekau, may Allah preserve him.

Interviewer: Are you prepared to enter negotiations with the government to stop the *jihād*?

AS: No, unless they surrender and rule according to the Islamic *sharī'a* or we die trying for that.

45

BEHEADING VIDEO BY CHADIAN FACTION OF BOKO HARAM[1]

(C. SEPTEMBER 2014)

[Summarized by Abdulbasit Kassim]

This video, which lasts about 12:27 min/sec, features approximately fifteen Chadians identifying themselves as JASDJ, most of whom have their faces covered, together with one uncovered spokesman. According to Reuters, the uncovered spokesman is Abdel Aziz, the leader of a Chadian faction of Boko Haram. Abdel Aziz gives Shekau's standard Arabic introduction, citing the following Qur'ānic verses: "And say: 'The truth has come and falsehood has perished. Falsehood is ever perishing'" (Q17:81); "Fight those among the People of the Book who do not believe in Allah and the Last Day, do not forbid what Allah and His Apostle have forbidden and do not profess the true religion, till they pay the poll-tax out of hand and submissively" (Q9:29); and "O you who believe, fight those of the unbelievers who are near to you and let them see how harsh you can be" (Q9:123). He also states that the goal of the group is either to attain martyrdom or victory in establishing the Islamic state, where the testimony of faith "There is no god but Allah" will be supreme.

In the video, there are three Chadian herdsmen, who are made to kneel in white clothing at their feet in the dirt. The herdsmen are identified as "Kanembuwa," the people of Kanembu, one of the Chadian ethnic groups. Although the viewer can see the knife, which is periodically rubbed against the heads of the victims, the man holding it has his face covered. Five of the armed men around him, however, are uncovered. The uncovered spokesman in military garb, Abdel Aziz, gives a short

Arabic speech where he explains that the herdsmen will be slaughtered because they aligned themselves with unbelievers. He then proceeds to read a statement in Boudouma, an Afro-Asiatic language spoken in the border area of Chad, Cameroon and Nigeria. In the second half of the video, Abdel Aziz switches to Hausa, explaining that the herdsmen were members of the Civilian JTF, who took some cows, and were captured while they were passing through the territory of the Islamic State at Kakuri on their way to Malam Fatori. He further threatens the governments of Chad, Niger and Cameroon.

Abdel Aziz recites from the Qur'ān:

> Indeed, the punishment of those who fight Allah and His Apostle and go around corrupting the land is to be killed, crucified, have their hands and feet cut off on opposite sides, or to be banished from the land. That is a disgrace for them in this life, and in the life to come theirs will be a terrible punishment. Except for those who repent before you overpower them. Know, then, that Allah is All-Forgiving, Merciful. (Q5:33–34)

Afterwards, he requests the knife, then proceeds to slit the throats of the three herdsmen. A copious amount of blood is seen during the last minutes of the video, attesting to the fact that this was not staged. He continues speaking in Boudouma while mentioning Goodluck Jonathan, Paul Biya, Idriss Déby, Obama and François Hollande, but mostly Déby.

The content of this beheading video is related to another video titled "Harvest of the Spies," released on 2 March 2015 by *al-'Urwa al-Wuthqā*, the media organ of Boko Haram before the group pledged allegiance to the Islamic State.[2] In "Harvest of the Spies," two people identified as Dauda Muhammad and Muhammad Awwal were beheaded for spying on behalf of a police officer named Saeed, who promised them 5,000 *naira* [$25]. "Harvest of the Spies" is Boko Haram's most unique video prior to its transition into Islamic State West African Province, and is its only video with French, Arabic and English translations, aside from Shekau's *bay'a* (swearing of allegiance) to the Islamic State (text 43).

Another related video titled "Exposing the Secrets of the Hypocrites" was released by Shekau's faction of Boko Haram on 14 March 2017 after the group split into two factions along ideological lines (see texts 71–4).[3] In the video, three males (Ibrahim from Uba, Ibrahim from Damboa, and Ali Madu) reportedly recruited by Nigeria's Directorate of Military Intelligence to infiltrate the group were executed (the first person was beheaded while the last two were shot at close range). The Boko Haram commander who supervised the execution said after his interrogation of the suspects, "Buhari [referring to Nigeria's president]: here are your spies whom you sent, but Allah exposed them to us. We will not set them free because Allah instructed us to kill hypocrites. We want to obey Allah by doing what he ordered us to do and desisting from what he asked us not to do. Let me be brief. You, the unbeliever, should understand that Allah will protect His caliphate whether you like it or not. He will surely protect His caliphate. Under your watch we will be victorious, God willing, and there is nothing you can do about it. This is all I have to say."

This video is significant for the fact that it was the first video released by the group where captives were paraded wearing the orange jumpsuit, a symbol of Guantanamo prisoners. Aside from the fact that the video shows the images of world leaders (Barack Obama, François Hollande, Vladimir Putin, Recep Erdoğan, Donald Trump and Bashar al-Assad) and the images of Saudi clerics, the clerics of al-Azhar as well as a Nigerian Izala cleric Shaykh Bala Lau, the video also shows the images of jihadi scholars such as the Jordanian Abu Muhammad al-Maqdisi, the British-based Hani Siba'i, and the Canadian-based Tariq 'Abd al-Halim, all of whom were portrayed as apostate scholars. The inclusion of Maqdisi, Siba'i and 'Abd al-Halim as apostates demonstrates that, in spite of Shekau's demotion as the Governor of ISWAP (text 71), his faction continues to support the Islamic State in its ideological rivalry with jihadi scholars sympathetic to al-Qaeda.

46

SHEKAU SAYS HE IS ALIVE AND WELL

(5 OCTOBER 2014)

[Trans.: Abdulbasit Kassim]
Available at: https://www.youtube.com/watch?v=zC0GJtoTttM

Shekau once again resurfaced and dismissed the claims of his death following the report of the Nigerian Army that he was killed in Konduga on 17 September 2014. In this video, Shekau confirmed the killing of the Nigerian pilot (Chimda Hedima), who was captured when Boko Haram members shot down a Nigerian Air Force jet (text 42). The full version of this video also shows graphic scenes of amputation, stoning to death, and beheading.

[*Shekau appears in combat fatigues and black runner boots, firing an anti-aircraft gun into the air.*]

Look at Shekau, who they killed with a *siwāk* (chewing stick). Maybe if someone dies, he will rise again. Unbelievers, you are in trouble! Allah has established an Islamic state for us. We are infuriating the unbelievers but making the believers happy.

[*Shekau speaking Arabic. Citations of Q8:30, 14:46, 3:54, 27:50–51.*]

And thereafter:

Know O unbelievers! Know O unbelievers! Know O unbelievers, Nigerian unbelievers and hypocrites! Know O unbelievers of the world! Know O unbelievers of the world—the unbelievers, transgressors, hypocrites—know that he who has understood these verses has, by the grace of his Allah, ascertained that he is the

335

victor, as long as he is sincere. Allah says: "Yet the evil cunning will only recoil upon its perpetrators." (Q35:43) "And we destroyed the houses and towers which Pharaoh and his people were building." (Q7:137) Allah says: "Whenever they kindle a fire for war, Allah extinguishes it." (Q5:64) "Then, Allah seized them from an unexpected quarter and cast terror into their hearts, so that they destroyed their homes with their own hands, as well as the hands of the believers. Reflect, then, O people of perception!" (Q59:2)

[...] This is what I want to say to the unbelievers and hypocrites, the Jews and Christians, the foreigners, and all those unbelievers, and those who want to do what they want to do to the religion of Islam: "See, then, what was the outcome of their scheming; we destroyed them together with all their people." (Q27:51) My statement concerns the killing of this unbeliever, this transgressor, who is the Nigerian pilot, and the bombing of their planes, and other statements in the Hausa language. Allah is great! Allah is great!

[*Shekau speaking Hausa.*]

My speech today which I would like to deliver to the Nigerian unbelievers, from Jonathan to the least important; those who are defending Nigeria—your lies, unbelief and hypocrisy have come to an end. It has come to an end, and in fact you have not started. You are liars. You said you killed me, do you think if you kill me you have killed the religion? This religion whose prophets they killed, yet the religion survives. Don't you know the Prophets Zachariah and John [the Baptist]? They were slaughtered in this religion. They burnt people in this religion. Don't you know *sūrat al-Burūj*? [*He recites Q85:1–10.*]

Look at it, if you do not know. My survival or death is meaningless to Islam's continuation. You are not sincere. You don't have anything onto which to hold. You don't have anything to say. Look at me alive—until the day upon which Allah takes my breath when I will die. Obama's love will not kill me, nor that of François Hollande, Benjamin Netanyahu, Ban Ki Moon, Queen Elizabeth, or the world's unbelievers, let alone Jonathan *jella*,[1] Kashim broomstick, let alone *bura-uba* mucus—nothing will kill me except my days come to an end.

You should do according to your wish. If you think what I am doing is not the right thing, even if you choose not to fight me, I will be annihilated—but you cannot destroy Allah's religion. I am here with my life. Some of you were asking: "Does Shekau have two lives?" No, O unbelievers! By Allah, I have just one life. The lies are many. My life is one. I am just a student, whose traditional school was burned. I did not die.

Look at your pilot [*video showing the slain pilot Chimda Hedima*] who flew your jet, the pilot who up till the present you have refused to reveal the truth of what happened to him. We are the people who shot him [down], and your jet, which has now crashed. This is not the only jet we shot down. We have shot down more than ten jets. Go to your airfields and check. Even if you conceal it, there is nothing you can conceal from Allah. Yes, we are the people who killed your pilot. Look at him, he is dead. We slaughtered and cut him. There is no one we would not cut.

We are people who in our religion, the Prophet's Companions killed 3,000 unbelievers in one day, such that a river became red like blood. We are people who in our religion, our Prophet slaughtered eighty or 80,000 Jews in one evening.[2] We are the people to whom Allah says: "Kill them wherever you find them and drive them out from wherever they drove you out. Sedition is worse than slaughter." (Q2:191)

Therefore, you are liars, and there is nothing you can do to us. There is nothing you kept for us in Konduga;[3] there is nothing you kept for us anywhere. Don't suffer yourselves. If at all you kept something in Konduga, is it a big deal? Look at us. We are the people who in our religion, the Prophet's Companions fought the unbelievers for a week. All the time they were firing, but did not turn back until Allah gave them victory.[4] This is the path we want to follow.

This is the path for which we beseech Allah to grant us steadfastness. We pray to Allah to make the heat of battle a sweet taste for us. And may Allah make us die in this religion. This is the speech to which I want you to listen. Therefore, you should understand that we are the people who killed your pilot. Shekau killed your pilot. Look at him explaining what transpired. At the time he finished his explanation, we held him for more than a week in our enclave. We studied the secrets of your plane— there are those among us who can fly the plane like it flew to the Pentagon [on 11 September 2001]. If you don't believe us, wait until we act. [*Shekau screams.*]

You are viewing Shekau as a lunatic without intelligence. You are liars. Where is the intelligence in you? We understood your ancestors, who said, "as long as the Muslims read and practice the injunctions of the Qur'ān, they will be powerful." We want to read the injunctions of the Qur'ān, so that we can become powerful. You are a liar, Jonathan.

What is my concern with the dogs' or pigs' language? The language I am proud of is Arabic—what is the English language? What is its origin? I don't have any concern for it. This is the speech I intend to deliver today. You are viewing me like a lunatic but this issue is beyond you. I am not the person who made it hard for you, it is Allah. This is the speech Allah destined I should deliver to you.

Therefore, look at me: I am alive because you said you killed me. We are here in our state, the Islamic state. We are here establishing the Qur'ān: amputating the hands of those who steal, killing the people who commit illicit sexual relations, and flogging the people who lie. We are implementing the Qur'ān in Allah's land. Or does the land belong to you? This is Allah's land, and He made it widespread for following the Qur'ān. He created the heavens so we can follow the Qur'ān, not the constitution. We do not know the constitution. We do not follow the constitution. And may Allah curse the constitution, may Allah curse democracy, may Allah curse Western education, and may Allah curse anyone who follows a path other than Allah's path.

47

SHEKAU SPEAKS ON CEASE-FIRE
AND THE CHIBOK GIRLS

(1 NOVEMBER 2014)

[Trans.: Abdulbasit Kassim]
Available at: https://www.youtube.com/watch?v=15Xh-rf2FoU

*On 17 October 2014, the former Nigerian Chief of Defense Staff, Air Marshal Alex
Badeh, announced a ceasefire agreement between the Nigerian government and Boko
Haram. Badeh's announcement followed a similar announcement on Voice of America
Hausa by Danladi Ahmadu, who claimed to be "the general secretary of Boko Haram."
Hassan Tukur, private secretary of President Jonathan, represented the Nigerian govern-
ment in the ceasefire negotiations, said to have been mediated by Chadian President
Idriss Déby. Part of the agreement included the release of the Chibok schoolgirls.
Although Déby claimed to have verified Danladi as Boko Haram's representative, the
ceasefire agreement fell apart upon this video's release. In it, Shekau denied any ceasefire
agreement, labeling Danladi an unbeliever who has no relationship with the group.
Shekau also said more than 200 out of the 219 remaining Chibok girls have converted
to Islam and been married off. He also gave information about the abduction of a
German national by the group, and ruled out future talks with the government, considered "illegitimate."*

*Videos featuring al-Baghdadi's speech from Mosul and that of Abu Muhammad al-
Adnani, with the Islamic State nashīds—most popularly "My Umma, Dawn Has
Arrived"—appeared at this stage. This mimicry of the Islamic State prior to Boko*

339

Haram's pledge of allegiance to the Islamic State (text 62) is exemplified by the 3 November 2014 video of Shekau's Friday sermon titled "Albishir" (Glad Tidings),[1] delivered in a style like the Friday sermon delivered by al-Baghdadi at Mosul in June 2014. In the video, Shekau affirms that the territory under Boko Haram's control now constitutes an Islamic caliphate. Afterwards he extended his greetings to the brothers in Islamic State in Iraq and the Levant, Afghanistan, Pakistan, Azerbaijan, Chechnya, Yemen and Somalia. The video switches to scenes of Boko Haram fighters imitating the Islamic State fighters by doing "wheelies" in a tank, and driving in a long convoy with the Islamic State flag held high, while the Islamic state nashīd plays in the background. In another 3 November 2014 video titled "Daular Islam" (Islamic State),[2] al-Baghdadi's sermon announcing his caliphate was featured in the opening scene. Just as the Islamic State documents life under its caliphate, some residents were interviewed about life under Boko Haram's caliphate, and the finale showed Boko Haram breaking Nigeria's border with Cameroon, the same way the Islamic State broke the border between Iraq and Syria. Boko Haram's portrayal of its doctrinal and military strategic contiguity with the Islamic State during this period manifests signs that the group was gradually moving to pledge allegiance to the Islamic State.

[Citations of Q9:52, 9:111 and 4:76.]

I do not intend to take much time in this speech. I am using this opportunity to send this message to the Nigerian *ṭāghūt* and others who are unbelievers, including the world's *ṭāghūt*. My speech is in Hausa, the language that is understood by many people, no matter how few. If it becomes necessary, there is nothing stopping me from explaining in either Kanuri or Fulani, but now let us explain to you briefly.

O people! You should know that it is Allah we are following and the path of His Messenger. This is the watchword we put in front of us. We are hoping to die on this path, gain tranquility of mind in our graves and an exalted position in the hereafter. We are praying to Allah just as He said: "There is no one of you but will go down to it [death]. That is for your Lord a decree which must be accomplished." (Q19:71) We will gain entry to paradise, and our desire is the highest peak of paradise, *firdaws* [paradise], and may Allah protect us.

O followers of the constitution! Have you forgotten what you said in your constitution, when we were preaching in Maiduguri? In your constitution, you said in section 8, paragraphs 1–3 in your accursed book, which you call the constitution, having now become law. Allah is king over human beings who deceive none but themselves in the world today. There is no shame—from your mouth, your radio and newspapers you declare that you are fighting against those who intend to establish an Islamic state? Don't you have shame? It is that constitution which prevented us from preaching in Maiduguri, so we emigrated from the town since Allah has decreed migration on us: "He who emigrates for Allah's cause will find on earth many a place of refuge and abundance." (Q4:100)

Have you forgotten? Today, you are sitting and claiming that we have a cease-fire with you? Through which medium? What type of cease-fire and with whom? Your Danladi, who is an unbeliever like you? If he falls into our hands today, we will not sleep until we slit his throat. When did we even know him, let alone allow him to claim that he is representing us? Who is Danladi in this world? Allah is all-Knowing and He is sufficient as a witness.

As a result, I am informing you that we did not agree on any cease-fire or dialogue with anyone. Rather, we are craving war, beatings and killing with guns the same way we crave *tuwo* with Maggi. This is our path and the path for which we fight. Our hope is not for any cease-fire, but to see that only the Qur'ān is being used for ruling on Allah's earth. This is the watchword we put in front of us.

The claim that we came together with the president of Chad, a Nigerian ambassador, and Cameroonians to agree on a cease-fire—where did we meet them? Your white man from Germany is presently with us, he is crying and if we like, we will slaughter him, cut him into pieces or gun him down. We are not afraid of anyone except Allah. This is our job.

Which day did they free the Chibok girls we abducted from their school? Those girls, Shekau abducted and took them to the place of his choice. Today, it is over six months [later]. Allah is far and above the unbelievers, the *ṭāghūt*, America, and the plane called "drone." Bastard! Allah is far and above everyone. If only the parents of the Chibok girls knew the current state of their children, they would not worry themselves. It will be good for you either to become Muslims or die in your pain and rage.

Don't you know that over 200 Chibok girls have become Muslims? Today, they have completed their reading of the first out of thirty parts of the Qur'ān? Today, they have finished reading *al-Uṣūl al-thalātha*[3] by themselves. In the middle of [the Gospels of] John, Luke and others, they have realized that Christians have distorted the gospel with lies. One girl among them was saying by herself that, by Allah, the religion of Islam is the truth. This girl is in form 6. Liars! We have married them off, so they are in the houses of their husbands. Shekau is the house of anger.

They are saying that Shekau is a title? Which title? Do you think we are practicing the traditional system? It is me, Shekau, whose father is Muhammad, and whose son is Muhammad, while my name is Abubakar. Shekau is still the same Shekau, the one who eats the unbelievers' hearts, since they insisted upon sinning against Allah.

Who created you? We did not agree on any cease-fire! We did not agree on a cease-fire with Chad, Cameroon, Niger, Nigeria, the ambassador of Chad, Africa, Asia, Europe, America, or the Assembly of Manipulators [United Nations]. We did not agree on a cease-fire with anyone. It is a lie. We will not do it. What is our business with any cease-fire? Allah says we should not agree to a cease-fire: "So do not weaken and call for peace, while you have the upper hand and Allah is with you. He will not stint you your actions." (Q47:35) It is the Qur'ān we are following, and no unbeliever will intimidate us. Now, you lack anything to do and are desperate to satisfy your elites, who are tired of you. They have understood your lies—the likes of Solomon Dalung, Abdullahi Wase, and Senator [Mohammed Ali] Ndume. They are tired of you, and have understood you are deceiving them and playing with their intelligence.

My actions are for the sole purpose of converting Allah's slaves to Islam. Whether you say it or not, what is my business with you? My goal is to please Allah. I left the house of my parents, my mother and father, and my relatives to come out and join up with those who want to promote Islam, that is "surely, the believers are brothers" (Q49:10), and you are there deceiving people with the claim of cease-fire. All praise be to Allah. I started fighting with a knife, while today I have destroyed more than twenty of your armored cars. Yet, they are saying Shekau is not a person, but a title.

I greet you, the orator, the grandchild of SSS, who studied in Israel, who belongs to the family of psychology, the descendants of biology, and the fools who pledge to "Nigeria, my country." Is that not what you said? You pledge to Nigeria, your country. I, Shekau, I pledge to Allah, my God. If you don't know, today you will know—I pledge to Allah, my God, to be faithful. This is Shekau. Bastards like you. This is my brief speech. This speech is enough for you, so you should repent, return to Allah and follow the Qur'ān. You will not be successful not following the Qur'ān, and stopping those who want to follow Allah. Anyone who rejects this, Allah will show him.

48

BOKO HARAM COMMUNIQUES WITH AFRICAN MEDIA

(18 NOVEMBER 2014–9 FEBRUARY 2015)

[Trans. David Cook]

Available at: https://azelin.files.wordpress.com/2015/02/jamc481_at-ahl-al-sunnah-li-l-da_wah-wa-l-jihc481d-e2809cpast-messages-from-jamc481_at-ahl-al-sunnah-li-l-da_wah-wa-l-jihc481d-to-the-muslims 22.pdf

These brief communiques were published by African Media, a jihadi media group administered by Abu Malik Shayba al-Hamad (see text 61). The communiques highlight the dramatic Boko Haram conquests of late 2014 into early 2015, and the amalgamation of the group with the Islamic State. Although not devoid of Islamic slogans and citations, for the most part these are propagandistic descriptions of the collapse of Nigerian authority in large sections of Borno and Adamawa states. 1 December marks a disassociation from the Kano Mosque attack of 28 November 2014 (text 49), symbolizing the rift between Shekau who carried out the attack and Nur (see text 72), while on 3 December there was an attack on the Izala and Sufi enemies of Boko Haram. These communiques are notable for their complete lack of Qur'ānic citations.

18 November 2014

By the grace of Allah, we now control several cities and villages in the two states of Borno and Adamawa. As for Borno State, we control most of its districts, and the

343

most important cities in it, including the cities of Bama, Gamboru, Banki and Gwoza. As for Adamawa State, we control the cities of Mubi, Maiha, Hong, Madagali, and Gulak. Two days ago, we took control of Gombe, which is very close to the state capital of Yola. But Allah's enemies feared for the state capital, so they concentrated their troops, rushed to the city, and sought to regain it from us. We are now located in the district of Gombe, and if Allah wills, we will return and enter it a second time.

We would like to inform our *mujāhidīn* brothers in every place that we are with them, heart and soul, and that all of us, *mujāhidīn* brothers, believe in the same method and creed. Our goal is one, which is to raise Allah's Word to the highest, and to implement Allah's *sharīʿa*. We will receive our *muhājirīn* brothers from every place—we are together, and our aim is one. All the land of Islam is one, the Muslims are brothers, and our land is their land. These are pictures of the town of Pulka, which is one of those belonging to the Islamic State in Nigeria. [*Pictures of the region.*]

20 November 2014

Today the brother commander Mulla Aba and his deputy Musa were martyred. They were from the earliest squadron of Muhammad Yusuf's students, and had set out in its jihadist trajectory from its first days. They had participated in all of the jihadist operations, and performed very well, being among the bravest of commanders. We consider them to be martyrs, but we do not presume anything before Allah.

They were both killed during the clashes that erupted in the Hong district by a tank bombardment that hit them full-on, while they were boarding a motorbike headed to destroy the tank.

Last news of the day: The brothers retreated slightly to a strategic and fortified district in the mountains between Mubi and Hong, and engaged in strengthening defenses, and preparing for other offenses in the coming days.

22 November 2014

Beloved ones in Allah, your brothers tried again to advance to the city Hong, but were then forced to withdraw a bit, and blow up the bridge that connects the *mujāhidīn* districts with those of the enemy. A few days ago, your brothers controlled the border city of Malam Fatori, between Chad, Niger and Nigeria. The brothers performed well in this battle, and killed a great number of the Nigerian *ṭawāghīt* soldiers. 200 of the cowardly *ṭawāghīt* soldiers fled to Niger.

Your brothers pillaged three tanks and twelve Dushkas, and a large amount of ammunition and light weaponry. There were a group of *ʿulamāʾ* and students of knowledge who spread throughout the liberated cities and villages to spread proclamation, and the correct creed among the masses. Praise to Allah that most of the Muslim masses understood monotheism, accepted the proclamation, and joined the ranks of the *mujāhidīn*.

The *mujāhidīn* have adopted the policy of winning hearts and minds in the cites they have entered. It is not lost upon you that your *mujāhidīn* brothers are lacking in military and administrative abilities, to administer and protect the new-born Islamic state. So where are you, O lions of monotheism and *jihād* experts? Hasten to us, and extend your hands to us in aid, for we are your brothers, and in the direst need of your help and expertise.

We are your brothers and the land is yours because it is the land of Islam, and all Muslims are its managers. Aid, aid, O men of Allah! Where are our brothers, the possessors of expertise in battle? And the military commanders? By Allah, our lands are big and wide, and we need believing men, and our immigrating brothers.

Where are those who are the men, when they call, they answer, "At your service," and when the general muster is sounded, they sally forth.

23 November 2014

This morning the *ṭawāghīt* army attacked the *mujāhidīn* viciously, and brought very strong forces. Prayer, prayer...

25 November 2014

Yesterday the enemies attacked the town of Mararaba, on the crossroads of the Michika–Mubi Road, with strong forces and tanks. The town near fell to the point that the people of Mubi feared that it would fall at the enemy's march against the nearby Mubi, and carry out a massacre against the Muslims because of their support of the *mujāhidīn*. This compelled the people to flee the city, but when the *mujāhidīn* saw the dangerous situation following the salvage of their equipment, they began saying "Allah is great!" in a loud voice, and divine providence and aid interposed, so the unbelievers retreated at the sound of *Allahu akbar*, and Allah cast fear into their hearts. They retreated at some distance to the strategic town of Mararaba.

But the danger still exists. We ask from our brother Muslims to implore with supplication, and abasement to Allah to help the *mujāhidīn*, and to repel the cunning of the unbelievers.

29 November 2014

Praise to Allah, O brothers in Allah, the situation of your brothers in the Islamic state in Nigeria is good. The *mujāhidīn* continue in their conquests and advance, as they are now preparing the provisions for taking over a strategic, importance city. Because of security concerns we will refrain from mentioning the name so we can surprise Allah's enemies. Prayer, prayer, O Muslims!

1 December 2014

We would like to give tidings to our brother Muslims in every place that Allah bestowed vast conquests upon us during the past two days. The first of these tidings: Our brothers, by Allah's grace, have reclaimed the cities of Mubi and Mararaba from the *ṭawāghīt*, and today the brothers conquered Konduga city,[1] and took much booty. They are now besieging Damaturu city.[2] There have been very violent clashes, and a *mujāhidīn* advance. They may push into the city today.

Brothers in Allah, Allah's enemies have been eagerly carrying out loathsome crimes in the cities, and have pinned them on the *mujāhidīn* to mobilize the people and to develop vigilantes against us. They have done this in Maiduguri city, and developed the vigilantes "Sticks and cleavers" (*Kato de Gora*) who have warred against us.

The latest crime that the *ṭawāghīt* fabricated was what happened in the Great Mosque in Kano city. We are innocent of it,[3] as Kano is not a city which the Stick People control that we would target it with a general massacre. Most probably the government is the one which carried out this crime, or the Shi'a, the Rejecters (*rawāfiḍ*), who are present in the city—those whose influence has grown there.

Maybe they are the ones who carried this out because of the religious strife—and there is precedent for that, and they have been amassing weaponry for a while. As for us, we do not carry out the likes of that, and everything that we carry out we proclaim it openly, and do not care [about the repercussions]. For example, we embrace the bombings of three days ago in one of the Maiduguri markets,[4] because Maiduguri city has declared war against us totally, and carries the sticks, cleavers, and buckshot weaponry, and has aided the Crusader government fighting us.

They were worse against us than the Crusader troops, as they arrested dozens of *mujāhidīn* and their families. Maiduguri people arrested our *mujāhidīn* and their families without accusing them of any fault, other than their waging *jihād* against the Christians, and tortured them, disgracing the [sexual] honor of their Muslim wives, beating them with cleavers and sticks until death, publicly in the streets and alleyways, to please the Crusader Nigerian government!

More than that, the inhabitants of Maiduguri joined with the Crusader Nigerian army to attack and fight us! Without exception they fought us, proclaiming their allegiance to the unbelievers, helping them in expelling, imprisoning and killing our brothers for five hours. When Allah gave us the victory we killed them, together with the Christian Army in the worst possible way, in vengeance for Allah, then for the blood of our brothers who they killed in cold blood, striking with knives and cleavers.

This is the truth of what happens with the apostate Stick Carriers, who are fighting against Allah and His Messenger. In every place, we find them we kill them—we did that to them in Bama and Gwoza, since its people were unbelievers, fighting, and we began to target them with killing and terror, not differentiating between them and the Christian Army. Whoever of them repents and gives up his weaponry we will accept his repentance. These are some of the road repairs in the cities we have conquered. [*Pictures*.]

3 December 2014

Just as with the other fighting groups in Allah's path throughout the world, a great deal of what the enemies publish about us is lies to defame our image, and to turn people away from us. Despite that, we clarify our method and creed, and disassociate ourselves before Allah from those lies ascribed to us. We are a *jihād* group according to the method and creed of the People of the Sunna and Jamā'a, and we disassociate ourselves from anything that is opposed to that method. We do not exclude the possibility of error or false exertion [in legal reasoning]. But our method is to return to the Truth, and to cling to it whenever it is clear to us, but from the beginning when we started this proclamation and clarification of the creed to the people, and fighting the Muslims' situation, we announced our disassociation from the unbelievers and their tails, and supported *jihād* and the *mujāhidīn* in the world.

We called the Muslims to hold to their religion and to prepare for *jihād* to liberate our land from the unbelieving Christian government. People shot the bow of enmity at us, and a flood of lies and calumnies poured at us—the first of which was that group from the filthy Murji'a calling themselves Izalat al-bida'a and claiming affiliation with the forefathers' method.

They saw in *jihād* destruction for the Muslims, and believed in the permissibility of entering the Parliament, and the legislative elections. The likes of them are the Bankrupt Brotherhood (*Ikhwanj al-muflisin*) (what is called the Muslim Brothers), so they began warning the people from us, and accusing us of ignorance, stupidity and haste, and put out about us that we were Kharijites sometimes, and other times that our leader was a Shi'ite rejecter or had Shi'ite ideas.

The last of their laughable lies was their claim that Imam Muhammad Yusuf was an American agent, and his interest was killing and dividing the Muslims, and sowing strife between them. Allah knows the truth of us, that we believe in the religion, the creed and the method of the righteous forefathers of the *umma*. They only revenged themselves on us because we believed in our Lord, took *jihād* as a method for our proclamation, and the liberation of our land completely, just as our ancestors did, at their head Shehu 'Uthman Dan Fodio. So, these [Izala] have flung themselves into the embrace of the unbelieving Christian government, then accused us of killing their leader called Shaykh Ja'far [Adam] as a lie, wrong and falsehood, without any proof—relying solely upon our opposition to him and disavowal of him for entering the religion of democracy, and the Parliament.

The second culminating sect is the polytheistic innovating Sufis, who are in abundance around us, who claim to be [part of] Islam, but believe in worship of saints (*awliyāʾ*) and working magic. When we waged *jihād* against them with our tongues and clarified the polytheistic nature of their actions in opposition to monotheism, calling them to put it aside, they attacked us by horse and foot, and claimed that we were declaring Muslims unbelievers. Allah knows that we do not declare any to be unbelievers other than those who Allah and his Messenger do, and those who commit one of the nullifiers of Islam, such as worshipping [entities] other than Allah, working magic and declaring their leaders holy, [thereby] raising them to divine status.

This is all prevalent among them, but they saw in our proclamation a popular conspiracy against them, and a downfall of their leadership by which they bilk the people of their possessions for nothing. Then they began with their slander: "These are a gang[5] of idiots, who declare the saints to be unbelievers and kill Muslims." There is no god but Allah, Allah is sufficient for us against them, and their hateful lies. The Christian government came and completed the game by means of the lying media, and its oppressing army. They began to kill Muslims in the middle of the night, ascribing their actions to us.

What these two sects were unable to do—being the extremist Tijaniyya Sufis and the Murjiʾa claiming to be according to the method of the forefathers (who are disassociated from them)—taking the Christian government's claims and lies that lack proof or evidence, other than hate and malice for us—ascended pulpits and in loud voices concocted accusations and lies of their lying Crusader unbelieving masters.

When the unbelievers saw that all of this was futile, not influencing our popularity among the people, they turned to force, and killed the Shaykh Muhammad Yusuf and most of his senior students, so we rose then, took up weapons and proclaimed *jihād* against the unbelieving Christian government. We proclaimed our goal: Liberation of the land from unbelief and application of Allah's *sharīʿa*, and defined our goals in killing just as our imam, Abubakar Shekau stated, which were killing the security and armed forces of the Crusader government and all the spies who assist them against us.

So, the enemy took refuge in a dirty tactic: every time we commence an operation and killed unbelievers, the unbelievers go to the Muslims' quarters, and kill every mature Muslim able to bear arms. Then the Crusader military commander will come, pretend to weep over the slain, and say: "This is not what we wanted, but the soldiers did this to protect people, while you bear half the responsibility as you allowed terrorists from your sons to kill soldiers. If you would not aid them, disassociate from them, and fight them, then this type of crime would not happen every time!"

The people have responded to the unbelievers' claims in some cities, and were happy to apostatize, and associate with the unbelievers, so they took up sticks, knives and small weaponry, and killed the *mujāhidīn* and their families. Even more, the shaykhs of the Murjiʾa and especially the shaykhs of the group of Izalat al-bidaʿa wrote legal opinions on our being unbelievers, such that "it is desirable to kill" a man of us each day because they see us as unbelievers! But see the Christians as friends! This is what has led us to announce fighting the Stick Carriers, their Mufti, and any who assist them. How many of the *mujāhidīn* have they killed, and our women's [sexual] honor have they defiled!

We are called JASDJ; as for the reasons, why they named us "Boko Haram," we never called ourselves that. It was only the unbelievers who gave that name to us, and the apostates from the innovating Sufi Izalat al-bida'a publicized it. The reason that led them to name us by that name was that we forbid study in the missionary schools, which are bankrolled by the Christian Western churches, that are spreading through the Muslim districts with the claim of spreading teaching. Muslim children study unbelief in them, denial of the divine, and decorate the Christian religion, the worshippers of the cross. They spread vice among the Muslims, encouraging the mixing between the sexes. So, we forbade study in these corrupting schools, and fought them, forbidding the Muslims from joining them, threatening the Crusaders working in them with death. So, the enemies stored this up, and claimed that we are forbidding teaching [as a whole]. But we do not forbid learning, technology or civilization; we only forbid unbelief and corruption. We do not permit a Muslim to call us "Boko Haram" so he does not help the unbelievers in their claims.

As for our stance, as to what is called "the Syrian division among the jihadi groups"[6] we dislike what is happening between brothers of religion, creed and method, and we call them to Allah's Book, and arbitration of Allah's law between, truce and assistance between them, unity of rank and belief.

5 December 2014

Allah has the praise and the grace, the Muslims' sons have exchanged the games of PlayStation and football for military exercises, after they finish their study sessions. These are pictures: [*Pictures.*]

The best thing is that their game was without supervision or command—they are only applying what they have seen from the *mujāhidīn*. This is their habit every day after finishing their study sessions. Whoever sees them doing this and their skill would think that they are outside of a military camp or that a trainer is overseeing them. Woe to the unbelievers from the next generation of the Muslims' children, the descendants of Shehu 'Uthman Dan Fodio!

6 December 2014

This is to remove the uncertainty concerning our killing masses and expelling other dwellers of certain cities like Gamboru and Bama, so we say:

These cities, most of their dwellers were Stick Carriers, and assisted the unbelievers. We warned them, again and again, but they went back to their ways, and even increased in their error to the point where the people of Bama for example went out with sticks and knives to the districts under our control, and demanded from the villagers to return from our proclamation, and accept stick-bearing against us. When the villagers refused, they killed them and burned their homes with those inside.

So, the *mujāhidīn* sent messages to them, warning them, asking them to repent and to stop associating with the unbelievers. But they refused. So, the *mujāhidīn* proclaimed that Bama city was fighting Allah and His Messenger, and when we entered it, we would consider all dwelling in it to be fighters—the men to be killed, while the women and children to be taken captive. We demanded that the masses leave the city and emigrate before we came, so whoever left left, but those who refused stayed, and the Stick People continued their crimes. For this reason, when we entered we revenged ourselves on them in general, expelling them, killing whomever we could of them.[7]

As for the people of Gamboru, their actions were more abhorrent than those of the people of Bama, but when we entered it we killed only the Stick Carriers and the army soldiers. We identified them by the eyes [spies] we had planted in the city. Some of the military took off their uniforms and wore civilian clothing, fled to the mosque next to the government [army] camp, thinking that we would not know them, reckon them to be civilians and leave them. But we, praise Allah, knew them and killed them inside their mosque, the Opposition Mosque (*ḍirār*).[8] We found their military identity cards with them.

As for the city masses, we pardoned them and demanded that they stay in their dwellings, but they refused and fled to Cameroon and Chad, either fearing us or fearing the unbelievers' return for revenge. We said to them: "There is no cause for fear, do not leave the House of Islam and immigrate to the unbelievers' dwellings ruled by constitutions." But they refused.

There are mass groups we drove out because of previous loyalties, their spying for the enemies, or especially if they were in a border town, adjacent to the unbelieving *ṭawāghīt*. We wanted to drive out the eyes [spies] that had been placed against us especially, and we had promised treachery and betrayal from that city's people.

We would hope from our brother Muslims that they would not believe the words of our enemies until they would investigate and learn the truth. If we killed people en masse, what would be the point of our leaving the peoples of the cities and villages we have entered? There are more than thirteen cities in our hands, dozens of towns, and hundreds of villages, with their people in their dwellings. Those, by Allah, who rejoiced in us have become *mujāhidīn*. The cultivators and herders when they have seen the enemy's movements have flocked to us, and informed us.

Just a few days ago, we began an offensive against the unbelievers, the people gathered to us with empty hands, while some of them carried sticks and knives, to block the unbelievers' advance with us. We have not compelled anyone to this, but their zeal for the religion and love for us led them to it.

9 December 2014

Has the report of the Nigerian pilot whom the brothers captured and slaughtered come to you? He came to bomb the Muslims in his airplane, but the *mujāhidīn* shot him down, when he ejected in a parachute. It was not long before the *mujāhidīn* were able to find his landing place—he landed in a village district nearby, but the cultivators were aware of him, and they gathered to capture him while shouting: "Unbeliever, unbeliever!" When he saw that, he prepared to fight them by hand, so they beat him with a stick until they broke his hand and skull. Then they bound him, and brought him to the *mujāhidīn*, who carried out Allah's ruling and killed him. This is only a small amount of what demonstrates the unity between most Muslims and the *mujāhidīn* in the Islamic State in Nigeria.

10 December 2014

Has the news of Nigerian prisons in Borno State reached you—how the brothers are tortured in them? They are given one bite of food alone morning and evening, and sometimes just one bite for the whole day. As for drink, water is denied them for long days, to the point where the Muslim prisoners drink their own urine because of the intense thirst. One of them [the Muslim prisoners], when he urinated, he would conceal it so that another thirsty person would not steal it and drink it! A Muslim prisoner would say to another: "If you allow me to drink a bit of your urine today, I will let you drink from mine tomorrow."

One of the brothers who was released from prison after the *mujāhidīn* broke in to free them said: "I urinated one night into a can, then slept, so my urine was stolen. I was thirsty, and could not find anything to drink!"

Imagine for yourselves a room four [meters] by six, packed with 200 Muslim prisoners, without air-conditioning, windows for ventilation, water in which to bathe or to perform *wuḍū'* (ritual ablution) [...] There is a pit into which the Crusaders throw several Muslims until the pit is filled. Then they leave them without food or drink until they die, then throw in others in their place. Of the *mujāhidīn* prisoners 3,000 were killed in one month from thirst, hunger and torture. This is the Crusader Nigerian dictatorship—then they blame us that we fight this dictatorial Christian government, which has neither religion nor this world!

9 February 2015

The message of our beloved has reached us, and we are in newfound agreement with the proclamations of the beloved Islamic State. We announce to you gladly that the Consultative Council of the Group [Boko Haram] is in the stage of mutual consultation and study, and that we will inform you shortly of the Group's decision concerning swearing allegiance to the Caliph of the Muslims, Abu Bakr al-Baghdadi. Give the peace greeting to all our *mujāhidīn* brothers, especially those of the Islamic State. Make sure our message reaches all Muslims, your brothers in Nigeria ask of you to make *hijra* to us, to help us in the administration of districts under our control, and to fight the alliance of the unbelievers.

49

MESSAGE TO THE EMIR OF KANO

BY ABUBAKAR SHEKAU

(15 DECEMBER 2014)

[Trans.: Abdulbasit Kassim]

Following the 28 November 2014 attack on Kano Central Mosque where more than 120 people died, the Emir of Kano, Sanusi Lamido Sanusi, urged the religious and community leaders to defend themselves in whatever way possible against Boko Haram. Sanusi also urged the residents of Kano, hunters and vigilantes, to arm and defend themselves against Boko Haram. In this video, Shekau did not claim responsibility for the Kano attack, but he condemned Sanusi as well as the followers of Islamic groups, whom he described as unbelievers straying away from Islam. Shekau said they should repent and practice Islam as understood by his group or face the consequences. This threat from Shekau is possibly what led to the suicide bombing against the Shi'a Muslims on 3 November 2014 during their procession marking the Day of Ashura.[1]

[*Citations of Q9:52, 9:111 and 4:76.*]

O honored brothers! O supporters of Allah! O people of [*sūras*] *Anfāl* and *Tawba*! We do not forget our pledge to Allah. Allah says: "Allah has bought from the believers their lives and wealth in return for paradise; they fight in the way of Allah, kill and get killed. That is a true promise from Him in the Torah, the Gospel and the Qur'ān; and who fulfils His promise better than Allah? Rejoice then at the bargain you have made with Him; for that is the great triumph." (Q9:111) [....] I am sending this piece of admonition firstly to my brothers, and secondly to the unbelievers, specifically the Nigerian unbelievers. Die in your rage! Allah will give victory to His religion. I am going to deliver this admonition in Hausa.

O people! Before I admonish my brothers, who are defending the religion of Islam; the religion of the Qur'ān, not the religion of democracy; the religion of the *ḥadīth* of the Prophet, not the religion of Western education; the religion of the Qur'ān, not that of the constitution; not the religion of Lamido Sanusi, Jonathan, Obasanjo, Atiku [Abubakar], [Ibrahim] Babangida, Obama, Bush, Clinton, François Hollande, and all other unbelievers.

Allah's religion—"The [true] religion with Allah is Islam." (Q3:19) So, you should listen, I am referring to you, the Emir of Kano. I am delivering this admonition because of your recent utterances. The Emir of Kano, you are late. You are just the Emir of Kano, the Emir of the bank,[2] and the Emir of money. You are Sanusi Lamido, Lamido of Fulani. You are the Emir of Kano. Is that how they practice the religion, the religion of democracy, the constitution, Western education and homosexuality? It is only Allah we follow. It is the Qur'ān we want to establish. This land is the land of Allah. Allah says, "Judgment is Allah's alone" (Q6:57) but you said, "Judgment is for the people alone." Our government is Allah's, by Allah and for Allah. Your government is of the people, by the people and for the people. We do not worship the people. It is only Allah we worship. It is only the Qur'ān we follow, and the law of Allah is what we seek to establish.

You are late. You said the "Civilian JTF" (*Kato de Gora*) should take up weapons and fight against us, right? "Civilian JTF," you should repent and follow the Qur'ān and the Prophet's Sunna. Our anger and hatred is only directed against those who oppose Allah. By Allah, the hunters you have lost! We are hunting those who oppose Allah. If you repent and join us to follow Allah's religion, defend the Qur'ān, the Prophet's Sunna, men and women's chastity and the establishment of the religion's laws, then you are our brother.

However, if you choose to follow democracy, the constitution, and Western education, you should join heads and even bottoms together [as a coalition]. Allah is great. Look at Shekau, he is in good health, but Allah protects him. Look at Shekau, he is an ordinary human being, but Allah protects him. "It was not you who slew them, but Allah; and when you threw it was actually Allah who threw, so that He might generously reward the believers." (Q8:17) This is our religion.

Emir of Kano, you are late. You even said that our victory is trivial. No! Your predecessors, who were also unbelievers like Abu Jahl, said the same thing. You can say that our victory is trivial since you are the Emir of Bank, and you worship the land. Your said our victory is trivial, when all we desire is for our blood to be spilled, and to be killed so that can gain the grave's tranquility and paradise. However, your ultimate desire is the establishment of democracy. You are late! I will not prolong my speech. This is a brief admonition which I am sending to you, Emir of Kano. You are late!

I came out to deliver this speech because of your recent utterances. You are a human being like me. You are serving the interest of people, while I am serving the interest of Allah. I am not praising myself. I don't see myself as important. Whoever is working for Allah's religion and thinks he is saved—such a person is in the state of perdition. I am seeking to be saved by Allah. "And those who give what they give while their hearts tremble for fear that they are returning to their Lord." (Q23:60) It is the Qur'ān we want to follow. We are students. If we follow the Qur'ān, through it we know how to treat our parents, help our brothers, live with our women, how to farm, engage in trading, and all other things. Even if we do not fight, when our days are over, we must die. This is our religion.

Now, do not think I am angry, just repent, and come and follow the religion. However, calling people to revolt against us because Americans made you the Emir of Kano—that is why you are angry with us, right? We want to bring back Allah's kingship. Oh, you are late! "Civilian JTF," you have lost. Hunters, you have suffered. The government, you have become enervated. The people of JASDJ, once their intentions are purified, they will be successful. And may Allah make us purify our intentions.

We are not praising ourselves. However, we attest to the truth of the Qur'ān and the sayings of Allah's Messenger. We do not follow any creed or ideology, except the Qur'ān and the Sunna. The Izala people are unbelievers, as are the Tijaniyya, the Qadiriyya, the Naqshbandiyya, the Shadhiliyya, the Mu'tazilites, the Shi'ites, and democracy is unbelief. The Saudi state is a state of unbelief, because it is a state that belongs to the Saud [family], and they do not follow the Prophet. The Ka'ba is Allah's house. The mosque of the Prophet is but a house. If Allah permits, we will go and perform the pilgrimage. The Saudi Arabians, since you have altered Allah's religion, you will enter hellfire. We follow the Qur'ān. We are the people of the Qur'ān and Sunna. We are not seeking after your praise. It is not until you say we are good people that we will become good people. The person who seeks people's praise is a liar. He is an unbeliever. We will kill, capture slaves, and sell them. [*Shekau screams his name while shooting into the air with a rifle.*]

If you don't know, this is Shekau. We are in a state of conflict with you, Emir of Kano, Jonathan and anyone who opposes Allah. Obama is a liar! Bastards like you are saying that you will annihilate us from the land. No one can annihilate us! [*Speaking Kanuri.*] What we are saying is that you should repent. Do you mean we will not practice our own religion? It is a lie! This is the speech Allah predestined me to deliver to you. You can go ahead, Civilian JTF. [*Speaking Kanuri.*] Civilian JTF and democracy are fighting us. By Allah, you should not sit, brothers. Come out, brothers! Kill! Slaughter! Torch them! This is the religion and by Allah we must practice it.

50

MESSAGE TO PRESIDENT PAUL BIYA OF CAMEROON

BY ABUBAKAR SHEKAU

(5 JANUARY 2015)

[Trans.: Abdulbasit Kassim]

In this video, Shekau addressed the government and people of Cameroon for the first time. This video was released several months after the President of Cameroon vowed to wipe out Boko Haram, following the abduction and subsequent release of ten foreigners and seventeen Cameroonian hostages, including the wife of Amadou Ali, the country's deputy prime minister. Shekau here threatens Paul Biya with a fate like his Nigerian counterpart.

"And should you fear treachery from any people, throw back their treaty to them in like manner. Allah does not like the treacherous." (Q8:58) [*Citing Q9:52.*] And all praise is due to Allah, who granted the *mujāhidīn*, the members of JASDJ, territorial expansion into Cameroon.

All praise is due to Allah, who saddened the unbelievers' grandfathers, such as Israel and Great Britain. And all praise is due to Allah, who has enraged the hearts of their kingpins—I mean, America and France—and He has placed trepidation in the hearts of their grandchildren and children. Why? Allah says: "We will cast terror into the hearts of the unbelievers on account of their associating with Allah that for which they have no authority," (Q3:151) such as democracy and other secular systems. Allah also commanded His servants in the Qur'ān to slay those who ascribe partners to

Him. Allah says: "Kill them wherever you find them and drive them out from wherever they drove you out. Sedition is worse than slaughter." (Q2:191) He also said: "And fight them so that sedition might end and that the only religion will be that of Allah. Then if they desist, Allah is fully aware of what they do." (Q8:39)

[Islamic opening] The Holy Prophet Muhammad said: "The best of people is a man who is holding the rein of his horse for the sake of Allah, while galloping towards the place wherever he hears a call for war or detects danger; he goes on forward, seeking martyrdom or death, wherever it happens. Then another man who retires with some sheep to a mountainside or a valley, performing prayer regularly, paying the alms, continuing to worship his Lord, until death overtakes him. He does not interfere in people's affairs, except to better them."

[Islamic opening]

And thereafter:

O Paul Biya! I am sending this message to you. I am the leader of JASDJ in the land of Africa called Nigeria. I am Abu Muhammad Abubakar b. Muhammad al-Shekawi. O Paul Biya! Repent to your Lord; otherwise you will see the suffering and sedition that will happen from our Lord who is capable of anything. O Paul Biya! If you fail to refrain from your evil actions, you will meet the fate of the Nigerian unbelievers, America, the hypocrites and the apostates. Verily, your soldiers cannot do anything by Allah's permission. Allah's soldiers shall remain victorious. Allah says in the Qur'ān: "Our Word unto Our Messengers has already gone out. They will surely be supported. And Our hosts are the true victors." (Q37:171–73) He also said: "Allah has decreed: 'I shall certainly vanquish, I and My messenger.' Surely Allah is Strong, All-Mighty." (Q58:21) He also said: "We shall support Our Messengers and the believers in the present life and on the day the witnesses shall arise." (Q40:51) And there are many other verses.

O people of Cameroon! You should know that a person does not become a Muslim except by disassociation from democracy and all other polytheistic acts. It is obligatory upon you to disbelieve and disassociate yourself from democracy. It is also obligatory upon you to declare disassociation from democracy's servants and helpers. Allah says: "They wish to submit their disputes to the Devil, although they have been commanded to denounce him; but the Devil wishes to lead them far astray!" (Q4:60)

Mujāhid, a Qur'ānic exegete, said: "*Ṭāghūt* is Satan or any entity set up by the people to judge between amongst themselves using laws not in accordance with the decisions of Allah and his Messenger." Ibn Qayyim says: "The *ṭāghūt* is everything through which man exceeds his limits—whether it is being worshipped, followed or obeyed." So, the *ṭāghūt* of every community is he from whom judgment is sought, instead of what Allah and His Messenger have ruled; or those whom they worship besides Allah, who they follow without proof from Allah, or who they obey, while not knowing if they are in accord with Allah's judgment.

MESSAGE TO PRESIDENT PAUL BIYA OF CAMEROON

O you who worship man-made laws and earthly constitutions! O bearers of the religion of democracy! O you gods who are ascribed as partners to Allah! We have disassociated from you and your path. We disbelieve in you, your polytheistic constitutions and your nationalistic parliaments. And hostility and hatred has emerged between us forever until you believe in Allah alone [cf. Q60:4].

I am telling you, Paul Biya, repent to Allah, otherwise you will see that your soldiers are nothing. Even the Nigerian soldiers could not do anything to us. Even if they were American soldiers they could not do anything to us, not even the entire world's soldiers. We are Allah's soldiers. We ask Allah to grant us steadfastness, and to make us among "those who fight for His religion and do not fear anybody's reproach." (Q5:54)

There is no deity worthy of being worshipped other than Allah, and I pray to Allah, the Lord of the Great Throne, to grace us all with guidance. May Allah bestow His prayers on Muhammad, as He bestowed them on Abraham and his kin. And may Allah defeat our enemies, give us victory over them, destroy their aircraft, drown their pilots, and have mercy on us.

I remain your brother in Allah, Abu Muhammad Abubakar b. Muhammad al-Shekawi, the imam of JASDJ in the land of Africa called Nigeria. This is a message to the leader of Cameroon, Paul Biya. You will see what you will see, with Allah's permission. We swear by Allah that we will remain true to what our Lord has commanded us to do. We shall not retreat from this until we die. Prayers and peace be upon Allah's Messenger, and praise be to Allah, the Lord of the worlds. I will now switch to Hausa.

This is a message to Paul Biya, the president of Cameroon. Even though you may be officially bilingual,[1] you should also understand my own language. If by Allah's grace, this message reaches you, O Paul Biya, president of Cameroon, you will understand my language. I am not delivering this speech on behalf of myself but on behalf of Allah. I am nothing. I am addressing you by Allah's will, the Creator of the heavens and earth, the trees, and all human beings. Remember that every soul will account for his deeds on the Day of Judgment, and even in the grave. We know that democracy is not Allah's religion. We know that the document you call the constitution which serves as your guide, your written laws used by your judges and lawyers, is not the way of the Prophet Muhammad.

As a result, your craftiness is a lie. "They schemed and Allah schemed, but Allah is the best of schemers." (Q8:30) What I am saying is there is no distinction between the poor, the monarchs, or the wealthy in Allah's sight, and whoever repents belongs to Allah. Allah will only embrace those who repent. The biggest virtue for an individual is repentance, while the biggest challenge is to dwell in sin. You will therefore see what you will see.

As for me, I am conveying a message. I may die anytime—even this evening because death is my dress. It is also your dress, you unbeliever, Paul Biya. Paul Biya and people of Cameroon, I am referring to you. I am warning you all, I am preaching to you all. Some of you claim to be praying and saying: "Only you do we worship, and only You do we implore for help," (Q1:4) and yet you follow democracy? You are saying "Lead us to the right path," (Q1:5) and yet you follow the constitution's laws and those of your country, all of which do not reflect the teachings of the Qur'ān. You say, "Lead us to the right path," while you are attending French educational institutions. You are aware that François Hollande is not a Muslim. Obama is not a Muslim. You know there is nothing Islamic in the Assembly of Manipulators [United Nations]. This is a global world based upon secularism. Do you expect us to sit down submissively and follow a cursed document [the constitution] and a book of feces? This is my brief speech in Hausa. [*Speaking in Kanuri and Fulfulde.*]

This is not our strength [*pointing to a rifle*]; Allah is the only source of our strength. [*Shekau waves the black flag.*][2] This is Allah's symbol, which is why we are displaying it for you to see. I am nothing, and only Allah is sufficient for me. I swear by Allah; Allah will grant us victory. As a result, we are not bothered by your lies. [*Shekau fires shots into the air with his rifle.*]

51

CHARLIE HEBDO

BY ABUBAKAR SHEKAU

(14 JANUARY 2015)

[Trans.: Abdulbasit Kassim]
Available at: https://www.youtube.com/watch?v=LzIAPmhuFK4[1]

In this eight-minute-long video, Shekau celebrated the attack on the French satirical journal Charlie Hebdo *on 7 January 2015, and reiterated Boko Haram's belief system and its vision to continue fighting. He also cited classical Islamic theologians to justify the group's ideology that whoever rules by a system of law other than the law of Allah is* ṭāghūt. *It is apparent that Shekau did not know details of the* Charlie Hebdo *attack in this video; more is given in text 52.*

[*Citation of Q9:52, 2:191, 8:39, and the* ḥadīths *cited in text 49.*]

O people of France! You should know that a person does not become a Muslim except through disassociation from democracy and all other polytheistic acts. It is obligatory upon you to disbelieve and disassociate yourself from democracy. It is also obligatory upon you to declare disassociation from democracy's servants and helpers. Allah says: "They wish to submit their disputes to the Devil, although they have been commanded to denounce him; but the Devil wishes to lead them far astray!" (Q4:60)

[*Citation of Mujāhid and Ibn Qayyim from text 50.*]

O you who worship the lying rulings, constitutions and nations! O bearers of the religion of democracy! O you gods who are ascribed as partners to Allah! We have disassociated from you and your path. We disbelieve in you, your polytheistic constitutions and your nationalistic parliaments. And hostility and hatred has emerged between us forever until you believe in Allah alone.

We are delighted. We are JASDJ in the African country called Nigeria. We are filled with joy over what happened in France. Allah is great! Allah is great! Glad tidings! Glad tidings, O brothers! Allah is great! Allah is great! We rejoice for what has befallen the people of France. We rejoice for the punishment that befell the people of France, their pains and afflictions as blood was spilled inside their own country. Allah is great! And I pray to Allah the Generous, Lord of the Great Throne, to bestow guidance and righteousness upon us all, and to bring piety to our souls and hearts, for He is the best purifier, and our Patron and Master. Indeed, He is a Hearer and Responder. We rejoice and are filled with joy for what has befallen the people of France in their country. And Allah is the one whom we beseech. It is You whom we worship and beseech. Guide us on the straight path—the path of those upon whom you have bestowed favor, not those who have evoked your anger or of those who are astray. Peace and blessings be upon Allah's Messenger. Praise be to Allah, Lord of the worlds.

52

MESSAGE TO THE WORLD ON BAGA

BY ABUBAKAR SHEKAU

(21 JANUARY 2015)

[Trans.: Abdulbasit Kassim]

Available at: http://jihadology.net/2015/01/21/new-video-message-from-boko-%e1%b8%a5arams-jamaat-ahl-al-sunnah-li-dawah-wa-l-jihad-imam-abu-bakr-shekau-message-to-the-world-on-baga/

This video is a follow-up to text 50. In it Shekau touted the success of the group in the raid on Baga and Doron Baga, and reiterated some of the key themes in its belief system. The inhabitants of these towns were almost all Muslims. In addition, Shekau chided the leaders of Nigeria, Niger, Chad and Cameroon for calling for international support against Boko Haram. This video marks the first public display of Nigeria's national flag being burned by Boko Haram. While reading a speech broadcast in French on Radio France, Shekau also stated that the French government is hostile to Islam and the Muslims. Shekau's spoken French is poor, but comprehensible. He was probably helped by Chadian members of the group. The final scenes of this video, which show a different speaker displaying the weapons the group acquired from the raid on Baga and Doron Baga, are akin to the April 2013 video on the raid on Monguno Barrack.[1]

[*Citation of Q9:52.*] And praise be to Allah who granted our *mujāhidīn* territorial expansion into the villages of Baga and Doron in the land of Nigeria; our *mujāhidīn* brothers, the members of JASDJ. And praise be to Allah, who saddened the unbelievers' grandfather—that is Israel and Britain. And praise be to Allah who angered their father—America and France—and cast horror in the hearts of their grandchildren and children. As Allah has said: "We will cast terror into the hearts of the unbelievers on account of their associating with Allah that for which they have no authority." (Q3:151) Who are those who have disbelieved? All of those who have disbelieved in Allah—and the unbelievers are the democrats and others.

And praise be to Allah who ordered the *mujāhidīn* to kill them in the Qur'ān. Allah says: "Kill them wherever you find them and drive them out from wherever they drove you out. Sedition is worse than slaughter." (Q2:191) Sedition is democracy, man-made laws, and foreign schools. "Fight them until there is no sedition and the religion becomes that of Allah. But if they desist, there will be no aggression except against the evil-doers." (Q2:193) [...]

[*Citations of the* ḥadīths *from text 49.*]

O people of this world! O people of this world! O people of this world! Hear these words from me. I send you my message. Who sends a message to you? He is the leader of JASDJ in the part of Africa called Nigeria, Abu Muhammad Abubakar b. Muhammad Al-Shekawi. O people of this world, repent to Allah: "O people, fear your Lord. Surely the clamor of the Hour is a terrible thing. The day you will witness it, every suckling mother will be distracted from the child she is suckling, and every pregnant woman will deliver her burden, and you will see people drunk, whereas they are not drunk; but the punishment of Allah is terrible." (Q22:1–2).

O people of America, perish in your rage. O people of Israel, perish in your rage. O people of France, perish in your rage. O unbelievers of this world, we uphold our religion, our doctrine, the doctrine of our Messenger. All those who have insulted our Prophet are unbelievers. And all of those who doubt their unbelief are also unbelievers.[2] All of those who infringe upon [insulting Muhammad] are unbelievers. O people of this world! Repent to Allah, or else you will see what our Lord who is capable of anything will show you. You will see the punishment and sedition that you will have. François Hollande, Ban Ki Moon, I do not call you by any name other than that which I have previously used, which is the Assembly of Manipulators [United Nations]—in Hausa, in the language of our locale.

You cannot do anything in this world, because this world was created by Allah for Him to be worshipped. Our Lord says: "Judgment is Allah's alone." (Q6:57) Allah says: "Whoever does not judge according to what Allah has revealed, those are the evildoers!" (Q5:44) And the All-Mighty also says: "O believers, do not take the Jews and Christians as friends; some of them are friends of each other." (Q5:51) The Prophet also said: "Whoever resembles a group is one of them."[3] If you do not renounce this evil, you will suffer the same fate as Pharaoh, and Thamud, Ad, and the other unbelievers who came before you—the polytheists, the apostates, and others. And know that Allah's soldiers are indeed the victorious ones.

MESSAGE TO THE WORLD ON BAGA

We, JASDJ, are those who fought the people of Baga, killing them thoroughly, just as He commanded us in His Book. We will not stop ever. We will not stop ever. We will not stop ever, until we die. Our doctrine is either victory or martyrdom. There is no god but Allah. You cannot do anything to us, by Allah's permission, because Allah's soldiers are the victorious ones. Allah says: "Our word unto our Messengers has already gone out. They will surely be supported. And our hosts are the true victors." (Q37:171–173). And He says: "Allah has written: 'I shall certainly vanquish, I and my messengers.' Surely, Allah is Strong, All-Mighty." (Q58:21) "We shall support our Messengers and the believers in the present life and on the day the witnesses shall arise." (Q40:51) Allah is great! And so forth are many verses.

Anyone who claims to be a democrat is an unbeliever. Anyone who resorts to man-made laws for adjudication is an unbeliever. And know that a person cannot become a Muslim without disassociating from democracy and other forms of idolatry, and renouncing them, just as we were commanded by Allah. As Abraham, Allah's friend, said: "We are quit of you and what you worship apart from Allah. Enmity and hatred have arisen between you and us forever, till you believe in Allah alone..." (Q60:4) There is no god but Allah.

You insulted our Prophet Muhammad and drew his image. Where did you find the image of our Prophet?! Where did you find the image of our Prophet?! *Charlie*, God damn you! *Charlie*, God damn you! François Hollande, God damn you, if you do not repent! There is no god but Allah. O people of Saudi Arabia! O people of Bahrain! O people of Qatar! O people everywhere! You are the Arabs. You are those who abide by democracy? After Allah has handed down the Qur'ān? In Mecca? Do you think— I will not complete my words. I leave you with this. Learn a lesson for yourselves. You will know what you know, if you saw us—I will not complete this either. You complete it. I have heard what you said, you are the speakers. Allah is great! Judgment is Allah's alone. There is no god but Allah.

Slaves of man-made laws and earthly constitutions, people of the religion of democracy, legislating lords, we turn to Allah disassociating from you and your faith. We reject you and your polytheistic constitutions and idolatrous assemblies, and "enmity has appeared between us and hatred forever until you believe in Allah alone." (Q60:4) We announce to all who claim to be with America, Israel, or François Hollande of France, that from anywhere we do not fear anyone but Allah. Allah commanded us in His Noble Book: "That indeed is the Devil frightening his follower; but do not fear them and fear Me, if you are true believers!" (Q3:175) We want to be faithful believers. We ask Allah to make us faithful.

Therefore, we do not fear anyone. With Allah's permission, not by our power— there is no dominion or power except through Allah. We do not kill anyone, except who He commanded us to kill. And Allah has prohibited polytheists from paradise. Allah says: "Surely, He who associates other gods with Allah, Allah forbids him access to paradise and his dwelling is Hell. The evildoers have no supporters!" (Q5:72) The polytheist is not forgiven in the hereafter: "Allah will not forgive associating [any other god] with Him, but will forgive anything less than that, to whomever He wills. He who associates [any other god] with Allah, has really gone very far astray!" (Q4:116) We heard what we have heard, and we want to revere Allah. Allah commanded his Messenger saying: "If you associate any others with Allah, He will frustrate your work and you will certainly be one of the losers." (Q39:65) This is our Lord's word: "Those they call upon, apart from Allah, do not create anything but are themselves created." (Q16:20)

[*Shekau speaking Hausa.*]

Jonathan, you are in trouble. Governors of Nigeria, you are in trouble. Look at these weapons; we acquired them in the towns of Baga and Doron. You are saying: "You don't have weapons," it is a lie. You simply do not have strength and power. Allah is the one with weapons. He is the one who says: "Be and it is." (Q3:47) What do we have in the first place? We started with knives and sticks, but today we have stood firm with resilience. Who are we to stand firm, if it were not for Allah's mercy? Jonathan, your followers are now cursing you. That is the consequence of following the people and unbelief. This is the end of it. Anyone who follows people will surely come to see that it is not pleasant. This is the end of politics. This is the end of democracy.

This attack we conducted is a low-scale attack. Did you not hear: "Marked from your Lord; and they were never far off from the wrongdoers." (Q11:83) By Allah, we are the people who carried out the attack. We will not withdraw. This attack is a low-scale attack. Wait and see. Are you not saying [Muhammadu] Buhari,[4] Jonathan? Do you think Buhari is a Muslim? An unbeliever! Mahamadou Issoufou, the president of Niger! You even paid a condolence visit to François Hollande, the grandson of *Charlie*. Mahamadou Issoufou, is this your work? You shall see the president of Niger.

Paul Biya, have you been gripped by fear to an extent that you are calling for support? Who will support you? Whoever decides to support you, Allah is above their support. Idriss Déby! The kings of Africa, you are late. You should descend on me now, I am ready. Look at the Nigerian flag. I will burn the flag, just like the way my brother burned it. Then, I will place the flag of "There is no god but Allah" instead of your cursed flag.

My final speech is about the report that was broadcasted in French on Radio France. At the time they blasphemed Allah's Messenger, they called the attention of the world to the fact that they are fighting Islam and the Muslims. They said when you hear mention of terrorists, "we are referring to Islam and Muslims." They broadcast in French on the radio. Look at it here written [*Shekau reads the broadcast message in French*]. They said when you hear mention of terrorists, "we are referring to Islam and Muslims." I read it in French and explained it in Hausa. Let me burn your flag and end my speech. This is the speech Allah has decreed for me to deliver to you. Look at the weapons we acquired from the raid on Baga and Doron Baga. These weapons are different from the ones in our possession before the raids. The weapons we acquired from Baga and Doron Baga are sufficient to wage war against Nigeria in its entirety, let alone Cameroon.

[*Shekau burns the Nigerian flag and replaces it with the black flag. This is followed by the burning of the Nigerian flag by another speaker while showing off the weapons that Boko Haram acquired from the raid on Baga.*]

53

INTERVIEW WITH OFFICIAL SPOKESMAN ABU MUS'AB AL-BARNAWI

ABOUT THE EVENTS IN THE CITY OF BAGA

(27 JANUARY 2015)

[Trans.: Abdulbasit Kassim]

Available at: http://jihadology.net/2015/01/27/al-urwah-al-wuthqa-foundation-presents-a-new-video-message-from-from-boko-%e1%b8%a5arams-jamaat-ahl-al-sunnah-li-dawah-wa-l-jihad-interview-with-the-official-spokesma/

From 3–7 January 2015, Boko Haram attacked Baga, a town on the border with Chad, and gained control over the military base of the multinational Joint Task Force. According to Amnesty International, the attack on Baga, which claimed as many as 2,000 lives, was the deadliest attack in the history of Boko Haram. Although the Nigerian military underestimated the number of casualties, Abu Mus'ab al-Barnawi, son of Muhammad Yusuf, in this interview explained the reasons Boko Haram attacked Baga and the strategic importance of the city to the group and the Nigerian military. This video and the next video (text 54) are unique for the fact that they were issued under a new media agency, al-'Urwa al-Wuthqā, and did not mention Shekau at all, while the style and contents of the videos carry many of the messages of Ansaru, protesting Muslim civilian deaths. It is likely that the speaker in this video represented a faction of Boko Haram that comprised of former Ansaru members who reintegrated with Boko Haram around this time. The decision to pledge allegiance to the Islamic State was achieved by the unification of Boko Haram's different factions, of which one was the faction that produced this video.

[Standard Islamic opening] All praise is due to Allah alone and prayers and peace be upon the one who is not followed by another prophet. It is the pleasure of the media establishment of JASDJ to present you with this meeting with the official spokesman of the group, Abu Mus'ab al-Barnawi, may Allah keep him.

Interviewer: Peace be upon you and the mercy of Allah and His blessings.

Abu Mus'ab al-Barnawi [AMB]: Peace and prayers of Allah and His blessings be upon you too.

Interviewer: Abu Mus'ab al-Barnawi, a lot of people talk nowadays about an important event in West Africa, meaning the establishment of the Islamic state here, and the liberation of the city of Baga, but most of the people who spoke about it have not gained real information about the formation of the Islamic state. That is why we want to ask you a few questions, and would like you to answer them specifically about the issues that are most controversial these days.

(First question) What is the importance of this city for you and for the Nigerian government especially, given the fact that many people do not know the position of this city or its importance in strategic or military terms? We ask you to please clarify that matter.

AMB: [...] First, this city lies to the northeast of Nigeria, near Lake Chad and it is important in terms of commercial and military value to the Nigerian government. As for its military value to the Nigerian government, that is because there is a coalition [of forces] in it with the states of Cameroon, Chad, and Niger, together with Nigeria, against our project of establishing the *sharī'a*, and it is a coalition designed to take control of Lake Chad, which is considered as one of the most important economic resources in the region.

As for its importance to us, this is because [control of] it removes that military presence from the lands of the Islamic state, and hence establishes the *sharī'a* of Allah in the region, and attains safety and security in it for the Muslims. It is known that those military complexes, if they are in a place, they corrupt it and injustice rules over it, so we, by Allah's grace alone, have managed to conquer this city and add it to the cities of the Islamic state in Africa. "The earth is Allah's and He gives it to whomever of His servants He pleases; and for the righteous is the happy end." (Q7:128)

Interviewer: (The second question) There are those who speak via the media defaming you and what you do by saying: "Enough of what 'Boko Haram' is doing and what they are doing, shedding Muslim blood." Are you really named "Boko Haram," and have you shed Muslim blood, or what is the truth?

AMB: Much of what the media publishes concerning the *mujāhidīn* is geared towards changing facts and spreading lies, especially via the media controlled by the tyrants. It is based on defamation wars against the deeds and saying of the *mujāhidīn*. And if they are not clarified, then truth is mixed with falsehood.

So, we say we did not call ourselves "Boko Haram," and our cause is not limited to the prohibition of democracy or Western schools. We are JASDJ, so that name "Boko Haram" is an attempt to change facts. We have come to give victory to the Sunna and to establish the governance of Allah on earth.

As for the accusation of shedding Muslims' blood, that is not true, and Allah is our witness. How is it that we fight Muslims, if we fight for their cause?! When we entered the city [Baga] there were people called stick carriers *Kato de Gora* [Civilian JTF]; they collaborated with the armies of the tyrants, carried their weapons, and stood by them. We fought those who fought us, and they know they fought us. When they saw our strength, they fled the city—some by water [to Lake Chad], and some to the forests. And yet we send them this message: those who fought or did not fight us, but who come to us in repentance will be forgiven and given safety and security, because we are an *umma* whose morals refuse to initiate harm against those who do not harm us.

Interviewer: (The third question) There are those who have no access to the internet or cannot access this video announcement, so how will you tell them about it? And how can they be assured that you would not kill them if they come? And how will they not fear your revenge?

AMB: Yes, there are many ways like printing readable pamphlets and publishing them on the internet. If some of them come towards us in repentance, we will send them to their brothers to tell them to come towards us in repentance. The best proof of this is in the cities which we entered, like Mubi, Damaturu and Pulka. We did not harm one single person there because they did not fight us. We only fight those who fight us. And if you are not with us then at least do not be against us. We want to free slaves [humans] from worshipping slaves [other humans] to worshipping the Lord of all slaves, and from the injustice of [false] religions to the justice of Islam, and from the narrowness of life to the breadth of life and the hereafter.

Interviewer: (The fourth question and it is the last.) We want you to explain your strategies to us, if we would want to enter a city after Baga to establish the law of Allah in it. Will this be a new strategy towards the inhabitants of Baga, or is it for all the cities that you conquer and whom you fight?

AMB: Yes, it is for all the cities. For instance, the people of Baga, they know that they fought us and when we went to them, they fled. Many of the people of the towns have not fought us, so they do not flee once we enter. For example, the people of Mubi and Damaturu welcomed us and glorified Allah in the streets [when we came]. And we have seen several examples of that, so that is why we advise them to repent, go home safely and to stand with us to defend themselves against the crusader campaign imposed upon the people by the evil crusader, the Nigerian government, may Allah curse it.

Interviewer: And finally, we want you to give a message to the coalition forces of Nigeria, Cameroon, Chad and Niger, and those who support them among the stick carriers *Kato de Gora*?

AMB: First, we would tell them to stop their evil. Otherwise just as you invade our homes, we will invade your homes. For example, Cameroon attacked us and so we attacked them. We would also tell Niger and Chad to stop standing against us, and we will not attack you. Otherwise as you fight us we will fight you, and we will wage a war against you of which you have already tasted its bitterness. So, withdraw your troops before you regret it when there is no chance for regret.

As for those who cooperate with them and support them, we tell them: return to the path of guidance and stand with your *mujāhidīn* brothers who left their families and homes only to defend you and your religion. And finally, as for those who talk about us in the media and who claim to be *mujāhidīn* and represent us: stop your tongues, and do not talk about something about which you do not know. If they want to talk, then listen to us and not about us. Allah says: "O believers, if a sinner brings you a piece of news, make sure you do not cause some people distress unwittingly." (Q49:6) Therefore, they should verify, before judging and regretting. So, verify before discussing us. Verify before saying that we shed Muslims' blood, and Allah knows best: "Allah has control over His affairs though most people do not know." (Q12:21)

Interviewer: Thank you. And that was brother Abu Mus'ab al-Barnawi, the official spokesman of JASDJ.

54

MESSAGE FROM A *MUJĀHID*

(28 JANUARY 2015)

[Trans.: Abdulbasit Kassim]
Available at: http://jihadology.net/2015/01/28/al-urwah-al-wuthqa-
foundation-presents-a-new-video-message-from-boko-%e1%b8%
a5aram-jamaat-ahl-al-sunnah-li-dawah-wa-l-jihad-message-from-a-
mujahid-1/

*In this video, the speaker reiterated the ideology of Boko Haram and also attempted to
make clear the targets and enemies of the group while simultaneously refuting the allegation that the group kills innocent civilians. On 25 January 2015, Boko Haram launched
a full-scale attack upon Maiduguri, the capital of Borno State and the base from which
they had been driven in July 2009. Although a total-warfare mode in Maiduguri
repelled this assault, Boko Haram did capture nearby Monguno and carried out more
attacks in Adamawa State during the following days.*

We just want to observe our rules and regulations from Islam. We do not want to
judge based on the constitution and democracy. The Prophet Muhammad instructed
us to adhere to Islam as it was laid down in the Qur'ān. Now, we cannot change our
religion, except when a person engages us in confrontation and kills all of us before
the constitution can be freely practiced. However, by Allah's power, killing us all is
not possible. This Islam will remain forever, by Allah's grace.

So, our purpose here is for the sake of Islam. We are not fighting because of territory, wealth, tribalism, or democracy. The reason we are all here is to practice the

sharī'a of Islam. We want to follow the Qur'ān and *hadīth*. What is the *hadīth*? It is what the Prophet encouraged us to do. So, let the whole world understand that we are not here to kill innocent people. We are not here to kill people who do not wrong us. The people we are fighting are those who contend with us that we cannot practice our Islam, except when we follow their form of religion [democracy].

It is for this reason we all came out with our weapons to fight. Whoever comes to us and contends with us that we cannot practice our own Islam, we will surely fight with that person. It is for this reason we are here. Nobody should blame us because we must practice our Islam. We are not going to fight anybody in any way, except a person who comes to us and encourages us to follow his own religion. So, we cannot follow any other religion, by Allah's power. We do not depend upon our weapons. We depend only on Almighty Allah who created us and created heaven and earth as well. He is our source of power.

We are not fighting because we possessed weapons. We depend only on Almighty Allah; He is the source of our power. Almighty Allah will guide us because we came out with our weapons to defend the religion [of Islam]. So, they should allow us to practice our religion. Whoever opposes us in the practice of our religion; from the broadcasting services, radio, or whatever, anyone who attempts to disrupt our practice of our religion, we will surely disrupt such a person. We will kill you wherever we see you. So, we encourage everyone to repent.

We call on all Muslims to come to us, and let us all organize ourselves and practice Islam so that no one will be killed. We will help individuals. We will train our children according to the way the Prophet Muhammad encouraged us. That is the main reason we are here. We are not here to collect money from the people. We are here to guard and protect Islam. Whoever comes here to fight us, we will surely fight that person. So, let the whole world understand this information. We are not fighting for anything apart from the *sharī'a* of Islam. Whatever the *sharī'a* prescribes for us to do is exactly what we will do. We will not do anything contrary to it.

55

ALLAH IS OUR MASTER

BY JAMĀʾAT ANṢĀR AL-MUSLIMIN FI BILĀD AL-SŪDĀN

(29 JANUARY 2015)

[Trans.: Abdulbasit Kassim]
Available at: http://jihadology.net/2015/01/29/al-hidayyah-foundation-presents-a-new-video-message-from-jamaat-an%e1%b9%a3ar-al-musliminfi-bilad-al-sudan-god-is-our-master/

Even after the declaration of the Islamic caliphate by Boko Haram, the charge against the group's attacks on innocent civilians impeded some members of Ansaru from aligning themselves completely with the group. In this video, Ansaru members explicitly demonstrated their opposition to Boko Haram's attacks on mosques, markets, motor parks and other public places, while simultaneously advocating for jihād *to help weak Muslims and to establish* sharīʿa *in Nigeria.*

And thereafter:

As you can see, we are JAMBS, a group waging *jihād* in this part of Black Africa called Nigeria. Our aim is to return the law of Allah on the land. Our aim is different from that of JASDJ (popularly referred to as Boko Haram) that attacks mosques, markets, motor parks and other public places. We do not kill any Muslim, nor do we attack the Muslims in the places of their day-to-day affairs.

375

We only wage *jihād* to help the weak Muslims who are being oppressed, just as Allah has brought us forth in this land. And it is known that we have carried out several operations, as you can see the result of one of our operations. Allah has gifted us with these items from a checkpoint where the masses are being oppressed. Their monies are collected for no just reason on the road between Bauchi and Jos.[1]

We are not killing innocent civilians. Our mission is to return the law of Allah on the earth and to reform the empire of 'Uthmān Dan Fodio, which was conquered by the colonialists. For this reason, *jihād* will not cease until the day of judgment. We will not stop until we return the law of Allah in the land and everywhere on the face of the earth by Allah's will.

This is our call and this is what we call upon the Muslims to know: *Jihād* is obligatory and every single [Muslim] person must give their own contribution with whatever Allah has blessed them. We also make it clear to the people that we do not kill any soul without a right. We do not oppress anyone. Our hope is that Allah will use us to remove from the Muslims this humiliation that has overwhelmed them, as we can see in other parts of the world such as France where they insulted the Prophet of Allah.[2] Allah said: "The Prophet is closer to the believers than their own selves." (Q33:6)

We will not sit back, fold our arms and watch while the Prophet's honor is being insulted. If we are alive, no human being, either a president or whatever status of unbelief he has attained, nothing will protect him from us. If we are still breathing we shall obliterate him by Allah's will. This is our aim. In conclusion, our call to the Muslims is to know that *jihād* is an obligation that Allah has placed on us so each one should give his own part as much as Allah blessed them. And as for those who cannot fight, then they should be firm in their acts of worship.

The reason why many people feel they cannot stand and fight is no other reason but their weakness in their faith. If *jihād* should be a thing that was impossible for the Muslims to execute, Allah would not have made it an obligation on them in the Qur'ān. Know our beloved brothers in Islam; come forth to *jihād* to raise Allah's religion on the way of the Prophet. This is our noble aim and our call. To the rest of the Muslims wherever they are, we beseech their prayers. We beg Allah to assist us in bringing an end to unbelief and oppression in this land and the whole world in general.

56

A MESSAGE TO THE AFRICAN LEADERS, SPECIFICALLY, IDRISS DÉBY

BY ABUBAKAR SHEKAU

(9 FEBRUARY 2015)

[Trans.: Abdulbasit Kassim]

Available at: http://jihadology.net/2015/02/09/new-video-messagefrom-jamaat-ahl-al-sunnah-li-l-dawah-wa-l-jihad-boko-%e1%b8%a5aram-abu-bakr-shekau-a-message-to-african-leadersespecially-idris-david/

Of all the opponents that the activities of Boko Haram had brought upon themselves by the beginning of 2015, the doughtiest were the Chadians. Boko Haram had initiated several operations threatening Chad, including the 28–29 December 2014 full-scale attack on Cameroon, close to the Chadian capital of N'Djamena. Thus, it was not a surprise when President Idriss Déby began to initiate military operations against Boko Haram first in Cameroon on 9 January 2015, and then into northeastern Nigeria on 16 January 2015. Obviously, these operations angered Boko Haram.

"Those to whom the people said: 'The people have been arrayed against you, so fear them.' But this increased their faith and so they said: 'Allah is sufficient for us. He is the best Guardian!'" (Q3:173)

All praise is due to Allah who decreed *jihād* as an act of worship. Allah is the one who decreed *jihād* as one of the most exalted acts of worship for His servants. He has bestowed glad tidings of two best outcomes upon His servants: either His servants attain victory or martyrdom (cf. Q9:52). And all praise is due to Allah, who implanted grief in the hearts of the tyrants and the leaders of Africa. All praise is due to Allah, who granted us territorial expansion into Chad, Cameroon, Niger, and other places where they [African leaders] claimed that we have been killed. We are ready and prepared for you, O people of unbelief.

All praise is due to Allah who bestowed *jihād* upon us for the sole purpose of the defense of the religion of Islam and the protection of our Muslim brethren. O people of unbelief! O people of democracy! O people who follow secular constitutions! O people who enroll their children in the colonial schools where they are being taught unbelief, polytheism and all other pernicious beliefs! We are the members of JASDJ. All praise is due to Allah, who bestowed upon us the splendid spirit of perseverance against the unbelievers such as Israel and Great Britain. And all praise is due to Allah, who has enraged the hearts of their kingpins—I mean America and France—and He has placed trepidation in the hearts of their grandchildren and children.

[*Citation of Q3:151, 2:191 and 8:39.*]

And thereafter:

O tyrants! O leaders of Africa! O leaders of Amnesty International, as you call yourselves!

You, Idriss Déby! You specifically, Idriss Déby! You lied in all the claims you stated in Chad. You did what you did, and you will see what you will see by Allah's permission, the Almighty. O Idriss Déby! Do you think that this battle is akin to the battle you fought in your country?[1] This battle is totally different from what you think. This battle is a battle for the defense of the Qur'ān and the authentic *hadīths*. This battle is a battle for the defense of the Muslims and all those who profess Islam so that they can acquire true knowledge about Allah and His prophets that is devoid of your own knowledge. Why do you think that you are a Muslim, after you have decided to impose ruling and judging by secular laws in your country and you relinquished ruling by the laws of the Qur'ān? You accepted the laws of [Barack] Obama and Ban Ki Moon, yet you are still deceiving yourself that you are a Muslim.

How can you call yourself a Muslim when you have become an infidel even though you pray, fast, give charity (*zakāt*), or travel for hajj [pilgrimage]? You are an infidel. Why? And a proof of this is because you have abandoned Islamic monotheism. There is no god but Allah alone. We pray to Allah to place us among those who fight in His path and do not worry about anybody's reproach. We don't fear anybody apart from Allah. We say that you are an infidel, and we will fight and kill you. We will not stop fighting you unless we witness the period when the Muslims adopt the Qur'ān for ruling and judging based on Allah's laws. This is our judgment and our intention. By Allah's permission, you should all watch out.

MESSAGE TO IDRISS DÉBY

O Idriss Déby! I am sending this message to you. I am the leader of JASDJ in the land of Africa called Nigeria. I am Abu Muhammad Abubakar bin Muhammad al-Shekawi. O Idriss Déby! Repent to your Lord and refrain from the actions you have chosen to embark upon. If you fail to refrain from your actions, then you are an unbeliever. If you fail to refrain from your actions, you will dwell forever in the bottomless pit of hell-fire. It is only Allah who will judge between us.

Surely, you will soon discern the liar between us. There is no god but Allah alone. Allah says in the Qur'ān: "O believers, do not take the Jews and the Christians as friends; some of them are friends of each other." (Q5:51) But you have taken the Jews and Christians as your brothers. My Lord is the Most Glorified, the Almighty. He is the One who has power over all affairs. You fabricate lies and you feed on lies. When did you come into Gambaru? When did you come into Malam Fatori? How are you going to kill us? There is no god but Allah alone.

O Idriss Déby! If you fail to refrain from your evil actions, you will be inflicted the same way you inflict. There is no doubt in what I stated. Wait! And I will also wait by Allah's permission, the Almighty. Allah says in the Qur'ān: "Our Word unto Our messengers has already gone out. They will surely be supported. And Our hosts are the true victors." (Q37:171–73) He also said: "Allah has decreed: 'I shall certainly vanquish, I and My Messenger.' Surely Allah is Strong, All-Mighty." (Q58:21)

He also said: "We shall support Our Messengers and the believers in the present life and on the day the witnesses shall arise." (Q40:51) There are many other verses which have been set forth as examples in this speech.

O people of Cameroon! O people of Chad! Repent to your Lord. You should know that a person does not become a Muslim except by disassociation from democracy and all other polytheistic acts. It is obligatory upon you to disbelieve and disassociate yourself from democracy. It is also obligatory upon you to declare disassociation from democracy's servants and helpers. And the evidence for this is what Allah said in the Qur'ān about the Prophet Abraham when he said to his people: "We are quit of you and what you worship apart from Allah. Enmity and hatred have arisen between you and us forever, till you believe in Allah alone..." (Q60:4)

There is no god but Allah alone. Let me deliver to you a very short speech. You dispatched 7,000 of your soldiers. Why not dispatch seven billion soldiers? 7,000 soldiers are small numbers. We can bring them down in succession. Why did you say you dispatched 7,000 of your soldiers? Unbelievers!

Verily, Allah's soldiers are the victorious ones. There is no truce between us until death. We will kill you and we will fight you. There is no god but Allah alone. Indeed, you are small. You dispatched 7,000 of your soldiers from different countries like Cameroon and Chad. Why not dispatch seven million or a billion or even a trillion soldiers? Allah is the One who bestowed victory upon us. Allah says: "There is no victory except from Allah." (Q3:126) He also says: "And when you called upon your

Lord for help, He answered you: 'I will reinforce you with a thousand angels following one another." (Q8:9) There is no god but Allah alone.

This is my message to you in Arabic:

To the slaves of man-made laws and secular constitutions! To the followers of the religion of democracy! To those who associate partners with Allah with man-made legislation!

We have disassociated from you and your path. We disbelieve in you, your polytheistic constitutions and your nationalistic parliaments. And there has emerged between us and you, hostility and hatred forever until you believe in Allah alone (Q60:4). We pray to Allah, the Noble and the Lord of the Majestic throne, to bestow upon us His bountiful guidance and steadfastness. We pray that He guides our souls from going astray and directs our hearts to what is right because He is the best purifier. There is no god but Allah alone. He is our guardian and protector. And He is the listener and the answerer. This is the statement that Allah has predestined that I will deliver to you in Arabic. Now, I am going to return to speak in our native Hausa language.

O people! O leaders of Africa! You should all rise to fight because you are so small. Your military campaign together with your soldiers is so small. The 7,500 soldiers you dispatched to fight against us is so small? We have risen to fight for Allah's religion, the Creator of heaven and earth, for the earth to be governed by His Qur'ān and not the constitutions with which you have chosen to govern the earth. Did you not understand the secret of my language to you?

You thought that this war you are fighting against us—even after we disclaimed the name Boko Haram and prefer to be called JASDJ—you thought that this war is akin to your war against the Biafrans. Idriss Déby! Do you think this war is akin to the Kanembu war you fought? You have lied, just wait and see. We do not benefit in our decision to fight you. We are only following the commands of Allah who instructed us to fight you and you have responded that you are not fighting against Allah but fighting against us.

One of you even went as far as saying that we are not Muslims. Liars! This is a big surprise. Is the democracy you are practicing part of Islam? Is the secular constitution you have adopted as a source of legislation part of Islam? You should take some time, sit on the chair and table in your living room, and think properly if the constitution your president has adopted as a source of legislation in Chad is part of Islam?

If the Prophet Muhammad were living in the world now would he practice it [Islam]? Secretary of Chad and Cameroon, go and conduct your research, likewise the ambassadors, and any other person interested in this issue. In fact, Africa is a small place. We did not initially commence our campaign with a focus only on Africa but the world in its entirety, and against those who do not believe in Allah and His messengers. It is either you become the servants of Allah or we kill you. This is exactly the instruction from the Qur'ān.

Indeed, you are a liar. There was never a period you came into Gamboru Ngala. You and your lackeys know this truth. But then even if you came into Gamboru Ngala, what is the big deal? This is the religion where the prophets were slayed. Are they not Allah's prophets? Did you mean that by their deaths they did not earn their victory? It is Allah's pleasure which is significant to us in this religion.

This is the religion where pious and great scholars were incarcerated because of their faith. Even [caliph] 'Umar was killed while he was performing his prayer. We are not speaking to you about murder, killing in the land, or fleeing from an area, but what we are speaking about is for you to recognize the fact that the heaven and earth belong to Allah alone. All the living beings playing on earth belong to Allah alone. The food that you all eat on earth belongs to Allah alone. Everything belongs to Allah alone and you do not have that authorization to adopt a different law to rule over a land apart from Allah's laws alone.

Allah has foreknowledge of your oppression; that is the main reason why He raised people all over the world who will fight to restore the supremacy of His laws on earth. Look at the People of the Cave and the People of the Pit (*ukhdūd*).[2] Allah spoke about them when He said: "They did not begrudge them except that they believed in Allah, the All-Mighty, the All-Praiseworthy." (Q85:8)

It is on this basis that I advise you once again that the 7,500 soldiers you have dispatched against us is a small number. You should listen to the advice of Shekau and add more than seven billion soldiers, because our own soldiers are more than the 7,000 soldiers you dispatched to fight against us. The number of your soldiers does not frighten us. The nature of warfare today is not all about jeeps, airplanes but it is about blood. It is either we attain victory or martyrdom. "Say: 'Do you expect for us anything other than one of the two best outcomes [martyrdom or victory]; while we wait for you that Allah will smite you with a punishment from Him, or at our hands. So, wait and watch, we are waiting and watching with you." (Q 9:52)

This is the Qur'ān that guides us in our campaign. So, stop spreading all your lies! Here I am the one who infuriates the unbelievers, the Jews, the Christians, the secularists, and others in Europe, Asia, and Africa, as well as the followers of democracy. Allah has kept me protected. This is my short speech to you. We are holding firm to our beliefs and creed. We are fighting *jihād* and we have established the Islamic caliphate.

O people of the Niger Delta! You should stop spreading your false lies. You and [Muhammadu] Buhari are both liars. All Christians are our enemies. We will kill you and all followers of democracy, except those who practice pure Islam. O people of the Niger Delta! You have lied. We do not have business with [Goodluck] Jonathan, Buhari and democracy except Islam. I pledge to Allah, my Allah, to be faithful, loyal and honest, to serve Allah with all my strength, to defend His unity and uphold His honor and glory. So, help me Allah. This is my religion.

57

APPLICATION OF THE RULINGS OF ISLAM IN THE ISLAMIC STATE IN AFRICA

BY JAMĀ'AT AHL AL-SUNNA LI-L-DA'WA WA-L-JIHĀD

(9 FEBRUARY 2015)

[Trans.: Abdulbasit Kassim]
Available at: https://www.youtube.com/watch?v=dZI2KlHvg9A

In this video, Boko Haram demonstrated the enforcement of its brand of sharī'a, *which ranges from whipping alcohol drinkers, to cutting off the hands thieves, to stoning adulterers to death. The content of this video is akin to another video entitled "Haddi a Cikin Daular Musulunci" ("Implementing Islamic Punishments in the Muslim State"), released on 13 December 2014.[1] In both videos, Boko Haram portrayed the realization of its vision, which was the unconditional implementation of their brand of* sharī'a *within their captured territories. These videos constitute documentaries of life under Boko Haram's caliphate.*

"Those who, if we establish them firmly in the land, will perform the prayer, give the alms, command the good and prohibit evil. To Allah belongs the outcome of all affairs." (Q22:41)

The enemies of Islam—the Jews, Christians, polytheists and their hypocrite minions—invaded the Sudanese state of 'Uthman Dan Fodio until they occupied the Muslims' lands, defiled Islam's sacred places, and exchanged Islam's law for the Crusaders' constitution and the rule of ignorance. This extended from their trashy ideas, but they were not satisfied, so conscripted soldiers to protect themselves. This situation spurred revolutionary hearts from the people of faith to strive to return Allah's law to Allah's land, so they established small states in many locations, which expanded at times and grew at times. Finally, Allah made it easy for our fighting brothers in the Islamic State to establish the caliphate's kernel in the Levant [*scene of Abu Bakr al-Baghdadi's sermon at the great mosque, Mosul*]. And in the same way, Allah made it easy for the fighters in the Sudan to establish courts that rule by Allah's law.

[*Scenes of the execution of Islamic punishments on alcohol drinkers.*]

"Anas reported that Allah's Apostle used to strike forty times with shoes and palm branches [in the case of drinking of] wine."

[*Scenes of the execution of Islamic punishments on fornicators.*]

"The adulteress and the adulterer, whip each one of them a hundred lashes." (Q24:2)

[*Scenes of the execution of Islamic punishments on thieves.*]

"As for the thieves, whether male or female, cut off their hands in punishment for what they did, as an exemplary punishment from Allah." (Q5:38)

[*Scenes of the execution of Islamic punishments on adulterers.*]

"Burayda reported concerning the stoning of Ma'iz,[2] 'A ditch was dug for him, whereupon the Prophet pronounced judgment concerning him and he was stoned.'"

[*Scenes of Boko Haram fighters doing "wheelies" in a tank and driving on a long convoy with Islamic State flag held high.*]

[*Excerpts from Yusuf's sermon "Come to Jihād".*][3]

58

INVESTIGATION OF THE NIGERIAN ARMY

BY JAMĀ'AT ANṢĀR AL-MUSLIMIN FI BILĀD AL-SŪDĀN

(10 FEBRUARY 2015)

[Trans.: Abdulbasit Kassim]
Available at: http://jihadology.net/2015/02/10/al-hidayyah-foundation-presents-a-new-video-message-from-jamaat-an%e1%b9%a3ar-al-muslimin-fi-bilad-al-sudan-investigation-of-the-nigerian-army/

This video by Ansaru is aimed at winning the hearts and minds of the Muslim community, and managing the increasing resentment against Boko Haram's indiscriminate violence. In this video, the group highlighted some of the abuses and human rights violations perpetrated by the Nigerian army, some of which had been documented by Amnesty International.[1] *Although both Ansaru and Boko Haram are steeped in the same jihadi ideology, unlike Boko Haram, Ansaru engaged in sustained efforts to win the sympathy and support of the Muslim population of Nigeria.*

Nigeria is the most economically endowed country, the most populous in West Africa, and it is being governed by a disbelieving system of democracy. Nigeria is a country plagued with different crises, mostly religious. Its leaders are oppressors who have no concern or regard for Muslims. The support of the Nigerian government for the minority Christians over the majority Muslims is glaring.

385

The ears of anyone who is acquainted with the news outlet is aware of this long-standing mass killing which the minority Christians have been perpetuating on innocent Muslims in various places, including the abduction of women and children in Yelwa Shendam, Plateau State, Nigeria. Allah says: "How [can that be]? If they overcome you, they will observe neither kinships nor pacts with you. They only give you satisfaction with their mouths, while their hearts refuse, and most of them are sinners." (Q9:8)

Eyes have not stopped shedding tears over the event [of people] eating Muslims' flesh during their end of Ramadan festival prayer in Jos in the presence of security agents who claim to protect the life and property of the citizens.[2] This is not different from what happened in Zonkwa and Gonin Gora in Kaduna State where Muslims were killed and even burned alive.[3] The ammunition and bombs of the Nigerian army have for long been responsible for the loss of many Muslim lives.

This has been the case and it is still happening in different places in this country, such as the killing of Muslim women and children in Bauchi, Maiduguri and Kano on 26–29 July 2009 under the command of Umaru Musa Yar'adua.[4] This is a proof of the atrocities of the Nigerian army. This kind of atrocity has not stopped, rather they have continued, especially in places which were affected by the Boko Haram crisis: "Nor will they cease to fight you until, if they can, they make you renounce your religion." (Q2:217)

As this video shows, the Nigerian army was slaughtering Muslims in Maiduguri. A leopard will not change its spots. This kind of terrorist act and disregard for human rights was repeated in Mundu village in Bauchi State under the guise of attacking the *mujāhidīn* of JAMBS, who had been living there for a long period of time in peace and harmony with the residents. Not once did they oppress them, but rather they stood as protectors for them against a gang of armed robbers who had made that place a haven.[5] The residents repeatedly reported this menace to the security forces but no action was taken.

The Nigerian army, under the unbelieving oppressor Goodluck Jonathan, descended on the people of Mundu during the morning of Saturday 6 to Sunday 7 December 2014, killing many people, and destroying houses and property. In a bid to appease their anger, after suffering a humiliating defeat in the hands of Allah's warriors, let us hear from the horse's mouth the victims of the atrocities committed by the oppressive Nigerian army.

Speaker 1: I saw the imam's house being burned with some copies of the Qur'ān, as well as my house.

Interviewer: Did you take anything out?

Speaker 1: No, we did not. We did not take anything out from the house. They completely burned my property.

This is a village market demolished by the Nigerian army. Who are the terrorists? The Nigerian army are the terrorists. We must fight them and prevent this type of killing.

386

Interviewer: Do they attempt to slaughter somebody?

Speaker 2: It was me they attempted to slaughter. They put a knife to my throat and said to me: "We will slaughter you now," so I said to them: "If I die today, one day you too will die."

Upon this we are calling on the Muslims to know that no one from amongst the security agencies or the politicians can give them a solution. The only way out is by following Allah's laws and performing *jihād* which Allah has obligated upon us: "You are enjoined to fight, though it is something that you dislike. For it may well be that you dislike a thing, although it is good for you; or like something although it is bad for you. Allah knows and you do not." (Q2:216)

Allah has raised for you those for whom your concern is their concern [Ansaru], those whose action is preaching to enlighten the Muslims and waging *jihād* in Allah's path to protect the lives and property of the Muslims—away from the actions of JASDJ (popularly known as Boko Haram) which conducted attacks on the Muslims and detonates bombs in their worship places, markets and motor parks, against the teachings of Islam. It is known that *jihād* was obligated to help the weak, as Allah stated in his blessed book:

"And why don't you fight for Allah's cause and for the downtrodden from among men, women and children, who say: 'Lord, bring us out of this city whose inhabitants are unjust and grant us, from You, a protection, and grant us, from You, a supporter." (Q4:75).

59

PROCLAMATION CONCERNING
THE AGGRESSION BEING LED
BY CHAD AGAINST JAMĀ'AT AHL AL-SUNNA
LI-L-DA'WA WA-L-JIHĀD

(14 FEBRUARY 2015)

[Trans.: David Cook]

Available at: https://azelin.files.wordpress.com/2015/02/jamc481_at-ahl-al-sunnah-li-l-da_wah-wa-l-jihc481d-boko-e1b8a5arc481m-22regarding-the-coalition-led-by-chad-against-jamc481_at-ahl-al-sunnah-li-l-da_wah-wa-l-jihc481d22.pdf

Text 45 proves that Boko Haram was already operating in Chad by summer 2014, and September at the latest, probably much earlier. There was a combined suicide attack against a Chadian village on 15 December 2015, although there was no official Boko Haram statement taking responsibility. After Chad began openly fighting Boko Haram at the beginning of 2015, the group responded by carrying out operations across Lake Chad, into Chad itself. However, the most spectacular operations occurred months after this proclamation—on 15 June 2015 N'Djamena, the capital of Chad, was targeted by suicide attackers, presumably from Boko Haram, and at least twenty-seven people were killed. Follow-up bombings took place on 27 June as well as another suicide attack on 11 July 2015.

The Chadian government has undertaken during these days a military alliance that was called by the states in the region to fight the *mujāhidīn* in the Islamic State to remove Allah's rule from the land of Nigeria. It claims that it undertakes this to defend its interests, but the veil has been removed from [Chad] and those who ally with it regarding their dislike of the Law of Allah, and its openly fighting Allah and His Messenger despite its claim to be Islamic. This is because the entire world knows that the JASDJ never once entered battle with the Chadian forces in the land of Chad, but that the Chadian forces were the ones who entered the lands of the State.

If we were one of those countries ruled by man-made laws owing allegiance to the Atheist Nations [United Nations] the entire world would have disapproved of Chad for its blatant interference in our land which we rule. But because the rule with us entirely belongs to Allah, the human demons refuse to do anything other than gather their masses and to call for war against us. This is for nothing other than because we have raised the emblems of Islam and our law is the Law of the Lord of Worlds, which has been removed from the land of Chad and other countries by the order of the cross and the Jews since the occupation of the Muslims' lands previously.

We say, asking for aid from Allah, and depending upon Him, that Allah promised us one of the two best outcomes: either victory or martyrdom: "Those who believe fight for Allah's cause, while those who disbelieve fight on behalf of the Devil (*tāghūt*). Fight then the followers of the Devil. Surely the guile of the Devil is weak." (Q4:76)

For we knew from the very first in which we went out to establish the Law of Allah that Allah's enemies would say about us what they said about Allah's Messenger: "magician, sooth-sayer, crazy," and we say to them that we are certain of the aid of Allah, and that martyrdom is more beloved to us than life, as you have tested of us previously.

You know that our love for death exceeds your love for life, and we say, in warning to the Chadian government, that even the Chadian Muslim people know that their government is causing them to enter a darkened tunnel because of their interference in our lands. The Almighty said: "Whoever commits aggression against you, retaliate against him in the same way." (Q2:194)

We are prepared to transfer our battles from Nigeria to the Chadian lands, even if it costs us everything. The Chadian Muslim people should know we would never target them until the Chadian government betrayed them by frightening them. We targeted the Chadian army which entered our lands, and believed that Allah would never allow the lions of monotheism to dominate over them. We are familiar with the Chadian army, which serves as agents and proxies in battle, every day it is in the Muslims' lands being deputized to fight by whoever pays it a few crumbs of this world.

Allah be praised! We hope for one of the two best outcomes, whether victory or martyrdom. Victory is only from Allah. We say to the Chadian opposition, and to the prisoners in the Chadian army: We have warned those who would take heed, so there is no blame on us when you enter our lands in continuing the civil war. As long as you do not take the hand of the Chadian tyrant, but leave him dragging your lands into war with us, let the tyrant know that ranks of martyrdom-seekers [suicide attackers] are awaiting orders from us to light up the land in vengeance for every martyr, and to protect the monotheistic state.

As for the government of Niger, it knows that our strike against it is in response to its aggression against our lands, so we say to it: The government of Chad will drag you to the bog of darkness, when you were in peace and safety. We never entered your lands at any time, but the tyrant of Chad refused anything other than enticing you that we were easy food for swallowing. If you refuse anything other than continuing the aggression and alliance with the government of Chad against us, then we will announce to you that the land of Niger is easier for us than the land of Nigeria. Transferring the war to the depths of your cities will be the first response to any aggression that occurs after this proclamation.

Lastly, we know that the Nigerien Muslim people reject wrong, and love Allah's *sharī'a*. We have witnessed their fervor about Allah's Messenger during the past days, and what they have undertaken for that. So we say: If the government of Niger aggresses against our lands, we recognize that it does not exemplify the Nigerien Muslim people in any way, but we advise them to forbid their sons from fighting in the ranks of the Nigerien army, for they would be fighting with their sons in a war that is not theirs, without benefit other than fighting Allah and His Messenger.

The Nigerien government knows that if we had wanted to transfer the battle to them, we could have done it previously, but when they held back, we held back from them. But they let themselves be seduced, and the Satan of Chad made it pleasant for them what they are doing. We are people of war, and our men seek death in response to the Messenger of Allah's words. [*From the English translation it seems that there is a section missing here on the virtues of the martyr.*]

We say to our Muslim brothers in every place that we in the JASDJ have undertaken to liberate the land of Nigeria from the rule of the Christians, the laws of creatures, and to apply the Law of the Lord of the creatures in accordance with the Book of Allah and the Sunna of His Prophet. Do not let the media deceive you by the proclamation of this war between us and the enemies of the Law of Allah that this is a war over land or this world, or that that we deny people the right to live. No, the life is the life in the shade of the Law of Allah, and our judgment is the judgment of every Muslim.

60

A MESSAGE TO THE UNBELIEVERS' LEADERS

BY ABUBAKAR SHEKAU

(17 FEBRUARY 2015)

[Trans.: Abdulbasit Kassim]
Available at: http://jihadology.net/2015/02/17/al-urwah-al-wuthqa-
foundation-presents-a-new-video-message-from-jamaat-ahl-al-sunnah-
li-l-dawah-wa-l-jihads-boko-%e1%b8%a5aram-abu-bakr-shekau-a-
message-to-the-leader/

This video follows the high point of Boko Haram's territorial control, and was issued shortly after its second major assault upon the Borno capital of Maiduguri on 1 February 2015. Shekau here threatens the upcoming Nigerian presidential elections, scheduled for 14 February. In the event, they were not held on time, but postponed because of the large territory controlled by Boko Haram. Already, however, the Nigerian army was beginning to roll back Boko Haram by the time this was issued, and had recaptured the town of Monguno, close to Maiduguri. Boko Haram was also overextending itself by attacking Chad overtly for the first time on 13 February. This video is also unique for the fact that it was the first video of Shekau produced under the media agency al-'Urwa al-Wuthqā, which signaled the unification of Boko Haram's factions prior to the pledge of allegiance to the Islamic State.

[Standard Islamic opening]

And thereafter:

You should know, O you Nigerian unbelievers and hypocrites; you should know, O you leaders of Cameroon, Chad and Benin, O you leaders of Africa—you must all know that whoever believes these verses, then by Allah's grace, he will realize that he is the winner as long as he is being sincere. Allah says: "Yet the evil cunning will only recoil upon its perpetrators." (Q35:43) Allah also says: "We destroyed the houses and towers which Pharaoh and his people were building." (Q7:137) Allah also says: "Whenever they kindle a fire for war, Allah extinguishes it." (Q5:64) Allah also says: "Then, Allah seized them from an unexpected quarter and cast terror into their hearts, so that they destroyed their homes with their own hands, as well as the hands of the believers. Reflect, then, O people of perception!" (Q59:2) There is no god but Allah. Allah is higher, more exalted. Allah is great and He has power over all things.

O you, prime minister of Niger, your senators, and whosoever is with you. O you, President of Chad, Idriss Déby and whosoever is with you. All of you have created a constitution that is organized with numbers and pages, and you established it as a rule of your government. You also made the people follow it; you made them follow it by force, by terrifying them with your prisons in which you jailed whoever opposes you. You know that all that your rulers do, the Holy Prophet Muhammad and his Companions would never dare to do the same if they were living in our time. Now you have imposed this rule on people. Even some of your traditional rulers and religious scholars did not remember or think about how Shaykh 'Uthman Dan Fodio ruled this land by following the Qur'ān. They would not even dare to say his constitutions and rules that you have today.

Yet, you are following and listening to François Hollande and you are imposing the rule of French people. And after all that, who gave you the authority to label some people as disbelievers? Who gave you the authority to say that the members of JASDJ are not Muslims? You are falsifying Allah's words.

Nobody can declare another person an unbeliever unless there is clear evidence that he is an unbeliever. We judge by the Qur'ān alone, and by following it we say what we say and do. The evidence of this is what Allah said in His Qur'ān: "O believers, do not take the Jews and the Christians as friends." (Q5:51) This is the word of Allah.

He also says: "Whoever does not judge according to what Allah has revealed—those are the unbelievers." (Q5:44) In other verses Allah referred to them as evildoers and transgressors. There is also a verse in the Qur'ān that says to the Prophet: "If you associate any others with Allah, He will frustrate your work and you will certainly be one of the losers." (Q39:65) Allah also says to all the prophets after He remembers and compliments them: "Had they associated [other gods with Allah], all that they did would have been nullified." (Q6:88) All these verses show that the wrong one will not win against the one on the right path.

And if you think that you are on the right path, sit and think about it, if all these rules that you are now using have been used by the Prophet before? Think about it,

A MESSAGE TO THE UNBELIEVERS' LEADERS

[and about] this democracy that came from America, France, Italy, Germany, Russia and the United Nations, which I prefer to call the United Nations of Atheists, because there is no one that can unite the hearts and make them as one, except Allah. Do you think in this way you will be saved in the scorching grave? O rulers of Africa! And you claim that you are Muslim!

O you Mahamadou Issoufou, the president of Niger! O you Idriss Déby, the president of Chad! Don't you see how [Goodluck] Jonathan has failed in his fight against us? Do you think that you came to fight the members of JASDJ? Take off the masks from your face, and then you will know that you are indeed fighting against Allah. The one who failed in his fight against us had initially thought that he is fighting us, but things became hard for him. It will be hard for you too, because we fight only with the guidance of Allah. We are not proud of our forces and our numbers. In fact, what number or forces do we even have to be proud of?

The intent of this message is to inform you that we are the ones who fought against you in Gombe. And only Allah knows what we found there, you don't need to know it. You are claiming that we do not know how to fight, but we forced your forces to flee from their bases and we freed our imprisoned brothers from the prisons where you oppressed them.

Praise be to Allah. These words are our reply to the current issues that have attracted a great deal of appeal from the people. We say that these elections that you are planning to do will not take place in peace, even if it will cost us our lives. Allah will not leave you to proceed with these elections even after us because you are saying that authority is from the people, to the people and for the people. Whereas Allah says that authority belongs only to Him, from Him and for Him.

So, we clearly see the unbelief of those who believe in democracy. We have no doubt in their unbelief. In fact, whoever doubts their unbelief is also an unbeliever. That is our religion. This message is not a message of declaring war on you, but a call for you to listen and obey Allah. Don't gather in the mosques to recite the Qur'ān while at the same time you are part of those who oppose His commands. And because of that, we are calling you, whoever comes and repents to Allah, and supports His religion, His book, and the Sunna of His Prophet; we will consider him as being part of us.

And whoever supports François Hollande and [Barack] Obama, as they previously supported [George] Bush and [Bill] Clinton and supported the Jewish State of Israel, and supports the unbelieving nations, he is an enemy to us and a target of our forces. We will enslave him and sell him in the markets. This is a message from Abu Muhammad Abubakar b. Muhammad al-Shekawi, the imam of JASDJ. We ask Allah to grant us steadfastness and to make us among those who fight for His religion and who do not fear anybody's reproach. And we ask Allah to bless us with good intentions. And may the peace and blessings of Allah be upon the Holy Prophet Muhammad. All praise be to Allah, the Lord of the world.

PART FIVE

WEST AFRICAN ISLAMIC STATE (2015–16)

Michael Nwankpa

With Goodluck Jonathan's replacement in May 2015 by the former military head of state Muhammadu Buhari (ruled 1983–85), who is a Muslim northerner, it was possible to hope that some of the lethargy in fighting Boko Haram would disappear. Indeed, Buhari made bold promises to this effect, both during his presidential campaign and afterwards.[1] However, as yet those promises have not borne fruit. Regardless of whether its self-proclaimed caliphate survives, Boko Haram has opened a new chapter in Nigeria's history. The group has not only challenged the contrived boundaries of Nigeria, but it has successfully enacted its brand of *sharī‘a* governance unconstrained by the constitutional laws of Nigeria over the territory it captured in northeastern Nigeria in 2014–15.

Boko Haram's intent has always been to destroy the people's livelihood and to impose a *sharī‘a* state. This is not the action of a group that seeks to win hearts and minds. But there is no evidence of ethnic or religious cleansing, as Boko Haram does not discriminate between Kanuris, Fulanis, Hausas and other Muslim ethnic groups. Nor does it distinguish between Muslims and Christians, or between the different Muslim groups. Shi‘ites in Nigeria have been specifically targeted by suicide bombers twice in recent years. The first attack was in Yobe State on 3 November 2014, leading to the deaths of fifteen people. The second attack happened a year later on 27 November 2015 in Kano, when a male suicide bomber rammed into a Shi‘ite procession, killing twenty-one people. Boko Haram has only claimed responsibility for the second attack.

However, the current Boko Haram leadership has not been able to articulate its objectives convincingly. Undeniably, the goal of establishing an Islamic society may

397

have guided the actions of the group under its founder, Yusuf. The political objectives of the group have become even more unclear with several factions having different motivations. External alliances and support from groups such as ISIS suggest that Boko Haram may be fighting Islamic proxy wars. This fact rings true if one considers how the group has turned against the local populace. The suicide bombing campaign since mid-2015 has targeted public spaces such as bus stops, markets, and particularly mosques. Frequent attacks on mosques parallel the regular attacks on Christians and churches in 2010–12 (less frequently targeted since that period). This fact supports the argument that the initial attacks on churches were a strategic diversion from what had always been an internal Muslim sectarian struggle for power dominance.

Perhaps it is time to adopt a cost-benefit counter-terrorism strategy, in addition to law enforcement and intelligence approaches. This will involve raising the opportunity or economic costs. For instance, adopting a defensive strategy that protects targets from easy attack from terrorists may increase the cost for the terrorists, and, consequently, deter them from attacking.

The Nigerian government and its external supporters may fortify security facilities (making it difficult for Boko Haram to attack and cart away weapons and ammunitions), and degrade Boko Haram's financial capabilities by blocking illegal arms trade routes (as well as freezing the assets of Boko Haram's supporters). It is however doubtful that the Nigerian government (with the military currently embroiled in multiple corruption scandals) will be able to achieve this goal alone, especially since it has not stopped the Niger Delta militants from selling their stolen weapons on the black market. However, the multilateral approach may offer some legitimacy to the Nigerian military, but the mandate of this force should go beyond an overt military solution.

There is a clear trajectory in Boko Haram's transition from Nigerian preachers to the West African Islamic State. While Boko Haram's ideology and pursuit of an Islamic state is somewhat constant, what is arguable is whether it would still have taken the path of violence if the Nigerian government with its military had not provoked it. There is abundant evidence to suggest that Boko Haram was planning for *jihād*, but this does not necessarily mean that it would have rejected other means of achieving its objective—which was to establish an Islamic state. It is noteworthy that Boko Haram has failed as yet to achieve its goal.

Although it once controlled some vast territory in northeast Nigeria, it has lost that territorial control to the combined military efforts of the regional MNJTF, made up of armies of Nigeria, Niger, Cameroon and Chad. Of greater significance was its ill-preparedness to administer the area it once controlled. Arguably, Boko Haram's attempt to seize control of the northeastern areas and its fleeting control over this territory may be read as a premature move forced upon it by the heavy-handedness of the Nigerian military, as much as that, perhaps, it never had the intention of establishing an Islamic state on that scale.

Whatever Boko Haram's intention was, and whether it would or would not have taken to violence, is irrelevant at this stage of the conflict. It is only useful to note that we are dealing with a deadly terrorist group with the sole objective of establishing an Islamic state. A more pertinent question to ask is: an Islamic state for what, and for whom? This question is loaded, as it encompasses the question of conflict between Boko Haram's local and global agenda, and its underlying quest for religious and political dominance over the Nigerian secular state and the traditional Muslim authority in Nigeria. Boko Haram is fractured into two broad camps: the Shekau-controlled camp and al-Barnawi's camp (text 70). Both camps represent the conflicting interests between a local and global Islamic agenda respectively.

There is a sense that Boko Haram, in my opinion, while sympathetic to the global plight of Muslims and the contest between a predominant Western (crusader) hegemony and a lost Muslim hegemony, is driven more by local (or more realistic) causes. It however needs the support (ideological, strategic and tactical) of global Islamic transnational groups such as al-Qaeda and ISIS to be able to face the Nigerian military. In the interview (text 52) Boko Haram tries, as in many other texts, to plug into this global campaign to pursue its own agenda. However, the extent to which it can perform its broader agenda as a franchise or affiliate of ISIS is yet uncertain. Despite such uncertainty, we cannot underestimate its capacity and willingness to carry out attacks targeting the West.

Yet, Boko Haram has not succeeded in appealing to Western foreign fighters in the same way that ISIS and other al-Qaeda groups such as AQIM and al-Shabab have. The most probable way to interpret this is that Boko Haram, despite its deadliness and transnational Muslim sympathies, is concerned with issues that are largely local. Boko Haram is therefore, first and foremost, a contest between different Islamic sects and groups in northern Nigeria. It is a challenge to the authority of the Sokoto Caliphate and an attempt to establish an alternative supremacist Islamic structure with political and religious control. This agenda will have little appeal for the global *jihād* community, hence Boko Haram's stretch towards transnational groups such as al-Qaeda and ISIS. But since Shekau swore allegiance to ISIS, we have yet to see a gruesome outcome of the alliance. What we have seen instead is the factionalization of the group and infighting between Shekau and the newly ISIS-endorsed leader of Boko Haram, al-Barnawi, the son of the late founder of Boko Haram, Muhammad Yusuf (texts 70–74). The factionalization of Boko Haram can again be interpreted as a contest between a local and a global agenda. We may see some trade-offs in the future, but so far, there has been an irreconcilable effort to combine these two agendas.

Boko Haram has shown capacity to attack Western targets and interests starting from the 2011 suicide-bomb attack on the UN Office in Abuja. But the number of attacks on foreign targets is negligible compared to other Salafi-jihadi groups such as AQIM, al-Shabab and ISIS. More so, the few attacks on foreign targets may have been coordinated with Ansaru (a faction of Boko Haram) in alliance with other regional terrorist groups that are more focused on a global *jihād* against Western interests. Possibly, Boko Haram's agenda is more locally inclined and premised on the historical case of 'Uthman Dan Fodio's *jihād* as evidenced by its overwhelming attack on local targets in Nigeria and neighboring countries of Chad, Cameroon and Niger. But it would be disastrous to underestimate Boko Haram's capacity to transform itself into a global Salafi-jihadi group with extended reach beyond northeast Nigeria and the West Africa region.

Boko Haram's military capacity and campaign have been degraded (although not fully defeated) due to the combined effort and increasingly improved military cooperation between regional forces and the MNJTF (Multinational Joint Task Force). We see another hiatus where the group is perhaps trying to transform itself and redirect its vision and define its target. The on-going leadership contest between Shekau and Al-Barnawi, and ISIS' public support for the latter, reveals the internal warring in Boko Haram. I believe Shekau's allegiance to al-Baghdadi was a political move—little more than a propaganda tool that offers some strategic benefit (and perhaps some tactical and ideological support) for Boko Haram's more localized ambitions. Hence, we may be seeing an attempt to fully integrate Boko Haram as a proxy for transnational terrorist groups such as ISIS. Once that process is achieved, which will entail eliminating Shekau, Boko Haram may directly threaten the West and Western interests in the same way as ISIS.

Prognosis

Boko Haram remains riddled with internal conflicts and contradictions. Understanding a group's rationality and its level of internal cohesion is essential to bringing the insurgency to a logical end. Hence, we might be able to separate its politically-minded members from its militant group.

Ultimately Boko Haram continues to suffer from major structural weaknesses that might eventually make the group more of a liability to the Islamic State than it is an asset. In the first place, the name of Boko Haram has become extremely toxic within the context of Nigeria (and other parts of West Africa). There is no evidence that significant sections of the northern Nigerian Muslims would join Boko Haram, even from those Salafi groups that could be sympathetic to the overall establishment of an Islamic state in Nigeria.

These attitudes have crystalized because of the ethnic composition of Boko Haram, and its continuing inability to make the leap from an ethnically-specific regionalism (specific to the Kanuris in Borno and adjoining states) to a more pan-Islamic or at least pan Hausa-Fulani identity that could (hypothetically) embrace significant portions of Muslim identity in the north. (There is no evidence that any Muslims from other regions of the country would be sympathetic to such an identity.) Another major reason for this failure has been the poor leadership skills of Shekau, who instead of establishing a broad-based leadership has concentrated on a personality cult strongly reminiscent of that of Joseph Kony from the Lord's Resistance Army (text 72).

In the second place, while the terrain of northeastern Nigeria favors, to some degree, the practice of guerilla warfare (being mountainous, forested, and remote), the major Muslim population centers of northern Nigeria are all located on a fairly flat plain. It is difficult to see how, other than by conducting urban warfare or through the complete collapse of the Nigerian government and armed forces, Boko Haram could possibly take root among the Muslim masses in these regions.

Thirdly, the methods of violence chosen by Boko Haram since the beginning of 2014 have been mass casualty attacks, involving bombings, suicide attacks in public places, and mass assaults upon both civilian and military targets. Although these methods are justified by the Salafi-jihadi method of warfare, none of them makes any attempt to differentiate between civilian and military casualties. It is due to this callous disregard for human life that Boko Haram has become so toxic.

Fourthly, and perhaps most problematically for the Islamic State, Boko Haram during its period of control (roughly corresponding to the year 2014 and the first few months of 2015) was not successful in establishing a viable state. Some efforts were made, such as the establishment of regulatory police, and the renaming of cities and towns, but in the end the Boko Haram state was not an attractant in the way the Islamic State has been. This unwillingness or inability to establish a positive example stands in sharp contradistinction to the method of ISIS, which has consistently given its fighters and even its citizens a state or at least an ideal for which to fight. Essentially, by abdicating its role in positive state-building during the period of its dominance, Boko Haram forced the people of the northeastern states to choose between its nihilism and destruction and the (admittedly problematic) Nigerian state, with all its corruption and inefficiency. It is not difficult to see what would seem preferable to any rational human being.

The trajectory of Boko Haram in the future remains a difficult one. On the one hand, as stated above, it is difficult to see how the group could expand beyond the boundaries it created for itself by the end of 2014. Religiously, ethnically, topographically and militarily, all the odds were against it. However, with Boko Haram now at a comparatively low point, it is also difficult to see how precisely the group might be eradicated either. Right now, it sits more or less on the border between Nigeria and Cameroon, and during the recent past has demonstrated its willingness and ability to carry out mass casualty attacks, usually suicide attacks.

The vindictiveness behind such attacks, directed against refugee camps and marketplaces (filled with apostates from Boko Haram's point of view), is appalling. Moreover, neither the Nigerian nor the Cameroonian government has the capability to completely root out Boko Haram, and there may very well be elements within the

Nigerian military that do not see such eradication as being something particularly desirable. After all, with Boko Haram in the picture, even if it is weakened, the Nigerian military has access to foreign and domestic support, the likes of which it has not enjoyed since the 1990s.

So it may be that the war on Boko Haram will remain at an impasse for a number of years, as the ideological and political imperatives of Boko Haram to rule have not disappeared, while its coercive ability is diminished. The Nigerian military has not demonstrated a willingness to fully eradicate Boko Haram, and the Cameroonian military is probably not able to do so.

61

JUMBLED WORDS AND AUTHENTICATION FOR THE IMPORTANT PERIOD PRIOR TO SHAYKH AL-SHEKAWI'S ALLEGIANCE WHICH MADE THE *UMMA* HAPPY

BY ABU MALIK SHAYBA AL-HAMAD[1]

(27 MARCH 2015)

[Trans.: David Cook]
Posted at: https://twitter.com/ifRk23 (suspended)

This document is presented as reminiscences by Abu Malik Shayba al-Hamad (@ shaiba_ha) of the Tunisian-based Anṣār al-Sharīʿa, who claims to have facilitated the union between Boko Haram and ISIS. Hamad appears to have been something of a clearing-house in connection with a wide range of West African and European groups, probably because Tunisia during the period 2011–14 allowed freedom to Salafi-jihadis. The document is placed here out of chronological order because it describes events that occurred in 2014 and early 2015. Only selections of the seven-page document are translated here, as the bulk of it concerns other groups in Africa. Note that it was the capture of the Chibok girls which provoked the admiration of the writer, and made him realize that Boko Haram is a truly jihadi group.

I have been charged for years with the task of establishing connections with the rest of the jihadi organizations and Islamic emirates in the name of the Anṣār al-Sharīʿa in

Tunisia, to coordinate and make assistance available to the extent our organization is capable, because of the relative free movement we enjoy and the abundance of abilities and cadres in several areas. [...]

This group was obscure, and subject to character-assassination—sometimes called Boko Haram, sometimes it was said that they are extremists, killing Muslims indiscriminantly, sometimes it was said that they are Kharijites (while the Nigerian government are unbelieving Christians), and sometimes they said that it is a [front] group for the security forces (*mukhābarāt*). It was odd that the group produced numerous publications, but these were unavailable at the known jihadi forums. [*He started being interested in Boko Haram during the early years of the Syrian civil war, but was distracted by the in-fighting there. Then he began to research Boko Haram and liked what he found.*]

It would declare even the Ikhwanj [Muslim Brotherhood] and the Murji'a unbelievers because they participated in democracy. [...] Then the blessed operation occurred that shook the entire world, which was the capture of dozens of Christian girls [at Chibok]. After it Shaykh Abubakar al-Shekawi stated in a famous proclamation that he would sell them in the slave market—and this, amazingly enough, according to my knowledge, was the first time someone revived the practice (*sunna*) of taking unbelievers captive. This enraged the hypocrites and the apostates completely, and the group became the talk of the entire world.

Palace [governmental] *'ulamā'* began criticizing and issuing proclamations to expel them from Allah's religion because of their denial of something known from the religion [slavery] and their forbiddance of it. But Shaykh al-Shekawi and his group, by Allah's grace, were another means to set the ranks apart and sift them, and division of the people into two camps: a camp of belief without any hypocrisy, as opposed to a camp of hypocrisy without any belief. [*Shekau continues to be admired by the writer for being willing to take stances that enrage the unbelievers as well as "false" Muslims.*]

When he appeared in a new video surrounded by the captured Christian girls, he said, smiling, "These captured Christian girls have converted to Islam." Probably the most enraging scenes for the unbelievers were the section where he chanted truthfully declaring the Murji'a, the democrats, the Tijaniyya and other deviant heretic sects to be unbelievers, fired rifle bullets in the air, and then threw [the rifle] on the ground to enrage them further to chant a *nashīd* repeating his name, which became their and their masters' worst nightmare!

[*He began to look for older videos of the group, finding one of the prison break—probably text 37. Groups from all over the Salafi-jihadi world were swearing allegiance to ISIS at this time, when apparently, he came across a thread in which someone from the media office of JASDJ gave contact information.*] I could not believe that this matter would be so simple and easy, but when I had verified that the man was indeed from the media office of the group [Boko Haram] I did the impossible: I wrote to him, but he did not reply. Then one night a message appeared from him in English, in which he said: "*Salām ʿalaykum*, my brother." I was so happy at this connection that I could not write, because I had hundreds of questions bursting from my fingertips, writing on the screen and sending immediately.

So, it started that day, the story of brothers, unknown to each other... [*But there was a linguistic problem: the contact spoke Hausa, and a little English and Arabic, while Hamad spoke Arabic and English, but no Hausa. Miscommunications abounded.*] Then, after a time, I asked him the question that every Muslim was asking at that time: "Have you sworn allegiance to the caliph of the Muslims?" He said something which pained my heart: "All of us are with the Islamic State [ISIS], and all of us want to swear allegiance to the caliph of the Muslims, but the leadership hesitates because of some doubts, while the Consultative Council (*majlis al-shūrā*) is studying the issue."

[*Hamad could sympathize to some extent; the same was true of his own Anṣār al-Sharīʿa in Tunis and several other West African groups. So, Hamad began to pray for his leader Abu ʿIyad al-Tunisi and Abubakar Shekau, so that the Muslims would be unified. The Boko Haram media contact told him that to upload videos he had to travel 300 kilometers. A 50-megabyte video would take nine hours to upload—which explains the low quality of early Boko Haram videos. After the establishment of al-ʿUrwa al-Wuthqā, the group's media outlet, though, the videos were of higher quality.*]

My Nigerian brother joked with me, preparing me for the news. He asked me for something which I could not do, and I said: "I will contact the ISIS brothers who will do that." He said: "I am afraid they will not assist me, because we have not sworn allegiance until now." So, I said to him: "How would they not assist you, when you are a Muslim asking them for help? It is impossible that any of our ISIS brothers would do that, as I know them, so if you want I will ask them on your behalf." He said: "Good tidings, my brother, I was joking with you. Soon you will hear news that will gladden both of us."

Then he informed me of the upcoming swearing of allegiance days before it was publicized. [The workers at Africa News] shed tears of joy at this news, and we prostrated to Allah in thanks. This blessed swearing of allegiance was broadcast, which the Muslims saw and heard. [...]

62

BAY'A (OATH OF ALLEGIANCE) TO THE CALIPH OF THE MUSLIMS

BY ABUBAKAR SHEKAU

(7 MARCH 2015)

[Trans.: Abdulbasit Kassim]

Available at: http://jihadology.net/2015/03/07/al-urwah-al-wuthqa-foundation-presents-a-new-audio-message-from-jamaat-ahl-al-sunnah-li-l-dawah-wa-l-jihads-boko-%e1%b8%a5aram-abu-bakr-shekau-bayah-jama/

It had long been anticipated that Boko Haram would swear allegiance to the Islamic State, if only because the former had been mimicking the actions of the latter for months by the spring of 2015 (see text 48). This oath of allegiance made it official, and completed Boko Haram's adoption into the larger family of Salafi-jihadi groups. An earlier indication of Boko Haram's adoption into the larger family of Salafi-jihad groups reflected in the mention of Abubakar Shekau alongside Nasir al-Wuhayshi of al-Qaeda in the Arabian Peninsula and Abu Zubayr of al-Shabab in Somalia in the letter on al-Qaeda/Islamic State rivalry written on 17 August 2014 by Abu 'Iyad al-Tunisi of Ansar al-Shari'a Tunisia to Ayman az-Zawahiri prior to Boko Haram's allegiance to the Islamic State. In what appears to be an unprecedented celebration of allegiance by Islamic State's provinces,[1] Boko Haram members were celebrated and the group was paraded as an epicenter in Sub-Saharan Africa. The significance of the declaration of allegiance from

Boko Haram was captured in the statement of the late Abu Muhammad al-Adnani in Dabiq, *the Islamic State's English-language magazine:*

> *And we bring you the good news today of the Khilāfah's [caliphate's] expansion to West Africa, for the Khalīfah [caliph] has accepted the pledge of allegiance made by our brothers in JASDJ. We congratulate the Muslims and our mujāhid brothers in West Africa on their pledge of allegiance, and we congratulate them on joining the caravan of the caliphate. So, rejoice O Muslims, for this is a new door that Allah has opened so that you may emigrate to the land of Islam and so that you may wage jihād. So, whoever is stopped by the disbelieving rulers, and prevented from emigrating to Iraq, Shām, Yemen, the Arabian Peninsula, or Khurāsān, will not be prevented—by Allah's permission—from emigrating to Africa.[2]*

Bayʿa [oath of allegiance] to Abu Bakr al-Baghdadi by Abubakar Shekau

[Standard Islamic opening]

And thereafter:

From your brother in Allah, Abu Muhammad Abubakar bin Muhammad al-Shekawi, the leader of JASDJ to the caliph of the Muslims, Abu Bakr Ibrahim b. ʿAwad b. Ibrahim al-Husayni al-Qurashi.

We are sending you this message, following what Allah said in the Qurʾān: "And hold fast to Allah's bond, all of you, and do not fall apart." (Q3:103) And what the Prophet said: "Whoever dies when he had not pledged allegiance to an imam [caliph] dies a death of ignorance (*jāhiliyya*)." In submission to the order of Allah, and submission to the order of the Prophet, peace be upon him, not to separate from each other and to stay united as a community of believers:

We announce our allegiance to the caliph of the Muslims Ibrahim b. ʿAwad b. Ibrahim al-Husayni al-Qurashi [Abu Bakr al-Baghdadi] and we will hear and obey him in times of difficulty and prosperity, in hardship and ease, and to endure being discriminated against, and not to dispute about rule with those in power, except in case of evident unbelief regarding that which there is a proof from Allah.

We call upon Muslims everywhere to pledge allegiance to the caliph and support him, as obedience to Allah and as their fulfillment of this era's absent duty [the caliphate]. We pledged allegiance to the caliph because of the interest of the Muslims in their religion and in their worldly affairs which can only be protected by an imam who looks after them according to Allah's laws, and fights the enemy of Islam and those who fight Allah's rule. This is the completeness of the religion with the Book that guides and the sword that favors victory. Allah is sufficient for guidance and victory.

Ibn Taymiyya said: "People must know that having to rule the people is one of the greatest duties of the religion. Indeed, the religion and the world for Muslims will never be complete without it. The interest of the sons of Adam will never be successful unless they are united under one banner as a community of believers. After the coming together of the Muslims as one community of believers, they must have a head, and it is not a problem even if the least group opposing the others unites for this cause."

We at JASDJ pledge allegiance because there is no cure to the Muslims' disunity except the caliphate. We also call all the Muslims to join us in this goodness, because it would enrage Allah's enemy. By Allah, our gathering under one banner under one imam is more detrimental to enemy morale than their gaining victory in the battlefield.

Allah is great! Allah is great! Allah is great!

To Allah belongs all honor, to His Messenger, and to the believers but the hypocrites do not know. And may Allah's blessings be upon our Prophet Muhammad, his family and his Companions. Your brother in Allah, Abu Muhammad Abubakar b. Muhammad al-Shekawi, the leader of JASDJ.

63

ARRIVAL OF THE CALIPHATE'S SOLDIERS IN WEST AFRICA

BY WILĀYAT GHARB IFRIQIYĀ

(2 JUNE 2015)

[Trans.: Abdulbasit Kassim]
Available at: http://jihadology.net/2015/06/02/new-video-message-from-the-islamic-state-arrivals-of-the-soldiers-of-the-caliphate-in-west-africa-wilayat-gharb-ifriqiyyah/

A mark of the post-allegiance to ISIS period for Boko Haram is the lowered profile of Shekau, who ceases to be the major focus of its public image. In this video, the two speakers alluded to the escalation of the conflict between Boko Haram and the Multinational Joint Task Force (MNJTF) comprising soldiers from Nigeria, Chad, Niger, and Benin. While mentioning the tensions and the context of distrust between Nigeria and her neighbors, the first speaker referred to the comment of the Chadian president, when he said that the fight against Boko Haram is being hampered by poor co-ordination between Chad and Nigeria. He also gave further information of the activities within the caliphate as well as detailed information concerning the soldiers killed in various clashes. This video should be understood within the context of Boko Haram's display of resilience against the operations of the MNJTF.[1]

First speaker

[Standard Islamic opening]

And thereafter:

We thank Allah for giving us the opportunity to send this message and to expose the liars—Nigeria and the armies of its allies—and what they have spread through the media. The main battle was fought on the frontlines, by jets in the sky, and with armored vehicles on the ground. But they chose the media as their principal weapon with which to fight us. But Allah knows the reality on the ground. I want to explain to the lying coalition partners who sent their armies against us—Nigeria, Chad, Cameroon, and Niger—that Allah said: "You think they are together, yet their hearts are at variance." (Q59:14)

We thank Allah. A few days ago, the president of Chad, Idriss Déby visited Nigeria and explained to the world that the reason they cannot defeat us is the problem of disunity amongst them. I swear that they will not defeat us, by Allah's permission. Most of our territory is still under our control, including Dikwa, Gamboru, Damasak, and other places. The Qur'ānic schools, markets, and mosques are still open. The people are going about their daily business as usual. But the armies claim, through the media, that they captured our towns and that they assaulted Sambisa [Forest] and killed us. I swear by Allah that I am talking right now from Sambisa. Here in Sambisa, you can travel more than four to five hours under the black flag of Islamic monotheism by car or motorbike.

We say again to our brothers that we are well, healthy and standing firm in the religion.

All praise and thanks are due to Allah, the One and Only. The Qur'ānic schools, *ḥadīth* schools, Arabic schools, and courses for technology, weaponry, and other fields of knowledge are carrying on securely. All praise is due to Allah. I swear by Allah that no one can demolish this religion. Even if they were to kill all of us here in Sambisa, if only one or two survived, they would rebuild the caliphate. And we are without number in Sambisa Forest. We are thousands of *mujāhidīn* here.

Finally, whoever believes that the Nigerian army has defeated us after seeing their false propaganda video, then know that we have battled them again and killed them. Here are the Nigerian military ID cards. The owners of these cards were killed by us, with Allah's help. This one's rank is lieutenant. His name is A.K. Shekoni and we killed him. If he is not from the Nigerian army, then explain to us where he is from? Here are more ID cards.

This is a small selection from among the many we have taken. We provide them [the cards] as proof. Know that we have collected numberless cards. Here you can see some of them. This is the end of what I have to say. May Allah support us and unite our hearts.

ARRIVAL OF THE CALIPHATE'S SOLDIERS IN WEST AFRICA

May Allah destroy our enemies and your enemies. May Allah support His religion. All praise is due to Allah, Lord of the creation. Exalted is your Lord, the Lord of might, above what they describe. And may peace be upon the messengers. And praise be to Allah, Lord of the creation.

Second speaker

Good news to our brothers all over the world. Allah the One and Only downed this Nigerian military jet through our hands this morning. This was not by our power and ability, but by Allah's power. Here are the pieces of the jet engine and other parts.

Here are its bullets, which were not fired but were exposed to fire and are now burning. Here is the jet propeller—everyone can see this. This is the jet. President of Nigeria [Goodluck] Jonathan, here are your goods. Idriss Déby of Chad, here are your goods. Mahamadou Issoufou of Niger, here are your goods. Paul Biya of Cameroon, here are your goods. Barack Obama of America, here are your goods. François Hollande of France, here are your goods. Benjamin Netanyahu of the Jewish state, here are your goods. O *mujāhidīn*!

Good news to you all. Good news again. Victory is from Allah. Here are the remaining pieces of the jet. Victory is from Allah. Allah is the greatest. All praise be to Allah.

64

'ID [AL-FITRI] PRAYER AND SERMON FROM WILĀYAT GHARB IFRIQIYĀ

(22 JULY 2015)

[Trans.: Abdulbasit Kassim]
Available at: http://jihadology.net/2015/07/22/new-video-message-from-the-islamic-state-id-prayers-and-a-sermon-from-wilayat-gharb-ifriqiyyah/

Another mark of the post-allegiance to ISIS era for Boko Haram is the increased focus upon Islamic devotion. This video consists of three interviews with Boko Haram members whose primary message is to state that the group continues to control its territory and can be considered part of the Islamic State.

'Id *Sermon*

Allah is great, all praises be to Him. O servants of Allah! You should know that the completion of the fasting in the month of Ramadan does not bring a period of abeyance to the actions and good deeds of a believer. This is so because the actions and deeds of a believer do not reach a state of cessation except with his demise. One of the most admirable deeds with which to embark, after the month of Ramadan's fasting, is the six [subsequent] days of fasting in the month of Shawwal.[1] The reward of fasting in the month of Ramadan followed by the six days of fasting is equivalent to the reward of a person who has fasted throughout a whole year. Those who faced constraints that inhibited them from completing the full Ramadan fast should make adequate plans to complete their fast.

Another admirable deed is to follow the guidance of the Prophet in his devotional night prayers, as it has been recorded that he routinely prayed eleven prostrations (*raka'āt*) every night during the month of Ramadan, as well as during other months of the year. You should also recite the Qur'ān and ponder Allah's words in the day and night so that you may prosper. Allah is great. The greatest significance of this occasion is the appeal to direct our souls and good deeds to the plight of the orphans and the indigent, for us to share our love with them. We also need to establish Allah's mandated rights concerning our parents and kindred and spread love and pleasantries among the Muslims.

'Id al-Fitr Speeches from the Members of Islamic State West Africa Province:

Speaker 1: [Islamic opening] Praise be to Allah, who brought us the day of *'Id* [festival] in safety and security. Indeed, Allah has bolstered our strength to observe the prayer of *'Id* despite the bellicosity of the unbelievers.

We pray that the people of unbelief find this day as a day of displeasure. We thank Allah who protected us during the *'Id* prayer while we prayed in safety and security. And we hope all our brothers all over the world pray in safety and security. We send special greetings to them. May Allah accept our deeds and join us together in paradise.

Secondly, I want to call on my brothers all over the world to stand firmly together in support of our religion. No matter what the unbelievers do to try to break our religion, they would not be able to succeed. Allah has promised that whoever follows His commands will surely be victorious. Indeed, this is a word of truth.

Speaker 2: [Islamic opening] We have completed our fasting in safety and security. We have observed the *'Id* prayer in safety and security. All praise be to Allah; all our brothers are in a good condition. Allah has supported us in establishing His religion. And may Allah make all our deeds for His sake.

And may Allah make the *'Id* celebration the cause of destroying unbelief and its people. My second message is to the Civilian JTF (*Kato de Gora*). Repent and turn to your Lord, so come and follow His path. We don't need you to follow us; we just want you to follow Allah's religion. And you should know that if unbelief could ever have defeated Islam, Pharaoh would have won.[2] So repent and return to your Lord. And I hope all our brothers overseas and all over the world performed the *'Id* prayer in safety and security. All praise to Allah, I testify that there is no deity worthy of being worshipped except Allah.

Speaker 3: [Islamic opening] To our brothers in Iraq, and those who are far away from us, we extend our homage, and pray to Allah to accept all our supplications. And to the unbelievers all over the world, you know we are here. We have not been driven out of the land [of Nigeria]; you should expect our coming by Allah's permission. Be prepared because you will soon hear from us and we will be coming from where you never expected, stronger than before. This is what I briefly have to say. All praise to Allah, I testify that there is no deity worthy of being worshipped except Allah.

65

MESSAGE TO THE NIGERIAN UNBELIEVERS

BY ABUBAKAR SHEKAU

(19 SEPTEMBER 2015)

[Trans.: Abdulbasit Kassim]

Available at: http://jihadology.net/2015/09/19/new-audio-message-from-
the-islamic-states-abu-bakr-al-shekau-message-to-the-infidels-of-nigeria-
wilayat-gharb-ifriqiyyah/

The lowered profile of Shekau in the post-allegiance to ISIS period for Boko Haram once again spurred the claim that he had been killed by the Nigerian army. In what can again be called Shekau's revival, not only did he prove that he was in good health, he also declared that the group's caliphate was extant and extended his homage to the Islamic State and its provinces. Shekau also dispelled the reports of the Nigerian army that the group had been defeated. While reiterating the belief system of the group, Shekau censured the Izala scholars and dismissed the report that the incarcerated members of the group had embraced revisionist ideas. A transcript of this lecture in French was published in Issue 6 of the Islamic State French Magazine 'Dar al-Islam'.

[Standard Islamic opening] This message is a rejoinder to the tyrants and their followers, the unbelievers and all the polytheists, from Abu Muhammad Abubakar b. Muhammad al-Shekawi, the leader of the ISWAP.

To my brethren in faith, wherever they may be, may Allah protect and guide you, and may He protect and guide me too. Verily, all praise and devotion belong to Allah who has made faith in Him, reliance on Him and working under His commands, the conditions for assurance that man will earn the taste and the reward of Allah's leadership both in this world and the hereafter. Allah has bestowed on His servants the ability to communicate and embrace the truth to the point that they can start reaping the fruit and taste of their unwavering tenacity in following the path of truth. You will know the true servants of Allah, those who propagate the truth, once you see them. May Allah make us part of His true servants.

Praise be to Allah, who has distanced all types of hubris from my tongue, and has made me a disciplined, obedient and humble servant. All praise be to Allah for the absolute blessing which He has bestowed on us. I testify that there is nothing worthy of being worshipped except Allah. No man has ever attained Allah's power and strength since He created the world and spread His servants over it. This is a truthful testimony filled with everything that Allah mandated and it is not from my own strength or power. I also bear witness that the Prophet Muhammad is a messenger and Allah's servant. The peace and blessings of Allah be upon him, his kin, his Companions and all the faithful servants who follow in his footsteps with the hope of a rewarding hereafter.

[...] Whoever holds firm to the dictates of the Qur'ān, the traditions of Prophet Muhammad, and follows the Companions' established path is together with us even if we have never met. Whoever follows the unbelievers' path, even if we gave birth to him or he comes from among us, he should know that he is our adversary and an unbeliever.[1] "We are quit of you, and what you worship apart from Allah. We disbelieve in you. Enmity and hatred have arisen between you and us forever, till you believe in Allah alone." (Q60:4)

I extend my homage to my brethren from the Islamic State in Iraq, Sham [Syria], in Yemen and the entire world. We are the group that has been erroneously labelled as Boko Haram, along with the claim that our weapons have been seized and we have been routed and defeated and now scattered and wandering in different places. I can assure you that we are in good health and the atrophied liars are the one who are unable to settle down. You can deduce that from my voice, which now sounds stronger and more energetic than ever before. This is Shekau.

We extend our homage to the Caliph of the Muslims in the Islamic State, Abu Bakr al-Baghdadi, the Commander of the Believers, may Allah protect and care for him.

We also extend our homage to the teacher of the believers, the honorable and venerable Muhammad al-Adnani, may Allah protect and care for him. We also extend our homage to the resolute Islamic scholars wherever they are, including those I do not know, to our brethren in Yemen and all over the world. We pledge our support for you our brethren. We will always stand by your side, with Allah's help. We do not make a distinction between our people and your people, wherever you are, our fighting brethren, we are all on the same path. Your *jihād* and our *jihād* are one. We are all treading on the same path to establish the Qur'ān and the traditions of the Prophet Muhammad. Our goal is to make supreme the word of Allah all over the world[2] and to earn the pleasure of Allah.

Here we are, in good health. We drink, eat, and slay the unbelievers daily. O brethren! Our *jihād* is incessant, as decreed by Allah. You should all be delighted. We are in good condition. They said that we have been routed, defeated, annihilated and our activities have come to an end. They are telling lies. Buhari, you have not yet earned your allotment of the money disbursed by Obama. Buhari, the money and business you run with them is unfinished. I am alive. Buhari, your business with François Hollande is without effect. Kukasheka, the avaricious baboon's tail, your desire has not been fulfilled yet.[3] Buratai, I know you fathomed what happened to you.[4] You know Kukasheka. Yes, of course, any blind man who competes in a stoning competition knows the risk of his vulnerability.

It is only Allah that knows when the blind [person] sleeps and He alone fathoms the reading of the deaf. I am communicating with you, Kukasheka. I know you are hearing my words—you unscrupulous liar! We pray that Allah Almighty will place us among those with whom He is pleased; "a people whom He loves, and they love Him, humble towards the faithful, but haughty towards the unbelievers. They fight in the way of Allah and do not fear anybody's reproach. That is a favor from Allah which He confers upon whomever He pleases." (Q5:54)

After expressing gratitude to my brethren, I will proceed to discuss the second point which is about the unbelievers, the polytheists, the hypocrites and the Civilian JTF (*Kato de Gora*). A great deal of work is ahead and we are still on the battlefield. O Nigerians! O Nigeriens! O Chadians, Idriss Déby! O Cameroonians! O people who have joined the alliance against the *mujāhidīn*, you are not worth Allah's finger. You absolutely know that your actions are antithetical to the actions of the Prophet. You know your actions are emblem of falsehood. "Die of your fury!" (Q3:119)

Would this not be a lesson for you, for Allah's sake? How many times have you killed Shekau, yet he is still speaking to you. Our Islamic caliphate is extant. We implement Allah's *sharīʿa* in it. We sever hands, whip the fornicators, imprison and slay based on the instructions from the Qur'ān. We implement the verses of the Qur'ān: "Whoever does not judge according to what Allah has revealed—those are the unbelievers" (Q5:44); "Whoever does not judge according to what Allah has revealed—those are the evildoers" (Q5:45); "He who does not judge according to what Allah has revealed—those are the transgressors." (Q5:47) We hope to be accepted by Allah as His true servants. May Allah protect us and save us from failure. Our Islamic caliphate is extant by Allah's permission.

Abu Muhammad Abubakar b. Muhammad al-Shekawi is the virtuous representative of Abu Bakr al-Baghdadi, the Commander of the Believers. Shekau is the nightmare of Buhari and Obama. Allah is great! Even if I die today, I am satisfied that my wish has been accomplished. The unbelievers are upset with me. I swear to Allah,

Buhari, you have been deceived. Your soldier, your liar, your apostate, I mean, Kukasheka, has lied to you. He and his soldiers have lied to you.

These bastards run without shoes when they have a physical encounter with us on the battlefield, but then they go back to fabricate lies. The hereafter is real indeed. Your army chief, Buratai will pay a hard price. I will not be explicit on this matter. You can obtain the full details of what I mean by asking Kukasheka. I swear by Allah he is aware of what happened to him and his soldiers. You will be nettled to know about this matter. All the rumors being spread by the *ṭawaghīt* on the TV and radio are all lies to prevent people from following Allah's path. They are all fabricated lies.

The third point is about the Izala members who are bent on dissuading the people in the villages from following Islamic tenets. Could anyone who claims to believe in the Qur'ān and the Sunna turn away from Islam and return to you in unbelief? By Allah, no, and I say 1,000 times no. That society that calls itself "the Society for the Removal of Innovation and Re-establishment of the Sunna" is now actively dissuading people from following the tenets of Islam; is democracy not a deviation from the tenets of Islam? Did you ever read or heard that the Prophet participated in democracy? You are just being unfaithful to Allah. There will certainly be more lingering explanations in the hereafter. On my part, I have successfully explained all the evidence that pertains to this world even if you fail to believe. Allah has already made your history known to me. You bastards!

The fourth point is about the statement of Buhari, the unbeliever, apostate and liar. He even tells lies about us saying that some of our brethren, who are being apprehended and detained in their prisons, have recanted their views and now understand that our action is erroneous. Buhari even stated that the so-called revisionists have started playing soccer. He uttered these statements shamelessly on TV and radio. Please, brethren take note of these lies. O brethren in faith! You should all pray to Allah. He has promised to judge between us and them in the hereafter, and will never let them be victorious over us. This is the promise of Allah.

Think of it, you have been fighting me for some years now, but today I come out again to you, bastards. Buhari, are you calling yourself a believer? As they wage their war against us, Buhari claimed that he will crush us in three months but now he has declared that it is no longer feasible to crush us within three months.[5] This retraction alone suffices as a proof for all their lies. Buhari, you should know that you are being duped and misled. May Allah help and protect us because nobody is spared of destruction. For those who fail to acknowledge the supremacy of Allah's laws, we will not stop declaring what Allah has commanded us to say to you. We are not being bombastic and we take refuge in Allah from the wrongs of our actions.

Why have you failed to comprehend? This is Buhari who has completely abjured ruling with Allah's laws, but rather he chooses to conform to the dictate of secular constitutions. He travels by plane following the Westerners and Europeans and he has also stymied all attempts to establish the supremacy of Allah's laws.

Was it not Buhari who announced that we have been crushed in all places? He said: "We have completely routed them from the forest called Sambisa."[6] Do you know why they keep re-inventing that name Sambisa? They want us to respond by saying; here we are in the Sambisa [Forest]. How would you know where we are? Are we shortsighted like you? Why have you chosen to talk only about Sambisa? Why have you refuse to speak about the Lake Chad and Damasak? You keep fabricating lies. Is it not funny how these people take arms, placing them in a forested area, and then take pictures which will later be displayed to the beguiled public on TV?

They always want to conceal their chicanery by pretending to have achieved a great feat in their fight against us. Even though the beguiled people are satisfied with their artifice, they will never be able to earn the pleasure of Allah. Our *jihād* is not limited to Sambisa [Forest], the Lake Chad or Africa, our target is the whole world. They even claim to have seized our weapons. If only their claim is true, how come we are still fighting and slaying them daily? Now, they also hold their meetings in a church when the Prophet proscribed eating food from a plate that was used by an unbeliever.

In conclusion, this is your brother in faith Abu Muhammad Abubakar b. Muhammad al-Shekawi, a native of the village of Shekau in Yobe State. Let me state here clearly for those who would listen. You are in deep trouble and there is more to come. We hope to spread Allah's laws to all His servants. May Allah accept our prayer and may He make this land a stepping stone in this struggle.

66

'ID AL-AḌḤĀ ATMOSPHERE
IN WILĀYAT GHARB IFRIQIYĀ

(28 SEPTEMBER 2015)

[Trans.: Abdulbasit Kassim]

Available at: http://jihadology.net/2015/09/28/new-video-message-from-the-islamic-state-id-al-a%E1%B8%8D%E1%B8%A5a-atmosphere-in-wilayat-gharb-ifriqiyyah/

With the lowered profile of Shekau following the swearing of allegiance to ISIS, there was a heightened profile for Boko Haram's spirituality. This video is part of that pattern.[1]

Allah is great, by the multitude of pilgrims who embarked on the pilgrimage in Mecca. Allah is great, by the multitude of pilgrims who circumnavigated around "the Ancient House" (*al-Bayt al-ʿatīq*).[2] Allah is great, by the multitude of pilgrims who set out for Mina praising Allah until they reached their destination in ʿArafat. As for what follows:

O you people! Fear your Lord as He should be feared, and safeguard your actions with the intention of doing what He loves and what pleases Him in life. It is noteworthy to have knowledge of the virtue of this day, the day of benignity, unity, togetherness, awe inspiring and exaltation. May Allah augment our wherewithal and progress. This is the day dubbed the day of the "Greater Pilgrimage." The Holy Prophet expounded on the virtue of this day. He commanded people in his sermons to strengthen their faith in and obedience to Allah.

We ask Allah Almighty to lead us in our war. We ask Him to grant us steadfastness in our intrepidity. We ask Him to grant us victory against the unbelieving nations. We ask Him to grant us the spirit of patience, fortitude and valor in the battlefields. We ask Him to help us to defend and protect the Islamic State. We ask Him to direct all our affairs to agree with the dictates of the Qur'ān and the Sunna. We do not possess any power except what He bestowed upon us. We do not possess any strength except by what He bestowed upon us. You are the Most Beneficent, the Most Merciful. O Allah! We ask You at this instant to not let a sin be unforgiven, a distress unrelieved, an illness unhealed, a debt unsettled, and to leave no learned [person] ignorant.

We ask You to guide those who have gone astray, and to accept our repentance and us as your obedient servants. We ask You to answer our prayers, make our sons good believers, and enrich the indigent. O Allah! By your mercy, make things easy for us and help us do anything that pleases You and is good for us in this world and the hereafter. O Allah! Cover our defects and make the truth clear. You are the One who has power over all affairs. Allah alone is sufficient for us, and He is the best disposer of affairs; and excellent is the Protector and excellent is the Helper. May the peace and blessings of Allah be upon Prophet Muhammad, his family, Companions, and all those who follow his path until the Day of Judgment.

'Id Speeches from the Members of Islamic State West Africa Province

Speaker 1: All praise be to Allah—we have successfully prayed the 'Id prayer. We extend our compliments to our brethren all over the world, in the Islamic State and all other provinces in the Islamic State. We extend our compliments to those who fight *jihād* in Allah's path and establish Allah's religion. By Allah's permission, we are on the same path with you just as you are also on the same path with us.

Speaker 2: May the peace and blessings of Allah be upon you, my Muslim brethren. All praise be to Allah, the One who destined for us to be among those who will take part in this act of worship, the prayer of 'Id and sacrifice of animals, which he has commanded us to observe. We pray to Allah to accept our act of sacrifice and good deeds. We extend a complimentary message to all our brethren, the believers and all those who fight *jihād* in Allah's path all over the world and those who are aiding the establishment of Allah's religion. Allah has made us among those in the world who will witness and take part in the *jihād* to attain victory for the establishment of Allah's religion.

We ask Allah Almighty to aid us in our struggle and *jihād* all over the world. My second message to my brethren and the Muslim *umma* all over the world is a reminder to fear Allah. Allah's religion will be established in this world whether you choose to aid the *jihād* or choose to abandon it for other worldly affairs. However, what is of benefit to you is for you to strive to be among those who are fighting *jihād* in Allah's path, doing what He loves and what pleases Him and turning away from the temptations of the world. Do not waste your time to engage in those actions that are not beneficial to you in this world or the hereafter. The unbelievers are deceivers who are deceiving the people of the world by their defiance and noncompliance with Qur'ānic dictates and instructions.

They are spreading fabricated lies with the claim that they have extirpated the *mujāhidin*. Allah will never allow such a situation to materialize or come into light. This is so because Allah has promised the victory of His religion and the establishment of an Islamic state all over the world. Your fabricated lies will never stymie or thwart our *jihād*. This is a promise from Allah that He will give victory to His religion through His servants. Allah has also promised that He will humiliate the unbelievers at the hands of the believers. We have established firm belief that Allah will aid the victory of His religion. We have no qualms. All commands belong to Allah alone. Allah's religion will never be extirpated.

The unbelievers who are fighting us will soon vanish from the world. It is upon you to come and take on Allah's religion. Your ability to fly in airplanes and ride cars is only possible by the command of Allah. He is the one who commanded His servants to be patient in the state of hunger. It is Allah who created you, the earth, the sky, the sun, the moon, the stars, and all other things and only He deserves to be worshipped. The world belongs to Allah, fear Him before your soul departs from the world. It is an obligation to be part of those who fight and aid the victory of Allah's religion. Allah has warned you to be wary of the luxury in this world which distracts you from aiding the victory of His religion.

Speaker 3: [...] As for what follows, all praise be to Allah who made it easy for us to witness this day of happiness which is the blessed day of 'Id, the day of animal sacrifice. May Allah accept all our actions and may He protect us all. Everybody is informed about our current state of affairs in Sambisa Forest and other areas under our control.

You have also listened to the threat from the *ṭawaghīt* who claimed that they have seized all the territories under our control including Sambisa Forest. They claimed that during their operation to take over Sambisa Forest, they found us in a state of hunger, panic and fear. We extend our gratitude to Allah and it is not our part to exaggerate our current stable state of affairs because as you can see it is obvious. By Allah's permission, all the forces of *ṭawaghīt* will soon face downfall and failure in their battle against us. We extend our homage to all our Muslim brethren in the Islamic State and all over the world. I would like to announce good news to all of you. All praise be to Allah; we are here in good health. All the statements you hear from the *ṭawaghīt* are fabricated lies. May the peace and blessings of Allah be upon us.

67

MESSAGES FROM THE CALIPHATE'S SOLDIERS IN WILĀYAT GHARB IFRIQIYĀ

BY MAN CHARI

(7 OCTOBER 2015)

[Trans.: Abdulbasit Kassim]
Available at: http://jihadology.net/2015/10/07/new-video-message-from-the-islamic-state-messages-from-the-soldiers-of-the-caliphate-in-wilayat-gharb-ifriqiyyah/

Following the declaration of bayʿa *(allegiance) by Shekau to Abu Bakr al-Baghdadi (text 62), this video is the* bayʿa *of the members of the group to the Islamic State, following the pattern of* bayʿa *of other Islamic State provinces (placing each other's hands around the speaker and repeating the pledge of allegiance to the Islamic State after the speaker). The bilingualism of this video reflects the growing unity between Boko Haram and the Islamic State. The Arabic version cites the complete Qurʾānic verses, whereas in the Hausa version they are paraphrased.*

[Arabic version]

[Standard Islamic opening]

And thereafter:

This is a message to the world in general and specifically to our emir, the Caliph of the Muslims Abu Bakr al-Baghdadi, may Allah preserve and protect him. We say:

may the curse of Allah be upon the liars. The unbelievers in Nigeria and the rest of the countries of unbelief are lying about us. They claim that some of our brothers became weak and turned over their weapons to the unbelievers, and that their number reached 200, and that they took more women and children.

This is an utter lie, slander, and baseless falsehood. This is part of the media war and the incursion of silly ideology. They have inherited this from their forefathers, the Jews. As the Almighty said about the tale of the words of the Jews to Jesus son of Mary: "And their saying: 'We have killed the Messiah, Jesus, son of Mary and the apostle of Allah.' They neither killed nor crucified him; but it was made to appear so unto them. Indeed, those who differ about him are in doubt about it. Their knowledge does not go beyond conjecture, and they did not kill him for certain." (Q4:157)

So, Allah denied them and responded with His word: "They neither killed nor crucified him; but it was made to appear so unto them."

We say to all the unbelievers from among the democrats, the secularists, and the apostates: Die in your rage! Die in your rage! Die in your rage! Wait for the glad tidings of what will harm you. Allah certainly supports His religion. We say to our *mujāhidīn* brothers everywhere: wait for the glad tidings that will bring you joy. You are part of us and we are part of you. We testify that the unbelievers and their minions the journalists have lied in their statements. All that they said about us is lies and slander.

We call on all the Muslims in West Africa not to be deceived by the unbelievers' statements. They must hasten to immigrate to the Islamic State and pledge allegiance to the caliph, and not accept dispersion and disintegration. Let them hold fast to the rope of Allah, as Allah commanded us in His Book: "And hold fast to Allah's bond, all of you, and do not fall apart." (Q3:103) Be patient amidst the harm of the unbelievers and wage *jihād* in Allah's cause, to make supreme the word of Allah and to earn the highest rank in paradise.

Allah said in His Holy Book:

"And those who emigrated in Allah's path, then were killed or died, Allah shall provide them with a fair promise. Allah is surely the best provider. He will admit them into a place with which they will be well-pleased. Surely Allah is All-Knowing, Clement." (Q22:58–59)

[*Group pledge showing the members of ISWAP placing each other's hands around the speaker and repeating the pledge of allegiance to the Islamic State.*]

We renew our pledge of allegiance to our caliph, the Caliph of the Muslims Abu Bakr al-Baghdadi. We say: we pledge to the Commander of the Believers, the Caliph of the Muslims Abu Bakr al-Baghdadi al-Husayni al-Qurashi, to listen and obey in times of difficulty and in prosperity, in hardship and in ease, to endure being discriminated against, and not to dispute about rule with those in power, except in case of clear unbelief, regarding which there is a proof from Allah. Allah is great! Allah is great! Allah is great!

At the end, we give our greetings to our *mujāhidīn* brothers all over the world, such as Ninawa Province, al-Raqqa Province, Salah al-Din Province, al-Falluja Province, Homs Province, Caucasus Province, Baraka Province, Libya Province, and the rest of the provinces with a blessed greeting. Peace be upon you, and Allah's mercy and blessings. Praise be to Allah, the Lord of the worlds.

[*Hausa version*]

[Standard Islamic opening]

And thereafter:

We want to send this message to the whole world, especially to the Caliph of the Muslims, Commander of the Believers, Abu Bakr al-Baghdadi. May Allah protect him.

And thereafter, the whole world should know that we, the *mujāhidīn* of the West Africa Province, constitute one of the provinces of the Islamic State. We are in good health. The leader of this province is Abu Muhammad Abubakar b. Muhammad al-Shekawi, may Allah protect him. We want all the unbelievers of the world to hear. May Allah curse all the unbelievers of the world.

The Nigerian unbelievers, and those of other unbelieving countries, tell lies about us, saying that a faction of our brethren has surrendered to the unbelievers, while also claiming that their number has reached 200. The unbelievers also claim that they hold many women and children from among us. They say that they have enrolled them in Western schools and made them understand that our doctrine is specious. These are some of their deceitful statements.

The fact is that all of this is lies. They were failing in their warfare and turned to the media. They failed to fight us with arms and resorted to propaganda. They rely on their weapons, whereas we have Allah and put our trust in Allah. Their logic is purely based on lies. The claims are false; they have not detained anybody from among us. We are here, in good health. We observe our religious duty, and carry out our *jihād*, and everything is going fine. There is nothing like distress affecting us.

The world should know. They inherited this kind of lie from their forefathers, the Jews. Their forefathers, the Jews, are already known to be liars. This can be understood from the word of Allah, glory to Him, the Exalted, when He stated that the Jews said: "We killed Jesus, the Prophet," when Allah raised Jesus to the heavens. They claimed to have killed Jesus, the Prophet, for the sake of deceiving. So, this is the kind of lie the unbelievers and Jews emulate in this present time.

But, Allah responded to them by saying: "No, they did not kill him. Nobody killed Jesus, the prophet, and they did not crucify Him either." (Q4:157) I hope it is understood. But, what happened was that they killed one of them [in his place]. They found someone who looked like Jesus, peace be upon him, and crucified him, saying that they had killed Jesus. So likewise, the Jews in the present time—I mean the supporters of democracy—also emulate their forefathers. That is why they make up those lies about us. They claim to have arrested this-and-that [person], but it is pure lie. We are in good health, and nothing happened to us.

We declare to the unbelievers of the world, the supporters of democracy, the secularists and the apostates, to listen. Listen, die in your rage! Die in your rage! Die in your rage! Furthermore, we bring you news about something that will annoy you even more. Allah, glory to Him, will indeed elevate His religion whether you want it or not.

To our *mujāhidīn* brothers, we say, O brethren, to you we bring good news that will please you. Allah, glory to Him, will elevate His religion. Wherever you are, you are with us and wherever we are, we are with you. We are together and let the unbelievers of the world die in their rage. Moreover, we say to all the unbelievers of the world, their followers and those who spread news on papers and on the radio, that they all tell lies. Everything they say about us is false. We are in good health, and the *jihād* is going well.

We call upon all Muslims, and especially the Muslims of ISWAP, which is a province of the Islamic State, led by Abu Muhammad Abubakar b. Muhammad al-Shekawi, to not be deceived by the lies of the unbelievers. Hasten and immigrate to the Islamic State. Hasten to follow Allah and His Messenger. Hasten to pledge allegiance to the Caliph Abu Bakr al-Baghdadi. Hold strongly to Allah's path. Hold fast to the rope of Allah. Hold fast to the Qur'ān and the ways of Allah's Messenger.

Exert forbearance during any adversity that may come from the unbelievers, for when you follow Allah's path, adversity comes little by little. The good thing is that those who have piety and faith in Allah will be victorious at the end. Allah said in His Holy Qur'ān that "those who leave the land of the unbelievers and immigrate to the Islamic state, to work for *jihād*, and are killed, Allah will indeed bless them with the best type of prosperity." Allah is the highest blessing who rightly rewards the one who has worked to promote His path. Allah will indeed place them in paradise. May Allah, glory to Him, accept us. Hasten to pledge allegiance to the caliph! Hasten to join the Islamic State!

[*Video reverts to the earlier section showing the members of ISWAP placing each other's hands around the speaker and repeating the pledge of allegiance to the Islamic State.*]

68

MESSAGE FROM THE *MUJĀHIDIN* IN WEST AFRICA TO THE *MUJĀHIDIN* IN SOMALIA

BY WILĀYAT GHARB IFRIQIYA

(14 OCTOBER 2015)

[Trans.: Abdulbasit Kassim]
Available at: http://jihadology.net/2015/10/14/new-video-message-from-
the-islamic-state-message-from-the-mujāhidīn-in-west-africa-to-the-
mujāhidīn-in-somalia-wilayat-gharb-ifriqiyyah/

Swearing allegiance to the Islamic State meant that to some extent Boko Haram began to be utilized by Islamic State as a proxy to obtain the allegiance of other African Salafi-jihadi groups. Although elements of AQIM and other West African groups had proved to be open to swearing, al-Shabab in Somalia thus far have proved to be resistant (for the most part—several sections of al-Shabab have declared allegiance). Boko Haram in this video is trying to exert its influence on behalf of ISIS. The influence of this video will later yield a result for the Islamic State as Shaykh ʿAbd al-Qadir Muʾmin, Abu Nuʿman al-Yentari and other members of al-Shabab pledged allegiance on 22 October 2015 to the leader of the Islamic State, Abu Bakr al-Baghdadi, thus switching their allegiance from al-Shabab to the Islamic State.[1]

[Standard Islamic opening]

And thereafter:

This is a word of advice and testament to our *mujāhidīn* brothers in Somalia, both the migrants and the helpers. We are calling on you to acknowledge that swearing allegiance to the caliph of the Muslims is an obligation. We are calling on you to declare your allegiance to the Caliph of the Muslims, Shaykh Abu Bakr Al-Baghdadi. The Holy Prophet Muhammad said: "Whoever dies without declaring allegiance to an imam [caliph] dies the death of ignorance (*jāhiliyya*)." It is obligatory on every Muslim, especially the *mujāhidīn*, to come under the authority of the Muslim community and its imam based on the saying of the Prophet to Ḥudhayfa b. al-Yaman: "Cling to the mainstream of the Muslims and its imam."

My brothers, you should also realize that coming together under the authority of a single imam brings numerous benefits for the Muslims. Among the benefits is the unification of the Muslims' voice. The Muslims will be able to project a single voice to the world. The unification will also put an end to partisanship, tribalism, racism and other ills that have become pervasive among the Muslims all over the world. Another benefit of the declaration of allegiance to the caliph of the Muslims is the rage to which it will bring the unbelievers, and the strength it will bestow on the *mujāhidīn*. You should know that the *sharī'a* of Islam forbids the multiplicity of different congregations, or different declarations of allegiance after the installation of an imam.

The *sharī'a* of Islam frowns upon such division and multiplicity. My brothers, please understand this point clearly. We are speaking the truth from where we are and it is obligatory upon every believer based on the saying of Allah: "O believers, whoever of you renounces his religion, Allah will certainly bring forth a people whom He loves and they love Him, humble towards the faithful, but mighty towards the unbelievers. They fight in the way of Allah and do not fear anybody's reproach." (Q5:54)

O brothers! We are calling you to follow the examples of your brothers who have declared their allegiance to the Caliph of the Muslims Shaykh Abu Bakr Al-Baghdadi, like your brothers in Sinai, Libya, Yemen and West Africa from JASDJ. In conclusion, I want you to exercise patience and endurance with each other. We should be careful not to think that we are not identical in tribe or nationalities. All Muslims are brothers because this is what Allah says: "Surely the believers are brothers." (Q49:10) I will end this message by extending our greetings to the Caliph of the Muslims Shaykh Abu Bakr al-Baghdadi and other *mujāhidīn* in the Islamic State. O Allah! Show us the truth and give us the strength to follow it. O Allah! Show us the falsehood and give us the strength to avoid it. O Allah! We pray to you and you are the Lord of the worlds.

69

MESSAGE FROM SHEKAU

(22 MARCH 2016)

[Trans.: Abdulbasit Kassim]
Available at: https://www.youtube.com/watch?v=HWzhr7dOyrk

After a half-year's hiatus, Shekau reemerged in a video which was erroneously inter-
preted by the Nigerian media as a call from him to end the group's campaign and
embrace peace. As the translation below shows, there is nothing in the video that suggests
surrender or an end to the violence. Rather, Shekau was simply acknowledging that he
received messages from his followers, while extending greetings to them and encouraging
them to be steadfast. There are some reasons to doubt the authenticity of this video. First,
unlike other videos of Boko Haram (after it became ISWAP), this video was posted on
YouTube. Second, the poor quality of this video stands out amidst the upgrade in Boko
Haram's video quality. This video shares more features with Boko Haram videos from
the period 2010–14. Third, Shekau also refers to himself as the leader of JASDJ, a title
defunct after the group's amalgamation with the Islamic State, and Shekau's becoming
emir of Islamic State West African Province. Fourth, the soft-spoken style of Shekau's
delivery in this video is quite different from his bombastic and taunting style in past
videos. The doubts surrounding the release of this video were laid to rest when the video
was countered almost immediately by another video produced by the media department
of ISWAP (see text 70).

"It was by a mercy from Allah that you dealt leniently with them; for had you been
cruel and hard-hearted they would have dispersed from around you. So, pardon

them, ask Allah's forgiveness for them and consult them in the conduct of affairs. Then, when you are resolved, trust in Allah; Allah indeed loves those who trust [in Him]." (Q3:159) [Standard Islamic opening]

And thereafter:

My honored brothers—may the peace and blessings of Allah be upon you. All praise be to Allah. O honored brothers! By Allah's permission, I have received your messages and have listened to your statements. I am Abu Muhammad Abubakr b. Muhammad al-Shekawi, the imam of JASDJ. I have received your messages and statements from my brothers, *mujāhidīn* fighting for Allah's cause without fearing anybody's reproach [Q5:54]. I am sending my greetings to you and reminding you to keep nurturing your souls with the fear of Allah. We pray to Allah to purify us and our intentions—accepting us to the highest place in paradise as *mujāhidīn* and martyrs. And may the peace and blessings of Allah be upon you. This is my face, my speech, and my message to you, my brothers.

My brothers, this is my brief message to you. It is a brief message which does not go beyond greetings. My joy and gratitude is unbounded such that I don't even know what to say, except that I say: may Allah reward you with goodness for all your deeds which are solely geared towards seeking His reward. Your greetings and messages have reached me from all of you who are working for Allah's cause—for example in the town we used to call the "land of Islam."[1] I also acknowledge all your efforts to unite with the army working for Allah's cause and His Prophet so that we can all stand before Allah and explain how we conducted our lives particularly in this era and condition in which we have found ourselves. We follow the teachings of our Prophet, who is the leader of all Messengers. We follow the Qur'ān, the most revered revealed book. We follow the Qur'ān and the Sunna.

We pray to Allah to grant us steadfastness to do what is right and work towards the right path. Allah knows best. This message is a message of greetings, gratitude and for you to see my face. Apart from this message, your messenger will relay to you any other message you are expecting to hear. My intention for this message is that if someone [an enemy] hears it, he will not hear more than greetings between us. For other things, only Allah knows, just as you have agreed and answered. For me, I have completed my part. This message I am sending to you, I did it purposely for you to see me. And may Allah protect our ranks from the hypocrites' infiltration of and from Satan, and may He grant us steadfastness on the path of worshipping Him. And may the peace and blessings of Allah be upon His Prophet.

From your brother in Allah,

Abubakar Abu Muhammad b. Muhammad al-Shekawi

70

"INVESTIGATE"

BY WILĀYAT GHARB IFRIQIYĀ

(31 MARCH 2016)

[Trans.: Abdulbasit Kassim]
Available at: http://jihadology.net/2016/03/31/new-video-message-from-the-islamic-state-investigate-wilayat-gharb-ifriqiyyah/

This video was released a week after text 69, which was erroneously interpreted as signs of weakness and defeat on ISWAP's part. In this video, the speaker, making a first-time appearance, spoke of the resilience of the members of his group in the face of the campaign by the coalition forces. He also attempted to disprove the media reports that the group had been defeated, saying this is a false victory proclamation contrary to the reality on the battleground. He further threatened those who fight against the group, and specifically mentioned the Nigerian President Buhari. It is noteworthy that the speaker identified Shekau as the leader of the group, and reaffirmed the group's allegiance to the Islamic State. This video goes a long way to prove that although the coalition forces might have technically defeated Boko Haram or ISWAP, the group does not see itself as being defeated.

[Standard Islamic opening] Verily, Allah's enemies hold conferences and meetings seeking solutions for the hole of despair and dejection in which they found themselves. They think they can free their proxies and allies from the caliphate's soldiers' assault. They gathered all their forces and threatened on the media, radio and internet that they will defeat the soldiers of monotheism, who have proven, by the grace of Allah, their resilience in the way they harm their enemies, and the losses they inflict in [terms of] lives, wealth and ammunitions in Nigeria, Cameroon, on the Niger border or Chad.

Their allied forces were shocked when they saw the *mujāhidīn*, and surprised by the steadfastness of the monotheists in the face of their crusader campaigns. Despite the alliance and cooperation with their apostate and Shi'ite minions it did not benefit them. The monotheists, on the other hand, have reaffirmed that victory is from none other than Allah. These campaigns have imbued them with steadfastness and determination to continue this path, until they purify the land from the unbelievers' filth and those who turn their backs on Islam.

It is a tradition of the unbelievers and apostates at every time and generation that when they feel hopeless in stopping the spread of the truth, they rush to organize schemes and spread lies against the *mujāhidīn* as a means of hindering people from following Allah's path. They follow the method of their polytheist ancestors who schemed day and night against Allah's prophets, the messengers and those who followed them, but did not attain their goal because Allah's cunning against them was faster. Allah says: "They schemed a scheme and we schemed a scheme, while they were unaware." (Q27:50)

Neither the unbelievers nor their apostate minions could extinguish Allah's light. This is the reason why they follow the path of hypocrisy by using the media and journalists to achieve a false victory. They portray Allah's enemies as men of determination, power and sternness, while hiding the true reality of the enemy, especially when they encounter the caliphate's soldiers face to face. If you do not believe us, ask those who fought us at Gudumbali and Geidam.[1] We in the West African Province say to all disbelieving sects: "Agree upon a course of action with your associates; then let not that course of action be a burden to you; then pass to me [your decision] and give me no respite." (Q10:71)

As a result, the [battle] days are between us. You will see our strength and sternness. Our war with you will not end by Allah's permission until you worship Allah and accept Islam. If you reject this and prefer arrogance, we will go forth under the command of the governor of West African Province, Shaykh Abu Muhammad Abubakar al-Shekawi, may Allah preserve him. Consequently, we will make your lives bitter: make your wives become widows and your children orphans. Your condition will become akin to the condition of the soldiers of the *ṭāghūt* in Iraq, Sham, Libya, Khurasan [Afghanistan] and Sinai, by Allah's permission.

You should know that your spreading of lies and rumors will only give us more reassurance that we are in accord with the truth. Therefore, you should know there will be no appeasement, pacification, peace or security if you fight Allah's religion: "We are quit of you and what you worship apart from Allah. We disbelieve in you.

Enmity and hatred have arisen between you and us forever, till you believe in Allah alone." (Q60:4)

We say to the *ṭāghūt* in Nigeria, Buhari, you should know that the Christians will not benefit you, nor will Allah's enemies benefit you, because they are weak and incapacitated. They will not be able to achieve what you want, nor will they come to your rescue if the *mujāhidīn's* knives reach your neck. You will regret, but at that time your regret will be of no benefit. Therefore, repent before we punish you—you should learn from the fate of your fellow *ṭāghūt*.[2] You will understand what we are saying in this land soon, in Aso Rock and Villa,[3] you shall see.

We say to the Muslims wherever you are what Allah said: "O believers, if a sinner brings you a piece of news, make sure you do not cause some people distress unwittingly, and so regret subsequently what you have done." (Q49:6) Be wary of their media, radio and internet, because they all follow the unbelievers' path and are managed by them. They broadcast only what suits the unbelievers' interests.

We say to the soldiers of the caliphate and the Caliph of the Muslims, Abu Bakr al-Baghdadi al-Qurayshi, may Allah preserve him: keep on with steadfastness, steadfastness, patience and patience. Victory comes with an hour's patience. Therefore, be firm in the face of your enemy, and seek help from Allah against them. Always mention the saying: "Allah suffices for us, and He is the Best Disposer of our affairs." This is the message that Allah decreed we would deliver now.

71

MESSAGE TO THE WORLD
BY ABUBAKAR SHEKAU

(3 AUGUST 2016)

[Trans.: Abdulbasit Kassim]
Available at: http://jihadology.net/2016/08/03/new-audio-message-from-abu-bakr-al-shekau-message-to-the-world/

In al-Naba newsletter no. 41 (of ISIS), Abu Mus'ab al-Barnawi, who had previously appeared in text 53 as the spokesman for JASDJ, was interviewed as the new governor of ISWAP.[1] In the interview, al-Barnawi discussed jihād in West Africa and how Boko Haram was founded, the reasons for its pledge to ISIS, and the nature of the war between the group and the MNJTF (coalition forces from Nigeria, Niger, Benin, Chad and Cameroon) together with the Civilian JTF. In addition, al-Barnawi also made clear the group's mission against Christianizing activities in Africa and answers some of the suspicions raised by Islamic scholars regarding Boko Haram. Although al-Barnawi mentioned Shekau as Yusuf's successor, he did not mention Shekau's present status or position. Shekau had previously been known as the governor of ISWAP. A day after al-Barnawi interview's was published, Shekau issued a ten-minute audio speech in Arabic and Hausa where he railed against his demotion from governor and the promotion of al-Barnawi as the new governor. In stating his refusal to follow al-Barnawi, Shekau explained the ideological differences between himself and al-Barnawi—particularly concerning the issue of judging Muslims who live in a land of unbelief. When al-Barnawi was asked a question about this issue in the al-Naba *interview he stated that:*

441

Even though Islam is not at their core, anyone who manifests Islam outwardly without any of the [ten] nullifiers [of Islam][2] is exempt from takfir, *not to speak of making his blood permissible. We have fought this extremism and we are still fighting it. On that basis, we do not target ordinary people's mosques, who are outwardly Muslims, nor their markets.*

On the other hand, Shekau believes that a Muslim who lives in a land of unbelief must disassociate himself from unbelievers and fight them in the land of unbelief. If he does not, then he himself is an unbeliever. In this audio, Shekau narrated how he sent eight letters to al-Baghdadi explaining the ideological difference between himself and al-Barnawi, but received no response. The altercation between Shekau and al-Barnawi demonstrates the differences in the Boko Haram hierarchy which had earlier led to the appearance of Ansaru.[3]

[Arabic version]

[Standard Islamic opening] A message from Abu Muhammad b. Muhammad Abubakar al-Shekawi. the imam of JASDJ in West Africa in the Islamic State, may the peace and blessings of Allah be upon you.

To the honored shaykh, the caliph of the Muslims, may Allah preserve and care for you, I ask Allah that this message reaches you while you are in the best of conditions, and that He will conquer through your hands and guide you to what is good. Amen.

My brothers in Allah, I received a message you sent regarding the selection of a new governor. My brothers, Abu Mus'ab al-Barnawi and those with him are saying that if a Muslim enters a land of unbelief, but does not manifest his enmity to the unbelievers there, he is not an unbeliever. However, we say that such a person is an unbeliever. Afterwards, they said that if he [a Muslim] does not show his enmity to the *ṭāghūt* who rules by [something] other than Allah's revealed law, he is not an unbeliever. However, we say that such a person is an unbeliever.

We found this in Allah's Book and the Sunna of His Messenger. We wish to follow the Sunna of our Messenger. Patience after patience, O shaykh! It is obligatory upon you to show us the truth of the matter in the Book, the Sunna and according to the understanding of the forefathers. Allah knows my brothers in Allah. As a result, we cannot follow a person who commits a major [act of] unbelief or polytheism, knowingly, with an explanation, and not based on misinterpretation. No, this is not possible. You do not know the condition of this group, yet we have sent you many letters, eight letters [in total], to show us the truth of this matter in the Book and the Sunna. However, you did not say anything [in response] nor did you answer, except for us to hear this news [of substitution].[4]

This is what the emir, the Caliph of the Muslims Abu Bakr al-Baghdadi, has ordered, Abu Mus'ab al-Barnawi. You have known him, and those with him. I sent you many letters explaining that their ideologies are false. This is so because their ideologies are based upon *irjā'* [postponement of judgment]. You asked me about this, so I responded to you in the languages of [Qur'ānic] verses and *ḥadīth*, and yet

I received no answer. Then I heard what I had known, that he engages in major unbelief and polytheism, and there is no misconception or misinterpretation. I heard this news which came from you, so what do you say of those who do this?

[*Hausa version*]

All praise be to Allah, and may Allah's peace and blessings be upon him after whom there is no prophet. I am the person known, by Allah's permission, as Abu Muhammad b. Muhammad Abubakar al-Shekawi. I am sending this message to the Muslims in their entirety in the world, including those who can understand Hausa, Arabic—or the message can be translated to any other languages for clear understanding. We have received the news being circulated and attributed to the people to whom we had earlier pledged our allegiance. Even though we are not against them, based on the message we heard in the world radio, we still hold our own ideology.

We know those people with whom we differ, and I have written on this issue long ago. We wrote up to eight letters between nine and ten pages long explaining that the ideology they [al-Barnawi] believe is based on *irjā'*. This is so because I am against the principle that someone can enter and live in the land of the unbelievers without manifesting publicly his enmity or hatred towards them. Where is the disassociation of which Allah has described in the Qur'ān?

Such a person, according to my belief, is not a Muslim—and this is the belief of the Sunnis which we hold. On the other hand, for them, they have agreed that it is permissible for a person to live in the land of unbelief while engaging in trading, even if they are not among those Allah has excused—such as weak people, those who are coerced, or those against whom you are on guard (cf. Q3:28). Their statement is doubt-free, so for us we cannot say it is only lip-service; it also extends to their actions. By Allah's permission, this is my explanation.

I want the world to know that we are still holding firm, believing in our ideology which is solely based on the Qur'ān and the Sunna of His Messenger. We will not turn aside or revolt, but will continue to remain upon Allah's path. It is compulsory to follow Allah's Book and the Sunna of His Messenger. We will follow it to the end. This is our position and we are still on the path of JASDJ. And may Allah help us and strengthen us to remain steadfast upon His path.

No matter what they call us, if you like you can call us Kharijites or Murji'a or whatever name you wish, even the Prophet said: "So try your guile on me, all of you; then then do not give me any respite." (Q11:55) They also told the Prophet that: "you are indeed a madman." (Q15:6) No matter what they call us, we remain what we are. No matter what they call us, what we aspire to achieve is to justify our ideology in the Qur'ān, the Prophet's *ḥadīth* and the understanding of the forefathers. This is ultimate because we have not turned aside.

In the future, we will not accept any emissary except one to whose sincerity we can attest upon Allah's path. In the first place, we sat [in discussion] but I was deceived.

They said I should write my ideology down, so if there is a mistake they will point it out and return it. Today, I found out that there are those following the unbelievers' principles, and they want me to follow them, even though the Prophet has prohibited us. "There is no obedience to a creature [human] resulting from the disobedience to the Creator." We are here upon Allah's path in the Islamic caliphate implementing the laws of Islam. We will continue to work for Allah's cause. This is our goal. Whoever caused this, there is no problem, if Allah wishes He will direct him onto the right path—otherwise may Allah protect us from his mischief.

72

EXPOSÉ: AN OPEN LETTER TO ABUBAKAR SHEKAU BY MAMMAN NUR

(4 AUGUST 2016)

[Trans.: Abdulbasit Kassim]

Available at: https://soundcloud.com/saharareporters/2016-08-04-audio-00000003-1

This video is a scathing attack upon Shekau and the direction in which he has led Boko Haram by Mamman Nur, one of the oldest veterans of the movement (see text 18). From summer 2015 through spring 2016 Boko Haram carried out a long string of suicide attacks, usually using young female suicide attackers, against mosques, market places, and refugee centers throughout the territories in northeastern Nigeria and northern Cameroon that it had controlled the previous year. Most probably, unless this was purely nihilistic violence, Shekau viewed these attacks as punishment for apostasy on the part of Boko Haram's former subjects. Those numerous attacks against refugee centers are particularly indicative, as most of the people living in them are originally from towns and villages that were controlled by Boko Haram and are still too dangerous to return to. Nur attacks Shekau's strategy in terms that are strongly reminiscent of al-Zawahiri's attack upon al-Zarqawi in 2005,[1] namely that it is Islamically problematic to deliberately target Muslim civilians, as well as being bad strategy overall. Most fascinatingly, Nur presents the inner workings of the core Boko Haram group around Shekau, in which the leader is presented as an arbitrary and capricious person, indifferent to civilian and mili-

tary needs, who regularly murders close associates for trivial offenses. Nur knew what he was talking about, as he apparently only barely avoided this fate himself. The description below is the closest yet to what life, at least in the upper echelons of the Boko Haram camp, was, and still is, like. It is obvious that Shekau has become drunk with power, and degenerated into a Joseph Kony-like figure, holding court in the Sambisa Forest, periodically killing off friends and supporters, and railing against everyone who opposes him.

I seek refuge with Allah from the accursed Satan, from his suffocation, his arrogance, and his evil insinuations. In the name of Allah, the Most Beneficent, the Most Merciful. [Standard Islamic opening]

[*Citations of Q3:102, 4:1, 33:70–71*]

And thereafter:

The truest of words is the Book of Allah and the best of guidance is the guidance of Muhammad. The worst of matters are those that are newly invented; every newly-invented matter is an innovation and every innovation is an error, and every error is in the Fire. And thereafter, may the peace and blessings of Allah be upon you.

We are grateful to Allah, who gave us the opportunity of understanding His religion in every nook and cranny, and every day, whether it is hot or warm. We thank Allah for giving us the opportunity of understanding the religion. Thereafter, this is a speech we will present, by Allah's permission, or should I say a [video] cassette as a message to Shekau. This is so because he released a cassette previously, so we were waiting for him to release it before we would release ours. We will also call the name of our own cassette "Exposé." The same way it has become a habit for him to expose people, we will also expose him. This is the tradition of the religion.

Whenever you reach a stage in which you begin to display egotism believing that there is nobody who can speak to you, Allah will bring people who will do so. Now, Allah has brought those people. Prior to this period, he [Shekau] would come out, saying whatever he felt like saying. No one would say anything as to whether what he said is true or false, right or wrong; everyone would just listen and say, "hmm, the imam has spoken," and proceed immediately to act.

Today, the reverse is the case, because the protocol has changed, it has turned its wrapper and is different. Just as I said in my previous admonition, Adnani said that: "Whoever changes, we will also change him." This is the tradition of the religion. After all, the religion is neither your father's or mother's, nor is it our father's or mother's. The religion belongs to Allah alone. Whoever plays with it will face the consequences alone.

We have promised Allah that we will worship Him alone and say the truth in all circumstances. That is what brought us to this point. He released a cassette saying that he has killed and will continue to kill because he has evidence [justifying] killing. We are not afraid of his threat of killing, because we agreed and came out [to fight] for the same purpose, namely killing. He has forgotten that we just came out of his room. If we had intended to kill him, we would have done so; since he was thinking that the security guards surrounding him are loyal to him, whereas they are loyal to us, not him. Now, in his house, we have the people who are loyal to us, unbeknownst to him. However, if he attempts to strike at us, they will strike him down there. That is how Allah carries out His affairs.

They consulted at night where he said that he heard about our decision to flee and emigrate (*hijra*) away from him. That is why he had tight security and specifically mentioned that if Mamman Nur comes in, they should allow him to enter, but he should not be allowed to leave. I entered and then walked out. You cannot play with Allah's affairs. It is not only me who walked out; eight other people did the same, even though they are members of his retinue. They walked out with me and we all came here. Two other people are on their way.

Therefore, the religion is beyond anyone's pride. You should not display selfishness. Once you start deceiving Allah's slaves,[2] who are practicing the religion with sincerity, there will surely be a day of exposé. Today is one of those days of exposé. We will practice our religion regardless—even if we will die, we will not abandon our religion. If you wish, you can kill or slaughter or eat [our flesh]. Did you not notice, Shekau, that we left, but our children and women are still in your house? Do you think we are afraid of death? We did not take anything, even a bag, except our guns. Whoever stands in our way, we will do away with him, but we will not strike at you. We will not strike anyone, but go and practice the religion.

In short, we were waiting for him to explain to us, since he said his cassette is on its way for everyone to hear. Before then, you know misconception is a delicate issue, so if we do not clear it up, many people who love the religion will be led astray. They will tell you that this person should be killed, and shedding his blood is permissible, whereas that is false. Allah in the Qur'ān has forbidden the killing of a soul without just cause, and I am not the person who said that.

The same way Allah has given us the permission to kill the *ṭāghūt*, even though they are His slaves, Allah says we should kill them so also are other slaves whom He forbade us from killing. In the Qur'ān Allah says: "And that you do not kill the living soul which Allah has forbidden you to kill except for a just cause." (Q6:151) Allah's Messenger said on the day of Mecca's conquest: "Which month is this?" They answered him that it is Muharram.[3] Then he said listen: "Your blood, your properties, and your honor are sacred to one another like the sanctity of this day of yours, in this city of yours, and in this month of yours."

Allah's Messenger forbade the spilling of blood among ourselves. He said: "The blood of a Muslim is not permissible, except if he commits any of three sins; the married man who committed illicit sexual relations." He is expected to be killed openly, not in a hidden place. It should be done openly, listen to what I am saying. He knows what I will say, it should be done openly. Everyone will witness the execution and the crime of Allah's slave will be explained to the people before punishing him

447

according to Allah's law. Everyone who loves the religion will be happy and not feel resentment. However, anywhere you see that they killed someone in a hidden place; you should know that there is something wrong on the ground. This is not the Islamic religion as we studied it.

For instance, when I entered his [Shekau's] abode, he called me and said that I should pledge allegiance to him, following his opinion. I thought all of you did the same, I said: "Yes, I pledge allegiance to follow your opinion." What if I said no and he had killed me? Would I be able to explain this to you? Later, I realized that his opinions cannot be followed. It will not work. Then we said: "We will not follow his opinion; rather we will follow Allah's Book and the Sunna of His Messenger, even if they will kill us, eat us or roast us after we decline to follow his opinions." We cannot allow these slaves of Allah to be in darkness. This message will reach him inside his house at Sambisa [Forest], by Allah's permission. We have couriers who will deliver it on our behalf. Whether he likes it or not, the message will reach him and he must listen to it. This is the nature of our affairs. I hope it is understood.

Allah has forbidden the killing of a soul except for a just cause. Allah's Messenger said: "It is better for the heavens and the earth to explode or be destroyed than killing a single believer." Surprisingly, this slave of Allah, Allah has tested him with the love of killing people. Don't you hear his cassette where he said: "I will kill, I will kill."[4] So if you kill, will you also live forever? You are also going to die. "And we did not grant immortality to any human before you. If you die, are they then immortal? Every living soul shall taste death, and we test you by evil and good as a temptation and unto us you shall be returned." (Q21:34–35) You should go ahead and kill, but sooner or later you will also die. No one will die unless the appointed time for him has come.

For example, look at us sitting here because the time of our death has not come and we are still alive. Look at Mallam Habib; he is sitting here with us. Look at Abu Fatima, who was also sent to be killed, he is here with us. Look at Ba Idrissa and Mustapha; Ikrimaya was sent to kill all of them, they are here sitting with us.

Whoever is not killed by Allah, you cannot kill him. Likewise, the person who Allah wishes to kill, even if no one lays hands upon him, he will die. That is the reason why when someone said: "I will kill you," another person replied to him: "Why are you in such haste?" Do you understand the Hausa used in this phrase? If it is time for me to die, I will die, and you do not have to kill me now. Is it not like that? So, slave of Allah, look at the numerous verses and *ḥadīths* that forbade the killing of believers. We promised Allah that we will practice the Islamic religion—that is why we left our parents, family, cars, houses and all our possessions and we emigrated to settle down in this forest to worship Allah. Therefore, how would we understand that we are not worshipping Allah; they are sinning against Allah and not worshipping Him, but then you expect us to support you?

Some issues are even related to creed and ideology. This man [Shekau] has introduced new ideology into our group that we do not know. For example, we were sitting in one of the mutual consultations we had. Well, I had initially mentioned that this speech will expose so many things, so there is no need to conceal the discussions in our consultation. In one of the consultations, they asked him, the Mallam who asked him, though you do not know him, his name is Mallam Mustapha Jere. He asked him that there are some people who were being chased by brothers [Boko Haram], so they fled, entering the unbelievers' land, fearing the brothers will harm them. What is the position concerning those people? He [Shekau] said: "They are unbelievers." He [Mustapha] said: "No, they are not unbelievers. They did not choose unbelief; they only fled out of fear." He [Shekau] said: "They are unbelievers." He [Mustapha] said: "Look at the explanation of Ibn Hazm."

Then I brought the explanation of Ibn Hazm, as perhaps he does not know that inside under the section of *al-walā' wa-l-barā*, Ibn Hazm said:

> The one who flees to the land against which we are fighting (land of unbelief) because he is afraid of injustice to which they might subject him in the Islamic state—[when] he did not fight the Muslims, did not help the unbelievers against the Muslims or among the Muslims, did not find anyone that can give him protection, there is no penalty upon him because he is in a state of necessity and was coerced, otherwise he would prefer to stay in the Islamic state.[5]

[Knowledge is an antidote to ignorance] This is an issue that deals with creed. Therefore, since it deals with creed, the ruling on *takfir* should not be dictated by you, because Islam is not your personal possession that you can admit or expel whoever you want. That is not the nature of our affair. It is only Allah who can dictate who is a Muslim and an unbeliever based upon evidence in the Book and the Sunna. This is the reason why when you travel and meet someone who says he is a Muslim, you do not have the right to call him an unbeliever, except if you find evidence against him. Allah says, "O believers, if you journey in the way of Allah, be discerning and do not say to him who greets you: 'you are not a believer,' seeking the fleeting goods of the present life. For with Allah are abundant gains." (Q4:94)

As a result, we will speak on what is certain in the religion. Why do you think we fled with our religion? We fled with our religion because *hijra* is an obligation and you must flee with your religion to a place where you can practice it. Have you forgotten that when we were in Yerwa,[6] Mallam Muhammad Yusuf delivered a lecture and an open letter the same way this lecture is an open letter to you?[7] Is it not so? In the open letter, he sent to the [Nigerian] president of that era, he said: "If you prevent us from practicing the religion, we will emigrate to a place we can practice our religion, but if there is no such place, we shall fight against you." So Shekau, what we are saying now is for you to leave us to practice our religion. We did not strike at you, your house and possessions, so you should leave us to practice the religion. If you decide to strike at us, we will also certainly strike back at you.

We are not the only people who seek the truth. There are many of Allah's slaves who want the same, even inside your house, your area to which you emigrated, and left us here, and even among your ten security guards, whom you selected. We have those who are loyal to us among them, but you are unaware. [We are not afraid of death] Engineer, you should listen, he does not know that as he is searching for a report on us, we likewise have his report. He sent his people to find out whether we have moved to another place. We are not there and did not go anywhere; we are here closer to you. This problem was caused by issues relating to creed.

Secondly, they are fighting people who are not supposed to be fought. For example, around the area of two rivers,[8] there is a town upon where hoisted the flags, yet they go there, fight them and confiscate their property. We were in the consultation meeting when he was informed and was admonished, but he refused to take any counter-measures. This is because according to his ideology, whoever is not with him are unbelievers and shedding their blood is permissible. We do not agree with such an interpretation and never have we understood Islam in that way. I hope it is understood.

Just like that they appropriate their property; they also find and kill little children. In some cases, they will find the yam-sellers in the towns[9] and detonate bombs amongst them. We are not bothered by the yam-sellers. Rather, we are bothered with killing the *ṭāghūt* for now. When we finish with the *ṭāghūt*, the yam-sellers will even fetch water for you. O Shekau! You don't have to kill them. Likewise, look at the way they are planting explosives and bombing the people even in the mosques! Look at the churches [as targets]! Look at the [military] barracks! This is a waste of Allah's property because we are not the ones who bought those explosives with our money. That is Allah's property, and He will ask us how it was utilized. Allah will ask you because we have disassociated ourselves from your actions, unless you repent. Today, if you say you repent and withdraw from those obnoxious misunderstandings, we will come back and say: "Shekau, we are with you, and you are our leader." Before now you were a leader, so do not start calling us rebels. No, you are indeed the rebel, because you refuse to follow the instruction of your leaders in Iraq [ISIS].

Thirdly, he is interpreting the Qur'ānic verses with his own opinion, and they spread those opinions via cassettes. For example, the saying of Allah: "Only those who do not believe in Allah and the Last Day will ask you [for exemption] and their hearts are in doubt. Thus, they vacillate in their state of doubt." (Q9:45) Shekau took this verse and misinterpreted it. This verse is not speaking about permission for going out to war. Look at all the exegesis. The reason I am saying this is because Ba Idrissa went to meet him with a book, face to face, and showed him the exegesis. He [Idrissa] told him that his interpretation is contrary to the [standard] exegesis, yet he [Shekau] refused to withdraw his interpretation. Then he [Shekau] said whoever said his inter-pretation is contrary to the exegesis—he stared at us with his eyes, but we were unafraid of him.

This verse is speaking about the hypocrites who refused to go to war. If they com-mand such a person to go to war, he will withdraw and seek an exemption by specious objections like "my head is aching," "my wife is so-and-so" or "my house is so-and-so." He seeks exemptions to be left at home. The verse is referring to these types of people, not the people who want to go out for war, O Shekau! I hope it is understood.

Therefore, do not interpret the Qur'ān for us based on your own opinion. This is just one example. There are numerous examples of his opinionated interpretation of Qur'ānic verses. Likewise, *ḥadīth* not narrated by the Prophet, he [Shekau] will say the Prophet narrated it. Sometimes, he will say that the opinion is the opinion of the imam. It is Allah's Messenger who said it, and he will claim it is inside Bukhari. Where did the Prophet say that? Go and research, slave of Allah! Go and study and seek knowledge from those who have it. Allah says, "So ask those who have knowledge if you do not know." (Q16:43) Therefore, we are not too arrogant to ask questions concerning issues we do not know. That is exactly what makes the Sunnis forge ahead. Have you forgotten the bounty that Allah has bestowed upon you? Were you like this before now? Have you forgotten when you were sitting in front of the door of Ibn Taymiyya Mosque,[10] with just two cloths [to your name]? You practiced asceticism, sitting under the tree, learning and reading about the religion, while abstaining from worldly issues? However, now that you have assumed the position of leadership, you are carried away with power to the extent of killing your fellow Muslims? Many people have been killed.

Fourthly, they are executing punishments not based upon Islam in their caliphate. That is the reason we do not reside there. There was a cassette showing the execution of punishments that was filmed in the barracks. Mallam Sani executed that punishment, as he was his [Shekau's] devoted follower. If he does not know, it is better for him to say he does not know. They brought out a person who took a ram and amputated his hand. Go and look at the previous cassettes, you will see it. They gave this man eleven rams [to watch], but then he sold one of them. They caught him and amputated his hand. No, this is a breach of trust and it does not call for amputation because it is different from stealing. Go and read Allah's Book and the Sunna of the Prophet for verification.

Likewise, in Bama, they executed different punishments unsanctioned by Allah. There was an instance we were sitting in the same place; I, Habib, Aliyu, Mallam Chari, Mallam Tahiru, five of us, and him, Shekau. Mallam Tahiru narrated to him that some of the slaves we captured and held in Bama, there are some among our people who abducted the female children and married them. When he opened his mouth responding, he said: "They should be killed." Eleven slaves of Allah were killed based on his command—all in the name of punishment, by stoning to death. Among the people killed are those who did not abduct the women from where they were kept, but rather married them from their parents' houses. You should read the Book, because this is a wrong judgment.

Were you not the person saying that the execution of a punishment can be rejected if there is a misconception? These people got married and did not commit illicit sexual relations. Yet, you went ahead apprehending these slaves of Allah, and stoned them to death to the point where one of them said: "If you execute this punishment upon us, you should know that you will never have peace, not just in the caliphate, but even your stay in the forest will not be peaceful." This is exactly what happened. That is an example of how they executed a punishment unsanctioned by Islam upon those slaves of Allah.

There are many other cases, these are just few examples. For instance, what Abu Ziyada is doing is even beyond what should be spoken about. They will capture people, kill them or amputate their hands. They complained to him [Shekau] that they are executing punishments unsanctioned by Islam in his area. In fact, someone sent the evidence to him in a cassette, and another person reminded him by word of mouth, but he refused to take any counter-measures because they are satisfying his government's wishes.

Furthermore, look at the issue of killing a soul without just cause. That issue is the greatest of all. Were you not the person who killed Mallam Ba`ana Banki, O Shekau? This man, to defend himself, even sang a *nashīd* for him [Shekau]. Were you not the person who killed this Mallam? We were with this slave of Allah right from the period we were at Yerwa. He was the leader of Banki, and we emigrated and fled together.[11]

However, since he entered your place, he did not come out again. You killed him— or are you not the person who killed him? Have you forgotten when I was asking you, O Shekau? I told you that his wives do not know until today whether their husband is here or not. Then he [Shekau] asked me: "Do you mean Ba`ana Banki? I don't know his whereabouts and he should be considered a missing person." Is this not what you told me? Were you not the person who killed him? This man was killed because of issues pertaining to the ceasefire and identity cards, but even if he had forgotten, you should have enlightened him. If he is ignorant, you should teach him. Would you not explain to a person if he does not understand? Rather, you captured a slave of Allah and killed him.

The second person is Mallam Abdulmalik, were you not the person who killed him? They call him Abdulmalik's father, the old father, and he is the leader of Kaduna. You killed him. You are always saying that you have evidence for killing people, yet you only kill them in secret. All the people I will mention by name were killed in secret. In Islam, it is not permissible to kill in secret. Look, let me tell you, even if this person is an unbeliever—today even if it is Buhari, if you tell him to come to your place and promise not to harm him, if he believes you, [comes], and you harm him, Allah will punish you. This is the rule of Islam, even if it is Buhari.

If you are fighting a war with the unbelievers, what did Allah say: "And should you fear treachery from any people, throw back their treaty to them in like manner." (Q8:58) Allah is speaking about an unbeliever in this verse. Yet, you will lure a slave of Allah who sees you as a believer like himself, and then you will drag him close by, but then kill him in secret. Which judgment of Allah have you ever seen that they executed in secret? Has the Prophet ever made any judgment in secret? Did the Companions do the same? Which leader has ever done this? You are saying that you are protecting the public interest? Which type of public interest is that? When the Prophet passed judgment on the hypocrites, did he kill them or leave them? He left them and they were never killed in secret. This is not the religion, Mallam!

There is a slave of Allah called Abu Amr Falluja. He was also killed simply because he was together with Abdulmalik. When he entered [Shekau's house], he never came out. Here in your center, there is also Ba Gomna, who was your blood brother. You apprehended him and killed him with your own hand. This is the time for disclosure Mallam! You killed him because he bought a house at Amchide.[12] Why would you kill a person because he a bought a house? He [Shekau] killed him with his own hand—look at the person who went there together with him. Ba Gomna was sitting on a motorcycle, so when Shekau came he fired at him with a gun, got on the motorcycle, and drove around the center [camp]. When they asked him the whereabouts of Ba Gomna, he said that he has not returned from the battle. It is a lie, as you killed him. You were the person who killed Ba Gomna, even though he was your blood brother. Really, is it religion you are practicing, slave of Allah? You are killing the leaders of war, but also killing religious scholars.

You were the person who killed Mustapha Chad and Kaka Allai inside your center as well. Go and ask the women about Mustapha Chad and Kaka Allai—they will tell you that they were martyred in battle, whereas the people outside will tell you that they were stoned to death. It is a lie. You were the person who killed them in Fath al-Mubīn.[13] You did not kill them directly. You called them having Aliyu place Pepe[14] in the house in which you stayed at Fath al-Mubīn. Pepe was sitting inside the house until they called Mustapha Chad or Kaka Allai. As he was arriving, Pepe fired at him and then they buried him. They called the other person Kaka Allai, who thought that Mustapha Chad was inside. As he was arriving, Pepe was hiding, but he also shot and killed him. Was that not how they were killed? War commanders! Since you killed these slaves of Allah, did you achieve any more victory? Will you not think? "Do they not see that they are tried once or twice every year? Yet they neither repent nor take heed." (Q9:126) Will you not think and repent for your sin?

You are killing the slaves of Allah simply because Mallam Chari and others are back-biting and informed you that Mustapha Chad was trying to divide the people? Which type of division did this slave of Allah initiate? This is someone who does not know anything other than fighting. In this place when the unbelievers were feeling enraged at Baga, he took his car without a windscreen, and plunged towards the unbelievers. Did you ever do such a thing? You are there sitting down, while these slaves of Allah bring guns, cars and posessions for you, yet you still go ahead and kill them deceptively, then lie to the people that you did not kill them.

Or you will say that you have evidence for killing them. You should bring your evidence. "Bring forth your proof if you are truthful." (Q2:111) What was their crime in the first place? Secondly, we will have to verify whether your evidence is credible or not. Is that how they implement Islamic judgment? Who is above Islamic judgment among us? Even if it was you against whom a punishment was rendered, we would bring you out to the stake, and execute the judgement. O Shekau, you should listen! Your followers who are striving to follow you. You were the person who killed these slaves of Allah.

It was here Aliyu understood that if he does not repent, things will go bad. This was exactly what happened. You made him kill some people, but he refused. We will reveal everything. This is the actual speech. You told Aliyu to kill some people, but he said he will not kill them. You argued with him and afterwards you removed him as the head of the army, and attempted to kill him. Aliyu understood that there is no one who would kill him except Pepe, since they both worked together.

Immediately you brought Pepe closer; he already knew the plot. How will I be trapped by a trap I know well? Aliyu is not a madman. Afterwards, you came out and said: "They are hypocrites," including me and the other brothers. You said we were being sent by the *ṭāghūt*. No, Mallam, maybe you are the person being sent by the *ṭāghūt* to come here and kill our leaders for us. We are not the *ṭāghūt*'s people nor did the *ṭāghūt* send us. We believe in Allah's Book and the Sunna. Whoever follows Allah's Book and the Sunna, we will follow him, but the person who does not follow them should not expect us to follow.

It was here that Aliyu understood he has a problem, so he was telling me that Mallam [Shekau] has obliged Pepe to kill people. That was exactly what Aliyu told me. They also killed Abu RPG and two other brothers. What was the crime of Abu RPG? You are all witnesses and you heard his cassette. He [Shekau] said Abu RPG is back-biting. So, is there a verse or *ḥadīth* that says if a person is back-biting he should be killed? Bring the evidence and say it now! There is none. Even the Kharijites did not pass such a ruling, let alone the Sunnis, or any book of *ḥadīth* where there is a ruling that a person that back-bites should be killed. And if you think of it, Abu RPG made a tremendous impact on this group. He assembled guns and other weapons, yet you caught and killed him by saying that he is a back-biter.

Thereafter, Pepe confronted Aliyu and attempted to kill him. The event occurred here, even though many people did not know. Your master taught you the job! There is no way you can outsmart him. When he made an attempt to kill him, Aliyu moved his hand faster and took him by surprise. Before then Aliyu was saying that if he kills Pepe, there is no one that Mallam [Shekau] can assign to kill people apart from Pepe—not even those two hypocrites who followed him, Mallam Chari and Mallam Tahiru, who are also involved in killing the slaves of Allah.

It was here Aliyu killed Pepe before fleeing. After this incident, he passed a ruling that Aliyu should be killed because he killed Pepe. However, the main issue is not that Aliyu killed Pepe—and everyone knows it, including the people with him. He said it is *qisas*, meaning retaliation. Is that how they carry out retaliation? Is it on the road where you shoot a person retaliation? What is expected is for the person to be captured, and the rulings read to them before execution. That is the way of Allah's judgment.

Were you not the person who killed Mujahid, Mallam Umar and Abu Maryam? Abu Maryam and Mujahid were killed when they went to the area under his [Shekau's] control. What was the crime of these slaves of Allah? What did they do to you? Is it that a person cannot tell you the truth? That is the reason why, when we realized that we cannot tell you the truth while we were close to you, lest you kill us, we decided to go far away telling you truth. Now it is impossible for you to kill us, so we will kill each other. Our reliance is on Allah. If it is about the army, everyone has his own army. If you wish, you can send your spy to come into our gathering, and try to kill us. It is a lie! If you have a spy, you should come to us, and wait for the consequences.

You were the person who killed Mujahid, Abu Maryam and Abdullahi Hudu. What was the crime of this slave of Allah [Abdullahi Hudu]? He had a dream, so after narrating the dream he was killed. He had a dream where Mallam Muhammad Yusuf said Shekau should abandon capturing slaves, and focus on fighting, otherwise he will not be victorious. That was the dream and after he narrated it, he was killed. Is this the religion of Islam? You are telling people that Hajjaj b. Yusuf also killed people—both the Companions and those who followed them.[15] Therefore, even if a leader is killing people, it is obligatory to obey him. No, Hajjaj b. Yusuf killed in the presence of the people while you are killing people in secrecy. The two situations are not similar and you cannot justify your action by citing Hajjaj b. Yusuf. Hajjaj b. Yusuf openly reads the crime of an offender and sometimes after reading the crime or offence, the offender will plead that they have repented and they will seek for his pardon and he will pardon them.

Here, before Mallam Umar came into your territory, he sent someone to me and told me: "Mallam, please help me tell Mallam [Shekau] that I have repented, even if I previously made a mistake, and I am not one of the people he is accusing." I told him: "Mallam 'Umar, this is a serious issue, so if something should happen to a believer, he is not expected to implicate his brothers. I will give you advice. You should rely on Allah, so if you have good intentions, Allah will accept you. If your days are not yet over, they will not kill you. You should manage to go to their territory since you know the route and you should send them your message." He managed to go to their territory, and sent a message of apology.

Shekau said that even though he had sent a message of apology, he would still be judged for making a mistake. Thereafter, he sent Mallam Chari to him. Mallam Chari came here to ask Iya Hassan for a cable and a shovel, but Iya Hassan told him there was none. He [Chari] later came with him [Umar] here to the valley of that river close to Alanbitre,[16] where Mallam Chari shot this slave of Allah. You Mallam Chari, is that how Allah's judgment should be executed? Are you worshipping him [Shekau]? He is making the slaves of Allah kill one another.

Today, if you are asked to kill someone, then tomorrow someone else will be assigned to kill you. O Shekau! You should gain some sense and wisdom. We have disassociated ourselves from your sin and offence. We do not support them. All my previous actions, either my advice or silence on issues where I was expected to speak out, I have repented for them, and I will not return. I leave you in your work. If you fear Allah, you should repent and return to Allah.

All of us here have rebelled from all those actions of yours. We are together with the caliphal state. We are not together with the unjust state, the state of killing, or the state that does whatever it wishes. We are together with the caliphal state. We are together with our leader, Abu Bakr al-Baghdadi, the successor of Allah's Messenger. We are together with him. Therefore, if you say you will not follow him [al-Baghdadi], you should know that you are the rebel.

Before now there were many actions taken by you where you refused to obey them. How many commands did they give you which you refused to follow? You are deceiving people. You even said that you regret pledging allegiance to them because you were compelled. He [Shekau] said it in a [video] cassette. At that time, we advised him to pledge allegiance, since it is obligatory to pledge allegiance to the caliph once he appears in the world. It is obligatory for every group to pledge allegiance to the caliph. At that time, we explained this to him, so he knew if he did not go ahead pledging allegiance we would break away from him to pledge our allegiance. He feared that we would break away, so that was the reason he pledged allegiance.

Listen to this clearly. You have killed Allah's slaves. The people I mentioned are few, but there are others about whom it is better not to make any comment. Your followers assigned to kill these slaves of Allah, if they obey you knowingly, you should know that they have worshipped you. You can check *Kitāb al-tawḥīd*. There is a chapter in the book that addresses the topic concerning anyone who obeys the scholars or leaders in forbidding what Allah made permissible or making permissible what Allah has forbidden. What is the status of such a person? This person has taken those scholars and leaders as gods besides Allah.

So why do you order people to kill someone when Allah did not make shedding the blood of that person permissible? You even bragged that you have evidence for killing people so you submitted our names for being killed. We are unafraid of death. I am repeating it again. Before now, the purpose of our coming out [to fight] is solely for the sake of the religion and it is not just us alone.

The night they came to wake me up, Allah's slave said: "Mallam, please wake up, do not sleep in this center. Please hurry and leave, because they had a meeting and plan to arrest you." I told him: "Mallam, please calm down. I am not the only person in this center and if I plan to leave, I cannot leave alone, because I will need to leave with the people so that we are together." Thereafter, I proceeded to wake Allah's slaves. You cannot know them, as they are there inside your house. There is nothing you can do to them, by Allah's permission, since you have chosen the path of injustice. The people who are unjust will never be successful, both in this world and the hereafter, when they repent.

Listen to this carefully. [*On worshipping humans by excessive obedience.*] Now, if you tell them they are worshipping Shekau, they will say: "No, we are not worshipping him." So, listen to the Prophet's explanation. Do they not forbid what Allah made permissible, whereupon you follow them, and do they not make permissible what Allah forbade, whereupon you follow them? For example, a believer's blood which Allah forbade being shed, but Shekau made it permissible, yet you followed him. 'Adı b. Ḥātim [in a *ḥadīth*] said: "Yes, we follow them," so the Prophet said: "That is the meaning of worship." Mallam! We came out to worship Allah alone. You should not make permissible what Allah has forbidden, nor forbid what Allah made permissible.

[*Citing* Fatḥ al-majīd *on the issue.*][17] [*Story of Usāma b. Zayd who killed someone who converted to Islam at the last moment, and was rebuked for it by Muhammad.*] You have killed all the commanders and yet are complaining that they are not fighting. Are you the person who killed the fighters? You killed the strongmen—those who know the art of war and the tactics and strategy of war. You have killed all of them, but they are there in paradise by Allah's permission. They are all martyrs.

[Nur cites Q69:44–46] Therefore, you should not personalize Islam. You cannot order that someone be killed because that person insulted you. You cannot order that someone be killed because someone criticzed you. You cannot order that someone be killed because they narrated a dream to you. Even if he dreamt that you are among the people of hellfire, what is expected from you is to do good deeds, so that they will have another dream where you will be in paradise. Killing them should not be the next line of action. Everyone should practice the religion. We came out solely for the sake of practicing the Allah's religion. Those misconceptions of yours and the killings you committed, there is no gain in them. Abandon them. Is it understood?

In addition, another issue, aside from that of killings, is the indifference towards the welfare of weak and vulnerable people. You do not care. You left soldiers, students, and women in a state of hunger, thirst and agony. It is not as if there is no food. There is food but he refused to give it to them. We know he eats chicken. During the last rainy season, twenty children died daily because of starvation. Fifteen children died because of hunger. Look at the pictures that some brothers took of those children. Many of them died because of hunger under your government.[18]

Look at the cassette when they told him about it. He [Shekau] said he does not care even if 1,000 of them die. Look at the cassette and everyone can listen to it. [*Nur plays the cassette of Shekau.*] Shekau said: "We did not give money so children are dying. Let them die even in their thousands. Am I the person who held them? Bastards! I can only do what is within my power. Did I come here to take care of babies? I am here to build the religion, but you come here telling me nonsense! Who told you that I should take care of children? Who told you I should take care of the *mujāhidīn*? If this is the reason they are talking, then you will have to take care of me as well. Is that what the Qur'ān says? What is your concern? What is your problem?"

If you say you do not care, on our own part we do care. Our Creator said we should take care of them to the point where Allah says: "And why don't you fight for Allah's cause and for the downtrodden, men, women and children, who say: 'Lord, bring us out of this city whose inhabitants are unjust and grant us, from You, a protector, and grant us, from You, a supporter.'" (Q4:75) One of the reasons fighting was made obligatory is to take care of weak and vulnerable people.

You are saying that Allah did not make that part of your responsibility. Mallam! It is your responsibility. The booty [you have] not for anybody's parents [but for the soldiers]. Let me read it for you to hear: "Indeed, the booty belongs to the *mujāhidīn*, Allah's soldiers, who are fighting." Do not allow Shekau to deceive you by saying that you do not have a right over him, and do not have share in the booty. It is his oblication to feed you. The people who are stationed to protect the borders of the land of Islam from the unbelievers' invasion are the people who should possess the booty. The Muslim soldiers and the people working for the soldiers who are protecting the borders of the land of Islam are the people who should possess the booty.

There are numerous explanations on the topic of the booty. I am not the person who wrote all these explanations, let alone that you would say: "These are Mamman Nur's opinions." This is an explanation according to the Shafi'ī legal school. There are even scholars who said that all the booty belongs to the soldiers alone. For example, if they bring booty of 20 million [*naira*], Shekau, you are expected to take a share that suffices for you and your household—either 2 or 3 million [*naira*] [$6,000 or $9,000].

The remaining money is to be shared among the soldiers for them to eat. These are the soldiers who, once they [officers] say "go!", are on the road. Now, soldiers did not go to war with you sitting there complaining. Why will they go when you cannot even give them common paracetamol? You are saying that Allah did not make that part of your responsibility. In the cassette, he even said that Allah says we should take care of him. Who will take care of you? [*Nur and his audience burst into laughter.*] In what verse did Allah say we should take care of the imam or the leader? In what verse did Allah say so? Bring the verse and do not deceive the people.

It is your responsibility to feed those weak children. It is their right to be fed, to be given drinks and clothes. That is why we said, since we know that we are close to you, you will give us money to buy chickens and foreign rice, but we said we are contented. Is that not true? If you move around on your motorcycle, you will not see Allah's slaves. Let me tell you, Shekau does not give them fuel to go to war. If you visit his center, you will see up to 500 gas generators[19]—yet he is telling the people that there is no fuel. It was because of his denial that a few days ago the generators exploded, and almost 700 gallons of fuel were destroyed by an inferno. So, will you not think? You are persistently in a state of denial—yet your house and the money could not be removed during the inferno. Will you not repent? Don't you understand? Expose! This is the nature of the religion. [*Nur and his audience burst into laughter.*]

Before now, whatever you say, we say "hmm," so how would you like us to do it, honored one? We had no option other than to say yes before they put a bullet in your head. Allah has brought the opportunity for us to talk. If you like you should hear, if you like your heart should break, and you should repent, since you are yet to die. If you feel arrogant and bitter about my speech, and say: "Mamman Nur has hurt me with the cassette he delivered." You can go haywire because you are on your own, even if you repent—you are still on your own. "He who performs a righteous deed performs it to his own advantage, and he who perpetrates evil perpetrates it to his loss. Your Lord is not unjust to His servants." (Q41:46) You must take care of these weak people. You must take care of these slaves of Allah.

Furthermore, another reason we fled from you is the fact that you do not follow the commands of your superiors [ISIS]. They instructed that you should not capture slaves from among the apostates, but you refused [their advice]. You came out challenging the caliph, and saying: "Who is he?" You were also quoting from the Qur'ān: "Except from their wives and what their right hands possess. [For these] they are not blameworthy." (Q23:6)

Let us even assume that taking slaves is permissible. Before now, it is obligatory to follow a leader only when what he commanded is permissible. If he instructs you to leave, you should leave. If it is a command from Allah, you will need to obey Allah. The Qur'ānic scholars have explained all these issues. The only people who do not understand are people who refused to study the religion or issues of jurisprudence. Allah has aided us to study minimally. You will deceive some people, but we will not be deceived. In the past, we kept quiet because we were afraid. Today, fear has come to an end because death is the finale. The gravest thing you can do is kill us. One day, 100 years from now, we will all gather in front of Allah for judgment.

They [ISIS] gave you a command, but you refused to follow it. What you are saying is not what they said. They said that since the apostates committed the offence of apostasy, they should be asked to repent, but they should not be captured as slaves. Even if it is a woman, and she becomes an apostate, you can only tell her to repent, but you cannot capture an apostate as a slave. If they refuse to repent, they should be killed. That was the explanation they sent to you, and we know the same way you know.

Yet, you spoke out because you have captured slaves, the children of Bama, for your selfish interest. They said that if they are unbelievers like the children of Chibok,[20] it is permissible to capture them as slaves. For apostates, however, the ruling, male or female, is killing unless they repent. That was the explanation the Islamic State sent to you. You came out and delivered how many cassettes on this issue? In your cassette, you brought the misconceptions surrounding the judgement of Abu Bakr and Umar [the first caliphs]. You said Abu Bakr went with the opinion that they can be captured as slaves, while Umar went with the opinion that they cannot be captured as slaves.

However, because at that time Umar was not the leader, Abu Bakr was the leader, Umar submitted to Abu Bakr. On this basis, you said your followers must also submit to your view. No, we are not the people in the conversation with you. It is you and your superior. Al-Baghdadi is the person in the position of Abu Bakr, while you are in the position of Umar. Since the leader said no, you are expected to leave your opinion and follow the leader. That was the explanation they sent to you and you should not deceive us.

Furthermore, the eighth issue is giving rulings that are not in accordance with Allah's *sharīʿa*. I have read some of his [Shekau's] rulings like the ruling of not feeding the soldiers. You will hear him saying [*Nur mimicking Shekau*]: "Allah says you should bring [food] and it is not me who will give it to you." When some people understood his speech, they go and tell him: "Mallam, we know that Allah says we should bring, and it is not Islam that should give us. However, now we do not have [anything], and if there is the bounty of Islam, we should be given from it." [*Nur and the people at his lecture burst into laughter.*] They are playing with him the same way he plays with them. He will reply to them that they have a good understanding—then he will take the bounty and give it to them. You are playing tricks on them, even though they are wiser than you. It is their right for you to give to them, but you refused to give to them. This ruling is un-Islamic.

Another ruling is the ruling that there is no consultation in Islam. It is un-Islamic. Allah says: "And consult them in the conduct of affairs. Then, when you are resolved, trust in Allah; Allah indeed loves those who trust [in him]." (Q3:159) Allah told the Prophet that "it is compulsory for you to consult your companions." This is how the linguist interpreted it. Any issue, you must consult them to the point the Prophet consulted the Companions on issues pertaining to his household, not to speak of the issue of religion.

In your case, there is no consultation and you just give orders unilaterally. Whatever you wish to do, you will say it is the opinion of the imam based on what the Prophet said, when the Prophet did not say it. This ruling that there is no consultation in Islam is false. The Qur'an says we should consult: "And those who answer their Lord perform the prayer—their affair being a counsel among themselves, and of what We provided them with, they spend." (Q42:38)

Allah says there is consultation, but you tell us there is no consultation. [*Someone in the audience screams: "It will not work!"*] Each time we attempt to speak about consultation you will hear him saying: "Mallam, remember I only need advice, no consultation." Now, we are saying that we will give advice, and speak about consultation. In fact, agreeing with [Shekau's] ruling that there is no consultation is sinning against Allah. If we go to the hereafter under your [ruling], we will not enter paradise, slave of Allah. Anyone who agrees with this ruling will be unsuccessful. That is why we had to leave, even though it hurts. We had to leave. You should stop issuing rulings that contradict Allah's *sharīʿa*. It is a mistake and you should repent! You should repent and ask the scholars.

At the time, we were proselytizing in Maiduguri before we dispersed.[21] Each time Mallam Muhammad Yusuf wrote the Friday sermon, he did not read it until he called us to sit and revise it together, slave of Allah. After we read it, he asked us what we think about the sermon, is it okay? We would tell him if it was okay because we were speaking to the [larger] world. We would tell him that "this section is okay, but the interpretation of this verse should be corrected." We were five or six who usually cross-checked each sermon before Mallam [Yusuf] mounted the pulpit to deliver it.

We all know, and you know, that you did not study to the level of Mallam Muhammad Yusuf. So why do you say you will not seek consultation from people and that they cannot tell you anything. There in Maiduguri, was it not at my place that you learned the art of Qurʾānic recitation? I am not trying to show off. I am just reminding you, so that you can listen. [*Nur and his audience burst into laughter.*] Expose!

The ninth issue is the refusal to give soldiers war materials. [*Nur asks the audience:*] Does he give them to you? [*Audience screams: "No!"*] Let me tell you, we know there are war materials, tankers, cars, guns and RPGs. We know, Shekau, that there are war materials, although you try to hide them from us. We were in the same center, yet he hides some things from us. What will you hide from me? [*Someone in the audience says: "Just give us our war materials!"*]

Look at Allah's slaves, seeking to fight solely because of Allah. Give them the war materials, but you have refused. You even swear by Allah that there are no war materials, but then told them they are expected to bring their own, and should not expect to be given anything. So how will you allow the Islamic State to be decimated? How many lands and towns did we hoist the flag of "There is no god but Allah" over, but because you refused to release these war materials, the unbelievers recaptured these lands—and you know you are the cause [of defeat]. You are the cause!

As a result, there are many issues to discuss, but this is just an introduction. We titled this lecture "First Disclosure." We will deliver the second lecture. If you deliver a [counter] lecture, we will respond with our own. If you refrain, we will refrain. If you strike at us, we will strike you. If you do not strike at us, we will not strike at you—and Allah knows that we have no intention of striking at you. That is why we came out here.

All these trials are the reasons we came out, and we do not see how our actions contradict Allah's Book or the Sunna of His Messenger. What you are telling people, that [they cannot oppose you] until they see obvious unbelief, is wrong [Do not obey leaders who contradict the book of Allah.]

It is not as if we are opposing the Islamic State; we are together with the caliph. The way we approach this issue is that, since you have a superior, we will submit our objections to him [al-Baghdadi]. Whatever they tell us is what we will accept as appropriate. We will forward our protests since you are also waiting for their message. If you repent and desist from your actions, we will reconcile ourselves with you. However, if you still maintain your old ways by saying [*Nur mimicking Shekau*]: "Mamman Nur, come, I will not harm you." No, that approach will not work this time. You should purify Allah's religion, purify Allah's slaves, sympathize with them, do not destroy them, mislead them, or make them deviate from Allah's path. You will go to heaven and meet with Allah. You should fear Allah.

This is the message. Open letter! It will travel to the world. It will travel to your center. This is the issue that spurred this lecture. Look at Allah's slaves when we were together, he thought that this affair is limited to a single person like before. [*Nur mimicking Shekau:*] "Follow him and kill him." Everyone will say yes and kill one or two people. Later, you will ask: "Where is so-and-so?" You will be told that they have been killed. Who is the leader who authorized the killing? You know they are cheating him.

There was an incident that occurred last year when they told us they are Shi'ites. "The properties of the town in which we resided were expropriated as booty and you are the cause." In the hereafter, you will provide justification for saying whether they are booty or not. You gave the ruling and you sullied our name in the mind of Allah's slaves. Allah will pay you back. We will not forgive you except if you repent. Allah says in the Qur'ān: "Indeed, those who love to see indecency spread among the believers will have in this world and the next a very painful punishment. Allah knows, but you do not know." (Q24:19)

As a result, you sullied our name in the mind of Allah's slaves, and now you came out repeating the same thing. You should go ahead; we will also respond. Slaves of Allah! Everyone should fear Allah. Anyone who hears this cassette should fear Allah. He should help himself and know that if he dies under this government, he has no excuse to present in front of Allah. Allah's Messenger said that when tribulations become pervasive, you should to go to the forest and hold firm to the branch of a tree till you die, which is better for you than to sit in the hub of evil.

We were sitting here for the usual consultation which we hold every three weeks, so they brought a report to him that if some fighters go to fight, there are townspeople who fornicate with their wives at night. Did you say anything about it? Did you take any counter-measures? Is it not your obligation to protect the fighters' wives and children when they go to war? They told you about what they are doing to the people of Iza,[22] did you take any counter-measures?

They asked you in the session we had with Adam Vitiri: "Is there an action a person can do that nullifies his allegiance?" You said: "There is none." They brought the verse about the soldiers where Allah says: "So he who breaks his oath only breaks it to his loss." (Q48:10) They read the verse to you, but you said your own interpretation is different. Was that not what you said? Is that religion? We are not with you, if you do not repent. I will stop here. Whatever I say that is correct, may Allah reward us, and may He forgive us for our mistakes or slips of tongue. This is it.

Everyone who hears or listens has sense. People are not insane for you to say what you like, then go back to sleep in your house with your wives and slaves. People have sense because Allah gave them sense and an understanding mind. Therefore, you should say whatever you like, so we also will respond and afterwards see who is truthful. Gone are the days when they cursed us, and you also cursed us, because you have a habit of cursing.

He was even reciting the verse of the Qur'ān in the front of people: "Except from their wives and what their right hands possess. [For these] they are not blameworthy." (Q23:6) Are they talking about slaves? Don't you understand? In his center, while he was teaching Allah's slaves, he was screaming: "May Allah curse you! May Allah curse you! May Allah curse you!" You are cursing people just on the issue of slaves. Abu Fatima will give a brief explanation. You should not think that we are alone in the forest. No, is Abu Fatima one of your commanders? No, he is the commander from the caliph [al-Baghdadi]. There are many commanders in his place, and all of them are loyal to us. There are other slaves of Allah as I mentioned, they are just watching you. If you strike at us, they will strike at you.

Lecture from Abu Fatima

[Standard Islamic opening] Praise be to Allah. My brothers who receive this message, we want you to understand us. Our coming out here is not for kindling tribulation (*fitna*). There are certain things that are going on in our religion, and specifically our creed, that have changed from what was preached to us, explained to us and by which we have developed. We went and explained to the best of our ability, but they insulted us all the time, and accused us of not following commands. I hope it is understood? We noticed some wrongdoings and went to explain to him as our leader—that is Mallam Abubakar Shekau. I hope it is understood?

We met you and conveyed our explanations to you. We also admonished you, but you took everything as disrespect. I hope it is understood. No, we saw that they have changed the original creed upon which we were trained. That is why we were looking for the way to restore our original creed. I hope it is understood. Brothers should not view our action as a sign of revolt. No, we stepped aside so that they can mend their ways before we return. We don't want to see the destruction taking place, lest we end up in perdition and go to heaven without rest. We have already said that we will not follow anyone until he follows Allah. I hope it is understood. We parted ways from our parents even though they suffered because of us, simply because we called them to the truth but they rejected it. No doubt, even if it is you, Mallam, if you leave Allah's path, we will part ways from you. I hope it is understood.

Brothers! You should understand that we did not revolt. Even if we revolt, we can only revolt against a caliph. Whenever there is revolution, it is the duty of the caliph to call us so that we will explain ourselves to him. We saw that there were errors in these issues, so then the caliph will remedy that and we will follow him. That is the tradition of the religion, and several scholars have written on these issues. If you correct your mistakes, then we will follow you. You should know that you are our leader, but now we are forwarding our objections to the caliph. People should understand us and should not take up weapons to fight against us. We do not want to pierce anyone with even a needle. If we had intended to fight, we would have started with Shekau for a long time. We do not want anyone to be hurt. Let us follow the religion peacefully, so that we can all achieve victory.

We are tired of being pursued by the unbelievers. It is because of all these issues that the unbelievers are pursuing us. We have deviated from Allah's path. Are we not the ones that in the past, twenty of us would go out raiding the security centers of the unbelievers to obtain guns for each one? Something must have happened that for almost a year we are being chased by these animals. We are seeing that if these issues are not resolved, there is no way we will become victorious. Have we become rebels? How come they will fight against the unbelievers and not achieve victory?

Brothers, if we are not animals, we need to sit and think. Why is it that we are being chased? The reason why these things are happening is because of the misconduct of Mallam Abubakar Shekau. If he mends all these issues, the religion's dignity will be restored. If the caliph instructs us to follow him, we will agree to follow him, but he should repent for his actions, and return to the religion. Let him return to *This is our Creed* upon which we were all nurtured, and the Prophet's methodology that was laid out by the scholars. If he returns, we will follow him. I hope it is understood.

We came out here for rectification. Why would we flee and leave Allah's slaves? He said we fled with his followers. By Allah, we did not flee. We only stepped aside to report you to the caliph, since reporting you to the caliph while within your [Shekau's] territory is tantamount to death. It will not be possible for us to report you to the caliph while we are still in your territory. Who will carry out the reconciliation? We explained this to you, but you did not make amends. Therefore, we stepped aside to report you to the caliph, who will then oversee the reconciliation. I hope it is understood.

We are together with Mallam Habib, Mallam Mamman Nur, and Mallam Abba. He [Shekau] has listed them as wanted. These people did not commit any offence, nor did they deliberately spill anybody's water. However, they wanted us all to be united and to return to our religion. We should unite and bring back the methodology upon which we were nurtured. These were the reasons that spurred them to come out. There is no one who will strike at them, nor will we. We will not strike at anyone. We would not have delivered this cassette if not for the fact that you delivered yours. However, since you intend to kindle sedition, we saw the need to deliver this cassette so that brothers can understand the issues on the ground.

Brothers, if you listen to this cassette, it is not meant to instigate you to fight him [Shekau]. Our goal is not to fight him. Even a pinch, do not touch him. By Allah, if we had intended to kill him, we would have killed him long ago. This is not to show off. If we had intended to kill him, we would have killed him, but we do not want even a pin to pierce him. Let us all come back, resolve these issues, and practice our religion. I hope it is understood. No one will strike at or arrest Habib or the likes of Mamman Nur, by Allah's permission. We have reported you to the caliph, Mallam Abubakar Shekau. Brothers! You should know that we have reported Mallam Abubakar Shekau to the caliph of the Muslims, and what we did is in accordance with the religion.

[You have invented a new creed] By the permission of Allah, whenever they send some people to you for reconciliation, if we observe we will not be deceived or cheated, we will come back and practice the religion together. You should return to the religion the way we understood it, whereupon we will join you and practice the religion together. Right now, we do not understand what you are doing. Most of the scholars who are with you know the truth, but they refuse to tell you, because they are afraid that you will kill them.

The scholars who told you the truth—you killed them. You planned to kill Mallam Abu Nazir. He told us how you attempted to kill him in a [recorded] cassette before Allah took him to prison for his protection. By Allah's permission, he will be released, and will join us to practice the religion. This is the reason why those scholars are afraid. There are some of the scholars who are now on their way coming [to join us]. They also prefer to step aside and after these issues have been addressed, we will all unite again.

This is not a revolt. Do not deliver a [video] cassette and say it is a revolt and call for bloodshed between us. We will not allow anyone to kill us nor will we strike at anyone. This is our mission. If our aim is bloodshed, we would have started long ago, but that is not our aim. We want to bring back sanity to the religion. Whoever wishes to understand should understand that our mission is not to bring destruction to the religion. If our goal is destruction or sedition, we would not have taken our wives and children to his place. We took them to him because we see the responsibility is his before our leaders commence the reconciliation between us. I hope it is understood.

If we had wanted to revolt, why would we take our women and children to his place? Why would we take some of our brothers to go and stay in his place? All those brothers we left with you, those in Timbuktu, Lake Chad, Gorgore, Machina and those across the road,[23] we want all of them brought back, so that we can all practice the religion together. No, we did not separate from you, brothers. We are with you.

This leader of ours is acting incomprehensibly, so we have reported him. Therefore, you should understand that we do not intend to kindle sedition. By Allah, if our mission was to kindle sedition, we would have started long ago. This is my explanation. I added this explanation so that the brothers can understand what is going on. Glory be to Allah, we seek His forgiveness, and we testify that there is no one worthy of being worshipped except Allah.

[As this book went to press, the Islamic State West African Province under the leadership of Abu Mus`ab al-Barnawi launched 'al-Haqa`iq Media Center' on 18 May 2017. The center produces Hausa version of the audio lectures from 'al-Bayan Radio' of the Islamic State and theological articles from al-Naba newsletter. Most lectures are delivered by Abu Mus`ab al-Barnawi and the themes are related to the contents of Mamman Nur and Abu Fatima's lecture.]

73

MESSAGE FROM THE SOLDIERS

BY MAN CHARI AND ABUBAKAR SHEKAU

(7 AUGUST 2016)

[Trans.: Abdulbasit Kassim]
Available at: http://jihadology.net/2016/08/07/new-video-message-from-jamaat-ahl-al-sunnah-li-l-dawah-wa-l-jihads-abu-bakr-shekau-message-from-the-soldiers/

This video continued to express resentment against Abu Mus'ab al-Barnawi's promotion as the governor of ISWAP by the Islamic State. In this video, the masked speaker, who had previously featured in several Boko Haram videos, spoke about his displeasure over Shekau's replacement by al-Barnawi, whom he accused of following an inauthentic Salafism. The speaker (later identified as Man Chari) declared that they would continue to follow Shekau, and threatened the Nigerian Chief of the Army Staff, Lieutenant General Tukur Yusuf Buratai, the spokesperson of the Nigerian army, Colonel Sani Kukasheka, as well as Nigerian President Muhammadu Buhari. In addition, the speaker said the group's adversaries should not rejoice over their internal differences because sooner or later they will be resolved and unified. In the second half of the video, Abubakar Shekau appeared, and challenged reports of his death. He also reiterated some parts of his audio speech (text 68), and vowed that they would defeat America and Nigeria.

[Arabic version]

[Standard Islamic opening] This is a message from the soldiers of JASDJ in West Africa, in the Islamic State, to the entirety of our *mujāhidīn* brothers around the world, and especially the leader of the believers, the Caliph of the Muslims, Ibrahim b. 'Awad b. Ibrahim Abu Bakr al-Baghdadi al-Husayni al-Qurayshi, may Allah preserve him and care for him.

The news was delivered to us through the unbelievers' media about the change to a new governor. On this issue we say, the man whom you appointed to this position does not follow a sound doctrine from authentic Salafism. On this basis, we will not follow him. Our leader, Shekawi, wrote to you eight letters in which he explained to you that those people follow the ideology of *irjā'*. You asked him about the meaning of *irjā'*, and he explained to you in his third message, but you did not respond. Before these issues, we had already informed you that they split away from us, becoming isolated from us, but you did not do anything. We have also sent you several questions, but did not receive any response from you—except that suddenly, we heard this news. As a result, we say that we are with our imam, Abu Muhammad b. Muhammad Abubakar al-Shekawi, may Allah preserve him.

There are other issues, but this is not the place to discuss them because they require secrecy. We say that we are still in accord with our allegiance, nor do we remove our hands from the pledge of allegiance to the caliph, but we will not follow the one who does not follow the doctrine of the Sunnis, nor do we want a mediator between us and the caliph, unless there will be a meeting with you, or an audio message from you, without a mediator. At that time, we will discuss those private issues that are not discussed at this moment.

Our second message is to the *ṭawāghīt*, the polytheists and the apostates, especially the *ṭawāghīt* of West Africa. Do not rejoice at the differences between us and our brothers, because we do not find such differences strange in Islam, and Allah will rectify the situation between us sooner and not later, by His permission. We say to you, O *ṭawāghīt* of the world, and especially you *ṭawāghīt* of West Africa: wait for the glad tidings of something that will harm you! Wait for the glad tidings of something that will harm you! Wait for the glad tidings of something that will harm you! By Allah's permission, you will very soon see what is beyond your expectation especially Buratai, you and Kukasheka, you will see surprising things by Allah's permission.

We announced to you that we have started the war against you. The *jihād* has just begun, the *jihād* has just begun, and the *jihād* has just begun! Die in your rage and wait while we enter the heart of your land. O you, the biggest *ṭāghūt*—I mean Buhari—you will see us in the heart of your land. In these coming days, by Allah's permission, you will see us in your alleged public area, called Abuja.[1] You will see us in these coming days, by Allah's permission, not by our power or strength but by Allah's power and His strength.

We will surely burn the flag of unbelief, which is colored green, white, green [the Nigerian flag], whereupon we will raise the flag of Islam, which is colored black, with the inscription "There is no god but Allah and Muhammad is Allah's Messenger" written in white. We will destroy all the slogans of unbelief and will uplift the Islamic slogans. We will implement the punishments stipulated in Allah's Book and the Sunna of His Messenger. These goals will become a reality by Allah's permission, and by His strength and power. We neither have power nor strength, but we rely on the victory from Allah which He bestows on whomever He wishes. He is the Almighty and the All-Wise. This is what Allah has made easy for me to say to you at this moment. All praise be to Allah, the Lord of the worlds. [*Chanting* takbīr *(Allah is great) with other followers*.] Die in your rage! Die in your rage! Die in your rage!

[*The Hausa version is exactly the same as above translation.*]

The Speech of Abubakar Shekau

[Standard Islamic opening] All praise is due to Allah, who decreed *jihād* as an act of worship. Allah is the One who decreed *jihād* as one of the most exalted acts of worship for His servants. He has bestowed glad tidings of two best outcomes upon His servants: either His servants attain victory, or martyrdom (cf. Q9:52). And may the peace and blessings of Allah be upon our master Muhammad, his family and his Companions.

And thereafter:

O my honored brothers! Glad tidings, by Allah's permission, the time for fighting has come. Now, the time for fighting has come. The time for fighting is upon us. O *ṭawāghīt* of Nigeria! O unbelievers of the world, especially the *ṭawāghīt* of America, France, Germany, and the *ṭawāghīt* of the Assembly of Manipulators [United Nations], as we say in our local language. Die in your rage! Die in your rage! Die in your rage! We have no need to fight our Muslim brothers; rather we will fight the unbelievers and only kill those whom Allah has commanded us to kill. We do not declare anyone an unbeliever except those who were declared by Allah. We are holding firm, following Allah's Book and the Sunna of His Messenger, based on the understanding of the forefathers.

Our scholars and shaykhs, be patient, patience after patience. O you unbelievers! Die in your rage! We will fight you, and we will defeat America and Nigeria. We believe in the verses of our Lord: "They will only cause you a little harm; and if they fight you, they will turn their backs on you, and will have no support." (Q3:111) Allah also says: "The case of those who took up another protector, apart from Allah, is like that of the spider who built a house. Truly, the most brittle of houses is the house of the spider, if only they knew." (Q29:41)

O you who wish for me to be dead! If my time has come, I will die by Allah's permission. Every soul shall die only by Allah's permission. "It is not given to any soul to die, except with Allah's leave, at a fixed time." (Q3:145) I am Ibn Muhammad—before I say Abu Muhammad b. Muhammad Abubakar al-Shekawi, the imam of JASDJ in West Africa.[2] I came out, by Allah's permission, to fight not only Nigeria alone, but the world in its entirety. Die in your rage, O you unbelievers! Glad tidings to you, my Muslim brothers! By Allah's permission, we are fighting the unbelievers until we see Allah's words uplifted (cf. Q9:41). This is what we want, by Allah's permission, to adhere to. We ask Allah to make our foothold and that of our brothers' firm. O Allah! Make our shooting accurate. [*Shekau shooting into the air.*] Nigeria will be defeated! O Buhari! Die in your rage! I am here, by Allah's permission.

74

SHEKAU RESPONDS TO HIS CRITICS[1]

(18 DECEMBER 2016)

[Trans.: Abdulbasit Kassim]

In this audio lecture, Shekau reiterated the ideological differences that led to the faction-alization of Boko Haram (see texts 70–72). Although this audio could be seen as a response to some of the allegations by Mamman Nur concerning him, specifically the allegation that he murders his close associates for trivial offenses, Shekau ends up more or less proving Nur's general accusation. Much of the audio concerns the plot of one Abu Ammar (or Baba Ammar) to undermine Shekau's leadership, and turns on the issue of the killing of Taasi'u, who supported Abu Ammar. Shekau defended himself by saying that the close associates he had killed attempted to undermine his authority, thereby violating the law they all pledged to follow. He stressed that no member of the group is killed without committing an offence. This lecture shows that Shekau is facing a crisis of legitimacy with other top echelons of Boko Haram, and there seems to be a competition by factional leaders to win the support of the mid-level and foot soldiers.[2]

[Standard Islamic opening]

And thereafter:

My brothers! May Allah's peace and blessings be upon you.

Today, by Allah's permission, we are in the month of Rabi' al-Awwal and the date is the eighteenth or nineteenth [17 or 18 December 2016]. What brought us here together: we are the people who proclaimed *jihād* for Allah with His Book and His Prophet's Sunna. We proclaimed the emulation of His Prophet's actions, and those of our predecessors backed by theological evidence just as they commanded us—and have preceded us to the House of Truth [the hereafter]. We are JASDJ, that is the name we called ourselves from the onset. Thereafter, Allah aided us in many ways until we finally came together and pledged allegiance to the Islamic State under the leadership of Caliph Abu Bakr al-Baghdadi.

Afterwards, we feuded with our brothers based on their introduced innovation which constitutes a [sign of] major disbelief. We believe that it is impossible for a Muslim to reside in the unbelievers' land without the public manifestation of his religion, and still claim to be a Muslim. This is not the practice of the Prophet [Muhammad]. Likewise, it is impossible for a Muslim who has not fought against an illegitimate ruler (*ṭāghūt*), who rules by means of a constitution, to claim to be a Muslim or for him to not be labeled an unbeliever. This is also not possible. These are the type of creeds they wrote to us with the claim that they emanated from the caliphate [Islamic State]. They said I should agree and work with these creeds because that is how the caliphate is governed. Afterwards I said that these beliefs, if I did not hear them directly from the spokesman of the caliphate, I will not accept them as truth nor will I agree to them or work with them. Whoever accepts these beliefs has committed apostasy (*ridda*). This is my creed. Let me explain clearly from now: women, men, and my brothers, it is the Qur'ān I will follow.

Thereafter, I said even if a woman is praying and fasting, once she participates in democracy, I will capture her the same way they capture Christian slaves in battles, because she is an apostate. This is the creed of our master Abu Bakr and other predecessors. There is no one who disputes this position and Allah knows best. Up until this moment, they said, it is not permissible for me to capture women participating in democracy, to fight them or to handle them as slaves. I replied to them that I will continue to capture and sell them just as our predecessors did. This is my creed.

Secondly, some brothers came to me when this disagreement intensified and they said they will support and aid me. They said I should rise up and come over to their region so that we can strive together for the religion of Allah. I agreed and left my own region for their place. Afterwards, Satan commenced his noise-making until people started confronting them, saying they are also so-and-so [guilty of Shekau's actions]. This was what the people were saying, and they wanted to come and hear the truth from me. I informed them that the tale they heard in a certain place, they are not expected to disclose it to their leader.

Now, they can see that we are actively working and everything is taking its shape. The brothers are on the frontlines and they are studying to wage *jihād*. Now, they want to sow the seeds of conflict between us, because whoever they see has become close to me for some days, they confront him with different doubts to ruin our relationship. I explained to them that they should be patient—let us stay together, but they said the disagreement is too intense. Abu Ammar said I should relieve him of his leadership. I explained to him that if I relieved him of his leadership, the people might conclude that dissension has broken out between us. If the people perceive doubts in you as a leader, that means we are not following in the footsteps of our predecessors. But if you agree with my leadership, you should be patient, let us stay together and I will do everything you want.

Allah did not allow my wish to see fruition. At last, He finally declined. This was what transpired and in the presence of everyone I explained what he said, but because of my integrity, I do not have to repeat it here. He said it with his mouth that they will never hear anything from him. This was what we concluded in the first meeting in his absence [*Shekau gives a recap of previous meetings.*] In the second meeting, we all sat together and I explained the deliberations of the past week.

Now, the third meeting concerned the issue of Man Chari,[3] Man Tahiru, the person they call Aribeka, and others whose issues were brought up in our conversations. This is the purpose of that meeting specifically, because they said Taasi'u was killed. This was what they said. They met Man Tahiru and Man Chari, and they told them that I will kill them—[thereupon] they packed their luggage and started searching for a place to hide themselves. This was what transpired so this is the private issue they want to make public. This is the purpose of our meeting. It has become necessary today for me to offer an explanation.

First, what is the reason for the killing of Taasi'u? Second, what is the reason for the impression that I would want to kill Man Chari and Man Tahiru? What led to the situation that Abu Ammar had some people camping in his place to confront me? What led to this situation? These are the clarifications that the leaders working for the establishment of *tawḥīd* must understand. This is the purpose of our meeting. Allah is the king. Allah knows best.

It would have been appropriate if Abu Asma'u and Mallam Abubakar Hairiya were present. Nonetheless, there is no problem using their names, based on what has already transpired. Likewise, it would have been appropriate if Abu Khalid were present, but there is no problem since I have mentioned their names. The third person is Alhaji Isa Akwe, and there is also another person called Abu Adam.

This is the breakdown of the problem [to be discussed]. Is this well understood? This is the sequence upon which I will speak about Taasi'u. There was nothing that brought Mallam Taasi'u and me together from the beginning. I did not know anything about him and he did not explain anything to me. The issues Abu Ammar informed me about Taasi'u or the conversation I had with him, now I am speaking about Abu Ammar and Taasi'u. Abu Ammar will listen to this cassette and he will realize what he said about Taasi'u with his own mouth, and also testify in the presence of Allah if he does not repent. This is sufficient for him, [meaning] Abu Ammar. You know what you said about Taasi'u. This is sufficient for you.

Let us go to the hereafter and finish this conversation there, or you should hide in your room and curse me and pray. Allah will accept the prayer of the oppressed, if indeed I oppressed you. Allah's Messenger told Mu'adh b. Jabal that there is no barrier between Allah and the prayer of the oppressed. You should hide while I also hide and pray to Allah. Even if what you are saying is driven by the protection of your integrity because you now have followers and you think you can satisfy your desire on me, Allah is sufficient for me. This is what I will say on the issue of Taasi'u. This is sufficient for me.

Furthermore, this issue of Taasi'u is not just about Taasi'u, me, you, or all of us. It is about the allegiance we have pledged. Whoever the law catches in this movement, we will not hesitate to implement the law and punish him. This is what we all pledged. So, Abu Asma'u and Mallam Abubakar Hairiya came and they were commanded to go to the town of Bula Yaga.[4] Alhaji Isa went to call them [to allegiance] and they came with their people. They came on foot. This is what really transpired and there was nothing hidden. They informed them that Mallam [Shekau] is calling them and they came. After they arrived, Alhaji Isa shared the news with me that they were arrested for something else, but the people who arrested them had already come and explained [the arrest] to me. Is this understood? Thereafter, we sat together with Abu Asma'u, and while I had initially wanted to speak, then I declined. I told them that since I was the person who had summoned them, they should start speaking about whatever they want to say while I listen.

This Mallam [Abu Asma'u?] started speaking. He said ten months ago, Mallam Taasi'u met him and said to him they have a mission for him. They told him that the mission will be carried out around Bauchi, and the name of the town is Falgore.[5] He informed them that if it is a command from Allah, he will proceed to carry out the mission. Carrying out the mission is between him and Allah. They told him that he should gather his belongings. I am repeating this word for word according to what they told him. I sat there crying and when disclosure became too disconcerting, I called Abu Khalid to come and sit and listen because he was the person who called me.

I was crying until he finished his explanation. Thereafter, he said Abu Ammar and Taasi'u are the people who conspired together and who instructed them to go to the place where they will wage *jihād* for Allah. That was how they left to the point that they stayed on the road waiting, while simultaneously fighting for up to three months.

Their activities were broadcasted on the radio and they overheard a number of things regarding the struggle for Allah's sake. Afterwards, they said they will not come again in the future. In the case of Mallam Abubakar Hairiya even in a dream, I did not hear about him until the day of the meeting. He also proceeded with his own explanation. Look at me with my shocked expression listening to what they said and how they plan to execute their mission. I told them that I am just hearing what they said in this room. This was what transpired.

Thereafter, I reached an understanding that this issue did not begin only today. I had been unaware for a long time previously. Can you give me a ruling from the Qur'ān? What is the ruling concerning those who are plotting different schemes without the knowledge of their leader? Go and verify it from Allah's Book! Last week, we studied this same issue; then we released our commentary on a cassette. Now, I am going to repeat it again to uphold the Book of Allah and the *ḥadīth*.

This was the same type of scheming they carried out during the period of 'Umar Mukhtār and 'Uthmān Dan Fodio. This was the same type of plot they effected against them. Allah's Messenger told us: "They will never gain victory over you, until you start fighting amongst yourselves."[6] This is the reality. They started this scheming. This was their action. They schemed more than did this, but I will only speak about this issue for now. Yet, they have persisted in their scheming.

Now, I am sitting here and you can see me. I know I bought these types of computers, Allah is my witness but the ones on the ground, they refuse to bring them for me. Now, I do not have a printer and my computer is broken, but go to their rooms, they lack nothing. I declined exposing them or saying anything about this issue because now we are striving for the religion, not for the acquisition of property. This was what transpired. A little exposé on the issue of Taasi'u.

Away from this issue, they started following people and explaining to them. Abu Ammar was the person that told me to be patient on the issue of Taasi'u. He told me he is aware of the scheme he is plotting. He said he will take him and keep him in his place to reach an understanding. "Be patient Mallam, we know everything." This was what he told me and I am repeating it on the cassette because now I see that you have turned black [like the devil]. You can go ahead and do anything you wish to do. This was what you told me. I replied to him that I agree and he can go ahead and do what he wants to do. This was the point he disconnected the phone conversation. On the phone conversation alone, I spent more than ten million [*naira*].[7] Allah is sufficient for me. This was what transpired and Allah is my witness this night.

Abu Khalid, Abu Asma'u and Mallam Abubakar Hairiya were sitting together, and I said because of Allah, "Abu Khalid, even by dreaming, I would never imagine that Abu Ammar is conspiring with Taasi'u." This was what I told Abu Khalid at that time. I told him to wait, let me take an oath with the hereafter while Abu Khalid, Mallam Abubakar Hairiya and Abu Asma'u were sitting [with me]. I told Abu Khalid to swear, if he can, that if Mallam Taasi'u is not conspiring with Abu Ammar, [if he is untruthful] may Allah deny him entry to paradise.

I told him to repeat that after me, but he said that indeed they are conspiring. I made this statement in this very room, and this land will testify on the Day of Resurrection [on my behalf]. This is the plot they were scheming together. According to the Islamic religion, if a person among you is creating division, even if he is a pious slave but not an unbeliever, he should be killed so that he can go and be in the Hereafter, while you continue striving for the religion. This *ḥadīth* is in [the collections of] Bukhari and Muslim. This ruling is the religion of Allah.

On this basis, you should all listen, I am the person who killed Taasi'u. Are you listening to my speech? You were saying that if he claimed that he did not engage in any plot, he should be summoned. Can someone kick-start a motorcycle now before daybreak and bring him [here]? No one should hinder the truth from us. Now, if there is anyone willing to go and bring Abu Ammar, they should go and bring him. This is my religion. Yes! You killed many people for the religion, and if you come here to tell me that, I will say it is acceptable. Is it today that you think is the time for you to reveal my secrets? Has this not been your desire? Let us go ahead and see.

On the issue of Mallam Chari and Mallam Tahiru, what was their crime for me to even desire to kill them? Since I left the center,[8] when did we ever meet with them? Mallam Chari and Mallam Tahiru, you should listen to me! At the time, I made the decision to leave, I told you that I am going to a locality where you will not see me; the reason for that is backed by religious evidence. You know the dissensions (*fitna*) they were causing, but you should be patient. I said these words in your presence and you replied to me: "May Allah aid me as you depart." Thereafter, I left. I believe you will understand if you recall my words.

What was your offence and why would I want to have anything to do with you? Is there anyone I killed who committed no offence? Is there anyone I killed and concealed the killing without providing an explanation? Nonetheless, if I execute an action for the advancement of the religion, you can go ahead and reveal my secrets, you are not my god. Yes! These indictments are not just against us, they want to ruin this path for us. They want to demonstrate to the people that I am engaging in different actions based on ignorance. They want to show the people that the path I am upon is not Allah's path.

Allah is my witness! Man Chari, which day did we convoke the past meeting? I informed Abu Khalid to inform the likes of Man Chari to attend the meeting because he is among the scholars. That was what I did. I was surprised they did not show up. Even before I came, I ask Abu Khalid, why did Man Chari not show up? He said they did not come and I did not say much. This was what I did.

Now, you heard what this slave of Allah said. In the past meeting, there was something that prevented them from speaking. If the situation is like that, then it means the people that attended have a different thought. It was not until they attended that they discovered that it was not what they assumed. Aribeka! Where did you hear that I killed Taasi'u? Who informed you? Which day did I meet with you? Is it permissible to work based on presumption in the religion? Firstly, who told you? You should go and confront the person who told you. Or are you thinking: if I said I killed Taasi'u, I will be attacked?

Even if I killed a hundred people, it is Allah who gave permission for them to be killed. This is my religion and this is the path I follow. As you know, if the law catches up with a person, the law must be implemented. Anyone you see killing someone, he also agrees to be killed. This is the religion in which we believe. Therefore, you should listen. I do not have resentment against Man Chari or Man Tahiru. We did not say anything against them. Since I changed my location, they have not seen me and this is the fact.

Thereafter, Abu Ammar, you were the person who came up with the issues pertaining to scholars, and the agreement to change the current arrangement. You removed Man Chari, and came to explain to me his deficiencies with suggestion of others that are better suited in the role of scholars. You implemented all these changes. You sat here and repented to Allah and vowed that nothing would be heard from you again, but now you are making an arrangement. It is permissible for me to speak about these issues now so that I can leave the world for you tomorrow since this is your own religion. On my part, I will strive for my religion and I will not change, even if it is inside a single room. I will not follow anyone who is engaging in acts of unbelief or religious innovation. This was the pledge we took and upon which we march forth.

If you are not knowledgeable, I do not view you with the evil eye, but you should repent because of Allah and strive for the religion. Today, you have revealed yourself. Let me inform you, if you were the person culpable of all the charges I am confronting you with in this speech, you have cheated me, thus Allah will not spare you even on the Day of Resurrection. Yes! I did not know anything about Abu Khalid. Everything they said about him, I have no knowledge about it, just the same way I do not know what is inside my stomach, and Allah knows best.

This is sufficient for me as an excuse in the sight of Allah, if not in the sight of the people. However, now because they are mentioning Abu Khalid and Abu Ammar, they want to ruin the people because of these two. Is this the intent? Now, you want us to focus on this type of explanation so that the unbelievers can hear, right? You want us to retract this type of conversation, and abandon the study of *tawḥīd*, right? This was the same thing they did in the past. However, one against whom no one plots or schemes cannot be on the right path.

[*Shekau explains the above conversation in Kanuri.*]

[*Shekau cites some Arabic sections of* al-'Aqidah al-Ṭahawiyya (The Creed of Imam Ṭahawi).]

"And we do not hold the rebelling against our rulers and those in authority over our affairs even if they oppress, we do not make supplications against them. And we hold that obedience to them is a part of obedience to Allah, the Mighty and Majestic, an obligation if they do not command with something sinful. And we make supplication for them that they be rectified and kept safe and secure."

"And we do not use the sword against anyone from Muhammad's community except upon whom it becomes obligatory to use it upon [someone]."

[*Shekau continues speaking in Kanuri.*]

This is what Allah has destined for me. The issue has been made clear both in Hausa and Kanuri. It is for this reason that I gave an elaborate explanation in Hausa because if I explain in Kanuri, it might be brief and some people will not understand. The explanation in Hausa is clear to everyone and you can identify the issues when the explanations are incomplete. The likes of this Mallam Shekau, who are the people conspiring evil against him? All affairs belong to Allah alone.

Allah is the one who understands the recitation of the dumb the same way He recognizes the sleep of the blind. Let us all go and testify in the hereafter. We will not abandon the religion. Whoever brings persecution and obstruction into our movement, we will punish him. We are following in the Prophet's footsteps and those of the pious predecessors. Let them detest us on this basis. Allah is the king.

[*Shekau explains the above conversation in Kanuri.*]

We did not persecute anyone. If you object to this assertion, speak out. On the speech of Abu Ammar, do not attribute doubt to his speech. If indeed he said it, we should put a condition so that someone will not later claim that Mallam is also operating based on assumptions. They can deny that they did not give the speech. If you did not give the speech and they attributed it to you, the doubt has been cleared between me and you. However, if indeed you said it, why did you not come to us initially? You should have come since they were also coming. Why is it that they must bring you? Why should we delay what we schedule to do during the midday and postpone it to the evening? This is our religion. What they wanted to do is to ruin everything and place trackers on us. This is the type of conversation they want. Take it! Let us wait for our Creator.

If there are no further questions, I will end the speech here. Whoever is credible, he can find a way for us to talk, even secretly. I am making a promise to Allah. O Allah! I will not harm anyone who desires further explanation from me. He should come forth. He should refrain from spreading falsehood about this religion without verse or *ḥadīth*. All wisdom belongs to Allah. If indeed you are sincere, now I have agreed to let us sit and engage in a conversation. Let him bring forth his conversation while I also bring mine. This is our religion. This is what I would like to explain to my brothers. You should be patient. We did not desire to expose all these conversations, but it has reached the level where they must be exposed.

[*A questioner asks Shekau a question in Kanuri.*]

[*Shekau's response:*]

What he referred to is the decision we made when we launched the struggle. We promised that there will be no further explanations, just execution of actions and implementation of *tawḥīd*.[9] Afterwards, this conflict of opinions ensued and it necessitated an explanation. Now, this issue has reached the level that I am expected to provide a detailed explanation. This is what the slave of Allah [the questioner] said.

So, what is better is for you to also rise and spread this explanation like the war. This is so because in the movement we said *li-daʿwa wa-l-jihād* [for preaching and fighting]. Therefore, even in the state of *jihād*, the proclamation must continue through various means. It is mandatory that we spread the proclamation. For example, this cassette I recorded tonight, it is important for people to listen to it. The cassette I recorded recently, it is good for people to listen to it. The cassette we recorded on the *dajjāl* [Antichrist] recently, based on the issue of the Resurrection, it is important for people to listen to it.

The cassettes I kept under my armpit, I made their stomach the same as mine,[10] even though they are the people who started this. Allah knows the arrangement we had with them. I have certainty, even if it is only for the arrangement we had with them, Allah will avenge me. Allah is the only One to be followed and *tawḥīd* is the same. This is the religion in which we believe. "Today I have perfected your religion for you, completed My grace on you and approved Islam as a religion for you." (Q5:3) By Allah, there is no unbeliever who can gain victory over us!

The hypocrites cannot be fought with any weapon other than clarification. You can go ahead and tell people. I believe you can hear him calling us hypocrites? I concur, since you have chosen to satisfy your desires with my speeches. Even if I did not call you a hypocrite, I will recite the [Qur'ānic] verses discussing hypocrisy with regard to you, because the Prophet Muhammad did the same thing. The verses are there in the Qur'ān.

All the verses in the Qur'ān mentioning the unbelievers are intended to alarm the believers. Today, even if you recite a verse of unbelief to a brother, because they have ruined the people, this kola [nut] is rotten,[11] so you will hear the brother saying: "he [Shekau] is reciting the verses of unbelief, so he is saying that you are an unbeliever." This is what they tell the people. Allah is the One who knows the intention of a slave. This is our religion. This is what Allah has destined for me.

Since this is the case, let us all gather, as I previously mentioned, even if our center will remain the same way, we should gather and strive for the religion. Whoever sees that we are truly following the religion should gather and strive on behalf of it. There is no persecution [here] and everyone should listen to this explanation. You should know if Allah predestined my death, I must die. If He predestined your death, you also must die.

Let us worship and pray. Whoever is engaging in actions based on ignorance, may Allah guide him. Whoever is deliberately causing conflict, may Allah take revenge for us. Whatever is apparent to us, even if it is coming from our children or ourselves, may Allah help us to implement the law. May Allah not make us the people who cannot implement the law amongst themselves, but who are striving to implement the law upon others. May Allah prevent us from being part of this category of people. Whether it is within our movement or outside the movement, we must implement the law. I will stop at this point. Allah knows best. When the recording finishes, I will save it. May the peace and blessings of Allah be upon His Messenger, his household and his Companions.

[As this book went to press, the internal schism between Abubakar Shekau and Mamman Nur/Abu Mus'ab al-Barnawi is nowhere near over. Shekau published two books and series of audio lectures where he expounded on the issues he discussed in this text. His books were published by Maktaba Wadi'u al-Bayan and his audio lectures were produced by 'Khairul Huda Media Center'. Both factions are still in active warfare with the Nigerian state. In conclusion, whether Boko Haram will survive this current wave of schism is yet to be seen, but for the foreseeable future this book's contribution lies in the detailed documentation of Boko Haram's trajectory from Nigerian Preachers to the Islamic State.]

NOTES

INTRODUCTION

1. http://abcnews.go.com/WNT/video/boko-haram-declares-joined-isis-29488051 (accessed 28 December 2015).
2. See texts 21, 25 and 26.
3. See Dierk Lange, *A Sudanic Chronicle: The Borno Expeditions of Idris Alauma (1564–1576)* (Wiesbaden: Franz Steiner, 1987), pp. 54, 63; See also Humphrey Fisher, *Slavery in the History of Muslim Black Africa* (New York: New York University Press, 2001), pp. 258–61, 263–66, 282–84, 287–94.
4. For a comprehensive biography of Uthman Dan Fodio, see F.H. El-Masri, 'The Life of Shehu Uthman Dan Fodio before the Jihād', *Journal of the Historical Society of Nigeria*, 2:4 (1963), pp. 435–448; Murray Last, *The Sokoto Caliphate* (London: Longman, 1967); Mervyn Hiskett, *The Sword of Truth: The Life and Times of the Shehu Usuman Dan Fodio* (New York: Oxford University Press, 1973); Ibraheem Suleiman, *A Revolution in History: The Jihad of Usman Dan Fodio* (London/New York: Mansell, 1986).
5. See Roman Loimeier, *Islamic Reform and Political Change in Northern Nigeria* (Evanston, IL: Northwestern University Press, 1997); Ousmane Kane, *Muslim Modernity in Postcolonial Nigeria: A Study of the Society for the Removal of Innovation and Reinstatement of Tradition* (Leiden: E.J. Brill, 2003). Ramzi Ben Amara, 'The Izala Movement in Nigeria: Its Split, Relationship to Sufis and Perception of Shari'a Re-implementation', Ph.D. dissertation, Bayreuth University, 2011. Yan Izala should be considered the mainstream of non-Sufi Sunnism in Nigeria today.
6. Muhammad b. Salih Ibn al-ʿUthaymīn, *Fatāwā al-ʿaqīda* (Beirut: Dar al-Jil, 1993), pp. 376–8.
7. E.g., Pantami (in Bauchi during 2006), text 1; For an overview of the debates inside Nigerian Salafism see Alexander Thurston, *Salafism in Nigeria: Islam, Preaching and Politics* (New York: Cambridge University Press, 2016), pp. 193–239. See also Abdalla Uba Adamu, 'African Neo-Kharijites and Islamic Militancy Against Authority: The Boko Haram/Yusufiyya Kharijites of Northern Nigeria', paper presented at the Islam in Africa Working Group of the African Studies Center, University of Florida, Gainesville, Florida, February 24, 2010, pp. 1–26; Anonymous, 'The Popular Discourses of Salafi Radicalism and Salafi Counter-Radicalism in Nigeria: A Case Study of Boko Haram', *Journal of Religion in Africa*, 42:2 (2012), pp. 118–44; Kyari Mohammed, 'The Message and Methods of Boko Haram',

Marc-Antoine Pérouse de Montclos (ed.) *Boko Haram: Islamism, Politics, Security and the State in Nigeria* (Leiden: African Studies Centre, 2014), pp. 9–32.

8. See Murray Last, 'From Dissent to Dissidence: The Genesis and Development of Reformist Islamic Groups in Northern Nigeria', in Abdul Raufu Mustapha (ed.) *Sects and Social Disorder: Muslim Identities and Conflict in Northern Nigeria* (Suffolk: James Currey, 2014), pp. 18–53; Toyin Falola, *Violence in Nigeria: The Crisis of Religious Politics and Secular Ideology* (Woodbridge: University of Rochester Press, 1998), pp. 137–162.

9. See http://www.blueprint.ng/2014/08/26/of-mutiny-and-crestfallen-troops/ (accessed 9 April 2016).

10. For example, the U.S. House Joint Committee on Homeland Security report of 30 November 2011: https://homeland.house.gov/hearing/subcommittee-hearing-boko-haram-emerging-threat-us-homeland/ (accessed 29 December 2015).

11. E.g., Abdulkareem Mohammed, *The Paradox of Boko Haram* (Kaduna: Espee, 2010), pp. 37–39, like so many holding to this idea, presents the facts of Nigeria's poverty, but makes no effort to prove that Boko Haram's appearance has any connection to it at all.

PART ONE: NIGERIAN PREACHERS (2006–2008)

1. E.g., http://www.ibtimes.com/number-nigerians-displaced-boko-haram-increases-21-million-international-organization-2083797; http://www.naijagistube.net/2015/11/28/president-buhari-releases-the-number-of-killed-and-displaced-people-by-boko-haram-so-far/ (accessed 29 December 2015).

2. Michael Nwankpa, 'The political economy of securitization: the case of Boko Haram, Nigeria', *Economics for Peace and Security Journal*, 10:1 (2015) pp. 32–39.

3. For overviews of the history of Boko Haram, see Dr Ahmad Murtada, 'Jama'at Boko Harām': Nashā'tuhā, Mabādi'uhā wa A'māluhā fi Nayjīriyā', *Qirā'āt Ifrīqiyya*, 13 November 2012, available at http://bit.ly/2qoUEAg (accessed 15 November 2016), English translation, 'The Boko Haram Group in Nigeria: its beginnings, principles and actions in Nigeria' is available at http://download.salafimanhaj.com/pdf/SalafiManhaj_BokoHaram.pdf (accessed 13 December 2016); also Mike Smith, *Boko Haram: Inside Nigeria's Unholy War* (London: I.B. Tauris, 2015); Virginia Comolli, *Boko Haram: Nigeria's Islamist Insurgency* (London: Hurst, 2015); and Andrew Walker, *Eat the Heart of the Infidel': The Harrowing of Nigeria and the Rise of Boko Haram* (London: Hurst, 2016) Alexander Thurston, *Boko Haram: The History of an African Jihadist Movement* (Princeton: Princeton University Press, 2018).

4. Global Terrorism Index, GTI, "Measuring and Understanding the Impact of Terrorism." *Institute for Economics and Peace* (2015), p. 2 available at http://economicsandpeace.org/wp-content/uploads/2015/11/Global-Terrorism-Index-2015.pdf (accessed 15 January 2016).

5. Jacob Zenn, 'The Islamic Movement and the Iranian Intelligence Activities in Nigeria', *CTC Sentinel*, 7:2 (2013), pp. 13–18; Alexander Thurston, 'Shi'ism and Anti-Shi'ism in Nigeria', *Maydan*, 15 May 2017, available at https://www.themaydan.com/2017/05/shiism-anti-shiism-nigeria/ (accessed 16 May 2017). See also texts 11 and 18.

6. See Roman Loimeier, *Islamic Reform and Political Change in Northern Nigeria* (Evanston: Northeastern University Press, 1997), pp. 288.

7. Loimeier, *Islamic Reform*, pp. 207–291

8. Zenn, 'Islamic Movement', p. 16; Thurston, 'Shi'ism and Anti-Shi'ism in Nigeria'.

9. Michael Nwankpa, *Boko Haram: Whose Islamic State?* Houston: James A. Baker III Institute of Public Policy, 2015, p. 8, available at https://bakerinstitute.org/files/9145/. For analyses of how Boko Haram appropriate the teachings of Dan Fodio see Abdulbasit Kassim, 'Defining and Understanding the Religious Philosophy of jihādī-Salafism and the Ideology of Boko Haram', *Politics, Religion & Ideology*, 16 (2015), pp. 173–200; Abdulbasit Kassim and Jacob Zenn, 'Justifying War: The Salafi-Jihadis Appropriation of Sufi Jihad in the Sahel-Sahara', *Current Trends in Islamist Ideology*, 21 (2017), pp. 86–114.

10. Mark Amaliya and Michael Nwankpa, 'Assessing Boko Haram: A Conversation', *Journal of Terrorism Research*, 5:1 (2014), pp. 81–87.

11. David D. Laitin, 'The Sharia debate and the origins of Nigeria's Second Republic', *The Journal of Modern African Studies*, 20:3 (1982), pp. 411–430.

12. On the connection, Abimbola O. Adesoji, 'Between Maitatsine and Boko Haram: Islamic Fundamentalism and the Response of the Nigerian State', *Africa Today*, 57:4 (2011), pp. 98–119.

13. Ali Mazrui, 'Shariacracy and federal models in the era of globalization: Nigeria in comparative perspective', *Democratic Institution Performance: Research and Policy Perspectives*, 63 (2005), pp. 63–75; Ruud Peters, *Islamic Criminal Law in Nigeria* (Abuja: Spectrum, 2003).

14. Philip Ostien, 'Sharia implementation in Northern Nigeria 1999–2006: a sourcebook', Vol. III: *Sanitizing Society* (Ibadan, Nigeria: Spectrum Books, 2007).

15. Roman Loimeier, 'Boko Haram: The development of a militant religious movement in Nigeria', *Africa Spectrum*, 47:2–3 (2012), pp. 137–155.

16. International Crisis Group, 'Curbing Violence in Nigeria (II): The Boko Haram Insurgency', *Crisis Group Africa Report N°216*, 3 April 2014, p. 7, available at https://www.crisisgroup.org/africa/west-africa/nigeria/curbing-violence-nigeria-ii-boko-haram-insurgency (accessed 10 April 2014).

17. Abu Usamatul al-Ansari 'A Message from Nigeria', *al-Risala Magazine Issue 4*, January 2017, p. 19, available at: https://azelin.files.wordpress.com/2017/01/al-risacc84lah-magazine-4.pdf (accessed 15 January 2017) For further analysis on the Nigerian Taliban see Jacob Zenn, 'Before Boko Haram: A Profile of al-Qaeda's West Africa Chief Ibrahim Harun (a.k.a. Spinghul)', *Militant Leadership Monitor*, 8:3 (March 2017), pp. 17–22.

1. DEBATE ON THE STATUS OF WESTERN EDUCATION AND WORKING FOR THE NIGERIAN GOVERNMENT BETWEEN MALLAM ISA ALI IBRAHIM PANTAMI AND MALLAM MUHAMMAD YUSUF MAIDUGURI

1. Mohammed, *Paradox*, pp. 58–68 cites two other debates (undated) with Ja'far Adam, and Idris Abdulaziz (of the Izala), but their contents are similar to this debate. Although the views of Muhammad Yusuf in this debate were largely drawn from his reading of the book

of Bakr ibn 'Abdallah Abu Zayd al-Ghayhab, *al-Madāris al-'Ālamiyya al-Ajnabiyya al-Isti'māriyya: Tārīkhuhā wa-Makhāṭiruhā,* Yusuf's ideas are similar to the position of Abu Muhammad al-Maqdisi on Western schools see *'I'dād al-Qāda al-Fawāris bi-Hajr Fasād al-Madāris,* available at http://www.ilmway.com/site/maqdis/MS_828 (accessed 15 December 2015). For an analysis of Yusuf's reading of Abu Zayd see Stephen Ulph, 'Boko Haram: Investigating the Ideological Background to the Rise of an Islamist Militant Organization,' available at http://www.scribd.com/doc/178672818/BOKO-HARAM-Investigating-the-Ideological-Background-to-the-Rise-of-an-Islamist-Militant-Organisation (accessed 16 January 2017). The views of Isa Pantami were further expounded in a publication *Is Boko Haram? Responses to 35 Common Religious Arguments Against Conventional "Western" Education* (Minna: Da'wah Institute of Nigeria, 2016).

2. Yusuf is hesitant to state absolutely that it is forbidden because he realizes that a verdict is more binding than an opinion.

3. Abu Muhammad al-Maqdisi made similar distinctions see Abu Muhammad al-Maqdisi, '*Kashf al-Niqab 'an Shari'at al-Ghab*', pp. 122–135, available at http://www.ilmway.com/site/maqdis/MS_38459 (accessed 16 December 2015).

4. Ibn Taymiyya (d. 1328) is the foremost pre-modern authority for Salafis, but during his own time, he was little respected.

5. Apparently, this statement is supposed to summarize an evolutionary development of the cosmos.

6. Pluto was demoted from being a planet on 24 August 2006.

7. A Saudi Arabian body.

8. At that time, Ibn 'Uthaymīn, who died in 2001, was probably the dominant figure on the Committee.

9. Mālik, *al-Muwaṭṭā'* (Beirut: Dar al-Fikr, 1989), p. 597 (no. 1651).

10. Joseph's previous master, in the biblical account Genesis 39:1, in the Qur'ān 12:30.

11. 'Abd al-Raḥmān b. Nāṣir Sa'dī, *Taysīr al-karīm al-Raḥmān fi tafsir al-kalām al-mannān* (an Egyptian scholar, active in Saudi Arabia from the 1960s till the present).

12. There are many versions to this tradition, but either Pantami is citing one that is obscure, or inexactly, because none of them begin with the formula he cites: see Wensinck, *Concordance* (Leiden: E.J. Brill, 1936–64), s.v., *umarā'*.

13. Approximately September 2005.

14. Nāṣir al-Dīn al-Albānī, the most prominent Syrian quietest Salafi scholar, d. 1999.

15. A major theologian and codifier who was close to Ibn Taymiyya, d. 1350.

2. TRANSLATION OF SELECTIONS FROM MUHAMMAD YUSUF: *HĀDHIHI 'AQĪDATUNĀ WA-MINHĀJ DA'WATINĀ*

1. Thanks to Alex Thurston for supplying us with a copy of the first edition of this text. Muhammad Yusuf published the second edition of this text on 13 May 2009 and a revised edition was published by *Fursān al-Balāgh and al-'Urwa al-Wuthqā* on 12 March 2015.

2. This is Yusuf and Shekau's standard opening; it is suppressed in all later transcriptions.

3. A symbol of Nigeria, in the National Assembly; http://www.nairaland.com/2545871/mace-weapon-power (accessed 1 June 2016).

4. Leader of the ancestor of the Islamic State, killed in Iraq 2006.

5. al-Bukhārī, *Ṣaḥīḥ* (Beirut: Dar al-Fikr, 1991), iv, p. 27 (no. 3017).

6. In English.

7. In English.

8. Lucien Lévy-Bruhl (d. 1939), author of important works on Africa (although now largely discredited). In the original his name and that of Durkheim are in parentheses.

9. Émile Durkheim (d. 1917), important sociologist and philosopher of religion.

10. Ibn al-Mubārak, *Kitāb al-jihād* (Sayda': al-Maktaba al-'Asriyya, 1988), p. 55 (no. 105).

11. In English.

12. E.g., al-Nawawī, *al-Nawawi's Forty Hadith*. Trans. Ezzedin Ibrahim and Denys Johnson-Davies (Cairo: Shirkat al-Amal, 1989), pp. 36–8 (no. 4).

13. al-Bukhārī, *Ṣaḥīḥ*, ii, p. 45 (no. 1088).

3. CLEARING THE DOUBTS OF THE SCHOLARS

1. A prominent scholar from Maiduguri who died on hajj in Saudi Arabia in December 2009.

2. Founded by Tahir Bolori and located on Imam Malik Street in Maiduguri.

3. Mallam Abdulwahhab Abdallah is a Togolese cleric based in Kano, a friend and collaborator of Shaykh Ja'far Adam see Andrea Brigaglia, 'Ja'far Mahmoud Adam, Mohammed Yusuf and Al-Muntada Islamic Trust: Reflections on the Genesis of the Boko Haram phenomenon in Nigeria', *Annual Review of Islam in Africa*, 11 (2012), p. 41; Thurston, *Salafism in Nigeria* pp. 169, 229, 232.

4. See text 1, part 8, where Yusuf was challenged because of his use of this tradition.

5. See his 2 April 2009 lecture 'Kungiyoyin Jihadi' which he delivered in Maiduguri as part of the series 'Dawla Uthmaniyya'. In the lecture, he criticized jihadi groups and attempted to discredit Muhammad Yusuf and his followers: http://dawahnigeria.com/dawahcast/album/dawla-uthmaaniyyah-dr-sani-rijiyar-lemu. (accessed 15 September 2016)

6. Dr Ibrahim Jalo Jalingo is referring to his book *Ithāf al-aḥibbat al-amjād bi bayāni khaṭai man ḥarrama al-tawazzufa taḥta al-ḥukūmāt al-Qā'imat fī al-bilād* (Jos: Ibzar Publishing Co., 2009), pp. 1–44.

7. A location that is part of the hajj ritual.

8. See text 20.

9. Indicating tight financial circumstances.

10. A mutual curse before Allah between two people or parties to reveal those who lie.

11. Yusuf is referring to Mallam Abdulwahhab Abdallah.

12. His full name is Safar ibn 'Abd al-Raḥmān Ḥawālī, a prominent Saudi scholar, associated with the *sahwa* Salafi movement, but today a mainstream figure.

5. WHO IS THE PROPHET MUHAMMAD?

1. Muslim, *Ṣaḥīḥ* (Beirut: Dar al-Jil, n.d.), vi, p. 23 (*kitāb al-umarā*). The tradition continues:

"They said: 'Shouldn't we fight them?' He said: 'No, as long as they pray,'" which denies the point here.

2. Meaning "Sun of the religion" and "Light of the religion" which have traditionally been common among Muslims.

3. A marabout is a Sufi holy figure; the exegesis given here is a strong attack upon Sufism.

4. It is difficult to understand what the reference is, as there are virtually no Jews in Nigeria, let alone in Maiduguri.

5. A mountain in Afghanistan where Osama bin Laden and other members of al-Qaeda took refuge during November 2001.

6. Apparently, a popular term for an armored car used by the security forces (Yusuf uses the English word), see text 43.

6. EXEGESIS OF *SŪRAT AL-TAWBA* (QUR'ĀN 9:9–16)

1. Cristiano Ronaldo, the football player for Manchester United and Real Madrid.

2. 'Umar al-Mukhtār, leader of the resistance against Italian colonial invasion of Libya in 1911–29, d. 1931.

3. Worth approximately £350 (GBP) in 1926 on the black market, wihich would be worth £18,320 in 2016 (= US$26,793). From the historical records, 'Umar al-Mukhtar was indeed offered 50,000 *lira* (al-Razi, *'Umar al-Mukhtār* [Beirut: Dar al-Madar al-Islami, 2004], pp. 119–29), so Yusuf must have had access to accurate information on this incident.

7. EXPLANATION OF THE MEANING OF ISLAMIC MONOTHEISM

1. Shekau appears to have taken this verbal tic from Yusuf, and abandoned it later.

2. A major Muslim mystic figure, to whom the doctrine of *waḥdat al-wujūd* (the unity of being) is ascribed, d. 1240.

8. EXEGESIS OF *SŪRAT AL 'IMRĀN* (QUR'ĀN 3:165–175)

1. See al-Haythami, *al-Zawājir 'an iqtirāf al-kabā'ir* (Beirut: Dar al-Ma'rifa, 1998), i, p. 341 (sin no. 109).

2. It is interesting that Yusuf's one certainty about the Bible is inaccurate.

3. In other words, doing the five prayers together rather than separately throughout the day.

4. Compare texts 40, 41.

5. See 'Abdallah Azzam, *The Signs of the Merciful One in the Jihad of Afghanistan*, at https://archive.org/stream/MiraclesOfJihadInAfghanistan-AbdullahAzzam/Signs_of_ar-Rahman_djvu.txt (accessed 25 May 2016).

6. On 24 November 1989 in Peshawar, Pakistan (two of his sons were with him). His murderers have never been identified.

7. Compare al-Bukhārī, *Ṣaḥīḥ*, iii, p. 269 (no. 2803).

8. al-Bukhārī, iii, p. 268 (no. 2797).

9. al-Tirmidhī, *Jāmi'* (Beirut: Dar al-Fikr, n.d.), iii, p. 106 (no. 1712). It is curious that Yūsuf does not emphasize the number of virgins more than he does.

9. BBC HAUSA SERVICE INTERVIEW WITH MUHAMMAD YUSUF

1. Thanks to Professor Abdulla Uba Adamu for supplying us with the audio.
2. For a translation, see W. Montgomery Watt, *Islamic Creeds* (Edinburgh: Edinburgh University Press, 1994), pp. 48–56.
3. Both by Ibn 'Abd al-Wahhāb.
4. A medieval Muslim heresiographer, d. 1153, today considered to have been an Ismaili.
5. By fall 2008 most prominent opponents of the polio vaccination had abandoned their opposition to inoculations. The BBC interview here may be focusing upon Yusuf as one of the hold-outs against the polio vaccine. For the basic arguments, see: *Polio Vaccine: How Potent?* (Kaduna: New Era Institute for Islamic Thought and Heritage, 2003), which argues that the polio vaccine was designed to sterilize Muslim women. See also Elisha P. Renee, *The Politics of Polio in Northern Nigeria* (Indiana: Indiana University Press, 2010), pp. 51–67.
6. The cumin seed, about which there is a vast amount of pious literature, e.g., Muhammad Mahmud 'Abdallah, *Khayr al-dawā' fi al-thawm wa-l-baṣal wa-l-'asl wa-l-ḥabba al-sawdā'* (Riyad: Dar al-Shawwaf, 1993).
7. Water coming from the well of Zamzam, close to the Ka'ba in Mecca.

10. FILM

1. This very highly literal understanding of entertainment is probably based upon Q33:4–5. For further discussion of the compatibility and incompatibility of Hausa films with Islam see Muhsin M. Ibrahim, 'Hausa film: Compatible or Incompatible with Islam?', *Performing Islam*, 2:2 (2013), pp. 165–179.
2. These were Muhammad's enemies.
3. A river in Paradise.
4. A suburb of Maiduguri to the northeast.
5. Apparently, a group of Shi'ites in the border town of Bama.
6. This dates this selection to approximately early December 2008, as the Muharram processions started on 29 December 2008.
7. al-Shahrastani, *Milal wa-l-nihal* (Beirut: Dar al-Fikr, n.d.), p. 114 (almost an exact quotation).

PART TWO: REACHING A VERDICT (2008–2009)

1. E.g., http://www.nigeriamasterweb.com/TalibanOfNigeria.html (accessed 25 September 2016), see text 3.

11. HISTORY OF THE MUSLIMS

1. The Ottoman Empire and France had close relations after the middle of the 1500s.
2. Muḥammad b. 'Abd al-Wahhab began preaching around 1744, and died in 1792.
3. The tradition being cited here is one of a family of traditions in which Muhammad states that succession to the office of caliph (or rulership in Islam) will remain in his personal tribe of Quraysh.

4. Muḥammad al-Amin al-Kanemi (d. 1837), a ruler of Borno, who fought against Dan Fodio's *jihād*.

5. 'Umar b. Muhammad al-Amin.

6. A basic Maliki legal text, by al-Khushani, d. 972.

7. On him, see Lange, *A Sudanic Chronicle*.

8. These were really slave raids.

9. Niger was ruled by the French, while Nigeria by the British, which was the reason they were separated.

10. First president of Chad, assassinated in 1975.

11. Ruled Chad 1979–82.

12. Ruled Chad 1982–90.

13. On 14 March 2006, there was a coup attempt against Idriss Déby.

14. Killed on 30 July 2005.

15. Al-Azhar, in Cairo in 970.

16. In 1967–70, the southeastern region of Nigeria tried to secede and took the name of Biafra.

17. Yusuf is pointing out that the purpose of the program is to transfer northern students to the south, and southern students to the north to create a sense of unity across the country.

18. JAMB (Joint Admission and Matriculation Board Exam) is an entry exam into tertiary institutions in Nigeria.

19. 'Alī ibn Aḥmad Ibn Ḥazm, who was a major iconoclastic Spanish Muslim scholar, d. 1064.

20. A Syrian scholar best known for his commentary on the collection of Muslim, and his *Forty Hadith*, d. 1277.

21. See text 2 for a translation of these texts.

22. Assassinated in 1949.

23. In Pakistan, founder of Jamaat-e-Islami, d. 1979.

24. A Salafi-jihadi group in Egypt during the 1970s that preached withdrawal from society.

25. Qutb was a leader in the Muslim Brotherhood who was radicalized while in prison, and became a leading ideologue, ex. 1966.

26. For counting the ninety-nine names of Allah.

27. Founder of the Islamic Novement in Nigeria, and the major Shi'ite figure in Nigeria.

28. Governor of Kaduna, January 1992–November 1993. The massacre is described in Falola, *Violence*, pp. 213–21.

29. He was later sentenced to death for his part in the killings, but was eventually reprieved.

30. Yusuf is referring to Isioma Daniel, a Nigerian journalist, whose newspaper article in 2002 where she commented on the Prophet Muhammad sparked the Miss World riot in Kaduna. A *fatwā* was issued on her and it was broadcasted by Mamuda Aliyu Shinkafi, the deputy governor of Zamfara State, on 26 November 2002. Shinkafi said in the *fatwā*: "Like Salman Rushdie, the blood of Isioma Daniel can be shed. It is abiding upon all Muslims wherever they are to consider the killing of the writer as a religious duty." See text 31.

31. On 7 March 1987, see Falola, *Violence*, pp. 179–81.

32. Most probably the Jos riots of 28–29 November 2008.

33. By 'Abd al-Rahman Luwayhiq, a Saudi author.

34. By ʿAbd al-Malik Jazaʾiri, covering the subject of the Algerian civil war.

35. Of Ibn Taymiyya.

36. Presumably in 2004.

37. Non-Muslim Nigerians?

38. See *Fatawa Islamiyya: Islamic Verdicts* (Riyadh: Darussalam, 2001), i, pp. 243, 255, 265.

39. The basic Salafi text in Nigeria. Gumi was the dominant figure in the Izala movement until his death in 1992.

40. It would be interesting to know specifically to whom he is referring. This theological tendency would be the equivalent of Dominion theology in the United States.

41. Compare text 28.

42. Possibly a member of the group.

43. The leader of Boko Haram in Katsina state.

44. Not identified.

45. Assassinated in 656.

12. ADMONITION

1. See http://allafrica.com/stories/200901130236.html (accessed 12 January 2016).

2. Generic Christian names.

3. In the south. Enugu here is a generic reference to the fact that a soldier's life is one of continual transfers without regard to one's place of origin.

4. Where Nigerian armed forces were stationed as peace-keepers.

5. Security forces of Izala.

6. Because of the abrogation of what Islam classifies as a previous revelation.

7. The most important among the messengers.

8. The idea that the constitution is based on man-made laws.

9. Abū Dāʾūd, *Sunan* (Beirut: Dar al-Jil, 1988), iv, p. 108 (no. 4297) "The nations are about to call out over you like hungry people call out over a bowl of food." See text 36.

10. Lawal Ningi Haruna, military governor of Borno state, August 1998–May 1999.

11. Anglican bishop, currently emeritus.

12. Probably a reference to the well-known tradition that "Islam began as a stranger, and will return to being a stranger" at the end of the world.

13. EXEGESIS OF *SŪRAT AL-BAQARA* (QURʾĀN 2:284–286)

1. A well-known recent biography of Muhammad by Ṣafī al-Raḥmān al-Mubārakfūrī.

2. There would often be only forty-five minutes to an hour of electricity in the evenings when I (D.C.) visited Maiduguri on 8–10 May 2009.

3. The *qunūt* prayer is a formal imprecation.

4. September 2008, probably the controversies mentioned in the BBC interview (text 9).

5. Cf. Q9:111.

6. Traditionally, this was Balaam (see Numbers 22–24).

7. From the description, Yusuf is talking about a *niqāb* which covers the entire body.

8. President of Nigeria, 2007–10.

14. WESTERN CIVILIZATION IS ATHEISM AND ANTI-ISLAM

1. Based on the text, which states that it was delivered two days after the exegesis of Baqara (text 13).
2. National Youth Service Corps (see text 11).
3. There are several reasons for this difference: one is that Muslim celebrations move around the calendar year, so they are difficult to place on an official calendar, and two, Shekau is ignoring the Muslim holiday that does have the character he is denouncing, which is the Prophet Muhammad's birthday (Mawlid al-nabī) because it is generally considered to be an innovation by Salafis.
4. Such as the "daughters of Allah" worshipped by the pre-Islamic Arabs.
5. Ibn Jibrin was a prominent Saudi scholar of the same generation as Ibn ʿUthaymin.
6. By Ahmad ʿAbd al-Qadir (below). However, the book does not seem to be on WorldCat.
7. Ibn Qayyim's *Badāʾiʿ al-fawāʾid* has been published in at least seven different editions, but none of the ones listed on WorldCat are from Dar al-Bayan.
8. See text 2.
9. ʿAbd al-Raḥmān ibn Ḥasan Āl al-Shaykh; the book is *Fatḥ al-majīd bi-sharḥ kitāb al-tawḥīd*.
10. Muḥammad al-Amīn ibn Muḥammad al-Mukhtār Shinqīṭī.
11. Flourished 1980–85.
12. Those who besieged Medina in 627, against whom Muhammad and the Muslims dug a defensive ditch.
13. A mistake, as the treaty of Hudaybiyya was in 628, and Abu Jahl died in 624 after the Battle of Badr.

15(A): GROUPING OF SERMONS OF THE IMAM ABU YUSUF MUHAMMAD BIN YUSUF JAMĀʿAT AHL AL-SUNNA LI-L-DAʿWA WA-L-JIHĀD

1. When President George Bush stated that "you are either with us or with the terrorists" in September 2001.
2. Ruled 717–20, sometimes considered to have been the "fifth" of the four Rightly Guided caliphs by Sunnis.
3. The rationalistic trend in early Islam, dominant during the ninth century, but largely defeated by mainstream Sunnism by the end of the tenth century. See text 9 for more explanation.
4. Ibn Taymiyya did no such thing: there were no Jahmiyya during his time, and he did nothing to fight the Shiʿites or the Mongols (who were no longer a serious threat during Ibn Taymiyya's life).
5. As well as negotiate with the Crusaders, with whom he enjoyed excellent personal relations. His nephew surrendered Jerusalem to Emperor Frederick II in a negotiated treaty.
6. It is awkward to mention Dan Fodio in Borno, since the Borno Empire under al-Kanemi fought the Fulani *jihād* to a standstill in 1811–12.
7. The end is the curse of Khubab against the unbelievers of Quraysh just before he was martyred.

16. *HĀDHIHI ʿAQĪDATUNĀ (THIS IS OUR CREED)*

1. Translator's note: *Titimi* is a Kanuri concept for folktales and story-telling at night. It is the most exciting moment for the young people, sitting while the moon is shining, and listening to stories told by their parents. Thus, for Shekau, commitment and loyalty will make *jihād* become as easy and exciting as telling a story.

2. There does not seem to be a verse which states this exactly, although the idea is in Q10:37.

3. The name of the founder of Boko Haram was Muḥammad [Yusuf], while his successor's name (the speaker) was Abū Bakr, exactly paralleling the early *umma*.

4. Translator's note: this is a veiled call to violence.

5. Appears to be the only place where Shekau uses this term. Is he really citing this from Ibn Taymiyya, though?

6. Could he be referring to Pantami (text 1)?

7. Referring to someone as a wizard or as a witch is a deadly insult throughout Africa.

8. This may be a reference to Samuel Zwemer, well-known missionary to the Muslim world during the colonial period.

9. In 1990–92.

10. Translator's note: a bald head here is a sign of wisdom, but also indicative of arrogance perceived as a product of knowledge.

11. This is a reference to the fact that in many local communities, many Muslims are adopting the wearing of suits, ties and wedding gowns during marriage ceremonies.

17. PROVISION OF THE MUSLIM FIGHTERS

1. In northern Nigeria, October–April.

2. al-Bayhaqī, *Faḍāʾil al-awqāt* (Beirut: Dar al-Kutub al-ʿIlmiyya, 1997), pp. 141–3 concurs.

3. Against the Persian Sasanians. The point of the tradition is the question of whether it is permissible to commit suicide in battle by attacking a superior force. Abu Ayyub takes the verse in a completely different direction.

4. It is difficult to know the historical circumstances to which Yusuf is alluding here in Algeria, perhaps during the period of ʿAbd al-Qadir (1832–47). Or perhaps he is referring to the Algerian civil war (1991–2003).

18. RETURNING TO THE QURʾĀN AND SUNNA:

1. Prior to the 2009 conflict, it was widely believed that Muḥammad (Mamman) Nūr was the third-in-command in Boko Haram. This is the only publicly available video where Nur was featured before the 2009 conflict. In the aftermath of the conflict, Nur, unlike Shekau, did not feature in any Boko Haram video or audio until August 2016 when he released "Open Letter to Shekau" (text 72).

2. Operation Flush to which both Yusuf and Nur allude throughout this text (and no. 19) was an operation supposedly designed to root out criminals along the roads of northern Nigeria. It turned out to be a mechanism by which security forces shook down locals for money.

3. From the period of the state established by Dan Fodio and his successors (1812–1902).

4. The last independent caliph of the state established by Dan Fodio.

5. On 27 April 2007, there was a supposed lesbian wedding in Kano (later denied), http://news.bbc.co.uk/2/hi/africa/6603853.stm (accessed 15 April 2016).

6. Probably the governor of Borno State, Ali Modu Sheriff (2003–11).

7. Presumably to increase the weight. Kola nuts are the sacral food of West Africa.

8. Throughout western Africa there are popular beliefs about protection, such as those documented in the Liberian and Sierra Leonean civil wars, see Nathalie Wlodarczyk, *Magic and Warfare: Appearance and Reality in Contemporary African Conflict and Beyond* (New York: Palgrave Macmillan, 2009).

9. Close to Jos.

10. Opening *sūra* of the Qur'ān, which is usually recited during prayers.

11. Presumably riding with three people on the motorcycle.

12. The very tradition Pantami asked Yusuf about in text 1, part 8, where Yusuf denied that he was continuing to use it because it was not attested in the mainstream collections (text 3). At moments of extreme tension among Sunni Salafi-jihadi groups, while overall, they aspire to only utilize "strong" well-attested traditions, they can fall back on those apocalyptic traditions which serve their purposes. Will McCants gives some examples in *The ISIS Apocalypse* (New York: St. Martin's, 2015), pp. 140–41.

13. A northern Nigerian rice-based dish.

15(B): GROUPING OF SERMONS

1. Used for brushing teeth according to the Sunna of the Prophet.

2. al-Bukhārī, *Ṣaḥīḥ*, iii, pp. 265 (no. 2787), 269 (no. 2803), 268 (no. 2797).

3. Three years prior to the first Boko Haram suicide attack Yusuf used this term. Until the summer of 2011 suicide attacks were completely unknown in West Africa.

4. The Arabicized version of the Greek word "paradise."

5. The first battle of Islam, in 624, fought against a Meccan relief detachment that was supposed to aid a caravan going to Mecca.

6. al-Bukhārī, *Ṣaḥīḥ*, iii, p. 284 (no. 2818).

15(C): GROUPING OF SERMONS BY MUHAMMAD YUSUF

1. Bruce Lawrence, *Messages to the World: The Statements of Osama Bin Laden* (London: Verso, 2005), pp. 133–138. For a detailed study of the intellectual responses of Muslims of Northern Nigeria to British colonialism see Muhammad S. Umar, *Islam and Colonialism: Intellectual Responses of Muslims of Northern Nigeria to British Colonial Rule* (Leiden: Brill, 2006) especially Chapter 2 "Responses to the Challenges of British Military Superiority," in which the author analyzes the Muslims responses in the form of different arguments for Hijra; Submission; Surrender; and Armed Confrontation, etc., pp. 64–103. Chanfi Ahmed also discussed those who made Hijra to Mecca and Medina see Chanfi Ahmed, *West African 'ulamā' and Salafism in Mecca and Medina: Jawāb al-Ifrīqī—The Response of the African* (Leiden: Brill, 2015).

2. Presumably, he is referring to the various slaughter trains that were exchanged between India

and Pakistan during the partition of summer 1947, during which Muslims slaughtered at least as many Hindus.

3. It is not clear what the Japanese had to do with Lugard. Perhaps Yusuf meant the Germans (*alman*), who did indeed colonize Cameroon.

4. Between 1921–74. Although the emperors of Ethiopia did forcibly convert Muslims to Christianity, this mostly occurred during the nineteenth century, not during the period of Haile Selassie. Forcible conversion to Islam has been commonly practiced recently, especially in the Sudan in 1989–2005.

5. Non-*halal* meat, especially bush meat (road-kill, etc), and its vendors proved to be a common target for Boko Haram during the following years.

19. OPEN LETTER TO THE NIGERIAN GOVERNMENT OR *DECLARATION OF WAR*

1. In 2009 one of the strongholds of the group.
2. Abubakar b. 'Umar Garba, who ascended in February 2009.
3. Aliyu Magatakarda Wamakko (gov. 2008–11).
4. In northeastern Borno State.
5. Muhammad Yusuf had previously delivered a lecture on funeral rites in Islam as an act of worship see https://www.youtube.com/watch?v=fpNvkflhByY (accessed 12 December 2015).
6. Perhaps one of the security personnel.
7. Inspector general briefly, June–July 2009.
8. Minister of the Interior, Nigeria from November 2015.
9. Israel was founded in 1948.
10. An AK-47 would have a 30-round magazine.
11. Nigerian political parties.
12. Presumably a nickname or perhaps a decal the soldier was wearing, perhaps with relation to the amateur radio network, http://www.ten-ten.org/ or the fertilizer called 10–10–10.

20. INTERROGATION OF MUHAMMAD YUSUF BY NIGERIAN SECURITY FORCES

1. Q96:1.
2. In the final pictures of him, Yusuf has a bandage around his left arm.
3. This transcript has been modified for English and clarity. It is available at https://naijainfoman.wordpress.com/2011/12/11/transcript-of-muhammad-yusuf-interrogation-before-he-was-summarily-executed-by-members-of-the-nigeria-police/ (accessed 30 September 2016).

PART THREE: MAKING NIGERIA UNGOVERNABLE (2009–2012)

1. See texts 11, 12, 14, and 18 for evidence that Boko Haram was already planning violence.
2. Murray Last, 'From Dissent to Dissidence: the genesis and development of reformist Islamic groups in northern Nigeria', Nigeria Research Network Working Paper, no. 5, March 2013

at http://www.soas.ac.uk/history/events/afhistseminar/06mar2013-from-dissent-to-dis-sidence-the-genesis—development-of-reformist-islamic-groups-in-norther.html; also Mazrui, op. cit.

3. http://www.nigerianwatch.com/news/1334-nigerian-senate-passes-new-anti-terrorism-act-with-death-penalty-for-offenders (accessed 31 December 2015).

4. The numbers are disputed: see https://africacheck.org/factsheets/factsheet-how-many-schoolgirls-did-boko-haram-abduct-and-how-many-are-still-missing/ (accessed 31 December 2015).

5. Global Terrorism Index, GTI, 2015.

6. Mazrui, 'Shariacracy', p. 65.

7. Ibid., p. 66.

8. Andrew Walker, *What is Boko Haram?* (Washington, DC: United States Institute of Peace, 2012), p. 8.

9. Jacob Zenn, 'Leadership Analysis of Boko Haram and Ansaru in Nigeria', *CTC Sentinel*, 7:2 (2014), pp. 1–9.

10. Nwankpa, 'The political economy of securitization', p. 35.

11. David Cook, *Boko Haram: A Prognosis* (Houston: James A. Baker III Institute for Public Policy Rice University, 2011), pp. 1–33, available at http://bakerinstitute.org/media/files/Research/535dcd14/REL-pub-CookBokoHaram-121611.pdf.

12. International Crisis Group, 'Curbing Violence in Nigeria', p. 21.

21. STATEMENT OF SANI UMARU

1. This translation has been modified and is available at http://www.vanguardngr.com/2009/08/boko-haram-ressurects-declares-total-jihad/ see also: "We will teach Nigeria a lesson" http://www.nairaland.com/310123/boko-haram-new-leader-teach#4354820 (accessed 27 April 2016).

22(A): DOCUMENTS FROM ADVICE AND SHARI'I INSTRUCTION

1. Abdelmalik Droukdel, leader of AQIM, formerly from the Algerian Jama'a al-Salafiyya li-Da'wa wa-l-Qital (GSPC).

2. One should note that major Boko Haram operations commenced immediately following this period, so it was very likely that this payment kickstarted the group.

3. Ansaru.

23. DECLARATION OF WAR AGAINST CHRISTIANS AND WESTERN EDUCATION

1. See text 14.

2. At this time Mallam Isa Yuguda (until 2015).

3. The two angels said to record the deeds of humanity.

24. MESSAGE OF CONDOLENCE TO THE *MUJĀHIDIN*

1. In a three-page communique titled "The Annihilation of the Muslims in Nigeria: A New

Episode in the Continuous Crusader War," released 1 February 2010, 'Abd al-Wadud said: "We are ready to train your children to use weapons and will supply them with all we can, including support, men, weapons, ammunitions and equipment, to defend our people in Nigeria, and to respond against the aggression of the Christian minority. So, push your children to the training fields and *jihād* to form the fighting and defending vanguards on behalf of the blood and honor of Muslims in Nigeria, which resists the declared Crusader war." Thanks to Jacob Zenn for providing us with the translation by NEFA Terror Watch. A news report in place of the since-deleted posting is available: http://af.reuters.com/article/topNews/idAFJOE6100EE20100201?sp=true (accessed 28 September 2016). Before 'Abd al-Wadud issued this message, Shekau had sent Khalid al-Barnawi and two other followers to meet with AQIM's brigade leader in Mali, Abu Zayd in August 2009 to request for training, funding and other financial and strategic communications support from AQIM, see "Letter from 'Abdallah Abu Zayd 'Abd-al-Hamid to Abu Mus'ab 'Abd-al-Wadud," (and text 22) Bin Laden's Bookshelf—ODNI, released January 2017, available at https://www.dni.gov/files/documents/ubl2017/english/Letter%20from%2Abdallah%20Abu%20Zayd%20Abd-al-Hamid%20to%20Abu%20Mus%20ab%20Abd-al-Wadud.pdf.

2. The raid of al-Damous uploaded: http://www.youtube.com/watch?v=HVB-6JcHucY (since deleted by YouTube). See 'AQIM Video Shows Ambush in al-Damous, Incites for Action', SITE Intelligence Group, 26 April 2010 available at https://ent.siteintelgroup.com/Multimedia/site-intel-group-4-26-10-aqim-video-raid-damous.html (accessed 16 November 2017). Prior to the video of al-Damous, al-Andalus media also featured a Nigerian, Abu Ammar al-Nijiri, in a training camp video 'Join the Caravan' which was released on 5 January 2010 see 'AQIM Video of Training, Incitement (Part 2 of 2)', SITE Intelligence Group, 5 January 2010 available at https://ent.siteintelgroup.com/Multimedia/site-intel-group-1-5-10-aqim-video-join-caravan-part-2.html (accessed 16 November 2017).

3. The al-Jazeera video titled "Nigerian Security Forces Kill Unarmed Civilians" can be accessed at https://www.youtube.com/watch?v=tlpZr8IRUcY; https://www.youtube.com/watch?v=T1hc1zKnLr0.

4. See https://www.youtube.com/watch?v=VQ1mPIk5T-M.

5. See https://videos.files.wordpress.com/tSjPuBwU/rsf4_std.mp4.

6. The early Muslim community was perennially short of mounts on which to travel to battle, so as Muhammad says in this tradition (see Bukhari, *Sahih*, iv, 266 no. 2790 for a version), this fact hampered the numbers participating.

7. Killed June 4, 2012 in Waziristan, Pakistan by a U.S. drone.

8. Baghdadi and al-Muhajir were killed on 18 April 2010.

9. These verses have been a locus for apocalyptic speculation about the U.S. since the 1980s, see Cook, *Contemporary Muslim Apocalyptic Literature* (Syracuse: Syracuse University Press, 2005), chapter 7.

10. Who was later to become the leader of the Islamic State.

25. LEAFLET FROM THE BAUCHI PRISON BREAK

1. We are grateful to Professor Abdalla Uba Adamu for providing us with the Hausa and English translation of this leaflet and the permission to include it in this anthology [translator's notes are his].

2. Translator's note: This is the first segment of a Hausa proverb "*in maye ya manta, uwar da ba za ta manta ba*." "*Maye*" is a person who has special powers to absorb his victim's souls. If a "*maye*" absorbs the soul of a child and promptly forgets he has done so, the mother of the child will not forget, thus: "if the perpetrator has forgotten (his crimes), the victim will never forget."

3. A reference to the 2010 Jos conflict where more than a thousand people were killed. The reference to the conflict in Jos (see text 11), intended to promote the image of the group as a vanguard fighting to defend the Muslims in Nigeria. The term "Suldaniya" would also be used by the splinter group "Ansaru" (see texts 32, 36–37).

4. Translator's note: The exact parlance, "*amma a hakan har za a samu wadanda su ka cuna Musulmi don a kashe ko a kama*", centers around the meanings given to the word "*cuna*", which means egging one person against another, or turning in (by an informant).

5. Near the Yankari Express bus station and the Emir's Palace.

6. Translator's note: This is in reference to the initial uprising of the sect in which many of their members were killed by security forces in Bauchi town on 26 July 2009.

7. Translator's note: The expression, "*dokin mai baki ya fi gudu*" means the "horse of the rider who can talk rides faster." Since the government (the rider) has greater access to the media (horse), it communicates its programs.

26. HAUSA *NASHID* "WE ARE NOT BOKO HARAM, WE ARE THE PEOPLE OF SUNNA"

1. See Gustav Nachtigal, *Sahara and Sudan: Kawar, Bornu, Kanem, Borku, Ennedi* (trans. Allan Fisher and Humphrey Fisher, London: Hurst, 1980), pp. 108, 267. It is odd that Boko Haram would use a Kanuri term in a Hausa *nashid*.

2. On 16 November 2002; see texts 11 and 31.

3. A Russian heavy machine-gun.

27. A LETTER TO OSAMA BIN LADEN LADEN'S DEPUTY

1. In his commentary on this letter, Jacob Zenn said, "This letter was not addressed to anyone in particular but by context of the letter it was likely intended for Droukdel to forward to al-Zawahiri or Atiyyatullah Abdurrahman al-Libi. al-Zawahiri had been more open than Bin Laden to enlist new affiliates, which was evidenced by al-Zawahiri's acceptance of the GSPC's affiliation with al-Qaeda in 2006 when Bin Laden presumably could have done so himself and of al-Shabab's affiliation with al-Qaeda in 2012 when Bin Laden declined to do so publicly before his death in May 2011. This may be why Shekau was advised to communicate with al-Zawahiri instead of Bin Laden on matters of 'joining the organization' of al-Qaeda. However, a loyal courier may have nonetheless delivered Shekau's letter to Bin

Laden, which is why it was found in his compound in Pakistan in 2011." See Jacob Zenn, 'Demystifying al-Qaida in Nigeria: Cases from Boko Haram's Founding, Launch of Jihad and Suicide Bombings', *Perspectives on Terrorism*, 12:6 (2017).

2. See Jacob Zenn, 'A Biography of Boko Haram and the *Bay'a* to Al-Baghdadi', *CTC Sentinel*, 8:3 (March 2015) pp. 17–21.

3. A Salafi-jihadi scholar located in the U.K. (deported to Jordan on 7 July 2013) noted for his religious support of extremists in Algeria and al-Qaeda.

22(B): LETTER FROM DISAFFECTED MEMBERS OF BOKO HARAM TO AQIM: CRITIQUING SHEKAU

1. Leader of the Algerian GIA 1996–2002, who became known for his *takfir* of all Algerians.
2. Al-Bukhari, *Ṣaḥīḥ*, viii, p. 113 (no. 7056).

28. MESSAGE FROM SHEKAU

1. See http://allafrica.com/stories/201007010432.html (accessed 12 December 2015).
2. Moses, after he had killed an Egyptian, see Ex. 2:11–14.
3. Apparently during this period Shekau was living in safe houses, and had not gone out into the field. This is the first time Shekau refers to himself in the third person, a standard sign of his burgeoning megalomania.

29. MESSAGE TO NIGERIA'S PRESIDENT GOODLUCK JONATHAN

1. This is the first suicide attack in Nigeria, see http://saharareporters.com/2011/06/26/story-nigerias-first-suicide-bomber-blueprint-magazine (accessed 28 September 2016).
2. See https://www.youtube.com/watch?v=WIcDglXJcvo; http://www.bbc.com/news/world-africa-14964554.
3. See https://www.hrw.org/sites/default/files/reports/nigeria1012webwcover_0.pdf (accessed 27 October 2016).
4. An in-law of the governor Ali Modu Sheriff, killed on 6 October 2010, see http://allafrica.com/stories/201010080326.html (accessed 28 September 2016).
5. See http://www.bbc.com/news/world-africa-12310536 (accessed 28 September 2016).
6. See https://sahelblog.wordpress.com/2011/03/28/nigeria-boko-haram-assassinates-another-anpp-leader/ (accessed 28 September 2016).
7. See http://saharareporters.com/2010/10/09/prominent-islamic-preacher-sheik-bashir-mustapha-killed-boko-haram-militants-maiduguri (accessed 28 September 2016).
8. See https://sahelblog.wordpress.com/2011/03/14/boko-haram-assassinates-prominent-muslim-cleric-in-maiduguri/ (accessed 28 September 2016)
9. See http://www.bbc.com/news/world-africa-13679234 (accessed 28 September 2016).
10. See http://allafrica.com/stories/201109060416.html (accessed 28 September 2016).
11. Village head of Bauchi (Kandahar) in Bauchi, killed on 22 October 2010, see http://allafrica.com/stories/201010250915.html (accessed 28 September 2016).
12. Younger brother of the Shehu of Borno, see http://www.bbc.com/news/world-africa-13618775 (accessed 28 September 2016).

13. See http://af.reuters.com/article/topNews/idAFJOE79O05K20111025 (accessed 28 September 2016).

14. See Ibn Hanbal, *Musnad* (Beirut: Dar al-Fikr, n.d.), iv, p. 103.

15. At that time, Ayo Oritsejafor (2010–15).

16. See for these speeches (28 December 2011 and 8 January 2012): http://www.bbc.com/news/world-africa-16462891 (accessed 28 September 2016).

17. Referring to President Jonathan when he admitted that members of Boko Haram have succeeded in infiltrating his government; he also believed that Boko Haram had sympathizers in government, see http://www.premiumtimesng.com/news/3360-boko-haram-has-infiltrated-my-government-says-jonathan.html (accessed 28 September 2016).

18. Referring to CAN president Ayo Oritsejafor, when he called upon Jonathan to allow Nigerians to carry arms and defend themselves. See http://www.pmnewsnigeria.com/2011/09/14/insecurity-let-nigerians-carry-arms-oritsejafor-tells-jonathan/comment-page-1/ (accessed 29 September 2016).

19. A mosque serving as a focus of opposition to Muhammad located to the south of Medina, and destroyed in approximately 630.

30. WE ARE COMING TO GET YOU, JONATHAN!

1. See http://www.vanguardngr.com/2012/03/boko-haram-menace-ll-end-in-june-jonathan/ (accessed 27 October 2016).

2. See http://www.bbc.com/news/uk-17305707 (accessed 27 October 2016).

3. See https://videos.files.wordpress.com/VKna05Hp/al-qc481_idah-in-the-islamic-maghrib-appeal-of-the-german-prisoner-to-his-government-save-my-life_dvd.mp4 (accessed 27 October 2016)

4. See https://azelin.files.wordpress.com/2012/03/al-qc481_idah-in-the-islamic-maghrib-22to-the-german-government-if-they-release-umm-sayf-allah-al-ane1b9a3c481rc4ab-then-we-will-release-to-you-our-prisoner22-en.pdf (accessed 27 October 2016)

5. See https://azelin.files.wordpress.com/2012/06/al-qc481_idah-in-the-islamic-maghrib-22on-the-killing-of-the-german-prisoner-in-nigeria22-en.pdf (accessed October 27, 2016); also http://www.bbc.com/news/world-africa-18278740 (accessed 27 October 2016)

6. See text 30; also http://af.reuters.com/article/topNews/idAFJOE82900F20120310 (accessed 27 October 2016)

7. See https://www.yahoo.com/news/video/boko-haram-video-kidnapped-french-145000298.html (accessed 27 October 2016).

8. See http://www.aljazeera.com/news/africa/2013/11/boko-haram-claims-it-kidnapped-french-priest-2013111519496392506.html (accessed 27 October 2016).

9. See http://www.aljazeera.com/news/africa/2014/04/two-italian-priests-kidnapped-cameroon-20144581312938177.html (accessed 27 October 2016).

10. Shekau repeated this in another video from 2013 which can be found at https://videos.files.wordpress.com/no6NflgX/imc481m-abc5ab-bakr-shekau-statement_std.mp4 (accessed 27 October 2016).

31. REASONS FOR ATTACKING *THISDAY* NEWSPAPER

1. See http://www.bbc.com/news/world-africa-17926097 (accessed 28 September 2016).
2. See text 11.
3. See text 26.
4. Said at the time to have been the spokesman for Boko Haram.
5. Northern-based newspapers.
6. http://saharareporters.com/
7. For the attack on Gombe State University, see http://saharareporters.com/2012/04/26/explosions-gombe-state-university-send-lecturers-students-fleeing (accessed 27 October 2016). For the attack on Bayero University, Kano: http://www.bbc.com/news/world-africa-17886143 (accessed 27 October 2016).

32. FORMATION OF JAMĀʿAT ANṢĀR AL-MUSLIMIN FI BILĀD AL-SŪDĀN

1. See https://www.youtube.com/watch?v=s6ATD6bLaBI; https://www.youtube.com/watch?v=aZ-6STrj2tI.
2. See http://jihadology.net/2013/01/22/new-statement-from-jamaat-an%e1%b9%a3ar-al-muslimin-fi-bilad-al-sudans-abu-yusuf-al-an%e1%b9%a3ari-claiming-credit-for-targeting-nigerian-soldiers-heading-to-mali/.
3. See http://azelin.files.wordpress.com/2013/03/jamc481_at-ane1b9a3c481r-al-muslim-c4abn-fi-bilc481d-al-sc5abdc481n-e2809ckilling-the-christian-prisoners-as-a-result-of-the-joint-nigerian-british-military-operation22-en.pdf.
4. See https://videos.files.wordpress.com/MfbYpZ8B/abc5ab-usc481mah-al-ane1b9a3c481rc4ab-22open-letter-to-the-governments-of-france-and-nigeria22_std.mp4; http://www.bbc.com/news/world-africa-20833946.
5. See http://azelin.files.wordpress.com/2013/04/jamc481_at-ane1b9a3c481r-al-muslim-c4abn-fi-bilc481d-al-sc5abdc481n-e2809cthe-charter-of-jamc481_at-ane1b9a3c481r-al-muslimc4abn-fi-bilc481d-al-sc5abdc481ne2809d.pdf.
6. See http://desertherald.com/jamaatu-ansarul-muslimina-fi-biladi-sudan-threatens-southern-kaduna-militant-group-akhwat-akwop/.
7. Groups are: Akhwat Akwop (a Kaduna-based Christian militia), OPC (O'odua People's Congress, a Yoruba group), Afenifere, a Yoruba vigilante group, Massob (Movement for the Actualization of the Sovereign State of Biafra), MEND (Movement for the Emancipation of the Niger Delta), IPC (Igbo People's Congress), IYC (Ijaw Youth Congress).

33. MESSAGE TO THE WORLD

1. Ibn al-Mubārak, *Kitāb al-jihād*, pp. 89–90 (no. 105).
2. Shekau is referring to the film *Innocence of Muslims* by Nakoula Basseley Nakoula. The film was perceived as denigrating to the Prophet Muhammad, and prompted demonstrations across Arab and Muslim nations, as well as in some Western countries.

34. CLARIFICATION OF THE FALSE REPORT ON NEGOTIATIONS WITH THE NIGERIAN GOVERNMENT

1. Thanks to Jacob Zenn for providing us with a link to this video. Some of the issues Shekau

discussed in this video were also discussed by Ahmad Salkida, the Nigerian journalist who has extensively covered the Boko Haram conflict in his twitter chat 'What Does Boko Haram Want' available at https://storify.com/jeremyweate/whatdoesbhwant (accessed 12 November 2017).

2. See http://saharareporters.com/2012/03/18/why-we-withdrew-boko-haramfg-talks-dr-ibrahim-datti-ahmad.

3. See http://saharareporters.com/2012/06/07/%E2%80%98boko-haram%E2%80%99-debunks-sheik-dahiru-bauchi-says-dialogue-ended-long-time-ago.

4. See http://allafrica.com/stories/201208270270.html.

5. See https://www.theguardian.com/world/2012/nov/01/boko-haram-peace-talks-nigeria.

6. See   http://www.reuters.com/article/us-nigeria-bokoharam-idUSBRE8AP11N20121126.

7. See http://www.voanews.com/a/nigeria-boko-haram-militants-announce-ceasefire/1592925.html.

8. See http://allafrica.com/stories/201302210151.html.

9. This video could not be accessed by the translator, but a link to a report on the video is available at http://www.premiumtimesng.com/news/122844-boko-haram-leader-abubakar-shekau-denies-ceasefire-in-new-video.html.

10. See https://www.youtube.com/watch?v=JUviaNT7kzE.

35. GLAD TIDINGS, O SOLDIERS OF ALLAH

1. See Neil MacFarquhar, 'Tape Ascribed to bin-Laden Urges Muslims to Stand with Iraq', *The New York Times*, 12 February 2003. Available at www.nytimes.com/2003/02/12/international/middleeast/12TAPE.html.

2. See Abu Bakr Naji, *Management of Savagery: The Most Critical Stage through which the Umma Will Pass* (trans. William McCants) (Cambridge: John M. Olin Institute for Strategic Studies, Harvard University, 2006), p. 37.

3. For further related materials, see https://www.youtube.com/watch?v=TSXWTPnyHak; https://videos.files.wordpress.com/IJXXkqWb/boko-e1b8a5arc481m-shooting_std.mp4; https://videos.files.wordpress.com/qSCyk0G0/boko-e1b8a5arc481m-group-training_std.mp4.

4. al-Bukhārī, *Ṣaḥīḥ*, iv, pp. 42–3 (no. 3062).

5. It is very interesting that Shekau would refer to Yusuf as a Nigerian.

36. DISASSOCIATION OF THE JAMĀʿAT ANṢĀR AL-MUSLIMIN FROM TARGETING MUSLIM INNOCENTS

1. Umar Tal, who established a brief empire through Senegal and Mauritania, and fought the French, d. 1864.

37. SERMON FOR ʿID AL-AḌḤĀ 1434/2013

1. This was al-Zarqawi's standard opening.

2. Text 36.

PART FOUR: BOKO HARAM STATE (2013–2015)

1. http://www.euronews.com/2015/02/08/nigeria-and-neighbours-announce-multi-national-force-to-confront-boko-haram/ (accessed 31 December 2015).

2. Steven Metz, *Rethinking Insurgency* (Carlisle: Strategic Studies Institute, U.S. Army War College, 2017), p. 52

3. Paul Wilkinson, 'The Strategic Implications of Terrorism', in *Terrorism and Political Violence: A Sourcebook*. Indian Council of Social Science Research (New Delhi: Har-anand Publications, 2000), pp. 19–49.

4. Metz, *Rethinking Insurgency*, p. 30. From my (M.N.) recent fieldwork, a holistic approach is well-received. There is not much point in addressing theological concerns without also addressing basic socio-economic conditions, which can be manipulated (of course concealing more religiously and politically inclined objectives).

5. http://www.newsforafrica.com/en/15-09-17/814715183008814715-boko-haram-kills-8-for-collaborating-with-cameroon-troops-voice-of-america.html (accessed 23 December 2015).

6. http://www.thetrentonline.com/dss-says-it-has-uncovered-boko-haram-sleeper-cell-in-abuja-statement-2/ (accessed 31 December 2015).

7. Global Terrorism Index, 2014, 2015.

8. http://www.aljazeera.com/news/2016/04/boko-haram-children-suicide-bombers-160412093755915.html.

9. Global Terrorism Index, GTI, 2014, 2015.

10. http://news.yahoo.com/boko-haram-kills-nearly-80-ne-nigeria-villages-005711494.html (accessed 23 December 2015).

11. Nwankpa, 'Boko Haram: Whose Islamic State'.

12. Ibid.

13. Amnesty International, *Our Job is to Shoot, Slaughter and Kill: Boko Haram's Reign of Terror in North-East Nigeria* (London: Amnesty International, 2015).

14. Judging from the numbers freed since spring 2015, the true number of captured women must be at least 10,000.

15. Amnesty International, 'Our Job is to Shoot'.

16. Amnesty International, 'Our Job is to Shoot'.

17. http://edition.cnn.com/2014/05/17/world/africa/cameroon-china-boko-haram/ (accessed 23 December 2015).

18. http://www.independent.co.uk/news/world/africa/life-as-a-boko-haram-captive-story-of-kidnapped-tribal-chief-and-family-gives-an-insight-into-10306123.html (accessed 23 December 2015).

38. RAID ON MAIDUGURI

1. Bayero was the emir of Kano, implying a high-status person.

2. This is a type of regalia commonly worn by imams, brides, traditional rulers and people of influence.

3. *Wubcham*a is a pseudonym for Imam Ibrahim Ahmad (1924–2014), the longest serving Chief Imam of Borno State and a member of the Borno Emirate Council.

4. In other words, black-listed.
5. Known as "necklacing."
6. Ibn Hanbal, ii, p. 218, "I [Muhammad] have come to you to slaughter you."
7. The current Nigerian minister for sports and youth development.
8. At that time, James Entwhistle. In the 92nd issue of its al-Naba newsletter, the Islamic State (IS) reported that its West Africa Province under the leadership of Abu Mus'ab al-Barnawi was responsible for the killing of nearly 70 'apostates' in an attack on an oil exploration team in northeast Nigeria see https://azelin.files.wordpress.com/2017/08/the-islamic-state-al-nabacc84_-newsletter-92.pdf p. 11 (accessed 17 November 2017).

39. HAUSA *NASHID* IN THE VIDEO "THE RAID ON MAIDUGURI"

1. This *nashīd* is from 13:53–19:00 in the video.
2. Probably the 5 February 2014 attacks during which eighty-two people were killed, see http://naijagists.com/boko-haram-latest-attacks-in-yobe-plateau-kaduna-states-kill-82/ (accessed 7 October 2016). "Their 'Id" might be a reference to Valentine's Day.

40. MESSAGE TO THE *UMMA*

1. Lawrence, *Messages*, pp. 104–5 (7 October 2001).
2. Derogatory, "your father's penis" (thanks to Carmen McCain for this identification).
3. See al-Bukhārī, *Ṣaḥīḥ*, vi, pp. 163–64 (nos. 5133–34).
4. Faith Sakwe.
5. One of the most committed enemies of the Prophet Muhammad.
6. Q85:4–8.
7. The practice of blood letting for medical purpose (*ḥajāma*).
8. A well-known northern Nigerian liberal, d. 1983.
9. Prime Minister of Nigeria, assassinated in 1966.
10. A night prayer, not obligatory.
11. Yahaya Jingir and Goni Gabchia are both scholars of the Izala movement.
12. All hallmarks of Salafism.
13. Former governor of Jigawa State.
14. On 16 September 2001. Of course, the Iraq war did not start until spring 2003.
15. Bukhārī, *Ṣaḥīḥ*, iv, p. 27 (no. 3017).

41. MESSAGE ABOUT THE CHIBOK GIRLS

1. See http://www.bbc.co.uk/news/world-africa-36321249; http://dailypost.ng/2016/11/05/breaking-another-chibok-girl-rescued-baby; http://saharareporters.com/2017/05/06/80-kidnapped-chibok-girls-freed-boko-haram; http://saharareporters.com/2017/05/07/photos-82-chibok-girls-boarding-helicopter-banki-abuja. Prior to the release of the twenty-one girls on 12 October 2016, Boko Haram issued a video on 14 August 2016 showing the girls and stating the conditions for their release; see http://jihadology.net/2016/08/14/new-video-message-from-jamaat-ahl-al-sunnah-li-l-dawah-wa-l-jihad-message-to-the-families-of-the-chibok-girls-and-f-g/ In the aftermath of the release of eighty-two Chibok girls on

6 May 2017, Boko Haram issued a video showing the return of the Boko Haram prisoners swapped with the girls: http://jihadology.net/2017/05/12/new-video-message-from-jamaat-ahl-al-sunnah-li-l-dawah-wa-l-jihad-and-prepare-against-them-whatever-you-are-able/ The group also issued a video showing five Chibok girls that chose to stay back with the group http://jihadology.net/2017/05/12/new-video-message-from-jamaat-ahl-al-sunnah-li-l-dawah-wa-l-jihad-chibok/

2. See http://www.telegraph.co.uk/news/worldnews/africaandindianocean/nigeria/10163 942/Extremist-attack-in-Nigeria-kills-42-at-boarding-school.html (accessed 27 October 2016). For Musa Cerantonio's support of Boko Haram's kidnapping of Chibok girls see 'Radical Preacher justifies Kidnapping, Slavery Threats', SITE Intelligence Group, 19 May 2014 available at https://ent.siteintelgroup.com/Western-Jihadists/radical-preacher-justifies-kidnapping-slavery-threats.html (accessed 16 November 2017).

3. See http://www.bbc.com/news/world-africa-24322683 (accessed 27 October 2016).

4. See http://uk.reuters.com/article/uk-nigeria-violence-idUKBREA1O1IO20140225 (accessed 27 October 2016).

5. See http://www.bbc.com/news/world-africa-29985252 (accessed 28 October 2016). For a timeline of Boko Haram attacks on schools and the abduction of students, see https://www.hrw.org/video-photos/map/2016/04/11/timeline-school-attacks-july-2009-july-2015 (accessed 28 October 2016).

6. al-Bukhārī, *Ṣaḥīḥ*, iii, p. 160 (no. 2517).

42. BEHEADING OF NIGERIAN AIR FORCE OFFICERS

1. Culled from the video "Sako Jirgin Yakin Nigeria."

43. DECLARATION OF AN ISLAMIC CALIPHATE

1. For Boko Haram's territorial control during this period, see: https://fulansitrep.com/2014/08/09/9th-and-10th-august-nigeria-sitrep-boko-haram/ (accessed 29 October 2016).

2. See http://allafrica.com/stories/201411070446.html (accessed 29 October 2016).

3. The final scene of this video is available: http://www.liveleak.com/view?i=305_1411967452 (accessed 30 October 2016).

4. Probably the 1 May 2014 attack, which killed nineteen.

5. Probably the series of attacks on 21–22 June 2014 in the villages around Kummabza, in which at least sixty women were taken.

6. Where approximately 200 Christians were slaughtered on 2 June 2014.

7. Probably referring to the massacre of the Banu Qurayza in Medina in 627.

8. Identifying as Muslims.

9. Shekau is most likely referring to this video where members of Civilian JTF were shown beheading suspected members of Boko Haram. See http://www.liveleak.com/view?i=499_1407274030 (accessed 28 October 2016).

10. The fall of Muammar Gaddafi in fall 2011 released a large number of weapons all over west Africa. Some of those were obtained by Boko Haram.

44.　INTERVIEW WITH A *MUJĀHID* ABU SUMAYYA

1. Published by Mu'assasat al-Ṣawārim (As-Sawarim Media Foundation).
2. Text 2.

45.　BEHEADING VIDEO BY CHADIAN FACTION OF BOKO HARAM

1. Thanks to Jacob Zenn for providing us with this video. Although this video is not available online, a report on the video can be accessed on the Reuters website: http://www.reuters.com/article/us-nigeria-violence-chad-insight-idUSKBN0IN1MG20141103 (accessed 16 June 2016).
2. See http://jihadology.net/2015/03/02/al-urwah-al-wuthqa-foundation-presents-a-new-video-message-from-jamaat-ahl-al-sunnah-li-l-dawah-wa-l-jihad-boko-%e1%b8%a5aram-harvest-of-the-spies-1/
3. See http://jihadology.net/2017/03/13/new-video-message-from-jamaat-ahl-al-sunnah-li-l-dawah-wa-l-jihads-abu-bakr-shekau-the-secret-of-the-hypocrites/ (accessed 13 March 2017).

46.　SHEKAU SAYS HE IS ALIVE AND WELL

1. Derogatory nickname for President Jonathan meaning someone/something who is wrapped around a woman (thanks to Carmen McCain for this identification).
2. The Banu Qurayẓa.
3. On the road between Gwoza and Maiduguri.
4. The Battle of the Ditch in 627.

47.　SHEKAU SPEAKS ON CEASE-FIRE AND THE CHIBOK GIRLS

1. See https://www.youtube.com/watch?v=nVDT85Es4zI (accessed 30 October 2016).
2. See https://www.youtube.com/watch?v=IvCc1vrTlRA (accessed 30 October 2016).
3. Written by Ibn 'Abd al-Wahhab.

48.　BOKO HARAM COMMUNIQUES WITH AFRICAN MEDIA

1. On the road between Bama and Maiduguri. Konduga had been raided on 14 February 2014, and fifty-one girls kidnapped, http://motherhoodinstyle.net/2014/02/20/boko-haram-kidnap-20-young-girls-in-konduga-massacre/ (accessed 26 October 2016).
2. In Yobe State, effectively cutting off Maiduguri, as Damaturu is located on the main Bauchi road.
3. Which may have been true, as these communiques were coming from the Nur faction of Boko Haram.
4. Probably the 25 November twin suicide attack in Maiduguri, which killed at least forty-five people.
5. Q26:54, said by Pharaoh of Moses and the Israelites.
6. Probably referring to the division in Syria between the Islamic State and Jabhat al-Nusra (and other jihadi groups).
7. For the massacre of the people of Bama, see http://www.liveleak.com/view?i=290_

1419258666; http://www.liveleak.com/view?i=575_1419006422; http://www.liveleak.com/view?i=ebe_1418914796; http://www.liveleak.com/view?i=115_1418995992 (accessed 27 October 2016).

8. See text 29, note 19.

49. MESSAGE TO THE EMIR OF KANO

1. See http://www.bbc.com/news/world-africa-29882218 (accessed 28 October 2016).
2. Lamido had been a banker before he became Emir of Kano in 2014.

50. MESSAGE TO PRESIDENT PAUL BIYA OF CAMEROON

1. Cameroon is officially bilingual, with a majority of the population speaking French and a significant minority speaking English.
2. This flag, although currently closely associated with the Islamic State, has its roots in 1990s Salafism.

51. *CHARLIE HEBDO*

1. This link is no longer available on YouTube.

52. MESSAGE TO THE WORLD ON BAGA

1. https://www.youtube.com/watch?v=El-O37TNIm4 (accessed 27 October 2016).
2. See Ibn 'Abd al-Wahhab's "Ten Nullifiers of Islam," (in the version by Ibn Baz), where this is the third nullifier: https://passtheknowledge.wordpress.com/2014/09/16/10-nullifiers-of-islam/
3. Ibn al-Mubarak, *Kitāb al-jihād*, pp. 89–90 (no. 105).
4. A candidate for the presidency of Nigeria at the time, seen by many as more likely to win against Boko Haram.

55. ALLAH IS OUR MASTER

1. This road has frequently been the site of checkpoints, as it is roughly the border between the Muslim-majority region of Bauchi and the Christian-majority region of Jos.
2. The massacre at *Charlie Hebdo* in Paris in which twelve members of the journal's staff were murdered by Muslims who swore allegiance to ISIS occurred on 7 January 2015 (see text 51).

56. A MESSAGE TO THE AFRICAN LEADERS, SPECIFICALLY, IDRISS DÉBY

1. The Chadian civil war.
2. Cf. Q18:9 (People of the Cave, the Seven Sleepers of Ephesus); 85:4 (People of the Pit, most probably some of the martyrs of Najran).

57. APPLICATION OF THE RULINGS OF ISLAM IN THE ISLAMIC STATE IN AFRICA

1. See https://www.youtube.com/watch?v=cnaYK5zXTlI (accessed 30 October 2014); also

https://videos.files.wordpress.com/voPz1hSs/the-islamic-state-22establishment-of-the-limit-upon-the-thieves-wilc481yat-gharb-ifrc4abqc4abyyah22_dvd.mp4 (accessed 1 November 2016).

2. Who was a self-confessed adulterer.

3. Text 15(B), starting with "During the previous week, these unbelievers [the police] shot our brothers with bullets..."

58. INVESTIGATION OF THE NIGERIAN ARMY

1. See https://www.amnesty.org/download/Documents/AFR4416572015ENGLISH.PDF; https://www.amnesty.org/download/Documents/AFR4433892016ENGLISH.pdf; https://www.amnesty.org/download/Documents/24000/afr440132011en.pdf.

2. It occurred on 29 September 2011 see http://newsrescue.com/birom-christians-eat-roasted-flesh-of-muslims-they-killed-in-jos-nigeria/#axzz46IqgBt59 (accessed 19 April 2016).

3. http://www.vanguardngr.com/2012/06/contemporary-ethnic-and-religious-crises-in-kaduna-state/ (accessed 19 April 2016)

4. Umaru Musa Yar'adua was president of Nigeria at the time (although incapacitated; he left the country three months later to receive medical treatment). The atrocities that are being described are the Boko Haram uprising in July 2009.

5. https://www.naij.com/345151-soldiers-raze-bauchi-village-kill-civilians.html (accessed 19 April 2016).

PART FIVE: WEST AFRICAN ISLAMIC STATE (2015–16)

1. http://thenationonlineng.net/buhari-boko-haram-to-be-crushed-by-december/ (accessed 29 December 2015).

61. JUMBLED WORDS AND AUTHENTICATION FOR THE IMPORTANT PERIOD PRIOR TO SHAYKH AL-SHEKAWI'S ALLEGIANCE WHICH MADE THE *UMMA* HAPPY

1. Shayba al-Hamad is a former member of Ansar al-Shari`a Tunisia and a pro-al-Qaeda poet and writer on prominent jihadist websites including Ansar al-Mujahidin, al-Fallujah and al-Tahaddi. He defected from Ansar al-Shari`a Tunisia and became pro-Islamic State and subsequently administered the Africa Media outlet that published Boko Haram Communiques (see text 48) and other military reports of Boko Haram's 'General Command' before Shekau's baya`a to al-Baghdadi. See Jacob Zenn, 'Wilayat West Africa Reboots for the Caliphate', *CTC Sentinel*, 8:8 (August 2015) pp. 10–16. We would like to thank Jacob Zenn for supplying us with this text.

62. *BAY'A* (OATH OF ALLEGIANCE) TO THE CALIPH OF THE MUSLIMS

1. The following Islamic State provinces issued congratulatory videos: Dijla, Raqqa, Halab, Janub, Homs, Khayr, Baraka, Shabwa and Furat.

2. See *Dabiq* (no. 8, April 2015), p. 15: http://media.clarionproject.org/files/islamic-state/isis-isil-islamic-state-magazine-issue+8-sharia-alone-will-rule-africa.pdf.

63. ARRIVAL OF THE CALIPHATE'S SOLDIERS IN WEST AFRICA

1. Another video with similar themes is available at: http://jihadology.net/2016/08/15/
   new-video-message-from-the-islamic-state-coverage-from-the-progress-of-the-battle-in-
   the-fortified-strongholds-of-west-africa-wilayat-gharb-ifriqiyyah/

64. 'ID [AL-FITRI] PRAYER AND SERMON FROM WILĀYAT GHARB IFRIQIYĀ

1. See al-Bayhaqī, *Faḍā'il al-awqāt*, p. 87 (no. 188, citing several sources).
2. While also meaning the biblical and Qur'ānic Pharaoh, the term is commonly used by Salafi-
   jihadis to refer to illegitimate governments.

65. MESSAGE TO THE NIGERIAN UNBELIEVERS

1. Compare al-Zarqawi, "*Mawqifunā al-sharaʿī min ḥukūmat Karzai al-ʿIrāq*," in *Kalimat
   mudiʿa*, https://www.ctc.usma.edu/posts/zawahiris-letter-to-zarqawi-english-translation-2.
2. Cf. Q 9:40, and al-Bukhari, iii, p. 272 (no. 2810).
3. Colonel Sani Kukasheka Usman, Director, Army Public Relations and spokesman of the
   Nigerian army.
4. Lieutenant General Tukur Yusuf Buratai, the 20th Chief of Army Staff of the Nigerian
   Army, apt. 17 July 2015.
5. See   http://thenationonlineng.net/buhari-boko-haram-to-be-crushed-by-december/
   (accessed 29 December 2015).
6. Close to the border with Cameroon, home to the primary bases of Boko Haram.

66. 'ID AL-AḌḤĀ ATMOSPHERE IN WILĀYAT GHARB IFRIQIYĀ

1. By the 'Id of 2016, the group has split into two factions but Shekau's faction released an 'Id
   video http://jihadology.net/2016/09/14/new-video-message-from-jamaat-ahl-al-sunnah-
   li-l-dawah-wa-l-jihad-a-blessed-id/
2. The Ka'ba.

68. MESSAGE FROM THE *MUJĀHIDIN* IN WEST AFRICA TO THE *MUJĀHIDIN* IN SOMALIA

1. See http://jihadology.net/2015/10/22/new-audio-message-from-shaykh-abd-al-qadir-
   mu-min-bayah-from-him-and-a-group-of-mujahidin-of-somalia-to-the-caliph-of-the-mus-
   lims-abu-bakr-al-baghdadi/; http://jihadology.net/2015/12/07/new-video-message-from-
   a-new-group-from-the-mujahidin-in-somalia-bayah-to-the-caliph-of-the-muslims-ibra-
   him-bin-awad-al-%E1%B8%A5ussayni-al-qurayshi/; http://jihadology.net/2016/01/12/
   new-video-message-from-the-islamic-state-message-to-our-brothers-in-somalia-wilayat-
   %E1%B9%ADarabulus/

69. MESSAGE FROM SHEKAU

1. Presumably Mubi (see text 42).

70. "INVESTIGATE"

1. See http://saharareporters.com/2015/10/08/nigerian-army-reinforces-troops-geidam-after-boko-haram-attack on 8 October 2015; http://icirnigeria.org/nigerian-military-covers-up-killing-of-soldiers-by-boko-haram/ on 16 February 2016 (accessed 1 November 2016).
2. Presumably Jonathan.
3. Nigerian presidential residence in Abuja.

71. MESSAGE TO THE WORLD

1. For the *al-Naba* interview with Abu Mus'ab al-Barnawi see https://azelin.files.wordpress.com/2016/08/the-islamic-state-e2809cal-nabacc84_-newsletter-4122.pdf, pp. 8–9 (accessed 1 November 2016).
2. See text 52, note 2.
3. Six weeks after this audio lecture, Shekau reappeared in a video on 24 September 2016 and identified himself as the leader of *Jamā'at Ahl Al-Sunna Li-L-Da'wa Wa-L-Jihād* in West Africa of the Islamic State and defended his group against the charges that he used *takfīr* on Muslims. See http://jihadology.net/2016/09/24/new-video-message-from-jamaat-ahl-al-sunnah-li-l-dawah-wa-l-jihads-abu-bakr-shekau-message-to-the-world/
4. Shekau being substituted for al-Barnawi.

72. EXPOSÉ: AN OPEN LETTER TO ABUBAKAR SHEKAU

1. https://www.ctc.usma.edu/posts/zawahiris-letter-to-zarqawi-english-translation-2 (accessed 6 November 2016).
2. Note that Nur uses the Hausa word *bawa* instead of the Arabic *'abd* which has usually been translated as "servant" throughout the text.
3. Nur made a mistake in this *hadīth*. All versions of the *hadīth* mention Dhu al-Hijja, not Muharram (both are sacred months).
4. See text 38.
5. A composite based upon Ibn Hazm, *Kitab al-muhallā*, xii, pp. 30–32. 123–5.
6. Yerwa is another name for Maiduguri.
7. Referring to text 19.
8. Possibly the Yobe-Komadugu Rivers.
9. Yams are a staple-food throughout Nigeria.
10. The original Boko Haram mosque in Maiduguri.
11. Banki is a town in Borno State that shares border with Cameroon.
12. Amchide is a town in Cameroon on the border with Nigeria.
13. Presumably one of the names by which Boko Haram renamed a town, probably in Borno.
14. Pepe appears to have been Shekau's executioner.
15. Hajjaj b. Yusuf al-Thaqafi (d. 714) was the cruel governor of Iraq for the Umayyads, who indeed killed Companions and other religious figures.
16. Unidentified.
17. Of 'Abd al-Rahman Al al-Shaykh.

18. Under the Boko Haram state.
19. For electricity. Because of intermittent power supplies, many Nigerians rely upon gas-powered generators.
20. Text 41.
21. After July 2009.
22. Unidentified location, probably in Borno State.
23. These places appear to be in northern Nigeria, close to the border with Niger. Perhaps the road here is the main Maiduguri-Potiskum Road.

73. MESSAGE FROM THE SOLDIERS

1. Abuja is a federal territory comprising the capital.
2. Note Shekau's slight uncertainty as to what to call himself.

74. SHEKAU RESPONDS TO HIS CRITICS

1. We would like to thank Jacob Zenn for providing us with this audio.
2. See the analysis in http://tempsreel.nouvelobs.com/monde/20170224.AFP8165/nigeria-le-chef-de-boko-haram-tue-l-un-des-commandants-pour-complot.html (accessed 16 May 2017).
3. Text 73.
4. Bula Yaga was once a hunter and he later became a member of Boko Haram and a commander in the group.
5. Falgore is a game preserve in southern Kano State; Palgore is a town further to the west. Both are at a considerable distance from Bauchi.
6. This appears to be a non-verbatim citation of a *hadīth*.
7. Approximately $31,687, most probably an exaggeration.
8. Shekau's primary location.
9. See texts 18 and 19.
10. In other words Shekau has chosen not to reveal sensitive recordings and kept them private.
11. Figuratively the verses of unbelief.

BIBLIOGRAPHY

Websites and materials cited purely for illustration are not reproduced in the bibliography as their full details are given in the notes.

Abū Dāʾūd, *Sunan*, Beirut: Dar al-Jil, 1988.

Adamu, Abdalla Uba, 'African Neo-Kharijites and Islamic Militancy Against Authority: The Boko Haram/Yusufiyya Kharijites of Northern Nigeria', paper presented at the Islam in Africa Working Group of the African Studies Center, University of Florida, Gainesville, Florida, 24 February 2010, pp. 1–26.

Adesoji, Abimbola O., 'Between Maitatsine and Boko Haram: Islamic Fundamentalism and the Response of the Nigerian State', *Africa Today*, 57:4 (2011), pp. 98–119.

Ahmed, Chanfi, *West African ʿulamāʾ and Salafism in Mecca and Medina: Jawāb al-Ifrīqī—The Response of the African*, Leiden: Brill, 2015.

Amaliya, Mark, and Nwankpa, Michael, 'Assessing Boko Haram: A Conversation', *Journal of Terrorism Research*, 5:1 (2014), pp. 81–87.

Amnesty International, *Our Job is to Shoot, Slaughter and Kill: Boko Haram's Reign of Terror in North-East Nigeria*, London: Amnesty International, 2015, available at http://www.amnestyusa.org/sites/default/files/nigeriabhreport2015.compressed.pdf.

Anonymous, 'The Popular Discourses of Salafi Radicalism and Salafi Counter-Radicalism in Nigeria: A Case Study of Boko Haram', *Journal of Religion in Africa*, 42:2 (2012), pp. 118–44.

al-Ansari, Abu Usamatul, 'A Message from Nigeria', *al-Risala Magazine Issue 4*, January 2017, p. 19, available at: https://azelin.files.wordpress.com/2017/01/al-risacc84lah-magazine-4.pdf.

Azzam, ʿAbdallah, *The Signs of the Merciful One in the Jihad of Afghanistan*, available at https://archive.org/stream/MiraclesOfJihadInAfghanistan-AbdullahAzzam/Signs_of_ar-Rahman_djvu.txt.

al-Bayhaqi, Ahmad b. al-Husayn, *Fadaʾil al-awqat*, ed. Khilaf Mahmud ʿAbd al-Samiʿ, Beirut: Dar al-Kutub al-ʿIlmiyya, 1997.

Ben Amara, Ramzi 'The Izala Movement in Nigeria: Its Split, Relationship to Sufis and Perception of Shariʾa Re-implementation', Ph.D. dissertation, Bayreuth University, 2011.

Brigaglia, Andrea, 'Jaʾfar Mahmoud Adam, Mohammed Yusuf and Al-Muntada Islamic Trust: Reflections on the Genesis of the Boko Haram phenomenon in Nigeria', *Annual Review of Islam in Africa*, 11 (2012), pp. 35–44.

al-Bukhari, Muhammad b. Ismaʾil, *Sahih*, ed. ʿAbd al-ʿAziz b. Baz, Beirut: Dar al-Fikr, 1991.

BIBLIOGRAPHY

Comolli, Virginia, *Boko Haram: Nigeria' Islamist Insurgency*, London: Hurst Publishers, 2015.

Cook, David, *Boko Haram: A Prognosis*, Houston: James A. Baker III Institute for Public Policy Rice University, 2011, pp. 1–33, available at http://bakerinstitute.org/media/files/Research/535dcd14/REL-pub CookBokoHaram-121611.pdf.

———, *Contemporary Muslim Apocalyptic Literature*, Syracuse: Syracuse University Press, 2005.

El-Masri, F.H., 'The Life of Shehu Uthman Dan Fodio before the Jihād', *Journal of The Historical Society of Nigeria*, 2:4 (1963), pp. 435–448.

Fakhry, Majid (trans), *The Qur'an: a Modern English Version*, London: Garnett Press, 1997.

Falola, Toyin, *Violence in Nigeria*, Woodbridge: University of Rochester, 1998.

Faraj, Muhammad 'Abd al-Salam (d. 1403/1982), *al-Farida al-gha'iba*, Amman: n.p., n.d.

Fatawa Islamiyya: Islamic Verdicts, Riyadh: Darussalam, 2001.

Fisher, Humphrey, *Slavery in the History of Muslim Black Africa*, New York: New York University Press, 2001.

Hiskett, Mervyn, *The Sword of Truth: The Life and Times of the Shehu Usuman Dan Fodio*, New York: Oxford University Press, 1973.

Ibn Ḥajar al-Haythami, *al-Zawājir 'an iktirāf al-kabā'ir*, Beirut: Dar al-Ma'rifa, 1998 (two volumes).

Ibn Ḥanbal, *Musnad*, Beirut: Dar al-Fikr (reprint of Bulaq ed.), n.d. (six volumes).

Ibn Ḥazm, *al-Muḥallā*, Beirut: Dar al-Fikr, 2001 (twelve volumes).

Ibn Maja al-Qazwini, *Sunan*, Beirut: Dar al-Fikr, n.d. (two volumes).

Ibn al-Mubarak, 'Abdallah, *Kitab al-jihad*, Sayda': al-Maktaba al-'Asriyya, 1988.

Ibn 'Uthaymin, Muhammad b. Salih, *Fatawa al-'aqida*, Beirut: Dar al-Jil, 1993.

International Crisis Group, "Curbing Violence in Nigeria (II): The Boko Haram Insurgency," *Crisis Group Africa Report N°216*, 3 April 2014, available at https://www.crisisgroup.org/africa/west-africa/nigeria/curbing-violence-nigeria-ii-boko-haram-insurgency.

Is Boko Haram? Responses to 35 Common Religious Arguments Against Conventional "Western" Education, Minna: Da'wah Institute of Nigeria, 2016.

Ibrahim, Muhsin M. 'Hausa film: Compatible or Incompatible with Islam?', *Performing Islam*, 2:2 (2013), pp. 165–179.

Institute for Economics and Peace, 'Measuring and Understanding the Impact of Terrorism', *Global Terrorism Index, GTI* (2014), available at http://www.visionofhumanity.org/sites/default/files/Global%20Terrorism%20Index%20Report%202014_0.pdf.

Institute for Economics and Peace, 'Measuring and Understanding the Impact of Terrorism', *Global Terrorism Index, GTI* (2015), available at http://economicsandpeace.org/wp-content/uploads/2015/11/Global-Terrorism-Index-2015.pdf.

Jansen, Johannes (trans. of Faraj), *The Neglected Duty*, New York: MacMillan, 1986.

Kane, Ousmane, *Muslim Modernity in Postcolonial Nigeria: A Study of the Society for the Removal of Innovation and Reinstatement of Tradition*, Leiden: E.J. Brill, 2003.

Kane, Ousmane, *Beyond Timbuktu: An Intellectual History of Muslim West Africa*, Cambridge: Harvard University, 2016.

Kassim, Abdulbasit, 'Defining and Understanding the Religious Philosophy of jihādī-Salafism and the Ideology of Boko Haram', *Politics, Religion & Ideology*, 16 (2015), pp. 173–200.

Kassim, Abdulbasit and Jacob Zenn, 'Justifying War: The Salafi-Jihadis Appropriation of Sufi Jihad in the Sahel-Sahara', *Current Trends in Islamist Ideology*, 21 (2017), pp. 86–114.

Kukah, Matthew H., and Falola, Toyin, *Religious Militancy and Self-assertion: Islam and Politics in Nigeria*, Aldershot: Avebury, 1996.

Laitin, David D., 'The Sharia debate and the origins of Nigeria's second republic', *The Journal of Modern African Studies*, 20:3 (1982), pp. 411–430.

Lange, Dierk, *A Sudanic Chronicle: The Borno Expeditions of Idris Alauma (1564–1576)*, Wiesbaden: Franz Steiner, 1987.

Last, Murray, *The Sokoto Caliphate*, London: Longman, 1967.

Last, Murray, 'From Dissent to Dissidence: the genesis and development of reformist Islamic groups in northern Nigeria', Nigeria Research Network Working Paper, no. 5, March 2013, available at http://www.soas.ac.uk/history/events/afhistseminar/06mar2013-from-dissent-to-dissidence-the-genesis—development-of-reformist-islamic-groups-in-norther.html.

Last, Murray 'From Dissent to Dissidence: The Genesis and Development of Reformist Islamic Groups in Northern Nigeria', in Abdul Raufu Mustapha (ed.) *Sects and Social Disorder: Muslim Identities and Conflict in Northern Nigeria*, Suffolk: James Currey, 2014, pp. 18–53.

Lawrence, Bruce (ed), *Messages to the World: The Statements of Osama bin Laden*, trans. James Howarth, London: Verso, 2005.

Loimeier, Roman, *Islamic Reform and Political Change in Northern Nigeria*, Evanston: Northwestern University Press, 1997.

———, 'Patterns and peculiarities of Islamic reform in Africa', *Journal of Religion in Africa*, 33:3 (2003), pp. 237–262.

———, 'Boko Haram: The development of a militant religious movement in Nigeria', *Africa Spectrum*, 47:2–3 (2012), pp. 137–155.

Malik (Ibn Anas al-Asbahi, Malik), *al-Muwatta'* (riwayat Yahya b. Yahya al-Laythi) wa-yalihi *Is'af al-mubatta' bi-rijal al-Muwatta'*, ed. Sa'id al-Lahham, Beirut: Dar al-Fikr, 1989.

al-Maqdisi, Abu Muhammad, *'I'dād al-Qāda al-Fawāris bi-Hajr Fasād al-Madāris'*, available at http://www.ilmway.com/site/maqdis/MS_828.

al-Maqdisi, Abu Muhammad, *'Kashf al-Niqab 'an Shari'at al-Ghab'*, available at http://www.ilmway.com/site/maqdis/MS_38459.

Mazrui, Ali, 'Shariacracy and federal models in the era of globalization: Nigeria in comparative perspective', *Democratic Institution Performance: Research and Policy Perspectives*, 63 (2005), pp. 63–75.

McCants, Will, *The ISIS Apocalypse: The History, Strategy, and Doomsday Vision of the Islamic State*, New York: St. Martin's, 2015.

Metz, Steven, *Rethinking Insurgency*, Carlisle: Strategic Studies Institute, U.S. Army War College, 2017.

Mohammed, Abdulkareem, *The Paradox of Boko Haram*, Kaduna: Espee, 2010.

Mohammed, Kyari, 'The Message and Methods of Boko Haram', in Marc-Antoine Pérouse de Montclos (ed.), *Boko Haram: Islamism, Politics, Security and the State in Nigeria*, Leiden: African Studies Centre, 2014, pp. 9–32.

BIBLIOGRAPHY

Murtada, Ahmad, 'Jama'at Boko Harām': Nasha'tuhā, Mabadi'uhā wa A'māluhā fi Nayjīriyā, *Qirā'āt Ifrīqiyya*, 13 November 2012, available at http://bit.ly/2qoUEAg.

Muslim, *Ṣaḥīḥ*, Beirut: Dar al-Jil, n.d. (four volumes).

Nachtigal, Gustav (d. 1885), *Sahara and Sudan: Kawar, Bornu, Kanem, Borku, Ennedi*, trans. Allan Fisher and Humphrey Fisher, London: Hurst Publishers, 1980.

al-Nawawi, Yahya b. Sharaf (d. 676/1277), *al-Nawawi's Forty Hadith*, trans. Ezzedin Ibrahim and Denys Johnson-Davies, Cairo: Shirkat al-Amal, 1989.

Nwankpa, Michael, 'The political economy of securitization: The case of Boko Haram, Nigeria', *Economics of Peace and Security Journal*, 10:1 (2015), pp. 32–39.

———, *Boko Haram: Whose Islamic State?* Houston: James A. Baker III Institute of Public Policy, 2015 available at https://bakerinstitute.org/files/9145/

Ostien, Philip, 'Sharia implementation in Northern Nigeria 1999–2006: a sourcebook', *Sanitizing Society (volume III)*, Ibadan, Nigeria: Spectrum Books, 2007.

Peters, Ruud, *Islamic Criminal Law in Nigeria*, Abuja: Spectrum, 2003.

al-Razi, al-Tahir Ahmad, '*Umar al-Mukhtār: al-ḥalqa al-ākhira min al-jihād al-waṭanī fi Libya*, Beirut: Dar al-Madar al-Islami, 2004.

Renee, Elisha P., *The Politics of Polio in Northern Nigeria*, Indiana: Indiana University Press, 2010.

Sanusi, S. L., 'Class, Gender and a Political Economy of 'Sharia'', *Weekly Trust*, April, 6:12 (2001), p. 2003.

al-Shahrastani, Muhammad b. 'Abd al-Karim, *Kitab al-milal wa-l-nihal*, Beirut: Dar al-Fikr, n.d.

Smith, Mike, *Boko Haram: Inside Nigeria's Unholy War*, London: I.B. Tauris, 2015.

Study of Terrorism and Response to Terrorism (START) (2015), Annex of Statistical Information: Country Reports on Terrorism 2014, http://startterrorismdatabase.pdf/.

Suleiman, Ibraheem, *A Revolution in History: The Jihad of Usman Dan Fodio*, London/New York: Mansell, 1986.

Thurston, Alexander, *Salafism in Nigeria: Islam, Preaching and Politics*, New York: Cambridge University Press, 2016.

Thurston, Alexander, 'Shi'ism and Anti-Shi'ism in Nigeria', *Maydan*, 15 May 2017, available at https://www.themaydan.com/2017/05/shiism-anti-shiism-nigeria/.

Thurston, Alexander, *Boko Haram: The History of an African Jihadist Movement*, Princeton: Princeton University Press, 2018.

al-Tirmidhi, *Jami'*, Beirut: Dar al-Fikr, n.d. (five volumes).

Ulph, Stephen, 'Boko Haram: Investigating the Ideological Background to the Rise of an Islamist Militant Organization', available at http://www.scribd.com/doc/178672818/BOKO-HARAM-Investigating-the-Ideological-Background-to-the-Rise-of-an-Islamist-Militant-Organisation.

Umar, Muhammad S., *Islam and Colonialism: Intellectual Responses of Muslims of Northern Nigeria to British Colonial Rule*, Leiden: Brill, 2006.

Walker, Andrew, *What is Boko Haram?* Washington, DC: United States Institute of Peace, 2012.

BIBLIOGRAPHY

Walker, Andrew, *'Eat the Heart of the Infidel': The Harrowing of Nigeria and the Rise of Boko Haram*, London: Hurst Publishers, 2016.

Watt, W. Montgomery, *Islamic Creeds*, Edinburgh: Edinburgh University Press, 1994.

Wensinck, Arent Jan (ed), *Concordance et indices de la Tradition Musulmane*, Leiden: E.J. Brill, 1936–64 (eight volumes).

Wilkinson, Paul, 'The Strategic Implications of Terrorism', *Terrorism and Political Violence: A Sourcebook*, Indian Council of Social Science Research, New Delhi: Har-anand Publications, 2000, pp. 19–49.

Wlodarczyk, Nathalie, *Magic and Warfare: Appearance and Reality in Contemporary African Conflict and Beyond*, New York: Palgrave Macmillan, 2009.

Yusuf, Muhammad, *Hādhihi 'aqīdatunā wa-minhāj da'watinā*, Maiduguri: Maktabat al-Ghuraba', n.d.

al-Zarqawi, Abu Mus'ab, *Kalimāt muḍi'a*, at https://www.ctc.usma.edu/posts/zawahiris-letter-to-zarqawi-english-translation-2.

Zenn, Jacob, 'A Biography of Boko Haram and the *Bay'a* to Al-Baghdadi', *CTC Sentinel*, 8:3 (2015), pp. 17–21.

———, 'The Islamic Movement and the Iranian Intelligence Activities in Nigeria', *CTC Sentinel* 7:2 (2013), pp. 13–18.

———, 'Leadership Analysis of Boko Haram and Ansaru in Nigeria', *CTC Sentinel*, 7:2 (2014), pp. 1–9.

———, 'Before Boko Haram: A Profile of al-Qaeda's West Africa Chief Ibrahim Harun (a.k.a. Spinghul)', *Militant Leadership Monitor*, 8:3 (March 2017), pp. 17–22.

———, 'Demystifying al-Qaida in Nigeria: Cases from Boko Haram's Founding, Launch of Jihad and Suicide Bombings', *Perspectives on Terrorism*, 12:6 (2017).

INDEX

517

INDEX

INDEX

INDEX

INDEX

INDEX